# WHOLE EARTH SOFTWARE CATALOG

## 28 PLAYING

*Strategy games, action games, computer sports, adventure and role-playing games*

## 46 WRITING

*Word processors, spelling and style checkers, typing tutor*

## 64 ANALYZING

*Spreadsheets, statistics programs, stock market programs*

## 78 ORGANIZING

*File managers, database managers, text organizers, computer organizers (keyboard enhancers)*

## 94 ACCOUNTING

*Personal finance, small business accounting, sophisticated accounting, tax programs*

## 106 MANAGING

*Integrated all-in-one programs, program environment integrators, project managers, vertical software (construction, energy, real estate, sales, psychiatric billing, law, farm, mail order)*

## 122 DRAWING

*Graphics hardware, business graphics, painting software, 2-D computer-aided-design, 3-D computer-aided-design*

## 138 TELECOMMUNICATING

*Home banking and shopping, investor services, online databanks, news services, electronic mail, computer teleconferencing/networking, bulletin boards (BBS), terminal programs, modems, file transfer programs, local area networks*

## 158 PROGRAMMING

*Languages, operating systems, software design library, software engineering, software maintenance, utilities*

## 175 LEARNING

*Simulations, problem-solving, math, reading, science, money handling, etc.*

## 192 ETC.

*Music, weaving, nutrition, exercise, astronomy, meditation, appliance control, slide show control, postal services, betting, artificial intelligence*

## 202 INDEX

## 204 MAIN INDEX

Quantum Press/Doubleday
Garden City, New York
1984

Copyright © 1984 by Point.

**Library of Congress Cataloging in Publication Data**

Main entry under title:
Whole Earth Software Catalog.
Includes index.
1. Microcomputers—catalogs. 2. Computer programs—catalogs. I. Brand, Stewart. II. Point (Foundation)
QA76.5.W494    1984    001.64'029'4    84-15096
ISBN 0-385-19166-9 (pbk.)

## INTRODUCTION

### IN WHICH THE BOOK ASSERTS ITS AGENDA, METHOD, & CREDIBILITY

STEWART BRAND: Computers and their programs are "embodiments of mind" (Warren McCulloch). Valuing thought, we value machines that mimic, enhance, accelerate thought. (We mistrust acceleration, with excellent reason). Something interesting and consequential is going on. The human frame of reference is ashift.

Computers and their programs are tools. They empower. They estrange. Their power was first generated and employed by institutions, originally in the various conceptual theaters of World War II (decrypting, weapon-aiming, command and control, bomb-blast modeling). Their power grew with governmental and commercial institutions after the war; they became a tool of institutional science and a major industrial product. But every few years they became ten times faster, smarter, smaller, and cheaper, and they still are doing that. By 1976 an individual could make one from a kit and try to put it to use.

With the coming of personal computers came a shift in the power balance. It may be that more accumulated code is stirring in the interests of individuals now than in the interests of institutions. It may be that more significant invention is coming from the hands of individuals. That's news that stays news, and good news at that, in the main. But there's a hilarious obstacle.

For new computer users these days the most daunting task is not learning how to use the machine but shopping.

Hence this book.

The impossible (and unachieved) task of the **Whole Earth Software Catalog** is to identify and comparatively describe all of the best personal computer products—especially software, where the most confusion reigns. Part of the impossibility is that those who know a program well don't have sufficient compara-tive experience; at the same time, the professional wide comparers don't have the deeper use experience. The only relief from the paradox is sustained discussion, gossip, and argument among the enraptured deeps and the cynical wides, and that's all this book is. It came to greater convergence of opinion than we expected.

Personal computers are skill machines. We took that as the organizing principle of the research and the book. Playing, Writing, Analyzing, Organizing, Accounting, Managing, Drawing, Telecommunicating, Learning, and that profoundest of skills, Et Cetera. For each, Barbara Robertson found and directed a Domain Editor to be responsible for all that appeared and failed to appear in that section, and to collaborate fully with the other Domain Editors. Thanks to talent and luck, it worked pretty well. One reader (you), one computer marketplace, one book—not an anthology.

In our software library are some 1,900 programs. We recommend 362 in the book. In our offices 25 assorted computers work for our living. We made the book with them.

The first question to ask any computer book is, "How out of date is it?" Publishing is much slower than the buzzing, blooming computer business, where last week's scoop is this week's shrug. Of course, we focus on the best, not the newest, and Doubleday did the printing in a breakneck six weeks—but how out of date? Mid-June, 1984, research congealed permanently toward ink.

Software has new versions all the time—version 1.3, then 1.4, then a major rewrite to version 2.0. Why can't a book do that? It can if the book is fully supported by a magazine, and this one is. Our **Whole Earth Software Review** comes out quarterly. If this **Catalog** is version 1.0, then the November '84 **Review** (our fourth issue) is version 1.1, followed by 1.2, 1.3, 1.4, and then a whole new **Catalog** in Fall '85, version 2.0. The book is part magazine.

Our EDITORIAL address is:

Whole Earth Software Catalog & Review
150 Gate Five Road
Sausalito, CA 94965
415/332-4335.

Electronically: The Source (PS0008); CompuServe (76703,436 or type GO WEC at any prompt); MCI MAIL (AKLEINER); ARPANET (@MIT = MULTICS.ARPA:Art@NJIT = EIES.Mailnet); or the EIES Network (accounts 866 or 226).

We missed some great products in this book. Tell us about them—comments, complaints, reviews, suggestions, articles; we pay for anything we print, including complaint letters.

The **Whole Earth Software Catalog** is part of Point, a non-profit educational foundation that has been making **Whole Earth Catalog**s since 1968 and the magazine **CoEvolution Quarterly** since 1974. More about Point's finances and procedures on p. 200.

## "ACCESS"

STEWART BRAND: The dense clump of information under the title of each program contains critical information you should scan first, like what machines the product runs on, what other hardware needs it has (joystick, two disk drives, color monitor, etc.), the price!, and whether it's copy-protected. Vast labor went into getting all this accurate (typically, three phone calls per product), so take advantage. The version number tells what stage in the program's evolution was available when we went to press in June '84. Since new versions are usually an improvement, don't buy an earlier number, do buy a later number if you find one.

# WHOLE EARTH SOFTWARE REVIEW

*The quarterly* Whole Earth Software Review *is subtitled "The Magazine of Fine Computing," in pursuit of the practice of personal computing as craft. Starting in November '84, the magazine also operates as an update supplement to this book.*

*In each issue the eleven Domains appear, each with its current list of recommended products, along with abundant discussion of the changes in the list since the* Catalog *and since the previous issue of the* Review. *Unlike the book, the magazine prints negative reviews. Unlike the book, the magazine is all color. Like the book, unlike other computer magazines, there is no advertising. Editor is Art Kleiner.*

*To order:*

*$18/year (four issues)*

*Whole Earth Software Review
P.O. Box 27956
San Diego, CA 92128*

*Phone orders with VISA or MasterCard: 800/354-8400.*

## "or COMPUTER LITERACY"

You'll find that phrase in the "access" part of book reviews. As a service to readers, all the books recommended in the **Catalog** are available by mail order from COMPUTER LITERACY BOOKSHOP, 520 Lawrence Expressway, Suite 310, Sunnyvale, CA 94086—the first (is it still the only?) all-computer-book bookstore in the land. See p. 201 for details. Point has no financial connection to Computer Literacy.

## STAFF

| | |
|---|---|
| **Editor in Chief** | Stewart Brand |
| **Editor and Research Director** | Barbara Robertson |
| **Managing Editor** | Matthew McClure |
| **Design and Production** | Dustin Kahn, San Francisco |
| **Production Assistants** | Karla Fung |
| | Barbara Gildea |
| | Walter Lynam |
| **Research Librarian** | Kathryn Parks |
| **Research Staff** | Clifford Figallo |
| | James Stockford |
| | Lyn Gray |
| | Karen Hamilton |
| **Research Assistants** | Anita Figallo |
| | Hank Roberts |
| | Cindy Craig |
| | Levi Thomas |
| **Domain Editors** | Tony and Robbie Fanning |
| | Rik Jadrnicek |
| | Art Kleiner |
| | Steven Levy |
| | Aaron S. (Woody) Liswood |
| | Marsha Mather-Thrift |
| | Sharon Rufener |
| | Robert Scarola |
| | Gerald M. Weinberg |
| **Contributing Editors** | Richard Dalton |
| | Charles Spezzano |
| | Dr. Dobb's Journal |
| **Production Liaison** | Elisabeth Folsom |
| **Line Editor** | Suzanne Lipsett |
| **Proofreading** | Hank Roberts |
| | Charles Sweet |
| | Susan Erkel Ryan |
| **Cover Design** | Rebecca Wilson |
| **Logo and Calligraphy** | John Proctianni |
| **Camera** | Don Ryan |
| **Office Manager** | Lyn Gray |
| **General Purpose Clerk** | Dick Fugett |
| **Doubleday Editor** | Philip Pachoda |
| **Literary Agent** | John Brockman Associates |
| **Printing** | Typesetting: Mackenzie-Harris Corporation, San Francisco |
| | Color Separations: Concept Color, Inc., Salt Lake City |
| | Film Production: Lithographic Consultants, San Francisco |

# SHOPPING
## TECHNIQUES OF SEARCH, EVALUATION, USE

STEWART BRAND: Software is a new enough kind of thing in the world that humans are still figuring out how to deal with it. Though it can be bought and sold, you can't see, hear, touch, taste, smell, eat, or burn it. On an unlovely flat artifact called a disk may be hidden the concentrated intelligence of thousands of hours of design, for which you are expected to pay hundreds of dollars, and which you can reproduce on your own computer with perfect fidelity in less than a minute, free.

Personal computers have an inherent outlaw element. This makes them enjoyable and creative and morally interesting. More on that in a moment.

All software does is manage symbols. Unlike letters and numbers on paper, the symbols reside in a marvelously fluid zero gravity noplace, where they dance with impeccable precision to your tune. Software articulates your intentions faithfully, but it eludes understanding. We treat the stuff (it isn't stuff) as if programs were just like the how-to books our **Whole Earth Catalog**s have been dealing in for years. They provide technique. They can transform lives. They sell cheap or dear. Some are better than others. This entire book is about finding the better ones.

Is shopping really worth the trouble? There are some 40,000 commercial programs for personal computers on the market, and they all work. Why not just grab the handiest and proceed? Because software, when it is used at all intensely, comes to feel like an extension of your nervous system. Its habits become your habits. The reason the term "personal" got stuck to these machines is, they become part of your person. Buyer beware.

### Strategies of shopping

**Acquire as little software as you can get by with, and stick with it.** That's hardware critic Richard Dalton's advice. It's easy to get so caught up in the constant onrush of improvements and "next generations" in the software market that you wind up forever getting ready to work instead of working. You can buy last year's computer cheap, get last year's software, which runs beautifully on it by now, take the month to get fully running with it, and then turn your back on the market for a couple years. Your system will pay for itself shortly, the rest is pure profit, and you're spared a world of distraction and itchiness.

**Buy the best.** That's Analyzing domain editor Woody Liswood's advice. "Get the top-of-the-line program in whatever area you are going to do work. If you don't, you will always wish you had and will eventually spend the extra money to get it anyway. If you are trying to solve a problem, buy the solution. Period." Take a look at Gerald Weinberg's analysis on p. 7. The price of a program, even if it's many hundreds of dollars, may be the least of your costs. A poor program for your purposes, which may or may not be cheap, will escalate the secondary costs, entangle you in its deficiencies, and can easily put you out of business. By contrast, the pleasure of driving a top program is as rich as driving a hot new car, at a fraction the price, and to greater effect.

**Use what your cohorts use.** If you have colleagues and they already have computers, you'd best blend into their system. It may well be, groan, WORDSTAR (p. 56) and DBASE II (p. 85), but the fact is, you'll be using each other's programs and files, and if you have an odd system you'll either be constantly translating or simply failing to communicate. The advantage of a group standard is the abundance of lore and sagacity about it that will have accumulated, saving you no end of lone bafflement.

**Base your hardware decision on your software decisions.** That's the conventional wisdom, but it's wise anyway. When users hear about a new computer, they ask, "What runs on it?" When they hear about a new program, they ask, "What's it run on?" No machine runs everything or even a majority of what's available. Check our Hardware section, p. 14, for the basic ultimate decision you'll have to make; then peruse the rest of the book for the programs that best meet your needs and budget, see what machines they run on, and return to p. 14 and your fate. That loop may be one of the best uses of this book.

### Criteria of software excellence

**Good software does an important job well.** The fundamental consideration when you're putting out this kind of money.

**Good software is transparent.** The term and idea emerged during our research on word processing programs, but it applies to all. Arthur Naiman, author of **Introduction to WordStar** (p. 57), said it best: "The writing tool I always dreamed of was one which would take my thoughts right out of my skull and put them on paper. The better a word processing system is, the closer it comes to this ideal. Thus the quality I look for most is **transparency**. By that I mean that the word processing program (and hardware) intrude as little as possible between you and your thoughts.

If I had to make a formula for transparency, I suppose it would look something like this:

$$\frac{power \times ease\ of\ use - fatal\ errors}{time\ required\ to\ get\ comfortable} = \text{``transparency.''}$$

In Naiman's formula "power" means the range of the program's capabilities—often called "features." "Fatal errors" don't hurt you or the machine; they may eat all or part of a document you're working on, which leads to swearing, repeated work, and distrust.

**Good software is structured like an onion.** Richard Dalton: "The ideal program is layered—simple and self-evident on the outside, with all the features anyone needs, but you can also dig into the program for progressively more complex layers." Most complex programs are horrors to learn—DBASE II (p. 85) is a classic. Most simple programs have no depth—PFS: WRITE (p. 54) comes to mind. The great programs have both simplicity and complexity—MICROSOFT WORD (p. 60), 1-2-3 (p. 67), and MACPAINT (p. 127) are examples in that direction. Programs should be like those Russian imperial Easter eggs by Fabergé, with the exquisite jeweled landscapes you peek into—attractive on the outside, magnificent within.

***Good software blends well with other software.*** You can't invite most software to the same party. If they speak to each other at all, they fight. Ideally, all of your "applications" software—writing, analyzing, organizing, accounting, managing, drawing, telecommunicating, and programming—would speak the same language and welcome interaction. They would be "command compatible" and "file compatible"—they would respond to the same instructions from you, and they could work comfortably with each other's documents. This is the great attraction of the "integrateds" like SYMPHONY (p. 111) and FRAMEWORK (p. 110), where a handful of applications are all in one program, but beware what Organizing domain editor Tony Fanning calls "the Decathlon effect"—"one function is done very well, and the others, usually including the data management function, are just fair." The **Whole Earth Software Catalog** gives extra points to programs whose files are in industry-standard formats so they're companionable with other companies' programs.

***Good software is well supported.*** "Support" refers to the cloud of information and other products around a program that give it a rich working context in the world. Some comes from the company's conscientiousness, some from the program's popularity. Good support: lots of machines run the program; lots of other programs will work with it; there are whole books on special applications; the program is routinely upgraded; and the company responds helpfully to users with problems. A typical spectrum of company support: users who call the makers of WORD PERFECT (p. 60) for help with a problem get thorough, friendly treatment; from the makers of MICROSOFT WORD (p. 60) they get indifferent treatment; from the makers of WORDSTAR (p. 56), no help at all—MicroPro won't take the call.

***Good software is not copy-protected.*** That's a somewhat controversial position on a highly controversial subject. Many manufacturers try to discourage "piracy" (wholesale copying) of their software by various protective devices. Fine. The problem is, if the users can't copy all or parts of the program easily within their own working environments, the tool is much less adaptable. Another vulnerability and another nuisance factor is added to a situation already chancy and problematic. Software is inherently a communication medium; sharing software is part of that. Buddhists talk about "Right Speech," "Right Livelihood," etc. We think there's a reasonable practice of "Right Copying," the Dave Smith Doctrine, which goes like this: "I've received copied software from friends. Most I played with for an hour or two, then erased. But in the cases of VOLKSWRITER, 1-2-3, DBASE II, and PROKEY, after trying them extensively and deciding that they would be useful on a continuing basis, I purchased them from a dealer." Smith is president of Smith & Hawken Tool Company. His approach, if widely enough taken, encourages manufacturers who don't copy-protect, thereby helping the user population, and satisfies both convenience and conscience.

***Good software is reasonably priced.*** Most isn't. Most spelling checkers cost upwards of $125. The best one—WORD PROOF (p. 62)—costs $60. Most word processors cost $300-600. One of the best—PC WRITE (p. 59)—costs $10. Because the prices are kept up by confusion in the marketplace, prices of software

will come down only when careful shoppers drive them down—it's already under way. Meantime, check out discount mail order, p. 23, and public domain (free) software, p. 25 and p. 202.

### Post-purchase advice

***Send in the warranty card.*** If it's a machine, you may well need the service. If it's software, the manufacturer will keep you informed of updates and offer very good exchange deals ($10-200) for new versions, which you should get. You already know the program, and it knows you; new versions won't violate that, they'll reward your loyalty.

***Never fight a problem in the system for more than an hour without making a phone call.*** First call the friend who has a system like yours. Then call the dealer who sold you the thing that isn't working. Then call the software company. Then call the hardware company. New systems don't work—especially if there's a printer or modem involved. It's not your fault. It's theirs; your responsibilty is to hold their nose to the fire until they fix your problem. Be of good cheer—systems work beautifully eventually, and you'll learn a lot that's useful getting there.

***The secret to succeeding with computers is to futz with them.*** BART EISENBERG: Push buttons, move text, insert lines, hit control characters, add dot commands, bring up menus, invoke commands and invoke more of them. Try it backwards, try it sideways, try it upside down. The method, if you can call it that, is vaguely scientific—in that you perform some action and observe the results. A playful attitude will get you further with these machines than weeks of serious endeavor.

***Join a user group for your machine.*** KEVIN KELLY: One of the most unreported grassroot phenomena in America must be computer user groups. I estimate there are at least 2,000 groups meeting right now. Each one serves a small regional area, composed of members in love with all microcomputers or only one brand. Despite the absence of a national association or newsletter, the groups have arisen independently in a similar form all across the country. There is a remarkable agreement of intent, purpose and style. Using our user group in Atlanta as an example, we meet once a month to discuss technical problems, flag new products, swap software, gossip, and co-op buy items like disks. We put out a monthly newsletter. Being more organized than many, we may ask experts or vendors to speak at the meetings. The chief purpose really is to fill the vacuum of information left by the rocketing advance of microcomputers—machines and software arriving light-years ahead of their instructions. User groups are the guiding hands across this stellar gap. The user groups also stepped into another vacuum—software review. Ollie asks if anyone has tried out any new software lately, and Andy gets up and says he's tried SCREENWRITER and it stinks. Well, SCREENWRITER has just lost 126 buyers right off the bat in northeast Georgia. More if you count the trickle effect. If the same number of people showed up for, say, peace or politics, with as much regularity, devotion, interest, and influence as they bring to user groups, they'd be running the country.

## THE PERSONAL COMPUTER BOOK

*The Personal Computer Book*; Peter McWilliams; rev. ed., 1984; 299 pp.; $9.95; Quantum Press/Doubleday & Co., Inc., 501 Franklin Avenue, Garden City, NY 11530; 516/294-4400: or COMPUTER LITERACY.

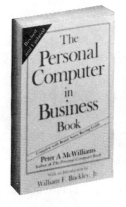

## THE PERSONAL COMPUTER IN BUSINESS BOOK

*The Personal Computer in Business Book*; Peter McWilliams; rev. ed., 1984; 299 pp.; $9.95; Quantum Press/Doubleday & Co., Inc., 501 Franklin Avenue, Garden City, NY 11530; 516/294-4400; or COMPUTER LITERACY.

## HOW TO BUY SOFTWARE

*How to Buy Software*; Alfred Glossbrenner; 1984; 648 pp.; $14.95; St. Martin's Press, 175 Fifth Avenue, New York, NY 10010; 212/674-5151; or COMPUTER LITERACY.

STEWART BRAND: These stand head, shoulders, and torso above the competition as introductory computer books. Peter McWilliams' two **Personal Computer** books because they are irreverent, accessible, current, and full of clear explanations and frequent sharp advice. Alfred Glossbrenner's **How to Buy Software** because it is the definitive text—the book we most strongly recommend as supplement to the **Whole Earth Software Catalog**. Everyone in our office uses it.

The McWilliams books are a publishing success story. Self-published until these October '84 editions from Doubleday, they were frequently updated and far more personal, funny, and judgemental of products than is the New York norm, and they sold like crazy. These editions, Peter's last, are completely revised with a full 100 pages more than before, which caught the new publisher by surprise and makes the cover price a bargain.

By way of update Doubleday will publish **The Peter McWilliams Personal Computer Buying Guide** in Spring, '85. Peter's final computer book is the one he's proudest of, and justifiably—**Computers and the Disabled** (1984; $9.95; Quantum Press, Doubleday & Company, Inc., 501 Franklin Ave., Garden City, NY 11530; 516/294-4561; or COMPUTER LITERACY). America has 36 million disabled. Most of them will find personal computers to be wonderfully enabling tools and this book a joy. For McWilliams' word on word processing, see p. 48.

Glossbrenner's amazing book has the best explanation I've seen anywhere of how personal computers work, put strictly in terms of a *shopper's* perspective. Dense with good information, the book is big and comprehensive but never heavy. Its rich sprinkling of tidbits and tips keeps you turning the pages looking for more. The book is divided, like ours, into chapters on each kind of software. The shopping advice is sound enough and general enough that it's surprisingly up to date for an early 1984 book. For Glossbrenner on public domain software, see p. 25; on telecommunicating, p. 140.

### Other books

The Book Company annually does **The Book of IBM Software 1985**, **The Book of Apple Software 1985**, **The Book of Atari Software 1985** (each $19.95; Arrays, Inc./The Book Division, 11223 So. Hindry Avenue, Los Angeles, CA 90045; 213/410-9466; or COMPUTER LITERACY) which have good evaluative comments on a fair range of programs. I wanted to review the brand new **Omni Complete Catalog of Software and Accessories** and **Omni Complete Catalog of Hardware and Peripherals** (each $12.95 from Macmillan Publishing Co., Inc., 866 Third Ave., New York, NY 10022; 212/935-2000; or COMPUTER LITERACY) but the publisher refused to let me see galleys, so all I can do is tell you about them and hope they're as good as the **Omni Online Database Directory** reviewed on p. 143.

---

*The purchase price of the program is probably the smallest expense . . .*

## HOW COMPUTER PROFESSIONALS BUY SOFTWARE

GERALD M. WEINBERG: Once upon a time, I wanted to be a high school track star. Fortunately, only one other kid in the school was *willing* to run as far as a mile, so I was assured a place on the team even though I couldn't run very fast. All the same, I often earned a medal in dual meets because the other schools were in the same situation—they had one good miler,

like my teammate, and one turkey. My strategy was to let *their* turkey trot himself out trying to keep up with the two leaders. At the three-quarter mark, I would usually pass him as he lay puking on the inside lane.

Track has come a long way in 35 years. In my day, girls weren't allowed to run a mile. Today, Eagle Junior High School has at least ten girls who can beat my lifetime personal best. In today's improved environment, my method of making the team simply doesn't work. And it's the same in software. When Apples first fell off the tree in the Garden of Eden, any software that could run a mile could make the team. Today, there may be a hundred packages that can go the distance, so we need more sophisticated selection methods.

Perhaps we can use the packaging as a criterion: Does he look like a miler? Does it look like a slick spreadsheet? Well, my running shirt says "Sub-4,"—under four minutes—but that's my time for the *half*-mile, so you know you can't believe what it says on the package. Perhaps we can use a trial run at the computer store? We haven't room to let him run, but look how well he lifts weights! No, we've all fallen for that one, too. There's really no alternative: To pick winners with any consistency, buyers have to learn sophisticated evaluation methods.

In my work consulting with large data processing organizations, I recommend a multistep selection method based largely on the work of Tom Gilb and Ken Orr. I use exactly the same method when selecting software for our little office, so I believe just about anyone can use it. The method resembles the way you'd produce a winning miler, and has four major steps: PREPARATION, MEASURING HEALTH, MEASURING FITNESS, and TRAINING.

## Preparation

The preparation step encompasses all the work you do before you even look at the candidates. Preparation itself has three substeps: define objectives, estimate investment, and budget for the decision.

Objectives—what you expect the software to accomplish—have to come first. If you don't know what you want, how can you hope to get it?

Of course, you might be lucky. The people who produced the package surely know your needs, don't they? They don't, but you still have another out, something psychologists call "cognitive dissonance." You may fall in love with your stupid purchase in order not to feel stupid. Cognitive dissonance lets you love *anything* you buy. If the product causes you immeasurable pain, you'll probably boast, "No pain, no gain."

If you're not into pain, though, try defining your problem before you start shopping for software solutions. Start with a general list of objectives, which you will later refine into more quantitative form.

The next step is to estimate your investment. A list of investment factors should look like this:

| | |
|---|---|
| Training | $_____ |
| Lifetime | _____ |
| Usage | _____ |
| Maintenance | _____ |
| The package | _____ |
| In-conversion | _____ |
| Out-conversion | _____ |
| Real Cost | $_____ |

On this list, *training* is the cost of preparing people in your firm to use the new software, and you must not forget those people who aren't yet around. To estimate complete training costs, then, you must estimate the next factor—*lifetime*, or how long you will use the package before replacing it. You'll also need to know the lifetime to estimate usage and maintenance investments. *Usage* is the cost of labor, space and supplies needed to operate the system. *Maintenance* is the cost of keeping it running—fixing bugs or working around them, installing new versions, or supplying enhancements to get exactly what you want.

Like the cost of the package, *in-conversion* is a one-time cost, independent of lifetime. In-conversion is the cost of changing over from your present system—reformatting your existing data files, for example, or modifying your operating system. *Out-conversion* is the cost of getting rid of the package when you go on to something bigger and better. Out-conversion can cost 100 times the initial package cost, as when you replace one programming language with a different version, or when you have accumulated hundreds of files that have to be translated.

When my office recently changed its word-processing software, these costs broke down roughly as follows:

| | |
|---|---|
| The package | $50-500 x 4 copies |
| Lifetime | 2 years |
| Training | 40 hours per person x 4 people |
| Usage | 20 hours per week per person (no difference in supplies) |
| Maintenance | 2 hours per week for one person |
| In-conversion | From $0 to cost of rekeying all files |
| Out-conversion | From $0 to cost of rekeying all files |

A hobbyist might set the labor cost at zero, making the package cost the only factor, but we're in business and have to put a price on our labor. Even at $10 per hour, the usage cost over a two-year lifetime would dominate all others; ultimately, according to the estimate, we'd wind up investing close to $100,000 in this word processor. The point of making such an estimate up front is not to be exact, but to gain a sense of what we're deciding and what alternatives we have. Given the above figures, a more efficient package that would save one hour per week per person would be worth at least $7,000. Therefore, our estimate tells us we can afford to consider rather "expensive" software that a hobbyist might not be able to justify.

The estimate also indicates the size of the decision we face. As a rule of thumb, I always budget 2 per cent of the estimated total cost for the decision process, and thus would be willing to invest several thousand dollars in making this choice. Without the estimate as a guide, this might seem an unreasonable amount to spend in deciding on one package. The hobbyist might allocate an equivalent amount of personal labor, but almost nothing in terms of out-of-pocket cost.

On the other hand, without the estimate as a guide, we might waste too much time on a decision. In certain circumstances—for example, when we needed a package that would be used sparingly by only one person for a limited time—it would be cheaper to buy the first satisfactory product that came to our attention. The estimate itself can usually be made with sufficient accuracy in fifteen minutes.

## Measuring Health

If only a few people can run a mile, each can be considered in some detail, but if many can, efficiency demands some initial qualifying heats. The same is true for packages. Where there are many candidates, I allocate about half the decision budget for eliminating the unhealthy, leaving half for picking the fittest from among the few remaining.

(continued on p. 8)

(continued from p. 7)

By "unhealthy" I mean "doesn't meet my objectives." For example, if I need a database manager that can handle multiple-disk files, I can immediately eliminate those that cannot. I won't be swayed by a sales pitch claiming "three times the speed"—what good is fast access if it can't handle my whole file? To avoid this kind of trouble at the point of purchase, potential buyers need to distinguish between functions and attributes. Functions are things the software *must* have; the question to ask here is "Yes or no?" (Is it there or isn't it?) Attributes are things it would be *nice* to have; the relevant question here is "How much does it cost?" It's obvious from this distinction why we look first at functions, then at attributes. If we're looking for triathletes (swim, bike and run), then we're not impressed by the marathon times of nonswimmers. As John von Neumann once put it, "There's no sense being precise about something if you don't even know what you're talking about."

In your search for office automation software, you might need such functions as: *Maintain* manuscript files; *Produce* printed manuscripts; and *Transmit* electronic manuscripts. So when you examine particular packages, you need to determine whether these functions are present or absent. Go down your list of specifications and ask "Yes or no?" for each one. If you need to, you can break down each of your specifications into necessary subfunctions. For instance, you might break down *Produce* printed manuscripts into: *Number* pages; *Extract* table of contents; *Print* letter quality; and *Provide* math symbols. Someone else might require line drawings but not math symbols. Only by successively and explicitly refining your own objectives will you avoid buying a package that perfectly fits someone else's needs.

Here are three universal standards that should head your list of objectives:
1. It must work.
2. It must work in your environment.
3. It must work in your environment tomorrow.

If you can't get "yes" answers to these three questions, asking about specific functions won't make much difference.

This may seem ridiculous, but I assure you it is not. I recently spent $25 for a financial application to work on my Commodore 8096. At that price, I couldn't afford too much investigation. The program was advertised to work with disk systems, but it came on a cassette. When I wrote to complain, the company replied that "all you have to do is transfer it from cassette to disk." When I wrote again to say that I didn't have a cassette drive, they wrote to say that I should "get someone in the neighborhood with a cassette drive to do it." My only neighbors are cows, and the nearest cassette-equipped 8096 is 60 miles away.

### Cheap Tests for Trouble

Nevertheless, I eventually did get the cassette transcribed (my in-conversion cost now exceeded the purchase price). The program never worked on disk, however, and an examination of the source code showed that it never *could* have worked with a disk system. In retrospect, of course, I should have dropped it the minute I learned what "works with disk systems" meant to the producer. Even if I had written off my $25 at that point and thrown the program away, I would have been way ahead of where I finally wound up after transcribing the tape.

If you're looking for a miler, you don't want someone who can't climb a flight of stairs without pausing for breath. Until there are enforced industry standards for software, you need to look out for quick signs of serious trouble. To start with, when a package doesn't install as advertised, send it back immediately for a refund—there are bound to be other faults.

Next, inspect all available written material for poor quality—a sure sign of danger. Errors in a product are like cockroaches in a kitchen—there's never just one, and they're never all in the same drawer. I recently received a mail advertisement for a spelling corrector. The ad contained two spelling errors. Three months later, the company folded. A friend of mine bought a statistical package. The manual contained an example giving the population distribution of various counties by sex and income. In one of the counties the distribution was 75 per cent males and 88 per cent females. The program was of the same quality.

Put prospective dealers to the test. If they can't refer you to actual users, look for another package—unless your objective is to be a software pioneer, complete with arrows in your back. If you get referrals from a dealer and discover that these buyers don't use the package, back off! But if they're using it and say they don't *like* it, don't be overly disturbed. At least they're using it. Ask them what specifically they don't like. You might not even be interested in those features.

Remember, too, that the software must *continue* to work in your environment, which is largely a function of the quality of the dealer. If your dealer doesn't answer calls, find another dealer. Dealers who won't respond to a sales prospect will never respond to a request for service. You can test dealers further by calling and pretending that you have already purchased the package but are having some difficulty. If they aren't helpful and courteous, look elsewhere. Also look for another dealer if you can't try out the system in the store, or if they don't seem to have a manual around for you to read. Finally, avoid any dealer who answers your questions by slapping you on the back and saying, "No problem!"

### Measuring Fitness

Once you have eliminated the candidates that can't run the distance, or are likely to have a stroke trying, you might find yourself with one or zero remaining packages. In that case, the decision-making process is essentially over. If you still have two or more packages to choose from, you can then begin to measure fitness by checking attributes. Generally, you can assess attributes with respect to three distinct variables: resources, satisfaction and lifetime. Resources are what the attribute will cost you—in money, time, people, space and supplies. Satisfaction is what you will get out of it—ease of use, performance, security, pleasure, inspiration, pride. Lifetime is how long the attribute will continue to yield the satisfaction your resources have bought—correctability, modifiability, portability, scope of application.

When you have written down the various attributes, you can use Tom Gilb's Mecca Method to measure the fitness of each candidate. First you attach a *metric* to each attribute. The figure shows a simplified example of three metrics you might assign to the attributes of an accounts receivable system. Each attribute is reduced here to specific quantitative measures. If you can't produce such a measure, then you don't have an attribute. Sometimes assigning a number value is difficult, but in those cases you'll always learn something important from the effort. For instance, "reliability" sounds nice in any system, but unless you translate it into something measurable, you'll be a sucker for the first smooth sales pitch.

| ATTRIBUTE | METRIC | GOAL | PERFORMANCE | GRADE | % WEIGHT | G×W |
|-----------|--------|------|-------------|-------|----------|-----|
| RELIABILITY | ERRORS TO CLIENT /INVOICES | 1/5000 | 1/1000 | .40 | 30 | .12 |
| COST | $$/INVOICES | 0.90 | .93 | .95 | 50 | .475 |
| PERFORMANCE | RESPONSE SECS / % ACHIEVED ( UNDER MAX-LOAD) | 2/95 | 2/90 | .75 | 20 | .15 |

overall grade = .745

Once you have the metrics, you must set a goal and assign a weight to each attribute to show what will be satisfactory and how important it is to you. Again, trying to assign these goals and weights will tend to expose your unstated—and thus dangerous—assumptions.

Once you're finished, you are ready to examine the actual candidates, making a score sheet for each. Take the grade sheet with you when you talk to a salesperson or to your friends and *use it as a checklist*. The sheet will keep you from being swayed by others' enthusiasm and from forgetting something important. Translating everything into numbers tends to bring blue-sky talkers down to earth. If you can't get the information to fill in your grade sheet, don't buy the package.

Each grade sheet will yield an overall score for its package. Use good sense in interpreting these scores. The difference between .745 and .750 cannot truly be significant in light of the rough nature of the calculations. If the packages are this close, you can flip a coin, or choose the one in the shiny box. But where the scores are, say, .49 and .75, the package with .49 will probably be much less satisfactory than the other. Still, never go against your instincts. If you're still inclined to buy the .49, even after you've compared the scores, it would be a good idea to reexamine your application of the Mecca Method. The package you favor might have an important attribute that you haven't identified explicitly, or perhaps one of its attributes is more important to you than you realized. Repeat the method as many times as necessary to get a good feeling about your decision, dropping out obvious losers each time. At the very least, each repetition will give you a better understanding of yourself, which is always worth the time invested.

## Training

Once you've chosen your potential champion, you've begun your relationship with the package. Choosing is not the same as purchasing, and you can often make up deficiencies in the package by negotiating with the vendor. In such a situation, the grade sheet can guide the negotiation by showing correctable weak spots. A friend of mine wanted a word processor whose spelling corrector graded low on speed. After seeing the grade sheet, the dealer tossed in a free stand-alone corrector. Another friend narrowed down her choice to two accounting packages that graded dead even. Using the grade sheets, she showed each dealer what he would have to do to raise his product's grade. In the end, she got a smart keyboard at half price to overcome one package's problems with keyed control sequences.

Even after making the purchase, you're still far from finished. Using a new package is very much like taking up running. Champions are made, not born, and the road to championship goes through four clearly identifiable stages: pain, stumbling, romance and realism.

In the pain stage, the package will seem impossible to use. You might need a lot of help from the vendor, who could suddenly be hard to find. Remember that only 2 per cent of your estimated cost was dedicated to the choice. Before long, your investment in the vendor's system will be a hundred times greater than the vendor's investment in *your* system. You can avoid a great deal of pain if you negotiate a 30-day money-back guarantee, giving the vendor an incentive to help you reach the stumbling stage.

In the stumbling stage, usage will be clumsy and inefficient, but you will probably have surpassed your vendor's knowledge. Now is the time to get in touch with other users. One good user group is worth fifty poor manuals. Other users can teach you about those obscure features you skipped when reading the manual—or that aren't even in the manual. A few minutes of discussion can save you many hours of work. Even so, you should now read the manual a second time, and a third. You may even begin to appreciate it, which is a sure sign you're falling in love with the package.

In the romance stage, you'll believe the package is the Olympic Games, and you are the gold medalist. Prospective buyers looking for information should steer clear of users in the romance stage. They can be identified by their inability to give any rational reply to the question, "What *won't* it do?" Most package users never graduate from the romance stage, because they are unable to overcome the power of cognitive dissonance. Who cares what it costs, as long as you *feel* like a champion?

To realize the full payoff on your investment, you must be able to identify specific shortcomings of the package for specific jobs. When you've reached this stage, that of realism, you've become the ideal referral for prospective buyers. You can help fill out *their* grade sheets, to find a package that meets *their* objectives. In fact, you'll be ready then to retire from racing and start coaching. Or to start looking for a replacement package of your own.

## MITHRIDATIC COMPUTER MAGAZINES

*Mithridatism—Tolerance for a poison acquired by taking gradually larger doses of it.— mithridatic.*
**The American Heritage Dictionary**

*Computer magazines are mithridatic. You always start with one, build up to doses which would kill a beginner, and probably end up immune to all of them. —Tony Fanning*

STEWART BRAND: Welcome to a field where the magazines are more important than the books. (Check p. 202 for indexes of each.) Books serve well for whole overviews (like this one, hopefully, and the ones on p. 6) and for specialized use (the likes of **RS-232 Made Easy**—p. 156), but books by themselves, including this one, are simply too out of date, and books don't *teach* as well as magazines do. Magazines give you the seething marketplace (some publications too heavy to read in bed because of their weight of advertising) and the voices of confusion and reassurance of users and reviewers and ware designers soft and hard. You can study a book; you wade into magazines.

At last count there were over 200 magazines about personal computers available via newsstand, hundreds more available by mail. A unique moment in magazine history, which will not last. Computer scientist Alan Kay notes that a new technology like this passes through phases—from novelty, to service, to appliance. "Oh boy," contemplates Art Kleiner, editor of our **Whole Earth Software Review**, "**Refrigerator Quarterly**."

All of the Domain Editors studied software reviews collected for them from dozens of periodicals and immersed themselves in the detailed market-watching that goes with trying to anticipate your situation and opportunities in the winter of '84-'85. The magazines reviewed here are ones that served us best and should do the same for you. Many of us have worked for and will work for various of these publications, so bear in mind that our judgement may be too intimate. We're reviewing our relatives, with relish.

*The industry, with glee . . .*

## INFOWORLD

**$31/yr (weekly); InfoWorld, 375 Cochituate Road, Framingham, MA 01701; 800/343-6474 or, in MA, 617/879-0700.**

STEWART BRAND: Our favorite, the source of the most conversation that begins, "Didja see in . . . ?"

ALFRED LEE: Two years ago I took a break from an accumulating burden of personal paperwork to drive across the continent with my family. I had already begun to suppose that a personal computer might help me fight my way out of the paper, and the long trip included trance-like stretches (e.g., Kansas) when I thought about all the wonderful things a computer at home might do for me. When we got back to New Jersey, my first trip to a computer store taught me in five minutes that I had no business out on the street with a credit card in my state of ignorance.

That same day I saw the tabloid **InfoWorld** perched between **Rolling Stone** and **Penthouse** at the local tobacconist. It changed my life.

At my level of experience, then and now, the breezy daily-newspaper style trivializes the subject matter, which is what I need. Makes me feel like I can hack it. At first I'd buy it at the tobacconist's whenever the cover motivated me, then every week just to read John C. Dvorak's column, then I subscribed. What I like best about Dvorak is that he walks over clichés as if over water, keeping his feet dry by **boldfacing the clichés**.

The news notes are compressed enough that I can get a feeling for microcomputer trends by osmosis. The weekly "theme" was more instructive when I was greenhorn than now. The reviews aren't more timely, descriptive, or reliable than in the monthlies, but four issues cover more new products than any four monthlies.

Few if any issues are "exciting," in the way a single issue of **Byte** or **PC Magazine** can hit several different topics that interest me. It's more lovable than great; I crawl into bed with it for two or three hours every week, then count the days until it comes round again. Reading **InfoWorld** was the first step I took toward mechanizing my professional life, and it's still an instructive hobby, still a serial guidebook to the industry.

DARRELL ICENOGLE: Even those who hate it read it. It captures the spirit of the fast-moving industry better than any other mag.

TONY FANNING: **InfoWorld** and **PC Week** are great! It's wonderful not being tied to the normal 3-4 month lead time which monthlies can't avoid. I like the sense of
A C C E L E R A T I O N  a weekly gives.

CHARLES SPEZZANO: The reviews in **InfoWorld** are too inaccurate too often for me to know when to take them seriously.

STEWART BRAND: The problem with the reviews, as with nearly all computer magazines, is that they're not comparative enough. Something will get blasted or praised strictly in its own terms; you can't tell if the reviewer has any experience with competing products. **InfoWorld** reviews are long and searching and cover hardware as well as soft, but you have to read carefully between the lines to get full value.

*Technical authority . . .*

## BYTE

**$21/yr (12 issues); Byte, P.O. Box 590, Martinsville, NJ 08836; 800/258-5485.**

BARBARA ROBERTSON: It covers the microcomputer field—particularly innovations—in depth. Technically accurate and objective, it's part of the history and well aware of the responsibility this implies.

STEWART BRAND: Barbara was a West Coast Editor of **Byte** before she came to Whole Earth. The magazine is for the profession, by the profession; many of the contributors are in the industry. No computer magazine has better covers or better cover stories behind them on the major trends in the business. Nobody has more immediate and thorough coverage of new machines. **Byte**'s long interview with the design team of the Macintosh was the best thing I saw anywhere on that machine, when everybody was covering it. Software coverage is techie—interesting but less useful to the buyer than others, and often late in the game. The controversial columnist here is science fiction writer Jerry Pournelle, whose writing is regarded by Tony Fanning as a "truly irritating extended advertisement for himself, his family, and his friends who just *happen* to be business associates."

*Everything for everybody . . .*

## POPULAR COMPUTING

$15/yr (12 issues); Popular Computing, P.O. Box 307, Martinsville, NJ 08836; 800/258-5485.

STEWART BRAND: In the shoot-out for top general computer magazine we prefer **Popular Computing** over the equally popular **Personal Computing**. The range, the carefulness, the writing quality, the general usefulness look consistently better to us, but a newcomer to the field may want both for a while, just to get up to speed. The magazine covers both home and business—large home, small business, you might say. The reviews tend to lack tooth.

*Binding the generations . . .*

## FAMILY COMPUTING

$17.47/yr (12 issues); Scholastic, Inc., P.O. Box 2512, Boulder, CO 80321.

STEWART BRAND: For me the tiredest question in the business is, "What use do computers have in the home?" Every month this magazine comes up with 100 pages or so of answer—stuff for the kids, stuff for home business, and home application goodies from party planning to cooking to home finance. It has brief but useful product reviews. If your family is unsure about whether getting a computer is worth the cost and nuisance, watch this magazine for a couple months and see if you're enticed. My hunch is that TVs divide the family somewhat, while computers connect it somewhat, since both kid and grownup may be equal beginners. But beware the resentment of anyone left out (many a wife, many a daughter, I am told).

*Kid power . . .*

## ENTER

$12.95/yr (10 issues); Children's Television Workshop, One Disk Drive, P.O. Box 2685, Boulder, CO 80322.

## K-POWER

$15.97/yr (7 issues); Scholastic, Inc., P.O. Box 2511, Boulder, CO 80322.

STEWART BRAND: For pre-teens and teens. Nice names. **Enter** is a tad more junior and welcomes the very beginner. **K-Power** takes the young obsessive toward hackerdom with wit and savvy ("How Teen Tycoons Take Care of Business") and carries some of the best game reviews (also see **St.Game**, p. 29). Both print contributions by their youthful readers.

*The bazaar . . .*

## COMPUTER SHOPPER

$15/yr (12 issues); Patch Publishing Co., Inc., 407 S. Washington Ave., P.O. Box F, Titusville, FL 32781-9990; 800/327-9926 or, in FL, 305/269-3211.

ART KLEINER: The heart of this newsprint tabloid is classifieds—used computers, mail-order software—and listings—user's groups, bulletin boards, and meetings. Range, nationwide. Features are uneven, but they cover each major type of micro and pick up on low-cost and public domain news that most other magazines miss. I've come to feel affection for it in a gritty technical kind of way.

*The shameless . . .*

## WHOLE EARTH SOFTWARE REVIEW

$18/yr (4 issues); Whole Earth Software Review, P.O. Box 27956, San Diego, CA 92128; 800/321-3333 or, in CA, 800/354-8400.

STEWART BRAND: Talk about self-advertisement. Since there's no chance of objectivity reviewing our own magazine, I'll try only to describe where we fit in the computer magazine spectrum. The definitive elements are: no advertising, non-profit. That makes the magazine small (**TV Guide** size), intense, judgmental compared to others. In a field driven by marketing, the **Review** works at connecting users and design people directly. The only computer magazine with a you're-on-it-or-you-aren't product recommendation list. The only computer magazine with a major book attached. Possible drawbacks: quarterly, new (one year old).

*The establishment steps in . . .*

## TIME-LIFE ACCESS: IBM

**$48/yr (12 issues); Time-Life ACCESS: IBM, P.O. Box 5652, Chicago, IL 60680; 800/621-7026.**

## NEWSWEEK ACCESS

**Single copy free to *Newsweek* subscribers on request; $2.95/newsstand; $3.50 direct; Newsweek, Newsweek Building, P.O. Box 403, Livingston, NJ 07039; 800/631-1040; 800/526-2595 or, in NJ, 800/962-1201.**

STEWART BRAND: Heh heh heh. This review feels like putting a tarantula and a scorpion in the same jar to see what happens. The two heavyweight American newsweeklies separately decide to spin off computer magazines, and they're both called **Access**. One of the disadvantages of publishing in New York.

The Newsweek entry looks like a natural—a slicky devoted to personal technology (video, audio, high tech furniture of all sizes, especially computers). All we have in June '84 is the pilot issue with Apple's Steve Jobs on the cover, but since the thing already paid for itself with advertising, it seems likely to persist at least till America's electronic obsession passes its chic peak. The project is attracting solid young journalists, the writing and editing are excellent. The magazine may help put computers in their place—somewhere between the telephone and the car.

Time-Life's **Access: IBM** is one of those nicely designed newletters for the executive scanner. Good idea, since there's not much available for the lay corporate PC user who is fighting the decades-old hegemony of the Data Processing department and is getting no help from IBM, who owns the DP department. Also handy for the small business user, who is never going to have a DP department. Product reviews are short, pointed, and good. Tidbits of advice everywhere, such as "Never use a phone line equipped with the **call-waiting** feature. If you use a modem on such a line, you will be disconnected when you receive another call." A 15-minute read max. I like it and use it. No ads; that means they sell your name and address and proclivity to upscale mailing-list renters.

*White water rafting on your IBM PC compatible . . .*

## PC WEEK

**Free to qualified subscribers; $120/yr (52 issues); PC Week, 15 Crawford Street, Needham, MA 02194; 617/449-6520.**

RICHARD DALTON: More comprehensive and better written (surprisingly) than either **PC** or **PC WORLD** who both seem to be trying for the statesman position in the PC/MS-DOS segment. **PC Week** is closer to **InfoWorld**; the others looking to out-**Byte** each other. Not unimportantly, it's free to "qualified subscribers," which seems to be people with an interest in the subject and residual eyesight great enough to at least scan the pictures.

ART KLEINER: Particularly from the corporate perspective there's no more lively, timely lookout point from which to watch the ongoing avalanche of new IBM PC-compatible products. They're not afraid to publish gossip and dirty rumors.

*Everything for the IBM PC-compatible . . .*

## PC

*PC (The Independent Guide to IBM Personal Computers);* **$34.97/yr (12 issues); PC Magazine, P.O. Box 2445, Boulder, CO 80321.**

STEWART BRAND: A year or so after the introduction of the IBM PC computer, **PC Magazine** split in two over a management/ownership beef, and the aggrieved "good guys" went away and started **PC World**. After two years of head-to-head competition, they're both alive and well—**PC** the more so, in our opinion. **PC World** does good things, like lengthy negative reviews of SYMPHONY (p. 111), WORDVISION (p. 58), and THE LEADING EDGE WORD PROCESSOR when everybody else is patting them on the head, and it's New Age nice, but **PC** has more goods more often (biweekly instead of monthly) more translatable into direct use. You'll need a sturdy shelf for back issues; July 10, a lean month, is 412 pages. **PC** and **PC Week** have different staffs, same owners.

*The user's voice . . .*

## SOFTALK

**Free to new Apple owners; $24/yr (12 issues); Softalk, P.O. Box 7039, North Hollywood, CA 91605; 800/821-6231.**

## SOFTALK FOR THE IBM PERSONAL COMPUTER

**Free to new owners of IBM compatibles; $24/yr (12 issues); Softalk/IBM, P.O. Box 7040, North Hollywood, CA 91605; 800/821-6231.**

STEVEN LEVY: One of the first things I did when I got my Apple II+ was to send my machine's serial number to **Softalk** for a free subscription. Ever since, I've devoured the magazine every month. Its ads are the definitive updated catalog of Apple accessories and software. Its not-quite-definitive (but informative anyway) "Top Thirty" programs tells me what's hot, and the smart-ass commentary on who's up and what's down gives valuable perspective. Most of all, **Softalk** makes me feel part of a community of Apple owners. Even though my free subscription has long expired, I renew yearly, with cash and pleasure.

STEWART BRAND: There's a bushel of Apple magazines, but none inspire the breadth of loyalty of **Softalk**. It has that home-truth hobbyist flavor that invented the Apple in the first place and still continues to nurture the product and the company years and millions of dollars later.

When the IBM PC had been around for a while, **Softalk** did a separate magazine for it and got similar almost-hobbyist following. Charles Spezzano: "**Softalk** has been the most consistently informative about the PC market since it came out in June of 1982. It's the only one I save all the issues of." No awe, no hype, nice inquisitive tone, more messing with code than some are comfortable with. When Phoenix Software came out with a potentially earth-shaking legal full-PC-compatibility device, **Softalk** had the story complete, early, and quiet.

*The hacker's voice . . .*

## DR. DOBB'S JOURNAL

*Dr. Dobb's Journal (Software Tools for Advanced Programmers)*; $25/yr (12 issues); M & T Publishing, Inc., 2464 Embarcadero Way, Palo Alto, CA 94303; 415/424-0600.

THOMAS SPENCE: Where **InfoWorld** is my meat and potatoes, I find **Dr. Dobb's Journal** is my monthly visit to a trade show "hospitality suite." Some months it is chips and dip and a Coke while other months it is cracked crab, caviar, and champagne.

**Dr. Dobb's** is very much a "hacker's" magazine and makes no bones about it. Until this year contributors were not paid for their efforts. Even now submitted articles and programs are placed into the public domain.

Its focus is still primarily on the 8-bit CP/M world although there are a few articles each month on 16-bit machines. **Dr. Dobb's** seems to have its finger on the pulse of the proletariat of the computer world, in that the majority of computer users still use 8-bit machines. As the 16-bit computers become more and more widespread I'm sure **Dr. Dobb's** will be there gradually shifting its emphasis to the more powerful machines. This steady-handed approach in a computer magazine is a welcome relief from the blowin'-in-the-wind feeling I get from most other mags every time a new computer comes onto the market.

I will probably never trash-can my **Dr. Dobb's** back issues, because they make excellent reference materials. Being that I am a programmer (software engineer?) by trade, I find back issues invaluable for finding tricks-of-the-trade subroutines.

STEWART BRAND: Dr. Dobb himself, itself, reviews utility programs on our p. 173.

## FREE COMPUTER MAGAZINES

KEVIN KELLY: Instead of searching for the Ultimate Computer Magazine, I sift through a pool of everyday computer magazines that flood to my house for free. What I do is take up every offer for a free trial issue of a new computer magazine by punching out the tab on the card and mailing it back. As per their instructions, when the invoice comes I write CANCEL on it, and keep the first issue. Since the subscription agency is usually in Colorado somewhere, I'll more likely than not get a second or third issue mistakenly sent to me after that. In the meantime the magazine has sold my name with great rapidity to other hatching computer magazines, and in no time I have several computer magazines appearing in my mailbox weekly.

All different kinds: for business, for kids, for publishers, for accountants, for schools, for librarians, and so on. A lot of the editorial is same-same but around the edges I get a nice sense of where and how actual programs and computers are being operated in daily use. And I get a rounded sense of the breadth of the frontier. I don't hear about things first this way, but I do hear new things splash into old terrain with the dull thud that says they are here to stay. It's kind of like watching the wake instead of the helm.

You really will get a mindboggling amount of computer junk mail this way, so beware.

*Macintosh essence . . .*

## MACWORLD

$24/yr (12 issues); PC World Communications, Inc., P.O. Box 20300, Bergenfield, NJ 07621; 800/247-5470 or, in IA, 800/532-1272.

STEWART BRAND: No magazine so reflects the quality of the machine it covers as elegant, inviting, intriguing, beautiful **Macworld**. The graphic content is Mac-generated, fluid and natural and part of the story in every article. It's revolutionary magazine making.

You get the magazine when you send in your Macintosh warranty card. If you're saving up for a Mac or still deciding whether to get one, **Macworld** would be worth studying beforehand. It works as an ongoing tutorial for the machine and the new programs and peripheral devices as they come on the market. Nevertheless it's not in thrall of Apple. The most damaging Apple story of mid-'84—that Macintosh software is visually distorted on the Lisa 2 machines—first appeared in **Macworld**.

*Industry newsletters . . .*

## WEEKLY MARKETING BULLETIN

£120/yr (52 issues); VNU Business Publications BV, 53-55 Frith Street, London W1A 2HG, England; Telex 23918 VNU G.

## RELease 1.0

$395/yr (15 or more issues); EDventure Holdings, Inc., 375 Park Avenue, Suite 2503, New York, NY 10152; 212/586-3530 for prepaid orders.

RICHARD DALTON: **Weekly Marketing Bulletin** comes from England and though it arrives about 10 days late, still contains more real news and intriguing industry gossip than any U.S. publication I've seen. Expensive at about $180/year (dependent on the current exchange rate), but it's fairly amazing how the clever Brits behind the publication stay so far in front, so far away.

STEWART BRAND: My favorite read is **RELease 1.0**, a pricey monthly from Esther Dyson, who writes with more intelligence per column inch than anyone else in the business—and with a high quaint humor. This sharp-eyed daughter of physicist Freeman Dyson treats the biz like a good field biologist might. She observes acutely, notes trends early, predicts boldly, and retains a wicked remote fondness for her obligingly complex subject.

## HARDWARE

STEWART BRAND: Which machine you buy is the most irrevocable and consequential decision you make around personal computers. 1) Whatever you get, you're eliminating utterly all the software that doesn't run on your machine. 2) You're making the biggest single expenditure of your system.

So: buy conservative. Buy a middle-of-the-road, popular machine with a wealth of software available for it—not too old, not too new. That preserves your options.

ALFRED LEE: If I have to live the next five years with one computer, let me live them with an unjealous one that lets me fool around.

STEWART BRAND: The most unjealous computers:
• Commodore 64—cheapest
• Apple IIe or IIc—most home software, and some business
• IBM PC and compatibles (Compaq, etc.)—most business software, and some home
• Macintosh—newest, juiciest software

Whichever road you choose eliminates the other three.

Before detailed shopping, there are some technical generalities to address. Not many. If you know a little about Memory, Storage, and Operating Systems, you know enough to shop intelligently.

**Memory.** Expressed in *K*, as in "You need 192K of memory in order to run 1-2-3 on that machine" or "CP/M machines like the Kaypro are forever limited to 64K." More K is better K, and costs more. Memory is sort of like the machine's consciousness—the amount of material it can hold in mind at once to think about and act instantly upon. Machines with larger memories can work with more complex programs and work conspicuously faster. Another term for memory in this sense is RAM—Random Access Memory. "The Macintosh gets a lot out of its 128K RAM." With some machines you can add more memory as you go (in the form of "cards"—circuit boards you can easily install yourself in "slots" in the machine), a handy way to keep up with growing ambitions.

**Storage.** "Old-timers will tell you. If users will maim for main memory, they'll kill for disk storage."—John Gantz, **InfoWorld**.

Also expressed in K. "How does the Macintosh get 400K on those 3½ inch disks when the Hewlett-Packard 150 only gets 270K?" The disk is where your information lives when it's not in active use. "Bigger" disk (more K), bigger program possible, also more room for your own data files—1K ( one Kilobyte) equals about 150 words of text; at 250 words per double-spaced page, a disk of 191K, like that on my Kaypro, will hold 114 pages.

There are only three consequential kinds of disk these days—the 5¼" "floppy" (Commodore, Apple, IBM, 160-360K); the 3½" "floppy" (more of a hardshell actually, HP 150 and 110, Macintosh, 270-400K); and hard disk (Apple, IBM, Macintosh, 5-200 + MB). Hard disk is what one aspires to. It measures storage in megabytes (MB), a million bytes (1,000K). "I cannot live without a hard disk. I really do not remember how I existed before. With 2.5 megabytes available for WORDSTAR and related spelling and grammar, and others, I am completely

spoiled. Floppy disks are OK, but hard disks are a necessity for a writer of books and other lengthy material. The additional storage and quickness of response will save you *hours* of frustration in working with large files."—Woody Liswood. (Note: Half the computer books on the market were written without benefit of hard disk. For writing it's a luxury; for accounting it's a necessity.)

**Operating systems.** This is the troublous realm of "compatibility." A program written for one operating system won't operate on another one unless it's translated, which is either a nuisance, expensive, or impossible, depending. This is where computer jealousy comes in. "The IBM PC is a lousy machine, but everything runs on it," said editor Barbara Robertson, on her way to buying one. The IBM's operating system, PC-DOS (generically, MS-DOS), is the closest thing we have to a standard these days, so software writers flock to it, and so do hardware manufacturers in the 16-bit generation. Ah.

There are three generations of personal computer hardware alive in the market just now. The oldest is 8-bit—Apple IIs, Radio Shack TRS-80, Commodore 64, Atari 800XL, CP/M 80 (an operating system) machines like Kaypro and Morrow. The current dominant is 16-bit—the IBM PC family and hordes of compatibles and sort-of compatibles. The cutting edge is 32-bit—Macintosh. Every now and then I understand the difference between 8 and 16 and 32 bit, but it doesn't matter to understand it, so I forget again.

Now then. Hardware shopping advice from an expert. Richard Dalton has been in the computer field for 17 years. He's a hardware buying consultant and editor of the office technology newsletter **Open Systems**. A founder of this **Catalog** project, he was the editor of the first two issues of the **Whole Earth Software Review** and is a continuing contributor there.

## HARDWARE: HARD CHOICES

RICHARD DALTON: This is June 1984 speaking. By the time you read this, there will have been changes in personal computing equipment. We've focused on general advice and direction, which shouldn't be seriously affected by the announcement of a new computer or even another "generation" of computer systems.

First reason: we at **Whole Earth** think there's more value in digging out the best in personal computing, not the newest. New products, especially hardware, are going to have problems. This was true of the vaunted IBM PC right after its announcement and frustrates our office today as we try to get the interesting new Mindset computer to cough up its excellent graphic capabilities, but can't because of a balky disk drive. That doesn't invalidate Mindset—they're just having predictable early production glitches.

FIRST RULE: ***Don't buy serial number "1" of any system (or anything close to it).***

Second reason: a new computer system that is revolutionary (the Macintosh is a good example) will not have enough software immediately available to satisfy the average buyer. It generally takes one or two years for the software producers to catch up with a new machine. We recommend Macintosh, but not as highly as six to twelve months from now. We expect a raft of software announcements during late 1984 for the Mac, but can't predict which kinds, their quality, utility, or overall value. It's a machine worthy of attention, so watch developments.

SECOND RULE: *Buy a computer that offers a number of choices in each software category (writing, organizing, drawing, etc.) that interests you.*

Since personal computers (and, of course, the programs that make the beasts work) are becoming more capable each year, a natural tendency is to hold back and await next year's developments. That's a valid approach *if* you don't have anything currently important to do that a personal computer would substantially improve.

A friend of mine with no personal computer experience spent about a month bugging computer dealers for advice on how to automate his 15,000-name mailing list he uses to market specialized seminar programs. He settled on a Televideo 802H computer and Selector V organizing software and wound up paying about $5,000. He had bumpy times at first: the computer's hard disk was replaced twice and the software wasn't as easy as he thought. The punch line, though, is the computer *paid for itself in six months*, based on what he no longer had to shell out to the service bureau that previously made address labels for his promotional mailers.

My friend would have been crazy not to buy some system. The benefits were quick to appear and the cash outlays, while significant, were justified. If more "efficient" personal computers appeared the day after he made his choice, it wouldn't matter.

THIRD RULE: *Think about what you can gain from a personal computer. If it's a lot, crash ahead. If you're uncertain, either wait or buy cheap and do some exploring.*

## WHOLE EARTH RECOMMENDED HARDWARE TOOLS

### (June 1984)

### EASY BUYS

Commodore 64, $500, p.16
TRS-80 Model 100, $599, p.16
Apple IIc, $1495, p.19
Kaypro 2, $1295, p.16
IBM PCjr, $1625, p.17

### SOMEWHAT HARDER BUYS

Morrow MD-1E, $999, p.16
Apple IIe, $1775, p.19
Tava PC, $2125, p.17
Compaq, $2995, p.17
Apple Macintosh, $2990, p.19
Leading Edge PC, $2895, p.17
IBM PC, $3045, p.17

### RELATIVELY DIFFICULT BUYS

Sanyo 555, $1399, p.17
NEC APC III, $2720, p.17
Hewlett-Packard 110—"The Portable," $2995, p.18
Hewlett-Packard 150, $3495, p.17
DEC Rainbow, $3995, p.17

*These considerations guided us in our selections:*

*• Computers should be buyable without the customer having an advanced degree in computer science. We include choices that we deem "easy," "somewhat harder" and "relatively difficult" to buy —for reasons noted in each system's review.*

*• When you buy a computer, you buy a company as well, which needs to be looked at as carefully as their product:*

*Do they provide good service and quick answers to your questions, directly or through dependable dealers?*

*Are they well managed and financially stable? The well-known failures of Osborne Computer and Victor Technologies aren't just microcomputer industry gossip. Osborne and Victor owners found themselves orphaned. This means a scramble for parts and repairs plus a limitation in future software product offerings.*

*Do they continually improve and enhance their systems?*

*• When two computers were similar, we went for the lower price. There's nothing wrong with the Radio Shack Model 4, for example, but it costs considerably more than the Kaypro 2 and offers no real advantage.*

*• The amount of software available for a particular machine carries great weight. You can't do without it unless you're a trained programmer or want to learn—a long-term project.*

---

*There is one true statement about microcomputers: NO MATTER WHAT YOU BUY, THE FIRST PERSON YOU MEET AFTER YOUR PURCHASE WILL TELL YOU THAT YOU SHOULD HAVE PURCHASED SOMETHING DIFFERENT.*

*—Woody Liswood*

*Disposable computer . . .*

## COMMODORE 64

JOHN SEWARD: The Commodore 64 is the BiC lighter of computers. It works great, but it's not destined to become a family heirloom. I've been writing software for the 64 ever since it was introduced and am familiar with its strengths and weaknesses.

Compared to the Apple IIe, the 64 has the same memory, an augmented version of the same processor, better color graphics and keyboard yet costs one-fourth as much. The Apple looks more substantial and has a well-deserved reputation for reliability, which Commodore lacks. Compared to the IBM PCjr, the 64 has a better keyboard, lower price, and will not run IBM PC software.

*The Commodore 64 at $200 owns the low end of the market and has been around long enough to attract plenty of software. Playing editor Steven Levy says it's even replacing the Atari 800 as the leading game machine. You can use it without a disk drive ($280) but you miss fine software if you do. It'll run with a TV, as here, but the Commodore monitor ($290) adds a lot. A good computer to mess with while you're deciding whether to mess with computers at all or while you're waiting for something ideal to come along. (Commodore Business Machines, Inc., 1200 Wilson Drive, West Chester, PA 19380.)*

*For students, journalists, executives . . .*

## RADIO SHACK TRS-80 MODEL 100

RICHARD DALTON: Sales of notebook-size computers are growing faster than those of desktop computers for a simple reason; they allow you to take your personal computing resource with you. The Model 100 is the largest seller in this category. It's the size and weight of a hardcover novel, has a usable keyboard and a built-in modem for telecommunicating. The screen's a bit cramped and the memory won't hold more than about 20 pages of text, but what do you want for a $600 base price?

*Radio Shack's TRS-80 Model 100 portable has forced the computer business to rethink what it's about. Well-designed, cheap, enormously popular, it continues to find new uses. ($599; Radio Shack, 1800 One Tandy Center, Fort Worth, TX 76102.)*

*The CP/M transportable bargain . . .*

## KAYPRO 2

RICHARD DALTON: Basically, Kaypro offers a pile of quality software (WORDSTAR, MAIL/MERGE, THE WORD PLUS, SUPER SORT, CALCSTAR, DATASTAR, PROFITPLAN, MBASIC-80, CP/M 80 ver. 2.2) at a substantial discount and throws in their computer for free. The complete package only costs $1,295; the retail value of the software alone is close to $2,000. That's why it's an Easy Buy. You unpack, plug in the power cord and start writing, organizing, calculating or programming.

Why shouldn't everyone buy a Kaypro 2? First, its CP/M 80 operating system gives a choice of thousands of programs, but little new software is being developed for it. Second, CP/M 80 is for business compulsives; little software is available for recreational or educational computer uses. Finally, its Z80 processor is limited to 64K memory.

*Our workhorse for this book has been the Kaypro 2. It looks like military surplus and is priced like it, and in some ways it is left over from former wars, since its CP/M-80 operating system is no longer a major contender. The value of the software bundled with it makes it practically a free machine. Newer Kaypros than ours have a pleasant high-resolution screen. ($1295; Kaypro Corp., 533 Stevens Ave., Solano Beach, CA 92075; 619/481-4300.)*

*CP/M desktop bargain . . .*

## MORROW MD-1E

RICHARD DALTON: George Morrow is one of the microcomputer industry's iconoclasts, and the company he founded builds computers that match his outlook. The MD-1E is a good example: decidedly unchic in appearance, it offers a standard CP/M 80 processor with 64K memory, single 380K disk drive, keyboard, monitor, and the highly regarded NEWWORD (p. 56) for $999.

No sex appeal, no sizzle, but if you use a computer mostly for writing, it may be all you ever need (except for a printer, which Morrow also sells cheap).

*The Morrow MD-1E is a righteous bargain at $999 and as obsolete as its CP/M operating system, which is limited to 64K memory. Since good business software is available, specialized users can take full advantage of its price. ($999; Morrow, Inc., 600 McCormick St., San Leandro, CA 94577.)*

*Big Blue . . .*

## IBM'S PC AND COMPATIBILITY

Personal computing changed direction when IBM announced their PC three years ago. Its 16-bit processor opened up broader vistas for software developers: they could write programs many times larger than the 64K maximum memories of the then-popular Apple and Radio Shack computers.

But the real impact was in marketing—a PC with IBM's massive organization behind it. By mid-1984, estimates were that 75-85% of all software being written was targeted for the IBM PC and compatible machines.

The computers that can use this burgeoning wealth of software share the MS-DOS operating system (IBM's version is PC DOS), but that doesn't simplify selection. More than 50 companies make MS-DOS computers. All of them claim to be "compatible" with IBM PC software. None of them are 100% compatible, though machines like Compaq, Tava, and Leading Edge are very close.

**TIP:** How do you tell if your favorite program is compatible on a Brand X machine? If a particular program is your main reason for buying a computer, go to a dealer and test it on the machine you prefer. It's the *only* sure way. Two popular programs used for testing IBM PC compatibility are 1-2-3 (p. 67) and FLIGHT SIMULATOR (p. 33).

IBM's competitors distinguish themselves by being faster and by offering more, especially better graphic attributes, a weak feature of the IBM PC. But improvements on the original can reduce software compatibility.

**The NEC APC III** has graphic capabilities that are twice as good as IBM's; the Hewlett-Packard 150 adds a touch screen; the **DEC Rainbow** has enhanced graphics, better communications and diskettes with larger storage capacity. But these excellent machines are among the least IBM-compatible systems and have less software to offer as a result.

The final departure point is price. Compared to an IBM FC, purchased at list price with all-IBM components, an equivalent Tava is about two-thirds the cost and Sanyo considerably less. The price difference reduces if you buy an IBM PC with other brands of boards and disk drives, but that makes purchasing and maintenance harder.

Our recommendations in the PC/MS-DOS world:

● If buying ease and minimizing your risks are your *only* concerns, trot down to IBM's Product Center and buy an all-**IBM** machine. You'll pay a lot to quell those concerns but it's the least-risk way to buy in this category.

● If money is a primary consideration, buy a **Tava.** Tava comes close to the generic PC. Compatibility is high, prices low and quality good. The **Leading Edge PC** includes some software and has a few more options yet retains close compatibility for a price significantly higher than Tava. It's sold by one of the largest hardware distributors, a plus.

● If money is the *only* consideration, pick **Sanyo.** You sacrifice a large part of PC-compatible software and expansion possibilities are limited, including memory, which can only be boosted to 256K. WORDSTAR (p. 56), CALCSTAR, INFOSTAR, and BASIC are thrown in for compensation. If your budget only permits Sanyo, decide whether you want a 16-bit machine or just a workable computer. You may do better with Apple II or Kaypro.

● If you can live with smaller savings and find a transportable system useful, **Compaq** has an excellent reputation for quality and compatibility. We know a number of people who selected Compaq over the IBM PC because they just liked it better. Its built-in monochrome screen (with graphic capability included rather than extra) is unusually easy to watch for long periods.

● Finally, the IBM PC doesn't fit everyone. Its being compatible may be less important to you than excellent graphics, in which case the **NEC APC III** is recommended. **DEC's Rainbow** is endorsed for people seeking a more powerful system with two-way compatibility—its two processors can handle MS-DOS or CP/M 80 software. Hewlett-Packard's 150 has good graphics and its touch screen makes it easy for neophytes to get used to personal computing.

*Widely discounted in price, the Tava has the most IBM PC compatibiity for the least money. Find out what software you want to use, see if it runs on the Tava. If it does, you can afford more software. ($1195; Tava Corporation, 16861 Armstrong, Irvine, CA 92714; 714/261-0200.)*

*Better than its reputation . . .*

## IBM PCJR

KEN MILBURN: At first glance the PCjr is disappointing. It's tiny: there's no room for expansion cards or more than one disk in the system box. The internal memory can't be expanded beyond 128K. The keyboard is workable, but slow and slippery.

Still, I can't think of another machine that meets so well all four (good) reasons for buying a home computer: "light" business, entertainment, education and communications. Graphics and colors are mightily improved over those in the PC, making the jr better suited to education, and entertainment. Capable business software will run on the jr and its files are compatible with PC DOS versions 2.0 and 2.1.

*The most conservative of buys is an IBM PC (right); the PCjr (left) is a slightly radical buy, due to its execrable keyboard and the fact that it's limited to 128k memory. The keyboard can be cured (p. 20); the 128K still includes the majority of great software that has been written for the IBM PC. Like the Apple IIe the PC is open architecture —you can adapt it forever. (IBM PCjr, $999; IBM PC, $1815; IBM, Entry Systems Division, P.O. Box 1328, Boca Raton, FL 33432; 800/447-4700.)*

The Sanyo 555 has limited compatibility with popular IBM PC programs and can't be expanded as much as other PC clones, but it's the low end of the price curve at $1399 list price with two disk drives. Discount sellers often knock another $200-300 off, making the 555 cheaper than Apple IIc or Kaypro 2. ($999; Sanyo Business Systems Corp., 51 Joseph St., Moonachie, NJ 07074; 201/440-9300.)

The Compaq is fully compatible with the IBM PC and comes with graphic capabilities. Its transportability keeps it more in use than a work station moose like the PC, and many find the 9-inch (diagonal) screen more readable than a big PC monitor. A 10-megabyte hard disk model, the Compaq Plus, is available in the same case. $2495; Compaq Computer Corporation, 20333 FM149, Houston, TX 77070; 800/231-0900.)

The NEC APC III is cheaper than the IBM PC, faster, and has far better graphics. Compatibility is somewhat less as a result. ($1995; NEC Information Systems, Inc., 1414 Massachusetts Ave., Boxborough, MA 01719; 617/264-8000.)

The Rainbow from Digital Equipment Corporation (DEC) is a genuine hybrid, capable of running both 8-bit CP/M programs and 16-bit MS-DOS programs. Its sprawling keyboard is an attraction to some. Particularly suited to tele-communications, the Rainbow is here being used for teleconferencing by the School of Management and Strategic Studies, La Jolla, California. ($2750; Digital Equipment Corp., 146 Main St., Maynard, MA 01754; 800/344-4825.)

The HP 150 "Touch Screen" from Hewlett-Packard is unique in how you control it. The cursor goes to where you touch on the screen; a touch on a command makes the command happen. Designers point out that a finger is more efficient than a mouse; among other things, you don't have to pick it up first. The HP 150 is solid, potent, not cheap, and not IBM compatible. Its 3½ inch hardshell disks are more compact than the old 5¼ inch floppies. ($3495; Hewlett-Packard, 1020 N.E. Circle Blvd., Corvallis, OR 97330; 800/367-4772.)

As you can tell by seeing 1-2-3 running, the Leading Edge PC is quite compatible with the IBM PC. Its one-third lower price is the attraction. ($2500; Leading Edge Products, 225 Turnpike St., Canton, MA 02021; 800/343-6833.)

Serious portability . . .

## HEWLETT-PACKARD 110— "THE PORTABLE"

RICHARD DALTON: Think of HP's 9-pound powerhouse as a quantum jump up from the TRS-80 Model 100 (p. 16)—in both price and performance. Cost is $2,995 and you get a lot more: 16 line x 80 column screen; 272K RAM and 392K ROM memory; built-in modem; sophisticated software and five extra pounds to lug.

That's all fine, but you should have use for the integrated software if the price difference is to make sense. The 110 comes equipped with 1-2-3 (p. 67), MEMO MAKER (a limited writing tool), and TERMINAL, a simple, powerful telecommunications program. All this will be replaced by a special version of the do-everything SYMPHONY (p. 111) when it becomes available.

If SYMPHONY doesn't suit you, other programs like MULTIPLAN (p. 70) and WORDSTAR (p. 56) are being modified for the 110. You load software and unload files via add-on boards to either an HP 150 or IBM PC compatible. It costs $175 for the HP connection and $125 for an IBM link. A standalone 710K disk drive serves the same purpose and costs $795.

The LCD (Liquid Crystal Display) screen is controversial. Characters are shaded for readability but the screen must be straight in front of you and tilted just right or glare is a problem. Contrast is adjustable over a wide range. At its best viewing point, I still wouldn't want to look at the screen for periods beyond an hour or two.

Overall, it's a high-quality way to have true desktop computer power in a package that's easy to carry. The price is prohibitive, though, if you don't get a tax break for using the 110 in business.

Hardware reviewer Richard Dalton falling further in love with the HP 110. It's got an 80-column x 16 line screen, a truckload of memory, modem built in, and Hewlett-Packard solid construction. ($2995; Hewlett-Packard, 1020 N.E. Circle Blvd., Corvallis, OR 97330; 800/367-4772.)

*For home and school and now at large . . .*

## APPLE II:
## OPEN AND SHUT CASES

The Apple IIe and IIc are direct-line descendants from the original that Wozniak and Jobs designed in a garage. Seven years later, the same modest processor is included, and care has been taken with operating system changes so buyers continue to have access to tens of thousands of programs written during the long Apple II dynasty. No other computer can make that statement.

The basic IIe, like its predecessors, is a starter kit, hence more "open." *You* decide about more memory, CP/M compatibility, a clock/calendar to time things, what disk drives to attach and what kind of monitor. This means self-education, comparison shopping and sometimes acute disappointment if your choices don't pan out. It's hard to argue with this philosophy since more than 1.5 million have been sold so far, but Apple took another route when they decided to birth the IIc.

The IIc was designed as a "closed" system, with a built-in disk drive, all boards inside and the case sealed shut. You invalidate your warranty if you open the IIc and muck about its internals.

First-time computer owners should give closed systems the most attention. Your choices won't be limited much and the selection process is simpler. Open systems offer more flexibility as you advance in skills, but unless personal computing is an exciting new avocation, you'll probably be better off keeping it simple the first time. That's why Apple made the change: to attract an even larger following with the IIc's simplicity.

It's tiny (7½ pounds), understandable (one of the better computer literacy courses comes with the IIc on six diskettes), and lives up to its advertising as "easier to set up than your average stereo system."

The machine costs $1,295, which includes a built-in 5¼" disk drive. Many people will want a second disk drive, which plugs into the IIc's back panel and adds $329. The IIc attaches to a TV (limiting text to 40 columns) or you can buy for $199 Apple's companion monitor that matches the IIc's design—elegant for a system in this price class. A mouse, joystick, and modem (300 or 1200 baud) are other options.

By the time you read this, the optional 80-column, 24-line LCD flat screen should be available. Expected to cost about $600, it will make the IIc one of the more powerful portable systems available for around $2,000.

*Inviting 32-bit dazzle . . .*

## MACINTOSH AND THE FUTURE

Apple's Mac tells us a lot about how personal computing will change. Inherently more powerful than any other mass production machine, it's unusually easy to use.

The secret is the software housed in the Macintosh. Every application program written for the Mac has a similar appearance to the user. Functions are selected by pulling down window shade-like menus with a mouse that positions the cursor and selects options as you glide it around your desktop. The mouse is a controversial beast. Some find it irritating, others fall in love and won't accept any other control device. Try it before you decide. Linked to appropriate software, it's a whole new way to interact wih a computer.

Mac's second major departure from other personal computers is its fine-grained, grey-scale graphic abilities. We know of no other computer that can be used to produce drawings as easily or that so encourages can't-draw-a-straight-liners to expand their creative repertoire.

All this newness has its price. Mac's software has been appearing slowly, and it will be a while before a selection is available that approaches either the PC/MS-DOS collection or that of its little brother, the II.

Test driving Mac is recommended: it may not come close to your needs (disk and memory limits currently exist); it may be fascinating and not have the software you want; or it may be what you always thought a computer should be and make all other systems pale.

*The state of the art in personal computers is Apple's Macintosh. It is the most user-enticing of machines in large part because it is the most graphic of machines. The mouse is an inherent part of its design, hence obligatory; be sure you like it before buying. Resolution of images on the screen (no color) is exquisite, and printouts on the Imagewriter are identical. Here you see the first game for the Mac, ALICE (p. 30). With its modest size and weight and handle in the top, the Macintosh is surprisingly portable. ($2495; Apple Computer, 20525 Mariani, Cupertino, CA 95014; 800/538-9696.)*

*Apple IIe (left) and IIc (right), open architecture versus closed architecture, same machine otherwise, running the largest library of software in the business. The IIe is more adaptable, but many of the things you might add, such as a card for 80-column screen (80 characters on a line instead of 40) and a card for the mouse, are already included in the IIc. Some things, like a card for CP/M programs, can never be added to the IIc. Once it gets its flat screen the IIc is truly portable. Runs on 12 volts—use it in a car or on a sailboat, or anywhere on attachable batteries. (IIc, $1295; IIe, $895; Apple Computer, 20525 Mariani, Cupertino, CA 95014; 800/538-9696.)*

FINAL RULE: *So that you know the machine and know that the one you're buying works, don't buy any computer unless you have:* ● *Typed on the keyboard for at least 15 minutes* ● *Started a program, ended it and started another* ● *Created a file and printed it* ● *Looked at the display and tested the system yourself (not a demo) for at least a half hour. If a dealer won't let you do the above, sheath your MasterCard and move on.*

STEWART BRAND: I find that when I'm asked by someone what computer to get for their work, I see if they have the $2,500 and the use to pay for it, and then suggest, "Get a Macintosh and grow with it. You'll understand the range of its capabilities as they emerge, and you'll enjoy playing with the hottest new software. If you've got immediate need for a full spectrum of application software, get an IBM PC or compatible, but be aware you may be using it for a doorstop in a year." Since a Macintosh arrived in the Whole Earth office it has been in constant use. People who would deal with no other computer stand in line to mess with it. "I am reminded of E.F. Schumacher's distinction between a *machine*, which requires users to adjust themselves to its rhythms, and a *tool*, which enhances its users' capacities. The Macintosh is clearly a tool."—Richard Conviser.

We're not recommending the Lisa 2s from Apple until it's clear that they can run Macintosh software without screen distortion (Mac pixels are square; Lisa's are rectangular). Better to wait for the enhanced (512K RAM, etc.) Macs to come.

Richard Dalton's CP/M strategy is an interesting one. Use the bargain Kaypro or Morrow machines for highly specific business applications and they'll quickly pay their way and you won't care about the software world passing you by. I would only add that you may want a Kaypro 4 ($1995, 400K disks instead of 191K) or Kaypro 10 ($2795, 10 megabyte hard disk, and still portable). I find the Kaypro 2 too cramped for comfortable writing—I'm always changing disks. Accounting on less than a Kaypro 10 is near impossible.

If you take advantage of the PCjr's relative unpopularity and good price, there is a cure for its atrocious keyboard. Pay the $209 ($160 or so, discount) and get a Key Tronic keyboard for it. Managing Editor Matthew McClure, who used to be a professional typesetter, says Key Tronic currently has the best of keyboards. They have two for the IBM PC, one with the numeric keypad and the cursor keys separated (essential for spreadsheet use), one more standard, both better than IBM's. There's also a Key Tronic for Apple IIs. They have versions for disabled users and for Dvorak believers—Dvorak is a more efficient layout of the characters on the keyboard, supported by some word processors, such as XYWRITE II+ (p. 61). (Key Tronic, P.O. Box 14687, Spokane, WA 99214, 509/928-8000.)

Keyboards and monitors are of the essence. They're the part of the computer that wear on your body day in and day out. Don't get a machine your fingers aren't happy with. One way to objectively test keyboards—in the store or with friends' machines—is with TYPING TUTOR III (p. 49), which tells you your words-per-minute rate as you mess with it. I *like* the Apple II keyboard better than the IBM, but TYPING TUTOR proved I'm a lot faster and make fewer errors on the IBM.

Monitors. It's an almost theological choice between high-resolution monochrome and lower-resolution color. If your computer life is strictly numbers and characters, monochrome will lessen the eyestrain. If you use graphics at all, color carries its own bonus of information. The color monitors we like for resolution and cost come from Amdek (Amdek Color-II plus, $799; Amdek Corp., 2201 Lively Blvd., Elk Grove Village, IL 60007; 312/364-1180). An RGB (red, green, blue) monitor is so much better than a TV screen that it's worth paying the extra couple hundred bucks, even with the cheapest systems.

## PRICES OF THE RECOMMENDED SYSTEMS

| SYSTEM | LIST PRICE | STREET PRICE | FIRST-YEAR COST | COMMENTS: |
|---|---|---|---|---|
| Commodore 64 | $500 | $390 | $450 | |
| TRS-80 Model 100 | $599 | $500 | $200 | Portable (4 pounds) |
| Morrow MD-1E | $999 | $900 | $600 | Includes NEWWORD |
| Kaypro 2 | $1,295 | $1,150 | $350 | Includes much software (page 16) |
| Sanyo 555 | $1,399 | $1,150 | $400 | Includes WORDSTAR PROF., CALCSTAR, INFOSTAR & BASIC |
| Apple IIc | $1,495 | $1,300 | $700 | Portable (7½ pounds) |
| IBM PCjr | $1,625 | $1,300 | $700 | |
| Apple IIe | $1,775 | $1,420 | $700 | |
| Tava PC | $2,125 | $1,600 | $1,000 | |
| NEC APC III | $2,720 | NA | $1,000 | 8MHz 8086 processor |
| Leading Edge PC | $2,895 | $2,700 | $700 | 7.4 MHz Processor; Includes LEADING EDGE word processor, Nutshell (database mgr.) |
| Macintosh | $2,990 | $2,695 | $900 | M68000 (32-bit) processor; mouse |
| Compaq | $2,995 | $2,300 | $1,000 | Transportable (28 pounds) |
| HP 110 | $2,995 | NA | $450 | Portable (9 pounds) |
| IBM PC | $3,045 | $2,300 | $1,000 | |
| HP 150 | $3,495 | $3,175 | $1,200 | 8 MHz processor; touch screen |
| DEC Rainbow (8/16-bit) | $3,995 | $3,000 | $900 | Dual processors |

NA–system is too new for discount price comparison

*What's included? Price shown for each system in the chart includes a keyboard, connections for a printer and communications, and a monochrome monitor—add $200-400 if you want color and deduct $200 if a standard TV set is used.*

*The real differences begin with memory: 32K for Radio Shack Model 100; 64K for Commodore, Kaypro 2 and Morrow MD-1E; 128K for Apple IIc and e, IBM PCjr and Macintosh; everyone else with 256K. Sorry, this isn't too tidy, but we're trying to show functional configurations that support available software. Similar problem with disk drives: one for Commodore, Apple IIc, Morrow MD-1E, and PCjr; all the rest have two.*

*The portable HP 110 is a special case: see page 18 for its components. Printers aren't included, as they run about the same for all systems, $200-2,000 depending on what features and printing speed you want.*

*LIST PRICE: the price established by the manufacturer. STREET PRICE: a mid-1984 price typical of what's charged by mail order firms and discount computer stores, often seductively lower than list. Street price shoppers should be knowledgeable about the system they're looking for and what kinds of internal substitutions (boards and such) a discounter may make in a system, which may affect serviceability.*

*FIRST YEAR COST: there's always more to buy after your initial purchase. This figure shows a reasonable amount to add for software, supplies (diskettes, paper, etc.) and repairs during the first year of ownership. It isn't the same factor for all computers: For example, Commodore software costs less per program than IBM PC; DEC includes a one-year warranty on its Rainbow, meaning no first year repair cost.*

The lingering hardware curse around personal computers is printers and their dubious compatibility. The safest thing to do is get whatever printer is most conspicuously compatible with your machine and the software you fancy and hook them up at the dealer's and run them.

CHARLES STEVENSON (head programmer and chief of printer configuration at MicroPro): At the low end—the slower, less expensive dot matrix printers—I'd recommend the C. Itoh 8510 (also known as the Prowriter 1) or their other models, the 1550, with a wider carriage, and the color version of the 8510. C. Itoh printers are workhorses at low cost ($350 and up) and unlike Epson and Okidata there are few compatibility problems within the product line. There is no such thing as a standard Epson MX80; that is, there are actually six MX80s, each different, and there's no way to tell which is which by looking at them. This means you can't simply select "Epson MX80" from a word processing printer menu and expect it to work. One of the six will; you have to try them to find out which. Okidata printers have a similar problem. (Prowriter 8510; $495; C. Itoh Digital Products, 55 Providence Highway, Norwood, MA 02062; 800/423-0300.)

In the lower speed, letter-quality printer range it's a toss-up. I'd go with the Brother HR-15 or -25 or the Silver Reed EXP-500 or EXP-550. Prices range from $600 to $1000; speeds are 12 to 23 characters per second. All four can handle Diablo escape sequences, which means that if "Diablo" is a printer choice in your word processor, you simply select it; no further configuration is necessary. (Brother HR-15; $599; HR-25; $995; Brother International Corp., 8 Corporate Place, Piscataway, NJ 08854; 201/981-0300 ● Silver-Reed EXP-500; $599; EXP-550; $699; Silver-Reed America, Inc., 19600 S. Vermont Ave., Torrance, CA 90502; 800/874-4885 or, in CA, 213/516-7008.)

BARBARA ROBERTSON: The new $495 ThinkJet from Hewlett-Packard is a delightful printer—fast, quiet, and portable (8" x 11½" x 3½", 6 pounds). Instead of mechanical printheads and ribbons, it uses a small disposable ink-filled cartridge ($10) that slides into a tray at the front of the machine. It paints characters on the paper by spraying ink through several tiny holes in the printhead. It's fast: 150 characters per second. Bold and underlining don't slow it down. Print quality is excellent. Not perfect letter quality, but the lines are much finer than dot matrix—and they're always the same. You'll never see faint characters from tired ribbons. The ThinkJet works with most computers. I think it's worth every penny for the peace and quiet alone. Clean thumbs and portability are bonuses. (ThinkJet; $495; Hewlett-Packard, 1020 N.E. Circle Blvd., Corvallis, OR 97330; 800/367-4772.)

STEWART BRAND: I think the notion of "letter-quality" printers is about as deep as "wood-quality" station wagons. Most letter-quality printers are expensive, gawdawful noisy, and huge, and they can't even do graphics, where all the action is with computers. Our favorite graphic printer is Apple's Imagewriter ($595; Apple Computer, 20525 Mariani, Cupertino, CA 95014; 800/538-9696), which makes the most of the Macintosh's capabilities. The very top graphic and color printers usually come from Hewlett-Packard (pp. 124, 126).

The bane within the curse is the cables that link printers and other pieces of your hardware; they *vary* invisibly and critically. Don't leave the store with equipment that isn't operationally cabled to each other. If your office deals with much variety, invest in a Smart Cable, which adapts to whatever it's connecting (Smart Cable 817 RM [male] or 817 RF [female]; $90; Smart Cable 821 [includes both male and female connectors on both ends]; $175; IQ Technologies, 11811 N.E. First St., Suite 308, Bellevue, WA 98005; 800/232-8324 or, in WA, 206/451-0232). It costs the equivalent of three stupid cables. The only other route is the good book, **RS-232 Made Easy: Connecting Computers, Printers, Terminals & Modems** (p. 156).

The future of personal computing increasingly belongs to portable computers.

We recommend the TRS-80 Model 100 over its close competition, the NEC 8201, primarily because of its on-board modem and good telecommunications and the fact that the 100 has more support. Besides the pervasiveness of Radio Shack stores, "there's an excellent online support group for the Model 100 on CompuServe (see p. 140) with a large library of downloadable software, including some quite useable utilities" (Louis Jaffe), there's an intriguing monthly magazine (**Portable 100**, $25/year, 67 Elm St., Camden, ME 04843, 800/225-5800), and a source of nice business application programs in the Portable Computer Support Group (11035 Harry Hines Blvd., No. 207, Dallas, TX 75229; 214/351-0564). The hacker action around this machine reminds me of early Apple IIs.

Competition for the full-service Hewlett-Packard 110 portable is coming rapidly. Sharp's PC-5000 is a contender. Control Data is supposed to have something remarkable rumbling down the chute, but every week brings new rumors of ware from somewhere. One of the battlefields is the flat screens, whether they will be liquid crystal like the HP-110 or brighter and more energy-draining electro-luminescent (EL) like the splendid GRiD Compass, which has been around the longest of the portables, serving the likes of astronauts and FBI agents, who could afford it (price coming down, now $4250-7995; GRiD Systems Corp., 2535 Garcia Ave., Mountain View, CA 94041; 800/222-GRID).

The first generation of personal computers led to the idea of the electronic cottage—a way to do business from home. The second generation suggests even more ephemeral uses.

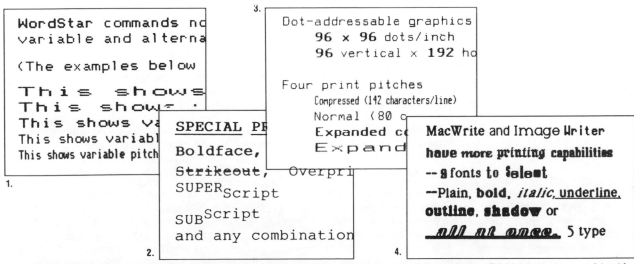

*Print quality from four printers. 1) C Itoh 8510 (Prowriter 1), dot matrix; 2) Brother HR25, letter quality, slow; 3) Hewlett-Packard ThinkJet, better than most dot matrix, but requires special coated paper for best results; 4) Apple Imagewriter, rich graphics, fine dot matrix.*

## BUYING

STEWART BRAND: It comes down to how you value your time. If you take the time to search out primo suppliers, you'll save certainly hundreds, maybe thousands of dollars. If life crowds you already and you have the dough, buy what you want over the closest counter and get all the service you can with it.

The strategies of buying in the next few pages (retail stores, discount mail order, public domain) go from expensive easiest to cheap hardest, and from least educational to most educational. Once you know the computer(s) you're interested in, the most effective single move you can make is to go to a User's Group for that machine in your area (computer stores can guide you to them), and listen and inquire. Along with the good information, you get relief—the group knows more than you could find out in weeks. And they'll be there when you get the machine home and find that your problems haven't gone away yet.

By and large you'll buy hardware at hardware places (thousands of dollars), software (and magazines) at software places (hundreds of dollars), and books at regular book stores—or mail order from COMPUTER LITERACY (p. 201). It's a fragmented, volatile market; that's part of the fun of shopping in it.

If you're using the computer for business, even if you don't succeed financially, it's a significant tax write-off—up to $7,500 in 1984, including software and peripheral gadgetry. Could be a saving of $2,000 on a $5,000 system, depending on your tax bracket and how much of your computer time goes to business use. As of 1985 the tax break is becoming more restrictive and complicated. Consult your tax adviser. While you're at it, check out software like TAX PREPARER (p. 104), PERSONAL TAX PLANNNER (p. 104), and MANAGING YOUR MONEY (p. 97).

Thieves love computers. Insurance costs on the order of $50-75 for $5,000 of stuff, with $100 deductible—worth it. Managing Domain Editor Tony Fanning, who had two computers stolen recently, has this advice. "You add an attachment to your homeowner's policy; if you do work at home, it's cheaper to get it as a business attachment. The AAA also apparently insures computers. Get insurance for 'replacement value.' Take photographs of the equipment and make copies of the receipts and give all that to the company. Be sure to inform them when you add to the system—send the receipts, etc. When you're robbed or burned or whatever, press hard on the company, but don't pad your loss estimates (surprise them). You have to get written replacement value estimates from stores, and the company will check them. They'll take out the deductible and 10% per year for depreciation, and you're back in business. Three times and they cancel. I'm getting one of those lock-down devices."

## First you shop for the store . . .
## BUYING AT STORES

STEVEN LEVY: The first and often the best place to look for software is in a retail store, either one specializing in software or your plain old neighborhood computer store. With a nearby store, not only can you switch faulty disks within minutes after you get home and find them not working, but you can use your phone to pester the clerk who so kindly served you. No long distance charges.

Too many stores, though, give inadequate service. The definitive example for me is the salesclerk who refused to leave his MISSILE COMMAND game when my mate and I tried to get his attention so we could spend $10,000 at his store buying two computers. With that kind of attention to big-ticket buyers, is it any wonder that people who merely want *software* are doomed to nonperson status at many computer stores?

Yet you should persist in finding a store that will listen to your needs, open packages of software for you, run the software on its machines, let you play with the software. Such a place more likely specializes in software than hardware, but if the place you bought your computer does not give you that kind of service, you probably bought your computer at the wrong place.

*Is the clerk a jerk?* Establishing a relationship with someone in the store can be a satisfying, fruitful experience. Some stores, of course, are not geared to this type of contact. Big-volume outlets, like New York City's well-known 47th Street Photo, trade off service for discounts that compete with the cheapest mail-order outlets. Yet even salespeople at 47th Street Photo, once you finish waiting in line to talk to them, will offer quick, knowledgeable advice. Stores like these are easily found by the large ads they buy in the local paper, with prices in the range of those offered in mail-order ads.

By perusing newspaper ads you might also find one for a store near you that seems to emphasize not only price, but desirable choices of machines or software applications. Another giveaway of a service-oriented store is mention of classes in using computers and popular programs. Often, fellow users will point you to a store where fair price meets conscientious customer support; some clever store owners have managed to be the default choice for software purchase by entire users' groups, just by paying attention to what people need and being around to answer questions and deal with problems. This is the kind of store where you might find your computer Godfather, and I suggest you persist until you find one or rule out all the possibilities in your area.

The guy you most want to cultivate is the store owner—he is the one most likely to be around when you drop in next week. The turnover at those places is incredible. If not the owner, settle for a manager. Don't give up on clerks, but it seems that once clerks reach an acceptable level of competence, they find a better job at a higher (better paying) rung in the computer field. Your best alternative might be a high school kid working in the store— freshmen especially, since they're not going anywhere for a while. Most often these kids got the job by hanging around the place and making it clear they knew more than anyone working there. They seem to have an endless curiosity about any problems you might encounter, and will devote marathon lengths of time to see something through to its solution. This is especially helpful in those seemingly trivial, ultimately baffling tasks like choosing the proper cable to connect your computer and your printer—a task which has the potential for disaster if you aren't in contact with a person who's done it before.

Make sure your store contact listens to you. Make sure you see software run—on your particular configuration—before you take it home. (If you have a very weird configuration, you might see the software run on something else and leave with a promise to immediately exchange it if it doesn't work—or perhaps make a phone appointment for your Godfather to talk you through the steps necessary to get the software running.) Make sure that the store can come up with several alternative packages to choose from and can explain the relative advantages of each. A good test would be an application that you already know: Can they explain *why* the three-hundred dollar word processor is worth three times the hundred-dollar program—for the needs you have described? If the program you're shopping for is a complicated one, find out how much help they're willing to give. Again, the store might give classes. If not, make damn sure the guy who sells you the program at least knows how to work it. At the very least, he should be willing to spend some time to understand how you might install the program on your system.

***The price you pay.*** The prices of software that we cite in this catalog are list prices, which only rarely are the cheapest available. You can often get sizable discounts by comparison pricing. It goes without saying that you should do this with hardware as well as software (almost everything I'm saying about software applies to computer buying at stores). A guide to the current discount prices on popular machines is the "Street Price Guide" found in the magazine **Creative Computing**. To find the rock-bottom levels in software, check out the prices in big mail-order houses like 800-SOFTWARE or Conroy La Pointe (below). (You can find their ads in magazines like **Byte** and **PC World**.) Then go to the store and see the software, feel it, get it explained to you—and find out what the store charges for it. Almost always it will be somewhat more than the mail-order house. Ten, even twenty percent discount isn't a big deal, but it can be up to *fifty* percent—*i.e.,* hundreds of dollars. In that case, see "Discount Mail Order," below.

The differential lies in the store overhead and support, some of which you've already consumed by taking up space and time by your browsing. Once you've spent time at the store going through programs and have made your choice, are you morally committed to buy at that store? Maybe, maybe not—your wallet and your conscience should decide. But you can also look at it this way—what kind of morons would spend an hour with you looking at spreadsheets, bid you goodbye when you say you'll "think about it," and two weeks (and no purchase) later, spend *another* hour with you looking at database programs?

If you want the support, you gotta support the store.

---

## *If you know what you want . . .*
# DISCOUNT MAIL ORDER

STEWART BRAND: They say 40% of software buying is done with mail-order outfits. I'm surprised it isn't more. For a mass market these goods are costleee. Is fingering the stuff in a store worth thousands of dollars?

You almost always wind up shopping by phone anyway, to see who has what you're looking for, to see who has the best prices—might as well try some of these 800 numbers. Often they'll have what the retail stores don't. Jim Stockford has been collecting experience, reports, and gossip on the subject for a year. It looks to me like the only advantage of buying retail locally is for the savvy and support of the dealer, right Jim?

JAMES STOCKFORD: Wrong. Mail order suppliers are in as good a position to provide support as your local retailers. They sell to a regional or national customer base and typically have a much broader selection of merchandise than any retailer could hope to stock in a storefront. Margins are low, but volume provides enough surplus to pay for a good staff. In fact, every good mail-order house has one or more technicians on the payroll who thoroughly understand the products the supplier stocks.

You can often get better information and advice over the phone from a qualified technician at a mail-order house than you can from a salesperson at a retail store. And if you take their advice and buy a product that is wrong for you, a good supplier exchanges it or refunds your money. The trick is to find a good supplier.

We have tried to give you a good start with recommendations culled from the networks, from reader response to our preliminary list in the first issue of the **Whole Earth Software Review**, and from our experiences. The painful part of this job is that there are so many good suppliers we couldn't list them all.

---

*Highly praised; IBM PC compatible computers, MS-DOS and CP/M software . . .*

## WILSON'S COMPUTER BUSINESS

**14 West Third Street, Suite 4, Santa Rosa, CA 95401; 707/575-9472.**

JAMES STOCKFORD: Best source for IBM PC compatible computers, peripheral devices, software for MS-DOS, CP/M, and Apple with Z-80 card. No other mail-order supplier has been praised so highly by so many people, including retailers. They have been known to refuse a sale when they thought the customer would have trouble. As a general hardware and software supplier there is none better.

---

*IBM, CP/M, Heath/Zenith software . . .*

## 800-SOFTWARE

**940 Dwight Way, Suite 14, Berkeley, CA 94710; 800/227-4587 or, in CA, 415/644-3611.**

JAMES STOCKFORD: I lightly panned their service in the first issue of the **Whole Earth Software Review**, but the mail brought strong support. I checked them out again, and I agree—their service *is* very good. Their newsletter is of high quality, and they are willing to research your needs pretty well for a big company. I give them high marks. (Suggested by Betty Corbin.)

---

*Peripheral hardware for IBM PC and Apple II, no technical advice, returns limited . . .*

## CONROY-LA POINTE

**12060 Garden Place, Portland, OR 97223; 800/547-1289 or, in Oregon, 800/451-5151.**

JAMES STOCKFORD: The only mail-order source I've found that sells the Apple IIe and IBM PC and XT machines themselves. Conroy-La Pointe is the best "plain vanilla" mail-order house. They're large, stable, have good prices and excellent delivery, but you'd better know what you're ordering—they don't give advice, and returns are limited to defects and mis-shipments.

*Commodore 64 . . .*

## A B COMPUTERS

252 Bethlehem Pike, Colmar, PA 18915; 215/822-7727.

JAMES STOCKFORD: Hardware and software for C-64, some Apple II and MS-DOS. Excellent technical support, low repair charges. If you have a problem with a product, they will exchange it or return your money. (Suggested by Milton Sandy.)

*Great deals on Apple hardware/software for members . . .*

## APPLE PUGETSOUND PROGRAM LIBRARY EXCHANGE

21246 68th Avenue South, Kent, WA 98032; 206/872-2245.

MARK COHEN: The Apple Pugetsound Program Library Exchange (A.P.P.L.E.) user's group has become a major hardware and software supplier to Apple II owners all over the world. To take advantage of the substantial discounts, you must become a member—dues are $26 per year with a $25 one-time initiation fee—but you get a monthly magazine, product catalog, and access to hotlines throughout the U.S., in Europe, and on The Source for free programming help from experienced, competent programmers.

*Hacker fodder . . .*

## MONARCHY ENGINEERING, INC.

380 Swift Avenue, Unit 21, South San Francisco, CA 94080; 415/873-3055.

JAMES STOCKFORD: Lots of chips at great prices. RAM in all sizes, logic and linear chips, PROM and EPROM chips, disk drives—these guys are Japanese-parts specialists with real good stuff, cheap. A great source for repair shops, consultants, and hackers.

*Macintosh, Apple II, IBM software . . .*

## STRICTLY SOFTWARE

P.O. Box 338, Granville, OH 43023; 614/587-2938.

JAMES STOCKFORD: Low prices, excellent advice (you're invited to call their technicians and ask questions) and service. They accept returns on most packages within 30 days. (Suggested by John Bryon.)

*TRS-80 hardware and software . . .*

## THE ALTERNATE SOURCE

704 North Pennsylvania Avenue, Lansing, MI 48906; 517/482-8270.

JAMES STOCKFORD: Low prices on commercially available software for most of the Radio Shack TRS-80 machines, some peripheral equipment (disk drives, printers, cables, interface cards, and CRT tubes), and a healthy sampling of their own software. They publish a newsletter and will develop software on a custom basis. Customer support and return policy is excellent.

They are beginning to broaden their line to include hardware and software for CP/M and MS-DOS machines. For users of the "less-compatible" MS-DOS machines, such as Sanyo or Leading Edge, they will try to find answers to questions—very valuable.

*Hardware/software for the disabled, doctors, hospitals and lawyers . . .*

## GOODRICH/HANSEN AND ASSOCIATES, LTD.

Bon Vista, Suite H-5, Morgantown, WV 26505; 304/599-8388; on The Source (p. 140) BBF203; on CompuServe (p. 140) 70355,1253.

JAMES STOCKFORD: This company primarily supplies hardware— synthesizers, voice recognition devices, protocol converters for printers, modems, and printers at low prices—and high-end legal, medical, and accounting software packages. They also provide custom hardware and software configurations for lawyers, doctors, accountants, and database aficionados, and offer a mini-feasibility study (generally at no charge) and low-cost or no-cost services for the disabled. (Suggested by Jonathan Sachs.)

*Peripheral hardware and software for TRS-80 and CP/M machines, emphasis on CAD, good for neophytes and special needs . . .*

## TOTAL ACCESS

P.O. Box 790276, Dallas, TX 75379; 800/527-3582 or, in TX, 214/458-1966.

JAMES STOCKFORD: Lots of experience with plotters, digitizers, and computer-aided design (CAD) hardware and software. This small shop mainly sells hardware peripherals and accessories such as printers, disk drives, cables, monitors, and so forth. Specialists in TRS-80 equipment, they also supply standard software products for all TRS-80 and many CP/M machines. Good telephone help before and after you order. Check with them if you have unusual needs.

*Typical price breaks from a mail-order supplier, in this case MicroFlash, advertising in the June 25, 1984, InfoWorld. On p. 61 of this book we suggest using the top word processor MICROSOFT WORD and its indispensable mouse with the Hercules Graphics Card to get a high resolution screen with 43 lines of text instead of the usual 25 on the IBM PC. List prices for the software, mouse and card total $994, plus sales tax if you buy locally. From this mail-order supplier you could get the same stuff for $717, saving $277, and no sales tax. Much larger discounts, to more than 50%, are common.*

*Kaypro only . . .*

## THE SYSTEMS HOUSE

Village Center, P.O. Box 617, Great Falls, VA 22066; 703/759-6800.

PHIL GAREY: They publish a small catalog filled mainly with software titles and some hardware for Kaypro owners. They don't accept credit cards other than American Express, but will ship C.O.D. If you have problems, they will exchange the product or refund your money.

JAMES STOCKFORD: Their electronic bulletin board service is loaded with public domain software. Call 703/759-6627.

*Computer supplies . . .*

## LYBEN COMPUTER SYSTEMS

1250-E Rankin Drive, Troy, MI 48083; 313/589-3440.

MICHAEL GILBERTO: Lyben is terrific for supplies: disks, paper, printer stands, and so on. Disks are competitively priced and there are frequent specials. Shipping is a flat $2 per order, except for large cartons of paper. My orders come fast.

*Dysan diskettes, add-on boards for Apples, technical expertise . . .*

## CALIFORNIA DIGITAL

P.O. Box 3097B, Torrance, CA 90503; 800/421-5041 or, in CA, 213/643-9001.

JONATHAN SACHS: California Digital is one of the few mail-order companies offering Dysan diskettes. Their prices are below list and they ship immediately.

JAMES STOCKFORD: In addition to having good disk prices, this hardware supplier (printers, disk drives, memory chips, add-on boards for Apple II machines, and diskettes) does such a thorough evaluation of hardware they have become a supply source and reference for equipment manufacturers themselves. Their support and return policies are excellent. They will adjust most ass-backward customer installations at no charge and will always repair or replace any defects at no charge.

*Nine-page report on mail-order buying practices . . .*

## MAIL ORDER REPORT

$2.50; Caverly's, Inc., 512 Bridle Court, Walnut Creek, CA 94596.

JAMES STOCKFORD: A dense collection of mail-order buying tips for computer products—nuts and bolts wisdom put together by a man who has studied mail-order suppliers for many years.

## HOW TO IDENTIFY GOOD MAIL ORDER SUPPLIERS

Check old magazines to see that an advertising supplier has been around for long enough to be stable. Call them up and ask questions: How long have they been in business, what do they carry, how do they handle returns, can they provide technical help? Place a few inexpensive orders at first. The process takes a while, but, as with anyone, you have to get to know them to develop a relationship. Use your credit card, so if calamity strikes you can ask the bank to reverse the charge made to your card. Don't bother reading about the horrors of mail-order ripoff; that's just sensationalism. With a little search, you will find wonderful people running excellent supply services. When you find them, tell us about them, and we'll help spread the word.

—*James Stockford*

*Annual listing and description of mail-order sources for computer supplies . . .*

## DISCOUNT AMERICA GUIDE

$3.50/issue; 51 East 42nd Street, Room 417, New York, NY 10017; 212/580-0541.

JAMES STOCKFORD: This guide lists mail-order purveyors of hardware, software, books and periodicals, accessories, and services, with a thumbnail appraisal of their business and a few pages that propose good buying practice. The computer guide is released in the fourth quarter of every year (other issues focus on music and audio equipment, sporting goods, crafts and sewing).

*Newsletter with frequent comments on suppliers, good info . . .*

## COMPUTERWHAT?

Corbin Consultants, Inc., 11111 Richmond Avenue, Suite 150, Houston, TX 77082; 713/781-7070. $12/year.

JAMES STOCKFORD: Well informed and easy to read, this 4 to 6 page newsletter provides a monthly comment on mail-order suppliers, new products, hardware, and software tips without any hype. When my copy gets to my desk, I stop everything and read it.

*Beat the system . . .*
# HOW TO GET FREE SOFTWARE

ALFRED GLOSSBRENNER: What's the best kept secret in the microworld? It's hard to say, but the existence of vast reservoirs of free, "public domain" software has to rank right up there with the unannounced products currently being developed in the backrooms at Apple and IBM. Most people aren't aware of it, but there are literally thousands of public domain (or "PD") programs available for virtually every brand of personal computer.

There are games, graphics, and music programs . . . word processing, database management, and personal finance . . . inventory, accounting, and educational software . . . VISICALC "templates" and dBASE II command files . . . plus scores of handy utility programs. All of them free—if you know where to look. You'll find some of the best sources described below. But first, some quick answers to some quick questions.

### Where Does Free Software Come From?

Though not yet widely recognized as such, there can be no doubt that the disk drive is the new printing press and the floppy disk the new medium. For an investment of as little as $500, *anyone* can write and "publish" a computer program. And from the beginning of the micro era in the mid 1970s, that's exactly what computer owners have been doing. Typically, a person will write a program and contribute it to his or her local computer users' group, along with a signed statement that officially places the work in the public domain. That means that it can be copied and distributed freely.

### Is the Free Stuff Any Good?

Yes. Some free programs are on a par with the very best commercial software. PC-WRITE (p. 59), a word processing program for the IBM/PC, PC/jr, and compatibles, is a case in point. Written by Bob Wallace, the architect of Microsoft Pascal, PC-WRITE can execute a search and replace up to five times faster than a leading program listing at $500, and I personally find it much easier to use. There is a 70-page manual (with index) on the disk for you to print out.

You can obtain a copy from one of the sources cited below. Or you can simply send $10 to Quicksoft, Mr. Wallace's firm, at 219 First N. #224, Seattle, WA 98109. If you like, you can place a telephone order and charge it to your Visa or MasterCard. Call 206/282-0452.

*(continued on p. 26)*

*(continued from p. 25)*

Naturally, not every public domain program is outstanding. With thousands—and in some cases *tens of thousands*—of programs, how could it be otherwise? You may not find all the whistles and bells you would like, and error-trapping can be a problem. But often you can add these features yourself. In fact, there is no better way to learn BASIC, assembler, FORTH, or Pascal than to start with the raw material of a public domain program.

In addition, almost all the public domain collections associated with each brand of computer contain utility programs that often have no commercial counterpart. Yet they can make using your micro so much easier that you won't be able to live without them. For example, a program called WASH presents a disk directory one file at a time. As each filename appears, you have the option of deleting, re-naming, or copying the file to another drive. WASH can be found in both the CP/M and IBM public domain, but similar utilities are available for most other computers (see p. 174).

## Where to Get it: Points of Access

### Users' Groups

Computer clubs and users' groups have traditionally been the primary collection and distribution points for public domain software. That's still true today, but many other sources have recently begun to appear.

If you belong to a local users' group, the "Software Librarian" is the person to see about getting copies of the programs in the group's free software library. If you've yet to join a group, contact your computer dealer for information about groups in your area. But don't worry if there isn't a group where you live. Many users' groups accept remote members and make their free software collections available by mail. The cost of membership ranges from $10 to $25 a year and usually includes a subscription to a monthly newsletter or magazine. Disks packed with free software are usually available for about $6, including the disk, disk mailer, and postage.

If you have an extra $24, I strongly advise using it to pay the annual membership dues for The Boston Computer Society (BCS). BCS is the world's premier computer users' group. There is simply nothing else like it, and with more than 12,000 members worldwide, it offers an excellent way to plug into the users' group network. More to the point, BCS serves as an umbrella for more than 35 special interest groups (SIGs) focusing on everything from Apples to Artificial Intelligence to Kaypros, Osbornes, IBMs, and UNIX. Virtually all of these SIGs maintain free software collections. For more information contact: The Boston Computer Society, One Center Plaza, Boston, MA 02108, or phone 617/367-8080 between 9:30 a.m. and 5:30 p.m., Eastern Time.

### Non-Users'-Group Sources

There are also a growing number of non-users'-group sources. Though it isn't always the case, these companies often offer public domain software on a "value added" basis. The "value" may consist of testing and debugging or adding additional features to the software. Or it may consist of preparing "collections" of PD programs designed for a particular application. Disks containing nothing but games or nothing but financial programs may be offered, for example. The cost per disk is usually slightly more than you would pay when ordering from a users' group. But since few users' groups classify their software by application, you might have to order several users' group disks to obtain all of the programs you want.

The American Software Publishing Company (ASPC) is a good example of non-users'-group source. Sheryl Nutting, the firm's president, estimates that ASPC has more than 10,000 public domain programs for Apple, Atari, Commodore, IBM, Texas Instruments, Timex, and TRS-80 computers. The software is available on tape or disk and the average cost is between 20 and 95 cents per program. For more information, contact the firm at: P.O. Box 57221, Washington, D.C. 20037 or phone 202/887-5834.

The Apple Avocation Alliance (2111 Central Avenue, Cheyenne, WY 82001) offers over 185 disks of Apple software, including Apple CP/M and Pascal, at a cost of $3 per disk ($2.55 if you order ten or more) plus $2 shipping and handling. This mail-order firm offers very good deals on hardware, commercial software, and supplies. The PD programs are listed at the back of the 150-page catalog. To obtain a copy, send $2 ($3 for shipment overseas) or phone 307/632-8561 between 8 a.m. and 5 p.m., Mountain Time, for more information.

You'll find inventory, checkbook balancing, and personal investment programs on Disk 044, a database management program on Disk 047, and communications and related programs on Disk 075. But if you're going to order only two or three disks, I suggest Disk 020 (SPARKEE), Disk 229 (ONE-KEY DOS), and Eamon Master 01. SPARKEE is a color graphics program that produces a different dynamic design each time you hit a key on your keyboard. ONE-KEY DOS makes Apple DOS 3.3 much easier to use. And the Eamon disk (there are over 40 of them in all) will intrigue any fan of ADVENTURE (see p. 41).

Commodore owners should consider contacting Public Domain, Inc., at 5025 S. Rangeline Road, West Milton, OH 45383, for a free catalog of free programs for the C-64, VIC-20, PET, and SX-64. Run by Bill Munch and George Ewing, this company specializes in "best of" PD collections. Programs are available on both tape and disk. The cost is $10, postage included, regardless of medium. Phone 513/698-5638; Visa and MasterCard.

There are many excellent programs in these collections, but one is so outstanding that it deserves special mention. It's called MONOPLE 64, and you'll find it on Disk C2. The program creates the Monopoly game board on your color TV, rolls the on-screen dice, moves your token, serves as the "banker," and keeps track of all your buy/sell transactions. I guarantee that if you have a C-64, you and a friend will spend hours playing this game. The same disk contains POKER (five-card stud), OTHELLO (like the board game), a logic game, a temperature conversion program, a bar graph generating program, and 20 other programs.

If you own an IBM or compatible, I suggest contacting the PC Software Interest Group (PC/SIG) at 1556 Halford Avenue, Suite #130, Santa Clara, CA 95051. This firm offers a 110-page catalog of over 135 disks of free IBM software. The catalog is $5.95, postage included, and disks sell for $6 each. (California residents, add 6.5% sales tax.) Visa and MasterCard are accepted, so you can order by phone if you like. Call 408/730-9291.

## HOW TO GET FREE SOFTWARE

*How to Get Free Software*; Alfred Glossbrenner; 1984; $14.95; St. Martin's Press, 175 Fifth Avenue, New York, NY 10010; 212/674-5151; or COMPUTER LITERACY.

STEWART BRAND: No one we know has a more comprehensive knowledge of software than Alfred Glossbrenner. His **How to Buy Software** (p. 6) and **The Complete Handbook of Personal Computer Communications** (p. 140) are the best of their kind. If you find what he's written here useful, you will want his new book, **How to Get Free Software**, which truly has chapter and verse on the subject. The major problem with public domain programs is finding out about them and finding where to get them. He takes care of both. (The minor problems are dealing with the sheer volume of choices and working without manuals.)

Alfred Glossbrenner is a regular contributor to the **Whole Earth Software Review** (p. 11).

---

Headed by Richard Petersen, this is one of the best-organized, most professionally run sources of free software in the entire public domain. In the not too distant future, it may very well become *the* source of free IBM software. There are simply too many excellent free programs to mention. Send for the catalog. You'll think you've died and gone to free software heaven.

CP/M users should consider contacting Elliam Associates at 24000 Bessemer Street, Woodland Hills, CA 91367. Phone: 213/348-4278 (evenings from 7:00 on; weekends anytime.) Bill Roch, the firm's president, offers virtually all the programs found in the huge libraries of CP/M users' groups. But unlike most users' groups, he can supply them in over 40 different floppy disk formats (excluding Apple and Commodore). Prices range from about $12 to $20 per collection, depending on the capacity of your disk format and the number of floppies required. Sending for the free catalog is an excellent way to get started.

Free CP/M programs of special note include BIZMASTER, a complete business software package occupying six single-sided eight-inch disks that formerly sold for $160 but is now in the public domain; DIMS—"Dan's Information Management System"—a file manager by Dan Dugan (**Microsystems**, a Ziff-Davis CP/M magazine, uses DIMS to keep track of its authors, articles, and other information.); ED (a full-screen word processor); READ (displays 24 lines of a file at a time and prompts you to hit ENTER for more); RECOVER or UNERA ("unerases" erased files); and XDIR (an "extended directory" utility that alphabetizes and presents disk files in three columns). The most famous free CP/M program of all is MODEM7 (p. 151), a communications program by Ward Christensen that has had a major influence on commercial communications software.

### Free Software Online

Speaking of communications, you should know that it is possible to obtain a large percentage of the free software available for your machine over the telephone. If your computer is equipped for online communications you can dial a free BBS (Bulletin Board System) or RCPM (Remote CP/M) system and "download" programs directly into your machine. The only other thing you need is a list of phone numbers, and you can obtain them from many computer magazines. Or you can subscribe to the "On Line Computer Telephone Directory" ($9.95/year; $15.95 for overseas shipment). The 400 to 500 phone numbers in this publication are tested and updated quarterly. Contact: OLCTD, P.O. Box 10005, Kansas City, MO 64111-9990.

You will also find huge collections of free software on the CompuServe Information Service (CIS). Available at many computer stores, a subscription is $50 and includes a manual and five free hours on the system. After 6 p.m., your local time, hourly charges are $6 for 300 baud service; $12.50 for 1200 baud. Call 800/848-8990 or, in Ohio, 614/457-8600, for more information (also see p. 140).

The free software on CompuServe can be found in the database sections of the more than 60 SIGs on the system. Many of these Special Interest Groups are devoted to a particular brand of computer. Because the documentation you receive may not explain how to use a CIS SIG, you may never know about all the free software unless you do the following:

1. Type GO PCS1 at any CIS exclamation prompt. This will take you to the Personal Computing Section.

2. Follow the menus until you get to "Groups and Clubs," then choose the SIG you want.

3. At your first opportunity upon entering the SIG, type XA0 at the prompt. This selection will not be on the menu.

4. That will take you to the XA0 database within the SIG. Once there, enter XA at the next prompt to produce a list of all available databases.

5. Choose a database and enter S/DES/KEY: followed by the keyword you would like to search for when scanning ("S") a program's description ("DES"). You might try BASIC for starters.

6. When you see a description that looks interesting, you can download the program itself by entering TYP followed by the filename at the next prompt.

### Conclusion

There are a number of other techniques to use on CompuServe. And if you subscribe to The Source, you'll find a host of excellent Apple programs in "Apple City" and SAUG, the "Source Apple Users Group" (type PUBLIC at the command level or follow the menus to User Publishing). There are also many other excellent users' group and non-users'-group sources.

But the information provided here will get you off to a good start. Once you enter the world of free software, you may never look back. Indeed, there may be no reason to, since the chances are you'll find that nearly everything you need is available for free.

# PLAYING

## Steven Levy, Domain Editor

STEVEN LEVY: There are by and large two kinds of computer owners: those who bought computers to play games and those who lie about it. The fact is that computers are almost by nature game machines. Even business applications, done correctly, become gamelike in their execution and manipulation, and it is the rarest of computerists who doesn't sneak a shoot-'em-up or an adventure onto the machine when the boss (or the superego) isn't watching. Not running games on your computer is like refusing to take your Ferrari out of first gear.

Literally thousands of games are available for computers, and most of them are mindless diversions. I don't object to mindless diversions now and then, and I include a few of the most relentlessly stupefying ones in my selection. But many computer games are much more: challenging brain-puzzlers that extend your problem-solving abilities, elaborate simulations that make you master of tiny universes, imaginative flights of fantasy that encourage you to create a persona within the machine, and tests of your own creative powers that secretly give you lessons on how the world works. All in the guise of play.

I make no claim that the games reviewed here are the definitive best of all those available. Games are not like word processors, where you choose the best you can find and use it. They're more like books, where you get involved for a while—sometimes to Proustian lengths—and then read another. Every game treated here, however, is great in its way. I found out about each one by asking people what games they really love to play. Sometimes I followed up by asking the suggestors to write about those games. Other times I liked the game so much I wrote about it myself. (You'll notice this happened a lot.)

The ideal game is fairly easy to get started on, but "deep" enough to give you new rewards as you keep playing. (The term "deep" here is borrowed from Trip Hawkins of Electronic Arts, a company that publishes some deep games.) The ideal game uses the computer fully but unobtrusively, and never feels like a chore. It makes you want to quit your job and play it all day, at least until you get sick of it. You don't get sick of great games quickly.

I categorize computer games under five loose headings.

***Strategy games***—there are two kinds of these. The first are simulations, notably those that re-create conflicts (the computer has modified the board-based war game). Then there are the pure *game* games—not translated-to-code chess but creations that owe their existence to the computer. I'm particularly inclined to this genre, since it is not only the most innovative, but also the one that promises the most mind-bending future developments.

***Sports and noncomputer games*** take advantage of the abilities of the machine to make familiar games into something entirely new, either by providing electronic playmates or by making things so easy you wonder why you put up with the original game before the computer came along. The sports games in this category beat the old board games all to hell when it comes to sports simulations.

In ***action games*** hand/eye coordination and quick reflexes are more important than the knowledge gained from a lifetime of study. Sometimes the action—and, yes, the violence—can be therapeutic. Often, though, action games are derivative, and their shallowness makes their $30 pricetags outrageous. I tried for a selection of the most absorbing, the ones with some elements of thought, the most graphically stunning, and the most slyly seductive of the bunch, including a couple of programs that give you a turn at designing games yourself.

***Adventure games*** exist only on the computer. They employ the logical branching patterns of the computer to pose elaborate puzzles. Almost all adventures, whether they are limited to text or are illustrated with colorful pictures, involve some sort of quest, with you giving instructions to the machine, usually in the

## WHY THIS SECTION COMES FIRST

STEWART BRAND: In our lives play precedes work. Play is a kind of pretend working where mistakes count but don't count. You lose points, maybe, and pride, but not livelihood, so you freely make mistakes, and you freely learn. For a growing majority of personal computer users—kids naturally, adults if they're smart—the first use of these machines is to play with them.

You're starting at the top. No programs push the limits of technique and design ingenuity of personal computers as thoroughly as games. No programs are as clever, as kind, as blatant, in reaching out to the user and compelling involvement. In the world of software development, computer games are invariably invoked as the ideal in "self-evident" program design. Elements that you will find in business application programs years from now are evolving in bright colors before your eyes in software like PINBALL

*Steven Levy*

CONSTRUCTION SET (p. 36) and CHOPLIFTER! (p. 35).

Steven Levy loves playing computer games. His research for his book **Hackers** (reviewed on p. 171) gives him perspective on the place of games at the cutting edge of computer artistry. His writing for **Rolling Stone** and **Popular Computing** (the column "Micro Journal") gives him perspective on their place in Current Events.

Computer games are treated in the press these days like popular films or TV or music, but something deeper is going on. Those aren't sports; this is. Those are for spectators; this isn't.

form of two-word commands ("Go east" or "Enter transporter"). This allows you to move through dozens of "rooms" on the way to slaying the dragon or finding the murderer. Frequently, you'll get stuck at a seeming impasse and find yourself making a long-distance call to an adventure publisher's hot line.

*Role-playing games* are not just variations on adventure games: They are the closest thing we have to truly interactive novels. Role-playing games, to quote documentation from one publisher, are those "in which the player assumes the identity of a character within the fantasy world of the game itself. Such a character is usually formed by assigning random values to special characteristics such as strength, intelligence, luck, or charisma. These characteristics in turn determine the capability of the character in combat, negotiation, and encounters with other beings." As you proceed, the value of the traits grows, making the characters more powerful. The games sometimes take hundreds of hours to play, and players develop intensely personal relationships with the characters they have developed. It's weird, but people have reported deep grief when some Orc of the Ninth Level wipes out a character after months of dungeon combat and questing. These are less games than ways of life for devoted addicts, yet the proliferation of computers has made this addiction far from uncommon.

## Shopping

When looking for games, try to see the program actually running in the store. Check out reviews in such magazines as **Family Computing** (p. 11) and **Creative Computing**, or in periodicals and books dedicated to your machine. (The Book Company's series called **The Book of Apple [Atari, IBM] Software** is excellent. Arrays, Inc./The Book Company, 11223 South Hindry Ave., Los Angeles, CA 90045; 213/410-9466; or COMPUTER LITERACY.) Usually the games on the bestseller list compiled by **Billboard** magazine or the Softsel distributor (some stores post the lists) will give you value.

## Hardware

I concentrate on four machines: the Apple, because it is the Apple; the Atari, because its exceptional graphics and sound make it the quintessential game machine, with the biggest selection of games available; the Commodore 64, because of its popularity and power; and the IBM PC, because a lot of people have one, and the game publishers have not neglected it. For those who own Kaypros, Morrows, and Osbornes and are kicking yourselves because you didn't know that Broderbund doesn't publish a CP/M CHOPLIFTER!, I've tried to do the best I can, but you have only yourselves to blame for the limited selection. Few excellent games are written for the Tandy TRS series, because (1) it's not a good game machine and (2) Tandy's restrictive attitude toward third-party software developers has kept innovators writing for other computers. I've generally ignored the (already obsolete) machines that do little more than play games, such as the VIC 20 and TI 99/4A.

Almost all the games reviewed are easily available from their publishers, but for games that are not (as in the case of public domain games and games available only on online services), the access section tells you where to find them. Often a game will come in versions for more than one machine; if play varies considerably from one version to the next, we mention it. The exception is when games run on the less powerful VIC 20 and TI machines; in those cases you can assume inferior play, unless we specify otherwise.

One final word: Wherever possible I've included the names of the game designers. The people who devise these delicious and edifying entertainments are artists and deserve recognition. Though I curse them when their creations draw my computer personae into dire and fatal fantasy catastrophe, I salute them here.

## Game Magazines

STEVEN LEVY: The cheekiest magazine in computerdom is **St.Game**, formerly known as **Softline**. Imbued with as much cheerful whimsy as the best of the games it considers in its well-written, informed reviews, this mag not only has the temerity (in an advertiser-supported publication) to call a game inferior when circumstances require, but will go an extra mile and *make fun* of the lousy game. The magazine polls readers annually to select a Dog of the Year. On occasion it will even make fun of entire software companies, as in its brilliant parody of the pompous ad that launched Electronic Arts ("Can a Computer Game Magazine Make You Cry?" asked the parody. No, but it can make a computer game magazine ad director cry: **St.Game** is much thinner than its siblings in the **Softalk** family.)

Obviously aimed at true gaming fans not wed to a particular machine (though games on Apple, C64, IBM, and especially Atari are just about the whole show here), **St.Game** cares as much about the gaming community as it does about the game. Software stars are profiled, and symposia on gaming issues (piracy, the future of interactive fiction) draw on the best minds of the industry. For the game purist, it offers not only advance looks at upcoming programs, but a comprehensive and current list of players' high scores for almost any computer game you could imagine. I find this morbidly fascinating if somewhat daunting: How can I be proud of achieving Level 8 on MARAUDER when I learn that Clark Alyea of Bloomington, Indiana, has accumulated more than half a million points on Level 21?

**Computer Games** magazine is slicker, but it too has the wisdom not to take itself too seriously. It contains valuable reviews, as well as a section called "Conversion Capsules," which lets you know what hit games look like after they're converted to run on different machines. Also useful are the features on how to score big on popular games. I never would have known that you could bomb a bridge *twice* playing BLUE MAX had I not read about it in the June 1984 issue.

A more staid publication specializing in computer games is **Computer Gaming World**. It is at its best at long analyses of complex games, including detailed strategies for doing well. For serious fans of strategy games, the subscription price of **CGW** is an investment in getting more out of some of these monster $40 simulation games they've been hacking away at.

**St. Game:** $12/yr (6 issues); St. Game, P.O. Box 605, N. Hollywood, CA 91602 ● **Computer Games:** $11.95/yr (6 issues); Computer Games, 888 Seventh Avenue, NY, NY 10106 ● **Computer Gaming World:** $12.50/yr (6 issues); Computer Gaming World, P.O. Box 4566, Anaheim, CA 92803-4566.

## WHOLE EARTH RECOMMENDED PLAYING TOOLS

### (June 1984)

### MAGAZINES (p.29)
**St.Game**, $12/yr
**Computer Games**, $11.95/yr
**Computer Gaming World**, $12.50/yr

### STRATEGY
ARCHON, $40, p.30
ALICE, p.30
LIFE, free/$10, p.31
MEGAWARS, CompuServe rates, p.31
OLD IRONSIDES, $39.95, p.32
BROADSIDES, $39.95, p.32
KNIGHTS OF THE DESERT, $39.95, p.32
OPERATION WHIRLWIND, $39.95, p.32
ROBOTWAR, $39.95, p.33
FORTRESS, $34.95, p.33
FLIGHT SIMULATOR, $50, p.33
FLIGHT SIMULATOR II, $39.95/$50, p.33
M.U.L.E., $40, p.34
THE SEVEN CITIES OF GOLD, $40, p.34
THREE MILE ISLAND, $39.95, p.34
SCRAM, $24.95, p.34

### ACTION
POLE POSITION, $39.95/$45, p.35
PITSTOP, about $30, p.35
CHOPLIFTER!, $34.95-$45, p.35
VYPER, $39.95, p.35
PINBALL CONSTRUCTION SET, $40, p.36
CROSSFIRE, $29.95/$34.95, p.36
DRELBS, $34.95, p.36
BOULDER DASH, $29.95-$40, p.37
MOONDUST, $34.95, p.37
LODE RUNNER, $34.95/$39.95, p.37
BLUE MAX, $34.95, p.38
REPTON, $39.95, p.38
OIL'S WELL, $29.95/$34.95, p.38
MINER 2049ER, $29.95-$50, p.38

### SPORTS AND NONCOMPUTER GAMES
MONTY PLAYS SCRABBLE,
    $34.95/$39.95, p.39
COMPUTER BASEBALL, $39.95, p.39
STAR LEAGUE BASEBALL,
    $29.95/$31.95, p.39

JULIUS ERVING AND LARRY BIRD
    GO ONE-ON-ONE, $40, p.40
PRO-GOLF CHALLENGE, $34.95/$39.95,
    p.40
SARGON III, $50, p.40

### ADVENTURE
ADVENTURE, $19.95/$24.95
    or Source rates, p.41
THE QUEST, $34.95/$39.95, p.41
ZORK I, II, and III, $29.95/$39.95, p.42
PLANETFALL, $50/$60, p.42
DEADLINE, $29.95-$60, p.42
TIME ZONE, $100, p.43
WIZARD AND THE PRINCESS, $29.95,
    p.43
EAMON, free/$10, p.44

### BOOKS (p.43)
**Wizisystem Manual**, $15
**Shortcut Through Adventureland**, $9.95

### ROLE PLAYING (pp.44-45)
WIZARDRY
    PROVING GROUNDS OF THE MAD
        OVERLORD, $50/$60
    KNIGHT OF DIAMONDS, $34.95
    LEGACY OF LLYLGAMYN, $39.95
ULTIMA II, $60
EXODUS: ULTIMA III, $60
WIZARD'S CASTLE, free/$10

---

## *Strategy*

*Moving the yellow square at left will pinpoint your next move against the forces of darkness in ARCHON. If you land on a square occupied by a blue piece, you'll be thrust into a fierce, arcade-like battle.*

*Two post-computer chess games . . .*

### ARCHON

**Westfall, Freeman & Reiche; Apple II family; 48K ● Atari 400/800/XL series; 48K ● Commodore 64 ● IBM PC compatibles; 64K; joystick; $40; copy-protected? YES; Electronic Arts, 2755 Campus Dr., San Mateo, CA 94403; 415/571-7171.**

### ALICE

**Steve Capps; Apple Macintosh; copy-protected? YES; price not yet set; Apple Computer, 20525 Mariani Ave., Cupertino, CA 95014; 800/538-9696.**

---

STEWART BRAND: Dungeons and Dragons meets chess, and I'm addicted. So far the computer is more subtle and violent that I am, but I'm gaining. (After maybe 50 games? My ladyfriend loathes both ARCHON and me.)

It's a chess-size board, the characters line up like chess people, and they move and capture, and that's the end of the resemblance. The two sides—representing the forces of Light and Darkness—have well-matched but quite different pieces. (About half are female, evenly distributed; this game mines a more chthonic vein of myth than chess does.) The mage on one side is a wizard, on the other a sorceress, each with equivalent but different talents of spell making, mobility, toughness, and weaponry. So it goes, through banshees, Valkyries, unicorns, basilisks, goblins, knights, archers, golems, trolls, and so on.

About half the playing board's squares vary with time through shades of gray, giving the advantage to Light or Dark players at different times. And capture is no simple matter. After your character lands on an occupied square, it must fight for it. The square suddenly fills the screen and your piece is locked in mortal combat, its lifeline shrinking each time the opponent strikes successfully. The game is won when all the enemy is eliminated or when one side occupies all five "power points" on the board. ARCHON is equally lively with one or two players.

STEVEN LEVY: ALICE, the first great Macintosh game, is a closer cousin to chess that ARCHON. With stunning 3-D animated graphics (you see chess pieces, even the cross-shaped cursor, get larger as they approach), a chessboard appears with pieces styled like Tenniel's looking-glass illustrations in Lewis Carroll. You pick a chess piece and your blond-haired Alice moves like that piece. You'd better move her quickly, because everyone on the board is after her and will jump her whenever possible. You, as Alice, can capture the other pieces, but since they move so fast, you gotta fake them out. Also, avoid a moving trapdoor—or trick the others into falling into it.

The mouse movements are easily mastered—send the cursor to your next move and click

(ALICE ignores illegal moves). The action is so fast here, you don't stop to enjoy the delightful albeit Mac-black-and-white graphics—you *get involved*, and get the best training ever for those five-second-limit chess games that some masters play. I think the Mac is going to be a great game machine, and ALICE is the first proof.

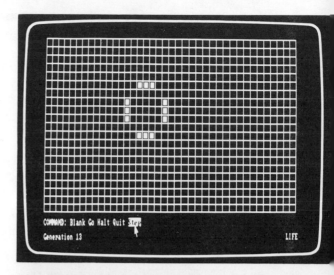

---

*Deceptively simple, infinitely deep . . .*

## LIFE

**John Conway; Apple II family ● IBM PC compatibles; $10 per disk; copy-protected? NO; Public Domain Software Copying Co., 33 Gold Street, #13, New York, NY 10038; 212/732-2565; IBM version also available from PC Software Interest Group, 1556 Halford Avenue #130, Santa Clara, CA 95051; 408/730-9291.**

STEVEN LEVY: In the November 1970 **Scientific American**, Martin Gardner introduced LIFE, a simulation conceived by British philosopher John Conway. It fired the imaginations of logicians, gamesters, and poetic mathematicians all over the world, but none were so excited as the first computer hackers, who could fully explore the mysteries suggested by what I consider the deepest of all computer games.

The rules to LIFE are elementary. Picture a grid. Each square is a "cell." Each turn of the game—called a "generation"— determines a cell's fate: A living cell bordering on two or three living neighbors survives. With fewer neighbors, a cell dies of isolation. With more, it's fatally stifled by overpopulation. A dead cell bordering on exactly three living cells is "born" and becomes a live cell.

LIFE works on many levels. On the simplest, it is fun to set up a pattern—a "colony" of LIFE cells—and move along generation by generation to see what happens. The patterns are often hypnotically beautiful until the

almost inevitable end: a stable "still life," a loop where a colony "pulses" between two patterns, or a blank dead screen. The exceptions to extinction are the rare self-replicating patterns.

One of the most fascinating hours of my life was spent before the computer screen of LIFE master and canonical hacker R. William Gosper, discoverer of the notorious "Glider Gun" (a deathless LIFE colony that snakes through the universe spitting off offspring). We raced through billions of generations of intricate patterns. Gosper says he "hacks LIFE" because it's one of the few remaining places where mathematical discoveries can be made. For those of us who are not world-class mathematicians, LIFE is still edifying, putting us viscerally in contact with the hauntingly beautiful nexus of logic and vision.

Gosper uses an intricate LIFE program fixed to run on the $60,000 Symbolics LISP machine, but versions of LIFE run on virtually every microcomputer. You can find a BASIC program for LIFE in many books.

Still, the ultimate microcomputer LIFE has yet to be written. It would be in superfast machine language and have lots of utilities, like zooming out to a larger grid or into a smaller section and slow-motion instant replay. Maybe because the game itself is public domain, publishers don't want to develop a program for it. Too bad—I'd buy one in a minute.

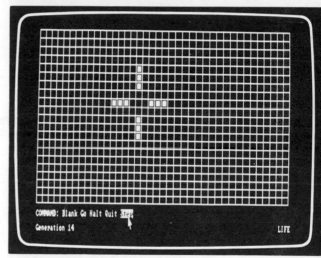

*After thirteen generations, what we have here is a "pulsar," alternating between these two patterns. Other results can be blank screens, "still life," or the very rare "glider gun," where you've generated life itself.*

---

*Shooting space ships via modem . . .*

## MEGAWARS

**All machines with modem & CompuServe Information Service hookup; available at regular CompuServe rates (see table, p. 140); CòmpuServe Information Service, 5000 Arlington Centre, P.O. Box 20212, Columbus, OH 43220; 800/848-8199.**

STEVEN LEVY: No single event in computer gaming has given me a bigger rush than my first MEGAWARS kill. I was sitting at a computer in Palo Alto connected by modem to the CompuServe host computer in Columbus, piloting a spaceship called Wolf. I was in the service of the Empire, locked in eternal battle with the Colonists (the usual epic scenario—I think computer games are single-handedly restoring myth to a central place in the hearts of young America). To put it bluntly, I destroyed the Colonist ship

Levant. Who the pilot was, I'll never know. A twelve-year-old in Georgia? A grandmother in Walla Walla? But that's interactive telegaming, and I think it's a wave of the future.

MEGAWARS is a variant of the old Star Trek computer game, where you moved across various sectors of a galaxy seeking to blow up unfriendly enemies while annexing the universe. This multiplayer CompuServe incarnation is complicated, and I didn't even attempt it until I had sent for the 38-page manual. (Like most CompuServe manuals that should have been sent to you in the first place, this is available at an extra cost via CompuServe's "Feedback" service.) After studying how to scan, move around, and confront my enemy, I logged on, ready to join the cosmic struggle, individual battles of which had been continuing for more than a year.

Since MEGAWARS requires you to join one of two sides eternally at odds, you automatically have partners, and they can communicate to you through "radio." It's a thrill to hear from real-life allies. Though the modem-received graphics are limited, I felt I was soaring. And when, after a few sessions, I could finally control the commands well enough to shoot down an enemy, I was ecstatic, though later I got wistful, wondering if I'd made some stranger feel really bad. There was obviously no way to take him or her out for a drink later to prove it was all in good fun.

Still, late at night when your friends are asleep, you can count on some MEGAWARS action on CompuServe (though at normal online rates it can get costly). Since you get "promoted" and get more powerful ships as you accumulate points, you have incentive to keep going. But even without that, the MEGAWARS lure is strong.

*Battle of the micro ships . . .*

## OLD IRONSIDES

**Richard Hefter & Jack Rice; Apple II family; 48K; paddles or keyboard; one disk drive; color recommended; $39.95; copy-protected? YES; Weekly Reader Software, Xerox Education Publications, 245 Long Hill Rd., Middletown, CT 06457; 800/852-5000.**

## BROADSIDES

**Wayne Garris; Apple II family; 48K ● Apple III ● Atari (all machines); 48K; paddle recommended; $39.95; copy-protected? YES; Strategic Simulations, Inc., 883 Stierlin Road, Bldg. A-200, Mountain View, CA 94043; 415/964-1353.**

STEWART BRAND: Qualifications to review these games, sir: I have read the entire Horatio Hornblower series of novels twice; I own a sailing vessel (sadly under-equipped with cannon); I know enough not to spit to windward, sir. I take great glee in these games.

Both of them reek of the salt, gunpowder, and blood of naval warfare of the eighteenth and nineteenth centuries—single-ship encounters of historic British, American, and French vessels. The BROADSIDES manual goes on to instruct you in how to design your own ships and capabilities, and the program will fight them accordingly. Electronic ship in a bottle.

Unlike many simulation games, these two play happily as action games. They pass the shout test: the aarrggh!s and oh no!s are more often within than at the game.

The two make a nice sequence. OLD IRONSIDES is the easier, faster, more engaging one, and it also sucks you into the fantasy quicker with its poster painting of battle, its "logbook" manual, its salty graphics and lettering on the screen. It is strictly for two players and works better with paddles than keyboard (so does BROADSIDES). Play involves a plausible, manageable, but challenging array of considerations—wind direction, powder availability, cannon damage, sail damage, ramming versus broadside attack, and so on. You can—unrealistically but interestingly— sail off the screen "into the fog" and cleverly navigate by compass to fire from there.

BROADSIDES goes far deeper. You have more commands, including speed, aiming (at sails or hull, at various ranges), kinds of shot, etc. There is a richer blur of play considerations viewed onscreen—wind speed (in knots) and wind direction, hull damage, crew losses, current speed, maximum speed available, distance to enemy, etc. And there are many more options of play—solitaire or two-player, level of complexity, and ship-design options. Also, a second phase of battle takes place when you grind your ships together and board the enemy. The screen switches to the two decks, and success becomes a matter of swordplay and sniper fire. It's more abstract and less satisfying than the cannon stuff; still, a fair amount of action is available, including cutting the grappling lines that hold the ships together.

OLD IRONSIDES you can try in a store to see if you like it; BROADSIDES takes longer to set up. OLD IRONSIDES is easier for younger players, visitors, or quick games. BROADSIDES tends to longer games and will probably have a longer play life in the house. Jolly tars will want both.

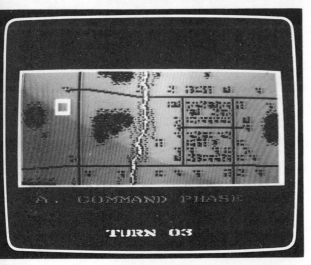

*A typically informative display of OPERATION WHIRLWIND, letting you know the status and position of your intrepid troops.*

*Extended campaigns for PC . . .*

## KNIGHTS OF THE DESERT

**Tactical Design Group; Apple II family; 48K ● Atari 400/800/XL series; 48K ● Commodore 64 ● TRS-80 Models I & III; 16K; cassette; $39.95; copy-protected? YES; Strategic Simulations, Inc., 883 Stierlin Rd., Bldg. A-200, Mountain View, CA 94043; 415/964-1353.**

## OPERATION WHIRLWIND

**Roger Damon; Atari; 48K ● Commodore 64; joystick; $39.95; copy-protected? YES; Broderbund Software, Inc., 17 Paul Dr., San Rafael, CA 94903; 415/479-1170.**

SHAY ADAMS: George "Blood 'n' Guts" Patton would snap to attention and salute. In KNIGHTS OF THE DESERT, a fanatically authentic simulation of the North African campaign, Rommel's tanks take on the Brits for control of the Sahara and a vital seaport, Tobruk. Every aspect of the conflict is re-created, from the strength and armament of actual Axis and Allied units (measured in terms of combat strength, operation points, and supply level) to the order of battle and arrival date of reinforcements.

The action takes place on a richly hued map overlaid with a grid of hexes: keyboard input moves infantry and tank and supply units. Most war simulations are similar in this, but KNIGHTS effectively adds a salient aspect overlooked by other games— logistics. Victory depends on more than just outmaneuvering and outgunning the enemy.

If your supply depots don't form realistic lines of support to the troops, supplied units lose corresponding points and can even be wiped out.

Though it might take a while for novice war-gamers to pick up KNIGHTS, individual settings allow "raw recruits" to even up the match when waging war against the computer or a human foe. If you're planning on playing solitaire, get out your Wehrmacht uniform— you have no choice but to command the Nazi forces in this version.

WILLIAM MICHAEL BROWN: WHIRLWIND looks much like every other war game: Move the little colored blocks around the big map— i.e., dullsville. What distinguishes it is that all the complications are in the actual play rather than the mechanics. Instead of having to learn the lineage and prejudices of the commanding officers of 152 different units before you can make an intelligent move, you're quickly trying to find elegant solutions to real military problems—like how to keep your tanks from outrunning your infantry, how to handle fringe fights without weakening your main assault force, how to take a town without being shot to pieces. While this streamlined quality will be most appreciated by war game aficionados, it's also perfect for people who want an introduction to what's best in war games: making tough decisions in tough situations. There are four levels of play, from ridiculously easy to incredibly hard, and an outstanding manual that lays the whole thing out for you in one read. If there's a user-friendly war game, this is it.

*Teaching your computer to fight . . .*

## ROBOTWAR

**Silas Warner; Apple II family; 48K; $39.95; copy-protected? YES; MUSE Software, 347 N. Charles St., Baltimore, MD 21201; 301/659-7212.**

## FORTRESS

**Patty Denbrook & Jim Templeman; Apple II family; 48K ● Atari 400/800/XL series; 40K ● Commodore 64; $34.95; copy-protected? YES; Strategic Simulations, Inc., 883 Stierlin Road, Bldg. A-200, Mountain View, CA 94043; 415/964-1353.**

RUSSELL SIPE: For years many fans of board war games and other detailed strategy games suffered a major obstacle to playing their beloved games: a lack of opponents. Then came the microcomputer—someone who plays *when* you want to play, *where* you want to play, and doesn't blow smoke in your face! But a computer makes a lousy opponent. Since it is not human, victory and defeat leave you with a distinctly antiseptic feeling.

But ROBOTWAR and FORTRESS have the best of both worlds. They permit human versus computer or human versus human competition at the keyboard, and they also permit humans geographically separated to fight it out tooth and nail.

In both, you can design a "player" that can be sent, on disk, to other gamers who can pit their creations against yours. In both cases the procedure involves "programming" a "player" who performs in the game according to the wisdom and insights you put in. In other words, these games allow you to train your army, fighter, team, and the rest.

ROBOTWAR players program "robots" to fight on a hi-res battlefield against other programmed "robots." The programming language looks familiar to anyone with even a rudimentary understanding of computer programming. Since the robot's "onboard computer" contains 34 registers to control location, direction, speed, damage checking, tracking, and so on, developing a true "contender" can take weeks.

The magazine I edit, **Computer Gaming World** (p. 29), sponsors an annual ROBOTWAR tournament. Contestants submit their robot creations on disks and show up for the computer slugfest. Grown men turn into raving maniacs or bowls of Jello in response to the fate of their creations.

FORTRESS is a game in the classic tradition of Go. The object is to build castles in order to control more territory than your opponent at the end of the game. Like many classic games, FORTRESS is easy to learn but requires much study to master. The interesting twist is that you can train a number of computer players to play against

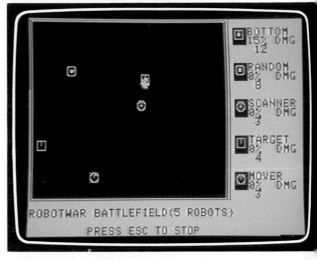

*The gladiator arena of ROBOTWAR, where your personal creation does battle, either with a computer opponent or a robot programmed by a friend or (more likely) enemy. Once the battle starts, you helplessly watch your progeny's travail—it's the first computer game to make you feel like a trainer at a cockfight.*

you—or other game players. Strategic Simulations, publisher of the game, runs FORTRESS tournaments, and I'm sure other play-by-mail tournaments will pop up in time.

---

*The pilot's point of view . . .*

## FLIGHT SIMULATOR

**Bruce Artwick; IBM PC compatibles; 64K ● IBM PCjr; 128K; one disk drive; color graphics adapter; $50; copy-protected? NO; Microsoft Corp., 10700 Northup Way, Bellevue, WA 98004; 800/426-9400.**

## FLIGHT SIMULATOR II

**Bruce Artwick; Apple II family; 48K (64K recommended) ● Atari; 48K ● Commodore 64; joystick recommended; $50 (limited feature version on cassette for Atari and Commodore; $39.95); copy-protected? YES; SubLOGIC Corp., 713 Edgebrook Dr., Champaign, IL 61820; 217/359-8482.**

DICK FUGETT: As the only instrument-rated pilot on the premises, I was chosen to check out FLIGHT SIMULATOR, but despite my ratings I wound up bending more aluminum (simulated) than any ten student pilots ever did. Being new to the IBM PC was part of the problem—success is based on keyboard skills as well as flying ability. But after a few sessions I could get in the air more often than into Lake Michigan. I discovered that hitting P (pause) freezes the action, letting me grab the manual and plan a proper response before returning to the drama. I'm quite sure that such a feature made standard on airplanes would be highly popular with pilots.

A split screen shows an instrument panel below and a view out the cockpit window above. The cockpit view can be in any direction, a nice feature but considerably limited by poor screen resolution. Don't expect anything more than a vague resemblance to passing scenery. If you have a monochrome monitor, don't expect *anything*—color display is mandatory here.

Of course, the most basic aspect of instrument flying is the "scan," that unnatural habit of continually shifting both the eyeballs and attention to cover all the instruments. Narrowing your focus to the artificial horizon and keeping the wings level is quite satisfying, but if you neglect air speed until you've passed redline, as the wings peel off the fuselage in the last dive you'll ever make, you'll be wishing you'd scanned better.

This program is by no means just a "game"; it could definitely aid in pilot training. From the navigational challenges of cross-country flight to IFR approaches, all with a choice of difficulty levels, there's plenty of juice here. Call it a $50 Link trainer and capitalize on the learning potential available.

STEVEN LEVY: I tried FLIGHT SIMULATOR II (by the same author) on the Apple, and was pleased by the same things Fugett liked, but as someone who is not flight rated, for

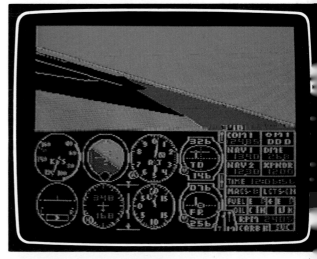

*Here, in the Apple version from SubLOGIC, you'll soon be worrying about how to land this thing.*

instruments or anything else, it took me an intolerably long time to figure out what in hell to do. Still, the program's obviously a super value, as its huge popularity indicates.

*Ninety-nine men set out, with four weeks worth of food, to explore this hunk of New World here and villages to the southwest. When they get to the villages, they will have to use caution and savvy to deal with the residents—and then again, they might initiate a massacre. All to find those SEVEN CITIES OF GOLD. The best way to learn about Columbus is to be Columbus.*

*Colonizing new worlds, past and future . . .*

## M.U.L.E.

**Ozark Softscape Designs; Atari 400/800/XL series; 48K ● Commodore 64; joystick; color monitor; $40; copy-protected? YES; Electronic Arts, 2755 Campus Dr., San Mateo, CA 94403; 415/571-7171.**

## THE SEVEN CITIES OF GOLD

**Ozark Softscape Designs; Apple II family; 48K ● Atari 400/800/XL series; 48K ● Commodore 64; joystick; color monitor; $40; copy-protected? YES; Electronic Arts, 2755 Campus Dr., San Mateo, CA 94403; 415/571-7171.**

BRADLEY MCKEE: In M.U.L.E., you and up to three other players choose the kind of alien you are (all very creative) and try to colonize a planet. The goal is to develop land and start your own business, producing either food, energy, Smithore, or valuable Crystite. Trouble is, you have to buy stubborn M.U.L.E.s (Multiple Use Labor Elements, natch) and pull them to your property to develop it.

The planet's currency is dollars; you can get 'em by gambling in the pub, buying or selling land, trading products in an auction (action-packed, as your opponents bid), and a few other things. Each turn, windfalls and calamities occur, appropriate to the interstellar-colonist scenario. This multiplayer game (playing it alone is a relative bore) is the first computer stab at the cutthroat, good-

time madness of Monopoly, and I think it's the best game since SPACE INVADERS.

STEVEN LEVY: Ozark Softscape's sequel to M.U.L.E. is called THE SEVEN CITIES OF GOLD, but it might better be called "Conquistador Simulation." This is the best blend of computer role playing, fun, and real history I've seen—its fascinating documentation contains a bibliography listing twelve history books. (Why isn't this review in the Learning section? Because I saw SEVEN CITIES first, and its ability to go either way shows that great software, thank God, makes taxonomies ridiculous.) Anyway, you're Columbus, Magellan, whoever, and you set off in your ships to explore the New World, or, if you like, an imaginary but realistically generated Western Hemispere. Cross the ocean (watch out for storms), and get your first big rush when you spot land. A new world!

The heart of the game is how you colonize—when you find a village on this uncharted continent or island, the screen picture changes from a map to a soldier representing your party. Natives surround you, and the way you behave (you control your party with intuitive joystick movements) determines their response—are these friendly folk who want to trade? Will movement set them to attack? The dynamic is only more absorbing because it's a consciously accurate replication of what the Spanish explorers really *felt* like going in there.

---

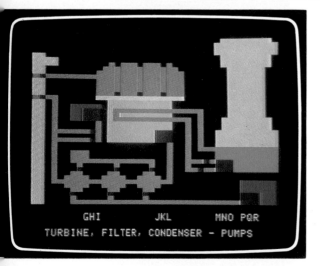

*The reactor setup in THREE MILE ISLAND. If you lose that water in the pumping system, say hello to China, and figure out what to tell the stockholders. If this looks strangely like the pictures you see in the paper to illustrate how a real nuke power plant works, don't be startled—Babcock and Wilcox should have used this to design their plants.*

*Run your own nuke plant . . .*

## THREE MILE ISLAND

**Richard Orban; Apple II family; 48K; $39.95; copy-protected? YES; MUSE Software; 347 N. Charles St., Baltimore, MD 21201; 301/659-7212.**

## SCRAM

**Chris Crawford; Atari 400/600/800XL; 16K; Atari 800; 24K; cassette; BASIC cartridge; joystick; copy-protected? YES; $24.95; Atari, 1312 Crossman Ave., Sunnyvale, CA 94088; 800/538-8543, or in CA, 800/672-1404.**

---

ROBERT SCAROLA: In THREE MILE ISLAND, you're the general manager of a nuclear power plant, responsible for overseeing all areas of the facility's operation. You must maintain a profit and must make sure, at all cost, that you prevent (gasp!) a *meltdown*. Your job is not easy.

All aspects of your system—time, temperature, pressure, electric power production, pumps, valves, turbine, steamer, filters, condensers, containment, and core vessels—are in a dynamic relationship with one another. You control them. Any change you make to one influences and modifies another. It's intense. The whole thing is alive and operating on the screen; parts move,

warning bells ring, liquids flow, and colors change as heat rises or sludge builds up.

It's easy to imagine you're really in a nuclear plant perched out on the edge of a fault line, fingers on the pulse of this most magical and dangerous of our modern wonders—but without real-world penalties for failures and mistakes. There should be more programs like this one.

STEVEN LEVY: Atari owners can enjoy the cozy experience of meltdown in their own homes, too. SCRAM is not as fixated with the financial bottom line of operating a nuke plant as it is with the real bottom line—keeping China Syndrome away from our door. SCRAM's plant is stripped to its bare bones, but the lesson still gets across, especially when you go from pure simulation into "game mode." There, when the earthquake hits, you wind up shuttling your hapless crew of 80 in and out of containment rooms until you're short of staff, solutions, and everything else but muttered prayers.

Aren't you glad it's only a simulation? Incidentally, there are 80-odd operating nuclear power plants in the U.S. that work just like these simulated ones.

# Action

**A play at the races . . .**

## POLE POSITION

Apple II family; 48K; disk drive; DOS 3.3 controller card; $39.95 ● Atari 2600; 16K; joystick; color; $35.45 ● Atari 5200; 16K; joystick; color; $41 ● Atari 400/800/600XL/800XL; $50 ● Commodore 64; joystick; color; disk $39.95; cartridge $45 ● IBM PC; 128K; color graphics; game adapter for joystick; $39.95 ● VIC-20; joystick; color; cartridge $45; ATARISOFT, 1312 Crossman Ave., P.O. Box 61657, Sunnyvale, CA 94088; 800/538-8543, or, in CA, 800/672-1404.

## PITSTOP

Atari ● ColecoVision & Adam ● Commodore 64; joystick, color; about $30; copy-protected? YES; Epyx, Inc., 1043 Kiel Ct., Sunnyvale, CA 94089; 408/745-0700.

STEVEN LEVY: Racing games are tried and true staples of electronic gaming. When you live in an electronic cottage, you want the illusion, at least, of driving somewhere. The computer allows you to tackle racecourses, the last stronghold against red lights and traffic jams. Best of the bunch is Atari's POLE POSITION. Originally a coin-op arcade game, the translation is particularly well done, with vivid, though not particularly varied, graphics. The virtues of a classic computer road race are intact, including intuitive joystick control (forward for low gear, back for high, left and right to steer), and the noises are suitably authentic, down to the louder churn in low gear. I also like the way you first take qualifying laps to get a position for the actual race.

After POLE POSITION's blazing graphics, the game PITSTOP was at first a comedown. There's no scenery: Le Mans looks like Monaco; if this is Tuesday, it must be Sebring. And in contrast to POLE POSITION, in PITSTOP actual contact with other cars does not result in a tragic end of game. Instead—got this—your tires wear out. You only get totaled when collective wear (you note this by a change in tire color) causes fatal blowout.

As the name implies, drivers must make pitstops to refuel the cars and change those dangerously worn tires. This part is more exciting than the actual race: You control a group of eager mechanics and your time is clocked onscreen. Only in a computer simulation can you find yourself more panicked when fumbling to change a tire than when you rear-end a Formula One car at 160 miles an hour.

**The classic helicopter hostage rescue . . .**

## CHOPLIFTER!

Dan Gorlin; Apple II family; 48K ● Atari; 48K ● Commodore 64; cartridge or disk; joystick required; $34.95 (disk version); $45 (Atari cartridge); $39.95 (Commodore 64 cartridge); copy-protected? YES; Broderbund Software, Inc., 17 Paul Dr., San Rafael, CA 94903; 415/479-1170.

STEVEN LEVY: The rarest of computer-game creatures—an action-packed hand/eye coordination extravaganza with a plot organically tied to the process of play. The seductive demo mode tells the story: you command a helicopter crossing enemy borders to rescue hostages. Obviously, you have to land to pick up the little fellows, who plaintively wave to you as you hover above them; just as obviously you have to avoid or shoot down the assortment of tanks, jet fighters, and killer satellites defending enemy territory.

Since you gain points only for hostages saved, your priorities are clear—lose as few hostages as possible. Don't engage in bloodlust. Just get those innocent people out of there! True, there is no "negotiation mode" to obviate the need for violence, but CHOPLIFTER! provides a much less vile scenario than 90 percent of its competitors.

Although CHOPLIFTER! is hard to beat, it is simple to learn. Your first "sortie" across the border is easy, with subsequent ones growing progressively harder. The graphics are sharp

*The rescuing helicopter here must not only take out that tank, but make sure your bombs or its rockets don't kill one of those cute li'l hostages. The burning fire in front of the barracks is indicative of the mindblowing detail in this Broderbund classic.*

and full of neat detail (though I'm not sure why the ground is pink). I've heard complaints that this hugely popular game is not much of a challenge to the extremely skilled arcader, and it *is* austere compared with some pyrotechnic wonders. But because the game constantly reinforces the life-saving role you're placed in, it's never boring.

**Blowing minds on the Mindset . . .**

## VYPER

Dan Browning; Mindset; 128K; joystick required; $39.95; copy-protected? YES; Synapse Software, 5221 Central Ave., Richmond, CA 94804; 415/527-7751.

KEVIN STEHLO: VYPER adds a new dimension to computer games—literally. Imagine playing ZAXXON in three dimensions, looking out the window of your ship instead of down on it. Realistic cities of a hostile planet zip past the way the trees do in that great chase scene in *The Empire Strikes Back*. The hostile craft you're tailing looms large, until suddenly you dive under it and streak safely past, zooming in and around and over buildings and firing at moving targets. Then you climb until the buildings' highest spires are tiny dots, and you must keep watch for the hostile high-altitude squadrons and their heat-seeking missiles.

VYPER is a breakthrough. Wait until you try flying through the twisting tunnel that leads to the final battleground. Even my friend Lee, an intellectual type who finds arcade games about as stimulating as "Laverne and Shirley," had to take a turn at the VYPER joystick.

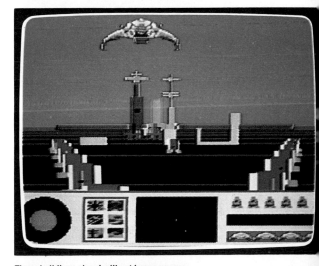

*Those buildings ahead will get larger as you swoop down into the city. Screaming fighter planes will come at you. You'll feel like bailing out. But first you must buy a Mindset computer.*

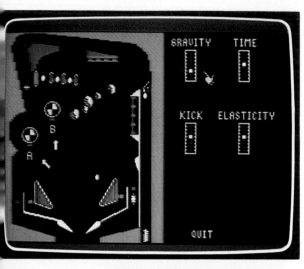

*In PINBALL CONSTRUCTION SET that little hand moves things around and gets things done by joystick. Mouse-like. After you build a pinball machine like the one on the left, you can exercise more power by changing gravity itself, as we're about to do here.*

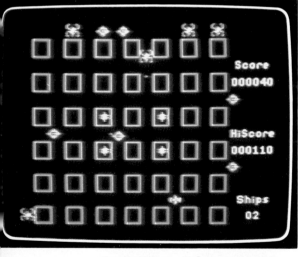

*Doesn't look like much? Try moving around the guy on the bottom row—while those other guys are coming at you from all four directions.*

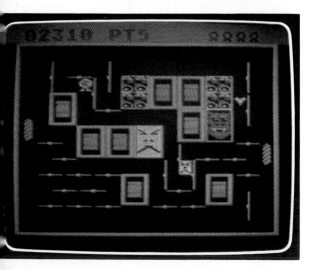

*Run through those swinging doors, avoid those frowning trollaboars, get the heart, and have a ball with DRELBS.*

*A universe of bumpers, flippers, and rollovers . . .*

## PINBALL CONSTRUCTION SET

**Bill Budge; Apple II family ● Atari 400/800/XL series; 48K ● Commodore 64 ● IBM PC compatibles; 64K; joystick; color monitor; $40; copy-protected? YES; Electronic Arts, 2755 Campus Dr., San Mateo, CA 94403; 415/571-7171.**

STEVEN LEVY: I've asked a lot of people who are crazy about computers just why it is they are so crazy about computers. They will hem and they will haw, but eventually it gets down to this: A computer makes you God. The only catch is that you have to learn to program before you can take command of the universe, and it takes more than seven days to learn to program.

PINBALL CONSTRUCTION SET makes you God in a few minutes. True, your universe is restricted to making pinball machines. But there is much to learn about pinball machines. There are series of targets to connect for creating bonuses. There are decoration schemes to consider. There are tactical variations that make subtle differences in play. You find this out as you build a pinball machine, try it out, debug it, make changes, and improve it. This trial-and-error process is something you might want to apply later on, when you learn programming, or anything else.

The method by which you build your machine is ridiculously simple—a little "hand" icon, controlled by your joystick, pulls bumpers, flippers, and targets to the pinball field. By pointing to other icons like a paintbrush, a screwdriver, or a little globe, you can add decorations, change the scoring or sound, create new shapes, and actually play your game. Since you are God in this universe, you can even change the pull of gravity to make the ball drop faster.

Everything works. (Well, sometimes a ball will go through a flipper—but who said Bill Budge was God?) Electronic Arts supplies a clear and detailed manual. If you hate pinball machines, you might not like this game. But, then, this program might make you like pinball machines for the first time.

*An addicting, quiet massacre . . .*

## CROSSFIRE

**Jay Sullivan; Apple II family; 48K ● Atari; 48K ● Commodore 64 ● IBM PC compatibles; 64K ● IBM PCjr ● VIC 20; $29.95 ($34.95 for cartridge); copy-protected? YES; Sierra On-Line, Inc., P.O. Box 485, Coarsegold, CA 93614; 209/683-6858.**

STEVEN LEVY: The archetypal author of a shoot-'em-up computer game is a wild-eyed eighteen-year-old who machine-guns lines of code like some kamikaze bomber. CROSSFIRE was written by a quiet, contemplative man in his forties, and it shows. What makes CROSSFIRE different is its seductive ability to immerse you in concentration, without the loud explosions or screaming sound effects that a more callow programmer might have inserted. Indeed, this is the quietest massacre you will ever indulge in.

As the defender of an abandoned city consisting of a gridlike layout of streets, you must be on the lookout from all four directions for aliens who can kill you by shooting little pellets or running into you. You must also move around the grid yourself, to avoid those aliens and get more bullets. Like some people I know, you might be tempted to splurge in long CROSSFIRE sessions. How these people do it, I don't know—the game is *hard*, and I'd estimate at least an hour's work at it was needed before you could last even a minute in the subtle yet deadly alien attack. But some folks get hooked and make CROSSFIRE a hobby.

*Cartoon capers on the atomic grid flip . . .*

## DRELBS

**Kelly Jones; Apple II family; 48K ● Atari 400/800/ XL series; 32K disk or 16K cassette ● Commodore 64; disk or cassette ● IBM PC compatibles; 64K ● IBM PCjr; joystick required; color recommended; $34.95; copy-protected? YES; Synapse Software, 5221 Central Ave., Richmond, CA 94804; 415/527-7751.**

MYRON BERGER: DRELBS is a curious little game: just two screens (that's all I've seen), simple graphics, but impossible to play only once. While I suspect that this fascination increases with the player's degree of youth, even "children" over 30 will find the game an entertaining challenge.

You are the drelb of the title. You are battling trollaboars on the atomic grid flip. In English now: you are a funny little square roaming around a board with swinging doors while being chased by (1) a square with a scowling face and (2) a tube that circles the perimeter shooting randomly. If you swing through doors properly, you can form an enclosed square, for which you will receive points and through which the square face cannot pass.

Squares with evil faces, girls screaming for help, windows on a scrolling background of forests eating rows of trees while robots shoot at you. . . . Rather than using a lot of ink to describe something that onscreen is apparent, intuitive, and fun, let me just say that DRELBS is, in a sense, the video version of billiards: a game of bare simplicity that is nevertheless captivating, entertaining, and challenging.

*Freeing the butterflies on 16 levels . . .*

# BOULDER DASH

**Peter Liepa & Chris Gray; Atari; 32K ● Commodore 64 ● IBM PCjr; joystick required; $29.95 (disk), $39.95 (cartridge); copy-protected? YES; First Star, Inc., 22 East 41st Street, New York, NY 10017; 800/223-1545 ● Apple family; disk; joystick; $40 ● ColecoVision/Adam; cartridge; joystick; $40 ● Commodore 64; cartridge; joystick; $35; MicroLab, 2699 Skokie Valley Road, Highland Park, IL 60035; 312/433-7550.**

SAM HILT: As Rockford, the subterranean hero of BOULDER DASH, you dig your way down through the dirt and rocks to the place where butterflies are trapped beneath a wall of boulders. When you finally find the way to release them (without killing yourself in the process), you must lure them back to the surface into the bubbling green slime, where they explode on contact and turn into jewels. These you must gather quickly in sufficient quantities to move on to the next level before your time has elapsed.

That's only one of sixteen scenarios, each so different from the others that the word "level" is insufficient to describe them. The documentation calls them "caves." Each one has its own logic and design, and each demands a unique solution to the basic challenge of acquiring gems before your time runs out. Game elements such as boulders, butterflies, amoebas, and explosions recur in various combinations, but the relationships

*Finally—a game you can chant to . . .*

# MOONDUST

**Jarron Lanier; Commodore 64; joystick; color; $34.95; copy-protected? NO; Creative Software, 230 Caribbean Drive, Sunnyvale, CA 94089; 408/745-1655.**

ART KLEINER: If this were still the psychedelic era, every game would be like MOONDUST. The points you score are somehow less important than the patterns and (especially) the music produced by the way you play the game. With the joystick, you manipulate a little white "spacewalker" with a bobbling head. His movement in turn affects, in obscure ways, the flight paths of six colored spaceships. By pressing the joystick button, you drop a little square colored "seed" on the playing field; then you try like hell to influence the spaceships to spread the seed's progeny, the "moondust," out across a shifting, mandala-ish target. The process feels like finger painting with somebody else's fingers. If you inadvertently bump your ship into your spaceman, you get knocked out and have to start over. My only complaint: the individual games end too soon. Restarting disturbs MOONDUST's hypnotic wavelike effect. Unlike other games, MOONDUST doesn't engage your adrenaline; it engages the part of your psyche that seeks to feel at peace.

among them change constantly and keep you guessing. Solutions may require speed and agility, careful observation of the movement patterns of fireflies, or deliberate plans for luring butterflies to their doom under an avalanche of boulders (BOULDER DASH is a disaster for lepidopterists). After an evening of play, you'll find yourself getting out of bed to try that one final strategy that occurred to you just before you drifted off to sleep.

BOULDER DASH also offers an exemplary approach to accessing different levels of game play. Don't you eventually hate those games that make you play through nine levels just to see the tenth? On the other hand, games that let you pick a level, any level, quickly lose pizzazz. Here, you can select any of four different caves as a point of entry, but the remaining ones are accessible only after you master those four. This prevents monotony while still making you fight and sweat for those privileged glimpses of hidden worlds.

*150 craaa-zzzy screens . . .*

# LODE RUNNER

**Doug Smith; Apple II family; 48K ● Atari; 48K ● Commodore 64 (disk or cartridge); joystick ● IBM PC compatibles; 64K; color graphics card ● VIC 20; cartridge; $34.95 ($39.95 for Commodore 64 cartridge); copy-protected? YES; Broderbund Software, Inc., 17 Paul Drive, San Rafael, CA 94903; 415/479-1170.**

STEVEN LEVY: I'm crazy about LODE RUNNER. It's a game I could play from the first five minutes and still have a great time with after wearing the disk to a frazzle by overuse. It's a "climbing" game, with its ladders, ropes, and leaps, but some of the maneuvers you need to make your stick-figurey little man advance to the next of LODE RUNNER's 150 (you read it right—one hundred and fifty) screens actually require . . . brace yourself . . . thought. So, in a sense, each screen is a puzzle that you must solve on the run. Literally on the run, because while your guy is dashing about digging holes with his laser drill, collecting treasures, and dropping from the ceiling, with the computer making weird *beee-yooooo* sounds, a cadre of enemy stick figures in constant Keystone Kop mode are in hot pursuit. If they catch you, you've had it. You can drill holes in the floor for them to fall into and eventually get buried in, but more figures will drop from the sky to replace them. There's hardly a moment's peace here.

Some of the screens are tough to solve. Others you can solve mentally but often screw up on execution. Playing sequentially, there is no way in hell I am going to see the 60th screen, let alone the 150th. (It takes me 20 minutes just to get to Screen 9.) But the game accommodates that complaint. For the weak

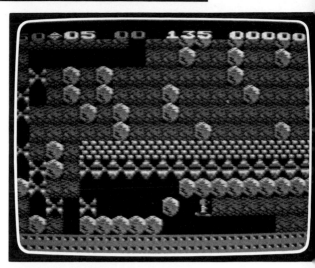

*To get those cross-shaped jewels toward the left, our hero Rockford must scurry out of the way of those boulders before he's crushed. Looks like he's about to be made into a pancake. Sixteen screens of this make for plenty of thrills in BOULDER DASH.*

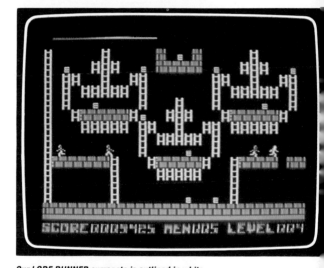

*Our LODE RUNNER surrogate is outlined in white, in virtual flight from those other fellows. He'll have to climb all over to get the little bundles of gold, then climb on to the next screen. There are 150 screens, and if you get bored with those, design your own.*

of resolve and reflex, one command advances the level, another gives you as many men as you want. Using these commands is surely a victimless crime, and they make LODE RUNNER constantly fresh and interesting; there's always a screen you won't have seen yet.

But LODE RUNNER doesn't stop there: it contains a mode that lets you actually *design* screens of your own. It sounds like great fun and good creative exercise, but I confess I haven't gotten around to designing new screens. Too busy being chased on the old ones.

Your ace, on the left, must now choose between bombing the boat (too late for that, probably), going after the plane on the right, or bombing that factory. I'd go for the plane and 100 points.

*The definitive WW-I ace game . . .*

## BLUE MAX

**Bob Polin; Atari 400/800/XL series ● Commodore 64; disk or cassette; joystick; color recommended; $34.95; copy-protected? YES; Synapse Software, 5221 Central Ave., Suite 200, Richmond, CA 94804; 415/527-7751.**

STEVEN LEVY: During the time I was working at the **Whole Earth Software Catalog** headquarters putting together this section, I was surrounded by hundreds of games for various computers. The game I played for pleasure during that time was BLUE MAX on the Atari. One afternoon Stewart Brand and I spent three hours taking turns at the throttle of a World War I biplane, shown onscreen from an overhead view with some 3-D perspective (provided by a shadow underneath that gets closer as you get lower). We could have gone longer.

There's a lot going on in this bombing game—much more than in its apparent inspirations, the ultimately boring space shootout ZAXXON (movement and perspective similar) and the repetitive dive-bombing orgy of RIVER RAID. Besides bombing bridges and factories (worried about the theoretical people inside? Don't buy this game. And don't pay your taxes), you have to monitor your fuel, altitude, and damage level; watch out for enemy planes and try to shoot them down; avoid anti-aircraft fire; stay alert for and bomb "primary targets"; find friendly airfields to land on (not easy!), refuel, and get repairs.

BLUE MAX is the type of game you master incrementally. There's so much happening in your foray into enemy territory that a perfectly simple error usually trips you up—the kind of error that makes you say "I can avoid that next time," thus ensuring a next time even if it's dinner time.

Blessedly, when you opt for replay, BLUE MAX does not force you to endure a drawn-out starting segment with animated titles and peppy theme music. Push the start button and you're off again.

---

*A trilogy of obsessions . . .*

STEVEN LEVY: Since a good percentage of computer games still appeal to the visceral rather than the cerebral, I thought it appropriate to mention just a few more of these.

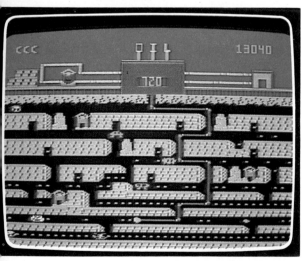

The pipeline is far down in this OIL'S WELL game, but if the player doesn't watch it, that blue "oozie" on the third row down will hit the pipe and ruin everything. Solution? Press that joystick button, and fast!

## REPTON

**Dan Thompson and Andy Kaluzniaski; Apple II family ● Atari (disk) ● Commodore 64; joystick; $39.95; copy-protected? YES; Sirius Software, 10364 Rockingham, Sacramento, CA 95827; 916/366-1195.**

STEVEN LEVY: When I feel like keeping my hand on the joystick "fire" button and ripping a bunch of interplanetary invaders to shreds, with a bit of extra adrenaline as the screen explodes in pyrotechnics, I go to REPTON. It is the most elaborate variation on the defender-type game, where a spaceship you control blasts away at enemies. It's important to get them soon, because the enemies are intent on building some kind of Superdome on your planet. Like all games of this type, the aliens will eventually prevail, but not before you obliterate lots of baddies with your arsenal, including the charming "nuke bomb," which lights up the screen with more *Sturm und Drang* than Wagner.

## OIL'S WELL

**Thomas Mitchell; Apple II family; 48K ● Atari; 48K ● Coleco; 64K ● Commodore 64 ● IBM PC compatibles; 64K ● IBM PCjr; $29.95 ($34.95 for cartridge); copy-protected? YES; Sierra On-Line, Inc., P.O. Box 485, Coarsegold, CA 93614; 209/683-6858.**

RANDI HACKER and GEORGE KOPP: OIL'S WELL is a highly addictive game combining PAC-MAN action with the features of an automatically retractable vacuum cleaner cord. Object: to slice out an underground maze with this Roto-Rooter-type device without letting the odd creatures who inhabit the maze drive over you. Only way to avoid them is to retract like a strand of spaghetti eaten by an unmannerly person (you do this by pressing the joystick button). Eight mazes, each tougher than the one before. You need joystick dexterity and nerves of steel.

## MINER 2049ER

**Bill Hogue; Apple II family; 48K; joystick, color; $40 ● Coleco Vision & Adam; joystick, color; $50 ● IBM PC compatibles; 64K; joystick, color; $40; copy-protected? YES; MicroLab, 2699 Skokie Valley Rd., Highland Park, IL 60035; 312/433-7550 ● Atari; 16K; joystick; $50; copy-protected? NO; Big Five Software, 14617 Victory Blvd. #1, Van Nuys, CA 91411; 213/782-6861 ● Commodore 64; joystick; $39.95 ● VIC 20; joystick; $29.95; copy-protected? YES; Reston Computer Group, Reston Publishing Co., Inc., 11480 Sunset Hills, Reston, VA 22090; 800/336-0338 ● Atari 2600; joystick, color; $25.00 ● TI 99/4A; joystick, color; $39.95; copy-protected? YES; Tiger Electronics, 909 Orchard, Mundelein, IL 60060; 312/949-8100.**

MYRON BERGER: MINER 2049ER had me sitting behind my Atari for several weeks, nudging my joystick for hours (days?) with the concentration and effort characteristic of brain surgeons. The plot: maneuver Bounty Bob through a maze of caverns, collecting mining supplies and trying to avoid the inevitable minions of evil patrolling the tunnels. The first three levels are simple enough to ensnare even the most innocent players. But then they are hit with dread Level 4: Bob must now climb inside caves by leaping onto ledges—tiny ledges. The dexterity necessary to pull this off must also be learned. In the higher levels you have to acquire a fine sense of timing. (There are ten levels in all, fewer in versions written for some low-power machines.) No longer in my obsessive period, I still enjoy playing MINER 2049ER every few months to brush up my skills.

# Sports and Noncomputer Games

*Word maniac's delight . . .*

## MONTY PLAYS SCRABBLE

**Apple II family; 48K; $39.95 ● IBM PC compatibles; 64K; $39.95 ● TRS-80 Model III; 48K; $34.95; copy-protected? YES; Ritam Corporation, 209 N. 16th Street, P.O. Box 921, Fairfield, IA 52556; 800/247-0043.**

DOUG GARR: One of my favorite Apple programs is MONTY PLAYS SCRABBLE, the computer version of the popular board game by Selchow & Righter. One reason I like it so much is because it is absolutely playable without the (oh, do I hate this word) documentation. I've watched kids who are far too impatient to read directions spend hours at it. They love the fact that they can cheat. If you insist a word is a word, there is nothing the computer can do about it.

You can challenge MONTY on any of four levels. Naturally, being a bit of a word maniac, I went right to "scholar," the highest level. With its 54,000-word vocabulary, MONTY is indeed difficult to beat. It took me several tries to win on Level 4, and then only after I used the ESC key to hurry MONTY's play. A marvelous feature of the program, this key prompts the computer to play the best word it's come up with so far in its process of considering the possibilities. MONTY is very strong on multiword plays, especially when he's holding lousy letters. Very often he will make a 25-point score with three or four distinctly obscure two- and three-letter words. You'd better learn the q's and z's if you want to beat him consistently.

You can challenge, but only with a hard-copy dictionary and an arbitrator. I have been challenged many times by MONTY: His image appears on screen; he looks left and right, almost embarrassed to bring up this nasty matter, and suggests that we "check that word." His suspicions have always been confirmed. I've never successfully challenged MONTY, though he supposedly bluffs.

MONTY will play up to three people, and he keeps score, quite honestly, for everyone. The screen display is comprehensive—the board, a tile-point count, and the player's letters on a rack with "rearrange" mode.

It's real Scrabble, and you don't have to swirl the tiles around after every turn.

*Strategy and a quick-reflex baseball simulation . . .*

## COMPUTER BASEBALL

**Charles Merrow & Jack Avery; Apple II family; 48K ● Apple III ● Atari (all machines); 40K with BASIC cartridge ● Commodore 64; $39.95; copy-protected? YES; Strategic Simulations, Inc., 883 Stierlin Rd. Bldg. A-200, Mountain View, CA 94043; 415/964-1353.**

## STAR LEAGUE BASEBALL

**Apple II family; $29.95 ● Atari; $31.95 ● Commodore 64; $29.95; joystick; copy-protected? YES; Gamestar, Inc., 1302 State St., Santa Barbara, CA 93101; 805/963-3487.**

STEVEN LEVY: I always figured that one of the easier translations of games to computers would be one of those replay-the-major-leagues-in-your-own-home systems that I played as a kid. Sure enough, in COMPUTER BASEBALL, the dice and stacks of charts are all on a single floppy disk, a much more pleasurable way to handle things. The graphics aren't much, but I'm happier knowing that the disk space is instead used for strategy features like hit-and-run, warming up a relief pitcher, and even the occasional ejection of a player by the computer umpire.

Like its pre-microchip predecessors, COMPUTER BASEBALL takes into account each ballplayer's batting stats, speed, earned run average, fielding prowess, and other data, so you can be sure when Mike Schmidt comes to bat you've got a good chance to go downtown (unless he's facing Juan Marichal—one of the infinite possibilities here). You can "manage" any of 26 World Series teams, order a disk of last season's real-life teams, or even construct your own, using the formula provided inside. COMPUTER BASEBALL works just as well in either one- or two-player variations (the computer is a fairly good manager), and I had enough strategy decisions (put the infield in? pitch around that slugger?) to keep me interested in all but the most absurd blowouts.

It's a much harder task to replicate the *action* of baseball than to merge strategy with actual game play. The best of the many games attempting this is STAR LEAGUE BASEBALL. The first time I booted it, I got the same delight I feel when first peering at the deliciously green infield of a major league stadium. The graphic representation is that good, as is the music that plays the national anthem and a catchy original number between innings. I think STAR LEAGUE is best as a two-player game—the computer simply doesn't make many mistakes, and I do, especially when fielding. The sparse manual promises that "throwing from base to base will soon be second nature to you," one of the biggest lies of the twentieth century. Score after my first game: Computer 73, Levy 1. But I stuck with it, and eventually I could

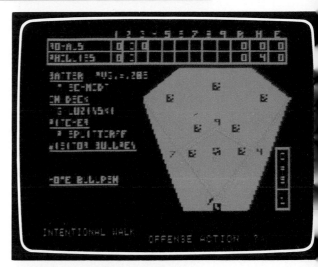

*In this replay of the 1980 World Series, the Phillies had second and third, one out, in the third inning of a scoreless battle. The COMPUTER BASEBALL manager "Casey" decided to walk Bake McBride and pitch to (gulp) Mike Schmidt (the real-life MVP in that series). Notice that the first and third basemen are playing "in" to cut off the run at the plate, while the shortstop and second baseman are deep enough for a possible double play. Did the strategy work? Yep—Schmidt bounced to short and started a DP.*

*The STAR LEAGUE BASEBALL stands are perpetually packed with noisemaking fans as the pitcher tries to hurl the ball past you. It'll take you a while to develop your reflexes to the point where you can hit it.*

make it competitive, inning by inning if not for a whole game.

The graphics and frills make this one worthwhile, but STAR LEAGUE BASEBALL's right fielder will consistently throw runners out at first on line drives over the infield—a faux pas that COMPUTER BASEBALL would never commit.

*Slam-dunkin' realism,
    playground pyrotechnics . . .*

## JULIUS ERVING & LARRY BIRD GO ONE-ON-ONE

**Bird, Erving and Hammond; Apple II family; 48K ● Atari 400/800/XL series; 48K ● Commodore 64 ● IBM PC compatibles; 64K; joystick; color monitor; $40; copy-protected? YES; Electronic Arts, 2755 Campus Dr., San Mateo, CA 94403; 415/571-7171.**

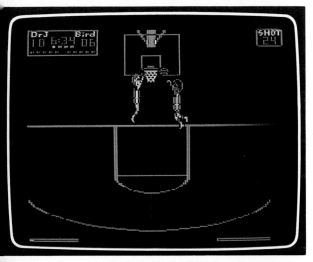

*Dr. J and Larry Bird go up for a ONE-ON-ONE rebound. Looks like J's got this one, but generally, Bird (on the left) will outrebound him, just like in real life. On the other hand, J's faster inside. Those "fatigue" lines in the foreground show that both have worked up a good sweat here and should call a time-out to rejuvenate.*

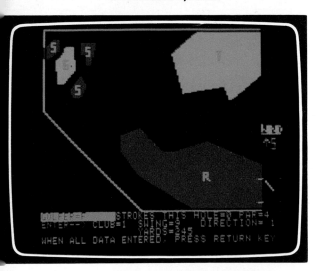

*A typical hole on the PRO GOLF CHALLENGE beginner's course. Beyond the rough and the trees is the green, protected by sand traps. Choosing the right club and the proper swinging speed is the easiest of your chores; you must then complete a difficult-to-master golf swing.*

STEVEN LEVY: My friend Basketball Joe is Sixers all the way and computers none of the way. "Come over," I said, "Doctor J's in a computer game." Say *what*? He came over, I booted, and the graphics were so good I didn't have to hem and haw and tell him the limits of the Apple. Sure, Doctor J and his opponent Larry Bird (white guy from Indiana, can play) look cartoony, but when they perform on the halfcourt, you can believe that they spent some days in the gym with the programmer making sure he got all the right moves. J in particular. "Wo!" said Basketball Joe.

I had been playing an hour a day for about a week, getting good enough to take on the computer on the "varsity" level (second of four) and picky enough to be complaining about the only flaw in the otherwise intuitive joystick control (hit the button to shoot but hit the button *quickly* to turn around— sometimes it doesn't work and you shoot when you don't want to). All in all, I was highly taken with Electronic Arts' conceptual leap: To do the best basketball game on a computer you don't do a whole basketball game—you take it to an elemental level of one-on-one, in-yo'-face play. With real characteristics of the two best hoopsters around (the computer Bird rebounds and shoots from outside better; the Doc does sky ballet), ONE-ON-ONE is on a level by itself as far as computer sports games go.

As one of maybe ten people in the country with a two-joystick Apple set-up (only in theory can you play two-player with stick and keyboard), I took on Basketball Joe, grudgingly accepting Bird (problem with the two-player game is, someone's got to be Bird). Joe hates computers so much he's usually awful at electronic games, but this time that madman beat me. I believe the reason is that he is a basketball player and I am not—the ultimate endorsement for ONE-ON-ONE.

STEWART BRAND: Levy is too modest to mention that he took on Electronic Arts' president Trip Hawkins in a semipublic bout of ONE-ON-ONE and beat him.

---

*In golf, the swing's the thing . . .*

## PRO-GOLF CHALLENGE

**Stuart Aranoff; Apple II family; 48K; joystick or paddle; $34.95 ● IBM PC compatibles; 96K; color graphics card; $39.95; copy-protected? YES; Avant-Garde Creations, Inc., P.O. Box 30160, 1907 Garden Avenue, Eugene, OR 97403; 503/345-3043.**

STEVEN LEVY: No golf game I've tried captures the action and subtleties of a golf swing nearly as well as PRO-GOLF CHALLENGE. The game succeeds so well, in fact, that you need a *lot* of practice to do it right. But, then, don't even veteran duffers whine and moan about their hooks or slices? Just as in real golf, of course, that all-important swing is the climax of a whole series of choices: which club to use, how hard to slug the ball, what direction to hit it in (take the wind factor into account—and on the greens make sure you note the lay). Hear that golf talk? I don't like golf, but the layers of complexity kept me at this game long enough to sound like Jack Whittaker whispering commentary at the seventeenth green.

The great thing about this package—and it qualifies as a package rather than merely a game—is that it knows how tough it is to acquire proficiency, and PRO-GOLF CHALLENGE compensates for this initial barrier by giving what may be the finest tutorial I've seen in an entertainment package. It walks you through a sample hole played by two golfers: an experienced guy named "Arnie," who does things the right way, and a clod named "George," who screws up much as you will until you've had a year or so of practice. Then there's a beginner's course, which is easier than the

tough selection of "pro" courses on the second side of the disk. If you only want the strategy part of golf and don't want to master the Zen of the hi-res golf stroke (which involves hitting the keyboard eight times to shift the club head precisely 22.5 degrees), there's an option to let the computer do the hitting for you.

My only complaints: the display lets you see only some of the holes at once—you have to toggle between views of fairway parts. And using the paddle (mandatory here) to determine direction of shot does not allow for the precision demanded in the swinging process.

Still, if I had world enough and time, I'd play so much PRO-GOLF CHALLENGE I'd get sufficiently good to hit the ball squarely, first time, every time. With maybe an occasional slice.

---

*Rediscovering chess with the computer . . .*

## SARGON III

**Don & Kathe Spracklen; Apple II family; 48K ● Commodore 64 ● IBM PC compatibles ● IBM PCjr ● Macintosh; $50; copy-protected? YES; Hayden Software Co., 600 Suffolk St., Lowell, MA 01853; 800/343-1218, or in Mass., 617/937-0200.**

PHILIP ELMER-DEWITT: After I got the (Broderbund) SERPENTINE monkey off my back and before I got hooked on LODE RUNNER (p. 37), I spent a couple of weeks compulsively playing chess with SARGON III, the latest version of Hayden Software's perennial bestseller.

I used to play a lot of chess with an old

college chum. He married and moved to Paris. I inherited his chess books but dropped the game. Until I bought this program. It plays at ten levels, from five seconds to hours per move. Also includes chess problems and famous games from the past. It put me right back into that barbaric place, acting out a collective fantasy left intact from the fourteenth century.

With a twist, SARGON lets you open up its head and peek at its systematic move generator as it tries every possible move at the rate of several dozen per second. Uncanny. Disturbing. Gruesome.

And ultimately it's a real spoiler, 'cause you soon discover that you can get the computer to suggest *your* best move. If it's better than what you had in mind, it's darned hard to ignore. Let that happen a few times and you find yourself watching a machine play with itself in an orgy of digital masturbation.

Whew.

One other thing: My wife didn't say anything at the time, but while I was hooked on SARGON, she seemed to warm up to my Apple—or at least she seemed a bit less cool. When I switched back to LODE RUNNER, we were back to square one. Apparently the chess game had the same effect on her that a pipe and tweed jacket have on some impressionable coeds.

Oh, yes. I did manage to beat that dumb computer a couple of times. The program's a sucker for a double pin.

## Adventure

*The first Adventure lives!* . . .

### ADVENTURE

**Don Woods & Will Crowther; 8″ CP/M ● DEC Rainbow ● Epson QX-10 ● Heath/Zenith ● IBM PC compatibles ● IBM PCjr ● Kaypro 2, IV, 10 ● MS-DOS compatibles ● Osborne ● Xerox 820; $19.95; copy-protected? YES; The Software Toolworks, 15233 Ventura Boulevard, Suite 1118, Sherman Oaks, CA, 91403; 213/986-4885 ● IBM PC compatibles and PCjr; 64K; color adaptor; copy-protected? NO; $24.95; Norell Data Systems, P.O. Box 70127, 3400 Wilshire Blvd., Los Angeles, CA 90010; 213/257-2026 ● any computer with 300/1200 baud modem on The Source at normal rates (see table, p. 140).**

STEVEN LEVY: The first time is always magical. At least it is for me. It was, classically, on a mainframe computer, and when I saw the now just-about-immortal words, "You are standing at the end of a road . . ." and typed my first command, GO EAST, I was hooked. At that time, the game was simply called ADVENTURE, because it had not yet become a genre. The act of using a computer was strange to me then, but ADVENTURE was not strange at all. By encouraging me deeper into the Colossal Cavern, by requiring me to light lamps, drive away snakes, avoid murderous dwarves, and get past the troll, ADVENTURE in essence invited me into the computer itself. The

further I got, the more I felt I was master of the keyboard attached to the billions of bits in that DEC-20. And the frustrating puzzles were much like some of the dilemmas that awaited me in the world of computing.

The consumer news is that the ORIGINAL ADVENTURE has lost none of its charm in microcomputer translation, even though its complexity and sophistication have been surpassed by some of its hundreds of children (a few of which we talk about on these pages). Knowing that this is the granddaddy of them all gives the concise yet unerringly significant descriptions of its more than 170 "rooms" almost biblical overtones. As a public domain program, ADVENTURE has many publishers, but I suggest that the best way to sample it is on The Source (see p. 140; just type PLAY ADVENTURE, and you're on), or better yet on some college computer (most have the game, though there might be a ban on playing it during heavy usage hours). The CP/M and IBM versions by Software Toolworks are among the very few that have voluntarily decided to give the authors a royalty.

Playing adventure games without tackling this one is like being an English major who's never glanced at Shakespeare.

---

*Bright graphics, punchy parser* . . .

### THE QUEST

**Snell, Toler & Rea; Apple II family ● Atari ● Commodore 64 ● IBM PC compatibles; $34.95 ● Macintosh; $39.95; copy-protected? YES; Penguin Software, 830 4th Ave., P.O. Box 311, Geneva, IL 60134; 312/232-1984.**

SHAY ADDAMS: Lots of adventures incorporate the word "quest" in their titles, but none can match the sprawling expanse of this "days of yore" scenario, which challenges you to track and slay an elusive dragon. You'll travel down vividly colored country lanes, discover ancient civilizations, combat lizard men, and ogle a scantily clad redhead while solving some clever puzzles.

The twist in this game is that your character is accompanied throughout by a tight-lipped knight-in-arms named Gorn. He has a mind of his own, and sometimes you have to convince him to do things he's not inclined to do.

I usually prefer Infocom's all-text adventures (p. 42) to the picture variety, but Penguin Software's atypically intelligent parser (the part of the program that interprets your typed-in commands) won me over. It accepts complete, even multiple, sentences—most

graphic adventures are hampered by two-word parsers that force you to depend on actions like LOOK ROCK. The high-res graphics are equally impressive, some of the most detailed you'll see in such a game. (Apple IIe owners with an extended 80-column card will be enthralled by a double hi-res version offering 560 X 192 resolution graphics.) Access time is brisk, so the 200 various scenes (twice as many as in most similar games I've tried) are quickly splashed across the screen.

Most unusual moment: when you encounter the aforementioned redhead, she drags Gorn into a back room. You see the door slam shut. After a while they reappear. No explanation offered.

STEVEN LEVY: I agree about Penguin's excellent parser and graphics. My favorite Penguin is TRANSYLVANIA, kind of a horror story in which you're chased by goblins and werewolves. The Macintosh version is easiest to play, since it keeps your most recent commands in view and fills in the screen fast. Art Kleiner has developed a strange affection for Penguin's COVETED MIRROR, in which your time limit as an escaped prisoner of the vile King Voar is emphasized by a steadily emptying hourglass.

*While setting out on THE QUEST, you visit the King, who's enjoying comfort you won't experience for quite a while. Meanwhile, your companion, Gorn, hooks up with a hot redhead.*

*The classiest adventures around . . .*

## ZORK I, II and III

**Marc Blank and Dave Lebling; Apple II family; 32K ● Atari; 32K; $39.95 ● CP/M machines including DEC Rainbow, DECmate, Kaypro 2 ● MS-DOS 2.0 machines (IBM PC format disk) ● NEC APC; CP/M-86 ● NEC PC-8000; 56K; CP/M; $50 ● TI 99/4A; 32K expansion; $39.95 ● TRS-80 Model I and III; 32K; (ZORK II & III); $39.95; copy-protected? YES; Infocom, Inc., 55 Wheeler St., Cambridge, MA 02138; 800/262-6868 ● Commodore 64 versions available only through Commodore dealers; $29.95 ● ZORK I for TRS-80 available through Radio Shack; $39.95.**

## PLANETFALL

**Steven Meretsky; Apple II family; 32K ● Atari; 32K ● Commodore 64; $50 ● CP/M machines (including DEC Rainbow, Kaypro 2, Osborne); 48K; $60 ● IBM PC compatibles ● IBM PCjr; 64K; $50 ● MS-DOS 2.0 computers (IBM format disk); $60 ● NEC APC; CP/M-86; $60 ● TI 99/4A; 32K expansion ● TRS-80 Model I and II; 32K; $50; copy-protected? YES; Infocom, Inc., 55 Wheeler St., Cambridge, MA 02138; 800/262-6868.**

## DEADLINE

**Marc Blank; Apple II family; 32K ● Atari; 32K; $50 ● CP/M machines (including DEC Rainbow, DECmate, Kaypro 2); 48K; $60 ● IBM PC compatibles ● IBM PCjr; 64K; $50 ● MS-DOS 2.0 computers (IBM format disk); $60 ● NEC APC; CP/M-86 ● NEC PC-8000; CP/M; 56K; $60 ● TI 99/4A; 32K disk expansion; $50 ● TRS-80 model I and II; 32K; $50; copy-protected? YES; Infocom, Inc., 55 Wheeler St., Cambridge, MA 02138; 800/262-6868 ● Commodore 64 version available only through Commodore dealers; $29.95.**

STEVEN LEVY: The Infocom company was started by people who saw the original ADVENTURE on an MIT computer and

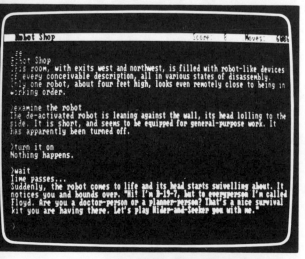

*A magic moment in PLANETFALL: your nebbishy character, after a couple hours of wandering around a deserted planet, finds a friend: a frisky robot named Floyd. The warm relationship you develop with this robotic fellow is indicative of the depth of all the Infocom games.*

respectfully tried to top it with ZORK. Now solely microcomputer-based, Infocom is known as *the* text-adventure company, and deservedly so. All its games accept full-sentence answers, and the prose is written by writers, or people who write like writers (same thing). Infocom seems to be aiming at a literate interactive fiction. Each of its products is top quality, with the most colorful documentation in the business, and each runs on a wide variety of machines.

CHARLES ARDAI: I think the three ZORKs are the most thrilling adventures produced. The dungeon scenario lets you do all sorts of Tolkienesque things: fight a troll; match wits with the eccentric Wizard of Frobozz; pull a sword from a stone; and of course slay a dragon.

ROE ADAMS: ZORK II is my favorite, because the quality of the puzzles is superior. Anyone can make a puzzle too contorted to solve—these are puzzles that seem incredibly complicated but in retrospect, after you figure them out, seem ridiculously simple. Once I got stuck at two different places in the game—an impassable ice cavern and a dangerous dragon. Eventually I noticed that when I hit the dragon one time, he ignored me. If I hit him three times, he fried me to death. But if I hit him only twice in a row, he got mad and followed me into the next room. Since I know that the Infocom people do things for a reason, I asked myself, "Where would I have a dragon follow me?" To the ice cavern! Sure enough, when we got there, the dragon saw his reflection in the ice—you know how territorial dragons are—attacked, and melted the ice. The resulting flood drowned him and I'd solved both problems.

RITA AERO: I found ZORK III the ultimate challenge. I played it on my Epson QX-10, watched closely by a friend who'd never seen an adventure game. A self-confessed hypochondriac, he constantly asked me to give the "diagnosis" command after we were wounded in a particularly gruesome swordfight with a hooded figure in Shadow Land. At one point he had to lie down and take deep breaths, hiding his queasiness by claiming to be frustrated with the slow pace of the game. Can't be done in one sitting, and one shouldn't try. In my continuing quest to confront the ZORK III Dungeon Master, I've been calling fellow wanderers in my local ZORK user's group. They not only give hints, but sell buttons that declare, "I'd rather be zorking."

RICHARD DALTON: Novice-to-intermediate-level PLANETFALL stars an inept junior officer in the Stellar Patrol who later gets an obtuse robot named Floyd as a sidekick—Floyd doesn't just show up; you have to find and activate him. This game is a good deal more human than the ZORKs, but since you wind up going through the same areas repetitively, the gags can get a bit stale. Balancing this, PLANETFALL's 600-word vocabulary allows you to give some fairly bizarre instructions and still escape the dreaded "I don't

understand that word" response. Packaging coup: you get three postcards from the planets you visit to send your friends—for example, the one from Accardi-3 that cites "the exotic anatomical charms of the Gabrillic Hyphenated Woman."

STEVEN LEVY: I'm lousy at reading detective novels; I invariably wind up peeking at the end to see who dunit. DEADLINE is the best antidote to that. Players have the same limitations and powers as a real detective; they're armed with dossiers and given twelve hours to solve the murder of industrialist Marshall Robner. The program lets you question suspects, confront them with evidence you've discovered, and gradually strip off the layers of deceit and scandal that permeate this sordid crime, which despite its hoity-toity mansion scenario is as steamy as *Chinatown*. Not only do you have to solve the crime, but you have to prove your solution is right—otherwise the perpetrator goes free, or even kills again. Other adventures leave me sighing for powers the computer doesn't have. This one leaves me dumbstruck at how much power the programmers have exploited.

Experienced Infocom-ers have told me I'd have had an easier time with the hard-boiled detective game THE WITNESS, more of a beginner's adventure than the intermediate-to-tough DEADLINE.

# Expert Adventuring

STEVEN LEVY: No one in the world is better at solving adventure or role-playing games than Roe Adams, author and review editor of **Softalk**. Companies hire him to play-test their games, and on occasion he's embarrassed them by finding the solution to their months-in-creation double-disk monsters in as little as twenty minutes. Here's how he goes about starting an adventure.

ROE ADAMS: Start with novice-level games. After you've solved four or five of those, you'll be ready for the intermediate and eventually the expert levels.

You have to learn how to "balloon-map." This looks something like an organizational chart, with a circle for each place your character can go, and a line leading up to each place he could go from there.

The first time through the game, don't *do* anything. Just go from each direction in each room and mark down what's there. Make sure you don't miss a direction. While it's tempting to try things out, hold back until you've mapped everything out. Then you can go back and open doors—probably with keys you know the location of already.

Keep trying options, save the game on disk often, and exhaust all possibilities. Sooner or later, the solution will become clear.

*The first microcomputer epic . . .*

## TIME ZONE

Roberta Williams; Apple II family; 48K; includes six disks; $100; copy-protected? YES; Sierra On-Line, Inc., P.O. Box 485, Coarsegold, CA 93614; 209/683-6858.

## WIZARD AND THE PRINCESS

Roberta & Ken Williams; Apple II family; 48K ● Atari (disk); 40K ● Commodore 64 ● IBM PC compatibles (ADVENTURE IN SERENIA); 64K; $29.95; copy-protected? YES; Sierra On-Line, Inc., P.O. Box 485, Coarsegold, CA 93614; 209/683-6858.

---

ROE ADAMS: TIME ZONE is the greatest adventure game ever written. Its breadth and scope are unsurpassed. We're talking about 39 interlocking scenarios (each one as complex as a complete adventure), and 1500 high-resolution "rooms," filling both sides of six disks (fortunately unprotected so you can copy them for the heavy use they will undoubtedly undergo). Each scenario takes place in a given place and time, and thousands of years of human history—past, present, and future—are spanned by this labyrinthine quest.

TIME ZONE is for expert-level adventurers only. Sierra On-Line estimates that a skilled player will complete it in about a year. The biggest problem in cracking it is perspective—since the scenarios interlock,

everything has to be done in the right order, as with a Chinese ball puzzle, where an erroneous move means failure is guaranteed (though you might not notice it for thousands of moves). In TIME ZONE, for instance, creating an anachronism—taking an object to a time period that preceded its actual invention—means you lose the object permanently. (You can take a hand mirror back to Cleopatra's time, but not a rifle.)

I solve adventures for a living, but TIME ZONE was my greatest challenge. I started on a Monday and, working for 20 to 22 hours a day (my wife Nan put food in front of me every so often), I finished it in a week. My pile of maps was two inches high. I was so taken with the game that I began "Vault of Ages," a PUBLIC conference on The Source (see PUBLIC review on p. 141) specifically intended as a hint exchange for people tackling this epic among adventures. So far more than 9000 people have accessed this conference.

STEVEN LEVY: While TIME ZONE is Roberta Williams's masterpiece, I use her WIZARD AND THE PRINCESS to initiate novices into the world of graphic adventuring. Some of the puzzles are kind of dippy, but this fairy-tale-style program (known to the IBM world as ADVENTURE IN SERENIA) has a sense of whimsy and wonder that has made it a favorite for three years.

*Spanning the breadth of human history, TIME ZONE is a ticket to meet and interact with all those figures you've heard so much about. Above, your first confrontation with the outlaw of Sherwood Forest.*

---

*What Do You Do When You're at Witt's End?*

## WIZISYSTEM MANUAL

Mike Nichols; 1984; 100 pp.; $15; also maps, $5/scenario; Nichols Services, 6901 Buckeye Way, Columbus, GA 31904; 404/323-9227; or COMPUTER LITERACY.

## A SHORTCUT THROUGH ADVENTURELAND

Jack Cassidy, Pete Katz, Richard Owen Lynn and Sergio Waisman; 1984; 167 pp.; $9.95; Datamost, 20660 Nordhoff Street, Chatsworth, CA 91311; 818/709-1202; or COMPUTER LITERACY.

---

STEVEN LEVY: Role-playing programs like WIZARDRY or ULTIMA are frighteningly complicated, forcing hours of play before you develop a character strong or smart enough to advance to higher levels. The challenge is so tough that a cottage industry has developed to lend support. Most commonly the vendors in this "cheat" industry work out of their homes, selling maps, hint sheets, or floppy disks with programs to "resurrect" slain characters (or, much to the dismay of purists, creating new supercharacters without "earning" the powerful characteristics). I've used some of the programs to create characters, and though they work well I can't recommend them, because the power corrupts—it's not as much fun to build your

character when you know you can create a more devastating one in five minutes.

On the other hand, one service I found not only helpful but fascinating in its own right was Mike Nichols's **Wizisystem** for the WIZARDRY games. It's a passionate rebuttal to the part of the WIZARDRY manual that states that the less said about rules and parameters the better. **Wizisystem** has plenty to say: Nichols has pondered the lessons of his hundreds of hours within the dungeons of the Mad Overlord, and he offers himself as your guide in this opinionated, chatty, 100-page opus devoted to the three WIZARDRY scenarios. It illuminates the WIZARDRY experience without taking any of the fun away.

When it comes to adventure games, most game publishers offer hints (not solutions) on the phone. But Infocom also sells colorful, cleverly packaged hint sheets—the hints don't appear unless you rub at them with a special marker. The best bargain to date in the adventure game-hint department, though, is a book called **Shortcut Through Adventureland**. At less than ten bucks, it'll take you through adventures, including the epic TIME ZONE. But have someone who's not working on the adventure read you a given hint—looking at the page yourself presents too much of a risk that you'll glance,

inadvertently or otherwise, at the secret to some dilemma you have yet to encounter.

From Nichols's **Wizisystem**:

### Notes on Character Classes

MAGE (minimum IQ 11, available to new characters). Mages are poor fighters but learn the spells that are most effective in combat. They are very limited as to equipment and can use only those magical items suited to their class and alignment.

THIEF (minimum agility 11, available to new characters). Thieves are not good for much besides opening chests, and they are not too skilled at that! They are lousy fighters and learn no spells. Since there are other means of dealing with chests, I suggest you do not have any thieves in your party. Case closed.

From **Shortcut Through Adventureland**:

When you see the werewolf on the screen, you can do one of two things: run away or kill him. We recommend you kill him at the first opportunity with the silver bullet from #6 and the revolver from #8. Otherwise he will follow you everywhere, making the game nearly impossible.

*Adventuring in the public domain . . .*

## EAMON

Donald Brown; Apple II family; $10.00/disk; copy-protected? NO; Public Domain Software Copying Co., 33 Gold Street #13, New York, NY 10038; 212/732-2565.

---

LYNN J. ALFORD: EAMON, a public domain fantasy, is an excellent role-playing system. Like many fantasy games, you give your name (or your favorite alias; mine is Lady Lynn) and the game will give you values for your charisma, hardiness, and agility. Then you're on your own.

There is no winning and losing in EAMON (except for losing your life). Sometimes you have to accomplish some specific task to leave the adventure, but that is rare. EAMON has lots of treasure, loads of monsters, and even an occasional damsel in distress. Don't attack every monster you meet until you've tried making friends—you might need a friend to help you survive the adventure. EAMON itself is more friendly than many other games of its ilk, because if you give it a command it doesn't know, it will tell you the commands it does know—wonderful to someone who once spent fifteen minutes trying to tell another game to put a raft in the river.

The EAMON system has a master disk, a dungeon-designer disk, and more than twenty games, each with its own story, some quite different from the others. I've completed some in a few hours; others take as much as twenty hours. Maybe the toughness varies according to how mean the author felt that day. The dungeon-designer disk contains a complete set of instructions for the beginning adventurer and a program that allows you to examine other dungeons and create new dungeons of your own.

I found EAMON in the library of the Carolina Apple club, copied it, and now make copies for friends. By doing this, I am following the instructions on the opening screen, which urges users to distribute this public domain program as freely as they wish.

---

# Role Playing

*This is the first thing you see when, after assembling your WIZARDRY party, you enter the Dungeons of the Mad Overlord. The next thing you'll probably see is a bunch of zombies wiping you out. After hours of experimentation, you just might be ready to fight demons and gremlins well enough to survive to the second level. After a few weeks you might realize you haven't talked to your family since you bought the game.*

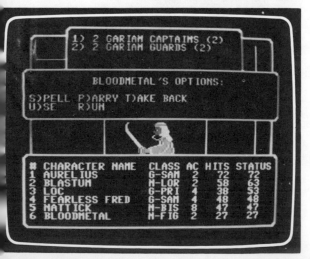

*Dungeons-and-Dragons brilliantly realized . . .*

## WIZARDRY

## PROVING GROUNDS OF THE MAD OVERLORD

Andrew Greenberg & Robert Woodhead; Apple II family ● Apple III; $50 ● IBM PC compatibles ● IBM PCjr; 64K; $60; copy-protected? YES; Sir-Tech Software, Inc., 6 Main St., Ogdensburg, NY 13669; 315/393-6633.

## KNIGHT OF DIAMONDS

Andrew Greenberg & Robert Woodhead; Apple II family ● Apple III; $34.95; copy-protected? YES; Sir-Tech Software, Inc., 6 Main St., Ogdensburg, NY 13669; 315/393-6633.

## LEGACY OF LLYLGAMYN

Andrew Greenberg & Robert Woodhead; Apple II family ● Apple III; $39.95 copy-protected? YES; Sir-Tech Software, Inc., 6 Main St., Ogdensburg, NY 13669; 315/393-6633.

---

WILLIAM MICHAEL BROWN: *The* classic. Sure, this trilogy is adolescent and gory and violent and weird. Just like the **Iliad**. It's also the most enduringly intelligent, even wry, Dungeons and Dragons-style role-playing game around, informed by a deep and sincere love of the fantastic. Like classic literature, the game has something to say about Good and Evil and the Meaning of Life—and since when have you booted a disk that addressed those human topics?

The three distinct games of the trilogy share basic D&D play mechanics: Create a few characters, equip them, and then send them into a multilevel dungeon—there to find better weapons and armor, gold, and other

*The third and most advanced WIZARDRY scenario, the LEGACY OF LLYLGAMYN, featuring a window-ing, Lisa-like display. Here you see the options available to your party before encountering that fierce looking fellow with the sabre.*

treasures; do battle with monsters; and discover a magic solution to various dangers threatening the kingdom of Llylgamyn.

All three games are linked: you create brand-new characters in PROVING GROUNDS; only survivors can go on to the quests in KNIGHT and LLYLGAMYN. The mechanics of creating and equipping characters are very simple, handled by clear menus. The core of the game is dungeon exploration: As your party moves around the maze, you see it as though you were inside it. Since you can rarely see more than a few steps ahead of the party, making maps is imperative (I usually do this on quadrille paper). Without a map you can get lost in only a few steps and are easy prey to monsters. While you're exploring, subsidiary menus at the side of the 3-D screen keep you posted on your progress. LLYLGAMYN, the most advanced of the trilogy, has a dazzling LISA-like windowing text-and-graphics display.

The dungeons are *fiendishly* designed: pits, traps, teleporting doors, and dark areas that make mapping incredibly hard; witty riddles and puzzles that appear as inscriptions on random walls or glowing in the air; odd statuary and furniture; enchanted swords and cursed rings; even entire individual structures, such as demon barracks and castles, tucked away in various corners. You're totally on your own in figuring out what any of it is for. Meanwhile, you've got to cope with more or less constant attacks from hundreds of varieties of marauding monsters. It's best to dip in a little way at first, try to grab some gold and not meet too many monsters; then dash up and rest before beginning again.

Like **Dune** or **Lord of the Rings**, WIZARDRY is a completely imagined, self-contained world. Anybody who buys PROVING GROUNDS may be on the way to a lifelong addiction. I'm a piker—I've only spent weeks on each installment. I've got a friend who's still at PROVING GROUNDS, even though he solved it almost a year ago. He claims he just likes hanging out down there.

*Role-playing quest marked by challenge and whimsy . . .*

## ULTIMA II

**Richard "Lord British" Gariott; Apple II family; 48K ● Atari (disk); 48K ● Commodore 64 (disk) ● IBM PC compatibles; 64K ● IBM PCjr; $60; color recommended; copy-protected? YES; Sierra On-Line, Inc., P.O. Box 485, Coarsegold, CA 93614; 209/683-6858.**

STEVEN LEVY: I admit to long sessions with ULTIMA II. In contrast to WIZARDRY's first-person perspective, here you get a bird's-eye view of the single character you create to do battle with evil Wizard Minax. But since dungeons are only a small part of your travels—you pass through towns, castles, seas, and outer space—the maplike graphics are just fine (though I would like to be able to turn off the shrill sounds, especially when monsters attack). Don't plan on finishing quickly, and count on lots of surprises and some tough challenges. This is second in a trilogy (ULTIMA I, the sluggish opener, is best left on the shelf) and as the following review implies, author Richard "Lord British" Garriott just gets better.

## EXODUS: ULTIMA III

**Richard "Lord British" Garriott; Apple II family; 48K; Mockingboard optional ● Atari; 48K ● Commodore 64 ● IBM PC compatibles; 64K; color graphics card; $60; copy-protected? YES; Origin Systems, Inc., P.O. Box 99, 1545 Osgood St., #7, North Andover, MA 01845; 617/681-0609.**

KEVIN STREHLO: EXODUS: ULTIMA III, the latest in Lord British's dense, almost rococo graphic fantasy adventures, expands on the considerable ULTIMA mythology. While your opponents in the first two ULTIMAs were clearly defined, EXODUS remains a mystery until the very end. So much the better. As you begin forming your characters (a party of characters, à la WIZARDRY, whereas previous ULTIMAs allowed you but a solitary gladiator), only one thing is certain: You're in for a long adventure.

EXODUS: ULTIMA III is quite a challenge: Lord British can put you through hell for a single lousy clue. But don't worry: It will begin to make sense eventually—if your characters survive. The game comes with three separate manuals and an unfinished map of Sosario, the fantasy world. The sheer bulk of the information makes it difficult to remember, as the clock of battle ticks away, exactly which command sends, say, a potent ball of lightning down the throats of your enemy. Was it the incantation of Mittar, or one of the supplications from the Liturgy of Truth? Make notes in the player-reference card, so you don't have to thumb through the documentation's medieval-flavored prose while your intrepid band gets pounded by a gaggle of giants.

The dungeons of ULTIMA III are much more interesting than those of the ULTIMAs that preceded it, and III has better graphics too, but its main strength is that it is even tougher to crack. (That's saying a lot—I know an accountant who's been trying to solve ULTIMA II for two years.) Penetrate III's inner sanctum without the proper exotic weapons, and you are but smoldering ash before the great dragons. Pay too little attention to tidal forces, and you'll never find the disappearing city of Dawn. There are many ways to fail, and only one way to win and discover the awful secret of EXODUS. That's why ULTIMA players are so fanatic—they have to be in order to finish the damn games. But even those who never finish seem to come back for more when the next ULTIMA hits the streets.

*ULTIMA III gives a colorful graphic display of your party, the surrounding geography, and the assortment of creatures that threaten your continued existence. Here you face off, à la the rumble scene in West Side Story, against a band of murderous Orcs.*

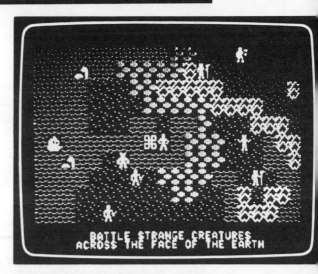

BATTLE STRANGE CREATURES ACROSS THE FACE OF THE EARTH

*A CP/M gem captured by modem . . .*

## WIZARD'S CASTLE

**IBM PC compatibles; $6.00/disk plus $4.00/order for shipping; copy-protected? NO; PC Software Interest Group, 1556 Halford Avenue #130, Santa Clara, CA 95051; 408/730-9291 ● CP/M, LOBO-DOS, MS-DOS, TRSDOS versions; $10.00 per disk; Public Domain Software Copying Company, 33 Gold St., New York, NY 10038; 212/732-2565 ● Public domain: available on various CP/M BBS by telecomputing; runs on CP/M, requires no extra graphics.**

RANDALL ROTHENBERG: When I purchased my Osborne I told friends and family I had but one purpose: mulching words. But in truth, I wanted to play games. Little did I know that CP/M would stand in the way of me and my secret desire. So few games! Nothing much stood between me and my wordsmithing.

Until I discovered telecomputing. Bulletin board systems (see Telecommunicating, pp. 148-149) opened up the game-playing world I'd missed. They also introduced me to a whole new set of frustrations. I'd spend 45 minutes downloading a massive game file, unsqueeze the damn thing, and load it, only to find that the version of BASIC in which it was written was incompatible with Ozzie's MBASIC.

Hence my joy over WIZARD'S CASTLE. I located it on the Technical BBS in Dearborn, Michigan. Although my version was written for the Heath, it runs flawlessly on the Osborne I. In the months I've owned CASTLE, it has provided so many hours of intrigue that I'm embarrassed to give an exact number.

In contrast with those in adventure games, CASTLE's maze is coherent, a cube-shaped three-dimensional fortress. Each time you play, the castle is randomly stocked with several hundred monsters (twelve kinds, from kobold to orc to gargoyle), treasures (eight varieties, each with the power to ward off a different spell), vendors, warps, sinkholes, books, and chests (the latter two items to be opened at the player's peril). The goal of the game is, first, to locate the Runestaff—in the possession of an unknown beast, which unfortunately must be slaughtered before it will relinquish it—and then to use the Runestaff's power to teleport into the (also unknown) room that hides the mysterious Orb of Zot. Oh, yeah: You've also got to get out of the castle alive.

Easier said than done. I won my first game ever only yesterday, after God knows how many attempts. It took me 1000 moves over three hours of playing time. The chief problem is the constantly shifting attributes of the player's character, which determine whether a player can attack a monster, cast a spell . . . indeed, stay alive. Slip below one point in any of the attributes, and be prepared to cross the Stygian gulf, my friends. In order to increase attribute points, gold must be found, treasures sold, and monsters—each of which guards a cache of some sort—slain. Additional points can be purchased from the sleazy vendors who infest the castle.

CASTLE has one additional attraction: On Technical BBS, it was accompanied by a separate superb documentation file, a rarity for CP/M public domain games. CASTLE's rules explain everything without spoiling the excitement of the unknown. I keep coming back for more. And now I love my Osborne.

# WRITING

## Stewart Brand, Domain Editor

STEWART BRAND: Said to account for more than 60% of personal computer use, word processing programs are doing to writing what pocket calculators did to figuring. Cue the testimonials:

JUSTIN KAPLAN (biographer): It's sexy, exhilarating, and addictive, as different from a typewriter as flying is from dog paddling. (From **Boston Review**)

CHARLES SPEZZANO: A good word processing program can change your whole attitude toward writing, while pens and paper keep you stuck in your old compulsive habits.

ANONYMOUS: Though not the first priority when businesses buy a computer, word processing becomes the justification for the whole system. (From **Boardroom Reports** and **Hillel Segal's Executive Computing Newsletter**)

MARGE PIERCY (novelist and poet): If I had to give up writing on my computer, I would feel I had returned to scraping letters in cuneiform on clay tablets . . . . The writing itself is far more serious than on the typewriter. There is no punishment for revising and revising again . . . . Writing on the screen has a fluidity that makes compromise with what you envision silly. (From **Boston Review**)

RICHARD WANDERMAN: Word processing is wonderful, period. It's hard to separate out the wonders of word processing in general from the wonders of a good program.

STEWART BRAND: That last one is our function here. General wonders first, specifics in a minute. There's a hidden greater advantage with writing on computers: you don't just write more fluidly, you *connect* more fluidly. With telecommunications (p. 138), text can flow into and out of your computer in torrents if you let it. The fact that you always have a copy of what you've written lurking on disk leads to all sorts of broadcast behavior, like sending mildly adapted copies of the same letter or article to many audiences instead of just one—either "personalized" informally by hand or in automated profusion with one of the "Merge" features.

Spellers are a blessing. The typos you can't see because you made them and the misspellings you can't see because you think they're right are fish in a barrel for the implacable software dictionaries. One of my favorites, WORD PROOF (p. 62), will offer synonyms when you're stuck for a better word—and even insert it for you. More subtle are the style checkers like PUNCTUATION + STYLE (p. 62) that will flag your awkwardnesses and clichés and suggest an improved usage. Outline programs, like THINKTANK (p. 92) and FRAMEWORK (p. 110), can accelerate the organization of your thoughts.

If there is a problem with writing programs, it is that we become too absorbed . . .

ALFRED LEE: I really do believe I go into something like a trance. When my wife intrudes to ask my opinion about buying a lamp, I just can't handle the weight of her other world unless I get up and turn my back on the screen.

ROBERT COWAN: I would not have been able to finish my 750-page book in 5.5 months without my word processing hardware, but the quality "seems" lower. I just can't put my finger on it. I know with my word processing I'm working "smarter, not harder." But what is it I have lost? What is it I have gained? The answer is right at the tip of my fingers . . . Did I almost state it earlier? I can't remember . . . The words have scrolled off the top of the screen and are being held deep within the crystal memory of a device I cannot understand.

STEWART BRAND: Writing is so extremely personal that people become identified with their word processing program and will brook no objectivity about it. Most people are still using the first writing program they learned. It's the native language of their fingers and all their files have sworn allegiance to its format.

STEVEN LEVY: I compare using a word processor to living with somebody. You go into it with all kinds of enthusiasms, and things are wonderful. Then, you see other word processors promising more. More features, friendlier style. The question is, is it worth tossing over a relationship in which you've invested months for a word-transpose toggle, an indexing function you'll use maybe twice, and a split-screen capability? A choice of a word processor is a major life-decision, and no one can afford (in terms of time, money, or emotional capital) to play the field.

STEWART BRAND: The bad news is, there's some 300 word processing programs out there; the good news is, with that many competing ferociously, the best are pretty good. We've been winnowing for a year. As usual, winnowing is done in part with biases. We're biased against programs that make writing and editing take place in different "modes," because it's too easy to lose track of what mode you're in, do the wrong thing, and then have to backtrack—that eliminated SELECT and moved BANK STREET WRITER (p. 184) to Learning. We're biased against programs that make formatting (preparing for printing) be a big, separate deal—that eliminated EDIX/WORDIX and hurt PERFECT WRITER (p. 55) and PC-WRITE (p. 59). We're biased toward "what-you-see-is-what-you-get" programs, where bold is bold on the screen, justified is justified, there's not a lot of command or format clutter, and page breaks are shown dramatically.

We're biased against slowness in all its forms—that eliminated VALDOCS and THE LEADING EDGE (if you can destructively backspace or overtype faster than the machine, you're bound to lose stuff and have to replace it) as well as SAMNA III (stops and goes to disk for even petty errands) and IBM's PC WRITER and DISPLAYWRITE2 (laborious menu sequences for everything). All of the programs recommended here are fast.

Our major criterion is that a program *wear* well. That the constant stuff goes easy—starting up, going in and out of files, printing, moving blocks of text, deleting words and sentences, knowing where you are in the document, being reminded of a rarely used command. Popular programs like MULTIMATE and EASYWRITER II lost out by being just a bit less smooth or reliable or potent than the competition we're recommending.

*Hardware.* All the best word processors are on the IBM family. Macintosh may challenge that by Spring '85. The Kaypro and Morrow are great bargains, but the top CP/M-80 programs are pretty clumsy, though powerful. Word processors on the Apple IIe & IIc are newer and more adroit. On any of these a hard disk is heaven for a writer. If you're on the move, get a portable such as the TRS-80 MODEL 100 or Hewlett-Packard 110 or possibly Apple IIc.

# WHOLE EARTH RECOMMENDED WRITING TOOLS

## (June 1984)

**The Word Processing Book**, $9.95, p.48

### COMMODORE 64
HOMEWORD, $70, p.52
OMNIWRITER, $70, p.52
TYPING TUTOR III, $50, p.48

### ATARI 800 XL
HOMEWORD, $70, p.52
ATARIWRITER, $100, p.53

### APPLE IIe, IIc
HOMEWORD, $70, p.52
PFS:WRITE, $125, p.54
WORD JUGGLER, $109, p.55

SENSIBLE SPELLER, $125, p.63
TYPING TUTOR III, $50, p.48

### CP/M-80
WORDSTAR, $495, p.56
NEWWORD, $249, p.56
PERFECT WRITER, $349, p.55
(with PLU*PERFECT), $39, p.55
THE WORD PLUS, $150, p.62
PUNCTUATION + STYLE, $125, p.62
COMPARE II, $145, p.63

### RADIO SHACK 100
SCRIPSIT 100, $40, p.57

### MACINTOSH
MACWRITE, p.54
MICROSOFT WORD, $195, p.60

### IBM PC COMPATIBLE
HOMEWORD, $75, p.52
PFS:WRITE, $140, p.54
WORDVISION, $80, p.58
VOLKSWRITER DELUXE, $295, p.58
PC-WRITE, $10, p.59
WORDSTAR, $495, p.56
NEWWORD, $249, p.56
WORDPERFECT, $495, p.60
XYWRITE II +, $300, p.61
MICROSOFT WORD, $475 (with mouse), p.60
WORD PROOF, $60, p.62
CORRECTSTAR, $195, p.63
THE WORD PLUS, $150, p.62
PUNCTUATION + STYLE, $125, p.62
COMPARE II, $145, p.63
TYPING TUTOR III, $50, p. 48

*WORDSTAR is the old and fading standard, supported by a legacy of machines, software, books, and fellow users. (NEWWORD is a WORDSTAR clone with significant improvements on the original at half the price.) MICROSOFT WORD may be the new standard, because it is the most powerful word processor on the IBM PC family, is surprisingly easy to learn and use, supports the elaborate capabilities of new and forthcoming printers, and is a link to the 32-bit world opened by Apple's Macintosh. WORDPERFECT is the most full-featured, relatively easy-to-use PC writing tool. VOLKSWRITER DELUXE is the most easy-to-use, relatively full-featured PC writing tool. XYWRITE II + is a bitch to learn, but it's fast, and it does nearly everything. Innovative, lonely WORDVISION is exceptionally handy for creative writers. PC-WRITE is fast and free and improving daily. PFS: WRITE is intelligently simple.*

*On CP/M-80 machines PERFECT WRITER's windows and buffers give awkward but rich editing power. On the Apple IIe and IIc WORD JUGGLER is breezy and fast. MACWRITE is highly decorative and easy on the Macintosh. OMNIWRITER has surprising power at low cost on the Commodore 64; so does ATARIWRITER on the Atari. Writers-at-large and telecommunicators have flocked to the portable TRS-80 Model 100 for its mobility, and they now have a good-printing program in SCRIPSIT 100. On nearly everything HOMEWORD is the easiest for kids and occasional writers.*

*The best of the spelling checkers is WORD PROOF (IBM family only). The most pervasive is THE WORD PLUS and its great style-checking companion, PUNCTUATION + STYLE. For most Apple II programs SENSIBLE SPELLER works well. CORRECTSTAR is the new speller for old WORDSTAR. Most mis-spelling is mis-typing; TYPING TUTOR III is the cure.*

# TRUTH THROUGH ARGUMENT

STEWART BRAND: Forgive the self-introduction. My perspective on the tools reviewed here is primarily that of an editor (16 years), secondarily a hack writer, thirdly an office-sharer. I don't have secretarial experience at all—the day-long dealing with other people's words in rigorously standard formats—and the section needs it. What is well represented is the experience of running small professional offices, thanks to psychiatrist Charles Spezzano and the several hundred members of his Society for the Prevention of Cruelty to Users (get the **SPCU Letter** for $36/yr from The SPCU Letter, 2261 Hudson Street, Denver, CO 80207; 303/388-2380). Spezzano has spent more time than I, weeks to months often, immersed in each of the leading word processors, sifting and sifting toward this section. On an EIES teleconference (p. 147) a good forty voices have been debating fiercely about these programs for over a year, 700 comments last I noticed, some of them reproduced here. The conversation now widens through this book; please join it.

*Stewart Brand*

Matt Herron

## TYRANNY OF THE NEW

STEWART BRAND: An interesting upstart coming on the Commodore 64 is SKIWRITER II (Ken Skier; Commodore 64 ● IBM PCjr; 64K; on cartridge with built in telecommunications; $69.95; Prentice-Hall, General Publishing Division, Englewood Cliffs, NJ 07632; 201/592-2000). Competitively priced with HOMEWORD and OMNIWRITER (p. 52), it comes on cartridge, so it can work without a disk drive or gives more storage if you have one. SKIWRITER's special talent is telecommunicating; it may be the best deal of all on the Commodore for that. Doesn't do bold; does do 22 pages of text.

The major battlefield of new top quality word processors is on the Macintosh. Something strong and good is supposed to be coming from Apple itself, which may or may not try to compete with MICROSOFT WORD (p. 61). By Spring '85 there should be half a dozen programs vying for position; I look forward to covering that in the **Whole Earth Software Review**.

MicroPro, the publisher of WORDSTAR (p. 56), is rumored to be preparing its successor for release in late '84. A difficult task. If it tries to be command and file compatible with WORDSTAR, it perpetuates that program's limitations. If it doesn't, where does that leave one million WORDSTAR buyers?

---

*Fixing the major source of word processing errors and slowness . . .*

## TYPING TUTOR III

**Kriya Systems, Inc.; Apple II family ● Commodore 64 ● IBM PC compatibles; 128K; copy-protected? NO; $50; Simon & Schuster, Electronic Publishing Group, 1230 Avenue of the Americas, New York, NY 10020; 212/245-6400.**

---

STEWART BRAND: This most miraculous of programs enables the machine to train you to use the machine at your optimum capability. There's no more fundamental computer skill than keyboard dexterity. With it, you can operate at program speed; without it, you're always fighting your way through your fingers to the work.

TYPING TUTOR III does for typers what the aerobics books did for runners—quantify the process, take it one part at a time, and constantly reward the budding athlete with distinct progress. Better still, this program

analyzes your performance in microscopic detail (thousandths of a second) and lets you know instantly how you're doing, so you adjust and improve without even thinking about it—Skinnerian reinforcement at its best.

Starting with the "home row" keys the program gives you a quick drill, reports your speed in words-per-minute (WPM) and number of errors, and on to the next lesson. It begins with a 20 WPM threshold; as soon as you master a letter at that speed, it gives you different letters; letters you're not fast with are repeated until you master them. You can stop any time, and the program will remember where you left off and what your skills are till next time (it will do that for a number of students simultaneously). You can get a graph any time that shows your proficiency with the various characters and also your detailed improvement (or decay) since last time you checked the chart. Whenever drill gets old you can go play Letter Invaders and zap incoming letters and letter combinations—the game picks up on your skill level and constantly challenges it. That's amazing. Why don't more games do that?

Training choices within TYPING TUTOR III include Alphabet Keys, Number Keys, Words Test, Numbers Test, Full Keyboard Test, Standard Speed Test (handy for employers), and a customization utility. The manual is simple and inviting. Since the program runs on nearly everything, it could be used in a computer store to help decide which machine and keyboard best suit you.

Of the dozens of typing programs available, this is still the top. The closest market competitor is MASTERTYPE (p. 187), which is more gaudy, more fun, less instructive, and copy protected (TYPING TUTOR III isn't). On the TRS-80 Model 100 there's a neat typing program, with game, called TUTOR + (copy-protected? NO; cassette; $50; Portable Computer Support Group, 11035 Harry Hines Blvd., Suite 207, Dallas TX 75229, 214/351-0564).

*The graph in TYPING TUTOR III shows every detail of how you're doing on the various characters (bottom row) in Words Per Minute, including improvement in performance since the last chart—it's usually dramatic.*

---

*Cheery, solid . . .*

## THE WORD PROCESSING BOOK

*The Word Processing Book (A Short Course in Computer Literacy); Peter McWilliams; revised edition, 1984; 299 pp.; $9.95; Quantum Press, Doubleday & Co., Inc., 501 Franklin Avenue, Garden City, NY 11530; 516/294-4400.*

---

STEWART BRAND: The most congenial of introductions to the wonders as well as intricacies of word processing is Peter McWilliams' classic, now updated and expanded for Fall '84. He's entertaining, instructive, and quite usefully judgmental about products. Though we're collaborators and friends with Peter, his shopping perspective is enough different from ours to be worth checking. If someone you know is considering word processing, this book can be an invaluable guide and encouragement.

## EXPLANATION OF FEATURES ON THE COMPARATIVE CHART ON NEXT PAGE (REASONS NOT TO BUY)

STEWART BRAND: Matrix diagrams like on the next two pages are common in computer magazines—it's one of the few ways they can compare software products without offending advertisers. This one aims to be more useful. It leaves out the common stuff that all our recommended programs do— wordwrap, justification, search & replace, hard disk compatible, etc.—and concentrates on their differences. The differences are selected to be the most important ones—"important" meaning that the absence of a certain feature may make the program useless to certain users (footnotes, decimal aligning) or may greatly reduce the ease-of-use for certain intensities of word processing (split screen, "undo" command, macros). Beware of buying a program with more features than you need; they'll only hinder and distract you. On the other hand, it's interesting to have a program that still invites exploration months after you've begun using it.

I threw in three all-in-ones—APPLEWORKS (p. 113), SYMPHONY (p. 111), FRAMEWORK (p. 110)—to compare their integrated word processors to these specialized ones. A typical dedicated word processor, CPT (p. 63), is added for perspective's sake.

CHARLES SPEZZANO: I divide the field of word processors into:

● *Lightweight*—strictly correspondence and memos;

● *Middleweight*—frequent writing of letters and reports or articles, but no need for advanced features like automatic footnotes or split-screens, no very long documents (over twenty-five pages);

● *Heavyweight*—a full complement of advanced features that will take you through articles and complex (varying formats) reports all the way up to books.

STEWART BRAND: Roughly from light to heavyweight, certainly from left to right . . . *Recommended to run on* . . . The machines that make the program worthy. *Not copy protected* For the user, copy protection is a nuisance, reducing adaptability of the program in your working situation. *Minimum memory required/maximum memory useable* The minimum tells if it'll run on your machine; the maximum tells if it'll take full advantage of your expensive acres of RAM. *Useable lines on screen* A critical matter for many; tunnel vision is the major restriction of computer writing; few available lines for writing makes it worse. *Maximum file size (double-spaced pages)* Estimated at 250 words per page (about 1.6K); if you do long documents and the program has short files, it better link files for printing. *Spellchecks easily with* . . . Some have their own proprietary spellers; some are comfortable with good generic

ones (see p. 62). *Telecommunicates easily with* . . . Same deal; if you telecommunicate much it is a major consideration, making PC WRITE and VOLKSWRITER DELUXE and XYWRITE II + stand out (see pp. 138-157). *Useable for programming* A surprising number of people use their word processor for writing code as well as text. *Blends easily with spreadsheets and databases* . . . A loose listing, pointing out companion packages and general compatibility.

*"Undo" command available* It means you can replace text you've deleted either inadvertently or because you wanted to see what the copy looked like without it; a boon. *Automatic reformatting* The text adjusts immediately around any changes you make instead of requiring you to request the adjustment; another boon. *On-screen page breaks/page numbers* If you're at all oriented to the printed document this becomes quite important; also an easy way to find your place in the text. *Split screen* Permits simultaneous viewing and editing of two or more documents or parts of documents; critical if you're blending texts; irrelevant otherwise. *Can print direct from memory* Handy for short-document people like me who don't want to have to save to disk (there goes speed and disk space) just to print out something ephemeral. *Continuously saves text/ automatically backs up files* Disaster insurance; I thought both were a mild nuisance until both saved hours of otherwise lost work; "continuously saves" periodically sips your text onto disk (with a tiny work pause, on some you can set the periodicity); "automatically backs up" keeps the previous draft on disk just in case—halves the available disk storage. *Macros available* Keyboard enhancers like PROKEY and SMARTKEY (p. 93) within the program that enable you to take shortcuts by putting routine text or routine command sequences under keys that you assign. *Mouse compatible* If you drive your cursor around the screen a lot, especially for editing, a mouse is fast, but it takes half your fingers off the keyboard.

*Links files for printing* Long files can get unwieldy, so it's better (and safer) to break them up; linking means a sequence of files can be printed out as one long document, with page numbers printed appropriately. *Merge capability* Personalized form letters usually; a monumental convenience; "conditional merge" permits automatic selectivity like "send to everybody in this list except the Californians"; at some point of volume you're better off with a full-scale file manager program like PFS:FILE (p. 80). *Page width possible* Especially if you're working with spreadsheets this can be crucial; otherwise irrelevant. *Decimal alignment/math capability* If you're doing columns of dollar figures, this'll make them line up; math is pocket-calculator level, usually less convenient than one. *Footnote capability* A major chore made easier; some offer the choice of end-of-text or same-page for placement. *Multicolumn formatting/whole columns may be moved* Handy for newsletters, reports and such; moving a column can be like Rubik's cube if the program doesn't help. *Can edit while printing/proportional printing* Lets you forge ahead writing while you're printing; proportional printing spaces *i*'s more narrowly than *m*'s, so the result looks typeset; pretty.

---

```
Bolding, underlining, flush right, and centering are all simple
to use: just press the bold, underline, flush right or center
key, type and it will be bolded, underlined,          flush right
                    or centered.
```

This is an example of **true proportional spacing.** In proportional spacing the capital W is wider than the small i. Each print thimble or wheel has a slightly different character width and placement (a character might be a bit to the left or right when compared with other characters).

*Ordinary versus proportional printing.*

| | Product | Recommended On | NOT Copy-Protected | Minimum Memory Required | Maximum Memory Useable | Useable Lines On Screen | Max. File Size (Double Spaced Pages) | Spellchecks Easily With... | Telecommunicates Easily With... | Useable for Programing | Blends Easily With Spreadsheets and Databases... | "Undo" Command Available | Automatic Reformatting |
|---|---|---|---|---|---|---|---|---|---|---|---|---|---|
| **LIGHTWEIGHT** | HOMEWORD $70 p. 52 | Commodore 64, Atari 800 Apple II, IIc, IIe, IBM PC, PCjr | | 64K | 128K | 15; can be 24 on IBM | 8; 24 IBM | HOMEWORD SPELLER, 39,000 words-$100; SENSIBLE SPELLER, 80,000 words-$125 | Anything (requires adding carriage returns) | | | ✓-"Undo" buffer, 2K maximum 3K on IIe | ✓ |
| | MACWRITE $195 with MACPAINT p. 54 | Macintosh | ✓ | 128K | 512K | 22 maximum (dependent on font size) | 10 | | MAC-TERMINAL $100 MAC-TEP (Public Domain) | | MULTIPLAN-$195 MICROSOFT FILE-$195 | ✓-can flick back and forth | ✓ |
| | PFS WRITE p. 54 | Apple IIe, IIc-$125 IBM PC/PCjr-$140 | | 64K Apple 128K IBM | 64K Apple 128K IBM | 22 | 16 Apple 20 IBM | PFS:PROOF, 100,000 words-$95 | With "Print to Disk" Function | | PFS:FILE-Apple $125 IBM $140 | | ✓ |
| **MIDDLEWEIGHT** | ATARIWRITER $100 p. 53 | Atari 800XL, 1200 | | 16-64K | 64K | 24 | 20 | ATARI PROOFREADER, 36,000 words-$50 | | | SYNCALL, SYNFILE, SYNTREND-$100 each | ✓ | ✓ |
| | OMNIWRITER $70, p. 52 | Commodore 64 | | 64K | 64K | 23 | 23 | ✓-30,000 words | | | MULTIPLAN (HESWARE)-$100 | | ✓ |
| | WORD JUGGLER p. 55 | Apple II, IIe-$189 Apple III-$229 | | 64K IIe 128K IIc, III | 128K | 23 | disk is limit | ✓-LEXICHECK, 50,000 words | Terminus-$90 | | PFS:FILE-$125 QUICKFILE-$100 | ✓ | ✓ |
| | PC:WRITE $10; $75 full registration p. 59 | IBM PC, PCjr | ✓ | 64K | 128K | 24 | 40 | WORD PROOF, 125,000 words-$60 | Anything | ✓ | PC FILE-$49 | | |
| | WORDVISION $80 p. 58 | IBM PC | ✓ | 96K | 640K | 20 | disk is limit | In "DOS FILE EDITOR" mode, w/ WORD PROOF, 125,000 words-$60 | In "DOS File Editor Mode," requires adding carriage returns | ✓ | | ✓ | ✓ |
| | VOLKSWRITER DELUXE $295 p. 58 | IBM PC, TI Professional, Tandy 2000 | ✓ | 128K | 640K | 24 | disk is limit | WORD PROOF, 125,000 words-$60 THE WORD PLUS, 45,000 words-$150 | Anything | ✓ | 1-2-3-$495; DBASE II-$495 SUPERCALC-$195; VISICALC-$99; MULTIPLAN-$195 | | |
| | PERFECT WRITER (CP/M Only) $349 (being changed); PLU*PERFECT $39, p. 55 | Kaypro 2, 4, 10; Morrow | ✓ | 64K | 64K | 23 | 35 floppy 130 hard disk | THE WORD PLUS, 45,000 words-$150 | Anything | ✓ | PERFECT FILER, PERFECT CALC-$249 each (being changed) | ✓ | |
| | WORDSTAR $495 p. 56 | Apple II, IIe, TRS 80, CP/M (Kaypro, Morrow), TI Professional, IBM PC, PCjr, HP 150 & 110, DEC Rainbow | ✓ | 64K | 64K | 14-22 | disk is limit | CORRECTSTAR, 65,000 words (MS-DOS only)-$195; THE WORD PLUS, 45,000 words-$150 | Anything (requires reformatting incoming text) | ✓ | INFO-STAR + $595 DATASTAR-$295 | | |
| | NEWWORD $250 p. 56 | Apple IIe, CP/M (Kaypro, Morrow) IBM PC | ✓ | 64K CP/M 96K MS-DOS | 180K | 17-25 | disk is limit | THE WORD PLUS, 45,000 words-$150 | Anything (requires reformating incoming text) | ✓ | INFO-STAR + $595 DATASTAR-$295 | ✓-Limit 100 characters; can be modif. by user | |
| | APPLEWORKS p. 113 | Apple IIe, IIc-$250 Apple III-$295 (Called III E-Z PIECES from Haba Systems) | ✓ | 64K | 128K | 20 | 56 | SENSIBLE SPELLER, 80,000 words-$125 | APPLE ACCESS II-$75 or other Apple terminal programs | ✓ | ✓ | | ✓ |
| | SYMPHONY $695 pp. 111 and 127 | IBM PC | | 320K | 640K | 20; 34 with Hercules Card | disk is limit | | ✓ | ✓ | ✓ | | |
| | FRAMEWORK $695 pp. 110 and 128 | IBM PC | | 256K | 640K | 21 | disk is limit | | 3rd party tele-communicators may be attached to program | ✓ | ✓ | ✓ | ✓ |
| **HEAVYWEIGHT** | XYWRITE II + $300 p. 61 | IBM PC | ✓ | 96K | 640K | 22 | disk is limit | WORD PROOF, 125,000 words-$60 THE WORD PLUS, 45,000 words-$150 | Anything | ✓ | 1-2-3-$495; VISICALC-$99; SUPERCALC-$195; MULTIPLAN-$195 | | |
| | WORDPERFECT $495 p. 60 | IBM PC, TI Professional; DEC Rainbow, Tandy 2000 | ✓ (except Tandy) | 128K 256K on Tandy | 256K | 24 | disk is limit | ✓-30,000 words | In "ASCII File Mode" | ✓ | DBASE II-$495; 1-2-3-$495; SUPERCALC-$195 | ✓ | |
| | MICROSOFT WORD p. 60 | IBM PC, DEC Rainbow, TI Professional, Tandy 2000-$375, $475 with mouse; Macintosh-$195 | | 128K | 256K | 19; 39 with Hercules Card | disk is limit | THE WORD PLUS, 45,000 words-$150 | In "Non-Formatted Mode" | ✓ | DBASE II-$495; 1-2-3-$495; SUPER-CALC-$195 | ✓ | ✓ |
| | CPT $5,000-$10,000 p. 63 | CPT | | | | 66 | disk is limit | ✓-72,000 words | ✓ | ✓ | DBASE II-$495; MSFILER$295; SUPERCALC-$195; MICROPLAN-$495 | ✓ | |

*Red indicates integrated program or dedicated word processor.*

| On-Screen Page Breaks/Page Numbers | Split Screen | Can Print Direct from Memory | Continually Saves Text | Automatically Backs Up Files | Macros Available | Mouse Compatible | Links Files For Printing | Merge Capability | Page Width Possible | Decimal Alignment/Math Capability | Footnote Capability | Multi-Column Formatting | Whole Columns May Be Moved | Can Edit While Printing | Proportional Printing |
|---|---|---|---|---|---|---|---|---|---|---|---|---|---|---|---|
| ✓/N | | ✓ | | ✓ | | | ✓ | | 78 columns | | | | | | |
| ✓/✓ | | | | | | ✓-requires mouse | | | 116 columns max. (dependent on font size & style) | ✓/✓ built-in calculator | ✓ | | | | ✓ |
| ✓/✓ | | ✓ | | | | | | PFS:FILE-Apple-$125 IBM-$140 | 78 columns | ✓/ | | | | | |
| Both in "Preview Mode" only | | ✓ | | | | | ✓ | | 132 columns | | | ✓ | | | ✓ |
| ✓/✓ | | ✓ | | | | | ✓ | ✓ | 250 columns | | ✓ | ✓ | ✓ | | |
| ✓/✓ | | ✓ | | | | | ✓ | ✓-conditional merge | 254 columns | | | | | | |
| | | ✓ | | ✓-with F1 command | ✓ | ✓-MOUSE SYSTEMS; MICROSOFT MOUSE | ✓ | | 160 columns | | | | | | |
| N/✓ | | ✓ | ✓ | | 5 "Phrase Keys" available-no commands | | | | 155 columns | ✓/ | | | | | |
| ✓/✓ | | ✓ | | ✓-suppressible | | | | ✓ | 250 columns | | | ✓ | ✓ | ✓-with DOS 2.0 | ✓ |
| | ✓ | | ✓-suppressible | | | | ✓ | | | | ✓ | | | | ✓ |
| ✓/✓ | | | | ✓-suppressible | | ✓-MOUSE SYSTEMS; MICROSOFT MOUSE | Only with MAIL-MERGE-$250 | MAIL-MERGE-$250 conditional merge | 240 columns | ✓/ | FOOTNOTE $99 (CP/M Only) Digital Marketing, 2363 Boulevard Circle #8, Walnut Creek, CA 94595 (800) 826-2222 | ✓ | ✓-Awkwardly | ✓ | |
| ✓/✓ | | | | ✓-suppressible | ✓-On IBM | | ✓ | ✓-conditional merge | 254 columns | ✓/ | FOOTNOTE $99 (CP/M Only) | | | | |
| ✓/✓- only when you ask for them | | ✓ | | | | | | ✓ | 336 columns | ✓/✓-in spreadsheet | | | | | ✓ |
| N/have to request | ✓ | ✓ | | | ✓ | ✓-MOUSE SYSTEMS | | ✓-conditional merge | 256 columns | ✓/✓-in spreadsheet | | | | | |
| | ✓ | ✓ | | | ✓ | | ✓ | ✓ | 255 columns | ✓/✓-in spreadsheet | | | | ✓ | |
| "Review Mode" Only/✓ | ✓ | ✓ | | ✓-if requested | | | ✓ | ✓ | 132 columns | ✓/✓ | ✓ | ✓ | ✓ | ✓ | ✓-But not right justification |
| ✓/✓ | | ✓ | | | ✓ | | ✓ | ✓-sorter extra $95 | 132 columns | ✓/✓ | ✓ | ✓ | ✓ | ✓-except on DEC Rainbow | ✓ |
| ✓/✓ | ✓-horizontal & vertical | ✓ | ✓ | ✓ | Format & Text, Yes; Command, No | ✓-designed for mouse | ✓ | ✓-conditional merge | 250 columns | ✓/ | ✓ | ✓ | | ✓ | ✓ |
| ✓/✓ | ✓ | ✓ | ✓ | ✓ | ✓ | | ✓ | ✓ | 240 columns | ✓/✓ | ✓ | ✓ | ✓ | ✓ | ✓ |

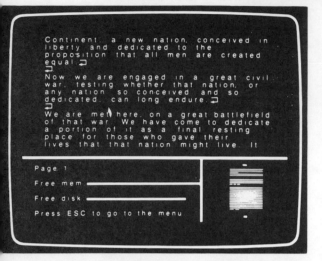

```
Continent, a new nation, conceived in
liberty and dedicated to the
proposition that all men are created
equal.

Now we are engaged in a great civil
war, testing whether that nation, or
any nation so conceived and so
dedicated, can long endure.

We are met here, on a great battlefield
of that war. We have come to dedicate
a portion of it as a final resting
place for those who gave their
lives that that nation might live. It

Page 1
Free mem _____
Free disk _____
Press ESC to go to the menu
```

*HOMEWORD's graphics make the program unique. When you're writing, images on the bottom of the screen show the amount of working memory left, the amount of disk storage left, and a "sketch" of each whole page as it will appear when it's printed—like a living miniature of your work. I found myself fascinated with it; no other program has such a thing.*

*Icons make it easy to learn, easy to remember...*

## HOMEWORD

**Tom Kain; version 1.0; Atari 800/800XL ● Commodore 64 ● version 1.2; Apple II family; 64K; copy-protected? YES; $69.95; Sierra On-Line, Inc., P.O. Box 485, Coarsegold, CA 93614; 209/683-6858 ● IBM PC, PCjr; DOS 2.1; 128K; copy-protected? YES; $75; IBM, Entry Systems Division, P.O. Box 1328, Boca Raton, FL 33432; 800/447-4700.**

STEWART BRAND: The most volatile part of the word processing market is the so-called "low end"—low-cost programs on low-cost machines for kids and beginners. Broderbund's BANK STREET WRITER ruled the roost in 1983 and is still loved by some. (Scarola defends it on p. 184 in Learning, where it may be defensible. The program was written for teaching writing—first you write, then you change modes and you edit. Being forced to work in two modes I find perpetually confusing.) In 1984 HOMEWORD took over. It costs the same, does more, does it easier, and, thanks to its use of graphics, it's easier to catch on to and to pick up again when you've been away from it for awhile. Though so far HOMEWORD has withstood challenges, such as Electronic Arts' CUT &

PASTE (cute but feeble), doubtless there's more to come (check SKIWRITER on the Commodore 64, p. 48).

The low-end programs may be cheap, but they're far from weak. HOMEWORD, like the others here, does wordwrap (you don't need to hit CARRIAGE RETURN at the end of a line, or even notice where the ends of lines are), does bold, underlined, and centered text, permits easy moves of blocks of text (as well as block delete and block copy), numbers your pages in sequence if you want, and automatically reformats your text around any changes you make (which is more than VOLKSWRITER DELUXE or WORDSTAR can manage). In addition it has an "Undo" command for bringing back deleted text,

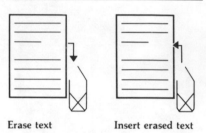

Erase text          Insert erased text

---

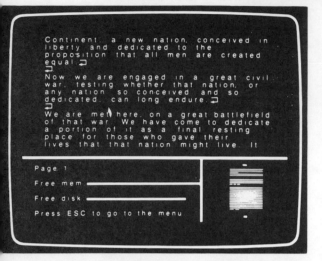
```
Omniwriter              name screenshot
On Page    1 of   1      Line  18 Col  39

The text of an OMNIWRITER document
shows little dots where there are
spaces--- a handy and rare detail.◄

It is hardly a what-you-see-is what-
you-print word processor.  This is
a  bold couple words .  This is
 underlined text .◄

→That's an indent (the arrow).◄

Unlike most Commodore 64 word
processors, words are not brok◄
en at line ends (I faked that one)
when the text is displayed in 40
columns, as here.  To see the text
in its full 80-columns, I would hit
a certain command and then scroll
sideways across the full wide text.◄
X (End of Page)
```

*Best on the Commodore...*

## OMNIWRITER

**Kevin Lacy; Commodore 64; copy-protected? YES; $70; HesWare, 150 North Hill Dr., Brisbane, CA 94005; 800/624-2442 or, in CA, 415/468-4111.**

STEWART BRAND: At present this is the dean of Commodore 64 word-processing programs, one you can do serious writing with. Why EASY SCRIPT from Commodore and PAPER CLIP from Batteries Included continue to sell for the Commodore 64 baffles me. They can't even manage to end lines on the screen without breaking words in the middle. At a similar price OMNIWRITER outclasses them both and includes a merge capability and a decent 30,000-word spelling checker (bless it, it'll tell you the number of words in your document).

In addition to its basic good sense OMNIWRITER is full of politenesses and clevernesses. Polite: a cue card which fits around your function keys; a good command reference card; choice of colors on the screen for text and background, easily changed to match your mood or the room's light; the file directory viewable even while you're writing. Clever: you can toggle quickly between 40-column width and 80-column (both have large letters—with the 80 you scroll sideways along the long lines) and you can write in both; tap "home," cursor goes to top of the screen, tap it again, goes to top of document; page breaks and page numbers are shown on the screen, and you can go to any page by its number. The up-to-23-page files can be linked for printing long documents. The program will blend in material from MICROSOFT MULTIPLAN (p. 70) and can go to 240 columns wide.

I wonder how many small businesses are being started on a shoestring with OMNIWRITER. No reason you couldn't.

automatically backs up files (so you always have the previous version of a document if, God forbid, you lose the current one), and links files for printing (which is fortunate, since files are limited in size to 8 double-spaced pages—24 pages on IBM). For checking spelling there's HOMEWORD SPELLER (30,000 words, $50) or SENSIBLE SPELLER (80,000 words, $125, p. 63).

HOMEWORD's major drawback is that only 15 lines of text are displayed at a time, because of all the screen space given to the icons, and because each format command in the text takes up an additional line. That is partly compensated by the page-sketch (see photo), and also by ready access to a screen-width full-80-column display of text as it will appear when printed (may or may not be legible in detail, depending on your system; you do all your writing in 40-column width, nice for those whose minds are young or whose eyes are old).

Another apparent drawback is that once you know your way around the icon commands, they get cumbersome. It takes nine keystrokes to move a block of text, for example. Fortunately HOMEWORD has a set of control-key commands (and a good reference card) that short-cut most

functions—a block move takes five keystrokes that way. On the IBMs you can suppress the icons entirely and get a full 24 useable writing lines on the screen.

Invitingly simple to enter, HOMEWORD becomes more sophisticated as you do, which is one of our measures of an outstanding program. The manual is good, and there's an audio cassette to talk you through your first session (always a delicate time).

---

*When you're messing with what you've written on HOMEWORD, a different set of images—called icons—are on the bottom of the screen. They become commands when you point the cursor at them. The basic menu includes "print," "edit," "file," "layout," "customize," and "disk utilities." Those lead to 28 other icon commands, each labeled with a word indicating its function. A good beginner's program should provide constant and easy rewards for using it, and it should always leave you certain about how to back out of a corner you wander into. HOMEWORD does both.*

Get document          Save document

---

*Best on Atari . . .*

## ATARIWRITER

**All Atari home computers; copy-protected? YES; $100; Atari, P.O. Box 427, Sunnyvale, CA 94086; 800/538-8543 or, in CA, 800/672-1404.**

---

STEWART BRAND: Like OMNIWRITER, ATARIWRITER is the kind of program that amazes old word-processing hands with the range of its abilities on a humble machine. It has no significant competition on the Atari. While not as fully capable as OMNIWRITER on the Commodore 64, it has some features that OMNIWRITER doesn't—an excellent manual, an "undo" command, and easy capability for proportional printing and double-wide printing. Notable limitations are the absence of bold lettering and the absence of overtyping as a way to change text (delete and insert is the only choice—my preference anyway). In "preview mode" 80 columns of text can be scanned across, but you can't edit without returning to 40 columns.

Educator Edna Mitchell runs an office at Mills College, Oakland, California, with ATARIWRITER.

EDNA MITCHELL: I had been struggling alone for many months to master WORDSTAR and had not yet become confident enough to trust any important or hurried writing to that program. Of course I knew how powerful it was, but it couldn't do it for me with the time pressures I live under daily. With ATARIWRITER I was delighted with the ease of producing material with different print types, justified margins, sub- or superscripts, underlining, and columns. I quickly learned to chain files, to reformat for printing, to move text and merge files and search for strings. I learned the hard way to watch for the limits of free memory in the Atari.

ATARIWRITER gets the user into the program instantly with a mini-overview—learn a little bit immediately and add the complex features later. It is this feature which enabled me to teach the process to my students and to others on my staff very quickly. I haven't yet given it to my secretary because I don't want to give up the computer and printer to her full-time use. Once one successfully begins to use a word processor it is inconceivable to be without it. It does not reduce the amount of paperwork I do; instead it increases it by making the production of words so easy and attractive.

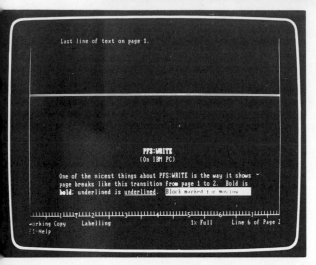

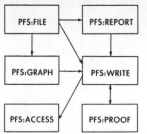

An advantage of PFS:WRITE is that it blends with a family of equally simple and effective programs—PFS:FILE (p. 80), PFS: REPORT (p. 81), PFS:GRAPH, PFS:ACCESS (p. 139), and its own 100,000 word speller, PFS:PROOF.

*Clean . . .*

## PFS:WRITE

**Apple IIe; 64K; 80 column screen; $125 ● IBM PC compatibles; 128K; $140; copy-protected? YES;**

## PFS:PROOF

**IBM PC/XT ● MS-DOS machines; 128K; 2 disk drives; copy-protected? YES; $95;**

**both from Software Publishing Corp., 1901 Landings Drive, Mountain View, CA 94043; 415/962-0191.**

STEWART BRAND: The enormous popularity of this program is well earned. It is living proof that for many of us, having lots of options in a program is not a feature, it's a bug. Keep it simple, right in the middle of what's most needed, and let the rest go by. I wish PFS:WRITE ran on my Kaypro—nearly all of my writing is short reviews and letters and is much better suited for PFS:WRITE than NEWWORD or PERFECT WRITER.

CHARLES SPEZZANO: PFS:WRITE is the obvious lightweight choice for someone who writes letters and nothing else. It is even more self-evident and easier to learn than VOLKSWRITER, has all the standard features plus automatic reformatting, and even takes the address out of a letter and automatically centers it on an envelope.

It is not, however, a flexible program. I once spoke to one of the men who wrote the program and he basically said that the design

and the popularity of the program revolve around the fact that it offers few choices, therefore requires few decisions. For example, although it is mostly a "what you see is what will print" program, if you force a page break, the screen no longer accurately reflects the page and line you are on. In fact, no real changes can be made within a document to deviate from the overall format you have chosen for that document. You cannot even temporarily change the left margin to indent a paragraph. The right margin cannot be pushed beyond column 80. If you create a header or footer, you get it on every page, including page one, whether you want it there or not, and the headers and footers all are centered. They cannot be flush left or right.

STEWART BRAND: That's fine with me. I'm much more concerned with words than format. I'd rather have a fiddle-free program that gets politely out of my way. An example of this program's built-in courtesy: I tried to save a document to a disk that had not been formatted for PFS files; halfway into the save the program stopped, told me the problem, and asked if it should format the data disk for me; when I said yes, it quickly formatted the disk, went ahead and saved the file on it, and returned me to the document, swift and pretty. Most programs would stop and ruin your day with a problem like that. There's even a feature in the Search function that tells you the number of words in your document—no other word processor that I know of does that within the program.

---

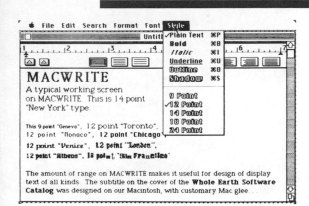

This snapshot of the Macintosh screen was made by the Macintosh itself and printed out on the Imagewriter.

*A revolution in word processing graphics . . .*

## MACWRITE

**Encore Systems; Macintosh; 128K; currently bundled with computer; copy-protected? NO; Apple Computer, 20525 Mariani Ave., Cupertino, CA 95014; 800/538-9696.**

STEWART BRAND: MACWRITE came bundled with the original Macintoshes to showcase the machine's astonishing graphic talents. In our office it was put to immediate work generating all posted memos, often combined with droll images from MACPAINT (p. 127). A

typical MACWRITE letter is one I got from a reader of our magazine **CoEvolution**: whenever he mentioned the magazine, he wrote it large type, italic, bold, outlined and shadowed—a fair approximation of our logo; we were so charmed he got extra-attentive service.

MACWRITE may grow with the 512K Mac, it may be absorbed by the next-generation Mac word processor from Apple, it may be supplanted by Mac versions of MICROSOFT WORD or PFS:WRITE. I hope they're all as inviting to the beginner as MACWRITE.

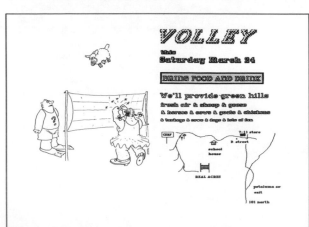

*Typical office use of MACWRITE. The map was done with MACPAINT. The drawing by James Donnelly was not.*

*Best on the Apple IIe and IIc . . .*

## WORD JUGGLER

Tom Gill; Version 2.6; Apple IIe; ProDos; 64K; $189 ● Apple III; SOS; 128K; $229 ● Apple IIc; ProDos; 128K; $189; copy-protected? YES;

## LEXICHECK

Tom Gill; Apple IIe; ProDos; 128K; 80-column screen ● Apple III; SOS; 128K ● Apple IIc; ProDos; 128K; copy-protected? NO; included with WORD JUGGLER;

both from Quark, Inc., 2525 W. Evans, Suite 220, Denver, CO 80219; 800/543-7711.

---

STEWART BRAND: One of the *handiest* programs I've seen, WORD JUGGLER, well translated from its origins on the bigger Apple III, has beat out APPLE WRITER IIe as the leading word processor on the IIe and IIc. It's probably at its best at either enhancing or replacing a secretary, since it specializes in handling correspondence adroitly—it has a full "conditional merge" capability for tailoring form letters, and its envelope addressing dexterity is second only to PFS:WRITE's.

Unlike many older programs on the Apples, WORD JUGGLER is quick—it was the very first product to take advantage of Apple's new operating system, ProDOS. Getting to and from disk, printer, current working document, and preview mode is always intuitively easy and fast. There is even a single command that converts your Apple to an expensive typewriter, where you type directly on the printer. And a single command prints a document direct from memory. With the program come 19 command-marked keys to unobtrusively replace ones on your Apple keyboard—a great help. I give WORD JUGGLER high points for transparency—you see the work, not it.

The included speller LEXICHECK deserves separate comment. Version 2.0 is a major improvement over previous incarnations. You can now look up words *while you're writing* to see if they're right. The dictionary will highlight the questionable word, suggest correct alternatives, and install any one you like for you. When checking a whole document (which can be done without having to store on disk first) LEXICHECK also tells you the number of words in the document. Among the 50,000 words, I was bemused to find "fuck," which is still missing from many printed dictionaries. The words seem to be assembled as word parts, so you can get some anomalies. When I asked the speller to look up "wifing," it said it was a valid word and offered as valid alternatives "wiling," "wiping," "wiring," and "wising." Oh well.

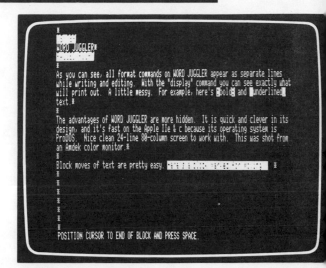

That LEXICHECK is included helps make WORD JUGGLER an exceptional bargain.

Also compatibly from Quark come TERMINUS ($89), a telecommunicator mentioned on p. 139, and CATALYST IIe ($149), which makes the Apple IIe (and presumably IIc) work happily with a hard disk. WORD JUGGLER is supposed to be comfortable with files from PFS:FILE (p. 80) and QUICKFILE.

---

*Strongest editing on CP/M . . .*

## PERFECT WRITER

Perfect Software; version 2.0; includes PERFECT SPELLER and PERFECT THESAURUS; CP/M-80 machines; 64K; $349 ● IBM PC compatibles; 128K; copy-protected? NO; $199; Thorn EMI Computer Software, 3187-C Airway, Costa Mesa, CA 92626; 714/751-3778.

## PLU*PERFECT WRITER

Mitchell and McKay; all Kaypros ● CP/M; copy-protected? YES (installation disk); $39; Plu*Perfect Systems, P.O. Box 1494, Idyllwild, CA 92349; 714/659-4432.

---

STEWART BRAND: The top contenders on CP/M machines like the Kaypro and Morrow (both p. 16) are WORDSTAR/NEWWORD (p. 56) and PERFECT WRITER. WORDSTAR is more mature but also somewhat decrepit; PERFECT WRITER has a split screen capability, multiple buffers (7) where you can park various documents or pieces of documents for easy shuffling, and sundry cutenesses such as a character transpose command, capitalizing commands, a great "undo" command, footnoting, indexing, etc.—heaps of features, but unfortunately their organization is also somewhat heaplike. Both programs are a pain to learn and remember. PERFECT WRITER also runs on IBM PCs, but it's outclassed there and not recommended.

Note: PERFECT WRITER for CP/M is in transition from version 1.0 to 2.0—due out in Fall '84 with price and performance improvements.

Most of us at Whole Earth who began with PERFECT WRITER because it came bundled with our Kaypros later converted to NEWWORD because it's easier for short documents, especially for printing, which is perpetually laborious with PERFECT WRITER. PERFECT WRITER is at its best with long or complicated documents, where its split screen, easier block moving and easier cursor moving can be put to work. And then there's the $39 blessing of PLU*PERFECT . . . [I'm about to bring in a paragraph from another file. With PERFECT WRITER it would be a breeze, not so with NEWWORD.]

RICHARD DALTON: I think PLU*PERFECT is probably the best value in writing tools. It turns the capable but clumsy PERFECT WRITER into a much more facile way to write. It changes PERFECT WRITER's personality so radically that I doubt if I would still be using PERFECT WRITER without this add-on.

STEWART BRAND: PLU*PERFECT is an enhancement program that cures some of PERFECT WRITER's lingering bugs and turns the Kaypro's keypad (the number keys on the right) into a set of short-cut function keys, nicely organized. The single key toggle for insert/overwrite, for example, replaces a 13-keystroke command sequence with PERFECT WRITER. There are also some wonderful public domain utility programs that come

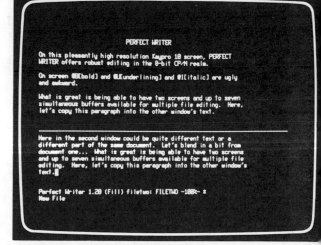

with PLU*PERFECT, such as D, the best of all directory displayers.

PERFECT WRITER is cramped on the Kaypro 2; you're better off with it on the Kaypro 4 or 10. It's no longer bundled with either the Kaypro (now has WORDSTAR) or the Morrow (now has NEWWORD). The other programs in the Perfect family—PERFECT FILER, and PERFECT CALC—are not very good. You can do your own spelling with THE WORD PLUS (p. 62). With its clean ASCII files PERFECT WRITER is good for telecommunicating.

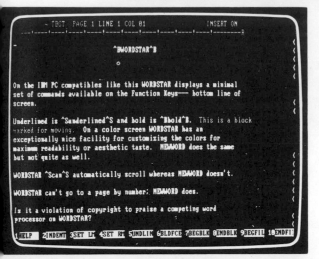

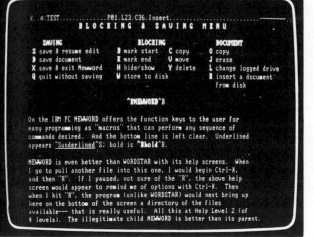

*The old standard, now controversial . . .*

## WORDSTAR

Version 3.3; CP/M-80 machines; 56K ● CP/M-86 machines; 80K ● IBM PC compatibles; PC DOS 1.1 (64K); PC DOS 2.0 (64K minimum, 128K recommended); copy-protected? NO; $495; MicroPro International Corp., 33 San Pablo Ave., San Rafael, CA 94903; 800/443-0100.

*Better, cheaper . . .*

## NEWWORD

Newstar Software, Inc.; version 1.29; CP/M-80 machines; 64K ● IBM PC compatibles; 96K; copy-protected? NO; $249; Rocky Mountain Software Systems, 2150 John Glenn Dr., Suite 100, Concord, CA 94520; 800/832-2244 or, in CA, 800/732-2311.

STEWART BRAND: You go into a computer or software store and ask about word-processing software. The clerk asks what you plan to use it for, listens closely to your description of your needs, and then recommends WORDSTAR. Most of the time that's the wrong answer.

Compared to other writing programs WORDSTAR is expensive, limited, slow, and difficult. Its major attraction is that there's so much of it out there—a million copies sold, they say, millions more copied. Indeed it runs on nearly everything, even new portables like the Hewlett-Packard 110 (p. 18), and a fair number of other programs try to blend with its peculiarities. Its minor attraction is that it's a friendly program, well co-evolved with its users over these many years (five or so).

A year ago a couple of renegades from MicroPro made a WORDSTAR clone called NEWWORD that removes many of the objections while keeping the same commands and file format. It's not expensive, less limited, even more friendly, and blends everywhere that WORDSTAR blends, but it is still as slow to use and difficult to learn as the original. It runs only on CP/M and IBM compatibles. What are NEWWORD's improvements over WORDSTAR? NEWWORD includes a conditional merge capability, whereas it costs $250 extra to get MAILMERGE with WORDSTAR. NEWWORD has an "undo" key (a major advantage, to my mind), document protection, search by page number, access to all user areas on hard disk, more helpful help messages, better printer support, nice micro justification, and a handier installation and tailoring procedure. On computers with graphics, like IBM and the new Kaypros, bold is bold on the screen and underline is underlined instead of ^Sunderlined^S.

What does WORDSTAR have over NEWWORD? Not much—it can edit while printing (spooling), and it works a trifle more easily with columns, including moving whole columns. Micropro's worthy new speller CORRECTSTAR (65,000 words, IBM compatible only, $195) doesn't work with

NEWWORD. In some reaches of the WORDSTAR empire it's still the best word processor available. I'd recommend WORDSTAR on Apple II and II + (with CP/M card, $139-290) and on the Radio Shack TRS-80. That's a lot of machines.

If you've got one of those, get WORDSTAR. If you're moving among many different kinds of machines, learn WORDSTAR. If your close colleagues have WORDSTAR on IBM or CP/M (that's my situation), get NEWWORD, so you can share advice and files. If you're word-processing to your own standard on IBM, get one of the programs on the next four pages. They'll work better for you.

Since WORDSTAR is everywhere, and is many people's first and apparently permanent love, as well as many others' deepest dislike, the subject needs fuller discussion. The floor is now open.

BARBARA ROBERTSON: WORDSTAR was the first word processor I used, and though I've tried and tested several others in the last four years, I still use it. WORDSTAR stays out of my way and never interferes with my work. Programs that make me stop, pay attention, change modes and take three or more steps before I can edit, use boldface or save or print a document waste my time and irritate me.

WORDSTAR is predictable and I trust it. I've never lost a document (though last month a deeply hidden bug prevented me from saving my latest corrections—I called; MicroPro has now fixed it). No, there's no little gauge on the screen to tell me how much disk space I have left. On the other hand, if I run out of space I can, without leaving the document, check the disk directory and erase an old file to make room.

To use one of Trip Hawkins' (Electronic Arts) criteria, it's deep. I've just scratched the surface. I customize the program a little (I don't like right justification and hyphen-help so I turn them off). With user patches, I could add special printer controls (to print "alternate" characters like the Greek alphabet or to change ribbon colors). Someday I intend to use the **Technical Support Reference Manual** to fiddle further with printer controls and special installation (although I might need to ask a programmer for help). I rarely use the non-document mode, but I have in the past to write commands that automatically run programs or to quickly edit a data file.

Hard to learn? Maybe. But it's easy to use, and once you learn the commands, they're hard to forget. Ask a WORDSTAR user his or her favorite command and I'll bet you get a quick answer. My favorites are QQB and QQZ. QQB reformats an entire document in front of my eyes, and QQZ starts automatic scrolling. I sit back, regulate the speed by typing 1 through 9, and read through my text, stopping, editing, and starting up again along the way.

DARRELL ICENOGLE: Power isn't the biggest collection of features possible. It's the *right* collection of features for a certain kind of person doing a certain kind of work. And they have to be at your right hand—not around the block and over a half-dozen menus. Look at the way WORDSTAR will stop whatever it's doing and accept a command when you want to give it. Or how it waits to see if you need a menu before it displays it. And how an easy install process will allow you to get virtually anything out of any printer.

FRED DAVIS: WORDSTAR is the best selling word-processing program because it's the best known, not because it's the best. It's the best known because so many people made illicit copies that it was easy to get ahold of. This is a good argument against copy-protection; illicit copies are free advertising that can make a program a *de facto* standard.

ARTHUR NAIMAN: In my estimation, WORDSTAR is one of the most poorly designed word-processing programs ever written—a huge, elaborate farrago of klugy patches, sort of like a Rube Goldberg machine gone berserk. All kinds of basic functions require disk access, thereby making the program fantastically slow (which it is even where disk access isn't involved; for example, its method of sending text to the printer is so clumsy that sometimes the printer has to wait for the computer!).

PETER McWILLIAMS: Do the readers of INTRODUCTION TO WORDSTAR know how its author feels about that program? My, my, my. It's like seeing Jerry Falwell marching in a gay liberation parade: refreshing, but surprising nonetheless.

By the way, your book is my favorite. Everyone in my office learned from it.

ARTHUR NAIMAN: Thanks for your kind words. My editor at Sybex does indeed know how I feel about WORDSTAR; in fact, one of my requirements before signing the contract was that I wouldn't have to use WORDSTAR to write the book.

CHARLES SPEZZANO: There are definite advantages to the IBM PC version of WORDSTAR, but the use of function keys seems to be an afterthought token gesture to IBM PC owners and doesn't really replace too many of those CTRL key commands. The main problem I am initially having with those is that I sometimes hit CTRL instead of shift key along with whatever letter I was intending to capitalize. Then something unexpected happens and I have to reach for my manual to see what I have done.

STEVEN LEVY: I hate the lack of a buffer, I hate the way WORDSTAR will open a new file if you get one lousy letter wrong when you call the file up (it should look; cut me some slack). It's clunky and weird and less fun as it goes along, and sometimes I press a wrong letter and it makes fun of me for calling up a program that MicroPro has written into it, but costs more. In other words, they dug a hole in it, and then when I fell in it, said that I should have purchased the optional manhole cover.

ALFRED LEE: The problem is that writing occurs in words, sentences and paragraphs, and WORDSTAR doesn't think that way. Although it sends the cursor left and right by character or word, it can delete by word only to the right. It can delete a line either way, but it cannot move or delete by sentence or paragraph. A keystroke won't take me to the beginning of a paragraph either. With WORDSTAR getting to the start of the paragraph is an important step, because that's where I usually want to press CTRL-B to reformat a paragraph after revising it.

RICHARD DALTON: What's wrong with WORDSTUFF besides Barbara's bug (after 5 years and a million users) isn't that it's clumsy, antiquated, illogical or techie. WORDSTAR COSTS TOO MUCH!!! You can wind up close to $1,000 by the time you add all the bits and pieces that aren't part of it and are in competitive products.

WILLIAM M. BULKELEY (**Wall Street Journal**, 26 March, 1984): WORDSTAR, an early word-processing package, is generally considered difficult to learn and more awkward to use than more recent programs. But it keeps selling—it has sold more copies than any other computer program—because retailers have learned to use and demonstrate it, and many are reluctant to learn a different system. Also, they like the high profit margins from its $495 list price, which is far more expensive than competitive systems.

STEWART BRAND: To end on a cordial note, one of the kindest attentions to detail in WORDSTAR (and NEWWORD) is the help screens. Many of them show up only when you start a command and pause in uncertainty. They can be set to four different levels of helpfulness (or lack of interference). Likewise, anytime you want to do something with files, the program automatically shows you the current directory of what's already on the data disk.

There is a potent remedy for the slowness of WORDSTAR and NEWWORD, which is caused by the programs constantly "going to disk" to get one thing or another. Install a "RAM disk" and load the program on it. Since it is an electronic circuit board *emulating* a disk, everything happens at electronic speed, faster even than with a hard disk. ("The improvement in response time is so dramatic that many people will not use WORDSTAR any other way."—Alfred Glossbrenner.) Costs a couple hundred dollars. Worth it.

*WORDSTAR is complicated enough to need a book to get you into it comfortably. Naiman's* Introduction to WordStar *is the best. (2nd edition, 1983; 208 pp.; $14.95; Sybex Computer Books, 2344 Sixth Street, Berkeley, CA 94710; 415/848-8233; or COMPUTER LITERACY.)*

*Write anywhere, even print . . .*

## TRS-80 MODEL 100

**$599 (8K model); $999 (24K model); 8K RAM expansion modules $120 each (capacity to 32K); Radio Shack, 1700 One Tandy Center, Ft. Worth, TX 76102; 817/390-3700.**

## SCRIPSIT 100

**Michael Stanford; version 2.5; TRS-80 Model 100; 5K; cassette; copy-protected? NO; $39.95; Radio Shack, 1800 One Tandy Center, Fort Worth, TX 76102; 817/390-3700.**

STEWART BRAND: The truly portable computers, called lap computers or notebook computers, usually have simple word processors wired into them—good introductory programs that are completely sufficient for many uses. The first to dominate and still the leader is Radio Shack's 100, with a fine word processor on board. (See pp. 16 and 153 for more information on the machine.) For telecommunicating, for notetaking, for first-draft writing it's outstanding. Beyond that . . .

JIM STOCKFORD: Radio Shack's built-in word processor is a terrific communicating tool except that it doesn't print worth a damn, beyond the crudest memo quality. SCRIPSIT 100 from the Portable Computer Support Group is an amazingly versatile formatting program that allows me to vary the widths of my side margins, the space at top and bottom of my page, double or single spacing, right justifying, centering, boldface, underlining, page numbering, footnoting, automatic dating, and quite a bit more. It comes with the clearest instructions I've ever seen. It loads from cassette and takes up 4.2K in the 100's limited memory.

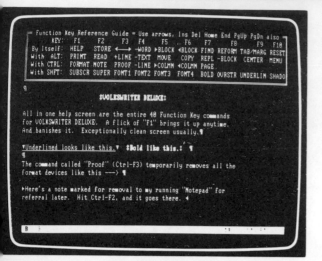

*The most elegant middleweight on IBM . . .*

## VOLKSWRITER DELUXE

Camilo Wilson; version 2.0; PC/MS-DOS; 128K; 2 disk drives required; copy-protected? NO; $295; Lifetree Software, Inc., 411 Pacific St., Monterey, CA 93940; 408/373-4718.

---

*What characterizes VOLKSWRITER DELUXE is its maximal use of the IBM PC's ten function keys. Taking them straight and combined with "Ctrl," "Shift," and "Alt," you've got 40 commands that do nearly everything, and one of them (F1) calls up a help screen with the full roster anytime. Makes for adept left little and ring fingers.*

STEWART BRAND: For quick learning and easy remembering, with strength enough for occasional professional use, nothing beats VOLKSWRITER DELUXE. It's more capable than PFS:WRITE (p. 54), faster than WORDSTAR/NEWWORD (p. 56). Its clean ASCII files let you use the best of the spellers and synonym finders—IBM's WORD PROOF (p. 62)—and it telecommunicates like a breeze.

CHARLES SPEZZANO: Small business owners and professionals who do their own correspondence will love VW DELUXE's ability to have you up and running in an hour, as well as the built-in and easy-to-use text merge feature. They will also appreciate the most self-evident editing, formatting, and printing procedures on the market. Students cannot go wrong with VW DELUXE. Anybody who needs foreign-language characters in

---

*Creative . . .*

## WORDVISION

T. Crispin & J. Edlin; version 1.1; IBM PC compatibles; PC DOS 1.1 or 2.0; 96K; copy-protected? NO; $80; Bruce & James Program Publishers, Inc., 4500 Tuller Rd., Dublin, OH 43017; 614/766-0110.

---

STEWART BRAND: WORDVISION stands alone. In some ways to advantage, in some to disadvantage. It's innovative and agile and a real buy—$80. By "agile" I mean it is fast and sure in use. It is especially suited to the creative writer, anyone who is thinking and writing at the same time. Author Jim Edlin is a writer, and it shows.

The well-named program takes every opportunity to be graphic. The manual is richly illustrated. So is the abundance of help screens. Thirty-two stick-on labels transform the IBM keyboard with bright colors and new capabilities everywhere, including the function keys (called "chameleon keys" by the manual—their function varies with what's going on). Since you *have* to use the labels, the keyboard is a bit veiled for other uses. After a year on the market, WORDVISION is still the only word processor that makes really intelligent use of color (though its icons serve perfectly well on monochrome screens, and the screen prompts will refer to function keys by their number rather than their assigned icon if you so configure).

Keyboard operation is arrayed in intuitive ways. Related function keys have related colors and are close to each other. The program *twiddles* handily. The erase and the cursor-forward and cursor-back functions can be accelerated to move by word, line,

sentence, or paragraph at a time using just a pair of accelerator keys. The "undo" key includes unmaking character deletes. While there are no "macro" keys that operate whole definable command strings, there is a set of five "quick phrase" keys to park your clichés on. If you often transpose letters (as I do), there's a special key to set them right, and there's another one to change lower-case letters to capitals and vice versa.

Limitations. Since the publishers, Bruce & James, are all but out of business (though the distributors, Simon & Schuster, are not), there's no directly compatible spelling checker or telecommunications program available or coming. (The program does easily convert to and from "DOS files," and they are completely compatible with spellers like WORD PROOF and any telecommunicator; you can work in DOS first, then convert and format after.) WORDVISION's unique format means that no keyboard enhancer such as PROKEY (p. 93) will work with it. Due to its format structure WORDVISION takes up twice as much space in memory and in disk storage as other word processors. So a 96K machine could only handle 8 double-spaced pages in a file, 26 pages on 128K, 50 on 256K. Since WORDVISION doesn't link files for printing, that may put a cramp on long manuscripts. There's a top limit of 50 files permitted on a WORDVISION disk. Finally, some critics have remarked that WORDVISION is too cavalier about letting you quit without warning that you may be losing unsaved text.

If WORDVISION's uniqueness matches yours, you've got a most potent instrument, but check carefully what it can't do and be sure you don't care.

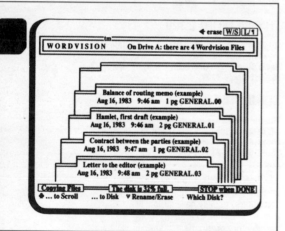

*Getting in and out of files with WORDVISION is slick and quick. File titles (up to 40 characters) look like they're on file folders, and they don't have to be typed out to load a file—you nab them with the cursor. Showing size of files by number of pages of text instead of bytes or kilobytes is typical of the program.*

When used with the right arrow key, (Vision) moves one word or sentence. or line or to the end of the paragraph.

Following the left arrow key, the pointer would move to the left or to the beginning of the paragraph.

their text doesn't have many other choices (WORDPERFECT is one, p. 60). A secretary will be disappointed with it (too limited). An academic will prefer the footnoting capability of WORDPERFECT, XYWRITE II +, or MICROSOFT WORD (p. 60).

STEWART BRAND: VOLKSWRITER DELUXE doesn't link files for printing, presumably because it doesn't need to—it can handle files up to a million bytes (1000K) "in case anyone wanted to write a sequel to **War and Peace** without any chapter breaks" (Spezzano). That doesn't affect the snap with which it flicks from screen to screen, but it does slow down the cursor a bit and makes loading and saving files a little slower. Another uncommon feature is the "notepad," which lets you quickly store thoughts, phone numbers, notes in a separate file that accumulates while you write.

Limitations. Reformatting of text you've messed with is by command rather than automatic; no split screen; no "undo" command; no macros. For many this may be part of the program's attraction. It is straight ahead, straight tasty vanilla.

VOLKSWRITER DELUXE wins with its ability to fit in—on nearly any IBM-style machine, with nearly any user, with nearly any program. Also check out PC-WRITE (this page) for similar qualities.

## STANDARD VOLKSWRITER KEYBOARD ARRANGEMENT

When you use the ALT key in combination with each of the following keys, you get:

| 1 | 2 | 3 | 4 | 5 | | 6 | 7 | 8 | 9 | |
|---|---|---|---|---|---|---|---|---|---|---|
| â | ê | î | ô | û | | £ | Pt | ƒ | ¥ | |
| Q | W | E | R | T | | Y | U | I | O | P |
| á | é | í | ó | ú | | ÿ | ç | Ç | ñ | Ñ |
| A | S | D | F | G | | H | J | K | L | |
| à | è | ì | ò | ù | | Ä | É | Ö | Ü | |
| Z | X | C | V | B | | N | M | | | |
| ä | ë | ï | ö | ü | | ¡ | ¿ | | | |

---

*Born free . . .*

# PC-WRITE

**Bob Wallace; IBM PC compatibles; 64K ● IBM PCjr; 128K; copy-protected? NO; $10—shareware, $75—full registration, ($25—commission to registered users who have had others register from their shareware); Quicksoft, 219 First Ave. North #224, Seattle, WA 98109; 206/282-0452.**

---

STEWART BRAND: This is becoming one of the most interesting programs in the **Catalog**. Its outstanding abilities as a text editor have been less reported than its marvelous distribution system, so we'll do the newsworthy access first and then get to the meat. You can pick up PC-WRITE free at your local user group or get it direct from the author for ten bucks. The manual is on the disk—print it out and you're in business. If you like the program enough to register with the author and pay a grateful $75, you really are in business. Copy your PC-WRITE freely to your friends; if any of them decide to register the copy and pay $75 to the author, you get a $25 commission back from him for each one. Besides the down-home business opportunity that goes with registration, you also get a bound copy of the manual, the next updated version (a significant value), and telephone support.

By cutting out all the middle people Bob Wallace is doing well by doing good. It's a bargain to you, a healthy income to him, and the program is the most rapidly evolving I've seen in the marketplace. He doesn't have to worry about competing with his inventory, because there isn't any, and there's no marketing and distributing people to cut him off from the satisfactions and dissatisfactions of his customers. The version 2.2 I'm looking at has come a great distance from what I saw

six months ago. By the time you read this he'll probably have added text merge, decimal alignment and footnoting to the program.

PC-WRITE is chock with good features like word-delete-left (with an intuitively correct CTRL-backspace), move by paragraph forward and back, character transpose, change capitals, a "bookmark" place marker, and the niftiest split screen alive. Bold and underline look that way on the screen, and if you've got color it's brightly tailorable. There's "undo" and macros and truly useful help screens. But its greatest strength is its blazing speed . . .

JOEL PITT (**PC**, Feb. 1984): PC-WRITE performs all its functions with unusual speed. When you scroll pages up or down, the new page appears instantaneously. The program jumps from the beginning of the text buffer to the end of the text in a second, even when editing a 60K file. By contrast, WORDSTAR takes nearly ten seconds to do the same thing, and MULTIMATE (widely lauded for its speed) takes more than three seconds. PC-WRITE replaced every occurrence of the word *the* with the characters *xxxx* in a 25K text in 57 seconds. The new version of WORDSTAR took more than 2½ minutes, and the task took MULTIMATE more than 8 minutes.

STEWART BRAND: The only major drawback with PC-WRITE is that you can't print direct from memory, and there's no on-screen page breaks or numbers (though there's a way around that, it's long), because you have to go to a different part of the program to print a file. This makes the program less desirable for short document use, but it's still a bunch easier than PERFECT WRITER (p. 55) in that. Wallace has managed to wedge PC-WRITE into the PCjr, where it should be a barn-burner.

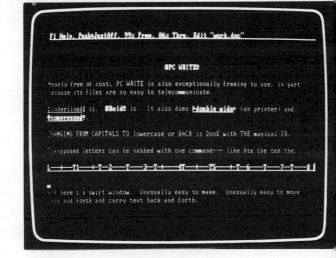

PC-WRITE has the purest ASCII files anywhere, so it blends sweetly with almost anything—speller (WORD PROOF would be my choice), telecommunicator, whatever. Combine it with other public domain programs like Jim Button's PC-FILE (p. 82) and Andrew Fluegelman's PC-TALK (p. 152), and you can travel a high-quality lowroad for practically nothing on the PC compatibles.

Radical.

## The Word-Processing Heavyweights

CHARLES SPEZZANO: WORDPERFECT for heavyweight word processing in the executive suite or professional office. XYWRITE II + for professional writers or professionals who write every day and will not mind a few days' break-in period in return for blinding speed. MICROSOFT WORD if you want the mouse or like a menu-driven rather than a command-driven program.

STEWART BRAND: I would put it: MICROSOFT WORD if you want industrial-strength editing, formatting, and merging capability along with exceptional ease of learning.

---

*Clean and powerful . . .*

## WORDPERFECT

Ashton & Bastian; Version 3.0; IBM PC/XT compatibles ● IBM PCjr ● MS-DOS machines; 128K ● Tandy 2000; 256K; copy-protected? NO, except Tandy 2000; $495; Satellite Software International, 288 West Center St., Orem, UT 84057; 800/321-4566.

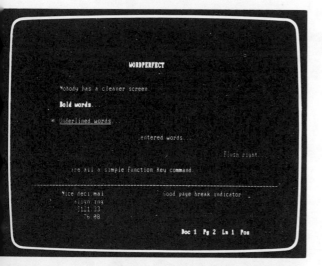

MIN S. YEE: WORDPERFECT was designed for the serious writer/editor/secretary/wordsmith who wants it all—and then some. Its features include extraordinary cursor control, macro definition, footnoting, mail merge (no additional cost), document assembly, hyphenation, end-of-page demarcation, extended Greek, math, and foreign character set, true proportional spacing, control of orphans and widows (bits of text left lonely at the tops or bottoms of pages), password security, user-definable defaults, dual document editing, a 30,000 word spelling checker (no extra cost) and a basic math package.

Editing functions are command-driven while formatting and file management commands are driven by menu. The "help" mode is so useful and clearly written that it can only be compared with the help screens in 1-2-3 (p. 67). Not only that, but when you want to call the folks at Satellite Software International for personal help, you can rest assured they will be there, cheery and willing. They'll even call you back.

CHARLES SPEZZANO: WORDPERFECT does everything WORDSTAR (p. 56) or MULTIMATE can do and functions much more smoothly than either one of them. Short letters can be centered vertically on a page. At the other end of the spectrum there is no limit on the size of document that WORDPERFECT handles easily. Reports with math and columns in them are created without any difficulty (they are almost impossible to work with using VOLKSWRITER DELUXE [p. 58] or WORDSTAR). The built-in speller and sorter makes WORDPERFECT a complete package for a one-person office with needs for record keeping and word processing, and a powerful component in a small business office with more demanding needs.

STEWART BRAND: With all that it's capable of, I'm impressed by WORDPERFECT's look of spareness. Sometimes it feels crippled to me, but crippled smart. Its major limitations are lack of an "undo" command and absence of split-screen capability. It partly makes up for that by offering two buffers you can jog between, somewhat crippledly—beats having to go to disk. I'd prefer a bigger speller. It's easier to learn than WORDSTAR or XYWRITE II +, harder than VOLKSWRITER or MICROSOFT WORD.

---

*Could be the new standard . . .*

## MICROSOFT WORD

Version 1.1; IBM PC/XT compatibles ● IBM PCjr; 128K; $375 ($475 with mouse); works better with color graphics card, best with Hercules graphics card ● Apple Macintosh; $195; copy-protected? YES; Microsoft Corp., 10700 Northup Way, Box 97200, Bellevue, WA 98009; 206/828-8080.

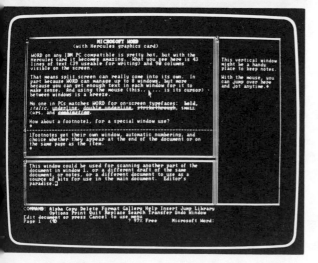

STEWART BRAND: What WORD has going for it: the greatest supermarket of word-processing features on personal computers, design from the ground up for fullest use of its mouse, easy-to-use menu-command structure (still good without the mouse), ahead-of-the-art support of printer hardware, direct linkage to the next generation of computers, the most formidable of publishers (who developed the very operating system the IBM PC family runs on), and a bargain, especially with the mouse.

WORD has all the features of WORDPERFECT and XYWRITE II + except math, password security, and indexing, and adds: an "undo" command of particular cleverness (you can see what it's holding), up to eight windows, the enormous acceleration of editing that goes with an adept mouse, "Style Sheets" that preserve arrays of formatting commands as ornamental as you like, a juicier macro facility (called "Glossary"—for text, not commands), elaborate conditional merge, continuous saving of text (Spezzano scorned that one because of the slight pause when it happens—until he turned off his machine without saving, one hurried evening, and the pauses paid off), automatic backup of files, support of 64 fonts on printers (my God), and on-screen display of bold, underline, double underline, italic, super- and subscript, strikethrough (for contracts), and my favorite, small caps.

Typically, programs with a lot of muscle are muscle-bound (SAMNA III and WORDMARC come to mind)—cumbersome, crowded, self-hindering. WORD is surprisingly light on its feet, quick and inviting to dance with. The complexities are kept relatively out of your way until you want them. Things you use all the time are simple and accessible. Speller support is THE WORD PLUS ($150, p. 62).

*Harsh, fast . . .*

## XYWRITE II +

**IBM PC/XT compatibles ● TI Professional; 96K; copy-protected? NO; $300; XyQuest, Inc., P.O. Box 372, Bedford, MA 01730; 617/275-4439.**

CHARLES SPEZZANO: XYWRITE II + traces its roots to ATEX, a company whose word-processing systems can be found in many high pressure newsrooms, and that's the flavor of the program. It babies you about as much as Perry White babies Clark Kent. There are no menus, the manual is mediocre, and the help screens are really just lists of the 150 commands.

XYWRITE II + is the most purely command-oriented PC writing tool on the market. That means once you get the hang of it, which really doesn't take long, you can fly. No mode changes are required to delete or move a sentence or a paragraph, just a quick series of commands. Most such editing commands are implemented with the function keys, in combination with the CTRL, ALT, and SHIFT keys. Many of the non-function key commands are mnemonics, like "AU" for Automatic Uppercasing of the character that immediately follows a period, question mark, or exclamation point. [SB: I find "AU" a slightly terrifying convenience, like wordwrap—leads to addiction and atrophy.] Like Dorothy Parker, who once said she changed seven words for every five she wrote, I erase a lot when I write. With XYWRITE II + I have the fastest, most comprehensive deleting system I have seen anywhere, allowing immediate removal of a character, the word the cursor is under, the previous word, all text to the end of the line,

all the text on the line, a sentence, or a paragraph. After any of these deletions, it instantly reformats your text.

XYWRITE II + also executes block moves as fast as or faster than any other word processor I have seen. There are a variety of ways to quickly mark a block, after which you can do almost anything imaginable to it, including storing it as a macro. Columns are handled just as easily. You can search forward or backward from the cursor, recognizing capitals or not, as you wish, and wildcards are allowed in a search string. Files are in pure ASCII.

The format of a document can be changed as often as you like by entering margin, line-spacing, or justification commands. You have to use a review command to see your text with footnotes (XYWRITE II + numbers these automatically and places them at the bottom of the right page or at the end of the document) and full justification on screen. The program offers three different kinds of screen splits—horizontal, vertical, and alternating.

XYWRITE II + 's extra features include a four-function math program, as well as the ability to generate an index or a table of contents—these may require some editing before final printing to avoid duplicated entries. You can remap the keyboard with PROKEY-like (p. 93) precision, and there appears to be a ready-made Dvorak keyboard available on the master disk. The program runs "around" DOS. You can jump from your current document to a DOS prompt instantaneously, run the word-count program from THE WORD PLUS package (p. 62), then exit back to where

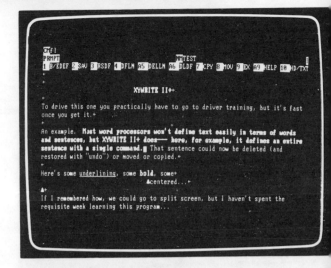

you were in the document in a flash. There will be plenty of room on your working disk for your favorite spell checker, since XYWRITE II + 's files only take up about 75K, with no overlays to slow things down.

At $300 XYWRITE II + is a great buy. If there was a contest between equally experienced users with different word processors, I wouldn't want to bet money against the person on XYWRITE II + being the first to finish writing, editing, and printing a document of any kind. That must be some sort of a bottom-line endorsement.

---

Drawbacks. WORD is copy-protected, groan, a nuisance. On-screen page breaks and numbers are muddy (you have to update them). The manual also is muddy, though big. Microsoft is publishing a series of books on WORD that help, but why aren't *they* the manual? Spezzano ran into two bad bugs in the program, consistently could not get through to customer service at Microsoft, and gave up on the product in frustration. Be sure to send in your warranty with WORD—they'll notify you about new versions of the program and you should get them. It's still evolving rapidly.

A number of hardware enhancements can supercharge WORD for you. The mouse, of course—which also works with MULTIPLAN (p. 70), 1-2-3 (p. 67), and VISICALC (p. 71). A RAM disk ($230 and up), 192K minimum, can greatly accelerate the speed of the program, same as with WORDSTAR/NEWWORD. With the Hercules Graphics Card ($499) you get 90 columns by *43* lines (39 writeable) on the screen. With a Hewlett-Packard Laserjet Printer ($3495) you get spectacular, publication-quality typesetting.

As WORDSTAR was the link between the 8-bit world of CP/M, Apple II, and Radio Shack TRS-80 and the 16-bit world of IBM and MS-DOS, WORD may be the link between the 16-bitters and the new 32-bit realm of the Macintosh and its forthcoming competition. WORD on the Macintosh should, we are told by Microsoft, be mostly the same as on IBM, except no Style Sheets (until the 512K Mac) and only four windows. It's supposed to be the first Mac program to support letter-quality printers. It's slower than MACWRITE (p. 54).

And that's as far over the horizon as we can look with this over-the-horizon word processor.

---

*With MICROSOFT WORD and one of the new Hewlett-Packard Laserjet Printers ($3495) you can do your own remarkably high-quality typesetting, sampled here. It could revolutionize the business, because the savings of time, money, errors, and aggravation can be enormous for the self-publisher.*

---

Microsoft Word lets *you* control the way your characters look: Underline, **boldface**, *italics*, superscript$^{abc}$ and subscript$_{xyz}$. Even SMALL CAPS and <u>double underline</u>.

Microsoft Word gives you the most advanced formatting tools available: Automatic footnotes. Snaking columns. Customized form letters with special messages for selected recipients.

With **Microsoft Word**, you can change page layouts as often as every page. YOU CAN MIX typefaces, *even with right and left justification*, as frequently as you want.

## Writer's helpers . . .
## *Spellers, Etc.*

STEWART BRAND: Nothing eases the central labor of writing. "*Tria digit scribit, totus corpul laborat*—three fingers write, but the whole body labors," complained a medieval scribe. But the mind-numbing janitorial periphery of writing can be eased considerably by the cheery robots of the craft—spelling checkers, style checkers, word counters, outliners, keyboard enhancers, and text databases.

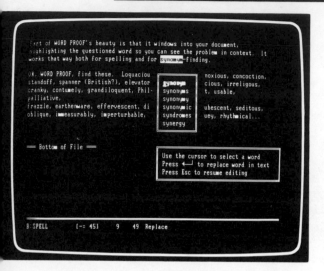

### *Best for spelling and synonyms on IBM . . .*
# WORD PROOF

**William Modlin and David Glickman; IBM PC compatibles; 96K; second disk drive required for synonym finder function ● IBM PCjr; 128K; copy-protected? NO; $60; IBM, Entry Systems Division, P.O. Box 1328, Boca Raton, FL 33432; 800/447-4700.**

STEWART BRAND: Interesting that this best of spelling checkers also has the best price, and from an unexpected publisher, IBM itself. The attractions are many. In a field where number of words in the dictionary is critical, WORD PROOF has a whopping 125,000. It's exceptionally easy to use. The bonus of synonym-checking is worth twice the price of the program. And WORD PROOF does its own rudimentary word processing, so you can finish doctoring a document with the program and print right out.

You pull up a text file (created with your regular word processor) and ask WORD PROOF to spell-check it—all done with simple menu commands. Your text is displayed, and if there's any word the program has doubts about, it stops and highlights the word. You can ask for a windowed list of possible correct spellings, cursor to one you like, and it'll instantly replace the incorrect one in the text, while the program goes on to the next word it doesn't recognize. You can get the same service by placing the cursor on any word in your text and asking (F3) about it. Likewise, put in the Synonyms disk, cursor to a word, punch F4, and you get a list of closely related words; indicate the one you like, it's instantly inserted, and on you go; I find this miraculous (supernatural, fabulous). No other spellers do it.

Most misspellings are actually typos. Spelling checkers catch both. What they can't catch is words disguised as other words— "than" or "the" instead of "then," for example.

WORD PROOF's major limitation is that it only allows 600 words to be added to its dictionary by the user, and it doesn't work with all word processors. Of the ones we recommend on the IBM, WORD PROOF works beautifully with HOMEWORD, PC-WRITE, VOLKSWRITER DELUXE, and XYWRITE II+; it works only in ASCII or DOS file mode with WORDVISION, WORDSTAR/NEWWORD, WORD PERFECT, and MICROSOFT WORD; and it works not at all with PFS: WRITE.

### *Ubiquitous . . .*
## THE WORD PLUS

**Wayne Holder; version 1.21; CP/M-80 and CP/M-86 machines ● PC/MS-DOS machines; 64K; copy-protected? NO; $150;**

## PUNCTUATION + STYLE

**Wayne Holder; version 1.21; CP/M-80 and CP/M-86 machines ● PC/MS-DOS machines; 64K; 2 disk drives recommended; copy-protected? NO; $125;**

**both from Oasis Systems, 7907 Ostrow St., San Diego, CA 92111; 619/279-5711.**

CHARLES SPEZZANO: THE WORD PLUS is a thing of beauty: simple, fast, accurate. The "Plus" part refers to a smorgasbord of writing aid programs that come with the spelling checker, including a tool for automatically hyphenating words, programs that help you solve crossword puzzles and jumbled word games, a general purpose word-counting utility, a program that locates and marks homonyms ("there," "their," "they're") in your text so you can decide if you used the write (rite, *right*) one, and a tool that keeps track of how many times each word appears in your document. Word count is indispensable.

The spell check program is a masterpiece. It is small enough to fit on the same disk with my WORDSTAR or VOLKSWRITER programs, so I do not have to change disks to use it. Despite this, it has a 45,000 word dictionary, and it's faster than most—1½ minutes to check a 1500-word file.

STEWART BRAND: THE WORD PLUS works much like WORD PROOF, except it's slower and feels a little more laborious. You have to ask it to show context of a questioned word, and it only shows a line, which often isn't enough for comfort. Of the word processing programs we've recommended, THE WORD PLUS works with WORDSTAR/NEWWORD (CP/M or IBM), PERFECT WRITER, PC-WRITE, VOLKSWRITER DELUXE, XYWRITE II+, and MICROSOFT WORD.

CHARLES SPEZZANO: PUNCTUATION + STYLE is by the same author. The PUNCTUATION part catches errors in punctuation and other inaccuracies, such as incorrect abbreviations, missing capitals at the beginning of sentences, repeated words (Paris in the the Spring), mixed upper and lower case letters (THe—it has a hell of a time with software names like WordStar and DesQ), unclosed parentheses, and misused numbers. The STYLE part has a list of phrases that are commonly misused in writing—clichés and phrases which are "awkward, erroneous, folksy, muddy, pompous, redundant, or wordy." Wayne Holder understands good writing and helps you achieve it.

STEWART BRAND: I have a feeling that word processing is encouraging sloppy writing, because it is so damned easy. This program is an antidote, embarrassing sometimes, but bracing. I don't think I've generated a single document over 200 words that didn't benefit from Holder's attention. If I now said something [necessitated] something, Holder would put brackets around it and suggest "required."

## Other Spellers

STEWART BRAND: Other spellers. WORD-STAR has a new companion, CORRECTSTAR, 65,000 words, $195 (from MicroPro, p. 56), only on 16-bit machines like IBM, not 8-bit CP/M, doesn't work with NEWWORD. Its special talent is finding words by sound. Woody Liswood: "That means you can type in the word as it sounds while you are typing and let CORRECTSTAR find the correct spelling for you later. It also reformats the file for you as it goes along, so you don't have to go back and do it later." Big improvement over SPELLSTAR.

On Apple II +, IIe, IIc the popular speller is SENSIBLE SPELLER, 80,000 words, $125 (Sensible Software, Inc., 24011 Seneca, Oak Park, MI 48237; 313/399-8877). It's good, but of our recommended word processors on the Apple, it only works with HOMEWORD, not with PFS: WRITE or WORD JUGGLER.

And now for something completely different (that revels in differences) . . .

JONATHAN SACHS: People who work with large, frequently revised documents often must keep track of the changes they make. For example, a writer may have to prepare a summary of all the significant changes in a new edition of a manual. Or an editor may want to know what a writer has changed between two drafts of a manuscript. For these tasks COMPARE II can be a major time saver. Many features add to its usefulness. It can write the summary of changes to a file. It can display the changed parts of the two files one after the other or side by side, or it can reproduce one file with "change bars" in the left margin to indicate where the other file differs. Available for CP/M-80, CP/M-86, PC DOS and MS-DOS, $145 (Solution Technology, Inc., Suite 400, 2000 Corporate Blvd., N.W., Boca Raton, FL 33431; 305/368-6228).

STEWART BRAND: If you like shortcuts you will love keyboard enhancers like PROKEY 3.0 and SMARTKEY (both p. 93). Nothing so tailors your machine and your software to your own work habits. Anything repetitive in your routine—sets of words, sequences of commands, or both—can be tucked under a single key and gleefully evoked by just touching it. Feels like money in the bank every time.

Creative use of outlining, for many of us only a grim memory from 7th Grade, is making a big comeback on computers, thanks to THINKTANK (p. 92). An all-in-one has been built around the outline idea, with a capa word processor as well as database and spreadsheet included—FRAMEWORK (pp. 110, 128). Another text-oriented all-in-one is INTUIT (p. 110). For general mucking about in your text files in supremely organized fashion, check out the databases that Tony Fanning calls "garbage bags"—DATAFAX (p. 90), SUPERFILE (p. 91), and NOTEBOOK (p. 91).

## For dedicated writers . . .
# DEDICATED WORD PROCESSORS

STEWART BRAND: If the main thing you do for a living is write, you may want the top professional tool available, figuring it'll pay its way. Dedicated word processors are a more mature technology than personal computers, and they do more and cost more. Why they're never covered in the personal computer magazines I don't know; we plan to survey them properly in the **Whole Earth Software Review**—Wang, Lanier, IBM Displaywriter, NBI, etc. For now here's a bit about one of the top ones. I note that Alfred **How to Buy Software** (p. 6) Glossbrenner drives a CPT.

FRED DAVIS: Raving starts here. The CPT dedicated word processor is a "typing machine"; the software and hardware are designed so that you don't need to know about computers. With its full page display the software works by imitating a typewriter as much as possible. When you start working, a new "page" is inserted into an imaginary platen and is "rolled up" to the first line of the page (using computer graphics). The letters appear as black characters on a white background. As you type, the imaginary sheet of paper advances a line at a time until the page is full, and then it is "ejected." The video display is exceptionally clear (only others that come close are Xerox 860 and Lisa) and my friends swear that it is easy on the eyes—they do 8 hours a day with no eye strain.

The CPT software is powerful—it does all the things you'd expect and a bunch of important frills (right-justification, footnoting, indexing, tables of contents, customizable spelling dictionary, telecommunications, CP/M emulation, etc., etc., etc.) Prices start at around $5,000 and go up to $15-20,000 if you add all the options—printer, hard disk, etc.

ARTHUR NAIMAN: The CPT 8100 (now the 8500) was by far the best word processor I evaluated in my book THE WORD PROCESSING BUYER'S GUIDE. It got a score of 94¾ on my obsessively detailed 100-point rating scale; the next closest runner-up (the Dictaphone Dual Display) got 85¼. The CPT can do just about everything (see chart, p. 50), and just about everything it does, it does well.

**CPT 8500; 1 console; full-page screen [black on white]; $4990; CPT Corporation, 8100 Mitchell Road, P.O. Box 295, Minneapolis, MN 55440; 612/937-8000.**

## ANALYZING

### Woody Liswood, Domain Editor

WOODY LISWOOD: Analyzing is probably what most of us think of when we think of computers. Why were computers "invented" in the first place? Answer: To manipulate and analyze large amounts of data in short periods of time.

#### Spreadsheets

The spreadsheet, or "calc" program, has been credited with creating the microcomputer marketplace. Prior to the introduction of VISICALC (p. 71) on the Apple computer in 1979 by Dan Bricklin, Bob Frankston, and Dan Fylstra, most microcomputers were thought of simply as game machines or machines only computer programmers owned and understood. Many folks credit the rise of Apple Computer to its predominant position in the micro world to the fact that VISICALC, when first released, was available only on Apples.

Spreadsheets can help you analyze any data that can be displayed in a row and column format. In addition to using the accountants' tools such as balance sheets, income statements, and profit-and-loss statements, with a calc program you can do regression analysis, correlation, and other statistical functions. You can derive and predict salary costs and merit budgets for home and business. If you think of a single file in a calc program as identical to a single page in a multiple-page report from a database, your micro can duplicate many complicated mainframe computer database reports as a series of identical spreadsheet applications.

The bottom line is this: The uses of spreadsheets keep growing as "limits" are stretched by new programs and new versions of old programs.

BARBARA ROBERTSON: Making the jump from budget charts on paper to, most likely, the same form on a microcomputer takes little imagination, learning, or adjustment, and the advantages are obvious. Typists no longer need a gallon of White-Out to correct a 30-page financial report because a change in one column affected rows of results. Analysts, managers, small-business owners, salespeople, and household budgeters can wonder "What if": . . . I reduced my expenses in July by $2000? . . . the loan rate were 12.3% amortized over 18 years rather than 13.4% amortized for 12? . . . it takes 56 people 35 hours a week to do the job in 43 working days and I have only 31 available? Plug in the numbers and get instant answers. Playing "What if?" is more fascinating and lively than a lot of computer games.

WOODY LISWOOD: When we started looking for spreadsheets to review and analyze, we came up with more than 35 products during the first go-through, including a portable "calc" machine (WorkSlate, p. 73) and some public domain programs (pp. 25-27). One fact emerged. Even though they all work and do about the same thing, even though there are more similarities among them than differences, and even though they all generate fierce loyalties in their users, they also differ significantly in style, memory capacity, speed of operation, and data management capabilities. Our recommendations are based on these differences.

#### Statistics Programs

Looking for statistics programs is not as complicated as looking for spreadsheets. There are fewer of them and they are so specialized that I doubt anyone would want one who did not already have some idea of what to do with them. These programs take data that you enter either directly or from a database or spreadsheet, and then perform various statistical tests to help you answer questions about the data and the relationships within the data. Before you buy a statistics program, read the documentation and sales literature carefully to be sure the program has exactly the capabilities you need.

#### Stock Market Programs

MATTHEW MCCLURE: Although no one really knows whether any kind of analysis is consistently effective at predicting stock performance, more than a dozen "systems" have one feature or another to recommend them, making them useful to professional investors and occasional dabblers. Most let you use data downloaded from networks (pp. 142-145), which saves lots of data-entry time. And most use only one or two methods of analysis. WINNING ON WALL STREET (p. 77) employs most of the popular methods. Be cautious—none of the methods is foolproof, and although these programs may help you rise above the novice level, they won't turn you into a pro.

#### Hardware

WOODY LISWOOD: Any time you're working primarily with numbers, you should have a keyboard with a numeric keypad as well as four arrow keys. That means the worst keyboards for calc programs are the ones that come with the IBM PC, the Apple II family, and the Macintosh. On the IBM PC keyboard, the arrow keys are on the number keypad, so you can't use both at once. You have to toggle a separate key to activate either the numbers or the arrows. The Apple II has only left-right, not up-down arrows, and it has no keypad. The Apple IIe and IIc have arrow keys but no keypad. The Macintosh has no arrow keys or keypad (I'm not sure that for real number crunching the mouse is better than arrow keys). A keypad can be purchased separately ($160) for all the Apples.

I use the EPS keyboard ($350) with my Apple II. For the IBM PC, the new Key Tronic keyboard ($255) with separate number pad and arrows would be appropriate.

The amount of RAM memory in your computer determines the maximum size of your spreadsheet (the number of rows, columns, and formulas). How big is your application? If you are contemplating no more than, say, 60 rows by 250 columns, you might like CP/M-based programs on 8-bit (Z-80) computers like the Kaypro 2, 4 or 10, and the Morrow Micro-Decision. However, to me, after a few weeks a spreadsheet of this size seems more like a scratchpad than a full-size calc program. Apple and IBM PC computers both allow larger memories and spreadsheets, but here you run into a different limitation. What good is a 512K spreadsheet in RAM when you can only store 360K on your floppy disk? If you have an Apple III with 256K, you can easily create a spreadsheet that exceeds the 160K available on the disk. When you get to these large-size applications, you need a hard disk drive. You want your storage capability to exceed the maximum size of your model and to hold, together on one logical drive, all the spreadsheets that make up your application.

## WHAT THE NUMBERS KNOW

STEWART BRAND: Spreadsheet programs have given me this peculiar vision of civilization. What I find new and wonderful about computerized spreadsheets is that you can have a vast array of meaningful numbers, and *all the numbers know about each other*. Change any one of them, and they all adjust immediately. They're positively ecological in that. The same goes for economies. Increasingly, all the numbers in the world know about each other. The value of your stock knows about the amount of change in my pocket as well as the turns of war in the Sudan and the quality of growing seasons in Colombia. The change in my pocket is ever alert to what you're deciding not to buy this week.

Computers are in the thick of that. A study I keep waiting for is a productivity analysis of what personal computers have done for the national economy in the last couple years—without any government intervention or even policy (except the decades of military research that invented the field in the first place—and the defending of patent rights). Some say that half of all IBM PCs, in their hundreds of thousands, are running just 1-2-3. Numbers—clever, quick, knowledgeable—boiling the stupidity out of countless business decisions. Interesting how essential the quickness is. It's 1-2-3's speed that put it on top.

BARBARA ROBERTSON: Woody Liswood has been using spreadsheet programs since the first month VISICALC (p. 71) appeared on the market and he's used nearly every spreadsheet program that's shown up since. He needs them for his business—he's one of the few (fewer than 100) "Certified Compensation Professionals" in the country, his specialty being "pay delivery systems" for large corporations.

**Woody Liswood**

With spreadsheet and statistics programs he sets up complicated models for job evaluations, salary planning surveys, regression analysis—and anything else he can think of. Since he recommends different computers and spreadsheet programs for different clients' needs, he's had to learn and teach them all. He's also a contributing editor for **Apple Orchard** magazine, where his reviews of a wide range of Apple software appear monthly, has his own product review magazine on The Source (key in PUBLIC 116) (p. 146), writes for **Popular Computing** and **Database Advisor**, has written a book, **Human Resources Information Systems, A Micro Computer Approach**, published by Potentials Group, Inc., in Cupertino, California, and teaches a graduate compensation course at Golden Gate University where he's Adjunct Professor. Good thing he already knew all the programs—otherwise he'd never have had time to shepherd this section.

## WHOLE EARTH RECOMMENDED ANALYZING TOOLS

### (June 1984)

### BOOKS AND NEWSLETTERS

**Dynamics of VisiCalc**, $19.95, p.71
**The IBM PC and 1-2-3**, $39.95, p.68
**SpreadSheet**, $42/yr, p.70
**SATN**, $50/yr, p.71
**Computerized Investing**, $44/yr, p.77

### SPREADSHEETS

1-2-3, $495, p. 67
SIDEWAYS, $60, p.68
SUPERCALC3. $395, p.69
SUPERCALC2, $295, p.69
SUPERCALC, $195, p.69

MULTIPLAN, $195, p.70
VISICALC, $99, p.71
VISICALC IV, $250, p.71
MERGECALC, $125, p.71
LOADCALC, $95, p.72
MAGICALC, $150, p.72
THE SPREADSHEET, $75, p.72
IACCALC, $85, p.72
WORKSLATE, $1195, p.73
TK!SOLVER, $399, p.73
TK!SOLVERPACK, $100 EACH, p.73
CALCSTAR, $195, p.74
MINIVC, free via CompuServe, p.74

### STATISTICS

DAISY PROFESSIONAL, $199, p.74
ABSTAT, $395, p.75
STATISTICAL CURVE FITTING, $65/$250, p.75
CURVE FITTER, $35/$95, p.76
SCIENTIFIC PLOTTER, $95, p.76
REGRESSION ANALYSIS, free, p.76

### THE STOCK MARKET (p.77)

VALUE/SCREEN, $495
WINNING ON WALL STREET, $700

## TYRANNY OF THE NEW

WOODY LISWOOD: Integration seems to be where everyone is headed. That means a single program does spreadsheets, word processing, database/file management, and telecommunications. SYMPHONY is the first major entry. The spreadsheet is still top caliber. Data management has been improved so it will give file managers a good run. The communications part gets the job done. The word-processing segment is adequate. The graphics section is workable. All in all, SYMPHONY will probably be a major factor in the marketplace. (More SYMPHONY on pp. 111, 127.)

The battle will be between single-function programs, specialists in their respective domains, and the integrated programs, jacks-of-all-trades but masters of few. The file-sharers seem to be led by MicroPro, which uses a standard comma-delimited ASCII file structure for its word processing (WORDSTAR, p. 56), its spreadsheet (CALCSTAR, p. 74), and its data management system (INFOSTAR +, p. 88).

MULTIPLAN (p. 70), as demonstrated on Macintosh, is another wave of the future. As of June 1984 it doesn't work. Pull-down menus using the mouse are its great claim to fame. However, if you are a serious user of spreadsheets who spends hours working at a keyboard, you might consider whether you always want to remove your hand from the keyboard, grab a mouse, go to a menu, point, then move back to the keyboard to get your work done. My personal philosophy is that any program which only allows mice, or any keyboard which has no cursor-control keys, may be great for learning, but ain't worth a damn for using. One cannot make a program so simple that anyone can learn it and at the same time have it be acceptable for the long-term business user. So, beware. Easy at the start may make for extreme frustration during day-to-day production use.

Spreadsheets in ROM (Read-Only Memory) are another part of the future wave. MULTIPLAN will be available on ROM for the TRS-80 Model 100. Other programs are sure to follow. That is significant: with the program on a chip, you'll have the available memory for your spreadsheet. 1-2-3 is available on ROM in the HP 110 portable (p. 18).

## *Spreadsheets*
### *Comparing the Big Four*

WOODY LISWOOD: When you need big features—a gigantic number of rows, sophisticated math, the ability to use the same program on a variety of machines, integrated graphics or data-management capabilities, you'll want to consider 1-2-3 (p. 67), SUPERCALC3 (p. 69), MULTIPLAN (p. 70), and VISICALC IV (p. 71). Many people use more than one spreadsheet.

### *Gigantic number of rows, sophisticated math*

If you need lots of rows of data and are in the IBM PC world, choose 1-2-3. 1-2-3 is the most talked-about program today and the one I recommend most highly. Some folks complain that it is slow. From my perspective, it is as good as any other program on the market. It can handle more than 2000 rows of data; the other spreadsheet programs normally limit their rows to 255. It could be classified as a true second-generation spreadsheet program (VISICALC being the original, first-generation product). The new all-in-one program from Lotus, called SYMPHONY (pp. 111 and 127), will increase the maximum number of rows to 8000. 1-2-3 owners can exchange 1-2-3 for SYMPHONY by paying the difference in price between the two ($200).

A second choice would be SUPERCALC3, if the company carries through with its promise to include 9000 rows in the new versions. Many people prefer the graph capability of SUPERCALC3 over that of 1-2-3.

If you are using a computer other than an IBM PC (or MS-DOS), you'll be limited to 255 rows in your spreadsheet. However, some programs let you link worksheets, so in effect you can work with more data than the size of one spreadsheet allows. MULTIPLAN (p. 70) shines in its ability to consolidate worksheets.

### *Using the same program on many machines*

If you use more than one machine now, or if you have a low-priced machine and want a spreadsheet that will be available on a higher-priced machine you might buy later, consider SUPERCALC, VISICALC, or MULTIPLAN.

SUPERCALC and SUPERCALC2 run under CP/M on Z80 machines like Kaypro and Morrow, and on Apples with CP/M boards; SUPERCALC, SUPERCALC2, and SUPERCALC3 run under IBM PC DOS and MS-DOS. SUPERCALC costs $195; SUPERCALC2 has added features for $100 more; SUPERCALC3 has everything in SUPERCALC2 plus graphics for $395. It's easy to go from machine to machine (or program to program), because all the programs use the same command setup regardless of the operating environment. SUPERCALC3 runs a close second to 1-2-3 as a recommendation. As of this writing, 1-2-3 is not available for CP/M or APPLE DOS operating systems, although Lotus is preparing a special version of SYMPHONY to run in the Lisa/Macintosh environment.

MULTIPLAN runs on most machines (including the Commodore 64) and so far is the only recommended program to run on the Macintosh. (We were unable to try a finished version of MULTIPLAN on the Macintosh, however, so we can't yet recommend it for that machine.)

VISICALC, the first spreadsheet program, was introduced on the Apple II and now runs on most machines, including the Atari 800. Since it was the first, it's well-supported, with templates, for specific applications sold as separate programs, and there are many books on how to use it. Both VISICALC and MULTIPLAN run on the Apple II family under Apple DOS, so you don't have to buy a CP/M card. VISICALC IV has an integrated graphics capability; MULTIPLAN doesn't. (MICROSOFT CHART, p. 129, adds powerful graphics capability to MULTIPLAN.)

### Integrated graphics and data management

1-2-3 was the first program to integrate graphics and spreadsheet data; SUPERCALC and VISICALC soon added graphics to their programs with versions called SUPERCALC3 and VISICALC IV. These programs all run only in the PC/MS-DOS environments. Many folks feel that the graphics in SUPERCALC are far better than those produced by 1-2-3, and unlike 1-2-3, SUPERCALC3 does not require a graphics board on an IBM PC. The Drawing section (pp. 122-137) has reviews of programs that produce graphs—often better than integrated graphics in spreadsheet programs—using data from almost any spreadsheet program.

Like SUPERCALC3, 1-2-3 has some data-management capabilities. This translates into "it can sort." SYMPHONY (pp. 111, 127) carries integration a step forward with up to 8000 rows available, additional data-management capabilities, including data-entry verification and report generation, a built-in word processor, and a communications program.

### Ease of use

1-2-3 has a good menu-tree structure, so you don't have to memorize a large number of commands; so does MULTIPLAN. But MULTIPLAN has an awkward way of referencing cells, which I find to be a problem. SUPERCALC runs from a command line (called up by typing a slash), which allows you to get to its functions without paging through a menu. VISICALC does this, too.

---

### Lots of rows, the premium multifunction package . . .

## 1-2-3

Version 1A; IBM PC/XT compatibles ● IBM PCjr ● IBM 3270 PC ● MS-DOS machines; 192K; graphics board required for graphics; 2 disk drives or hard disk; $495; copy-protected? YES; Lotus Development Corp., 161 First St., Cambridge, MA 02142; 617/492-7870.

SALLY GOTTLIEB: This program hit the top of the best-selling software list shortly after its introduction in late 1982, and stayed there throughout most of 1983 and 1984, with good reason. It was the first spreadsheet program to include graphics capabilities along with many powerful features such as large spreadsheet size, consolidation of spreadsheets, many built-in math functions. It also had a macro feature (so you can type in a series of commands, save them, and then do the whole command sequence again at any time by pressing one key on the keyboard). It's also one of the fastest spreadsheet programs on the market.

The ads bill this program as an "integrated spreadsheet, database and graphics package." Buyer beware! Although 1-2-3's database allows simple sorting and selection, it has no true report generator, data entry or data validation functions. It's a stretch to call this a database. (See the Organizing section for recommended database managers [pp. 85-89].) Likewise, the graphics are crude compared to those of most graphics packages on the market and require a graphics board in the IBM PC.

BARBARA ROBERTSON: For number people, standard IBM PC monochrome monitors have better character resolution than color monitors— but this configuration rarely includes a graphics board. IBM PCs with color monitors do have a graphics board. Graphics boards start at about $600. Compaqs have graphics capability as standard equipment.

SALLY GOTTLIEB: 1-2-3 has a very good online tutorial, which helps ease a beginner into its many features. Although menu-driven, 1-2-3 is a complex program. If you have a secret hankering to be a programmer, you will love the tricks you can play with the macro feature. If you don't, you probably won't find much use for them.

WOODY LISWOOD: I feel that 1-2-3 has one funny anomaly. When moving rows or columns of data, the program writes the new data on top of any found in the new column or row, and the old data is lost. Other programs, when moving data, push aside the old to make room for the new, and preserve both. When you first use 1-2-3, you will make the mistake of moving data without first creating a space. After overwriting some data once, however, you will probably never do it again.

CHRIS WOLF: I have complaints about design features that work against the natural feel. The command menus in 1-2-3 exhibit inconsistent behavior. Sometimes when you complete a command sequence you wind up back in "ready" mode; other times you drop back one, two or three menu levels; still other times you stay exactly where you are and must quit explicitly to complete the sequence. Some menus have no "quit" option, so you have to press the escape key to go back one level. This is especially confusing for beginners.

Any error that occurs in "command" mode drops you back to "ready" mode, and you have to go back through the menu tree to where you were to complete what you wanted to do—especially annoying if you simply make a typo in a cell, range, or file name where any decent program would tell you it was an error and let you try again. This is really rude behavior from a $500 package.

The graphing feature in 1-2-3 is quite nice, but it just makes me wish it were better. The biggest problem is the program's inability to draw dotted or dashed lines.

DICK YORK: The thing that's missing from most financial statements is cash flow projections. With 1-2-3, I can do cash flow projections of the type usually only affordable by large corporations. These projections tell me what to expect; they also inspire confidence in potential lenders concerned with "ability to repay." This is particularly important when sources of income are complicated.

I use graphs a great deal to look at relationships. I often don't even print them, but find the ability to simplify information valuable. Putting our consolidated cash receipts in the form of a pie chart shows sources of income and how the total is derived more clearly than a page full of numbers—lenders can see relationships and interrelationships easily.

I also use 1-2-3 to keep track of cash flow for a portfolio of selected properties, since none of the property-analysis programs I've found will deal with more than one piece of property at a time. I take basic information from our tax returns (my CPA is about to get a modem, so soon, I hope, I won't have to re-enter all the data), then enter debt totals. The spreadsheet model shows rental income, expenses, debt service, and various rates of return evaluations; it produces a cash flow for the entire portfolio. When we're considering buying or selling a piece of property, I add it

*(continued on p. 68)*

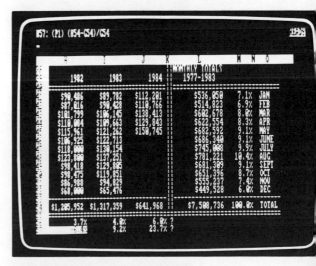

*1-2-3 has a versatile spreadsheet with variable column widths. Turn the page to see a printout of this cash-flow analysis.*

*(continued from p. 67)*

to (or subtract it from) the spreadsheet and immediately see how the proposed transaction affects the entire portfolio.

The application pictured calculates how much rent I expect to receive from a business that leases a building from me and how much I'll owe on the land I lease from someone else. Since the amount of rent is based on gross receipts, my income and expenses vary from month to month. Using 1-2-3, I discovered what seems to be a very accurate way to predict my cash flow. When I entered monthly receipts over a period of several years, divided each year's totals by each month in the year and looked at the results in a pie chart, I found to my surprise the pie charts for each year looked identical—it turned out that each month's percentage of the annual gross varied by less than a tenth of a percent each year. May 1981 was 9.1%; so were May 1982 and May 1983. With this information I can predict monthly and annual receipts with a fair degree of accuracy.

Of course, as we get further into the year, these projections become more accurate. Meanwhile, I have an ongoing picture of how much rent I'll owe and how much they'll owe me, and I can compare this year's projections to last year's figures to find the percentage of increase or decrease. With this information, I can compare sales per year to the inflation rate and chart the comparisons with a line graph. I also look at how the business is doing compared to the cost-of-living index and gross national product.

## SIDEWAYS

**Version 2.01; IBM PC compatibles; 64K; IBM, Epson, Okidata, Prism, or ProWriter printers; copy-protected? NO; $60; Funk Software, Inc., P.O. Box 290, Cambridge, MA 02238; 617/497-6339.**

DICK YORK: I use SIDEWAYS to print the spreadsheet, and it does exactly what its name implies: prints the spreadsheet sideways on continuous form paper, so the spreadsheet can have as many columns as you want. The database for this property has five years of information so far. It's a 20-year lease and I expect to keep adding information for the next 15 years, and keep printing the added columns with no problems. SIDEWAYS doesn't print the graph, but I rotate it 270 degrees in 1-2-3 to match the printout.

*Learning . . .*

## The IBM PC and 1-2-3

*The IBM PC and 1-2-3*; James E. Kelley, Jr.; 1983; 306 pp.; $39.95; Banbury Books, 353 West Lancaster Ave., Wayne, PA 19087; 215/964-9101; or COMPUTER LITERACY.

WOODY LISWOOD: I found more tips and lucid explanations about 1-2-3 in this book than I ever expected I could find anywhere. If 1-2-3 drives you crazy with its multitude of commands and its vast potential, this book presents the features, along with samples on a disk of the functions, that are somewhat arcanely explained in the 1-2-3 documentation. The disk contains, among other things, a project-scheduling template, which shows you how to do critical-path scheduling without having to purchase that type of program. That alone makes this book extremely valuable for the business user. (For other scheduling programs and project-management programs, see Managing, pp. 106-121.)

*Real-life business analysis with 1-2-3.*

### < > GROSS SALES

| | 1976 | 1977 | 1978 | 1979 | 1980 | 1981 | 1982 | 1983 | 1984 | MONTHLY TOTALS 1977-1983 | % | |
|---|---|---|---|---|---|---|---|---|---|---|---|---|
| JAN | | $58,948 | $59,827 | $66,987 | $75,404 | $94,616 | $90,486 | $89,782 | $112,201 | $536,059 | 7.1% | JAN |
| FEB | | $53,491 | $59,218 | $65,244 | $71,144 | $89,282 | $87,016 | $90,438 | $110,766 | $514,823 | 6.9% | FEB |
| MAR | | $58,871 | $70,065 | $79,398 | $83,810 | $102,680 | $101,799 | $106,145 | $138,413 | $602,678 | 8.0% | MAR |
| APR | | $58,510 | $69,122 | $77,007 | $83,709 | $114,459 | $110,084 | $109,663 | $129,843 | $622,554 | 8.3% | APR |
| MAY | | $64,477 | $76,851 | $78,010 | $99,977 | $126,054 | $115,961 | $121,262 | | $682,592 | 9.1% | MAY |
| JUNE | | $63,810 | $76,942 | $89,775 | $101,500 | $124,675 | $106,925 | $122,713 | | $686,340 | 9.1% | JUNE |
| JULY | | $70,973 | $85,250 | $101,036 | $110,546 | $129,029 | $118,000 | $150,154 | | $745,908 | 9.9% | JULY |
| AUG | | $72,263 | $85,553 | $105,522 | $123,483 | $135,349 | $123,800 | $137,251 | | $781,221 | 10.4% | AUG |
| SEPT | | $65,254 | $77,580 | $99,277 | $98,855 | $112,120 | $98,418 | $129,805 | | $681,309 | 9.1% | SEPT |
| OCT | | $65,775 | $70,267 | $90,604 | $102,501 | $103,923 | $98,475 | $119,951 | | $651,396 | 8.7% | OCT |
| NOV | $29,156 | $56,642 | $61,244 | $79,307 | $88,796 | $87,431 | $86,988 | $94,829 | | $535,237 | 7.4% | NOV |
| DEC | $44,562 | $54,354 | $60,482 | $74,482 | $54,420 | $72,314 | $68,000 | $65,476 | | $449,528 | 6.0% | DEC |
| TOTAL | $73,718 | $743,368 | $852,401 | $1,006,559 | $1,094,165 | $1,288,932 | $1,205,952 | $1,317,359 | $491,223 | $7,508,736 | 100.0% | TOTAL |
| INFLATION RATE | 3.7% | 6.9% | 9.2% | 12.8% | 11.8% | 7.1% | 3.7% | 4.0% | 6.0% ? | | | |
| SALES/% INCREASE (PER. YEAR) | | 14.7% | 18.1% | 8.7% | 17.8% | -6.4% | 9.2% | 23.0% ? | | | | |

```
                        PROJECTED ANNUAL GROSS FOR 1984:      JAN    $1,571,659
                        (BASED ON HISTORICAL DATA,            FEB    $1,595,152
                         AVERAGED, THEN DIVIDED INTO          MAR    $1,641,018
                         CURRENT YTD.)                        APR    $1,620,516
                                                             MAY
                                                             JUNE            @SUM(J41..J45)
                                                             JULY
                                                             AUG
                        THIS YEAR   LAST YEAR   % INCREASE    SEPT
                                                             ACTUAL 1984
PROJECTED SALES INCREASE:     $1,620,516  $1,317,359   123.0%
PROJECTED SYH NET:              $52,667    $42,814    123.0%
PROJECTED YHJU NET:             $81,026    $65,868    123.0%
(BASED ON CURRENT YR/MO.)
YHJU NET TO LAST YR.                       $379,123
YHJU NET (PROJECTED) THIS YR.  $460,148

COL INDEX (ALL ITEMS) 1977-84 (177 TO 305)           172.3%
(   ) GROSS SALES (1977-84 PROJECTED)                211.4%
GNP 1977-84 (2000-3400)                              170.0%
```

### (   ) GROSS SALES
**INFLATION vs. SALES INCREASE**

Legend: □ ANN. INFLATION RATE   + % INCREASE IN SALES
(years: 1976 1977 1978 1979 1980 1981 1982 1983 1984)

*Great graphics . . .*

## SUPERCALC3

Version 2.0; IBM PC/XT compatibles; 96K required, 128K recommended ● TI Professional; 128K; copy-protected? NO; $395;

## SUPERCALC2

Version 1.0; all CP/M machines; CP/M-80; 48K required, 64K recommended ● CP/M-86, PC DOS and MS-DOS machines; 64K required, 128K recommended; copy-protected? NO; $295;

## SUPERCALC

Version 1.12; all CP/M machines; CP/M-80; 48K required, 64K recommended ● CP/M-86, PC DOS and MS-DOS machines; 64K required, 128K recommended; copy-protected? NO; $195;

all from Sorcim Corp., 2195 Fortune Dr., San Jose, CA 95131; 408/942-1727.

SALLY GOTTLIEB: SUPERCALC users will feel right at home with SUPERCALC3, Sorcim's latest addition to the bewildering array of spreadsheets on the market. It has the same straightforward simplicity as SUPERCALC, plus integrated graphics that make it a worthy competitor of 1-2-3 (p. 67). Spreadsheets created by SUPERCALC, SUPERCALC2, or SUPERCALC3 load and operate with no changes from one version to the other.

The graphics are delightfully easy to use. One keystroke switches from spreadsheet to graph on the screen, so you can see your graph as you build it. Unlike 1-2-3, SUPERCALC3 does not require a graphics board to have this capability on an IBM PC.

The user manual, which contains ten lessons for the beginner, is remarkably good. In general, the program is straightforward and easy to use. Sophisticated users (*i.e.*, programmers-at-heart) will prefer the complexity and elegance of 1-2-3.

WOODY LISWOOD: SUPERCALC runs a close second to 1-2-3 in our recommendation because it operates in both CP/M and PC DOS environments and because many folks think the graphics are better. Its announced 9000-row capacity might have bumped SUPERCALC3 into the top recommendation were it not for Lotus's new SYMPHONY.

BARBARA ROBERTSON: SUPERCALC's features include ones typically found in spreadsheet programs: automatic recalculation, replication (copies formulas), cell protection, formatting for dollar amounts, whole numbers and scientific notation, and the ability to have two parts of the spreadsheet onscreen at the same time (in windows). Formulas include arithmetic (add, multiply, divide, subtract), exponentiation (raise to a power), and relational operators (equal to, not equal to, less than, greater than, and so on). Also, it lets you combine formulas with conditional expressions (or, and, not, and if). Among the built-in functions are ones that let you calculate absolute value, net present value, averages, counts, exponential value, logarithms, maximum, minimum, sine, cosine, tangents, arctangents, square roots, and pi.

SUPERCALC2 has all the features and functions of SUPERCALC plus formatting options for a floating dollar sign, imbedded commas, macro capability, bracketed negative numbers, and zero amounts expressed as blank cells. SUPERCALC2 can sort by column or row, can consolidate total spreadsheets or parts of spreadsheets, and has date and calendar functions. In addition, it can show results as percentages and print spreadsheets doublespaced.

SUPERCALC3 has all the features of SUPERCALC2 plus graphics and data management. All three SUPERCALCs give you a maximum of 63 columns and 254 rows per spreadsheet; however, SUPERCALC3 is being upgraded to have more columns and, as noted above, 9000 rows.

*ANDREA SHARP: In addition to all the obvious uses a calc program has for spreadsheets and accounting, I have noticed I tend to use mine as much as possible for other small tasks that may or may not require arithmetic functions per se, but do require organization of material on a page for presentation.*

*Since you can easily set up the columns and cells to appear as you want, I find using SUPERCALC2 as a form of tabbing very convenient. Insertions and deletions are easy, which makes rearranging information on a page quick.*

*My husband, Daniel, likes SUPERCALC2 because it "executes" commands. He can write a command file and have it automatically update other files and perform other repetitive processes. Someone can run these routines without knowing how to use SUPERCALC2.*

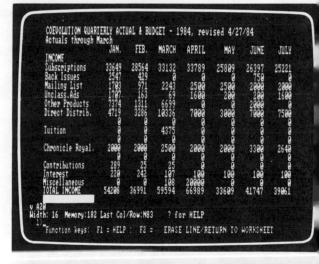

*Change one or two numbers, and calculate an entire set of salary ranges for your company. Data is entered in the MidPoint column. Then you select the starting percentage for your range spread as well as the percentage difference between adjacent spreads. SUPERCALC3 does all the rest.*

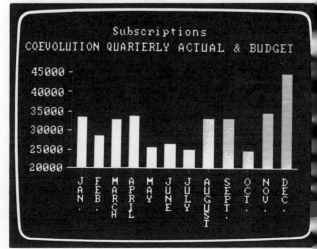

## BOOKS AND A NEWSLETTER

One of the best features of the spreadsheet market is the multitude of books containing instructions and sample worksheet models. There are books about 1-2-3, VISICALC, SUPERCALC, and MULTIPLAN, as well as others. But you really don't need to purchase a book written specifically for your program to get good use from its worksheet models. For example, all the recommended spreadsheet programs use some type of code to indicate a range of cells—say, A1, A2, A3, A4, and A5. In VISICALC you use three dots to simplify the entry (A1 . . . A5); in SUPERCALC, a colon (A1:A5); in 1-2-3, two dots (A1 . . A5). Since the logic is similar, you can take examples from a book written for VISICALC and simply substitute the correct codes for the spreadsheet program you're using.

If a book has a model you find interesting, try it. You'll find it better using the tools, techniques, and tips mentioned in these books than spending hours with the program trying to self-discover those same devices.

SpreadSheet; $42/yr (12 issues; includes membership); $7.50/issue to non-members; InterCalc, P.O. Box 4289, Stamford, CT 06907.

**SpreadSheet**, a members-only newsletter published by the International Electronic Spreadsheet Users' Group (formerly VisiGroup), was originally focused solely on VISICALC. I've watched it grow from a Xeroxed single-sheet letter to a typeset edition. The tips are good and the example spreadsheets are workable. The newsletter now tries to cover all spreadsheets.

—*Woody Liswood*

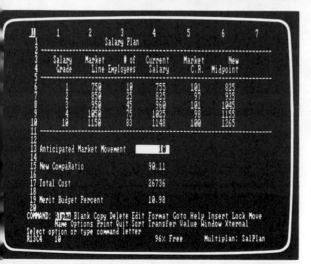

*Best at consolidating worksheets . . .*

## MULTIPLAN

Apple II family; 64K ● Apple III ● CP/M-80 (with SoftCard System); 128K; other CP/M-80 machines; 56K ● IBM PC compatibles and MS-DOS machines; 64K ● Macintosh; 1 disk drive; copy-protected? YES; $195; Microsoft Corporation, 10700 Northup Way, Box 97200, Bellevue, WA 98009; 206/828-8080 ● Commodore 64; 1 disk drive; copy-protected? YES; $99; Human Engineered Software, 150 North Hill Drive, Brisbane, CA 94005; 415/468-4111.

WOODY LISWOOD: MULTIPLAN is also a close runner-up to 1-2-3 (p. 67). It advertises itself as a second-generation spreadsheet. It is available on almost all machines in almost all operating environments. Like 1-2-3, MULTIPLAN has a well thought-out menu structure, so you don't have to memorize slash commands as in VISICALC or SUPERCALC.

*A salary plan determines the appropriate percentage merit budget for a coming year. Not a lot of work after you have things set up. After you enter the required data, you change the market movement assumption and this MULTIPLAN spreadsheet will tell you the appropriate merit budget needed for that set of employees.*

*Cindy Craig used MULTIPLAN on the Mac to create a readable draft of the chart on pp. 50-51. She had never used a spreadsheet before.*

There's one "feature" of MULTIPLAN, however, that I find abominable—the way it refers to cell locations. Most other programs designate rows and columns as numbers and letters, so you know when you are in cell A1 (the junction of column A and row 1). So when you are in C1 and want to reference A1, you type A1. In MULTIPLAN, however, you keep *track* of rows and cells that way, but enter and keep all cell *references* in relative notation. This means that when you are in C1 and want to refer to A1, you must type C-2 R—translation: "go back two columns and stay in the same row." Such expressions make it very difficult to read logic flows, so you always end up pointing with the cursor rather than typing in the relative location. MULTIPLAN shines, however, in its ability to consolidate worksheets.

MULTIPLAN allows you to use alphabetic names for groups of data. So you might label the "results" column in a worksheet as RESULTS and then build a consolidated worksheet using the RESULTS from ten other worksheets. To do this, you would design the original ten worksheets, then design a consolidated worksheet that instructs MULTIPLAN to place the RESULTS column from each of those other worksheets in the correct column in the consolidated worksheet. What happens if you make changes in, say, three of the original worksheets? Load the consolidated worksheet and it automatically adjusts, using the new data.

*The original . . .*

## VISICALC

Apple II family; 48K ● HP-125, -150, -9826, -9836 ● IBM PC/XT compatibles ● IBM PCjr ● TRS-80 Models II, III, 4, 16; copy-protected? YES; $99;

## VISICALC IV

IBM PC/XT compatibles; 128K minimum; 192K preferred; graphics card required for graphics; copy-protected? YES; $250;

both from VisiCorp, 2895 Zanker Rd., San Jose, CA 95134; 408/946-9000.

WOODY LISWOOD: VISICALC is the program that started it all. There are versions for most machines and in most operating environments. The older versions lack the features of the newer versions, but all work. VISICALC IV for PC/MS-DOS environments comes with a program called STRETCH CALC, which, like 1-2-3 and SUPERCALC3, provides graphic capabilities.

Because VISICALC is the granddaddy spreadsheet program, a large number of useful templates and utility programs work with it.

The term "template" indicates the rows, columns, formulas, and other data used in specialized spreadsheet applications. Since many of these applications are rather complicated, a market has opened up, and you can now purchase templates to solve many problems in finance, statistics, and mathematics. Many of the books that provide instruction about the various programs also come with disks containing templates. If you have a membership in The Source (p. 140), you can download some VISICALC templates from the Product Review Magazine (key in PUBLIC 116 and download the template file).

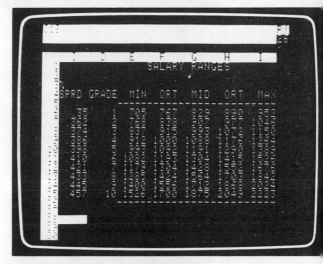

*A merit budget payout matrix is hard to calculate by hand but easy to what-if with VISICALC. You need to enter the percentage of each of your employee groups in the appropriate categories, then, as you test possible new merit percentages, this VISICALC spreadsheet will show you what your over-all percentage payout would be.*

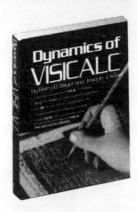

*Expensive but good newsletter . . .*

## SATN

*SATN* (Software Arts Technical Notes); Software Arts Products Corp.; bi-monthly; $30/6 issues, $50/12 issues; SATN Subscriptions, P.O. Box 100, Newton Lower Falls, MA 02162.

WOODY LISWOOD: Software Arts, the original producers of VISICALC, publishes this newsletter about VISICALC. The editors make no attempt to explain other spreadsheets. The newsletter is very expensive for the volume of information it contains, but it gives a good set of tips and techniques as well as limited spreadsheet models illustrating the use of the various functions. I still subscribe to this one, but if the cost continues to rise, I plan on not renewing.

*Advanced functions . . .*

## DYNAMICS OF VISICALC

*Dynamics of VisiCalc;* Barry D. Bayer & Joseph J. Sobel; 1983; 225 pp.; $19.95; Dow Jones-Irwin, 1818 Ridge Rd., Homewood, IL 60430; 312/798-6000; or COMPUTER LITERACY.

WOODY LISWOOD: This is one of the few VISICALC books that does not have a variety of models. Instead, the book concentrates on teaching the reader how to use many of the advanced functions found in the *almost* most recent version of VISICALC. I say almost, because I received a review copy of the book at the same time I received a review copy of VISICALC IV for the IBM PC. The book does not cover the new commands made available by the addition of STRETCHCALC (graphics, etc.). Maybe next edition?

*VISICALC represented a new idea of a way to use a computer and a new way of thinking about the world. Where conventional programming was thought of as a sequence of steps, this new thing was no longer sequential in effect: When you made a change in one place, all other things changed instantly and automatically.*
—Ted Nelson

*VISICALC should stand with the printing press, the steam engine, the harnessing of electricity, the development of immunizing agents for virulent diseases, and with computers in general and the microcomputer specifically as a milestone along the path of progress.*
—Al Tommervik, **Softalk**

*Combining VISICALC worksheets . . .*

## MERGECALC

Laurence Chapman; Version 3.0; IBM PC/XT compatibles ● IBM PCjr; 128K; copy-protected? YES; $125; Micro Decision Systems, Box 1392, Pittsburgh, PA 15230; 412/276-2387.

DON SCELLATO: This utility program operates on VISICALC worksheet or template files, allowing the user to add them together, subtract one from another, divide or multiply them by a selected number, and add or subtract a number from them. You can add together all the segments of an activity to provide an overall analysis or generate variance-analysis reports along with percent- and time-change reports. Since a worksheet in one file can be divided by a worksheet in another, you can also, for example, get a "percent of total company" analysis report for one segment of a company, or a "percent of total market" analysis for a company.

To use MERGECALC, however, the layouts of all the worksheets and models to be manipulated as a set must be identical. You are working with different versions of identical templates, so the only difference between the templates will be the input data, not the formulas or grid locations of your data. You select files you want to include, and MERGECALC assigns a number to each. You can then enter formulas such as 1 + 2 + 3-4 or 2*12 (number 2 file multiplied by 12 file). MERGECALC can work with either "logic" (VISICALC models) or DIF files. The resulting format can be the same as that of the original files, a two-decimal format, or an integer (whole number) format throughout.

*Moving text into VISICALC...*

## LOADCALC

**Laurence Chapman; version 4.0; IBM PC/XT compatibles ● IBM PCjr; 128K; copy-protected? YES; $95; Micro Decision Systems, Box 1392, Pittsburgh, PA 15230; 412/276-2387.**

DON SCELLATO: LOADCALC converts print format and text files into Data Interchange Format (DIF) files, which may then be used by VISICALC and other programs that read the DIF file format. The program can also convert print files generated by time-sharing systems like The Source (p. 140) or a mainframe computer into DIF files.

File conversion is simple. The program allows you to select specific data from the text or print file to be included in the new DIF file. LOADCALC's screen display closely resembles a VISICALC screen and the program uses the same slash (/) to enter mnemonic abbreviations for commands. Special features include automatic selection of the columns to be moved into a new file as they are scrolled across the screen, selection of files by scrolling through a list of names, and the ability to load a file you want converted into a predefined worksheet. LOADCALC is easy to learn. The manual is brief but adequate. Help is easily available onscreen.

## DATA TRANSFER

There are a variety of ways to get data into your spreadsheet. The most common is just to type it in as you are developing your application. However, you may wish to read data from a database or another spreadsheet. The two most common methods are by means of DIF (Data Interchange Format) files and comma-delimited ASCII files. The DIF method of transferring data is sponsored by Software Arts, the original developers of VISICALC; there are a multitude of programs that all input and output data in the DIF format.

Comma-delimited ASCII files are a second way BASIC programs might use to store their data. In this method, each field is separated by a comma and alpha-numeric fields containing special characters are normally surrounded by quotes. A wide variety of programs also accept input from and output to these files.

Many spreadsheet programs will input (but not output) spreadsheets that were created by competitors' programs. The most common format to be accepted is VISICALC format. Second most common is MULTIPLAN.

*—Woody Liswood*

---

*For the Apple II family ...*

## MAGICALC

**William Graves; Version 2.165; Apple II family; 64K; copy-protected? YES; $150; ARTSCI, Inc., 5547 Satsuma Ave., North Hollywood, CA 91601; 213/985-2922.**

## THE SPREADSHEET

**William Graves; Apple II family; 48K ● Apple III in emulation mode; copy-protected? NO; $75 to members only ($51 membership: $26/1st year dues, $25 initiation fee); A.P.P.L.E., 21246 68th Ave. South, Kent, WA 98032; 206/872-2245.**

## IACCALC

**William Graves; Apple II family; 48K ● Apple III in emulation mode; copy-protected? NO; $65 for members (membership fee: $30), $85 for non-members; International Apple Core, 908 George St., Santa Clara, CA 95050; 408/727-7652.**

DON SCELLATO: MAGICALC is currently available from three different sources under three different names. The product is the same in all cases, but the price varies significantly. A.P.P.L.E. and International Apple Core have lower prices for paid members of their organizations.

MAGICALC is very similar to the Apple DOS 3.3 version of VISICALC and the original version of VISICALC for the IBM PC.

MAGICALC can use VISICALC models and data files, which means the experienced VISICALC user can easily move from one program to the other without retyping entire models, although a few changes are sometimes required to move formulas from MAGICALC into VISICALC.

MAGICALC's menu offers Calculate (the spreadsheet program itself), File, Format, and Configuration subsystems, and the option of "Booting the next program." A spreadsheet can hold 16,002 cells (63 columns, 254 rows), although unless you have 512K RAM memory, you can't access all the cells at once.

MAGICALC has thirteen built-in math functions and seven built-in logic functions. It provides "Lookup," minimum and maximum value selection, and the use of "not, or, true, and not available" criteria for displaying values in particular cells. It has a single built-in financial function—Internal Rate of Return—and no built-in date functions.

In addition to working well with VISICALC, MAGICALC's DIF files can be used by other Apple II programs, such as Apple II business graphics, DB MASTER (p. 83), and PFS:GRAPH which saves keying data into other programs.

It's an excellent spreadsheet program, offering the user more file handling and formatting options than the basic versions of VISICALC. However, MAGICALC has no built-in trigonometric functions; it can't display 70 columns of characters without a video expansion card; nor can it be configured for 80-column display on a number of video expansion cards.

WOODY LISWOOD: MAGICALC, available in a number of incarnations, is the recommended program in the Apple DOS environment. It lacks some of the advanced mathematical functions of the original VISICALC program. However, for normal use it has most of what you will need as well as the advanced features found in the second-generation programs (variable column widths being the most important).

---

*A program should be self-evident. You look at it and you know what to do. Spreadsheets like VISICALC are the classic example. All you need is a crib sheet for commands and you can fumble around nicely.*

*—Richard Dalton*

*A portable spreadsheet machine . . .*

# WORKSLATE

**$1195; CommPort; $195; MicroPrinter; $295; Convergent Technologies, 2441 Mission College Blvd., Santa Clara, CA 95050; 408/980-9222.**

WOODY LISWOOD: I fell in love with my WorkSlate. Here was what I had always wanted: a portable calc machine that weighed only a few pounds, fit in my briefcase, allowed me to work on planes, and needed no separate storage package. It also helped me show clients how interactive computing using calc programs could save them time and money and help them solve their day-to-day problems.

In addition to being a dedicated calc machine, WorkSlate has a number of interesting functions. Hook it up to a phone line and you have a speaker phone. Keep your numbers in a phone list and WorkSlate will dial them for you. Belong to The Source or CompuServe (p. 146) or other network or online databases? The built-in modem allows easy access, once you've entered the proper codes, numbers, passwords, and special commands. The built-in microcassette recorder will both act as your dictaphone and store your templates; while you are saving a template, you can also record a voice message to be played when you next load the template. Forget your calculator? The

WorkSlate has a special mode that acts just like it (assuming you know Reverse Polish Notation). Don't remember what you were going to do today or tomorrow—or what you did yesterday? A special time-management book is built in as a template—and there's a built-in alarm.

WorkSlate is a fantastic machine for what it does. But it has some limitations that make it less than perfect. The good things first.

WorkSlate has a great way of handling storage. There are five user areas in memory. Each area can expand to take over the entire available free space. Five templates can be stored on each microcassette. The first part of the tape is a directory; you designate where on a tape you want to place templates when you store them. No worry about overwriting previous work.

There are two options for printing out data. You can use Convergent's small, portable, battery-powered pen printer, or you can purchase a communications port and talk directly to any printer using parallel or serial outputs.

Now the limitations. The key to this multifunction machine is "how good is the calc program?" I have used all versions of VISICALC (p. 71), all versions of SUPERCALC (p. 69), 1-2-3 (p. 67), MAGICALC (p. 72),

CALCSTAR (p. 74), and MULTIPLAN (p. 70) extensively. WorkSlate has four limitations that make it less effective than any of the calc programs for desktop micros.

First, WorkSlate has a limited memory. Second, WorkSlate is missing some (in my opinion) critical math functions. It lacks the square root and log functions, for instance. Both of these are necessary for many types of data and statistical analysis. Third, the sort routine is virtually useless, since it will only sort rows containing whole numbers, not formulas. Fourth, the keyboard is smaller than normal (okay, you do get used to it), it lacks a shift key for your right hand (if you are a touch typist, this will drive you crazy), and the designers eliminated the number row over the keyboard in favor of a single ten-key pad on the right. They themselves probably never entered a cell reference like A1. There is no return key. There is, however, a key labeled DO IT.

If you don't sort, log, or square, you will find that you can create the same types of financial and analytical templates with WorkSlate as with any of the other programs. WorkSlate runs like a dream. As I write this I have used WorkSlate for about two solid months and have never had a failure or a problem with the unit or the tape.

---

*Complex problem solving . . .*

# TK!SOLVER

**Apple II family; 64K ● IBM PC/XT compatibles ● MS-DOS machines; 128K; copy-protected? YES; $399;**

# TK!SOLVERPACK

**Mechanical Engineering, Financial Management, Introductory Science, and Building Design & Construction, runs on same systems as TK!SOLVER; copy-protected? YES; $100 each;**

**both from Software Arts, 27 Mica Lane, Wellesley, MA 02181; 617/237-4000.**

DON SCELLATO: TK!SOLVER is a useful tool for people who must frequently solve complex mathematical equations, have no desire to write complicated programs in BASIC or another language, and do not want to work within the constraints of electronic spreadsheet programs.

If you are an engineer, architect, statistician, chemist, physicist, navigator, astronomer, or financial or statistical analyst whose job involves the solution of complex formulas and the frequent use of mathematics, TK!SOLVER is a program you should examine. It's extremely easy to learn and use. I would even recommend that high school students

studying science and advanced math look at the program. College math students would find it a useful tool.

It solves complex mathematical problems, creates tables of various parts and results of a formula, and makes rudimentary plots of the data generated. Although the graphics output of the program is adequate for someone working with math, it is not presentation quality.

TK!SOLVER uses a very logical and simple approach to solving problems. You begin by setting up a Rule Sheet—a list of equations or formulas to be solved. As you enter rules, each variable in an equation is automatically transferred to a Variable Sheet. The Variable Sheet is particularly important, since it is used to enter known values in the equations on the Rule Sheet. Equations can be supported by a table of conversion factors or further defined by use of a Unit Sheet (which interlocks with the Rule and Variable Sheets). A Global Sheet can be used to set printing defaults and turn the automatic transfer of variables on or off.

Once you have entered rules and known variables, you can solve for unknown variables in the equations. The "Direct Solver" produces a series of guesses that

lead to a solution by trial and error. You provide the problem to be solved and the first guess at the correct answer. Press the ! key, and the program solves the equation based on the first guess. It then replaces the first guess with the first solution. Press the ! key again, and the process is repeated until the proper solution is reached.

By setting up a List Sheet for repetitive solutions to the same problem, you can make the process happen automatically. The List Sheet describes each list of data required for the solution of a problem, with further subsheets used to define the known elements of each list. The problem can then be solved for each item in the list. If the problem must go further than required on the Rule Sheet, a User Function sheet can be used to define specific functions or numeric relationships.

TK!SOLVER is produced by the same folks who invented VISICALC and uses a similar command structure. The manuals are clear and complete. Optional TK!SOLVERPACKs have equations for solving common problems in particular fields such as introductory science, mechanical engineering, and financial management.

*MINI-VC lets you stay on top of your financial situation even in remote areas like the racetrack.*

Free for Model 100 owners . . .

## MINIVC

**TRS-80 Model 100; 24K; free to members of CompuServe's (p. 140) Model 100 SIG (PCS-154); membership in the SIG free to CompuServe members.**

WOODY LISWOOD: There are a number of calc programs available for the TRS-80 Model 100 (p. 16). When you compare price to features, however, the winner is the MINIVC program, available as a free public domain program on the TRS-80 Model 100 Special Interest Group (SIG) on the CompuServe Information Service (CIS) network (p. 140). If you are on CIS, you'll find the SIG by typing GO PCS 154 at the main prompt.

The cost is right: $000.00.

MINIVC has the right features. It is modular in approach, and you do not need to add the code (and can delete the code) for any features you do not need. This is important, for with less code you have more memory available for your spreadsheet.

MINIVC can ABS (absolute value), INT (integer), SQRT (square root), ROUND (round off), SUM (add all or part of a row or column), and AVG (find an average). A second module adds MIN (find the minimum value in a list), MAX (find the maximum value), MOD, FIX, PI, EXP (exponentiate), COS (cosine), LN (natural logarithm), TAN (tangent), SIN (sine), ATAN (arctangent), as well as Boolean operators. You can also replicate both absolute and relative numbers, insert and delete, transfer and edit your data. In other words, MINIVC can do the same sort of things that many of the other calc programs can do. That is more and better (in my opinion) than the programs for the Model 100 that cost you your hard-earned dollars. By the time you read this, author Woods Martin (CIS number 70235,232) will probably have added more features.

Well, if it is free, what is the problem with it? One complaint is that you see each of the cells being addressed during recalculations, which takes a long time to do. This is a BASIC program, not a machine-language program. Also, I would like to have adjustable column widths. Other than that, no problems. It has all the features you might want, considering the limited (32K) memory on the machine.

---

Statistical functions and WORDSTAR compatibility . . .

## CALCSTAR

**Version 1.46; CP/M-80 machines; 48K ● IBM PC compatibles and MS-DOS machines; 128K; copy-protected? NO; $195; MicroPro International Corp., 33 San Pablo Ave., San Rafael, CA 94903; 415/499-1200.**

WOODY LISWOOD: CALCSTAR from MicroPro uses most of the same keyboard responses as the entire line of MicroPro products (based on WORDSTAR p. 56). Its main disadvantage is that it always displays menus. It shows only ten rows on the screen because the other fourteen possible rows are taken up by menus. You can adjust it, but only to a fifteen-row screen. The most recent release makes use of as much memory as you have in your PC/MS-DOS machine. It also has built-in statistical functions, such as regression analysis, not found in other programs. CALCSTAR's best feature (and the reason it's on this list) is that it communicates with the INFOSTAR+ (p. 88) data-management system, forming an integrated environment (WORDSTAR, INFOSTAR, CALCSTAR) using the same comma-delimited ASCII format. Thus you can transfer data among the word processing, database, and spreadsheet programs. (Versions of all three are available for CP/M and PC/MS-DOS operating systems.)

# *Statistics*

Best value for Apple II owners . . .

## DAISY PROFESSIONAL

**Apple II family; DOS 3.3; 48K; copy-protected? NO; $199; Rainbow Computing, Inc., 8811 Amigo Ave., Northridge, CA 91324; 818/349-0300.**

WOODY LISWOOD: Funny name, you think, for a statistics program. Well, DAISY stands for "Data Analysis and Interactive Statistics." For the money, it's a best-buy among statistics programs.

DAISY's two data-entry routines are among the best I have used with a statistics program. The first is standard with BASIC programs: You define your $X$ and $Y$ variable names, then the program asks you to enter your data one entry at a time. The second option is a calc type of entry model, in which you can enter data in a row-and-column format and use arrow keys to move around—a very, very good feature. In addition, DAISY has full editing capabilities within the matrix of data.

All the features of the program are accessed with four-character codes for more than 100 commands. If you are familiar with statistics, I would rate DAISY as user friendly. Otherwise, you might have to look up a command or data request in the documentation—or even a statistics textbook—before you are certain that you are responding correctly. Documentation is complete and explains each of the commands in a reasonably lucid style. DAISY's HELP command gives you a list of available commands grouped according to function; INFO gives you a full description. If you enter a command that cannot possibly work, given where you are in the program, DAISY reminds you that if you are unsure of your next move, you can use the HELP and INFO commands to get more information.

DAISY makes use of the extra memory in the Apple IIe and will use various 80-column cards including the Videx Videoterm and Ultraterm boards.

DAISY also does graphics: sequence plots, histograms, scatter plots, semilog on both $X$ and $Y$ axes, and log-log scatter plots. You can save the plots to print with your favorite graphics program (see Drawing, p. 122-137).

What statistical wonders does DAISY perform? Transforms on a column basis: mean, standard deviation, variance, standard error, minimum, maximum, range, sums, frequency tables, histograms, covariances, correlation, partial correlation, auto-correlation, Spearman rank correlation, Kendall rank correlation, Kendall partial rank correlation, and Kendall coefficient of concordance. It runs tests about mean and about a given value, performs analysis of variance one-way or two-way, analysis of variance for regression, Chi-square, *t*-test, Cochran Q-test, Mann-Whitney U-test, Friedman two-way analysis of variance, summary statistics, regression coefficients, Durbin-Watson statistics, beta weights, fitted and residual values, and simple or multiple regression. DAISY uses all subsets of possible independent variables, uses all subsets of a given size, goes forward or backward in a stepwise regression, and sweeps a variable in or out of a regression.

Also . . . handles exponents, integers, inverse, natural logs, logs, base 10, absolute values; adds, multiplies, divides, raises to powers, calculates cumulative totals and differences, and can lead or lag the data. DAISY creates new columns of data for the fitted and/or residual values of the regression.

*Accepts data from many sources . . .*

## ABSTAT

**Version 3.03; CP/M-80 machines; 56K ● IBM PC compatibles or MS-DOS machines; 128K; copy-protected? NO; $395; Anderson Bell Co., P.O. Box 191, Canon City, CO 81212; 800/225-5550.**

WOODY LISWOOD: Although this program does not have all of DAISY's features, it has an impressive number, and unlike current versions of DAISY, it runs in the PC/MS-DOS environment as well as in CP/M.

ABSTAT doesn't have curve fitting (see CURVE FITTER, p. 76); you have to determine in advance the maximum number of variables you'll need; you must always use upper-case letters; and the editing capabilities are very weak. But the program works rather well, it's reasonably well designed and easy to use, has enough statistics to solve many problems, and you can transfer your data to it from a multitude of sources. This means you do not have to re-key data already entered into other programs when you want to perform statistical analysis on it.

In addition, ABSTAT can automatically create bar graphs and plots of the data. They aren't the high-resolution plots you might be used to, but they get the point across. Because they are created with "alpha" print characters, you don't need a plotter—you can use any printer. ABSTAT reports can be printed in 132 or 80 columns, displayed on the screen (80 columns), or stored as a disk file so you can edit them later with a word processor.

You select commands via a menu, or, if you know what you want to do, you can avoid the menu by giving direct commands. You can type ? for help at any time; adding a command name gives you information about that command.

With ABSTAT's command file (macro) option, you can use a word processor to create files of commands, name them, and then (if they are all valid ABSTAT commands in the proper order), once you bring your data into ABSTAT and give the program your command file name, the system will run by itself. The command file can turn on your printer and perform all the analysis you might need while you are out drinking coffee with your friends.

ABSTAT comes with a demo file and demo command file, and I would recommend that the first thing you do is run that command file and let ABSTAT take you through a sample set of commands and screen displays.

What does ABSTAT do? Functions include Create a new file, Fetch an existing file, Edit, Save, Transform the current data set, Add variables from another file, Transform a variable from another file, Append data from another file, Print, Generate random numbers, Sort, Read an ASCII data file, and Read and Write a DBASE II (p. 85) data file.

Statistical commands include one-way and two-way analyses of variance, Chi-square goodness of fit and Chi-square two-way contingency table, correlation coefficients (*r*) matrix, means, standard deviation, modes, values, frequencies, percent and *z*-scores, Mann-Whitney U-test, variable pair mean test, population mean test, *t* test for paired observations, probability commands, simple and multiple linear regressions, Spearman rank correlation matrix, and cross-tabulation.

The latest version of ABSTAT has a new command, called Miss, which handles missing values on a casewise, listwise, pairwise, variable-wise, or "include all" basis.

*ABSTAT really worked well on this rank order correlation. I did this same matrix with DAISY and it took more than 45 minutes to sort each row before it actually processed the data. ABSTAT finished the entire affair in just under 5 minutes.*

## Curve Fitting

WOODY LISWOOD: Most of the charting programs designed for on-screen graphics or to drive digital plotters come with built-in statistical functions. These are normally regression functions that will calculate and plot a regression line when you enter in a scattergram. PRIME PLOTTER and CHART MASTER are examples of these programs. While they're fine programs, we are not reviewing them here because their primary function is graphics, not statistics.

*For lap computers . . .*

## STATISTICAL CURVE FITTING

**Gavilan; 128K ● HP 110; 128K ● IBM PC/XT compatibles; 128K; $250 ● NEC PC-8201A ● TRS-80 Model 100; 24K; $65; copy-protected? NO; American Micro Products, Inc., 705 North Bowser, Suite 125, Richardson, TX 75081; 214/238-1815.**

WOODY LISWOOD: The best statistical package for these three popular lap computers is STATISTICAL CURVE FITTING. Not only does this program have many of the statistics from the full size microcomputers, it displays a graphic curve that fits on the small screens in a most professional manner.

```
COMMAND: SRANK

                    SPEARMAN RANK
                *** CORRELATION MATRIX ***

    VARIABLES:
    1  K        1.00000
    2  P        0.965180    1.00000
    3  R        0.964069    0.958539    1.00000
    4  PT       0.994018    0.978825    0.981867    1.00000
    5  GD       0.989396    0.977747    0.983244    0.996776    1.00000
                   1 K          2 P         3 R         4 PT        5 GD
```

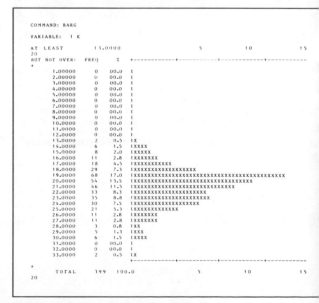

*ABSTAT constructs bar graphs (above) and plots of the data—not the fancy hi-res plots you might be used to, but they get the point across, and they print with any printer.*

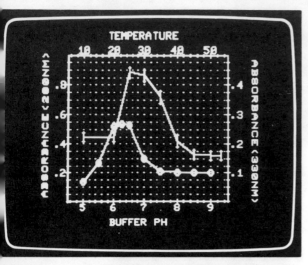

CURVE FITTER and SCIENTIFIC PLOTTER are two Apple-based programs that work in tandem. Some consider the curves produced by Scientific Plotter to be some of the best available. In addition, you can print these graphics on your dot matrix graphic-capable printer or on selected digital plotters.

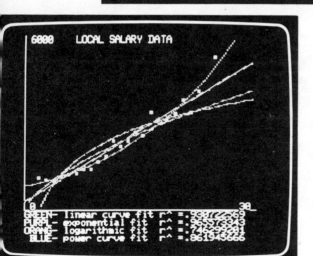

REGRESSION ANALYSIS, a free public domain program available from most APPLE USER GROUPS, calculates the best fit line for Power, Linear, Exponential, and Log curves. It also graphs your data for you and, if you have the correct dot matrix printer, it will print those graphs for you as well.

*Professional, technical . . .*

## CURVE FITTER

**Apple II family; 48K; $35 ● IBM PC/XT compatibles; 128K; color graphics board required; $95; copy-protected? NO;**

## SCIENTIFIC PLOTTER

**Apple II family; 48K; disk drive; $25 ● IBM PC/XT 128K; color/graphics adaptor board; $95; copy-protected? NO;**

**both from Interactive Microware, Inc., P.O. Box 139, State College, PA 16804; 814/238-8294.**

WOODY LISWOOD: If you do curve fitting and also need to generate high-resolution plots of your data, then you must— repeat, *must*— have CURVE FITTER and SCIENTIFIC PLOTTER as part of your program library.

These programs are designed by technical folks to be used by technical folks. Some engineers we talked with felt that these programs were the only "professional" plotting programs on the market.

*The price is right, too . . .*

## REGRESSION ANALYSIS

**Apple II family; 48K; available through Apple User Groups; copy-protected? NO; International Apple Core, 908 George St., Santa Clara, CA 95050; 408/727-7652.**

WOODY LISWOOD: If all you need to do is curve fitting (determining which type of curve—linear, exponential, logarithmic, or polynomial—best fits a particular data set), the best program is free. That is, if you have an Apple. A program called REGRESSION ANALYSIS is (or should be) in the user library of your local Apple User Group. This program takes data sets and produces regression curve fits for linear, exponential, logarithmic, and power curves; graphs those curves singly or together on a screen; and then prints out those screens on a printer.

Regression analysis.

Once you figure out how to use CURVE FITTER, the ease of operation and error trapping are superb. I tried to get the program to bomb and couldn't. You can enter data by keyboard, disk, or other means. You can then manipulate the data, transform it, or do almost anything else to it before you generate the curve fit. Along the way you can generate high-resolution plots.

A curve-fitting procedure can contain between 25 and 1000 data points. The program first generates a scatter diagram of the data you entered. Then, after you fit your curve through the data, it lays a dotted line through the scatter diagram. You can save any of the pictures as you go along or use another graphics program to print them on a graphics printer. (I use a Grappler Board with an Epson MX-80 printer.)

Because the program code is not protected, you can modify it to your heart's content. In fact, specific areas of the program are left open so you can put in the data-manipulation techniques you need. I added my own printer-initialization routines so I could print graphics as part of a normal work session without having to save the graphics as pictures first.

SCIENTIFIC PLOTTER accepts data from CURVE FITTER with no problems whatsoever, though it's somewhat difficult to use because of its flexibility. You can address any individual pixel on the screen and put anything you want there—special symbols, numbers, lines, dots, and so on. However, once you've learned SCIENTIFIC PLOTTER, you'll find you can do quick-and-dirty graphics very quickly. You can even identify end points of the X and Y graphs using game paddles or a joystick. It works and it speeds things up. In fact, command sequences go as fast as or faster than many of the available graphic programs that require almost the same number of responses to give you someone else's version of what you need for your graphic display (and still require you to enter your data into the other programs). SCIENTIFIC PLOTTER lets you add five lines (255 characters each) of fancy labels to each graph.

I tested the program by generating 38 separate graphics for related data and then printing and converting them to overhead projector slides that would overlay each other with perfect registration during presentation. It worked fine. The program works better than any graphics program in my library. It only does curves, but it does them well. At the price, I think it is a best buy—if you go in for this sort of thing.

SCIENTIFIC PLOTTER, too, is unprotected, and the authors encourage you to modify it to meet your specific needs. As in CURVE FITTER, you have easy entry to BASIC, DOS, and other sections of the program via built-in control sequences. New versions support various digital plotters. You can purchase the special printer disks separately.

## *Analyzing the Stock Market*

MATTHEW MCCLURE: When I was a securities analyst fifteen years ago, I helped build a regression model to predict the stock market. I was working with some economists at Stanford who explained the Random Walk theory of stock prices—which says essentially that stock prices can't be predicted mathematically—and then proceeded to develop a model that worked. Once we knew what the market as a whole was going to do, we could pick industries that were likely to accelerate rapidly in a bull market, or ones that would be resistant to the weakness of a bear market.

We picked our industries according to "fundamental" considerations, as opposed to "technical" ones. Fundamentals are things like price/earnings ratio, market share, annual sales, dividend yield, debt capital, financial strength, percent return on net worth, and projected growth rates. Technical analysis is based on the axiom that a trend will continue until it changes; it is concerned with how prices fluctuate in a market, essentially independent of the kind of company or industry being evaluated.

Having chosen industries that looked attractive for the kind of market we expected in the next six or nine months, we would pick companies that looked fundamentally sound. Then we would do some technical analysis—to determine which ones seemed to have the most market potential. We made our money on service charges based on performance, and we consistently outperformed the market.

Now there are tools for personal computers that make this whole process comparatively painless. Anyone who is considering playing the market should consider investing in these programs. They won't give you the edge that the pros on Wall Street have, but they will give you good, valuable methods for making investment decisions.

---

*Fundamentals, for investors . . .*

### VALUE/SCREEN

**Version 2.1; Apple II + , IIe; 64K; 2 disk drives; 80-column card; printer recommended ● IBM PC/XT compatibles; 64K; 2 disk drives; parallel printer recommended; $495 annual subscription; 2-month trial, $49; Value Line, Inc., 711 Third Avenue, New York, NY 10017; 212/687-3965.**

MATTHEW MCCLURE: For automating analysis of securities fundamentals, VALUE/SCREEN is excellent. Enter your criteria for selection from the 32 available variables—computer stocks with price/earnings ratios less than 10 and dividend yields greater than 8%, for example—and you'll get a list of stocks that meet them. If the list is too long, refine your criteria further, eliminating those with a low percent return on net worth, for example, and ordering the resulting list by financial strength rating.

VALUE/SCREEN's data is updated monthly on disk; it's not as current as what you could get from Dow Jones News/Retrieval, but it's got a lot more information.

---

*Technical, for traders . . .*

### WINNING ON WALL STREET

**Apple II family; 64K; Grappler board and compatible printer; 2 disk drives; Hayes micromodem ● DEC Rainbow 100; 192K; DEC printer; compatible modem ● IBM PC/XT compatibles; 192K; color/graphics board; 2 disk drives (one may be hard disk); copy-protected? NO; complete package $700; separately: Trader's Data Manager, $200; Trader's Forecaster, $250; Trader's Accountant, $350; Summa Software Corp., P.O. Box 2046, Beaverton, OR 97075; 503/644-3212.**

MATTHEW MCCLURE: This is the program I would get if I were only getting one. TRADER'S DATA MANAGER lets you automatically download securities information from Dow Jones News/Retrieval (p. 142). Then it will produce a graph of the stock's behavior—the traditional high, low, close, and volume chart (H/L/C/V) or a special chart of an indicator graphed against volume or against another indicator.

It is TRADER'S FORECASTER that makes the package worthwhile, though. In addition to the staid H/L/C/V graph, it also uses such reliable methods as moving average, weighted moving average, exponential smoothing, and least square fit to produce informative graphs. Technical analysis tools include speed resistance lines, trading bands, on-balance volume, relative strength, and point-and-figure analysis. The Proprietary Matrix Projection Formula uses sophisticated analytical techniques to predict the "next high" and "next low" prices—sell and buy signals, respectively.

With all these tools, the best technique is to try as many as possible. If one gives you a buy or sell signal, get confirmation from another before you act.

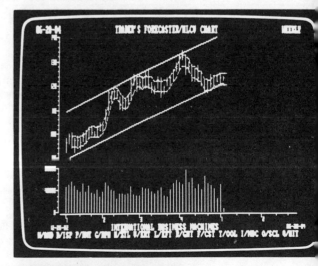

*WINNING ON WALL STREET draws moving averages and mid-channel support/resistance lines like these for IBM, whose price broke through the support lines (a sell signal). The stock's price went down $20 after this signal.*

---

Commodity traders will be interested in obtaining price data via modem from Commodity Systems, Inc. (CSI, 200 W. Palmetto Park Road, Boca Raton, FL 33432; 800/327-0175 or, in FL, 305/392-8663) and update data files. Participating brokers will pay the CSI fee for their clients. For more on online services for investors, see p. 142.

---

*Newsletter for the Money SIG . . .*

### COMPUTERIZED INVESTING

**$44/year (6 issues), $22/yr to members ($44/yr); American Association of Individual Investors, 612 North Michigan Avenue, Chicago, IL 60611; 312/280-0170.**

MATTHEW MCCLURE: Using a microcomputer to improve your investing skills is a new trick. **Computerized Investing** is a newsletter for those who can afford to keep up with the latest software for investors, traders and speculators—or can't afford not to. Its reviews are knowledgeable and newslettery. But even better, the Member Software Services let you download software, and point you to good public-domain investment software. Nine subgroups around the country meet to exchange ideas about investment theory and computers.

## ORGANIZING

### Tony and Robbie Fanning, Domain Editors

TONY AND ROBBIE FANNING: Information bombards us—much more than we care to, or can, sift through and remember. Only ten percent of every ton of paper going by carries interesting information. Five percent of that is useful, and we might want to look at one percent of it again. How do we find that one percent? We organize. We make lists, alphabetize and prioritize them, group similar kinds of information into piles, and throw out the garbage.

To do this, we use mundane organizing tools—pencil and paper, paper clips, forms and questionnaires, little pads of stickum-backed yellow notepaper, 3″ by 5″ cards, file folders, fluorescent highlighting pens, Rolodex files, notebook section separators, and file cabinets. And we use tricks like outlining, patterning, and shuffling. We grow used to the limitations of our tools and tricks—we know we can't easily store a particular item under several references, or automatically reshuffle a filing system, or quickly make a list of what's in a cabinet drawer.

Organizing programs can help sift information more flexibly. They exchange the familiar paper activities for new formats: lists, files, fields, records, databases, and even "computer environments." If you find the terms confusing—computer mavens might call your address book a "database"—don't worry. These programs do only a few simple, dumb things. They store away information. They sort it for you. They let you pick out what specifics you want to look up or print out.

You probably already know what you want to do—manipulate a mailing list, organize your research notes, manage a small business—but you don't know which program fits your needs. To help you choose, we divided organizing programs into two rough categories—*little boxes* and *garbage bags*.

*Little boxes* (called "file managers" if they're simple, "database management systems" [DBMS] if they're complex) are designed to organize structured information that can be arranged so it all looks alike—for example, rows in a table of figures or entries in a phone book.

Within this category we included two "flagship" programs—PFS:FILE and DBASE II—the standards against which we compared the rest of the candidates. If you're unfamiliar with the computer terms used to describe organizing tools, be sure to read these reviews first. Then look at the other reviews to pick a program appropriate to your particular needs.

When you shop for this type of organizing program, play the numbers game. Find out the limits of a data-management

## DATABASES WILL EITHER BURY YOU OR UNBURY YOU, IF YOU LET THEM

STEWART BRAND: My theory of old age is that people decay and eventually die from having too much stuff to remember. Nephew's wife's mother's name. The percent the IRS is interested in of your rental property depreciation. Dozens of potentially guilt-producing birthdays. When you go to have a new thought, there's no place to put it.

I can't tell yet if personal computers are helping or hindering our beleaguered lifework of Keeping Track. They certainly offer help; they even deliver it. But it may be one of those the-more-you-do-the-more-you-do things. The more the computer is remembering for you, the more you have to remember what it's remembering. Like the illusion of the Paperless Office a couple years ago—electrons were going to replace ink in the workplace. Ha. The busy little electrons helped generate more paper than ever. To good effect? Maybe. Maybe even probably. But people are not, I notice, working less, or agonizing less.

I'll bet next year we'll be reviewing a kind of program that scarcely exists yet—the dedicated database for home and office. MICRO COOKBOOK (p. 195) is headed in that direction. Bird books and tree books and flower books should soon be on software, with fulsome illustrations (videodisc please), the perfect way to "key" down the very subspecies of Mitigated Flycatcher that inhabits your part of the county. Meanwhile all we have is general purpose databases of increasing muscle.

*Tony and Robbie Fanning*

Matt Herron

Tony Fanning has been watching them come on for decades. Now involved in Research & Development planning at Hewlett-Packard (who makes the "Touch Screen" 150 computer and portable 110 [both on p. 18] and PERSONAL CARD FILE [p. 83]), he started with computers 23 years ago programming an insurance company's first plunge into Data Processing. He's been in Silicon Valley since 1969, spent a couple years at SRI International before going to HP. Robbie Fanning edits and publishes a quarterly newsletter for thread-benders called **Open Chain**, on stitchery and such—she uses DBASE II and WORDSTAR to keep it organized. Together they've written eight books on quilting, running, and personal time management.

You may ask what program they used to organize Organizing. They used manila envelopes and 3″ by 5″ cards in little stacks on the floor. Personal computers can look deep and snaky into your information, but they still have tunnel vision.

program: its maximum number of files per database, records per file, fields per record, characters per field. (We list those statistics for every program recommended here.) Ask yourself, "How long will I keep my computer? How long will I use this program?" If the answer shows that you'll outgrow the program soon, consider alternatives.

We call the second category of organizing programs *garbage bags*. Sometimes called "text organizers," they handle unstructured information of varying sizes, shapes, or types—such as quotations from books or research notes.

More than any other type of program, organizing tools require powerful or expandable computer equipment. A good rule of thumb: if the computer system requires you to use your home TV for display, stick to 3" x 5" cards. It'll be less frustrating. For business use, a mainstream computer—IBM PC/compatible, CP/M, Apple—and two disk drives are musts. Expect soon to find yourself considering a hard disk and extra RAM (memory), especially if you depend on fast look-up capability. If you manage a lot of information, budget a lot of time to learn how to do it right.

## WHOLE EARTH RECOMMENDED ORGANIZING TOOLS

### (June 1984)

**BOOK**

**Everyman's Database Primer,**
   $19.95, p.86

**LITTLE BOXES**

PFS:FILE, $125/$175, p.80
PFS:REPORT, $100/$125, p.81
PFS:SOLUTIONS, $20 each, p.81
OFFIX, $99, p.82
PC-FILE III, $45 contribution, p.82

**OTHER FILE MANAGERS**

PERSONAL CARD FILE, $150, p.83
DB MASTER, $350, p.83
VERSAFORM, $389/$495, p.84

DATA + , $60. p.84
SORT2 + , $29.95, p.84

**BIGGER LITTLE BOXES**

DBASE II, $495, p.85
QUICKCODE, $295, p.86
DBPLUS, $125, p.86
R:BASE 4000, $495, p.87
R:BASE EXTENDED REPORT WRITER
   (XRW), $150, p.87
CONDOR III, $650, p.88
INFOSTAR + , $595, p.88
ASAP FIVE, $275, p.89
SEQUITUR, $795, p.89

**GARBAGE BAGS**

DATAFAX, $249/$299, p.90
SUPERFILE, $195, p.91
NOTEBOOK, $150, p.91
THINKTANK, $145/$195, p.92

**ORGANIZING YOUR
   COMPUTER ENVIRONMENT
   (p.93)**

PROKEY, $130
SMARTKEY II, $90
VIDEX ENHANCER II, $149

## TYRANNY OF THE NEW

TONY FANNING: Some organizing programs are so new they haven't run up enough of a track record to analyze. Other formerly not-too-hot programs have reappeared in what might be hot new versions. In either case, it would be premature to recommend these preannounced programs, since they haven't been used in real-life situations, though they all have an air of promise or excitement. Should one of these programs intrigue you, watch the news, read the magazines (especially ours), and ask friends before you take the plunge. The only thing they have in common is they all sound good so far.

FRAMEWORK—an integrated environment from Ashton-Tate, with outlining functions like THINKTANK's;

ALADIN—a re-do of one that's been around the CP/M world a while;

POWERBASE—claimed to be an easy-starter DBMS;

TI IOR—another "idea processor" of uncertain capabilities;

DBASE III—The upgrade of DBASE II (p. 85), designed for 16-bit processors (such as the IBM PC);

SYMPHONY—will 1-2-3 (p. 67) now have real data management, or continue to be half-assed about it?;

DAYFLO—an integrated computer environment; desktop metaphor; needs hard disk and lots of memory;

KNOWLEDGEMAN—the current implementation is curiously unfinished although the design is good;

MACFILE—can a tombstone with a mouse and stiffy disks find your info?

## Little Boxes
### "Beginner's Luck"

TONY AND ROBBIE FANNING: Some simple organizing programs stand out as remarkable values. You may not wish to organize your whole business using them, and you may outgrow them quickly. But they'll introduce you to ideas that will let you master more flexible industrial-strength programs later. Or they might be exactly what you need in themselves. We call the first group of file managers "beginner's luck," because they're easy to use and understand.

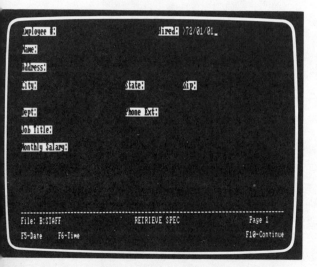

**First you "paint" your PFS:FILE form on the screen . . .**

**Then you can use it to control lookup, printing, and other functions.**

---

*Our flagship program: good for beginners, maybe all you need . . .*

## PFS:FILE

**Apple II family; $125 ● Apple III; $175 ● Apple Macintosh; $125 ● DEC Rainbow ● Gavilan ● HP 150 ● IBM PC/XT compatibles ● IBM PCjr; $140 ● TRS-80 Models III & 4; $125 ● TRS-80 2000; price not available (TRS-80 versions distributed only by Radio Shack) ● TI Professional; $140; copy-protected? YES; Software Publishing Corp., 1901 Landings Drive, Mountain View, CA 94303; 415/962-8910.**

---

**Number of files permitted per database: 1**
**Records per file: 1000 max (Apple); 2200 max (PC/MS-DOS)**
**Fields per record: 50-100/page; up to 32 pages/record**
**Characters per field: 840 (Apple II); 1680 (others)**

---

PETE WENDELL: It does everything I need it to do easily and relatively quickly. And it's so simple that even my boss can use it.

PHILIP ELMER-DEWITT: Give my vote for PFS:FILE. It makes the kind of list-keeping most people do palpably easier. Still sells like hotcakes today after years on the market. I did my wedding on it (chapel seats, lunch plates, gifts, thank you notes—the perfect use for a home database)—and even my wife learned to love the printouts.

TONY AND ROBBIE FANNING: PFS:FILE is one of the simplest organizing programs to learn because bells and whistles were designed out of instead of into it. It's an ideal starter for learning about data management, and in itself it's good for just about anything you could do with paper forms, as long as the job isn't too big. (In fact, its vocabulary is that of familiar paper forms rather than the

more common, mind-deadening vocabulary of data processing.) Like forms, PFS:FILE works well when the information being organized is all of the same type: names and addresses, order information for customers, etc. You can make the blanks in its forms any size and fill them with any type of information (numbers, letters, or a combination); thus it can keep track of good-sized but discrete chunks of text, like comments, quotations, or recipes.

---

The information you type into these forms (one form after another) is stored in a data file that might cover employee information for your little company, gardening books in the university library, customers of your custom sewing business, or (if you were a fat New York detective) a bedding history for your orchids.

Setting up forms in PFS:FILE is so easy that you must remind yourself to design the form carefully, because the blank form controls all the other PFS:FILE functions, such as printing or making changes. For instance, to look up a piece of information on the screen, or print it on paper, you simply fill in the specifications on the same blank form. To ask for all employees earning more than $1000 a month, type ">1000" in the item "Salary." You can combine conditions to select exactly the records you want. You can look at the information on the screen, print it, or delete it.

PFS:FILE is fairly powerful, but it achieves its simplicity by limiting its capabilities—a standard tradeoff with organizing programs. When searching for forms to update, print, or delete, PFS:FILE has two speeds. The normal speed is sufficient for a small number of forms in your data file, but it slows down when the number gets large. If you will usually search by one item, make it the first item on your form, and the search will go faster because PFS:FILE uses that item as an index to narrow down the range of data it searches through.

PFS:FILE can't use more than one index at a time. Also, it can't use more than one disk for a data file, so the number of forms you can track at once on a floppy-disk system is limited to about a thousand. But you can use the program on a hard disk, which relieves both the speed and capacity problems somewhat.

---

If you outgrow PFS:FILE, you have to learn a new vocabulary to move on to more powerful programs, which usually use data-processing talk.

**NAMES FOR OBJECTS**

| PFS:FILE Talk | DATA PROCESSING Talk |
|---|---|
| Form design | Database structure |
| Data file | Database |
| Form | Record |
| Page | Screen (of data) |
| Item | Field |
| Index | Key field |
| Report | Output, reports |

*For convenience and calculations . . .*

## PFS:REPORT

**Apple II family ● Apple III ● Apple Macintosh ● DEC Rainbow ● Gavilan ● HP 150 ● IBM PC/XT compatibles ● IBM PCjr ● TI Professional; $125 ● TRS-80 Models III & 4 (distributed only by Radio Shack); $100; copy-protected? YES; Software Publishing Corp., 1901 Landings Drive, Mountain View, CA 94303; 415/962-8910.**

TONY FANNING: If PFS:FILE fits your needs, you'll probably need the separately sold PFS:REPORT, which increases the kinds of reports (printouts) your data files can produce. PFS:FILE keeps its printout capabilities simple, requiring you to design your form with items in the order you want them printed; if the first item on the form is a zip code and the name is next, that's the order it has to print. It also makes you type in the printout specifications each time, even if they're always the same.

PFS:REPORT can rearrange the items in a printout and save your printing formats for later use. It can also perform calculations like totals, subtotals, averages, and subaverages in a printout—to print a monthly summary of customer activity that averages the dollars spent per customer, for instance. It can group items by a particular characteristic—first the customers who bought your X-widget, then the Y-widget buyers.

SHARON RUFENER: I met the PFS: family at the offices of the San Francisco Fair & Exposition, an urban version of a county fair, where everything got done on a crash basis by an understaffed group of workers up to their armpits in paperwork.

They had an Apple III with a hard disk and the PFS: software and didn't know what to do with them. Being complete computer virgins and terrified technophobes besides, they needed help, even with what might be the world's friendliest software at their disposal. And since these people needed to be self-sufficient in the future, I had to teach them to design and create their own systems. I also trained various part-timers to use those systems.

With PFS:FILE and REPORT, we scheduled paid and volunteer time for hundreds of Fair workers; we sent mass and selected mailings; we monitored the entire floor plan, including space available and billing; we kept track of contest prizes and payments; we printed status reports for state officials; and we coordinated hundreds of phone calls to media contacts without anybody slipping through the cracks.

Eventually even the most computer-phobic staff member refused to give up her computer, and they got another Apple so everyone could get work out. It's a good thing we used PFS:—if we had used DBASE II or the like, the Fair never would have happened.

### EMPLOYEE INFORMATION

| SALARY | NAME | ADDRESS | DEPT |
|---|---|---|---|
| 1,400 | J STRIBLING | 1801 LAWNDALE LOMAS, CA 91075 | SALES |
| 1,625 | J M STONE | 33 SPARKS AVE TACOMA, CA 92071 | MANUFACTURING |
| 1,700 | I JONES | 45 ELM TIOGA, CA 96832 | FINANCE |
| 1,850 | M K TALENT | 202 S ALMA HALLEN, CA 91001 | MARKETING |

### INVENTORY

| PART = | DESCRIPTION | QTY | PRICE | TOTAL $ |
|---|---|---|---|---|
| 23 | ¼" DRILL | 170 | 29 25 | 4,972 50 |
| 25 | ½" DRILL | 125 | 18 50 | 2,312 50 |
| 83 | 5" BOXES | 100 | 0 50 | 50 00 |
| 87 | 8" BOXES | 250 | 1 25 | 312 50 |
| TOTAL | | | | 7,647 50 |
| COUNT | 4 | | | |

### MONTHLY SALES STATUS

| TERRITORY | REP | QUOTA | SOLD TO DATE | % QUOTA |
|---|---|---|---|---|
| EAST | BROWN | 200 | 150 | 0 75 |
| | JONES A | 200 | 135 | 0 68 |
| | TAYLOR | 175 | 132 | 0 75 |
| | AVERAGE | 191 | 139 | 0 72 |
| | TOTAL | 575 | 417 | |
| WEST | JONES, J | 225 | 175 | 0 78 |
| | PARDEE | 200 | 110 | 0 55 |
| | AVERAGE | 212 | 142 | 0 66 |
| | TOTAL | 425 | 285 | |
| AVERAGE | | 200 | 140 | 0 70 |
| TOTAL | | 1,000 | 702 | |
| COUNT | 2 | | | |

*PFS:REPORT can create more complicated printouts than PFS:FILE.*

*Easier yet . . .*

## PFS:SOLUTIONS

**Apple II family ● Apple III ● DEC Rainbow ● IBM PC/XT compatibles ● IBM PCjr ● TI Professional; $20 per application. Twelve applications: Stocks, Home Budget, Disk Library, Home Inventory, Mail List, Employee, Payroll, Ledger, Invoices, Inventory, Checks, Tickler; copy-protected? YES; Software Publishing Corp., 1901 Landings Drive, Mountain View, CA 94303; 415/962-8910.**

TONY FANNING: There are always busy or just-plain-scared people who want only to get the job in front of them done, not to learn a general-purpose tool to create a specific tool to do that job. If you're one of them, and the PFS: family isn't simple enough for you but you'd still like to use it, you could try PFS:SOLUTIONS, a collection of predefined specific applications used in conjunction with PFS:FILE and PFS:REPORT. The titles read like the definitive list of business/home organizing activities: Home Inventory, Inventory, Checks, Disk Library, Employee, Home Budget, Invoices, Mail List, Ledger, Payroll, Stock$, and Appointments Tickler.

Each PFS:SOLUTION disk contains a form design, some sample forms for practice, and three to seven report designs. You can use these well-designed form and report "templates" as is, or modify them to your specific applications.

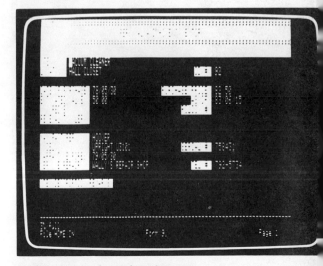

*This home inventory form and reports you can print from it are pre-designed PFS: SOLUTIONS. All you need to do is enter information.*

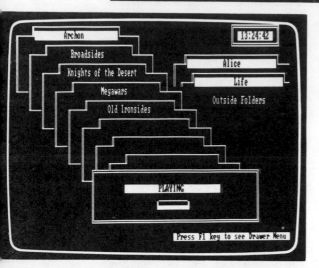

*Once you have opened a drawer, the screen displays the file folders now in the drawer. To the right are the folders you have taken out of the file cabinet. Tutorials are available for each OFFIX function.*

*Right before your eyes . . .*

## OFFIX

**DEC Rainbow ● HP 150 ● IBM PC/XT ● NEC APC ● TI Professional ● TRS-80 Model 2000 ● Victor 9000 ● Zenith Z-100; copy-protected; YES; $99; Emerging Technology Consultants, Inc., 2031 Broadway, Boulder, CO 80302; 303/447-9495.**

**Number of files permitted per database: 2**
**Records per file: limited by disk size; up to 1,000,000 characters**
**Fields per record: 50**
**Characters per field: 250**

CHARLES SPEZZANO: This "personal office system" mimics so well what most of us have seen all our lives—an office with a file cabinet—that my wife Jill and I often understood what to do next without instruction. There are really no commands anywhere in the program. The first thing you do is open a drawer in the file cabinet and select a folder, using arrow keys and a single letter. Each drawer can hold 100 folders, each

folder one form or document created with the word processor.

OFFIX can search a data file (drawer) for up to ten fields simultaneously and then sort by one of the ten—alphabetically by state, for example. You can send the information you've looked up to the screen or print it as a report. The only calculation it will do is total a column of figures, though.

The better I get to know OFFIX the more I like it and the more useful it seems for getting anything, anyone, any office better organized. It's a great basic starter program for almost any home user, professional office, or small business.

---

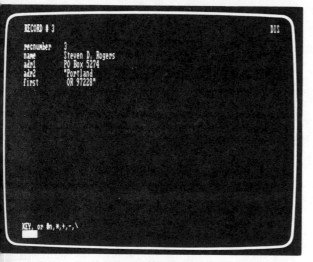

*PC-FILE III has features not found on more expensive file managers. This mailing list record was "imported" to PC-FILE III from a MAILMERGE file, putting it in the database without rekeying.*

*Count the features and divide by the cost . . .*

## PC-FILE III

**IBM PC compatibles; 96K; copy-protected? NO; $45 contribution for disk and updates; ButtonWare, P.O. Box 5786, Bellevue, WA 98006.**

**Number of files permitted per database: 1**
**Records per file: 10,000**
**Fields per record: 41**
**Characters per field: 65**

JIM CELONI, S.J.: When I first wanted to catalog my diskettes, I used my text editor, creating a file with a one-line record for each disk. To look up a program, I used the editor's search command; to update the catalog, I edited the file.

When I read about PC-FILE III, I wrote to Jim Button for my free copy; a week later I was so happy with it I sent a contribution. With PC-FILE I could update my file, sort it by any collection of fields, find records matching any specification, and format and print a report about any diskettes. A computer-novice friend of mine, using PC-FILE III, created a name and address file and printed three-across mailing labels the same day.

PC-FILE III is easy. You give commands by pressing a function key or typing the first few characters. Report formatting directions are cryptic but well-documented. The manual, included as a file on the diskette, is excellent: explains everything, defines terms, and gives examples without being condescending.

The program prompts you for new data clearly, though it flags input errors with only a "beep." It can fill in some fields such as date and time automatically. You can retrieve the most recently changed entry or the one just before it. Passwords can keep a file secure. PROKEY it isn't (p. 93), but ten "smart" keys (ALT-0 through ALT-9) can represent up to 75 characters each for speedy data entry or single-keystroke command sequences.

Reports can include totals, other calculations, and text. You can sort fields by more than one characteristic (for example, employee names in alphabetical order within each salary level). You can send reports to a file and save report formats for continual use.

PC-FILE III's data limits are reasonable, since the file must be on one disk drive. If I approached the limits, I'd buy R:BASE (p. 87). PC-FILE III is fast enough; for big files I use a RAM disk. I run it with 128K, a double-sided drive, and an 80-column color display (you can specify foreground and background colors). You can move data between PC-FILE and VISICALC (p. 71), 1-2-3 (p. 67), MAILMERGE (p. 56), and other programs. It's also compatible with the other two major "shareware" programs—PC-WRITE (p. 59) and PC-TALK (p. 152). When you count the features and divide by the cost you get a very big number.

Programmer Jim Button answered my questions promptly and incorporated suggestions into new versions. I look forward to his planned PC-CALC and PC-GRAPH.

## *Other File Managers*

TONY FANNING: With controls less complicated than a 747 jetliner, you can organize information, select from it, sort it, and print it. Each program in this section is powerful enough for "mid-range" organizing but conceptually simple enough to learn quickly. (Also see JACK2, p. 112, with a good file manager in its all-in-one package.) Remember that what is simple enough to learn quickly may be as quickly outgrown.

*Touch and roll . .*

## PERSONAL CARD FILE

Version A.01.02; HP 150; 256K; $150; copy-protected? NO; Hewlett Packard, 11400 Wolfe Rd., Cupertino, CA 95014; 800/367-4772.

Number of files permitted per database: 1
Records per file: 550 max; limited by disk space
Fields per record: limited by screen size
Characters per field: 80 max

TONY AND ROBBIE FANNING: Apart from the fact that you can point to the screen to have information instantly expanded out and displayed, PERSONAL CARD FILE operates much like PFS:FILE. It's great for quick card-file-like look-up by people who use a computer routinely at work.

CLIFF FIGALLO: On the screen you see a facsimile of a rotary card file showing index tabs. Touch the "rollers" and the cards spin by. Touch a card's "tab" and the entire card appears on the screen.

You can search on any field, and very quickly on the card file's key field (displayed on the tab). You can look up a person or business by touch, and the program will automatically dial the phone number (with a Hayes-compatible modem). PCF will print data on a card-by-card basis, including the entire image of the index card. It has limited reporting capabilities, however, and once data is entered changing the format is not advisable. Still, PCF is a natural for the HP 150's touch capabilities.

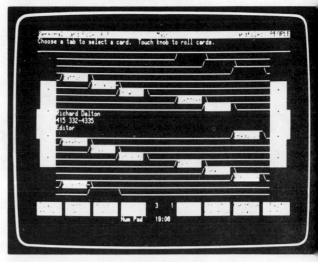

*Touch a handle to roll the card file; touch the tab to select a card.*

---

*For files spread over several disks . . .*

## DB MASTER

Version 4 Plus; Apple II family; 64K; 2-4 disk drives; copy-protected? YES; $350; Stoneware, Inc., 50 Belvedere St., San Rafael, CA 94901; 415/454-6500.

Number of files permitted per database: 1
Records per file: 5-10 megabytes (50-100 disks)
Fields per record: 100 (1020 characters)
Characters per field: 100

TONY FANNING: This upgrade of a file manager popular in the Apple computer world for years has many convenience features and copious documentation. Like most file managers, DB MASTER allows you only one data file; unlike most, it lets you spread that file across many diskettes. With such a large file, you'll want three or four drives or a hard disk unless you don't mind swapping diskettes constantly. (A hard disk requires a special edition of the program).

You define the data structure with a form that you build on the screen. Later you construct similar forms, called Master Reports, for searching, printing, and updating. Searching is not particularly fast except with the primary index key, which can be a combination of fields. It offers three levels of password protection and it can pull bite-size chunks out of long data entry forms so you can update a few fields without having to press hundreds of carriage returns. This makes DB MASTER 4.0 useful in office situations where one person designs a system and other people use subsets of it.

We recommend DB MASTER on the Apple (see MAGICALC, p. 72). The IBM PC version, called ADVANCED DBMASTER, is much more complex, fulsomely documented, and slow, though it is competently implemented. You can probably do better with R:BASE or another database manager (pp. 85-89).

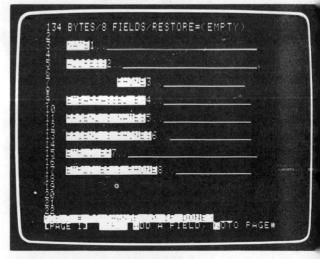

*The bottom few lines of every DB MASTER screen are reserved for ever-changing, helpful prompts that lead you by the hand through a myriad of choices. This program falls between the easy-to-use, limited file managers (such as PFS:FILE) and the more difficult, flexible database managers (RBASE:4000).*

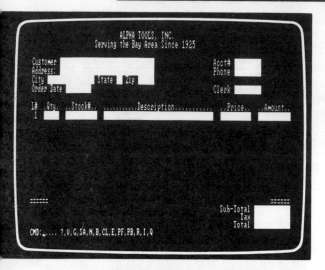

*If your business depends on forms for information collection, VERSAFORM will be the quickest way to automate the process. Somewhat clunky and rigid compared to other database managers, but light years faster than manual paper shuffling.*

*An organized form
of record keeping and billing . . .*

## VERSAFORM

Version 2.7; Apple II family; 64K; 2 disk drives or hard disk ● Apple III; 128K; $495 ● IBM PC compatibles; 128K ● MS-DOS machines including TRS-80 2000, Wang, DEC Rainbow, TI Professional; 256K; $389; templates: Legal/Office Manager; $249; Purchase Order, Invoicing; $50; Mailing List, Cash Receipts, Expense Journal, Checkwriter; $39.95; Job Cost; $80; copy-protected? NO; Applied Software Technology, 170 Knowles Drive, Los Gatos, CA 95030; 408/370-2662.

---

Number of files permitted per database: 1
Records per file: limited by record and disk size
Fields per record: limited by screen size (approx. 50/Apple II; 75/Apple III, IBM PC)
Characters per field: user-specified

---

TONY FANNING: Don't throw away your old paper forms—with VERSAFORM you duplicate them as input screens and report formats. Once set up, people familiar with the paper versions can easily use the electronic versions with little training. As a standalone program VERSAFORM can make business a lot easier, but moving information from it into other programs (like a word processor) is difficult. Also, because VERSAFORM is written in the UCSD Pascal p-system, it doesn't interact easily with programs or files in your operating system. P-system programs are often slow, and VERSAFORM is no exception.

THOMAS R. PIPER: If followed literally, without too much thinking or conceptualizing, VERSAFORM can help a variety of businesses do their workaday tasks. For example, a local coal company runs more than $20 million of its transport tickets each year on forms designed and implemented by a low-paid secretary. They track 45 drivers and 30 trucks going to 25 major vendors.

They weigh each load of coal and store customer names, billing and receiving addresses, truck numbers, driver numbers, gross weights, road taxes, reclamation taxes, sales taxes, discounts, and other shipping information, as well as variable prices of different coal grades. They continue to be amazed and delighted with what they can accomplish.

VERSAFORM's look-up tables and business-form "calculators" work superbly for the coal company's invoicing. Later, the firm uses the reports from the same data files to manage its operations. For example, a "hauled tonnage between repairs" report is a prime indicator for each truck (sort of like reporting on mean time between repairs for computers); a driver's work-history report can be calculated for payroll (since drivers are paid by the load and mileage, not by time or on salary). I wish VERSAFORM'S fields were bigger, but its report generating is nice.

---

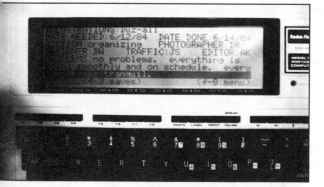

*You can take your file manager with you: DATA + and the TRS-80 Model 100.*

*Put a filing system
on your lap-sized computer . . .*

## DATA +

TRS-80 Model 100; 16K minimum, 32K recommended; also available for Olivetti M-10 as DATA10; copy-protected? NO; $60;

## SORT2 +

TRS-80 Model 100; 16K minimum, 32K recommended; also available for Olivetti M-10 as SORT10; copy-protected? NO; $29.95;

both from Portable Computer Support Group, Inc., 11035 Harry Hines Blvd. Suite #207, Dallas, TX 75229; 214/351-0564.

---

Number of files permitted per database: 1
Records per file: 60 with 10K; more with more memory or if records are smaller than maximum
Fields per record: 16 max
Characters per field: 249 max

---

JIM STOCKFORD: A word on the great convenience of filing systems on lap-sized computers: the computer itself can be carried down rows of shelves for the tax-time countdown, or taken to the field or library for data collection. At the worksite you can enter data into fields presented by the screen, and from there on the program does the work.

Isn't that better than walking around with a notebook and returning to the office to key everything in?

So far, these two programs from the Portable Computer Support Group are the best we've seen for the Radio Shack Model 100. DATA + is a standalone filing system that allows you to print labels, listings, and forms; sort records on any of the sixteen fields by alphabetical or numerical order; and incorporate fields into text files. It also has an Add: feature that creates files and reports from unrelated records. With the built-in search features of the Model 100, DATA + is as good as many of the filing programs that run on desktop computers.

If you use DATA + for your work, you should get SORT2 + as well. It sorts DATA + files by any field. It can sort alphabetically (recognizing upper-case letters ahead of lower-case letters if you wish) or by number, and it has an astonishingly low 1K memory requirement.

The manuals are beautifully simple. The factory support is friendly and immediate. Together, DATA + and SORT2 + provide an excellent filing, sorting, and printing tool at an awfully good price.

## *Bigger Little Boxes:*
### *Database Management Systems*

TONY FANNING: Database management systems (DBMSs) perform all the functions of the file managers and more. But they're not easy. What distinguishes them from file managers? They simultaneously process information from more than one file, and they're often programmable, letting you query them about that information in a variety of ways.

With a database manager, you can store information in several data files and still have access to all the data in all the files, creating new files (or reports) that combine items selected here and there from any of the data files (which are often called "databases" for these more complex programs). The word used (and often misused) to describe this data handling ability is "relational"; it refers to the ability to combine (or "relate") information from different files that are set up in the form of tables. For example, you can combine address information from one file and sales information from another to create an invoice, if customer names are common to both.

Database management systems are direct descendants of the monster data-processing programs that once lived only on corporate mainframes. They usually require something uncomfortably similar to programming to do their tricks— including getting the information back out of the database. This makes them extremely flexible and adaptable, but often frustrating for nontechnical users. They may exact a long apprenticeship, but if you need flexibility and industrial-strength information management, you'll be glad you have a DBMS.

There are only three choices for beginners when it comes to these serious programs. (1) Decide right now that your organizing job is big and that you ought to devote a large amount of effort (and maybe a large amount of money) to mastering a powerful program. Then go do it. (2) Maybe you aren't cut out to be a computer programmer. Get someone else to set it up for you, and be happy that you can use it. (3) Forget it. You don't need the difficulty that accompanies this kind of complexity.

We're beginning to see new approaches, such as "natural language" add-ons that let you ask for information in English instead of programmer talk. They'll probably make personal computer DBMSs easily useable. We're also beginning to see good database managers included in all-in-one packages (see OPEN ACCESS, p. 109). But we're not there yet.

---

*The flagship, against which all others must be measured (batteries not included) . . .*

## DBASE II

**Version 2.4; Apple II family ● Apple III ● IBM PC/ XT compatibles ● most CP/M machines ● most MS-DOS machines; (contact dealer or Ashton-Tate for specific machine compatibility); copy-protected? NO; $495; Ashton-Tate, 10150 W. Jefferson Blvd., Culver City, CA 90230; 213/204-5570.**

---

**Number of files permitted per database: 2
Records per file: 65,535
Fields per record: 32
Characters per field: 254**

---

TONY FANNING: You can't even talk about personal computer databases without mentioning DBASE II. Even satisfied users will tell why it's the most frustrating program in the world: it's so damn useful—but it's slow; it's so hard to figure out how to do what you want—but you can ... eventually. Despite its limitations, just as with the IBM PC, DBASE became the standard against which we must measure all others, because of the widespread, consistent support that exists for it—it's a marketing success. There's love/hate from everyone who's used it.

Many people who think that "DBASE" is the generic name for any database management system buy it only to find they can't understand it because so much of it is a programming language. Their next step is to take a course; DBASE II courses form a minor industry. There are also about a dozen books

on it so far. And there are outboard programs ("batteries not included") to make it faster where it's slow and easier where it's hard (see "the DBASE family" this page). DBASE II is to database programs as WORDSTAR is to word-processing programs.

Unlike such "free-form" programs as PFS:FILE, DBASE II requires a rigid data structure. You must tell it the name of a field, what kind of data will go into it (text, numeric, or logical), and how many characters the field will occupy. Data entry is reasonably easy (WORDSTAR users will recognize the editing commands), but how do you find the information once it's in? Simpler file managers prompt you or give you a form to fill in. DBASE II gives you a dot. Period. You must type in DBASE II commands just as you would in BASIC. Just as with BASIC, you can string together a series of commands in a file and feed the file to DBASE. But isn't that programming? Right. Flexible if you understand it, frustrating if you don't. Many who have shelled out full dollar for the program never do understand it.

Though DBASE II is a relational database management system, in practice you can only use two files at once. It requires little memory, but sorting is slow, report capabilities are fairly rudimentary, and it requires programming for practically all but the most simple reports. Think long and hard about how you want to interact with DBASE before you buy it. If you don't want "custom" processing, you might want a simpler file manager, or one of the other DBMSs reviewed in this section.

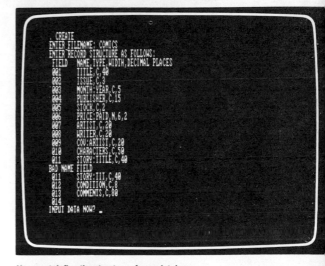

*You must define the structure of your database rigidly before DBASE II can accept data.*

*(continued on p. 86)*

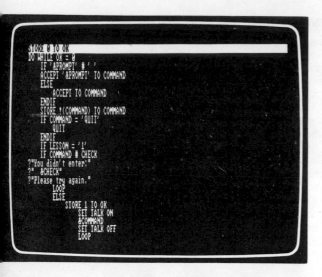

*(continued from p. 85)*

LOUIS JAFFE: PFS:FILE and its REPORT cousin are easy to learn and use (great for teaching beginners) but very limited in total capabilities compared with DBASE. DBASE is a full-fledged, high-level programming language for data manipulation. DBASE programs can be quite cranky to set up and debug, but they make possible all sorts of customized applications. Despite misleading ad campaigns that label it "user friendly," however, DBASE is really best employed by a trained programmer. It's very dependable, having been debugged through several revisions, and there is a large and growing library of DBASE programs, many in the public domain, which are useable without modification by any computer running DBASE.

*DBASE II's programming language makes it extremely flexible, but many people will find it difficult to learn.*

JIM WHITESCARVER: It is the only package I've found that does just about every data-conversion task you're likely to need on a micro. Any report you can print to a file can be loaded into DBASE. If your data outgrows your spreadsheet, you can load it into DBASE. You can capture a report on your micro from a remote host and load it easily into a DBASE file. You can reformat it, and use the data with CBASIC, MBASIC, and 1-2-3 if desired. I'd sure like to find a low-cost DBMS that can do even some of the tricks that DBASE does, but I haven't found one yet.

TONY FANNING: Now that DBASE III is with us, the remaining DBASE II bugs may never be fixed.

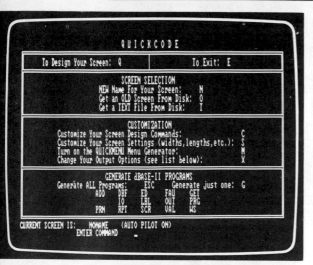

*QUICKCODE lets you "paint" an entry screen and automatically creates DBASE II programs for entering, searching, printing, and modifying data. This main menu gives you some idea of the program's flexibility.*

## THE DBASE FAMILY:

### QUICKCODE

**Version 2.1C; most CP/M machines; 64K ● version 2.2; IBM PC/MS-DOS machines; 180K; copy-protected? YES; $295; Fox & Geller, Inc., 604 Market St., Elmwood Park, NJ 07407; 201/794-8883.**

### DBPLUS

**Version 2.0; most CP/M machines; 64K ● most MS-DOS machines; 128K; copy-protected? NO; $125; Humansoft, 661 Massachusetts Ave., Arlington, MA 02174; 800/451-2502.**

### EVERYMAN'S DATABASE PRIMER

*Everyman's Database Primer*; Robert Byers; 1982; 295 pp.; $19.95; Ashton-Tate, 10150 W. Jefferson Blvd., Culver City, CA 90230; 213/204-5570; or COMPUTER LITERACY.

TONY FANNING: DBASE II is a strange mixture of flexibility and incompleteness. You can program it to do damn near anything, including creating input menus and very complex report programs. But you may not want to take the time or effort to do it. An army of add-on packages now do this for you.

QUICKCODE allows you to "paint" menus and formats on the screen; it then generates DBASE II programs that you can use for data input and report output. As with most program generators, the result is slower operation. And it doesn't really remove the need to understand the DBASE language. The cost can be high, too. I know one sad person who paid about $1000 for DBASE and QUICKCODE so she could generate a menu-driven application that PFS:FILE could easily have handled for $150.

Since DBASE II was originally written for 8-bit micros and never really rewritten for higher capability machines, even its 16-bit versions are slow when sorting. DBPLUS's main attractions are a flexible fast sort and the ability to compress DBASE files (for storage) to less than half their original size. DBASE III claims to remedy the sorting problem. (Many other specialized add-ons and extenders exist, including interfaces for graphics, statistics, and scientific applications.)

Books explaining personal computer programs are an industry in themselves; a large subindustry is books explaining DBASE II. The clearest is **Everyman's Database Primer**. It uses DBASE as an extended example while it teaches the basics of data management with simplicity and humor.

*A faster, more helpful new contender . . .*

## R:BASE 4000

**Version 1.1; IBM PC/XT compatibles ● HP 150 ● DEC Rainbow ● TI Professional; 256K; $495 ● Burroughs computer; CTOS ● NCR computer; BTOS; $795; copy-protected? YES; Microrim, 1750 112th N.E., Bellevue, WA 98004; 206/453-6017.**

**Number of files permitted per database: 40
Records per file: 2.5 billion (limited by file size of operating system)
Fields per database: 400
Characters per field: 1500**

WAYNE CHIN: R:BASE is far easier to use than DBASE II. Its help and prompting facilities make life easier for the new user. Querying facilities match those of DBASE II; basic report-generation capabilities and relational operations are better. R:BASE removes the severe limitations that DBASE II puts on the size of a database and the number of records in it, so the user doesn't have to worry about such details.

But DBASE II has one significantly better feature: The user can define command files that can save lots of keystrokes or build fairly sophisticated applications. R:BASE has a command-file capability, but these commands are limited to what can be typed in from the keyboard. DBASE II provides additional constructs such as IF-ELSE, DO-WHILE, and DO-CASE, that allow for flexible programs that respond automatically to some situations.

TONY FANNING: R:BASE selects at about the same speed as DBASE II and sorts better than twelve times faster on unindexed files. R:BASE has a good help facility, a moderately good demo and tutorial, consistent report generation and input screen building (though a little puzzling the first time through), and a very good set of relational operations. R:BASE can prompt you for most commands; it takes some getting used to, but once you grasp the syntax it becomes quite simple and does not get in the way. Although the writers apparently hoped to reach a less sophisticated audience, the documentation is written in language for programmers. For practical use, you'd better have a serious, "industrial strength" job to do, and you'll need a hard disk.

R:BASE interfaces to RIM (a mainframe relational database manager), MULTIPLAN, VISICALC, 1-2-3, WORDSTAR, MAILMERGE, and packages with ASCII files (including DBASE II).

CLIFF FIGALLO: What first attracted me to R:BASE was its pedigree. In its mainframe incarnation, R:BASE was used by NASA in the space shuttle project and underwent its field testing and debugging there. In its present form, it is a smooth-running, well-thought-out program.

We use it in the research department of the **Whole Earth Software Catalog** to order, receive, process, catalog, disseminate, and track our permanent and temporary holdings—software, books, and hardware included. I definitely recommend using it on a hard disk, not a floppy based system.

It took some trial and error before the database was set up the way we wanted it, but the nicest thing about R:BASE is its forgivingness. It allowed us to radically modify our file structure and field lengths without having to rebuild or re-enter the database.

The syntax of its "English-like" command language took some getting used to: "SELECT ALL FROM VENDORS USING VNAME ADDR1 WHERE VSTAT EQ CA." The optional "prompt screens" helped us avoid syntax confusion during the learning stages. Microrim's natural language option, CLOUT, allows you to state the same command as, "Gimme all the California vendors."

*R:BASE help screens are always just a few keystrokes away.*

*If you aren't sure exactly how an R:BASE command works, it will prompt you through it.*

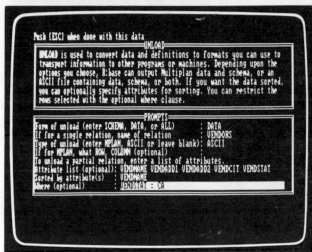

## R:BASE EXTENDED REPORT WRITER (XRW)

**IBM PC/XT compatibles ● HP 150 ● DEC Rainbow ● TI Professional; 256K; ● Burroughs computer; CTOS ● NCR computer; BTOS; copy-protected? NO; $150; Microrim, 1750 112th N.E., Bellevue, WA 98004; 206/453-6017.**

WAYNE CHIN: R:BASE XRW adds report-writing capabilities far beyond those provided in the standard package. XRW's user interface is consistent with R:BASE's—menus are used and online help facilities are available upon request. Users do not have to write a program to generate reports, as they must with DBASE II, although some "programming" may be necessary. The body of a report can refer to more than one database; subsets and sorting are allowed; and limited arithmetical computations can be made. The report can be directed to the printer or to the screen.

|  | STATEMENT | |
|---|---|---|
| 02/01/84 | RIM FUEL COMPANY | PAGE 1 |
|  | 1234 GASOLINE ALLEY | |
|  | BELLEVUE, WA 98001 | |

FOR:

Norris Aviation Service
1432 Airport Way
Renton,    WA 98026

| DESCRIPTION | DATE | QUANTITY | PRICE | AMOUNT |
|---|---|---|---|---|
| Aviation Fuel | 01/13/84 | 15000 GAL | 2.159 | $32,385.00 |
| Lubricant, 10w-30 M/Oil | 01/14/84 | 180 CASE | 24.0 | $4,320.00 |
| Lubricant, 30W HP | 01/17/83 | -04 CASE | 18.00 | -$72.00 |

|  |  |
|---|---|
| Total: | $36,633.00 |
| Tax: | $2,564.31 |
| Previous Balance: | $1,085.22 |
| Amount Due: | $40,282.53 |

*Complex tabular reports are XRW's forte.*

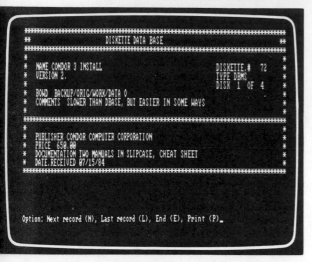

```
*******************************************
**              DISKETTE DATA BASE         **
*******************************************
*                                          *
*  NAME CONDOR 3 INSTALL        DISKETTE.# 72  *
*  VERSION 2.                   TYPE DBMS      *
*                               DISK 1 OF 4    *
*  BOWD  BACKUP/ORIG/WORK/DATA O                *
*  COMMENTS  SLOWER THAN DBASE, BUT EASIER IN SOME WAYS *
*                                          *
*                                          *
*  PUBLISHER CONDOR COMPUTER CORPORATION    *
*  PRICE  650.00                            *
*  DOCUMENTATION TWO MANUALS IN SLIPCASE, CHEAT SHEET *
*  DATE. RECEIVED 07/15/84                  *
*******************************************

Option; Next record (N), Last record (L), End (E), Print (P)_
```

*Like many file managers and DBMSs, CONDOR can find information for you when you fill in a screen form.*

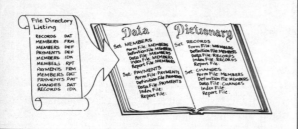

*CONDOR's manual explains how the program's Data Dictionary groups files into a dataset, speeding up sort/select operations. CONDOR also lets you modify the Data Dictionary directly, without a lot of hassle.*

*Hey! Look over here! I can do that, too. Hey, guys . . .*

## CONDOR III

**Version 2.10; computers using 8080/8086 microprocessors; PC DOS, MS-DOS, CP/M-86, Xenix, TurboDos; 80K ● Version 2.11; computers using Z80/8080 microprocessors; CP/M-86, CP/M, MP/M-80, CDOS, TurboDos, PC DOS, MS-DOS; 64K; copy-protected? NO; $650; Condor Computer Corp., 2051 S. State St., Ann Arbor, MI 48104; 313/769-3988.**

---

**Number of files permitted per database: 1**
**Records per file: 65,534**
**Fields per record: 127**
**Characters per field: 127**

---

TONY FANNING: CONDOR III is similar to DBASE II in operation, scope, and (in the mid-range) capability. It, too, allows commands for searching, updating, sorting, and so on, to be strung together into programs, although DBASE offers more in its programming language. While CONDOR allows more fields per record and is slightly easier to use than DBASE II, it is generally considered slower and less flexible, and it is not as widely supported. Documentation is both copious and uneven—not unusual for a DBMS.

JOHN RICKS: After about 30 hours learning CONDOR on my DEC Rainbow, I am fairly proficient. I develop maintenance management systems for a large pulp mill. The first was a mill lubrication program with several thousand entries and more than 250 pages in the finished report. CONDOR III has a very good report writer; when I need a new application of CONDOR, I design the output report first, then set up a data record to match the report. This takes about 20 minutes to prepare on the computer before I can input data.

DAVID DEGENER: CONDOR III operates by commands—42 in all, but you use no more than a dozen very often to enter, change, and manipulate data. The commands are reasonably easy. For example, to change a group of records in a dataset (CONDOR's term for a data file) you name the fields and specify their content. For example: "UPDATE dataset WHRE field1 IS blue AND field2 IS red." With "Select" and "Project" you can create new "result" datasets from records or fields in existing datasets. "Join" can combine information from two datasets with different structures when they have at least one field in common. "Sort" can arrange records alphabetically or numerically by as many as 32 fields at once.

CONDOR's fields are too short to manage much text, but the program is good at manipulating numbers. "Compute" fills one field with a value computed from other fields. "Stax" does statistics. "Tabulate" summarizes, giving you totals, averages, and maximum and minimum values. And "Post" operates across datasets to replace, add, or subtract the contents of one dataset's fields with the contents of the same fields in another dataset—an extremely useful command for business applications.

*If WORDSTAR is your idea of wonderful, you might like this . . .*

## INFOSTAR +

**IBM PC/XT compatibles; 96K ● MS-DOS computers including TRS-80 2000, DEC Rainbow, TI Professional; 96K; hard disk recommended; copy-protected? NO; $595; MicroPro International Corp., 33 San Pablo Ave., San Rafael, CA 94903; 415/499-1200.**

---

**Number of files permitted per database: 255**
**Records per file: 65,535**
**Fields per record: 245**
**Characters per field: 120**

---

TONY FANNING: INFOSTAR comes from MicroPro, the WORDSTAR (p. 56) people. It can easily move reports to WORDSTAR for editing, and its control-commands are similar to WORDSTAR's (though confusingly not identical). If you have other packages in the -STAR family (like CALCSTAR, p. 74), you might want it, since data can be transferred among them. Or you might want something cheaper and easier to use.

INFOSTAR's large records, fast sorting, extensive reporting, and data-entry controls may make it attractive to some, particularly in production environments. But its confusing complexity may turn others away. The creation of databases and sophisticated reports is definitely not for beginners, though once it's set up, novices can use INFOSTAR.

BILL GUNS: My first impression is that any database manager that requires three manuals is daunting. That is also my second, third, and fourth impression.

*Automatic starter,
    automatic transmission . . .*

## ASAP FIVE

**IBM PC/XT compatibles; 192K; copy-protected?
YES; $275; ASAP Systems, Inc., 2425 Porter St.,
Soquel, CA 95073; 800/247-2727 or, in CA,
800/345-2727.**

---

**Number of files permitted per database: no limit
Records per file: 65,534
Fields per record: no limit
Characters per field: 40**

---

CHARLES SPEZZANO: Although I have
semimastered several database management
programs, I continued to manage my
hundred or so psychiatric patient records and
300 newsletter subscriptions (SPCU; see
p. 47) with only a good memory for the
location of papers and an occasional frantic
search for misplaced information. I'm a
database resister, rather than a connoisseur.
But I like ASAP FIVE very much.

ASAP is a relational database management
system with an automatic starter and
transmission instead of a crank and clutch.
Although it comes with an eighty-page
manual, the twelve-page tutorial and one-
page "mini manual" are probably enough to
get you up and running. Onscreen helps
guide you the rest of the way. ASAP asks you
straightforward questions, gives clear
directions, and does as much of the work of
data storage and retrieval as I can imagine a
program doing.

.Other database systems demand a high
degree of organization from you before you
even use them, but ASAP allows you to be
extremely disorganized. Like my real-life
habits, my ASAP databases are heaping
masses of information until I ask ASAP to pull
one together in some specific way. Then it
gives me a particular set of facts in a second,
or a longer report in a minute. It further
tolerates my personal disorganization by
allowing me easily to redefine fields and field
entries, records, files, and report formats
without losing any data. I did not have to
learn to think like a database in order to use
ASAP. I think like me and it thinks
databasically.

ASAP's "Custom Reports" are designed in
question-and-answer procedures;
rudimentary word processing functions are
included for creating a "free-form" area of the
report. You can modify Custom Report forms
to add, delete, or move data and free-form
text as many times as you like. You can't
stack commands (it doesn't have a query
language), but with ASAP FIVE you don't
need to.

I asked Tom, a real estate agent, and George,
a CPA, both of whom use ASAP daily, for their
impressions. Tom, who had never used any
other program on his IBM XT, was entering
real data into ASAP after two hours of
practice. George uses ASAP for everything
from complex client tax records to his stamp
collection. He and his staff are currently
entering 300 time sheets a week, and as they
approach a thousand records, the search time
for a single record still appears to be in the
half-second range.

*Your friends all have short names—Ron, Jimmy,
Nancy, Henry—so you set up a seven-character
first name field. Then you meet Zbigniew
Brzezinski. With one function key (F9 = MODIFY
FIELD), ASAP FIVE lets you expand any field length
on this data entry screen. Zbigniew fits!*

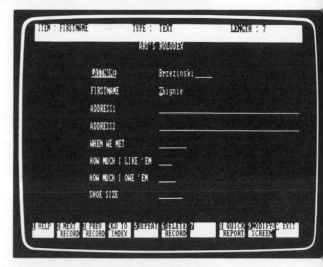

*A little slow, but handles text nicely . . .*

## SEQUITUR

**Version 3.20; IBM PC/XT compatibles; 256K;
copy-protected? NO; $795; Pacific Software
Manufacturing Co., 2608 Eighth Street, Berkeley,
CA 94710; 415/540-5000.**

---

**Number of files permitted per database: 750
Records per file: no limit
Fields per record: 1024
Characters per field: no limit**

---

TONY FANNING: SEQUITUR is another
serious DBMS, and the very definition of a
relational database management system. It
has several likable features: you can enter/
manipulate data in two forms (see picture);
you can add text to its variable-length fields
as an afterthought; you can easily create
detailed tabular reports of great complexity;
and you don't need to write programs, since
everything is presented in tables. You trade
this flexibility for speed (MS-DOS machines
barely give SEQUITUR the resources to do its
job; 68000-based micros might make it a joy
to use). You really need to be dedicated, since
all this is explained with "relational-DBMS
talk." A pleasant program for programmers;
masterable by nonprogrammers with some
effort.

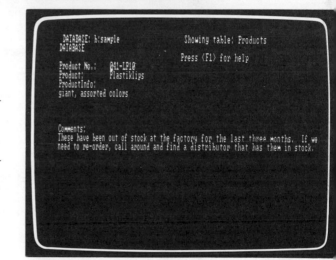

*SEQUITUR displays data in either tabular
form . . .*

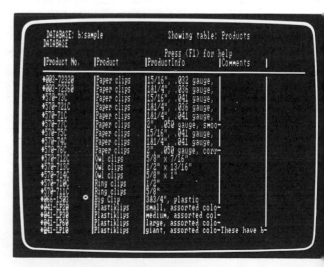

*. . . or in expanded form. Large text fields are
easy to handle.*

## *Garbage Bags*

TONY FANNING: Much of what we really need to organize—words, notes, ideas—can't be categorized precisely enough to fit into tables or other rigid structures. Nor can we organize them easily with word processors, which are really tools for formatting our words on paper, not for cataloging, saving, searching, and combining them in idea blocks.

But there are programs that manage text in many of the ways that a file manager handles structured data, and there will be many more in the future. These new programs for helping us corral what we really love—our thoughts and ideas—are much more fun to use than the cut-and-dried file managers and DBMSs we might need to organize our businesses.

There are three types of "garbage bags." First are programs like SUPERFILE and DATAFAX, which we might call indexers—they're electronic highlighting pens. They allow you to organize blocks of unstructured information—like long text passages—by marking key words and phrases within them. You can quickly retrieve a whole text item later by knowing only one of the key words or phrases you marked it with. They're especially suited

to academic scholarship, and probably won't satisfy a more general need.

Then there are file managers that can handle blocks of text easily, allowing you to create (almost) free-form screens for entering information. PFS:FILE (p. 80) can do so within its limitations, but freer-form text-file managers like NOTEBOOK let us lay out an entry-screen form and later search for any word or phrase we entered in it.

A few database management systems, like SEQUITUR (p. 89), are designed for organizing text as well as structured data. Because text can be of any length, such a DBMS must permit fields of any (variable) length, and dealing with this complication can slow performance down considerably.

Finally, there are outlining tools, like the remarkable THINKTANK (p. 92) and FRAMEWORK (p. 110). They let you arrange headlines and chunks of text in an outline form, with subordinate headline/text chunks visually "indented" under others. You can then move text easily by moving the headline associated with it—great for brainstorming and rearranging presentations, articles, manuals, and general documents.

---

*Like a highlighter pen . . .*

## DATAFAX

**Version 2.6; Apple II family; 64K; $249 ● Version 2.7; Apple III; $249 ● IBM PC/XT; Pascal; 64K ● Corvus Concept ● Sage; $299 ● Version 3.0; IBM PC/XT; MS-DOS; 96K; $299; copy-protected? NO; Link Systems, 1452 2nd Street, Santa Monica, CA 90401; 213/453-8921.**

---

**Number of files permitted per database: 3000**
**Records per file: 255**
**Fields per record: limited by screen**
**Characters per field: limited by screen**

*You can enter text into DATAFAX randomly (without fields) and go back later to search for key words—all recipes with "1 cup cream" in this database, for instance. Though it's not shown here, you could highlight individual words for easier sorting later.*

GIL SYSWERDA: DATAFAX (version 2.4a) is one of the most useful programs I have. It absorbs all the little facts I want to remember but don't know how to file. It allows very easy updating, retrieval, format-free data entry, and error recovery. It also comes with a built-in text editor. DATAFAX will not allow a database to span volumes, and volumes cannot span diskettes, but volumes can be as large as 16 megabytes, so if you have a hard disk . . . .

The logical organization within DATAFAX is that of a folder. There can be as many folders per database as will fit. Each folder contains pages, of which, again, there can be any number.

Each page contains exactly as much information as will fit on one physical screen. You enter data into pages with a text editor. There are absolutely no format restrictions except those you invent yourself. When you save folders, you save them with associated key words. These key words either come from the text (you point them out to the system) or are arbitrarily entered.

You find folders by specifying key words in logical combinations, and can display, print, or edit them. If the system is used as intended, most folders contain only one page, and that page contains only a few lines. The key words hold things together.

If I read a magazine article (I read a lot) that I think I might want as a reference later, I enter onto one DATAFAX page the source of the article, the topic, and a very brief summary. I then key word it in every possible way. If in the future I want to know what articles

(books) I have read about topics X and Y, I can find out in seconds from DATAFAX.

CHARLES SPEZZANO: Record retrieval in DATAFAX is very sophisticated. You create intricate strings of key words connected by "ands" and "ors." You can use ranges and wild cards and nested parentheses for sorting. If you know the key word, you can find a record in two seconds. Key words do not have to be added in a separate step after you create a record. Any word in your text can be easily tagged as soon as you have typed it. All these key words go into a list into which you can also add words not in the record itself.

JAMES V. MCGEE: Using DATAFAX is like writing a note to yourself and highlighting all the words you might use later to retrieve the note. You can start a new database without any prior planning; just load in a disk and start entering and filing data. You can let the structure evolve as your information does.

System performance is generally good, but setting up a new disk (which you must do before entering any data) is frustratingly slow. When I timed it, it took well over five minutes. If you are sufficiently impatient you may never wait to use the program itself. Also, because it runs under the UCSD p-system, DATAFAX uses the disks much more heavily than PC DOS programs, resulting in slower operation.

The manuals are extensive and well written in a refreshingly human and personal style. They describe other users' experiences and suggest a variety of clever ways to take advantage of DATAFAX's unusual design philosophy—in enough depth to trigger your own thinking on potential uses.

*Free-form notes, bibliographies . . .*

# SUPERFILE

CP/M version for Apple, Kaypro 2, 4 & 10, Osborne 1 and Executive, Xerox 810, 8-inch format; 64K ● PC DOS/MS-DOS version for IBM PC compatibles, Eagle, TI Professional, Zenith 100; 64K; copy-protected? NO; $195; FYI, Inc., 4202 Spicewood Springs Rd. #204, Austin, TX 78759; 512/346-0133.

Number of files permitted per database: 100/disk
Records per file: limited by disk storage capacity
Fields per record: 250 keywords/record
Characters per field: 64 characters/keyword

TONY FANNING: SUPERFILE (and its more expensive big sister, FYI 3000) lets you index free-form blocks of text created with your word processing program, rather than requiring data that's organized into fields and records. One regrettable limitation is its need to re-index whenever you modify a text block.

However, it can index over more than one diskette, so a group of references can grow to a fair size and still be searchable.

PAUL DECHOW: SUPERFILE is good for managing notes and making bibliographic records. Its biggest improvement in its new version is the automatic re-indexing feature, allowing data from a new file on the data disk to be indexed into an existing database by a quick and easy menu-driven procedure. Other recent improvements include an automatic check of dictionary and index files whenever you start it to make sure these files are intact and in good working order; a utility that appends parts of files to the ends of other files without writing over them; and the ability to keep up to 100 datafiles on single disk (of course, databases can be made up of many disks), which takes advantage of higher-capacity disk systems.

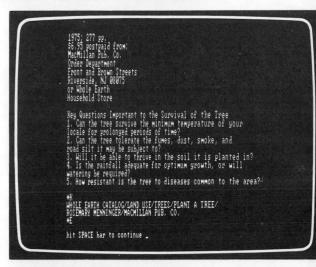

*SUPERFILE scans text created by a word-processor for key words and phrases, then sorts and indexes them—as here, in excerpts from books reviewed in* Whole Earth Catalog.

---

*For CP/M computers . . .*

# NOTEBOOK

CP/M-2.2 machines including Kaypro 2, Epson QX 10, Morrow; 64K ● IBM PC compatibles; PC DOS, CP/M-86; 128K ● MS-DOS machines including Victor 9000, NEC, Eagle, DEC Rainbow, Zenith Z-100; 128K; copy-protected? NO; $150; Digital Marketing, 2363 Boulevard Circle, Walnut Creek, CA 94595; 800/826-2222.

Number of files permitted per database: 1
Records per file: limited by disk capacity
Fields per record: 20
Characters per field: 500 (CP/M); 4000 (CP/M-86 and MS-DOS)

CHARLES SPEZZANO: NOTEBOOK stores and retrieves text. A single record can hold up to 32,000 characters, divided among up to 20 fields. It offers online help, sorts records by any field, and allows you to edit records without damaging the database. You can retrieve records using any item in any field. The word processor uses WORDSTAR commands, and NOTEBOOK will read WORDSTAR files.

Drawbacks: You cannot change data files from within the program; you have to exit first. NOTEBOOK is not the easiest program to

use. There is no word-wrap feature in the word processor; each line accepts only 57 characters and the program beeps to warn you at the 54th character. To get more than 57 characters into a field you must first go into insert mode and then press the return key at the end of every line.

Unlike DATAFAX, which is menu driven and organized around your selected key words, NOTEBOOK interacts with you by question and answer. You go to a "select" screen, which lists all the field names in your data file. You then pick a field, and tell NOTEBOOK the search parameters for that field: since NOTEBOOK's forte is text material, you often select simply by telling it to find all those records with a particular word in that field, but you can also select by functions, such as equal to, not equal to, greater than or equal to, less than or equal to, greater than, and less than. You can also sort on two fields.

DATAFAX has a much better editor than NOTEBOOK, but handles each screen of information separately. With NOTEBOOK, the whole document is continuous.

TONY FANNING: We recommend NOTEBOOK only for CP/M computers. On MS-DOS computers, go with DATAFAX or PFS:FILE.

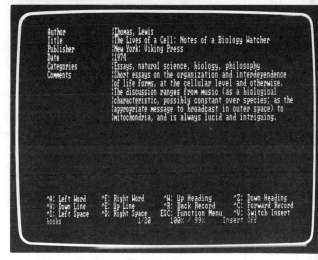

*NOTEBOOK lets you fill in text into large fields, and use the same form to search for the text.*

You can expand your THINKTANK outline easily by pressing the + key, or . . .

. . . collapse your outline so you can see the big picture.

*Outlining with both sides of the brain . . .*

## THINKTANK

**Version 1.001; Apple II family; 64K; $150 ● Apple Macintosh (THINKTANK 128); $145 ● IBM PC/XT compatibles; 256K; $195; copy-protected? NO (Apple II); YES (others); Living Videotext, Inc., 2432 Charleston Rd., Mountain View, CA 94043; 415/964-6300.**

TONY FANNING: Shortly after I started using full-screen editors (nowadays called "word processors"), I discovered that the way to write with them was to start typing one-liners to prime the pump, then indent some and move them under others. Sort of like making an outline. Then I typed in between the one-liners until I said what I needed to say. Then I agonized and rearranged, using fairly clumsy block moves. Then I edited.

Later I was introduced to "patterning" by Tony Buzan (**Use Both Sides of Your Brain**, E.P. Dutton, 1976). This kind of organizing is topologically equivalent to outlining, and visual to boot. It generated lots of beginnings for me, but I can't write much on a pattern, and recopying the pattern into outline form is a nuisance.

THINKTANK on my IBM PC combines the best of both methods. When I use it, I start with a blank screen with the word HOME at the top. I furiously type one-liners ("headlines") at the screen. These are the basic ideas of the outline I will create, if I already have a good idea of the structure of my ideas. If I don't, and this is where TT really helps, it's stream-of-consciousness outpouring. I think of this as my brainstorming phase.

After a while I notice that some ideas in the headlines are contained in others, and I simply move them under the main ideas using the cursor-control keys. It's as easy as shuffling little bits of paper, but gives me a far greater feeling of a growing structure. Soon I have subordinate ideas neatly indented under other ideas, perhaps to many levels of subordination. It begins to look like an outline.

Every headline followed by subordinate ideas has a + (plus sign) in front of it, and every headline with none has a − (minus sign). If I position the "bar cursor" over one of the plussed headlines and press the minus key, all subordinate material disappears (I can bring it back with a plus). This neatly lines up all my main topics. If one seems out of order I can easily move it. If something's missing I can add it, or drop down a level and promote what was a subordinate idea to mainhood.

At any point I can enter text as "paragraphs" attached to any headline. In fact, I can import whole files of text from outside my "outline." I can move big chunks of ideas around, and I do. When I'm done I can print out, or view, or file the outline to any depth of detail, or the entire document with all text. Neat.

What's it good for? Starting to write. Writer's block. Refining expositions or presentations. Keeping notes that you can use later. Brainstorming. Revenge on your seventh-grade English teacher, who taught you what an outline is, but never taught you how flat-out useful it can be.

PHILIP ELMER-DEWITT: Best use I've found so far: to lay out the stories I write for **Time** magazine. **Time** pieces tend to be highly structured, so it helps to know where you're going before you start. My thoughts, alas, tend to issue forth helter-skelter, bearing little resemblance either to normal human discourse or to the shape of a typical **Time** feature.

So the night before I'm scheduled to write a story, I type my ideas into THINKTANK as they arise. Then I use the program's outlining features to rearrange them, putting the A's with the A's and the B's with the B's. The key ideas tend to bubble to the highest levels of the outline while the supporting details fall to lower levels.

When I'm done, what I've got is a list of key or topic ideas buttressed with my best quotes and anecdotes. Then I write, using the outline as a guide. Even when I forget to refer to the outline, it seems to shape the story. On occasion I've gone back to look at a THINKTANK file I'd forgotten about and found the resemblance between topic ideas and finished **Time** paragraphs uncanny.

Once I used the program to outline a speech. I found I didn't even have to flesh it out on a word processor; simply spoke *ex tempore* from the THINKTANK printout.

I don't think I ever got the hang of outlining back in high school. I tended to lose my structure in the flood of illustrative detail. Now that this program has made outlining something of a game, I'm much more likely to do it. Perhaps that's the key.

## Organizing Your Computer Environment

TONY FANNING: Shortly after you start doing more than one thing on your personal computer, you will notice that the computer becomes a place. Like your desktop it gets messy. Like your car it has unlovable features. But the real trouble arrives as you start to use more than one computer program. For example: the universe of programs is divided into two camps: one, the "Wonderful Destructive Backspace" camp, believes that when you stretch your right pinkie to hit the "backspace" key it should delete the last character you typed and then back the cursor up; the other, the "Terrific Non-destructive Backspace" camp, believes that the cursor should back up without deleting. Either would be easy to live with if it were the only one.

But no-o-o, life isn't that easy. Very popular programs like DBASE II (p. 85), WORDSTAR (p. 56), and PFS: FILE (p. 80) believe in the Non-destructive Backspace. Your operating system, which you use between programs, probably uses the Destructive Backspace, and so do a whole slew of other programs like 1-2-3 (p. 67). To move between programs, you have to shift gears as in a Model T on the hills of San Francisco. You may have noticed. Are you crazy yet?

When you get to this state, you understand what "computer environment" means, because yours is messed up. The problem: all programs act different from all other programs unless someone has taken the effort to make them operate similarly. Your solution? You can stay within a family of interlocking programs (for example, PFS:, -STAR, VISI-, MULTI-), turn to the Managing section (pp. 106-121) and look for an integrated "all-in-one" or an integrator (such as DESQ)—or you can take control of the environment. What if you could redefine what the backspace key does, so that it always does the same thing no matter what program you're using? What if you could redefine *any* key combination (say, CONTROL-SHIFT-N) so that when you pressed it, it would send your program any string of characters (say the phrase "non-destructive backspace")? That's what a "key-changer" program does for you. Some do a lot more.

---

*Organize your MS-DOS/CP/M computer environment . . .*

## PROKEY

**Version 3.0; IBM PC compatibles; copy-protected? YES; $130; RoseSoft, 4710 University Way N.E., No. 601, Seattle, WA 98105; 206/524-2350.**

## SMARTKEY II

**CP/M 80 machines ● CP/M 86 machines ● PC/MS-DOS machines; copy-protected? NO; $90; Software Research Technologies, Inc., 3757 Wilshire Blvd., Suite 211, Los Angeles, CA 90010; 213/384-5430.**

---

ART KLEINER: "Key-changers" are customizing tools. They'll organize confusingly diverse programs into a single syntax; they'll streamline strings of complex commands (macros) into one keystroke; they'll turn numeric keypads, like those on the Kaypro, into usable function keys; they'll toss in frequently-used bits of boilerplate text.

TONY FANNING: The simplest differences between programs can be deadly. I use two programs daily. In one, a CONTROL-Y restores deleted text; in the second, a CONTROL-Y deletes the line the cursor is in. How many times have I deleted lines forever when I thought I was bringing back text? Many. With PROKEY, I redefined what CONTROL-Y does so that now it always does the same thing.

ART KLEINER: We recommend two keychangers: PROKEY for PC/MS-DOS computers and SMARTKEY for CP/M systems. They're better documented and more flexible than KEYNOTE, KEYSWAPPER and SPEED KEY. SMARTKEY runs on PC/MS-DOS computers, but the following comparison shows why we pick PROKEY. SMARTKEY does have two advantages: it's not copy-protected, and its manual is the first I've seen brilliant enough to make me want to credit the author—Paul Golding.

RICHARD PLATT: PROKEY uses about 10K of resident memory; SMARTKEY about 2.25K. Additional memory (in 1K increments) must be allotted as you add macros. Only if you create an extensive library of boilerplate paragraphs are you apt to run into trouble storing PROKEY in your memory.

Most of your macros will be created on the fly in the middle of a program; for boilerplate, use a separate word processor and store the text as a macro. SMARTKEY and PROKEY both allow you to do this, but with SMARTKEY, if you make a mistake in a particular string of commands, there's no turning back—you must start over. With PROKEY you can at least backspace and correct your error. And PROKEY lets you combine previously defined macros within your new one, another real time saver. What's more, you get instant feedback with PROKEY; your commands are interpreted and executed as you record your keystrokes. With SMARTKEY, you're never sure if you made a mistake until you use your macro later.

A unique feature of PROKEY is its "One Finger OFF/ON" mode, which allows disabled people with limited mobility (or just a mouth-stick) to, for instance, type control characters by pressing CONTROL, then (instead of simultaneously) the following key.

Certain programs will not run with PROKEY; the manual mentions VISIFILE, WORDVISION, XYWRITE, and "certain terminal emulators." And acknowledges problems with some ramdrives and spoolers, including Quadram's. The SMARTKEY manual mentions only that it's not compatible with XSUB and DESPOOL by Digital Research.

PROKEY includes sample on-disk macros for WORDSTAR, VISICALC, BASIC, and DBASE II. SMARTKEY includes samples for WORDSTAR, PERFECT WRITER, SELECT,

screenwriting, and the Kaypro numeric keypad in a separate book they sell, **Screen Smarts** (Paul Golding; 2nd ed., 1984; 120 pp.; $15.95; Central Computer Products, 860 Central Ave., Fillmore, CA 93015; 805/524-4189; or COMPUTER LITERACY). Both include Dvorak keyboard files. Articles listing macro configurations for particular programs (especially WORDSTAR) appear frequently in **PC World** and **PC** magazine, most often written by PROKEY users. Whatever the relative merits of PROKEY and SMARTKEY now, they're in stiff competition. Watch for updates.

---

*Apple II + keyboard enhancer . . .*

## VIDEX ENHANCER II

**Apple II family (requires Revision 7 or greater motherboard); $149; Videx, Inc., 1105 N.E. Circle Blvd., Corvallis, OR 97330; 503/758-0521.**

---

DR. DOBB'S JOURNAL STAFF: The VIDEX plug-in board gives the Apple II + a 128-character type-ahead buffer and a 512-character keyboard redefining capability. VIDEX's auto-repeat function adds on to the Apple's repeat key; if you hold a key down along with the repeat key, it really zips. VIDEX gives you all printable characters, like "curly brackets"—{ }—and it's not too hard to remember where they are once you learn them. VIDEX works with every program we've tried. Some of us like it better than the Apple IIe keyboard.

TONY FANNING: An army of single-purpose programs can also help organize your computer environment—cataloging your diskettes, helping you browse through hard-disk files, back up your files, etc. These programs are reviewed under "Utilities," p. 174.

## ACCOUNTING

### Marsha Mather-Thrift, Domain Editor

MARSHA MATHER-THRIFT: Lots of us have fantasies about gentle-hearted computers that work patiently all night at quarter's end and tax time, efficiently organizing stacks of calculations scribbled down during the course of the year. Although it's true that computers were designed to save enormous amounts of drudgery, it's easy to be taken in by visions of instant invoices and automatically paid bills. The truth, as every computer initiate knows, is not so rosy.

But fantasy is close to truth, and what's true here is the idea that computers *keep things in place for you.* Busy offices have a way of swallowing important papers—especially client charges and billings that need to get out on time to keep a small business solvent. Good accounting software not only keeps things in place, it saves time in repetitive entry and calculations as well as in locating errors and running calculator tapes. Being able to track expenses, materials, and labor hours is probably more vital for my small firm than it is for a vast corporation like Bechtel. And it's more vital still for the company that maintains an inventory and depends on stocking the goods in greatest demand. Accounting software can save you money, let you know quickly if you're losing money, and help you plan better ways to save in the future.

Yet businesses are as unique as people, so the problem is to choose an accounting system flexible enough to fit individual requirements. A retail farm-equipment business isn't likely to have the same accounting needs as a nonprofit organization or a law office. Even the fellow who builds cabinets to sell at wholesale prices probably won't share accounting needs with his neighbor who builds half a dozen custom-paneled interiors a year.

Computer-store salespeople, who often present themselves as consultants, are really creatures of the sales trade. Most of them don't understand quite what it is that makes your business unique, and most are unwilling to recommend software they don't happen to sell—a basic flaw in their consulting role.

In this section, we've set out to give you a range of accounting packages to mull over. We've left out software that merely duplicates your checkbook or tracks expenses and taxes in a limited way. And we've ignored spreadsheet programs that many people will tell you are complete enough to fill small-business needs. (They aren't. We've covered these in Analyzing, pages 64-77, where use value catches up with cost.)

At the most basic level—personal finance—we've included programs (DOLLARS AND SENSE and MANAGING YOUR MONEY) that offer order-loving creatures a chance to organize their financial existence from birth to retirement. For the more complex needs of small business bookkeeping, we've included some inexpensive accounting packages (BOOKS!, BPI, and THE ACCOUNTING PARTNER) which provide most standard functions and reports. We've isolated good tax preparation and planning programs for home and business. Then, for those who require interactive accounting and a variety of special reports, we've taken a look at more sophisticated packages (PEACHTREE and IUS EASYBUSINESS) that are well worth the investment for retailers (and others) who depend on inventory control and discount buying to beef up profit margins.

### *Buyer Beware*

Treat your search for good business software the way you would

---

STEWART BRAND: Accounting is so much of the essence, we pretend it isn't by making fun of accountants. To get a realistic sense of how important the matter is to your business or home, imagine that you've had a set of accounting programs working for about six months and you decide it's the wrong set. The extended agony of transition to new accounting software—what Jerry Weinberg calls "out-conversion" on p. 6—is a measure of your dependence. The same is true, of course, of your accounting *people.*

I rank accountants with librarians—unsung heroes and heroines of civilization, worth far more to us all than lawyers, architects, doctors, and others in the glory trades.

BARBARA ROBERTSON: Marsha Mather-Thrift is particularly well-suited to oversee this section. She's currently juggling two careers: researcher and office manager for an international consulting firm, and writer of fiction—short stories and a novel. Occasionally, when she has time, she does free-lance work (like this section of the [nonfiction] **Catalog** or book reviews for the **San Francisco Chronicle**) while managing the finances of her enterprise along with those of her family. With no time for false promises, she brings a critical and cautious eye to programs claiming to whisk accounting problems away.

Marsha realized early that computers would be necessary at the pharmaceutical consulting firm where she works. There a small number of people process tons of information for U.S. and European clients trying to win FDA approval for their formulas. She began automating their office with CompuCorp's dedicated word-processing system and had just begun evaluating accounting programs for the office when I asked her to take on our Accounting domain. (She settled on BOOKS!, p. 100.)

I was astonished when she said she'd give up her fiction-writing hours for a few months and, with six-month-old Caitlin in backpack, take on the project. And delighted . . . she had exactly the perspective I wanted for the section, and lord, can she research and write—important qualities for a domain whose copy deadlines fell in the middle of income tax season.

*Marsha Mather-Thrift*

an exciting but dangerous safari. Listen to advice from local experts, but keep your mind on your own crucial needs. Here are a few ideas.

### English

Every accounting program worth a second glance should have a manual in plain English that doesn't send you searching through volumes for set-up instructions. If you have employees, this is especially crucial, or you'll end up as an unwilling participant in the computer-support business.

### Flexibility

Look for flexibility in the areas where you need it most. If your business requires tracking interest on overdue debts, for example, make sure accounts receivable can "age" balances at several different rates. (Most in the upper price range age at 30-60-90 and over 90 days.) If you have extensive accounts payable and can save money by making early payments, make sure your accounting system can provide you with reports that summarize stock on hand, discount payment dates, and vendor payment history. (OPEN SYSTEMS will do this.) If you bill clients each month for services rendered, check to see that your invoicing will let you tailor a description of services for each individual client job. (BOOKS! does this.) It's also a good idea to go over your needs with your accountant and decide where you stand to gain the most from improved management.

### Support

Retail software dealers seldom have the staff to provide attentive follow-up. Some vendors—the IBM Product Center, for instance —have a ten-day trial and return policy. If you can't take the program out of the store, make sure before buying that you look it over several times, get some references from people who are using it, and find out what backup you can expect from the manufacturer. (A direct phone call to the company can tell you a lot about what to expect in the way of future support.) Some programs, like CHAMPION, are sold in a demo version that will allow you hands-on testing before you buy the whole system.

### Safeguards

Safeguards against loss of data are crucial in accounting, especially in multi-user situations where a single file must be simultaneously shared by two operators. You can run a crude safety test by having two people attempt to access the same file at once.

Some safety features can create complications. Programs that follow standard accounting practice won't allow you to delete or edit entries. Instead, you must enter reversing entries to correct errors (it's the standard embezzlement-discourager). This is no problem if you are an accountant and can juggle figures in the general ledger, but it can be a serious drawback for less agile users.

Once you've isolated your software candidates, eat, sleep, and work with them until you know exactly what they will and won't do. The highest cost of automating your accounting system lies in the time it takes to set up your reports and chart of accounts and enter your data. You don't want to do that work twice.

### Hardware

A really workable accounting system requires a lot of disk space

—in most cases, a hard disk (Corvus is one of the better ones). Putting your accounts on fifteen or sixteen floppies might be an interesting challenge at first, but you can be sure it will be a headache later. For relaxed small businesses, though, floppies may be entirely practical. PEACHTREE ACCOUNTING, for example, is designed with this in mind. If you don't yet own a computer system, plan on buying one with as much memory as you can afford. Don't plan on doing anything but the simplest home accounting with less than 128K. Screen resolution and keyboard set-up are also important considerations if you work long hours on your machine. And nearly every accounting program requires a 132-column printer. Some home finance programs produce acceptable reports on an 80-column printer, but only if it has a compressed print mode.

Remember: Think about the areas where you need increased control in your business and focus on those. If you don't already own a personal computer, find the right software first. Plot out what the computer will actually save you in tracking down figures and producing invoices and checks. Then choose the program that covers your major needs. Make sure you won't have to make radical changes in your accounting system to use it, but be ready to bend a little.

Think about how much you may have to pay your CPA to double check your figures. Make sure the audit trails are good enough that you can easily follow each item through its travels from entry to postings to reports. And just to be safe, it's not a bad idea to keep dual books for the first few months—until you know that your program works the way you hoped it would.

### Books, magazines, and search services

Books and magazines are still the most useful resources for finding what you want in software. For approximately $150, a computer search service like SOFSEARCH (San Antonio, Texas) can provide you with lists of available software narrowed by application or computer. Good magazines, such as **LIST**, do the same and are cheaper, but they require more effort from you. For specifics, track down product reviews. (Most reviews are uniformly enthusiastic, so read between the lines.)

If you're a beginner, start with **The Personal Computer in Business Book**, by Peter McWilliams (1984; 299 pp.; $9.95; Quantum Press, Doubleday & Co., Inc., 501 Franklin Avenue, Gardon City, NY 11530; 212/053 4490), a good general purpose book with a glance at accounting and a useful section on hardware. Another entertaining and helpful (though slightly dated) guide is Nicholas and Sharon Rosa's **Small Computers for the Small Businessman** (1980, 344 pages; $16.95 from dilithium Press, 8285 S.W. Nimbus, Suite 151, P. O. Box 606, Beaverton, OR 97075; 800/547-1842). **How to Buy Software**, by Alfred Glossbrenner (reviewed on p. XXX), is the best we've seen anywhere for mapping the software-search territory as a whole. If you know what you want and simply need more particulars, Sheldon Needle, an accountant with several years of corporate experience, has written **A Guide to Accounting Software for Microcomputers** (1984, 147 pages; $75 from Computer Training Services, 5900 Tudor Lane, Rockville, MD 20852; 301/468-4800)—an expensive, in-depth analysis of Champion, Peachtree, BPI, State of the Art, and others. For accountants who are ready to plunge into the PC world, two good books are available: **Microcomputers for Accountants**, by Theodore Needleman (1983, 186 pages; $14.95 from Prentice-Hall, Englewood Cliffs, NJ 07632; 201/592-2640), and **Computers in Accountants' Offices**, by Gordon E. Louvau and Marjorie E. Jackson (1982, 132 pages; $25 from Lifetime Learning

Publications, 10 Davis Drive, Belmont, CA 94002; 415/595-2350).

All of these books are available by mail order from COMPUTER LITERACY. For ordering information, see p. 201.

Among magazines, **Business Computer Systems** is one of the best sources for articles on real estate software, general-ledger software, and tax-preparation programs. **Interface Age** regularly runs reviews written by a CPA. **Small Business Computers** contains inventive articles on everything from local area networks to accounting packages for crop dusters. Also, be sure to check local user groups and professional organizations for special seminars and demonstrations.

**Business Computer Systems**: $35/yr (12 issues) or free to qualified business people; Cahners Publishing Co., 221 Columbus Avenue, Boston, MA 02116; 617/536-7780.
● **Interface Age**: $21/yr (12 issues); Interface Age Magazine, 17000 Marquardt Avenue, Cerritos, CA 90701; 800/423-6665; or 213/926-9544. ● **Small Business Computers**: $14.97/yr (6 issues); Small Business Computers, P.O. Box 638, Holmes, PA 19043. ● **SOFSEARCH**: $50/yr *plus* (1) corporate plan: $150/6 searches; (2) pay-as-you-go: $35/search; SOFSEARCH International, Inc., Route 20, Box 3572, Gladiolus Drive, Fort Meyers, FL 33908; 800/531-5955; 813/481-4994.

## WHOLE EARTH RECOMMENDED ACCOUNTING TOOLS

### (June 1984)

### PERSONAL FINANCE PROGRAMS
MANAGING YOUR MONEY, $200, p.97
DOLLARS AND SENSE, $165, p.97
FINANCIER II, $195, p.98
HOME ACCOUNTANT, $100, p.98
MONEY STREET, $100, p.99

### SMALL BUSINESS PROGRAMS
THE ACCOUNTING PARTNER, $395, p.99
PEACHPAK 4 ACCOUNTING, $395, p.99
BOOKS! THE ELECTRIC LEDGER,
    $345 to $745, p.100

BPI GENERAL LEDGER, $595, p.100

### PRICEY AND SOPHISTICATED
THE BOSS FINANCIAL ACCOUNTING
    SYSTEM, $1595, p.101
PEACHPAK 8 ACCOUNTING SYSTEM,
    $750 per module, p.101
THE CHAMPION, $495/$595 per module,
    p.102
IUS EASYBUSINESS SYSTEMS,
    $595/$795 per module, p.102

REALWORLD ACCOUNTING,
    $348/$695 per module, p.103
OPEN SYSTEMS, $695 per module, p.103
GREAT PLAINS HARDISK ACCOUNTING,
    $595 per module, p.104

### TAXES (pp.104-105)
TAX PREPARER, $250/$295
PERSONAL TAX PLANNER, $99
MICRO-TAX, $195/$2000
MASTER TAX PREPARER, $1695

## TYRANNY OF THE NEW

By the time you read this, a revolution will be under way in the world of accounting programs. For some years people have been transporting cumbersome ideas and sluggish languages from the old world of minicomputer accounting to the new world of micros; but gradually the spread of micros to all levels of business has begun to democratize things. Obligatory security features were part of the old order, but not all accounting programs need the traditional guard dogs. Batch entry, mandatory control reports, and passworded payrolls get in the way of small-time business. Requiring them is like keeping a boat on your back porch in case of a tidal wave. New programs are getting faster, friendlier, and more flexible. If money management continues to move in this direction, maybe the rest of the world will follow.

Here are some of the newest developments. (By the time you read this, even these may be old hat.) Continental Software is putting out a compiled BASIC version of their hot seller, THE HOME ACCOUNTANT; Atari is putting out two home-finance programs of its own—BORROWING MONEY and SAVING MONEY. Great Plains has come up with a true multi-user

version of its excellent HARDISK ACCOUNTING. IBM PCs using the Corvus disk will link up in a local area network that will take full advantage of new Great Plains features. At some point, the company intends to hook up Apples as well. (More on local area networks on p. 157.)

Systems Plus is working on new modules—inventory and payroll—for BOOKS! THE ELECTRIC LEDGER. A word-processing program is also on the horizon. Realworld is entering the true small-time operator market with its SMALL BUSINESS BOOKKEEPING. If this new program is easier to use than REALWORLD, it could be an important new entry in a quickly burgeoning market.

IUS, while maintaining the integrity of its solid old traditions, is moving into this area too, hoping to give BPI a run. The new IUS programs will be especially user-kind, files will automatically expand when necessary, and a new integrating tool, EASYPLUS, will ensure that the IUS programs all communicate nicely.

And finally, that already indispensable program, MANAGING YOUR MONEY, will be on its way into every home via PCjr and Macintosh versions. Check to see if I'm wrong.

## *Personal Finance Programs*

*A lot more than home accounting . . .*

### MANAGING YOUR MONEY

**Version 1; IBM PC compatibles; 128K RAM; color monitor recommended; $200; copy-protected? YES; M.E.C.A., 285 Riverside Ave., Westport, CT 06880; 203/222-1000.**

KEN USTON: MANAGING YOUR MONEY is the most comprehensive and easy-to-use home-finance package I've run across. In addition to performing conventional checkbook and budgeting functions, MANAGING YOUR MONEY forecasts cash flow, estimates income taxes, tracks net worth, and calculates gains and losses on investments.

But that's not all. MANAGING YOUR MONEY evaluates family life insurance needs, suggests income tax strategies, prints checks, and calculates rates of return on tax shelters and rental properties.

The programs are designed to be learned without the user's manual. Although other software manufacturers have made this claim, MYM is one of the few packages that totally succeeds.

Better yet, MYM programs are completely integrated. A check you write to the doctor is not only deducted from your checking account balance but is also reflected in your budget, income tax deductions, and net worth.

For insurance planning, MYM calculates your mortality. No armchair advisor, it tells you how much insurance to carry and makes suggestions about where to purchase it. The tax section estimates income taxes at any time of the year and allows you to do tax planning. The retirement programs factor in such variables as taxable savings, pension plans, IRA and Keogh portfolios, rates of inflation, and your income tax bracket. There's an equally good investment program.

If you, like me, have been thinking, "One of these days I'm going to get my finances in order," MYM might be the program to finally get you going.

MARSHA MATHER-THRIFT: MANAGING YOUR MONEY is in a category all by itself. It's not just another home accounting program, it's a financial consultant. If you need advice, buy this one.

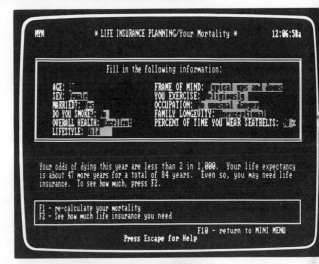

*A hot new trend—celebrity software. Bestselling author Andrew Tobias (The Only Investment Guide You'll Ever Need) offers new bits of canny advice in MANAGING YOUR MONEY. After repeated use, the recommendations get a little old, but even so, the program sets the new standard in home finance software. Fully interactive files (they talk to each other) cover everything from savings accounts to retirement plans.*

---

*Speed, flexibility, and a great capacity . . .*

### DOLLARS AND SENSE

**Apple II family; 48K; $100 • IBM PC compatibles; 64K; 2 disk drives; $165; copy-protected? YES; Monogram, 8295 S. La Cienega Blvd., Inglewood, CA 90301; 213/215-0529.**

FRED SALAND (Shoreline Software, San Rafael, CA): After a long and frustrating search for a good home-money manager, I finally found DOLLARS AND SENSE. It isn't good . . . it's great.

The program lets you categorize transactions into 120 different accounts and enter monthly budgets for each one. You can add and rename accounts or delete unused accounts at any time. Transactions can be flagged for tax returns. Even after using this software for five months, I had used only 92 accounts, and I'm *compulsive* about detailing my financial affairs.

Speed and capacity are the greatest selling points. DOLLARS AND SENSE is written in PASCAL and operates at lightning speed compared with the competition. Moving from menu to menu is fast. Data entry is done by the screenful instead of line by line. Up to 2000 entries per disk can be stored on an

Apple. You can also correct or add transactions from previous months at any time. (THE HOME ACCOUNTANT won't let you add transactions after you've closed out a month.) D&S's editing function, which works like that of a word processor, is the best I've seen.

The program was designed to be easy to use, and it's a success. It always displays your options so you can back out of any process gracefully.

A few shortcomings: In printing checks, the payee isn't saved, and repeat payments have to be re-entered. Some users have mentioned that disk drives must be perfectly adjusted in order for transactions to be saved. This might be a result of the operating system or of Monogram's copy-protection scheme.

For personal finances, though, the package is nearly ideal. I haven't said DOLLARS AND SENSE is the simplest program to use, but it's worth the extra effort. For the investment, you get speed, flexibility, and results.

MARSHA MATHER-THRIFT: In the personal finance world, DOLLARS AND SENSE is a star. It's better designed than HOME ACCOUNTANT, light years faster, and the documentation looks like a million bucks.

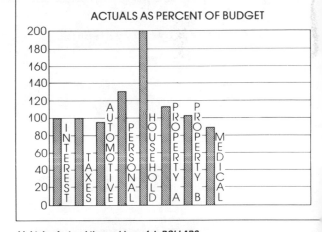

*Lightning fast and thoroughly useful, DOLLARS AND SENSE surpasses HOME ACCOUNTANT in everything but forecasting and range of machines on which it runs. For home budgeting, choose exotic colors for bar graphs that show at a glance what you spend on household items or your automobile. You may discover, as I did, that those harmless little trips to used-book stores add up.*

```
                BALANCE SHEET FOR YEAR-TO-DATE
                ------------------------------
                     JANUARY to DECEMBER

                      Yr. Begin  Period End  Difference  Budget  Variance
Current Assets
  CITIBANK-CHECKING        597       1903       1306
  BANK OF BOSTON-CHECK      29         29          0
  BANK OF BOSTON-SAVGS     622        622          0
  POCKET CASH               85        135         50
  STOCKS & BONDS         35000      35100        100
  CITI NATIONAL CD       15000      12900      -2100

    Total Current Assets  51334      50689       -644        0      -644

Fixed Assets
  PROPERTY VALUE        120000     120000          0        0         0
  AUTOS                  18000      18000          0        0         0

    Total Fixed Assets  138000     138000          0        0         0

Other Assets
  MORTGAGE-TAX               0       2300       2300     2300        -0
  PAYROLL WITHHOLDINGS       0      15199      15199    15000       199

    Total Other Assets       0      17499      17499    17300       199

    Total Assets        189334     206188      16854    17300      -446

Current Liab
  CREDIT CARD - VISA      -606       -280        325
  AMERICAN EXPRESS        -110       -222       -112

    Total Current Liab    -715       -502        213        0       213

Long-Term Liab
  MORTGAGE-PRINCIPAL    -80000     -79000       1000     1000         0
  AUTO LOAN - BMW       -10000      -6666       3334     3333         0

    Total Long-Term Liab -90000     -85666       4334     4333         0
```

*A double-entry bookkeeping system is a must for producing business balance sheets your bank will accept. FINANCIER II is the one personal finance program that offers low price, a complete accounting package, and business quality reports.*

*Versatile, easy to use, and expandable . . .*

## FINANCIER II

**Version 2.10; DEC Rainbow ● IBM PC/XT compatibles ● TI Professional ● Wang; MS-DOS 2.0; 192K RAM; 2 disk drives or hard disk; copy-protected? NO; $195; Financier, Inc., 2000 West Park Dr., P.O. Box 670, Westboro, MA 01581; 617/366-0950.**

FRED SALAND (Shoreline Software, San Rafael, CA): FINANCIER II is a personal and small-business software system for accrual or cash-based double-entry accounting. That means it will work for both lazy and ambitious users who want sophisticated fiscal management. So far, this sounds pretty much like HOME ACCOUNTANT or DOLLARS AND SENSE. But the folks at Financier, Inc., have spent a lot of time designing a program that is versatile, relatively easy to use, and *expandable*. While HOME ACCOUNTANT limits you to 100 categories and D&S to 120, this program can support any number of categories. It goes one step further and permits you to classify each category into current and fixed assets, long- and short-

term liabilities, and so on. That's a definite plus in a business setting.

Where does this very sophisticated package fit in? It's more complete than HOME ACCOUNTANT. It's slower than DOLLARS AND SENSE, but does have enhanced tax coding, memo fields, and easy payables and check writing. FINANCIER II probably falls slightly above D&S for usefulness and a few steps below a general-accounting package like PEACHPAK or BPI, since they can be upgraded to full accounting systems as your business grows.

MARSHA MATHER-THRIFT: FINANCIER II has less flash, but a few more refinements than programs like HOME ACCOUNTANT and DOLLARS AND SENSE, including a tax preparer/planner (at a separate cost) that can actually print forms. It's more expensive than D&S and HA, and not terribly fast, but a good buy if you have complicated personal business.

```
       ** THE HOME ACCOUNTANT **
              V. X.XX
             MAIN MENU

   1. TRANSACTIONS
   2. GRAPHS
   3. PRINTED REPORTS
   4. PRINT CHECKS/ACTIVITY REPORT
   5. BUDGET
   6. EXTEND DATA DISK
   7. START NEW YEAR
   8. HARDWARE/START NEW SYSTEM
   9. EXIT

        ENTER SELECTION (1-9)
```

*HOME ACCOUNTANT is a household word—at least in the electronic cottage. It runs on more machines than any finance program in its price range and offers a no-frills set of graphs and reports. HOME ACCOUNTANT PLUS, the IBM version, has a forecast module that teaches the tricky art of future budget planning. If you do nothing more than predict returns on a savings account, you'll still find HOME ACCOUNTANT's orderly thinking a godsend.*

*A home-finance manager with reports for every occasion . . .*

## HOME ACCOUNTANT

**Apple II family; 48K ● Atari; 48K ● Commodore 64 ● Epson QX-10; 64K ● IBM PC compatibles; 128K ● Kaypro 2 & 4; 64K ● Osborne 1 & Executive; 64K ● The Professional; 128K ● TRS-80 Models 3 & 4; 48K ● Wang PC; 256K; $150 ● Zenith 100; 128K; copy-protected? Varies with computer; $100; Arrays, Inc./Continental Software, 11223 S. Hindry Ave., Los Angeles, CA 90045; 213/410-3977.**

ROBERT D. KOLB (Micro Support, Sausalito, CA): My accounting needs are rather simple, because I have only one checking and one savings account. But having spent hours sorting through boxes of receipts and past bank statements, I was delighted to find a software product to help organize my financial mess. Oh sure, I always know my current balance or whether I've paid my electric bill, but whenever I have to review past payments, I have to do a couple of hours of tedious work.

It took me about 60 minutes to set up HOME ACCOUNTANT, from formatting disks to entering checkbook records. This included reading through the documentation, which is not quite as easy as it should be for novices.

Since I had never really taken the time to set up a budget, I decided to try it. Then I got so ambitious that I created two credit card accounts and an expense account.

HA can handle up to five accounts with a maximum of 100 categories each. Searching for transactions is simple and painless. You can search by date, check number, payee, amount, budget category, memo, or any combination for any period. And the program is reasonably fast, despite the fact that HA is written in interpreted BASIC. (A compiled BASIC—and faster—version for IBM PC is in the wings.)

There are plenty of reports, including budget and net worth. Also, you can print comparative income and balance sheets and choose specific areas for reporting (ie. all checks to the landlord). Graphs allow limited forecasting—for example, the future value of an investment after assumed rates of return and inflation have been calculated.

If I keep using HOME ACCOUNTANT, who knows? Those valuable investments might even be mine.

MARSHA MATHER-THRIFT: Although it is cumbersome, HOME ACCOUNTANT has the invaluable ability to funnel information to Continental's low-priced TAX ADVANTAGE (which does not, however, print forms). It also runs on nearly every computer ever made. HOME ACCOUNTANT PLUS (the IBM version) also has one of the more complete forecasting modules available. Every home finance program should have one of these.

*I once created a pie chart out of last month's spending. Found that I spent three times more money on books than any other personal item. The next month I started using my library card and spent the extra dollars on clothes and a good haircut. Felt great!*

*— Barbara Robertson*

*While most households could greatly use the bill-juggling processes (called "Accounts Payable Management"), there is at present no really simple program that handles it on a casual basis with zero learning time.*

*—Ted Nelson*

*A cheap, useful home-finance manager for Apples, and soon for IBM . . .*

## MONEY STREET

Apple II family; DOS 3.3; 48K; copy-protected? YES; $100; Computer Tax Service, P. O. Box 7915, Incline Village, NV 89450; 702/832-1001.

MARSHA MATHER-THRIFT: If you like things simple, then MONEY STREET's your program. It's less trouble than most other programs in its price range and will do a lot more than organize your desk-drawer accounting system. It's also inexpensive and can easily be learned in half an hour. There are 99 codes for dividing up tax categories, income categories, loans to friends, and so on. Design revolves around one main entry screen and a back-up help screen in case you forget code numbers. By far the best thing about the whole program is its avoidance of detail for detail's sake.

MONEY STREET prints fifteen different reports (in one standard format). It also keeps cumulative totals for each category, a handy quick-reference feature if you want to know where your money is going.

There are things MONEY STREET won't do. It won't let you invoice, print checks, print reports by code category, or forecast, and you have to buy an additional disk to sort, copy codes, and make back-ups of the program.

# Small Business Programs

*A sensible double-entry small-business system . . .*

## THE ACCOUNTING PARTNER

Version 1.22; IBM PC/XT compatibles; 128K RAM • CP/M-80 and CP/M-86 machines; 64K RAM; 2 disk drives or hard disk,132 column printer; copy-protected? NO; $395; Star Software Systems, 20600 Gramercy Pl., Torrance, CA 90501; 213/538-2511; modules available: G/L, A/R, A/P, payroll.

## PEACHPAK 4 ACCOUNTING

Apple II family; 64K; Microsoft Z-80 card • CP/M; all machines • IBM PC compatibles; 2 disk drives; 80-column display; copy-protected? YES; $395; Peachtree Software, 3445 Peachtree Rd. N.E., Atlanta, GA 30326; 800/554-8900; modules available: G/L, A/R, A/P.

JAN PEHRSON, M.B.A., C.D.P. (Datalink, Novato, CA): Most small-business bookkeeping systems are a combination of spit and baling wire. Staff never quite keeps pace with growth, and there's little time to keep track of the precise figures that go into the monthly payables and quarterly financial statements. A lot of businesses don't even use quarterly statements. In fact, plenty of owners run "successful" companies by frequently asking, "Just how much do we have in the bank, anyway?" Then the accountant (if there's a good one) picks up the pieces at the end of the year.

THE ACCOUNTING PARTNER is one of those sensible accounting systems that can change all that. It's a double-entry system complete enough for businesses that don't require elaborate inventory control. For retailers, there are plenty of options for vendor payment and purchasing—enough, at least, to give you an extra inflation hedge through discount buying. THE ACCOUNTING PARTNER also includes accounts receivable and an invoicing module to track sales and to age overdue accounts. And you can do a sales analysis on products by item file, invoicing your items at five different prices.

Similar to Peachtree's PEACHPAK 4 in price, design, and applications, THE ACCOUNTING PARTNER has a couple of features you can't get with PEACHPAK. First, it interfaces with the STAR LEGAL TIME AND BILLING PROGRAM, which makes it a good candidate for attorneys and consultants. Also, THE ACCOUNTING PARTNER's journals are divided into three simple categories: cash disbursements, cash receipts, and a general journal. You get all the standard reports, but with more comparisons and groupings than PEACHPAK allows. And one of its most far-sighted features is a function that permits small companies to print checks straight from the general ledger check-disbursements journal.

Still, victory doesn't go entirely to THE ACCOUNTING PARTNER. Despite its easy set-up, good documentation, and freely offered 800 number, there is no index or error glossary to help you through the rough spots. The general ledger will not summarize departments into divisions as PEACHPAK's will. A/R allows only balance forward accounting, so you can't check detail on invoices for previous months. This might be fine for a five and dime, but not for most inventory-maintaining businesses. It also costs $50 per quarter to get the benefit of Star's direct advice. From the company's point of view the fee is probably a good way to get rid of malingerers, but it's not terribly practical for customers who can't put their businesses on hold while breaking in their new accounting pals.

You don't have to be an accountant to use this program, but you'll have to act like one if you want to make any corrections. Reverse entries are your only way out of errors. Also, THE ACCOUNTING PARTNER is not entirely interactive, so you'll have to post transactions in a separate maneuver, but at least you can rely on the accuracy of your figures this way.

Still, despite all this, THE ACCOUNTING PARTNER will, as it claims, haul you out of the Stone Age. It's a cinch to give you a better idea of how your books are being kept. And you won't be likely to discover, as someone who recently hired us did, that you've been losing money invisibly for the last six months.

MARSHA MATHER-THRIFT: If you've got a growing small business and limited cash flow, then THE ACCOUNTING PARTNER and PEACHPAK 4 can offer low price now and an easy move up to more sophisticated accounting software from the same manufacturer later. (Also, see PEACHPAK 8, p. 101.)

```
•••••••••••••••••••••••••••••••••••••••••••••••••••••••
                  The Accounting Partner
           (c) 1983 by Star Software Systems
             Enter/Sort/Post Transactions Sub-Menu
•••••••••••••••••••••••••••••••••••••••••••••••••••••••

    Code      Function

     1)    General Journal Transaction Entry

     2)    Check Disbursements Journal Transaction Entry

     3)    Cash Receipts Journal Transaction Entry

     4)    Daily Journal Transaction Sort & Register

     5)    Post Sorted Journal Transactions

•••••••••••••••••••••••••••••••••••••••••••••••••••••••

        Enter Code Number of Choice (or 0 to return): 1
```

*ACCOUNTING PARTNER has three simple entry screens (cash receipts, cash disbursements and general journal). These help to separate financial transactions and cut down chances for error.*

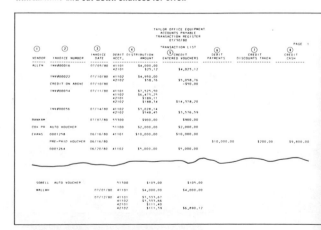

*A good vendor file can save time in tracking balances due to creditors. Due date notations also help to prevent nasty phone calls about overdue bills. And entries for discount dates flag payments that can save lots of money.*

*BOOKS! is a novice businessperson's dream. A bookkeeping tutorial and ten simple charts of accounts streamline initial setup. A report (such as the one above) provides a tidy summary of outstanding debts with balances aged at four different rates. Overdue bills can quickly sink busy or inexperienced entrepreneurs, but with BOOKS! you can instantly monitor cash and receivables.*

*For the old-fashioned bookkeeper . . .*

## BOOKS! THE ELECTRIC LEDGER

**Version 1.01; IBM PC/XT compatibles; 128K RAM; 2 disk drives or hard disk ● most CP/M-80 & -86 machines; 64K minimum RAM; copy-protected? NO; $745 for complete package or $345 for basic module plus $75-150 for additional modules; Systems Plus, Inc., 1120 San Antonio Rd., Palo Alto, CA 94303; 415/969-7047.**

DENNIS JOW: BOOKS! is a program with a revolutionary approach. The screen is a graphic simulation of the familiar journal worksheet (with columns for debits and credits) designed to make the changeover from paper to machine an easy task. One section of the screen shows the register or account presently active, while another section gives prompts which show the transaction to be performed. The system even suggests automatically whether the entry is to be debit or credit, based upon what is usual for that type of transaction.

BOOKS! is closer to textbook accounting than any other system on the market. It's a double-entry system with G/L, A/P, A/R functions, and includes options for invoicing, check writing, recurring entries, and budgeting (including job cost). Accounts receivable will print open item ageing reports and detailed aged or balance forward customer statements. It will also handle any number of customers you wish.

One of the nicest features is the chart of accounts for the general ledger. There are pre-designed charts for ten different types of businesses—wholesale, retail, personal, manufacturing, construction, and others. You can modify any of these charts to your own specifications.

BOOKS! is a program meant for ease. The reference manual has a section explaining the theory of double-entry accrual accounting and there is a tutorial.

This is one of the better accounting programs on the market, although I have heard some complaints. At least one person I know felt the report capabilities weren't adequate and that the program lacks some flexibility. But if you're dreading the day when you'll need to convert all your paper files to electronic, then be sure to take a look at BOOKS!

MARSHA MATHER-THRIFT: BOOKS! combines old-fashioned bookkeeping formats with the newest software "windowing" features for a totally fresh approach to small business accounting.

---

```
              CORNER HOME IMPROVEMENT CENTER
                     TRIAL BALANCE
                     JUNE 30, 1985

                                         PAGE 1
-------------------------------------------------
CURRENT ASSETS
   1010  REGISTER CASH                   128.99
   1020  CASH ON DEPOSIT                    .00
   1021  CITY NATIONAL                 8,255.67
   1022  COMMERCIAL USA                  252.29
   1110  ACCOUNTS RECEIVABLE          5,065.33
   1120  PREPAID INSURANCE               56.32
   1130  EMPLOYEE ADVANCES              449.50
   1140  RETAINAGE ON CONTRACTS           .00
   1150  INVENTORY                   25,674.11
   1160  CONSTRUCTION IN PROGRESS         .00
   1180  LABOR CONTROL                    .00

FIXED ASSETS
   1510  FURNITURE & FIXTURES        10,274.26
   1520  MACHINERY & EQUIPMENT       48,179.86
   1550  ACCUMULATED DEPRECIATION     4,316.04-

OTHER ASSETS
   1800  DEPOSITS                     7,466.58
   1830  PREPAID INTEREST            11,585.40

CURRENT LIABILITIES
   2005  DEPOSITS ON CONSTRUCTION         .00
   2010  ACCOUNTS PAYABLE            13,061.25-
   2030  SALES TAX PAYABLE            1,592.80-
   2040  FICA PAYABLE                  215.35-
   2050  FEDERAL INCOME TAX W/H        269.87-
   2060  EARNED INCOME CREDIT             .00
   2070  STATE INCOME TAX W/H          101.12-
   2080  NEW YORK CITY TAX W/H          23.34-

LONG TERM LIABILITIES
   2620  NOTES PAYABLE-EQUIP         66,237.32-

CAPITAL
   3010  CAPITAL STOCK               24,500.00-
   3050  RETAINED EARNINGS            7,071.22-

INCOME
   4011  SALES                            .00
```

*The workhorse of small business accounting, BPI requires month-end closings and audit reports. Trial balance (above) gives you a quick summary of all your general ledger accounts—a handy tool for quickly assessing cash and excessive spending.*

*A workhorse for small businesses, flexible and expandable . . .*

## BPI GENERAL LEDGER

**Version 1.10; Apple II family; Lisa ● IBM PC/XT compatibles; PC DOS ● most MS-DOS machines ● most CP/M machines; copy-protected? NO except Apple II; $595; BPI Systems, 3423 Guadalupe St., Austin, TX 78705; 512/454-2801. Call BPI for specific machine compatibility and requirements.**

PAUL WALHUS, business systems consultant: BPI was started by the owner of a chain of grocery stores in Austin, Texas, who needed accounting systems to run his stores. He teamed up with a programmer and created a product that Apple, Commodore, and IBM fell in love with. The product caught on and sold more than 100,000 copies in two years.

It doesn't take knowledge or expertise in computers to use BPI. This is truly a program for the small business. Besides a general ledger module, BPI offers accounts receivable and payable, inventory control, payroll, job cost, church management, association management, and time accounting for lawyers.

The programs are easy to use, well-supported, well-documented, relatively bug-free—but slow—and the menus are always consistent. You can stack up commands in the BPI "queue" menu and enter data in several journals without going back to the main menu. And you can do the same with the reports. This shorthand data entry saves a lot of keystrokes.

BPI is written in BASIC, which accounts for its lack of speed. The Apple III version is written in Pascal and runs at a faster clip on a hard disk. The system will let you keep a whole year's transactions on a Profile hard disk.

One drawback: BPI is a month-to-month accounting system. However, it is possible to transfer information to APPLEWORKS (p. 113) or VISICALC (p. 71) files with a program called GENCALC (Business Machines and Systems, Box 1010, Bolinas, CA 94924). There, data can be worked up for budgeting, ratio analysis, and projections.

Most important, BPI is an expandable system. And the additional programs for churches, associations, and lawyers offer a range of eccentric flexibility that's hard to equal.

MARSHA MATHER-THRIFT: BPI has outsold other accounting programs in this price range. It's dependable and offers a lot of options (such as legal time and billing and job cost) that you won't find in similarly priced programs.

## Pricey and Sophisticated

*Full-featured and carefully designed . . .*

### THE BOSS FINANCIAL ACCOUNTING SYSTEM

John Burns and Sally Craig; Version 1.21; IBM PC compatibles; 128K ● most MP/M machines; 64K; 2 disk drives or hard disk; copy protected? NO; $1595; Balcones Computer Corporation, 5910 Courtyard Dr., Austin, TX 78731; 800/531-5483; system includes G/L, A/R, A/P; also available: inventory accounting ($1095), payroll ($795), and time billing ($795).

JOHN R. SOWDEN, JR.: Unlike most software packages, THE BOSS's manual lists its program writers right up front. So it was my first impression that if somebody was taking responsibility for it, the whole program must be well put together. I wasn't wrong. When I called Balcones (via an 800 number), the first person I talked to fully understood the program—and also had a strong knowledge of accounting.

The manual is well-written and the system offers a number of features for easy use. You can create your own function keys, for example, so if you want you can easily design your command keys to resemble those of MicroPro's WORDSTAR, which is helpful if your staff is already familiar with WORDSTAR commands.

Another help is the preset chart of accounts. You can delete the accounts that don't match your operations and add ones that do. Ordinarily, setting up a chart of accounts is one of the most time-consuming and complicated tasks in computer accounting.

There are lots of flexible features, too. THE BOSS allows you up to ten transaction categories per entry. If ten isn't enough, Balcones performs an accounting sleight-of-hand by allowing one of these entries to refer to a temporary account that makes another ten entries available.

The system has three levels of password security, and there are excellent error-detection features to warn you if your disk is bad or your hardware malfunctioning.

Balcones also gives you a chance to test what they're selling. You purchase the demo disks and manual. If you buy the package within 30 days, the demo charge is credited and the company sends you unrestricted disks along with a new reference manual that covers the program in even greater detail.

MARSHA MATHER-THRIFT: THE BOSS is a leader in outstanding system safeguards. It's a good multi-user program, and it's the only one recommended in this price range that offers a general time and billing package.

*A fine, market-tested integrated system . . .*

### PEACHPAK 8 ACCOUNTING SYSTEM

Version 2.0; Apple III with Profile hard disk ● DEC Rainbow 100 ● Eagle; 64K ● IBM PC/XT compatibles; 128K ● Televideo ● TI Professional; 64K; all require 2 disk drives or hard disk; copy protected? NO; $750 per module; Peachtree Software, 3445 Peachtree Road NE, 8th Floor, Atlanta, GA 30326; 800/554-8900; modules available: G/L, A/R, A/P, sales invoicing, inventory control, payroll, job cost, fixed assets.

JAN PEHRSON, M.B.A., C.D.P. (Datalink, Novato, CA): If you don't care much for frills and want a good easy-to-use accounting system, PEACHPAK 8 ACCOUNTING SYSTEM is one of the best buys on the market. My firm installs business software and trains people to use it, so we've spent lots of time looking for programs that give small businesses the power and flexibility they need. We found PEACHPAK 8 several years ago and still think it's dynamite. Recently, we converted a small pest-control business from its old manual system and found that set-up and training on PEACHPAK 8 took only four and a half hours of our time. That's the kind of miracle small, understaffed companies are looking for.

PEACHPAK 8 is similar to PEACHPAK 4 (p. 99) but a lot more powerful. Available components include job cost, payroll, order entry, and a general ledger for CPAs. The system is truly modular and written in compiled BASIC, which means it's fast, and you can be sure it's well-tested. Peachtree is the third largest software manufacturer in the country, and the company has a solid reputation for both user and dealer support.

PEACHPAK 8 is less complicated than OPEN SYSTEMS (p. 103) and more flexible than IUS (p. 102). A systems file lets you choose the way you want to handle editing and control reports. If you're very security conscious, this may not be the system you want, but in most businesses with 20 or fewer employees, people know each other well enough to make a locked-up program unnecessary. The series has two levels of password security, and I really think that's sufficient.

PEACHPAK 8 offers all the standard accounting features, such as balance sheets and income statements. You can do custom invoicing by using PEACHTEXT 5000. All modules feed directly to the general ledger, and trial balances can be run. Accounts payable allows open invoices and aging on balances due (with a 30/60/90-day format); it also provides an unusual and extremely useful cash-requirements forecast. Payroll includes a subscription service for updated tax tables, so you never have to key in new information as the laws change.

Describe PEACHPAK 8 in one word? It's *accessible*. It won't teach you accounting, but it will make it inviting to learn.

MARSHA MATHER-THRIFT: We recommend PEACHPAK 8 for small businesses interested in doing accounting on a floppy disk system.

*Stuck with expanding business and a floppy disk computer system you can't afford to trade? PEACHPAK 8 was designed to ease your dilemma. Although any accounting system performs best with a hard disk, PEACHPAK keeps disk-swapping to a minimum. You get plenty of standard business reports, nonetheless, including a departmental income statement (above). A vital aid in comparing departmental profit margins for combined sales and service operations.*

*THE BOSS accounting system is well-designed for safety and ease of use. Error messages warn if disks or programs function improperly. A short form chart of accounts report helps in coding items to the proper account before entry. Balcones clearly dreams up its programs with ordinary users in mind.*

## Extreme ease of use . . .

## THE CHAMPION

**Version 3.4; CP/M-80, Apple DOS machines; 64K; $495 per module ● PC DOS, MS-DOS, CP/M-86 compatible machines; 64K minimum; $595 per module; copy protected? NO; Champion Software Corp., 66 S. Van Gordon, Ste. 155, Lakewood, CO 80228; 303/987-2588; call Champion for specific machine specifications and compatibility; over 75 configurations; modules available: G/L, A/R, A/P, inventory, payroll.**

```
            DATA BASE RESEARCH CORPORATION
            STATEMENT OF FINANCIAL CONDITION
                    JUNE 30, 1982
                      PAGE   1
                       ASSETS

CURRENT ASSETS:
  PETTY CASH                              150.00
  CASH IN BANK - CHECKING            332,464.15
  CASH IN BANK - SAVINGS             269,000.00
  TOTAL CASH                         601,614.15

  TOTAL ACCOUNTS RECEIVABLE                0.00

  INVENTORY - FINISHED GOODS         164,246.00
  TOTAL INVENTORY                    164,246.00

  TOTAL CURRENT ASSETS               765,860.15

FIXED ASSETS:
  COMPUTERS                          101,400.00
  FURNITURE & FIXTURES                17,300.00
  TOTAL FIXED ASSETS                 118,700.00

  ACCUMULATED DEPRECIATION            -5,500.00
  FIXED ASSETS (LESS DEPR.)          113,200.00

OTHER ASSETS:
  TOTAL OTHER ASSETS                       0.00

  TOTAL ASSETS                       879,060.15

               LIABILITIES & EQUITY

CURRENT LIABILITIES:
  ACCOUNTS PAYABLE - TRADE           242,951.79
  TOTAL ACCOUNTS PAYABLE             242,951.79

  FEDERAL WITHHOLDING PAYABLE          4,389.79
  FICA WITHHOLDING PAYABLE             1,059.44
  STATE WITHHOLDING PAYABLE              658.79
  MISC PAYROLL DEDUCTIONS                250.00
  TOTAL TAXES PAYABLE                  6,358.02
```

ANDREA SHARP (Whole Earth bookkeeper): Bookkeeping must have been one of the tasks for which computers were conceived. And Champion has put together a five-module accounting package that makes bookkeeping a bearable activity. You can use the modules —general ledger, payroll, accounts payable, accounts receivable, and inventory—together or as stand-alone functions. The amount of disk storage you have will determine what you can run together and how many months you can run concurrently. These programs are not suitable for small computers. On a Kaypro 2 (190K disk drives) I could only run the general ledger module for one month at a time.

The program will automatically produce financial reports—just like the ones your accountant gives you (although you cannot create a *customized* budget or financial report directly). But herein lies the one complication of using such software. You need to think like an accountant to set up your chart of accounts and general ledger unless you want to use the standard one Champion provides.

I sure got an instant education going through the set-up procedure on my own. Once that was done it was easy street. A program like this does such niceties as post all your payroll

*Because it's written in DBASE II, CHAMPION accounting is the fastest and most expandable system in the upper price range. If you rely on your accountant, you must normally wait until year's end for a statement of financial condition. With CHAMPION, you can produce on-the-spot reports any time during the year.*

deductions to the proper accounts in your general ledger while you are printing out your payroll checks. When all modules are used, this is a true order-entry system that updates inventory.

CHAMPION is designed to be extremely easy to use, with an extensive manual that is coordinated with the menu-driven program. There are on-screen help functions available throughout, and a recovery procedure should a program crash.

Champion Software Corporation lets you purchase its package on a money-back basis. Under the agreement, you can make just 200 entries but use all aspects of the package. If you want to keep it, the program is released to you via a "security code" that allows you to continue without losing any work. It's also guaranteed for one full year. All software should be sold this way.

Once your system is set up, even a temporary employee could come in and do your bookkeeping for you. This is one of the major advantages of a system like this. There are audit trails for all activities, and any accountant could make sense of the system— which rescues you from the potential tyranny of an idiosyncratic bookkeeper.

MARSHA MATHER-THRIFT: If you need a purchase order module, CHAMPION is the program that has it. Companies with a lot of employees and purchases to keep tabs on should consider the value of a program like this one.

---

## Security conscious accounting with excellent support . . .

## IUS EASYBUSINESS SYSTEMS

**IBM PC/XT compatibles ● TI Professional; 64K; $595 per module except Payroll ($795); copy protected? NO; Information Unlimited Software, 2401 Marinship Way, Sausalito, CA 94965; 415/331-6700; modules available: G/L, A/R, A/P, Inventory Control and Analysis, Order Entry, Payroll.**

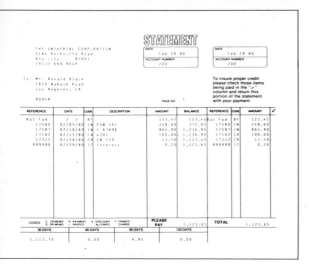

*Invoices in many programs require you to use quantity and unit cost categories whether you manufacture, sell retail goods, or service clients. This can make an excellent accounting system useless if your business requires a more flexible invoicing format. IUS EASYBUSINESS invoicing is more flexibly-designed than most, and slated for further improvements.*

JAN PEHRSON, M.B.A., C.D.P. (Datalink, Novato, CA): IUS puts out one of the most useable small-business accounting programs in the currently available herd. It's a kind of maiden aunt among accounting software, decidedly trustworthy and predictable even though its design is a little behind the times. Modeled on the old minibatch design, it is extremely safe, but for my tastes a little cumbersome to use. Still, all this caution does have its benefits. IUS has excellent error-detection capabilities, enhanced by easily understood messages and a "catastrophic error" warning to stop you dead in your tracks when hardware or software malfunctions occur.

Set-up goes quickly, despite the fact that this is a complicated accounting system. There are good instructions for allocating file space

on disks and setting up your chart of accounts. The manuals are small enough to fit on a desktop or shelf (a plus if you've ever tried to wrestle one of the damned things put out by most software companies), and *readable*.

Despite its accessibility, IUS offers plenty of flexibility and power. It can handle multiple departments and divisions using a twelve-digit account number (but can't consolidate multiple companies). Available reports are strongly management-oriented, offering such niceties as cash-flow monitoring and reports from the Inventory module that track order progress. The financial reporter, included in the general ledger module, makes report generation an art.

It's also good to know that IUS has a reputation for excellent support. IUS is as easy to reach as your next-door neighbor— and a good deal cheaper to consult than your accountant.

MARSHA MATHER-THRIFT: Consider IUS if you're looking for an accountant's dream of a program that will give you excellent safeguards against errors in data entry. It's easier to use than OPEN SYSTEMS, but less flexible than PEACHPAK 8.

---

*Minicomputer ancestry and volume . . .*

## REALWORLD ACCOUNTING

Version 3.0; PC DOS; MS-DOS; CP/M-86 machines; 128K (256K recommended); CP/M, TURBODOS, MmmOST, UNIX, XENIX; 64K; hard disk; 132-column printer recommended; $695/module except Sales Analysis ($348); call for specific machine requirements and configurations; copy-protected? NO; RealWorld Corporation, Dover Road, Chichester, NH 03263; 800/255-1115; modules available: G/L, A/R, A/P, payroll, order entry, inventory control, sales analysis.

---

LEROY TAVARES: REALWORLD GENERAL ACCOUNTING is not the accounting software for someone who wants to do household accounting or keep the books of a cottage business, but it is ideal for wholesalers and distributors who do volume sales, have a large inventory, and deal with numerous customers and vendors. In addition to the Basic Four—G/L, A/R, A/P, and payroll, modules are available for sales analysis, inventory control, and order processing. The program is derived from a minicomputer accounting system and has been on the market for ten years, so it is well-tested and predictable.

This is a double-entry system, but transactions can be easily edited in order to balance entries prior to posting, unlike some systems that require data from each entry *session* to be in balance.

All reports, except the customized G/L financial statements, are pre-designed and ready to run. They require a printer capable of printing 132 columns. The 3.0 version of

REALWORLD provides a way to install control codes in order to use the compressed print feature of most popular dot matrix printers. It's mighty handy being able to compress these wide reports onto a standard 8½" page without fooling around.

The program is written in COBOL, a widely-applicable computer language. A multi-user version has been introduced for a number of local area networks. Because of the number of programs and data files for each module, I highly recommend a hard disk.

This software is easy for both non-computer and non-accounting people to operate. Installing a module, however, is not so easy. Neither is the layout of a financial statement or setup of payroll tax computations. You need knowledge of accounting principles and conventions to configure each module to your specific accounting practices. Even then, you may want to discuss setup options with your accountant.

REALWORLD is available only through dealers and, because it is complicated to set up, a good dealer is invaluable for proper installation. Certain dealers are licensed to take the original COBOL source code and rewrite it to fit unique business requirements. Such flexibility makes REALWORLD an inexpensive route for acquiring custom accounting software without the risk of hiring someone to develop your accounting system from scratch.

MARSHA MATHER-THRIFT: REALWORLD is a complicated but excellent system for wholesalers and retailers. It also gets high marks as a good general ledger for use by scrupulous Certified Public Accountants.

*Good payroll software is expensive but invaluable if you have numerous employees whose hours and job rates vary from month to month and year to year. Realworld puts out well-tested software with excellent safety features. A data integrity program helps detect hardware-caused errors before you store any faulty information. You won't have to worry about undetected errors that can bring IRS wrath upon your company's head.*

---

*Once it's set up it's the top of the line . . .*

## OPEN SYSTEMS

Version 3.0; Apple III ● DEC Rainbow ● IBM PC compatibles with 128K ● Wang PC ● Xerox ● multi-user machines including Televideo; Novell; TI; PC Sterns; Sperry; copy protected? YES; 10 megabyte hard disk recommended; $695 per module; Open Systems, 430 Oak Grove Rd., Minneapolis, MN 55403; 612/870-3515; call for specific machine compatibility and requirements. Modules available: G/L, A/R, A/P, inventory, sales order processing, payroll, job cost, interpreter, team manager.

---

JAN PEHRSON, M.B.A., C.D.P. (Datalink, Novato, CA): Flexibility is a great virtue, but too much flexibility in program design can cause trouble. OPEN SYSTEMS runs on nearly every operating system imaginable, handles multiple companies, departments, or profit centers, and is designed for multiple users. OS has more functional capability than just about any other major accounting package, but there's a trade-off. It's written in interpreted BASIC (slow, and you need the interpreter) or COBOL. This is not the program to choose for your IBM PC dual-floppy system, and probably not the program for you if you can't afford an accountant with

computer experience to install it for you.

OPEN SYSTEMS is a totally interactive accounting system that has Purchase Order, Inventory, and Job-Cost modules. Its "Team Manager" module also provides a data dictionary of 800-plus elements that can be used to infinitely customize reports. The program has been around since 1976, and it has a great many sophisticated functions.

The manuals are imposing, colorful, and confusing. Initial set-up requires that you program option and interface switches—an annoyance—but this lets you make configuration choices, such as whether or not you care to do automatic posting from accounts receivable to the general ledger.

OPEN SYSTEMS is an accounting Cadillac. If you've got the resources to get it going, you can take it nearly anywhere you please.

MARSHA MATHER-THRIFT: If you have an enormous number of specific accounting needs or just one particular need that no one seems able to meet, look at OPEN SYSTEMS. This program has more modules and reports and features than anything else we've seen.

```
          JOB PROFITABILITY REPORT

JOB ID              FROM 001
                    THRU 100
MANAGER             FROM 01
                    THRU 10

   PICK
1. COMPLETED JOBS
2. IN PROCESS JOBS
3. NOT YET STARTED JOBS
4. ALL OF THE ABOVE
4

   SORT BY
1. JOB ID
2. MANAGER ID
1
INCLUDE PHASE DETAIL? YES
```

*Job costing is one of the tasks computers do best, but only a handful of accounting programs include full-featured job cost modules. OPEN SYSTEMS has one of the best. Good job software can provide instant oversight that will help prevent major and minor cost overruns on a variety of complicated projects.*

## Hard disk on the Apple III . . .

### GREAT PLAINS HARD DISK ACCOUNTING

**Version 3.0; Apple IIe; 64K; hard disk ● Apple III; Profile hard disk ● IBM PC/XT; copy-protected? NO; $595/module; Great Plains Software, P.O. Box 9739, Fargo, ND 58109; 701/281-0550; modules available: G/L, G/L with financial reporting & budgeting, A/R, A/P, payroll, inventory management with point-of-sale invoicing.**

EUGENE KRAMER, C.P.A.: GREAT PLAINS is a system with an abundance of useful features. It allows flexible formatting of financial statements and prints these at any time during the month or year. It allows four, seven, or ten digit account numbers. Account descriptions can be up to 30 characters long. (Unfortunately, GREAT PLAINS permits only twelve accounting periods per year, not thirteen.)

The system provides data security through password protection. Executives can use system-wide passwords while departmental employees can be given passwords for selected accounts only. All password and other security features are superb.

The documentation is also excellent. So is the telephone support, which is handled by people who specialize in each of the various applications.

The GREAT PLAINS GENERAL LEDGER meshes smoothly with other GP accounting programs: accounts receivable, accounts payable, and payroll. Inventory handles point-of-sale chores such as pricing and sales tax. A job cost module will soon be available, too.

GREAT PLAINS accounting programs are written in PASCAL, which requires its own operating system. They run easily on the Apple III. To adapt these programs to IBM's PC DOS, Great Plains supplies an intermediary system called Bubble DOS.

If you are willing to buy a hard disk, this is an excellent accounting system at a reasonable price.

MARSHA MATHER-THRIFT: GREAT PLAINS is head and shoulders above other accounting programs for the Apple III. It's great on IBM, too. And, we've heard nothing but good reports from longtime users.

---

```
Prepare Returns (On-screen)
  1) New Name (Active Filename)    12) Schd W      (Married Cpl Ddn)
  2) Form 1040        (Main Form)  13) Form 2106   (Employee Expns)
  3) Schd A       (Itemized Deducn)14) Form 2119   (Residence Sale)
  4) Schd B        (Interest & Divs)15) Form 2210  (Tax Underpymnt)
  5) Schd C        (Business Profit)16) Form 2441        (Child Care)
  6) Schd D         (Capital Gains) 17) Form 3468    (Invstmt Credit)
  7) Schd E        (Supplmnt Income)18) Form 4562      (Depreciation)
  8) Schd F          (Farm Income)  19) Form 4797     (Supplmt Gains)
  9) Schd G     (Income Averaging)  20) Form 5695     (Energy Credit)
 10) Schd R&RP     (Elderly Credit) 21) Form 6251       (Alt Min Tax)
 11) Schd SE      (Self-emplmt Tax)
 Which do you choose (Esc=exit)?  1
```

*No more late-night scrambles to the Post Office for overlooked forms and schedules. TAX PREPARER supplies 90% of the paperwork most people need for returns. It's a preparer, a planner, and all-around April 15th wizard. A personal tax preparer that's good enough for professionals to use.*

```
-----------------------------------------------------
ENTER, CHANGE, OR REVIEW WORKSHEET
-----------------------------------------------------
  ALTERNATIVE         ----1---  ----2--- ----3--- ----4--- ----5---
                        1983      1983     1983     1983     1983
1 Filing Status           .         .        .        .        .
2 Exemptions             ..        ..       ..       ..       ..
3 Wages & Salaries    -T ........  ........ ........ ........ ........
                      -S ........  ........ ........ ........ ........
4 Two-Earner Earned Income-T ....  ........ ........ ........ ........
                      -S ........  ........ ........ ........ ........
5 Interest            -T ........  ........ ........ ........ ........
                      -S ........  ........ ........ ........ ........
6 Dividends           -T ........  ........ ........ ........ ........
                      -S ........  ........ ........ ........ ........
7 Int & Div Exclusions-T ........  ........ ........ ........ ........
                      -S ........  ........ ........ ........ ........
WORKSHEET:
-----------------------------------------------------
       J)ump, C)alculator, T)ax plan, R)esults,
       G)row, S)ingle entry, W)orksheet layout,
                H)eadings, ESC, ?
-----------------------------------------------------
```

*THE PERSONAL TAX PLANNER is a tool for making investment decisions, solving real estate rent-or-purchase dilemmas, deciding job changes, and even restructuring settlements from lawsuits.*

---

## Two things are certain . . .

### TAX PREPARER

**Version 84; Apple II family; 64K; $250; ● IBM PC/XT compatibles; 64 K minimum ● IBM PCjr ● TI Professional; 128 K; $295; copy-protected? NO; Howard Software Systems, 8008 Girard Avenue, Suite 310, La Jolla, CA 92037; 619/454-0121.**

WOODY LISWOOD: Death and taxes are inevitable here in the U.S. But TAX PREPARER almost makes tax preparation fun. It helps you look at your taxes in a logical manner, helps you prepare the proper documentation for your return, and also allows you to "what if" your return to see how various options, deductions, and whatnot might affect the taxes you pay.

I've used the TAX PREPARER in various versions for the past three years. It generates schedules and data that are accepted by the IRS. There is also a provision for batch data entry, if you are a business using TAX PREPARER for a number of clients.

The documentation is complete and to the point. I find that the program is very easy to use and mostly self-explanatory.

Remember how many times you had to transfer data from form to form when you did your taxes by hand? No longer. TAX PREPARER automatically moves data into other areas and forms that use it. This means that if you make a change or a correction, all else is corrected automatically.

The program's best feature is the itemized lists that you can prepare as detail for each appropriate line item in each form. If your household is like mine, having some income property, a self-employed income, two kids in daycare, and so on, you will appreciate sitting down with the computer, going through your bags of receipts, entering them, and printing out the entire form at one sitting.

MARSHA MATHER-THRIFT: TAX PREPARER is expensive, but it's the best personal tax preparer around. In fact, it's so good professionals can use it. So why hire them if you can do it yourself?

---

## Schemer's helper . . .

### PERSONAL TAX PLANNER

**Version 1.0; Apple II family; DOS 3.3; 64K ● IBM PC/XT compatibles; PC DOS; 128K; $99; copy-protected? Apple: NO; IBM PC: YES; Aardvark/McGraw-Hill, 1020 N. Broadway, Milwaukee, WI 53202; 414/225-7500.**

JOHN OVERTON, attorney: Sooner or later, most of us have the odd thought that if we refuse to spend most of our time thinking about the tax consequences of our daily lives, we will inevitably be penalized every April. Enter PERSONAL TAX PLANNER—a cheap, easy-to-use, effective means of modeling tax

## TYRANNY OF THE NEW

By the time you read this, some of the products we have covered may have bitten the dust, and new winners we haven't heard of yet may be sweeping the marketplace. This is a volatile, high-stakes game, especially in the area of integrated, all-in-one packages.

We have taken some advance looks at products not yet ready to go on the market (SYMPHONY, p. 111, FRAMEWORK, p. 110). These reviews had to be tentative, since we couldn't give the products a real-life workout.

Some things are still on the horizon for us as of June '84. A new publisher called Breakthrough Software in Novato, California, has three interesting packages promised for late 1984 for the IBM PC, PCjr, and PC XT. (1) SOFTOFFICE, which uses handsome icons and windows (à la Macintosh) and works with only seven (!) commands. It will integrate word-processing, spreadsheet, and database functions. (2) ABC, a database that does word processing. Each "field" in a database record can expand to contain an entire document. Interesting. (3) TIME LINE, a project scheduler and time manager. This program will do project-management analysis by task, human resource, or time.

Project management is another area where new products are rapidly emerging. One that people are waiting for is MACPROJECT, a Macintosh version of the highly acclaimed LISA PROJECT.

Expect a lot of action for the Macintosh. Major software developers are hurrying to bring out versions of their most popular products for the Mac. Lotus, predictably, is working on a SYMPHONY-like package for the Macintosh.

Portable lap computers are also on the frontier for integrated software. SYMPHONY, for example, was designed to be on a chip and may be expected on portables soon.

OVATION is an integrated system with word processor, spreadsheet, graphics, file management, and communications. It is highly touted for its ease of use, simplicity, and smooth integration. It looks like a head-on competitor to JACK2 in the quick-'n'-easy realm. It's more powerful and more expensive—and it requires top-of-the-line hardware. It comes in color and you can have windows if you wish. (IBM PC/XT or TRS-80 2000; 512K; hard disk; copy-protected? YES; $795; OVATION Technologies, 320 Norwood Park South, Norwood, MA 02062; 617/769-9300.)

## WHOLE EARTH RECOMMENDED MANAGING TOOLS

### (June 1984)

**INTEGRATED PACKAGES**

OPEN ACCESS, $595, p.109
FRAMEWORK, $695, p.110
INTUIT, $395, p.110
AURA, $595, p.111
SYMPHONY, $695, p.111
JACK2, $495, p.112
THE INCREDIBLE JACK, $129, p.112
JACK REPORT, $99, p.112
APPLEWORKS, $250, p.113

**INTEGRATORS**

DESQ, $399, p.114
MEMORY/SHIFT, $99, p.114
THE DESK ORGANIZER, $298, p.114

**PROJECT MANAGEMENT SOFTWARE (p. 115)**

HARVARD PROJECT MANAGER, $395
MILESTONE, $295
THE CONFIDENCE FACTOR, $389

**"VERTICAL" SOFTWARE FOR BUSINESSES AND PROFESSIONS**

EXACT DIMENSIONS!, $80, p.116
THE MASTER BUILDER, $800/$1250, p.116
CONSTRUCTION MANAGEMENT, $5995, p.117
CALPAS3, $795, p.117
MICROPAS, $795/$895, p.117
SUNPAS, $400, p.118

LEAD MANAGER 1.0, $350, p.118
THE REAL ESTATE CONSULTANT, $275, p.118
THE SALES EDGE, $250, p.119
PSYCHOLOGIST'S BILLING SYSTEM, $525-$550, p.119
PERSONAL LAWYER SERIES, p.120
WILLS, $80
POWER OF ATTORNEY, $70
RESIDENTIAL REAL ESTATE LEASE, $100
PROMISSORY NOTES, $70
VERDICT, $995, p.120
LITIGATION MANAGER, $750/$2000, p.120
FARM LEDGER PRO, $425, p.121
MAIL ORDER PRO, $695 to $1995, p.121

---

liability, and a tool for making investment decisions, solving real estate rent-or-purchase dilemmas, deciding job changes, and even structuring settlements from lawsuits. PERSONAL TAX PLANNER does not do your taxes for you or help you keep track of your income and deductions, but simply answers that powerful query, "What if?"

The program is essentially two programs of similar format: "alternative mode" and "projection mode." Alternative mode enables the user to compare the present-year tax consequences of up to five different courses of action, employing any of 48 different variables. For instance, is it preferable to realize a short-term capital gain of $5000 or a long-term capital gain of $4000? Projection mode allows the user to project tax consequences into the future as far as five years, thus making it possible to calculate balloon payments, pay raises, inflation, and other time-dependent situations.

Although my law practice is primarily copyright and intellectual property, complicated tax issues often arise. A client may need to know whether it's preferable to negotiate for a large advance or for a larger royalty payable in future years.

An accountant's time for this costs (conservatively) about $50. If the TAX PLANNER can answer these questions for you, the program pays for itself.

MARSHA MATHER-THRIFT: Other tax-planning programs, like Sunrise Software's TAX MINI-MISER, offer more sophisticated calculating features but cost three times as much. If you don't like to part with your money, TAX PLANNER is a secure bet.

*A significant time-saver for the professional tax preparer . . .*

### MICRO-TAX

**Version 1.0; most CP/M machines ●IBM PC compatibles; 2 disk drives or hard disk; Level I (Individual Package) $195; Level II (Professional Package) $1,000; Level III (Partnership/Corporate Package) $1,000; Level IV (Overseas Tax Package) $2,000; copy-protected? NO; Microcomputer Taxsystems, Inc., 6203 Variel Avenue, Suite A, Woodland Hills, CA 93167; 818/704-7800.**

J. WILLIAM PEZICK: MICRO-TAX cuts my work time by 20-30 percent, and that's absolutely critical during tax season. The biggest single time-saver is the carry-over to state tax forms. MICRO-TAX repeats the federal data on the state form, and then allows quick review. You need only enter the figures that have to be changed.

A good tax-preparation program should give you flexibility in entry, a wide range of schedules, good carry-forward features, and, most important, reliable updating and support. MICRO-TAX scores well on all points. It provides 35 federal and numerous state forms, including Foreign Tax Credit, Alternative Minimum Tax, and Limitation on Investment Interest Expense. It also has a very serviceable depreciation module.

The program is fully integrated and clearly designed with the professional in mind. Level I contains fourteen of the most commonly used schedules, Level II covers at least 95 percent of the professional tax preparer's needs. The company also supplies up-to-the-minute information via an electronic mailbox on Taxnet through The Source.

*MICRO-TAX provides 85-90% of the tax forms necessary for professional preparation of federal and state tax returns. The company ships updated software that incorporates the most recent tax law changes regularly in January each year. Tax preparers can save loads of time entering repeated data and use those free hours to take on new clients.*

I've prepared tax returns for ten years and used MICRO-TAX for three. In addition to all the preparation-time benefits, MICRO-TAX has also given me another deduction—after April 15 every year I'm now in business as a computer consultant.

*A dynamic tool for the tax professional . . .*

### MASTER TAX PREPARER

**Version 83.3; IBM PC compatibles; 192K; 2 disk drives; also formatted for computers running CP/M, MP/M, Xenix, TURBODOS or MmmOST; 64K; (call for specific machine compatibility and requirements); copy-protected? NO; $1695; CPAids, 1061 Fraternity Circle, Kent, OH 44240; 216/678-9015.**

DEE KLEIN, E.A.: The MASTER TAX PREPARER program is a logical system that allows easy direct entry during client interviews, something my clients seem to enjoy. This also makes on-the-spot refund and liability estimates possible.

No matter how you do your returns, MASTER TAX PREPARER is a program worth considering when you set out to buy. It has been out long enough to mature, and each year's update contains added features. The most recent is a diagnostic that summarizes the data to be printed and encourages that last-minute check for an IRA or other recently added item. Another is a client fee program that maintains billing information and tabulates the final fees for services.

MASTER TAX PREPARER is comprehensive enough to be used as an interview tool or a tax planner. It's a dynamic tool for the tax practitioner who has decided to prepare computerized returns in-house.

MARSHA MATHER-THRIFT: These two are neck and neck for best professional tax preparation programs. MICRO-TAX offers the most variety and costs less, but MASTER TAX PREPARER offsets all that with its yearly features innovations.

*MASTER TAX PREPARER entry screens duplicate tax forms and schedules. Since the program is interactive, the totals you enter on schedules leap instantly forward to appropriate lines on master returns. Most tax software does this, but MASTER TAX PREPARER makes sure the important items also get into your client billing file.*

## MANAGING

### Sharon Rufener, Domain Editor

SHARON RUFENER: This section evaluates software that helps you manage your data, your business, your computer, and your life.

We'll cover the *integrated* all-in-one packages—usually containing a word processor, spreadsheet, data manager, and more. This is the direction the software marketplace is currently taking—some developments are already here; many are still on the horizon. Integrated packages reviewed are AURA, INTUIT, JACK2, OPEN ACCESS, FRAMEWORK, SYMPHONY, INCREDIBLE JACK, APPLEWORKS.

We also cover some *integrators*—programs that act as umbrellas over groups of programs. They tie together programs so that two or more can be run simultaneously and pass data to each other. MEMORY/SHIFT and DESQ are the integrators we review.

A similar function is performed by the operating systems that provide an integrated environment—the LISA, WINDOWS, and CONCURRENT DOS (p. 174). These are reviewed in other sections.

Then, there are integrator programs that tie together only families of products. EASY PLUS (coming in late 1984) will do it

for IUS programs (EASY WRITER II, etc.). STARBURST integrates WORDSTAR and other MicroPro products and lets you do a form of programming to control the flow of a job. There is also VISI-ON, a mouse-driven windowing integrator for the VISI-group of software (VISICALC, p. 71, VISIWORD, etc.). The manufacturer is hoping other vendors will adapt programs to run under its system. We are not recommending VISI-ON or STARBURST, mainly because they integrate so few attractive programs. However, if you are wedded to one of their products, you might consider their integrator.

The section also covers software packages designed for managing your business activities, such as appointment tending and project scheduling. The packages we review are DESK ORGANIZER, HARVARD PROJECT MANAGER, CONFIDENCE FACTOR, and MILESTONE.

Finally we have what's called *vertical software*—all-embracing packages for particular businesses and professions. The number of software products for specific business needs is already vast and is still growing. Specialized vertical packages tend to be more expensive than the integrated packages, raising the question, Why not get a general-purpose all-in-one package instead of one tailored to your type of business? Several reasons. It's a major undertaking to design a complete business system yourself and it's expensive to hire a consultant to do it for you. And integrated packages generally lack the capability for creating "single-entry" accounting systems, where you enter an item only once and the program automatically posts the data to the appropriate files.

## WANT IT ALL NOW?

STEWART BRAND: Of course you want it all now. That's why you bought a computer. To increase your productivity by making your work faster, easier, and more connected to itself. You do not wish to spend your day helping machines translate code, endlessly manipulating a file received over the phone so you can edit it with the WORDSTAR you're stuck with, remembering which of your programs speak to each other and which don't, remembering the different command incantations you must make here and there, searching manuals for the fragment of arcana that will break the data logjam between your spreadsheet and your database.

The promise of relief from all that is what makes this domain one of the fastest moving in the marketplace. The integrateds promise (and mostly deliver) the ability to have most of your computer operations all in one program. The integrators promise (and mostly don't deliver) the ability to have a facile over-program connecting all your existing application programs. The verticals promise (and charge royally for) a package suited precisely to your business.

*Sharon Rufener*

BARBARA ROBERTSON: Domain Editor Sharon Rufener has been involved on all sides of information management. As an office manager equipped with typewriter and adding machine (for a branch of the Frank Lloyd Wright Foundation, the architecture firm that carries on Mr. Wright's work), she struggled with manual paperwork systems. As a COBOL programmer and system designer for banks and clothing manufacturers, she mastered the intricacies of big mainframe systems, while getting a law degree and passing the California State Bar. Now, as a consultant to small businesses, including County Fair organizations, securities marketing firms, and software dealers, she relishes the creativity of the micro world, where, she says, "hardware, software, and users are closer together." Deeply concerned about the quality and usefulness of software from the user's point of view, Sharon is an appropriate seamstress for this crazy-quilt section.

## The Integrateds

SHARON RUFENER: One message keeps coming through from our reviewers: "If I had seen this integrated package first, I would never have bought my word processor, spreadsheet, and database. This is all the software a person needs!"

So why *did* they buy their standalone software? Because before Spring 1984, almost no all-in-one packages on the market integrated all three main functions into one smooth and easy system. Now a lot of products do it. Some also offer graphs, telecommunications, and a procedural programming language. An additional advantage of these packages is their use of a single set of common commands, which makes learning the whole system as easy as learning one program. And the packages sell for significantly less money than it costs to purchase the equivalent applications separately. It looks like integrated systems are going to make many standalone word processors, spreadsheets, and file managers obsolete.

### What Are Integrated Packages Good For?

With an integrated package, you can produce more varied documents than with a word processor alone. It allows you to include lists, calculations, and in many cases graphs, all on one printout. That can be useful for bills, estimates, proposals, business plans, analyses, research reports—any communication involving numbers or lists.

Also, integrated software handles form letters more elegantly than do word processing programs with mail-merge capabilities. A database module handles a name/address file in a friendlier, more versatile fashion than, say, WORDSTAR (p. XXX) with MAILMERGE. You enter your addresses and other data into a form on the screen. You can then select and sort records from that file before merging them into the form letter.

In an integrated program, you can automatically select activities and transfer data between them. You could, say, store transactions (such as sales) on your database, send the numerical data to the spreadsheet, and use totals from the spreadsheet to generate graphs or charts, illustrating, for instance, how this month's sales compare in detail to last month's.

### What Aren't They Good For?

Integrated packages are not good for setting up complete single-entry accounting systems to run a business. Transactions will not automatically post to more than one file. Further, "password" file security and data validation for error-trapping, which every good accounting system should have, generally are non-existent on the integrateds. Also, most integrateds are not programmable, a definite disadvantage where a business system

is to be used by clerical workers or others who can't take the time to learn the whole thing and who need a preprogrammed set of procedures to control separate phases of the job.

### How Good Are the Integrateds?

The newer ones appear to be very good indeed. Each element in a package is usually as easy to use as the friendliest standalone equivalents. However, the first integrated packages, such as CONTEXT MBA and T-MAKER, suffered in varying degrees from their earliness—murky manuals, cryptic commands, and a certain awkwardness of execution.

It's possible to generalize a bit in evaluating the separate modules in integrated software. The word-processor modules, for example, range from medium-featured to minimal—usually in accordance with the package price.

The spreadsheets are generally quite powerful. INTUIT has the easiest and most elegant spreadsheet in existence.

The databases are generally simple, friendly little single-file data managers, about equivalent to PFS:FILE (p. 80). OPEN ACCESS has an actual relational database that can tie together more than one file.

The end-products of the graphics capabilities, when present, range from simple ones to dazzling 3-D charts and graphs (OPEN ACCESS). Generally, the graphs are the offspring of a spreadsheet, but some products can generate them from the database as well (AURA, JACK2).

### Which One Should You Buy?

Which one? It depends—first, on your hardware, then on your needs. If you have a CP/M system, then T-MAKER ($275; T/MAKER Co., 2115 Landings Drive, Mountain View, CA 94043; 415/962-0195), which we have not included in our recommended products, is about your only choice. It's not as chummy or as elegant as most of the others, but it should suffice.

For the Apple computer, the INCREDIBLE JACK is a good, cheap little program for home use. APPLEWORKS will serve the needs of a small business nicely.

There's more choice in the IBM realm. We recommend INTUIT for large documents: Its automatic outline structuring is perfect for research reports and documentation writing. JACK2 is best for quick summaries illustrated with figures and charts. OPEN ACCESS has the most powerful spreadsheet and graphics for serious number crunching. AURA, FRAMEWORK, and SYMPHONY all promise that they will be programmable, to let you create prefab minisystems for entering data and generating reports.

*Lots of options,
    but spreadsheet prevails . . .*

## OPEN ACCESS

Version A1.00; IBM PC/XT compatibles ● Tandy
2000; 192K; copy-protected? NO; $595; Software
Products International, 10240 Sorrento Valley Rd.,
San Diego, CA 92121; 619/450-1526.

ERNIE TELLO: OPEN ACCESS has six
programs integrated into one system—
database, spreadsheet, word processor, 3-D
graphs, communications, and appointment
scheduler. An incredible value for the price.
Information in one of OPEN ACCESS's
modules is available in the others, and you
can "import and export" data (move files
back and forth from outside programs). It's
all menu-driven with command windows
opening at each step to display your choices
and an executable command language to
control the show.

The word processor is more than minimal. It
has block moving, find-and-replace,
justification and margining, mass mailing,
and the ability to use data both from the other
modules and from outside programs as well.

The "information manager" (database) offers
powerful query capabilities and streamlined
record and screen design. Not so great: fields
are limited to 40 characters, and redesigning
existing files is difficult.

The spreadsheet, with 216 columns and 3000
rows, is more powerful than most, including
1-2-3. It lets you sort columns, block off
areas, and make reference to other models. A
unique feature is the ability to do "goal
seeking," where you enter the result you want
and get the program to recalculate an
"independent variable."

The 3-D graphics module is spectacular and
impressively fast. Also, you can make "slide
shows" by scheduling a sequence of various
graphs in different formats: pie charts, line,
bars, and overlays—up to four on the screen
at once.

The communications module lets you
transmit data or documents without leaving
the OPEN ACCESS environment. It works with
acoustic, direct-connect, or intelligent
modems, local networks, and mainframe
hookups. It can do automatic dialing.

The time manager is a useful appointment
calendar and scheduler. There's also a
calculator window for quick calculations.

SHARON RUFENER: If spreadsheeting is your
heaviest need, this champion number
cruncher and chart maker is the one to buy.
And it has a true relational database that can
tie five files together at once. But
telecomputing heavies beware: the
communications module has a limiting
feature—both the sending and receiving
computers have to be running OPEN
ACCESS.

*Here's how the integrated all-in-one package
OPEN ACCESS works. Let's get some data from the
database. (This is the only integrated package
with a relational database instead of a single-file
manager.) We can move some figures from the
database into a spreadsheet. Then we can do
"goal-seeking": plug in the totals we want, and it
will recalculate backward. The spreadsheet totals
can be displayed as a graph (it's a 3-D graph—no
other all-in-one product has that). And, finally, we
can use the word processing module to write a
summary and wrap it all up into one report.*

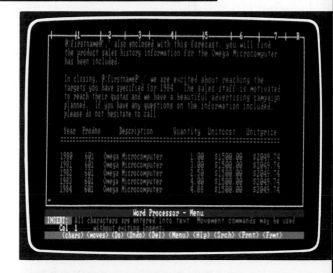

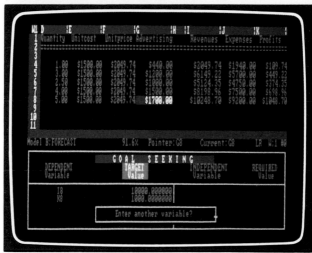

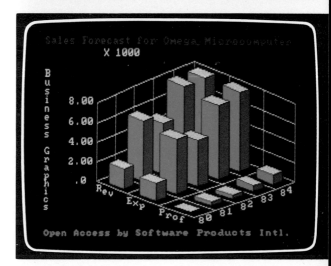

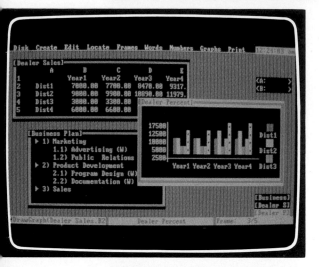

FRAMEWORK uses an outline format to group and display files relating to a particular job. It will display several of its integrated functions (word processing, spreadsheet, database, and graphics) in windows—you can shuffle the windows around and work on the contents in the top one.

*An all-in-one geared to text work . . .*

## FRAMEWORK

**IBM PC/XT compatibles; 256K; copy-protected? YES; $695; Ashton-Tate, 10150 W. Jefferson Blvd., Culver City, CA 90230; 213/204-5570.**

PHILIP ELMER-DEWITT: First impressions of pre-release FRAMEWORK: a very sweet program, with a fast 'n' easy spreadsheet, passable word processor (see the table on p. 50), superfast bar grapher, and a little toy database program.

You get into the program through pull-down menus and windows. The best window of all gives you an outline straight out of Living Videotext's THINKTANK (p. 92), where each line in the outline represents a graph, spreadsheet, list, or text. This puts the whole program into another dimension, one its competitors have yet to explore.

What FRAMEWORK lacks: a communications program (but you can patch in your own.)

What it's up against: Lotus, which gives 1-2-3 owners its 5-in-1 SYMPHONY (including communications) on trade-in for another $200.

What it's got going for it: Ashton-Tate's name (DBASE II, etc.) and clout. And an impressive demo.

SHARON RUFENER: Looks like there will be a battle of the giants between Lotus and Ashton-Tate in the integrated arena. FRAMEWORK is supposed to offer "tight coupling with DBASE II" (p. 85), giving it a built-in head start with the owners of that best-seller. It also has a programming language, which ought to make it popular with a grateful army of consultants and applications developers who have been earning their livings off DBASE II.

The central concept in FRAMEWORK is a file directory in the form of an outline that ties everything together. You hang your files, forms, documents, etc. into appropriate spots in the outline. The contents of one or more levels can be displayed in "frames" (which resemble "windows" remarkably). You can move data from here to there, cut and paste, and overlap, shuffle, expand, and shrink the frames in true windowing style.

You get a goodly selection of graph styles, and (thank you, Ashton-Tate!) you don't need a graphics board or color monitor for it. The database module has less power but more speed than DBASE II.

One very interesting feature—you can use a Search and Replace command in *any* of the modules. Like the spreadsheet. Like the database. Amazing.

INTUIT's super-easy spreadsheet can be automatically generated from database records, including the titles for the rows and columns. The spreadsheet understands English. Tell it to "ADD SALARIES THROUGH MISC. EXPENSES GIVING TOTAL EXPENSES." It will automatically add all the applicable blocks of cells and create the TOTAL line.

*An intuitive manuscript organizer . . .*

## INTUIT

**Martel Firing; IBM PC/XT compatibles; 256K; copy-protected? YES; $395; Noumenon Corp., 512 Westline Dr., Alameda, CA 94501; 415/521-2145.**

SHARON RUFENER: INTUIT was originally developed as a solution to a real-world problem—managing and producing reports for large research projects. This unique system has no menus or complicated commands, yet it is extremely powerful and simple to use.

INTUIT thoroughly integrates word processing, spreadsheets, and file management. You can zing and zap data back and forth among files, cut and paste, and hop from one activity to another with great agility. The directory, which integrates the system, is a multilevel list using descriptive phrases instead of shorthand file IDs. You make your selection with one keystroke.

The word processor alone is worth the price. It has all the standard features a serious wordslinger would want. It even takes care of widows and orphans—those awkward dangling lines at the bottoms and tops of pages. The formatting concept puts it in a class of its own—it creates an outlining structure that lets you enter text at any level, with appropriate indentation and optional automatically numbered headings for each level. If you are writing something that has

chapters, sections, paragraphs, subparagraphs, and lists, the headings and formatting are done automatically.

INTUIT has the ultimate in spreadsheets—not the biggest or the strongest, but the most elegant, and you can learn to use it in about fifteen minutes. You talk to it in English: ADD RENT THRU MISC. EXPENSES = TOTAL EXPENSES will give you the bottom line for a block of numbers. It will even create the TOTAL EXPENSES row for you if you haven't already set it up—good intuition.

You can set up and execute nested spreadsheet procedures (this is almost a programming language), and the spreadsheet is reasonably large—200 rows by 65 columns or vice versa, and you can "tilt" it either way, back and forth. A graphics capability will be available for INTUIT by the time you read this.

The file manager is standard and straightforward—a good place to stash your names and addresses and keep transactions. It can serve as a mail-merge adjunct to the word processor: you can add records to a file by entering data into the form letter. Or, alternatively, crank out form letters using selected records from an existing data file.

Those looking for superpowerful number crunching might look elsewhere, but if you need a workhorse of a word processor, say for technical writing, and a no-sweat spreadsheet, look at INTUIT.

*Power and flexibility
in an integrated package . . .*

# AURA

Version 1.0; IBM PC/XT compatibles; 256K; color graphics board required for graphics capability; copy-protected? YES; $595; Softrend, Inc., 2 Manor Parkway, Salem, NH 03079; 603/898-1896.

KEN MILBURN: Sometimes a software company will find itself deservedly famous for a single applications program, and will take advantage of its reputation by releasing a series of substandard applications so it can boast a "family" of programs. AURA seems to promise what those companies don't deliver—a single software package that does all the basic office tasks and is so well integrated that the commands are the same in each application, and the files you create in one application program are easily shared with the files you've created in another. And all in a package that's so easy to learn that I found myself zipping through it without glancing at a manual.

Note that I say "seems to promise." I am reviewing a prerelease copy of AURA, and am trusting that the few bugs I found will be corrected, and the program will stand up to heavy daily use.

Still, the program is exciting enough to talk about now. It's especially notable because its components are powerful, yet its logical, menu-driven process can take relative novices by the hand and lead them into the serious stuff. Help screens for most functions are accessible in two keystrokes.

And the components? The database is one of the finest single-file information managers

I've come across, most reminiscent of DB MASTER (p. 83). You can search data on any word in the file! You can generate a report laid out exactly to your specifications in less than ten minutes. These reports can even be used to fill in preprinted forms. You can create as many data-entry screens per file as you wish, and each screen can have up to four pages. This one segment might be worth the full system price.

The word processor is all the word processor most offices will need (though it has no spelling checker). Documents can be of any length, and data from the other applications can be inserted anywhere.

The spreadsheet is similar in size and design to Microsoft's MULTIPLAN (p. 70). More than 50 preprogrammed functions come with it. Look-up tables are possible, so information can be pulled into the spreadsheet when your conditions are met.

In graphics mode, you can specify which information from a spreadsheet you want charted and how you want it presented and labeled. You can choose data from the database as well, or simply input data onscreen. Best of all, you can create free-form graphics and diagrams to illustrate reports and presentations.

It's possible to "program" AURA for specific applications and save the commands for later execution. The promise is exciting. Softrend is offering an unbelievable amount of convenience, power, and flexibility for the money.

SHARON RUFENER: Softrend is a new company, and it remains to be seen what

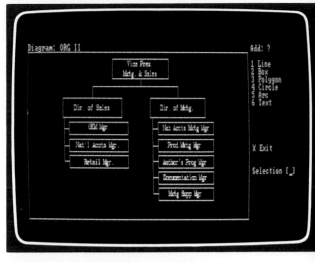

*AURA does the usual integrated functions (word processing, spreadsheet, database, and graphs) and, in addition, adds a unique feature: free-form graphics. Here we have used the graphics program (something like MACPAINT) to make an organization chart.*

support it will offer for this major product, whose test version promises so much. This is the only integrated package we've seen with a graphics capability beyond generating charts and graphs. You could use this to make organization charts and flowcharts or to embellish your printouts with original artwork. Another noteworthy feature is AURA's ability to fill out preprinted forms—very nice for people who routinely use standard forms.

---

*The spreadsheet that communicates . . .*

# SYMPHONY

IBM PC/XT compatibles; 320K; color graphics board required for graphics; copy-protected? YES; $695 ($200 credit given for 1-2-3 trade-in); Lotus Development Corp., 161 First St., Cambridge, MA 02142; 617/492-7171.

SHARON RUFENER: In all of baseball history, only Johnny Vander Meer threw two no-hitters in a row. Lotus Development is attempting the equivalent by following its perfect-game 1-2-3 (p. 67) with the further integrated all-in-one SYMPHONY—an improved version of its current winner beefed-up with a real word processor, a versatile telecommunications capability, and a powerful and programmable command language. We are reviewing it in its prerelease form because we know it will be prominently on sale by the time you read this.

Here are some observations on the demos we have seen.

RIK JADRNICEK: SYMPHONY has profound potential for building turnkey models—preprogrammed applications, ready to use off the shelf—and I don't think that much of the modules' power was lost in the integration.

BARBARA ROBERTSON: To get the most mileage out of it, you have to think like a programmer. You have to know what result you want and work backward from that. Also, to really make SYMPHONY sing, you need 512K of memory.

ART KLEINER: The telecommunications capabilities offer some interesting possibilities for applications. One of the biggest problems with communications is compatibility—and it looks like they thought that out very well. It should be possible to set up a bulletin board with it—you can dial in

and get into the database. Also, you can access a remote database and store data for your own later use. For instance, you could program it to run at night, dial up Dow Jones and pull in the data, and present you with charts in the morning.

STEWART BRAND: The word processor is a good middleweight—but no speller (yet). Also no "Undo" command, no onscreen page breaks, no automatic reformatting; it does bold and italic, superscript and subscript, but they don't show on the screen (see the table on p. 50). The complete integration with telecommunications, however, is a boon.

SHARON RUFENER: I'm not ready to say that SYMPHONY will be the breakthrough in its field that 1-2-3 was. In fact, I doubt it. But the upgrade deal for Lotus customers and the communications capabilities make it a must-see program for those looking for an all-in-one.

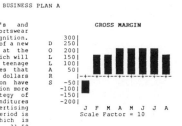

BUSINESS PLAN A

DESCRIPTION: Our men's and lady's line of athletic sportswear had good brand name recognition. We are particularly proud of a new line of swimmer aimed at the affluent teenage market which will be promoted by a famous teenage idol. Experience indicates that additional promotional dollars spent later in the season have minimal impadct in generation more sales, therefore, a strategy of declining advertising expenditures is proposed. Total Advertising Dollars budgeted for the period is 12.50 million dollars, which is expected to generate 31.50 million dollars in sales.

GROSS MARGIN

```
      300 |
D     250 |
O     200 |
L     150 |
L     100 |
A      50 |
R      --+--+--+--+--+--+--+--+--
S     -50 |
     -100 |
     -150 |
     -200 |
          J F M A M J J A
          Scale Factor = 10
```

|  | JAN | FEB | MAR | APR | MAY | JUN | JUL | AUG |
|---|---|---|---|---|---|---|---|---|
| ADV. $ SPENT | 3500 | 2625 | 1969 | 1477 | 1008 | 831 | 623 | 467 |
| CUM. ADV. $ | 3500 | 6125 | 8094 | 9571 | 10579 | 11410 | 12033 | 12500 |
| SALES $ | 3569 | 5354 | 4819 | 4337 | 3903 | 3513 | 3162 | 2846 |
| CUM. SALES $ | 3569 | 8923 | 13742 | 18079 | 21982 | 25495 | 28657 | 31503 |
| PRODUCTION COSTS | 968 | 1304 | 1173 | 1056 | 950 | 855 | 770 | 693 |
| GROSS MARGIN | -899 | 1425 | 1677 | 1804 | 1945 | 1827 | 1769 | 1686 |

(In thousands of $)

CUMULATIVE ADVERTISING DOLLARS VS. CUMULATIVE SALES DOLLARS
(IN THOUSANDS OF DOLLARS)
Bar 1= Cum. Adv. $/Bar 2= Cum. Sales $

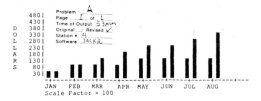

*JACK2 says it can create "cut and paste" documents, like this one, combining text, calculations, spreadsheet and graph, faster and easier than any other software product can. To prove the point, they have been holding public contests—and winning.*

*Like a jackrabbit . . .*

## JACK2

**Version 1.0; IBM PC/XT; 128K; copy-protected? YES; $495; Business Solutions, Inc., 60 E. Main St., Kings Park, NY 11754; 800/645-4513 or, in NY, 516/269-1120.**

SHARON RUFENER: In the spring of '84, JACK2 (they use a rangy jackrabbit for a logo) challenged its integrated-package competitors, such as CONTEXT MBA, 1-2-3 (plus a word processor), and the VISI-ON group to a series of races over some short obstacle courses from the business world. Contestants were given specifications for three one-page business plans, which they were to produce within 90 minutes. The documents called for a little word-processing with imbedded calculations, a little spreadsheeting, and two graphs apiece. Halfway through the race, changes were handed to the contestants—just as a real boss would do 40 minutes before the Big Meeting. As of the third in the nationwide series of compute-offs, JACK2 was still winning handily. This was an educational, imaginative, and gutsy way to publicize a product.

JACK2's word processor has the usual features a person spoiled by a powerful word processing program wants to see: word-wrap, justification, centering, search-and-replace, underlining and highlighting, and variable column set-ups. Especially useful for newsletters, JACK2 can handle multicolumn formats, and its word-wrap is column-sensitive.

The spreadsheet capability is large enough for anyone who doesn't work for the IRS or NASA. You get up to 1024 rows and 1024 columns (where would you find a printer to deal with *that*?). You can optionally address cells by name rather than coordinates—that is, MARGIN = SALES − COST. And you can set up "IF . . . THEN . . . ELSE" types of commands to orchestrate spreadsheet activities.

The graphs are unartistic but adequate bar and scatter styles. They can chart numbers from the file manager or from a form letter as well as from a spreadsheet. When you change any numbers the derivative is automatically revised.

The file manager has the usual forms-design, sort, and select capabilities. There are up to 1024 fields per record and a whopping 15,000 characters per field, so you can use it for storing text. You can also change the record formats at any time.

Though individual components here are not as strong as the best standalones, JACK2 is the champ at quick cut-and-paste-type jobs. Also, the file manager, with its enormous capacity, has interesting possibilities for storing text—research notes? product descriptions? notes of meetings? You can fit about five single-spaced pages into one record! And those with limited memory space should note that JACK2 requires but 128K to get you hopping.

*Apple all-in-one for home use . . .*

## THE INCREDIBLE JACK

**Version 1.3; Apple II family; 64K; 2 disk drives; copy-protected? YES; $129;**

## JACK REPORT

**Version 1.0; Apple II family; 64K; copy-protected? NO; $99;**

**both from Business Solutions, Inc., 60 E. Main St., Kings Park, NY 11754; 800/645-4513 or, in NY, 516/269-1120.**

SHARON RUFENER: THE INCREDIBLE JACK (of all trades) truly lives up to its name. For the incredible price of $129, this all-in-one integrated package has some features you won't find in the Cadillac of word processors or the Lincoln Continental of database managers. On the other hand, some features are totally lacking, which you should note before buying.

What JACK does, it does supremely well and with a minimum of fuss. Seamlessly, it joins together text, spreadsheet calculations, and record-keeping data management. You can combine any or all of the capabilities to produce a document. The exemplary documentation is written for regular humans, the tutorials cover all the bases, and the whole thing can be mastered in a day.

JACK's perfectly acceptable word processor has the easiest text moves and deletes I've seen, as well as other niceties, including page numbering and titles at the top or bottom of each page. It makes form letters a snap and lets you include numeric calculations in the body of the letter. You can manually enter the data needed to complete the form letters or merge it from one of JACK's data files.

However, a lot of the features found in more serious word processors are missing in THE INCREDIBLE JACK. You don't get underlining, boldface, automatic centering, or search-and-replace. Unlike its similarly named stablemate (JACK2, above, which is a totally different program running on the IBM), JACK won't win any speed races.

The file management feature is as simple as anything around. You define the file by designing a form on the screen, as in PFS:FILE. This layout is used for data entry, record selection, and display. But again, there are limitations. In this file manager you get no totals, subtotals, or counts on the figures in the files. It will do calculations within a record but not across a file.

JACK has a companion software package called JACK REPORT, which solves some of the limitations of the file manager. With REPORT you can produce printouts in column-and-row format (one line of data per record with the specified data fields lined up in rows). You can sort, count, total, subtotal, or average things. All in all, JACK REPORT is a nice, basic little report generator. And, true to the JACK philosophy, it is incredibly easy to use.

*State-of-the-art integration for the Apple . . .*

## APPLEWORKS

**Rupert Lissner; Version 1.1; Apple IIe/IIc; PRODOS; 64K; 2 disk drives; copy-protected? NO; $250; Apple Computer, 20525 Mariani Ave., Cupertino, CA 95014; 800/538-9696; also published as III E-Z PIECES; Rupert Lissner; Apple III; 128K (256K recommended); hard disk recommended; copy-protected? YES; $295; Haba Systems, Inc., 15154 Stagg Street, Van Nuys, CA 91405; 818/901-8828.**

CHARLIE CLEMENTS: At last, a program that makes my IIe seem indispensable.

In this integrated package, everything is menu driven. The user works on an electronic desktop, a wonderful metaphor that allows even the least experienced user to learn intuitively to "move" with the program. Makes my IIe feel like a LISA, kind of.

The word processor is not as muscular as APPLEWRITER but more than compensates by its elegance of use (see the table on p. 50). The cursor is easier to move than in any other word-processing program I've worked with.

While no slouch, the spreadsheet is less powerful than its full-blown parents, VISICALC and MULTIPLAN. Adequate for small businesses and individuals.

The database is reminiscent of PFS:FILE in the way it lets you design your own files. One of the most remarkable features is the Zoom command, which allows you to get all the information in the database on the selected record.

Had APPLEWORKS been available when I got VISICALC and APPLEWRITER, those two

programs would never have made it home with me.

PAUL WALHUS: APPLEWORKS has an almost gamelike appeal—you glide effortlessly from one function to another. The manual is written in warm and cuddly Apple style. The screen menus are clearly labeled, with pictures of file folders stacked on top of each other. Help screens are readily available. It gets files from its "desktop" and goes from application to application with lightning speed. You can have twelve files of any description on your desktop at the same time.

With cut-and-paste you can highlight a block of text, move the cursor to where you want it inserted, hit return, and your words leap into their landing place, no matter which application you target. Easy, obvious, and admirable!

APPLEWORKS convinced me that I had a power tool that would do all the jobs that formerly required an assortment of programs. This may be the most powerful Apple program of all time.

SHARON RUFENER: Seems the choice for Apple owners is between this wonder and INCREDIBLE JACK. APPLEWORKS won't run on IIs and II + 's, but those with IIe's and c's (Apple alphabet soup here, sorry) might consider APPLEWORKS well worth the $120 differential.

*APPLEWORKS does the big three: word processing, spreadsheet, and file management. It has an easy, gamelike appeal—options take the form of a desktop filled with files to choose from. You can zoom in on all the data you have filed on a particular subject.*

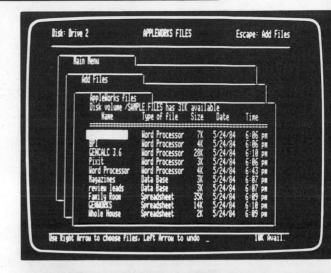

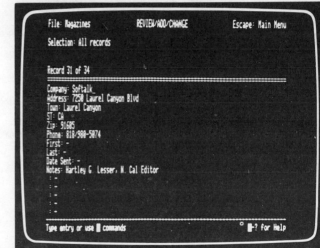

## Integrators

SHARON RUFENER: Wouldn't it be wonderful if you could integrate your favorite programs into one system? Ideally, you'd merge the powerful word processor you have finally mastered with your high-powered database, and then tie in all your carefully created spreadsheet files.

DESQ and MEMORY/SHIFT are programs making that promise. They vow to integrate any MS-DOS programs—a tough vow to keep, since your favorite programs probably come from different manufacturers. If you are going to run programs without exchanging data—say you are viewing your notes in one window and writing something in another—there should be no problem. Same if you simply want to cut and paste a document together from things you see on the screen. But getting standalone applications from different manufacturers to cooperate fully— swapping data as if they were blood relatives—is tricky stuff.

No wonder the claims of these "we can integrate anything!"

programs are often inflated. If you want to swap data among files, you are going to have to know an awful lot about the programs and their file formats—probably more than the program documentation will tell you. Installation and testing can be a chewing-gum-and-baling-wire ordeal, and if you don't like heavy-duty technical challenges, you had better forget the whole thing. The installation of systems such as DESQ looks like a promising new area of endeavor for computer consultants.

An integrator is not a good, cheap alternative to an integrated all-in-one package. Integrators require lots of memory and usually a hard disk, so you may have to purchase extra horsepower. If you don't already have the applications you want integrated, you will have to buy them too.

If you are starting from scratch, you will probably find an all-in-one integrated package easier, cheaper, and more satisfactory. However, if you have already mastered a favorite program, stored a lot of data in its files, and don't want to begin again, then an integrator like DESQ or MEMORY/SHIFT makes sense.

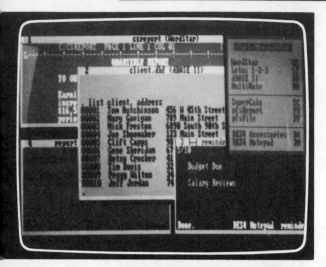

**DESQ is an umbrella kind of a program which integrates existing programs into one system. Tie together your word processor, database, and spreadsheet programs and you can run these programs together and make a cut and paste document. Or send data from one file to another. If you add a telecommunications program, you can transmit your work-product somewhere else. Like an umbrella it can be a bit awkward.**

*A multicolored juggling act for well-muscled systems . . .*

## DESQ

**Gary Pope; IBM PC/XT compatibles; 256K plus sufficient memory for largest application program running under DESQ; 5MB hard disk; copy-protected? YES; $399; Quarterdeck Office Systems, 1918 Main St., Santa Monica, CA 90405; 213/392-9851.**

SHARON RUFENER: DESQ *looks* like a dazzler. Up to nine windows in magnificent technicolor and a mouse to move it all around and click the pieces into place. You can, if you wish, specify the color you want for your word-processor window, your spreadsheet, and so on—or just let DESQ do your color coordinating.

DESQ is also smart. It will "learn" a series of commands and let you execute them later. It will also let you create forms, menus, and your own help screens for tailor-made applications.

DESQ will run almost any program, but that "almost" can be a killer. It can't handle anything that doesn't run under DOS or that bypasses DOS BIOS—VISI FILE, for instance. It can't referee between programs that are

fighting each other for the same file or modem, or insist on inserting themselves into the same place in memory.

DESQ can juggle data. It does this flawlessly in the screen environment—cut and paste is no problem. It can usually send things from one window into another program without difficulty if the data is in ASCII text format, or if the sending and receiving files are the same type. It can save up to 22 screens' worth of data and deposit it where you want it. What it doesn't handle smoothly is transferring incompatible data directly from one file to another. If you don't want to go through a lot of technical hassle, send your data via the screen—it's more tedious but more foolproof.

DESQ is for you if your hardware system is well-muscled, you want to get your favorite programs on speaking terms with each other, and you don't mind spending $400 to make it happen.

*A computer "secretary" for $298 . . .*

## THE DESK ORGANIZER

**Collopy, Huesman & Milner; IBM PC/XT compatibles; 128K; copy-protected? NO; $298; Warner Software, Inc., Dept. 2, 666 5th Ave., New York, NY 10103; 800/223-0880.**

DAVE SMITH: In my small and rapidly growing mail-order business, operations were getting complicated and I needed to hire a secretary to keep up with it all. With THE DESK ORGANIZER, I was able to justify buying a second computer to be my secretary.

Here's how I work with my "secretary" on a daily basis: THE DESK ORGANIZER has integrated into my Compaq some of the clutter that was on my desk. It has a clock that chimes every hour and a calendar that can be paged through by day or month. It tracks appointments and reminds me with alarms or chimes. It has a Rolodex-type cross-indexed filer that can also be used to dial phone numbers. Included are a four-register floating-point calculator, and notepads that can be time-stamped, cross-referenced, filed, and printed out. Putting it into background mode allows me to use other software as it continues to remind me of appointments. It does not make coffee.

*Cheap substitute . . .*

## MEMORY/SHIFT

**Jonathan More; IBM PC/XT compatibles; 128K minimum; copy-protected? YES; $99; North American Business Systems, 642 Office Parkway, St. Louis, MO 63141; 800/325-1485.**

CHRIS GILBERT: For only $100 you can have a cheap substitute for such big-ticket integrated systems as LISA or VISI-ON. Like them, MEMORY/SHIFT allows you to run several programs simultaneously and to transfer data between them. If you have a color-graphics card and a second monitor, MEMORY/SHIFT will display a different program on each screen.

MEMORY/SHIFT was a Godsend for me in my job of designing instructional materials for computer programs. With it, I can place the program I'm writing about—say 1-2-3 (p. 67) or MULTIPLAN (p. 70)—in one partition, and do the writing/designing in another partition, using WORDSTAR (p. 56). I've even gotten fancy and split the writing in two by creating a third partition; I use one for the instructor's class notes and the other for the participants' materials.

BOB HALL: MEMORY/SHIFT is appropriate for users who routinely transfer data from one program to another, but it requires that you understand how the receiving program operates (it thinks the data is coming in through the keyboard). MEMORY/SHIFT works particularly well with data from a spreadsheet going to a word processor, but not the other way—I transferred data from VISICALC (p. 71) and SUPERCALC (p. 69) to the MULTIMATE word processor and it worked very well, but sending data from MULTIMATE did not work at all.

SHARON RUFENER: MEMORY/SHIFT got a bad review in **PC** magazine by a reviewer who pushed the program to the maximum and succeeded in getting it to crash and lose his data. Chris Gilbert used it to run only two or three programs at once and had no problems whatsoever. Bob Hall's comments illustrate the pitfalls of interprogram integration. Since this is tricky business, you should try to test out the combo you want before buying—if you can. However, $99 isn't a bad price for a gamble.

## Project-Management Software

SHARON RUFENER: You don't have to go to business school to learn how to schedule and manage projects—the following programs can do the trick. Whether you're a building contractor, software developer, magazine publisher, or just someone who needs to juggle tasks, time, and resources, you should take a serious look at project-management software. MBAs will tell you about the three different approaches to project management —GANTT, PERT, and critical path method. Too complicated to differentiate here—just rest assured that there is software to support all three.

Besides the following programs, we've been hearing announcements of more to come. And if you have an Apple LISA you should consider LISA PROJECT— some people say it's worth the price of the machine.

---

*Project management . . .*

## MILESTONE

**Organic Software; Version 1.13; CP/M-80; 64K ● CP/M-86; 128K ● IBM PC compatibles; 128K ● MS-DOS; 128K ● UCSD p-System; 128K; copy-protected? YES; $295; Digital Marketing, 2363 Boulevard Circle, Suite 8, Walnut Creek, CA 94595; 415/947-1000.**

---

STEWART BRAND: Someone loaned me a copy of MILESTONE, a critical-path method scheduling program. I nibbled at it tentatively, like a cat. It's pretty inviting. Soon I was inventing tasks and durations and prerequisites and pay levels, and the thing lined them up neatly, and correlated them, and prominently displayed the critical path of tasks that *had* to be done in sequence and the minimum time that would take. "Wanna print out?" it offered. "Sure." The printer snarled for a full minute, and I had a four-way analysis of the whole operation.

Instant scheduler. I'd messed around the subject of critical-path method for years, read and reviewed the books, spoken well of the technique. Now I was doing it. Power. Not just to me: to anybody in the shop who wanted to use the clarity and flexibility of a mutually made and understood schedule.

---

*The dean of project managers . . .*

## HARVARD PROJECT MANAGER

**Versions 1.0 (reviewed) and 1.16; IBM PC/XT compatibles; 128K; copy-protected? YES; $395; Harvard Software, Inc., 521 Great Rd., Littleton, MA 01460; 617/486-8431.**

---

MELVIN CONWAY: The HARVARD PROJECT MANAGER is the leader in the project management field, at least as far as the MS-DOS contenders go. It has a set of easy-to-grasp, menu-driven functions, graphic representation of bar charts and calendars; split screen capability; horizontal and vertical scrolling; and it also cost- and time-tracks each task. All necessary stuff to keep track of the project.

With HPM, you can feel free to try out different scenarios, a freedom seldom exercised when you do these things manually. While the program does not entirely eliminate tedium—you still have to enter and edit the data—once that is over, everything is at your fingertips for tracking, reporting, and figuring out how the inevitable glitches in a project will affect your deadline.

The manual is well organized and easy to follow. Besides letting you know how to use the software, it contains a valuable tutorial on project management.

---

*A versatile, unorthodox project manager . . .*

## THE CONFIDENCE FACTOR

**Falconer, Hermann & Newman; most CP/M machines; 64K ● IBM PC compatibles; 128K ● MS-DOS; 128K; copy-protected? NO; $389; Simple Software, 2 Pinewood, Irvine, CA 92714; 714/857-9179.**

---

JO-ANN STURTRIDGE: "Yes, you could do this manually with paper and calculator, but would you?" is the question THE CONFIDENCE FACTOR asks. This is a project-manager-style problem solver for tasks you would ordinarily decide by mentally balancing various factors and finally making a gut decision. THE CONFIDENCE FACTOR works by different means: decision trees, best alternative, risk simulation, linear programming, best course of action, critical-path method, and yes/no decisions.

THE CONFIDENCE FACTOR is geared toward business use, but it has unlimited personal uses too. Which car should I buy? Should I open a pottery studio? It forces you to prioritize your thinking by having you assign relative values to factors influencing your decisions. The best course of action becomes obvious—it is even highlighted!

---

BOB HALL: Features? HARVARD PROJECT MANAGER has PERT charts, GANTT charts, and critical path analysis. Up to 200 tasks can be assigned to any one project. The program will automatically roll up task durations and costs and build a "summary schedule" of the entire project. Changes made on lower level charts, including any overall changes in critical path, will be reflected at the higher level.

One problem I found was in producing printouts. You can rotate a report and print it lengthwise down the page, but this is s-l-o-w. It's necessary, though, for producing long charts without scissors and tape.

HARVARD PROJECT MANAGER is a significant improvement over VISI SCHEDULE (the previous champ), and should be considered by the user who wishes to automate the display and tracking of medium to large projects.

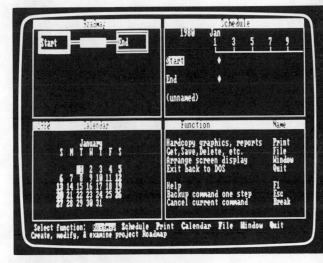

**HARVARD PROJECT MANAGER helps keep your project under control. The windows here show a project "roadmap" (PERT chart), a schedule, a calendar, and a menu to select the next function.**

## "Vertical" Software for Businesses and Professions

SHARON RUFENER: We have included some software for specific businesses in this section, but lack of space prevents us from covering the gamut of business activities. To paraphrase the late Mae West, "So many products, so little time!"

Obviously, the computer can transform any business. Perhaps the first package any professional should get is accounting software, to keep track of money and possibly to handle billing. After that, you can try software that helps you analyze the way you use your resources and make your profits. Such a package enables you to get control of your business by making planning and management more effective. Finally, you might find some programs to actually *automate* your activities! There are programs that help architects design buildings, that churn out legal documents, and that play the role of a savvy sales manager to show salespeople how to deal with their leads.

If you are ready to take the big plunge, look for a comprehensive package. Much more than a bookkeeper, it will provide a complete system for running your business. This can be a real plus if your enterprise has been suffering from disorganization. It can be a liability if your current system's methodology is inconsistent with the software package you would like to get.

Cost in these applications is secondary to effectiveness: even the most expensive microcomputer hardware and software system will probably cost less than the salary for one person to handle your paperwork for one year.

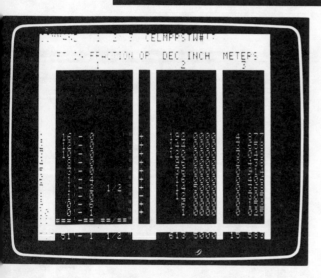

### For the builder's toolkit . . .

### EXACT DIMENSIONS!

**Version 1.0; Apple II family; 64K ● IBM PC compatibles; 64K; copy-protected? YES; $80; Aspen Inchware Corp., P.O. Box 3203, Aspen, CO 81612; 800/824-7888 (ordering) or 303/925-3734 (information).**

GREG MALKIN: For those who design or build things, I've found a great little item to add to your tool box. It's called EXACT DIMENSIONS! and it's been very useful to me in my engineering work.

*It's a calculator. It's a spreadsheet. It's a translator from feet to inches to metric, from fractions to decimals, and back again. It's EXACT DIMENSIONS!, an inexpensive and handy little program for the designer or builder.*

Imagine that you are building a house and you need to calculate the length of a wall, taking into account doorways and other openings. By hand, such calculations are slow, tedious, and prone to error. With EXACT DIMENSIONS! this problem is as easy as writing down the measurements.

The program calculates dimensions with feet/inch/fractions, decimal inches, and meters. It will also automatically convert from any one of these formats to another. The display is spreadsheet style. As you enter or change figures, the total is updated. You can print out the worksheet and add notes and titles to provide a complete written record of the calculations.

SHARON RUFENER: Another fine calculating aid for builders is the mechanical engineering template for TK!SOLVER (p. 73).

### Construction management for the little guys . . .

### THE MASTER BUILDER

**Smith and Omeara; version 1; Apple II family; 64K; $800; version 2 (for larger businesses), $1250; copy-protected? YES; Omware, 140 High St., Sebastopol, CA 95472; 707/823-7783.**

KIRBY ODAWA: Whether you're a general contractor or a moonlighting handyman, THE MASTER BUILDER could become your most useful tool. It will balance your books, generate financial statements, create job estimates, track job costs, and maintain your payroll records, while you concentrate on getting the job done.

Although it is not a sophisticated accounting package, this program provides a simple system for recording payables (including subcontractors) and receivables (although you can't age them). Financial reports include a check register, general journal, balance sheet, trial balance, general ledger, and profit/loss statement. An exciting feature is the program's ability to update your job-cost records automatically when you enter financial transactions related to a particular job.

You can create job estimates by entering the number and price per unit of up to 195 different items. Then you can save your old estimates and use them as templates for creating new ones.

Best of all, this program is as straightforward as a 16d nail. The screens appear as a series of questions or statements to which you respond, and always include explicit instructions about how to proceed. The manual was thoughtfully written, and includes helpful suggestions.

Unless you want to get fancy with your accounting system, this program is the one to get you out of the office, fast.

SHARON RUFENER: This program is too limited for major projects—you can store costs for only 195 items—but it should serve as a handy and inexpensive tool for the small builder. A version for the IBM PC is due this fall.

*Heavy duty construction tool . . .*

## CONSTRUCTION MANAGEMENT

**Version 4.0; IBM PC/XT compatibles; 192K ● TRS-80 Models III and 4; 48K; modem and 5MB hard disk recommended; copy-protected? NO; $5995; Small System Design, Inc., 1120 Oakdale Place, Boulder, CO 80302; 303/442-9454.**

JOE TROISE: What's this? More than $5900 for *software*?

Well, as the tired old adage goes, you get what you pay for, and what you're getting is a package that can control just about every facet of the construction business.

I have used the CONSTRUCTION MANAGEMENT package for a year. It was put together in conjunction with builders, and the software reflects its "on-the-job" origins, being developed in part by people who know how to swing a hammer.

The system is divided into three major components—job control programs, payroll programs, and accounting programs—which work together to keep track of your business, from comparing bids with actual costs to handling your checking accounts. The net effect of all this interconnection is that every cost you incur, every penny you spend, is accounted for and incorporated into records and reports that not only store the data but logically interpret it for you. This gives you an accurate assessment of your business's financial health. By making one entry into the payroll program, you print a check for an employee, calculate all the deductions, compute the tax records, create accounting records, add the payroll costs to the appropriate jobs, and update your billing file.

Included is a word processor (LAZYWRITER, which is a good one). Upcoming additions to the package include critical path scheduling and a materials take-off function, both of which are tasks generally found only in very expensive systems.

This package is a bit intimidating, but it comes with excellent documentation. The writers assume that you know how to run a computer, that you know accounting, and that you can competently provide the large amount of cost information that you must tediously enter (but just once) from whatever bid books or life experience you have. So plan to spend a few days plugging that information in.

True, you will have spent upwards of $10,000 by the time you buy all you need in software and hardware. But this package is not merely an "aid" to your business. It literally runs the whole show, with you in the director's chair. Make damn sure you're ready for that. If you are, no building package I am aware of even comes close in terms of price, power, and reliability.

---

*Energy analysis, plain and fancy . . .*

## CALPAS3

**Version 3.13; IBM PC compatibles; 256K; 8087 math co-processor and hard disk recommended; copy-protected? NO; $795; Berkeley Solar Group, 3140 Martin Luther King Jr. Way, Berkeley, CA 94703; 415/843-7600.**

## MICROPAS

**Nitler & Novotny; CP/M-80 machines; 64K; $795 ● PC/MS-DOS machines; 128K; $895; copy-protected? NO; Enercomp, 757 Russell Blvd., Suite A-3, Davis, CA 95616; 916/753-3400.**

DOUGLAS MAHONE: It used to be nearly impossible to do sophisticated energy analysis of buildings, but now there are some very good analysis programs for microcomputers that can be used by architects, engineers, builders, and equipment installers, especially those who plan on using passive solar heating. However, you still have to know what you're doing to make an accurate analysis.

The programs reviewed here share a common ancestry: a mainframe program called CALPAS. This program was written to comply with California energy codes, and since California has taken the lead in energy efficiency requirements, a building that passes the California Code would almost certainly be in compliance in any other state.

CALPAS3 is a mainframe program translated down to a small computer. It runs in (ugh)

batch mode, using input data prepared on a word processor. It models the building's energy performance for *every hour of the year*, using detailed weather data for your location. The calculations take anywhere from 25 minutes to an hour and produce an impressive array of reports, which also take a long time to print out. It takes so long to run that the author recommends you set it up to churn on and on overnight.

In MICROPAS, the mathematical procedures are greatly simplified to speed up the processing. There are lots of menus and fill-in-the-blanks data-entry screens. It is easy to change data previously prepared to input. Added features of this program are the nice graphic printouts to accompany the tabular reports, and a simple self-running demo program. But MICROPAS calculates only six weeks' worth of hours; one each for the summer and winter seasons, plus four for the swing seasons. Simplification here means less precision than with CALPAS3.

Neither program has a well-written manual, and both assume that you understand energy modeling and can choose the correct input assumptions. Both companies offer training classes, and these represent good investments in time and money even if you already know the energy-analysis field.

MICROPAS is definitely easier to get into and runs much faster, but some people who've used them both extensively tell me they end up preferring the more powerful CALPAS3.

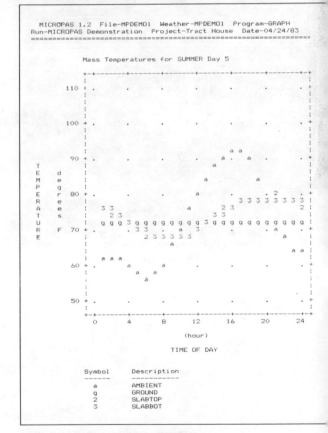

*A picture worth pages of numbers. MICROPAS, an energy-analysis program for building designers, illustrates how efficient your building will be.*

*Solar design on the Apple . . .*

## SUNPAS

Version 4.0; Apple II family; 64K ● Apple III ● Apple Lisa ● IBM PC/XT compatibles; 128K; copy-protected? YES; $400; Solarsoft, Inc., Box 124, Snowmass, CO 81654; 303/927-4411.

BILL SMITH: SUNPAS answers questions every solar designer faces: How much energy will a building need for space heating? and How will changes in the design affect its energy performance? Unlike CALPAS or MICROPAS, SUNPAS is based on research done by the Los Alamos Scientific Laboratory and uses the "solar load ratio" (SLR) method of solar calculation. Using a hand calculator for the job is tedious, open to error, and discourages experimentation and recalculation. With SUNPAS you can redo an entire calculation within 30 seconds.

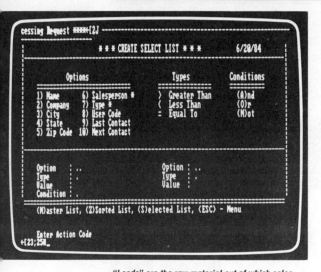

*"Leads" are the raw material out of which sales are fashioned. LEAD MANAGER will keep track of them for you and tell you who to call today.*

SUNPAS allows you to specify virtually any variable related to a building's energy performance, except heat-recovery ventilation (air-to-air heat exchangers), large changes in thermal storage, and heat loss through basements.

One of the nicest features is the graphic output. Many similar programs give you tables of numbers to stare at, but SUNPAS provides lots of visual output summarizing the data. Tabular data is available to accompany all graphs.

Don't expect to get this package up and running quickly. With a little patience and hard work, however, you can build your project with the confidence that the structure will need a minimum amount of heating energy, and will stay warm in the winter and cool in the summer. It is cheaper to make mistakes on paper and on the computer than to cast them into concrete.

*Taking care of salespersons' paperwork . . .*

## LEAD MANAGER 1.0

Jim Brant; CP/M-80 machines; 64K ● MP/M machines; 48K ● PC/MS-DOS machines; 64K; copy-protected? YES; $350; Systems Plus, Inc., 1120 San Antonio Rd., Palo Alto, CA 94303; 415/969-7047.

ROBERT SALMONS: LEAD MANAGER is a database system designed to be used by a salesperson while on the phone. It is something like a mailing-list program, showing a prospect's name, address, and phone number, and a user code. In addition, it shows the name of the salesperson assigned to the lead, the type of business activity the lead is involved in, date of last contact, date for the next contact, history, and any free-form notes you'd care to add.

Sorting and selecting with LEAD MANAGER results in all kinds of efficiencies. A sales manager can sort by salesperson to see how the troops are producing. A salesperson can easily find out what leads to contact in a given day. Because it is capable of producing hard copy, LEAD MANAGER has the very real management benefit of making salespeople deal with paperwork in a timely and accurate fashion.

The package is reasonably well documented, and it has a demo and tutorial that convey a good feel for this program. LEAD MANAGER can interface with word processors for mass mailings—a really a nice set-up (even though I hate to do anything to encourage more junk mail in my mailbox).

*Keeping track of real estate . . .*

## THE REAL ESTATE CONSULTANT

Jim Yee; Apple II family; 64K ● CP/M 2.2 machines; 64K ● CP/M-86 machines; 64K ● IBM PC/XT compatibles; 64K ● PCjr; 128K ● TRS-80 computers; 64K; copy-protected? YES; $275; CONSULTANT Systems, Inc., 3704 State St. Suite 311, Santa Barbara, CA 93105; 805/682-8927.

DICK YORK: While searching for a good real estate analysis program for my own professional use, I turned up a lot of losers. I finally found THE REAL ESTATE CONSULTANT, a program that actually works, has good documentation, and produces a meaningful end product.

All the programs of this genre produce similar output: a cash-flow rate of return and/or an internal rate of return, both before and after taxes, based on your tax rate. Some handle depreciation better than others; the recommended program allows several kinds of depreciation within one analysis.

THE REAL ESTATE CONSULTANT surpasses the competition in a number of ways. It gives you a lot of control over the variables; it makes clear what input is needed; and it makes moving from function to function a simple matter. In other words, here's a program that lets you feel you are in control and that it is working for you, not the other way around.

Syndications, partnerships, creative financing, amortization, depreciation (supports longterm investors, buyers, sellers)—it's all here. The only program most real estate brokers and investors will need.

*A controversial sales tool . . .*

## THE SALES EDGE

Version 1.0; Apple II family; 48K ● IBM PC compatibles; 128K; copy-protected? YES; $250; Human Edge Software Corp., 2445 Faber Pl., Palo Alto, CA 94303; 800/624-5227 or, in CA, 800/824-7325.

RICHARD DALTON: THE SALES EDGE is not easy to assess. It is claimed to be a way for salespeople to succeed with prospective buyers. The program uses fairly standard psychometric techniques to gather information, first about the salesperson, then about the client. The result is a set of recommendations about how the salesperson can communicate with and, of course, sell the prospect on the widgets or whatever the company is making.

THE SALES EDGE hasn't been around long enough to be thoroughly tested in real-life situations. Are the theories that underlie the program valid? *Does it work?* Will it help a salesperson get the message across to the client, deal with objections, and close the sale? We need to know if it improves a salesperson's ability to communicate with prospects; if it engenders more confidence (an important issue by itself); if it enables salespeople and managers to communicate more effectively—a critical side-issue, often ignored.

Considering the expense of other sales aids, also flimsily justified, $250 for THE SALES EDGE is worth a try. For the psychological edge, if nothing else.

CHARLES SPEZZANO: THE SALES EDGE is less sophisticated psychologically than it pretends to be, but it does offer new salespeople a way to organize their thinking about a particular prospect, and this could prove very valuable.

Sometimes any theory or plan of action is better than none at all.

STEVEN LEVY: Reading about this program gives me the 1984 creeps. What are these salesmen selling? Does the program care? Does the program publisher care? Do the unsuspecting clients get a program to regain their "edge"? This is software only a Social Darwinian could love.

SHARON RUFENER: The same folks have another product called THE MANAGEMENT EDGE "to develop tailored management strategies" in dealing with subordinates. What's the next area to get the computerized psych-out treatment?

*The controversial SALES EDGE is designed to give you a psychological edge over your clients. Fill out their questionnaires about yourself and the other party and it will tell you how to deal with that person.*

---

*Billing for psychiatrists and psychologists . . .*

## PSYCHOLOGIST'S BILLING SYSTEM

Dr. Jerome Blumenthal; Versions 2.5 (reviewed) and 4.0; Apple II family; 48K; $525 ● IBM PC compatibles; 256K; $550; copy-protected? NO; Teller, Bailey Associates, Inc., P.O. Box 7240, Boulder, CO 80306; 303/258-7258.

FRED KADUSHIN: As a clinical psychologist in private practice, I have looked for ways to reduce my paperwork. The PSYCHOLOGIST'S BILLING SYSTEM (PBS) is geared to help me accomplish this goal. It is designed to keep a record of patient charges and payments and at the end of the month to print patient statements and/or insurance bills. The program can calculate interest on overdue accounts, if indicated.

PBS is a billing program and not a complete accounting package. However, it does perform its intended function quite well. Its main sections are menu-driven, and help is provided on the screen. In some cases it tries to fit a lot of information onto each screen and at first this can be a little confusing.

Don't plan on sitting down and having this system running in a couple of hours. Initial

data entry may take a while. You need to create a fee schedule, a list of commonly used diagnoses, and a list of frequently used hospitals.

Overall, it is a powerful program for the money. The only reason I didn't buy a copy on the spot was that it won't run on my IBM PC. The next version will.

CHARLES SPEZZANO: We psychologists have different needs from other medical professionals. We see far fewer patients, and we see them on a regular and repetitive basis. Most of us practice alone and don't have staff to handle our paperwork for us. Our record keeping and billing is relatively simple—we may send out about 2 bills a month.

Is it cost-effective to computerize? I don't think so. Yet PBS seems to get disorganized people organized. As one person told me, "I didn't have a system before, now I know just what to do." And another person said, "It took a while to get into, but now I couldn't live without it." PBS has some nice features: It fills out insurance forms, does billing reminders, and produces a quarterly summary that is useful for tax reports. And the way PBS is written pretty much reflects the way we do business.

```
                    PROMISSORY NOTE

$20,000                                    Marin City, CA
                                           June 29, 1984

    For value received, the undersigned promises to pay to First
Ethereal Bank or order, at 1234 Union Street, San Francisco,
California, the sum of $20,000 with interest thereon from July
29, 1984, at the rate of 13% percent per annum: upon the demand
of the holder hereof.
    If this note is not paid when due, the undersigned promises to
pay in addition all costs of collection and reasonable attorney's
fees incurred by the holder hereof on account of such collection,
whether or not suit is filed hereon.
    This note is secured by a security title agreement, executed
on June 29, 1984 in favor of First Ethereal Bank, and covering an
IBM 360 mainframe computer system.
    Each maker consents to renewals, replacements, and extensions
of time for payments hereof before, at, or after maturity,
consents to the acceptance of security, if any, for this note,
and waives demand and protest. All payments made hereunder shall
be made in the lawful money of the United States.
    Executed this _____ day of _____,
_____, at Marin City, CA.


                              By_____
```

*Want to be your own lawyer? The PERSONAL LAWYER series of programs lets you write your own customized legal documents. Here is a Promissory Note (a legalized IOU)—the program will do everything but sign it.*

*Your IBM replaces your lawyer . . .*

## PERSONAL LAWYER SERIES

## WILLS

## POWER OF ATTORNEY

## RESIDENTIAL REAL ESTATE LEASE

## PROMISSORY NOTES

**Douglas B. Jacobs, Attorney; IBM PC/XT compatibles ● PCjr; 128K; WILLS, $80; POWER OF ATTORNEY, $70; RESIDENTIAL REAL ESTATE LEASE, $100; PROMISSORY NOTES, $70; copy-protected? YES; Lassen Software, Inc., P.O. Box 1190, Chico, CA 95927; 916/891-6957.**

JOHN OVERTON: Like most attorneys, I have reservations about "self-help" legal products. The PERSONAL LAWYER series is presented as a way to be your own lawyer and let your computer generate your legal documents for you.

Even standard situations, like the ones covered by this group of programs, can have ramifications not foreseeable by laypeople. Although some legal information is included with the programs, you do not get personalized advice from products like these, so I cannot recommend their use by the unsophisticated. Caveat emptor!

The programs consist of menus and questionnaires asking you to plug in data peculiar to the situation. You can also select from various scenarios of what you want to accomplish. The programs will then tailor their basic documents to your needs. They are very easy to use and can be executed in about the time it takes to explain your situation to an attorney.

Besides being low-cost alternatives to using a lawyer, these programs are good document-drafting tools for lawyers themselves. They can help relieve the tedious task of typing lengthy documents, and I found them easy to modify with WORDSTAR.

*Legal billing for small firms . . .*

## VERDICT

**McIntyre and Paff; CP/M and CP/M-86 machines; 64K ● IBM PC/XT compatibles; 128K; copy-protected? NO; $995; Micro Craft, Inc., 2007 Whitesburg Dr., Suite F, Huntsville, AL 35801; 205/534-4190.**

DOUG SORENSEN: A lot of legal billing systems are simply not very good; even the best are far from perfect. Lawyers make up quite a small software market, and publishers like to invest their resources where it will bring the greatest return. So we get warmed-over general accounting packages and "cottage industry" software. Poor documentation, program bugs, limited capabilities, and high prices are common. Surprisingly, the more expensive systems rarely offer much more than the least costly.

VERDICT is at the low end of the price range, yet it provides a generally adequate capability for the law office of fewer than ten attorneys. VERDICT has been around long enough to be well debugged. It is one of the few systems that does not require a hard disk, but it will run faster with one.

It primarily expedites billing, and it also produces several rudimentary management reports. Prebills can be printed for the attorney's review and adjustment. A nice feature is the inclusion on the prebill (not on the final bill) of an aged account summary for each case (that is, how much this client owes you and for how long). The prebill also shows hypothetical charges for flat-fee and contingent-fee accounts—the value of the time expended if billed at straight time.

It's a solid and serviceable program at a reasonable price.

*"Litigation support" running on micros . . .*

## LITIGATION MANAGER

**IBM PC/XT compatibles; 128K; 10MB hard disk recommended; $2000 (9,000 documents per case), $750 for "Junior" version (3,000 documents per case); copy-protected? NO; Institute for Paralegal Training, 1926 Arch St., Philadelphia, PA 19103; 800/628-3232.**

DOUG SORENSEN: "Litigation support" has become a generic term for the computerized organization of factual material within the context of a given court case. The classic example is the indexing and cross-referencing of documents for use at trial. Until recently it was the exclusive province of trial lawyers handling cases large enough to support the substantial costs of computer service bureaus providing this service. LITIGATION MANAGER attempts to change all that.

The heart of any document-control system is its "document surrogate": someone must review each document individually and attempt to capture its essence. The LITIGATION MANAGER form provides for 19 types of information. The information can be retrieved using any combination of these fields, or by searching for a particular word in the free-form summary portion.

The publisher offers demo disks and will give a full refund within 30 days if you are not satisfied.

*Computing down on the farm . . .*

## FARM LEDGER PRO

**Conrad, Randolph, Rybolt & Vint; Apple II family; 48K; 2 disk drives recommended ● IBM PC compatibles; 128K; copy-protected? Apple: YES; PC: NO; $425; Harvest Computer Systems, 102 S. Harrison St., Alexandria, IN 46001; 317/724-4429.**

WILLARD WINTERS: Currently, very few farmers use computers, but I hear from those who do that they finally feel like they are managing and making decisions for the future rather than just going from day to day.

FARM LEDGER PRO is an excellent and flexible program. You should use an accountant to assist in setting up beginning inventories, cash values of assets, depreciation schedules, etc. But after that, the program will produce a financial statement, valuable both to manage the business and to take to the bank to get financing.

Many farmers use more than one checking account, and they may have more than one savings account. The program provides for this, and it can write your checks for you. You can account for borrowed money and record your payments.

I like the principle of noncash transfers, which means that I can take into account the grain I don't sell but do use for feed. Although the manual is excellent, setting up will require considerable time. I think it is time well spent. This would be a good program for accounting firms servicing farmers, as well as for farmers interested in keeping their own records.

---

*My husband and I use computers. They were supposed to make life easier. But now we work harder than ever before. It's our choice. The computer has only made that choice much easier for us.*

*—Arielle Emmett*
*in* **Personal Computing**

*All-purpose aid for mail-order businesses . . .*

## MAIL ORDER PRO

**Michael Lindeberg; CP/M-80 machines; 64K ● IBM PC compatibles; 128K; $695 (PRO 1, 500 orders/day), $995 (PRO 2, 999 orders/day), $1495 (PRO 3, multi-user), $1995 (PRO 4, 32,000-name mailing list); copy-protected? NO; Professional Publications, P.O. Box 199, San Carlos, CA 94070; 415/593-9119.**

BEN ELLISON: My mail-order business is heavy with paperwork: invoices, shipping labels, shipping costs, inventory adjustments, charge-card or check processing, mailing lists—you get the idea. If a customer calls with a question about an order, I'm scrambling in a box of invoices. It's enough to make a mail-order entrepreneur frightened of growth.

Many of us have lashed together some sort of homebrew order processing/inventory-tracking/list-management system, but constructing a complete system is murder. I, for one, tend to get quite envious when I examine the paperwork churned out by, say, L.L. Bean's mainframe.

MAIL ORDER PRO seems a solution. It's a single-entry system: customer and order information is entered once and everything after that is automatic—paperwork preparation, inventory updating, back ordering, accounting, shipping manifests, and mailing-list maintenance. Order entry is easy and straightforward. There is extensive error checking. Shipping zones and costs are calculated for a wide variety of shipping methods.

You can process mail orders in a batch and phone orders right on line. Information about back orders can be obtained immediately. Numerous labels, forms reports, and letters are available. This program could be the core of a highly efficient, reasonably priced computerized system.

SHARON RUFENER: Not only mail-order companies, but any company that does a lot of mailing might want to take a look at POST MAN (p. 197).

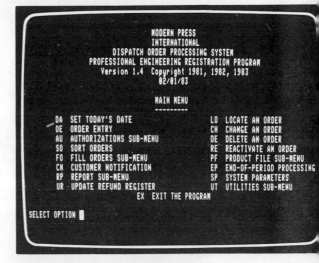

*If you're buried under the paperwork details of a mail order business, MAIL ORDER PRO will take care of business for you. Customer lists, inventory, back orders, order entry—it's all here.*

---

*I am a design chauvinist. I believe that good design is magical and not to be lightly tinkered with. The difference between a great design and a lousy one is in the meshing of the thousand details that either fit or don't, and the spirit of the passionate intellect that has tied them together, or tried. That's why programming—or buying software—on the basis of "lists of features" is a doomed and misguided effort. The features can be thrown together, as in a garbage can, or carefully laid together and interwoven in elegant unification, as in APL, or the Forth language, or the game of chess.*

*The difference between the design that is just right and the design that is not just right is the same difference Mark Twain pointed out for words. The difference, said Twain, between the word that is just right and the word that is not quite right—"is the difference between the lightning and the lightning bug."*
*—Ted Nelson*

*Bringing computers into the home won't change either one, but may revitalize the corner saloon.*
*—Alan J. Perlis*

*Clean your display screen. Go ahead. You'll be amazed at how dirty it is. You'll also be amazed at how much brighter the display is after you clean it.*
*—Jim Stockford*

## DRAWING

### Rik Jadrnicek, Domain Editor

RIK JADRNICEK: Stick around if you like to doodle, draw cartoons, illustrate books, draw block diagrams or flowcharts, do space planning, develop advertising copy, design circuit boards, design buildings, or create any other casual or professional drawings. In this section you'll discover microcomputer software and hardware useful for graphic art, drafting, and design. Computer-aided design (CAD) is swiftly coming of age on microcomputers . . . at last, you really can draw with equipment that's reasonably priced.

Why are graphics programs becoming such an important part of a business software library? Ever catch yourself reading a magazine backwards? I do, and I suspect I'm in the majority. Perhaps it's simply the more natural, quicker path to the "bottom line" in this age of information overdose. I look at the pictures first, read the captions, look at any charts I find, and then if I'm still interested I read the text. It's the same with business reports. But before microcomputer graphic programs were available, a business had to hire an artist to depict the bottom line in full color. Today, bar charts and line graphs pop out at the push of a button.

Like a good word processor, a good graphics processor will soon be a mainstay of your software library. Microcomputers have placed the masterful control of numbers and text at our fingertips, and now they can give us that same degree of control over pictures.

BARBARA ROBERTSON: Word processors and spreadsheets were a giant step up from typewriters and adding machines, as typewriters and adding machines were a giant step up from handwriting. But picture processing has never had a mechanical middle-step equivalent to a typewriter or adding machine. With picture processing, you leap straight from pen on paper into the magical world of microcomputing: brush and canvas with a brain. In picture processing, just as in word processing or spreadsheet analysis, you can cut, copy, move, erase, and save all or pieces of your creation to be used again in a variety of forms. But you can also shade, texture, expand, contract, zoom in to toy with what was once just a speck on the screen; draw a straight line without a ruler; vary the size of your pencil, pen, or brush; paint with a palette of colors—and change anything in the blink of an eye. While word processors rarely turn hacks into writers, picture processors could make artists out of doodlers. It's so much fun . . . more than you ever dreamed would be possible. And you never have to get out the turpentine or even an eraser.

## THE FUTURE DRAWS NEAR

STEWART BRAND: Every month personal computers have more memory and more storage at less cost. All programs benefit to some degree, but the ones that gain the most are the graphic programs, because it's taking them over the barrier between impossible and possible. And once possible, these programs are going to take off, I believe. Personal computer users are biased toward graphics, feel rewarded by them, and reward them right back with enthusiastic market support.

As a result, stuff in the Drawing section is probably neck-and-neck with Managing (the integrated packages) as one of the fastest-moving nags in the software horserace. Our coverage, necessarily, lags behind. Fortunately, Rik Jadrnicek covers the cutting edge of the field professionally, so he is able to report in detail on microcomputer graphic capabilities that may seem on the other side of the impossible barrier to many of us now but are rapidly coming within financial reach as we speak.

BARBARA ROBERTSON: Rik waited, watched, impatiently, yearly, for microcomputer graphics. Bought one of the first Apples and VISICALC (p. 71) for the analytical capabilities (a house designer and builder, he was immersed in the vagaries of California's real estate market), but mostly because he could create charts. He quickly discovered two things: analysis that formerly took hours happened in five minutes on the Apple; and he had a knack for fiddling with programs and sharing his enthusiasm. A true entrepreneur, he turned this sideline into a business, giving seminars on spreadsheet modeling, reviewing software for magazines, putting together systems for small businesses. Meanwhile, he kept

*Rik Jadrnicek and family.*

searching the marketplace for graphics packages he could use to draw architectural plans, to paint. About a year and a half ago it all clicked together—sophisticated drawing software landed on microcomputers. And Rik was ready. His clients are now artists, architects and designers. Is he content? Nope. Now he's tapping his feet waiting for software that lets him play with movies on the monitor—fully three-dimensional animated pictures of the world moved onscreen from a camera, created with the microcomputer, or both—an altered reality. I think he'd even like to carry this bit of magic in his briefcase. Who knows? Maybe he'll review it in the next **Catalog**.

STEWART BRAND: Humans drew before they wrote. For much of our brain, I suspect, drawing *is* thinking. It may be that computers will be releasing that brainpower in the next few years, as we learn to express ourselves graphically as easily as we use the car or telephone. I don't know that we'll get back to the exquisite artistry of the beasts drawn on the walls of the Lascaux Caves, but I wouldn't rule it out either.

RIK JADRNICEK: Drawing software falls neatly into three categories: *painting* (for artists), *two-dimensional drawing* (for architects, engineers, space planners and drafters) and *three-dimensional solids modeling*. You'll find all three in this section, in that order.

Putting together computer-aided design systems is my profession, so sorting through myriad graphics hardware and software in search of the ultimate graphics computer configuration is my journey. Welcome.

## WHOLE EARTH RECOMMENDED DRAWING TOOLS

### (June 1984)

### INTEGRATED GRAPHICS HARDWARE/SOFTWARE (pp.126-127)

MINDSET, $2458
LISA, $4495
MACINTOSH, $2495

### INTEGRATED SOFTWARE WITH GRAPHIC TRENDS

SYMPHONY, $695, p.127
FRAMEWORK, $695, p.128

### BUSINESS GRAPHICS (pp.128-129)

BPS GRAPHICS, $350
FASTGRAPH, $350
GRAPHWRITER, $395/$595
MICROSOFT CHART, $125
EXECUVISION, $395

### PAINTING SOFTWARE

FLYING COLORS, $39.95, p.130
4-POINT GRAPHICS, $195, p.131
KOALAPAD, $110/$150, p.131
MOVIEMAKER, $50, p.131
MOUSEPAINT, $99/$149, p.131
LUMENA, $400/$2500, p.132
EASEL, $1250/$2500, p.132

### 2-D COMPUTER-AIDED DESIGN (CAD)

PC-DRAW, $395, p.133
ROBO-GRAPHICS CAD-1, $1095, p.133
CADPLAN, $495/$1900, p.134
AUTOCAD, $1000/$1500, p.134
VERSACAD, $1995/$4995, p.135
CADAPPLE, $1795, p.135

### 3-D COMPUTER-AIDED DESIGN (CAD) (pp.136-137)

ENERGRAPHICS/PC, $350
3DESIGN, $249
ADVANCED SPACE GRAPHICS, $1695/$1995
CUBICOMP CS-5, $9700

### BOOKS (p.137)

**Graphics For The IBM PC,** $28.50/$50 with disk
**Graphics Primer for the IBM PC,** $21.95
**PC Graphics,** $15.95
**Graphics Programs for the IBM PC,** $14.95

## TYRANNY OF THE NEW

RIK JADRNICEK: The future is colorful and exciting. Graphics software and hardware are becoming more sophisticated and at the same time prices are rapidly falling.

DAZZLE DRAW from Broderbund does animation on the Apple IIc and IIe. Tritek has a new product called 3DESIGN3, billed as a significant up-scaling of both the capabilities and price (to $800) of 3DESIGN (p. 136). 3DESIGN3 should be able to do things like sweep out 3-D volumes using a 2-D surface (for example, making a doughnut out of a circle by swinging it at arm's length) and includes printer and plotter support.

### *Video Digitizing—Animated Hard Copy*

Videotaping is an excellent way of recording images you produce with a computer. You may also want to take an original video image and edit it with your computer. A variety of hardware and software is appearing on the market to do that. The FAX640 Image Digitizer from SCION Corporation changes standard (RS-170) video images to 640 x 480 pixel grayscale images you can edit with your microcomputer—at the rate of one frame per half second. The LIVE640 Live Video Card goes the other way, transferring microcomputer drawings in full color to (MTSC) video images, four of which can be overlaid for creative slides. Time Arts, Inc., developers of EASEL and LUMENA (p. 132), has come up with a way to edit video images using the SCION hardware. You can take a picture of someone with a video camera, then edit the image using your computer. The PC-EYE software/hardware combination displays video images on an IBM PC for editing there.

SCION Corporation, 12310 Pinecrest Road, Reston, VA 22091; 703/476-6100
● PC-Eye; Chorus Data Systems Inc., P.O. Box 810, 27 Proctor Hill Road, Hollis, NH 03049; 603/465-7100.

*(continued on p.124)*

*(continued from p.123)*

These are a few items I ran across at the National Computer Graphics Association conference in Anaheim in May 1984:

***Graphics Boards:*** Lots of good IBM PC graphics boards are coming on stream, like the reasonably priced Cono-Color 40 board for $695 put out by Conographic Corporation. There is much software to support this high-resolution color graphics board that has a fast and unique way of handling curve generation and is worth looking into. The Revolution board by Number Nine Corporation is finding more software support. It offers a 1440 x 1440 color display for the IBM PC (although it uses two slots). This multiported board, which uses the NEC 7220 graphics coprocessor, will become a popular graphics board. Vectrix Corporation has announced its new Midas color graphics board for the IBM PC: $2995 provides 512 colors out of a palette of 4096 in 672 x 480 resolution. It uses an Intel 80188 microprocessor and an 8-megahertz NEC 7220 processor.

***Graphics monitors:*** With all the changes being made in graphics boards and display technology, a flexible monitor is almost essential. The Electrohome ECM 1301 high-resolution color monitor, for $1500, seems to fit the bill. It provides a 25-megahertz bandwidth with horizontal frequency switch-selectable from 14.5 to 25.5 kHz. NEC is putting out the NEC PC KD 651, a high-quality color display for less than $900. During these times of nonstandardization, you may need to change your horizontal frequency from board to board and application to application.

***Output devices:*** Along with the Diablo Inkjet printer at $1350, Tektronic's new TEK 4695 and TEK 4691 color graphics copiers ($1600-13,000) are worth looking at. Hewlett-Packard introduced the HP 7550 eight-pen graphics plotter ($3995) with automatic sheet feed of 8½" x 11" or 11" x 17" stock and an increased pen speed of 31.5 inches per second (twice that of the 7470A and 7475A models).

***Graphics software:*** A new painting software program has been introduced on the new Vectrix IBM PC graphics board; it's currently called both PAINT PAD and THE PAINT PROGRAM. It retails in the area of $900—too bad the Vectrix board costs so much. The ARTRON PC-2000 paint software put out by Artronics Incorporated will run on the Number Nine Revolution board. Retail looks like $14,995 for the board and software, but no one seemed to be sure. The software is very sophisticated—but let's get realistic on the price. Artronics also offers an IMAGE-GRABBER, a video digitizer and frame-grab device including circuit board, software, color filters, TV camera, copystand, and miscellaneous fixtures, all for an additional $9995. Designboard 3D is a new $750 3-D software package for the IBM PC produced by MEGA CADD, Inc. CADMASTER, a $1795 two-dimensional drafting software package by Datagraphic Systems, looks intriguing; it comes with an optional $2155 bill-of-materials function. The CARRIER E2000 CAD system from United Technologies appears powerful and interesting; a training program is offered with purchase. 3Design 3-D software is offering an interface with the two-dimensional AUTOCAD drafting program. AutoCAD announced an Intgraph (mainframe CAD system) interface and the availability of architectural, mechanical, and electrical shape libraries for their programs.

***Input Devices:*** GTCO has introduced the new Micro DIGI-PAD 6" x 6" and 12" x 12" digitizer tablets. The tablets are light, thin and inexpensive (less than $500) but they don't sacrifice on precision. Micro Control Systems, Inc., introduced the Perceptor 3-D digitizer, which provides interactive 3-D graphics capability through dual RS-232 ports. It makes 3-D ($X, Y, Z$) coordinate data accessible at a rate of 7 points per second.

---

*It begins with instruments . . .*
## Hardware Elements of Graphics Computers

RIK JADRNICEK: Understanding the hardware required to produce computer graphics can help you understand the evolution and potential of computer graphics software.

In a nutshell, you begin to draw using a graphic input device and/or the computer keyboard much as you would a brush or pencil and paper. The computer records your efforts on a floppy or hard disk, while the software provides you with a palette of colors and brush types, T-square, triangle, compass, grid framework, and a variety of other drawing tools. A graphics board (also called graphics processor or frame buffer) translates your work into an image on a black-and-white or color graphics monitor, which is something like a TV set. Printers, plotters, cameras, and video then provide ways of producing a hard copy of your work. You, the artist, have the eye—the computer and its devices (or peripherals) are simply media to serve you. I have to keep reminding myself of that.

*It adds $3000-4000 to the price of an IBM PC, but jazzing up the desktop micro with specialized drawing equipment turns it into a full-fledged CAD system. This photo shows a typical configuration: IBM PC plus a $1400 GTCO digitizing tablet (precision input), $1290 MicroVitech CUB graphics monitor (high-resolution screen display) and a $1095 Hewlett-Packard 7470-A plotter (high-resolution output).*

## The artist's helper . . .
## Computers (CPUs)

As microcomputer graphics become more popular, most new computers appearing on the market will come from the factory equipped with graphics capability. For example, Lisa, Macintosh, Mindset, the TI Professional, and many of the IBM PC lookalikes now arrive with built-in graphics. This is a welcome development, since outfitting a computer for graphics can be expensive, confusing, and time consuming.

Still, you may prefer or need to customize your own graphics computer for greater image resolution and higher quality color capability than you would get stock from the factory. For example, many graphics cards (discussed below) are available for IBM PCs, STD-BUS, and S-100 systems. If you choose this route, make sure all the hardware is compatible prior to purchase.

The software also must support the hardware you are using, so be careful. In general, try to go with software that is not tied to a single piece of hardware, but rather supports a variety of hardware devices. For example, using the same software you should be able to change computers, graphics cards, monitors, mice, digitizers, printers, or plotters in the future and take your work with you. Think about it . . . you should also be able to share your work with people using different types of hardware.

## The drawing instruments . . .
## Input Devices

You use an input device to enter data into the computer much as you use a brush to apply paint to a canvas.

The *keyboard* is often used alone in drawing with computers. You enter either by drawing coordinate points using numbers or by using the arrow keys to move a cursor (like a cross hair) on the video screen. DELTA DRAWING (p. 189) for the IBM PC and Atari, for example, uses the keyboard exclusively. All drawing elements are entered as data points and relative distances using the keyboard. Often this method is cumbersome, but I know some engineers who will use only the keyboard for data entry, claiming that it is more natural and accurate for their work. Ideally you will use a combination of the keyboard and one of the input devices described below.

*Joysticks* are used for games and as elementary drawing input devices. In general, you can use one to scribble on the monitor, but don't expect to use it easily for precision drawing.

*Trackballs* are often used for games and are gaining in popularity. Rolling a ball socketed in a case, you can control the speed and direction of a cursor on the screen. The trackball still sacrifices precision, but it is great as a pointing device.

*Light pens* and *touch pens* let you draw directly on the surface of the monitor (see PC-DRAW, p. 133). They are direct and seem to make sense until you try to trace a drawing or draw with a high degree of precision . . . imagine holding a drawing up to the monitor and tracing over it. These tools are best for basic drawing and pointing at menu choices. Some computers, like the HP-150 (p. 18), let you use your finger instead.

*Mice* provide you with a cursor on the monitor that scurries around the screen (often randomly) as you move the device on a tabletop or metal sheet. Your eyes watch the cursor while your hand moves the mouse; surprisingly, there's no coordination

problem. The cursor marks an active area on the video monitor and you press a button on the mouse to draw or choose a function (see the discussions of Macintosh, p. 127, and Mindset, p. 126). These rodents tend to be temperamental and only moderately precise. Again, it is not practical to use them for tracing an existing drawing on the table.

A *digitizer* is like a drafting table and pencil. Digitizers come in a variety of sizes, from the notepad-size KOALAPAD (pp. 131 and 184) to a backlighted architectural 48 x 48 inch drafting-table size. They also vary in degree of accuracy. Digitizers provide a way to draw very precisely with a computer (see AUTOCAD and CADPLAN, p. 134). You can lay an existing drawing on the surface of most digitizers and accurately trace it into the computer using a *stylus* (a pencil-like device) or *puck* (a mouse-like device with its own cross hairs and buttons). I strongly recommend a digitizing tablet for professional drawing needs.

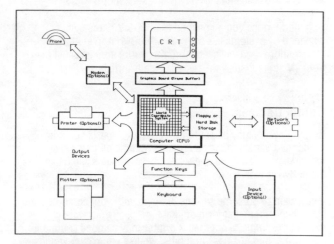

The basic, functional elements of a CAD system. I used AUTOCAD (p. 134) running on a Compaq computer to do the drawing, then printed it with a Hewlett-Packard 7475 plotter ($1895).

## The artist's palette . . .
## Graphics Cards

If your computer does not already have graphics capability, you may need to purchase a graphics card (a circuit board you install in the computer); they come in all shapes and sizes. This is where the greatest improvement is being made in the area of computer graphics hardware. The cards are becoming more sophisticated and cheaper at the same time.

In general, these cards determine the number and quality of the dots of light (pixels) that appear on your graphics monitor. The images you see are really made of hundreds of pixels. The more pixels, the higher the resolution and clearer the image. (If you look at a magazine photograph with a magnifying glass, you will see that it, too, is actually composed of very tiny dots of color — an example of a very high resolution image.) The cards must be compatible with your computer, monitor, and software, so be careful to match things up.

Graphics produced on standard Atari, Commodore, Apple, or IBM PC with a standard graphics card have a resolution of about 300 x 200 pixels, so the images normally look jagged and somewhat crude. With a good graphics board and compatible software and monitor, you can get 600 x 400 dots to represent your image (the suggested minimum for professional work). Inexpensive 1024 x 1024 resolution on micros is just around the corner.

*The canvas . . .*
## Graphics Monitors

Graphics monitors, also known as "CRTs" (for Cathode Ray Tubes) come in a variety of flavors. Often a graphics monitor will accompany your computer. This is another case of hardware increasing in quality and decreasing in cost.

At some point you may want to start getting familiar with terms like RGB (red, green, blue), analog or composite video, dot pitch, band width, scan rates, and interlace. However, not to worry. Just make sure—preferably before you buy it—that the monitor you choose is capable of working in harmony with the rest of your hardware and software. At least check out the difference between an analog and a digital graphics board and the different monitors they require. If your board sends an interlaced signal be sure you get a monitor with long-persistence phosphors or the image will flicker. Check it out.

In general, once you go beyond the 300 x 200 resolution provided by systems like the standard IBM, Apple, Atari, or Commodore, you will need a monitor more sophisticated than your TV set to display the results. Again, prices are falling.

*The artist's copy machine . . .*
## Output Devices

Output devices may be anything from a dot matrix or ink-jet printer to a variety of the pen or electrostatic plotters currently on the market. Find the one that suits your needs and make sure the software works with it.

If you want to do some serious drawing with your computer, you should consider what form of final hard copy your work will take. For example, a dot matrix printer may be good enough for draft prints and business graphics, while a pen plotter would be more suitable for an architect wanting to produce 24 x 36 inch drawings. A graphics artist may prefer working with photographs or video images on the monitor. With painting software, which can produce millions of different colors, you may be able to use only photography or video to record your work satisfactorily. Again, it is always good to involve yourself with software that can support a variety of output devices should your needs change.

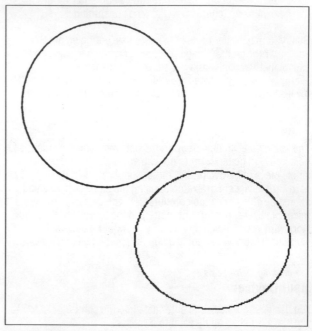

*Notice the difference in the smoothness (resolution) of each circle—the bottom circle from a dot-matrix printer, the top circle from the HP 7470-A plotter. Plotter resolution is typically .001 inch.*

---

*Mindset is the first microcomputer with built-in color graphics and animation capability. You could probably buy extra boards for your IBM PC and get it to work as well, but if graphics are your goal, why bother? Mindset runs many IBM PC programs, you don't have to add boards, and it costs less.*

*A trend . . .*
## Integrated Graphics Hardware/Software

For those of us who want to simply take the computer out of the box and draw, there is hope. A variety of computers continue to appear on the market that not only have graphics capability, but come with graphics software as well. You can spend your time learning how to use them rather than how to put together a compatible system from scratch.

*The beginning of animation at home . . .*
## MINDSET

$2458; Mindset Corporation, 617 N. Mary, Sunnyvale, CA 94086; 408/737-8555.

RIK JADRNICEK: The Mindset computer is designed for graphics—it's an IBM PC compatible that teams up the Intel 80186 processor chip and a powerful proprietary graphics chip.

You get standard IBM 320 x 200 color-graphics resolution—higher if the software allows—and a total of 16 colors at a time from a palette of 512 colors. It's fast. An entire graphics screen can be redrawn within 1/60th of a second—without you seeing it happen. The speed, combined with Mindset's "postage stamp" method of animation, makes possible great, smooth-flowing animation like that in good video games.

The more technically inclined folks will be glad to know that the special chip also provides graphics primitives capable of powerful animation, including support of dithering, elimination of zero bytes in images, collision detection, fast polygon fill, rectangular clip, and stereo sound capability, to name a few.

This computer provides both an inexpensive way to run standard IBM PC computer applications software and a delightful way to explore the world of computer-aided design and animation.

*A black-and-white beginning
and a black-and-white miracle...*

## LISA

Lisa 2/5; $4495; Lisa 2/10; $5495;

## MACINTOSH

$2495;

both from Apple Computer, 20525 Mariani Ave., Cupertino, CA 95014; 800/538-9696.

RIK JADRNICEK: A good example of the ''no muss, no fuss'' computer is Apple's Lisa with LISADRAW, one of the best things about the package. Apple's Macintosh (p. 19) is Lisa's smarter younger brother. Mac's screen is smaller (9 inches versus Lisa's 12 inches), but Mac's square pixels make the images seem sharper, so the smaller screen is still easy on the eyes. (Lisa's pixels are oblong.) Both computers use the Motorola 68000 processor chip and come with a mouse (Mac has no cursor keys) but Mac seems faster. Mac comes with MACPAINT, as wonderful in its way as LISADRAW.

*Irresistible...*

## LISADRAW

## MACPAINT

Bundled with Lisa and Macintosh computers. Apple Computer, 20525 Mariani Ave., Cupertino, CA 95014; 800/538-9696.

LYNN CELOTTI: LISADRAW is particularly good for instant designs that have a fair degree of mathematical precision—for architects, space planners, and those who draw flowcharts. MACPAINT, on the other hand, is better for freehand, aesthetically pleasing drawings—more for artists than architects. While MACPAINT has bit-by-bit control for detail, shades, and tone control, in LISADRAW objects stay together as a unit, so they're easier to move around (for example, architects wanting to move furniture from one room to another). The larger Lisa screen can be an advantage. One customer of ours, a film producer, draws storyboards on Lisa; the screen is large enough to have text on one side, picture on the other. Doing the same thing with MACPAINT would be difficult, for unlike Lisa, Mac can run only one program at a time; but then MACPAINT has many type fonts, styles and sizes. Early Lisas were slow, but it's now hard to pick which of the two family members is faster. You can use MACPAINT on the Lisa, but so far (June 1984) Apple hasn't modified the software for the Lisa—the image doesn't fill the screen and it's distorted—sort of putting a VW engine in a Ferrari. (You can't run LISADRAW on the Mac, but a MACDRAW is coming.)

RIK JADRNICEK: MACPAINT is the perfect example of the speed you can get out of a

pixel-based drawing system (see Painting Software, p. 130) that does not have to create a vector database or drive a 24 x 36 inch plotter (see 2D Software, p. 132). Its purpose is to paint the screen and print the screen image to a dot matrix printer, and this it does very fast and very well.

MACPAINT gives you an impressive set of drawing tools. You can sketch freehand and draw precise lines and circles using an assortment of pen styles and a variety of fill patterns. An electronic eraser can be customized to any size. You can move parts of a drawing around, zoom into areas to take a more detailed look at your work, ''lasso'' an object and drag it across the screen—all very impressive and powerful features. Drawings can be merged with MACWRITE (p. 54) documents... the list of advantages goes on. Keep in mind that in spite of its power and flexibility, MACPAINT produces only black-and-white drawings and (so far) the drawing can be printed only with Apple's ImageWriter and only in one size. If this is all you need, fine; the system will serve you well. Also remember that, in general, Apple computers can share their graphics work only with other Apple computers, owing to what is called a ''proprietary'' operating system. This limitation may be inconvenient if you plan to share work with people using different computers.

*Imagewriter, the companion printer for the Macintosh, reproduces the screen graphics with unusually close fidelity. Resolution is typical of a dot matrix printer. Considering Imagewriter's capabilities, the $595 price tag is reasonable. The cartoon print-out is from a design partly shown onscreen in the previous picture—the first MACPAINT endeavor by cartoonist Jay Kinney.*

*MACPAINT is the most seductive Macintosh feature and a highly evolved program based on several-year-old LISADRAW. It provides a variety of tools for painting black and white pictures—even an eraser to undo mistakes. Best of all, you pick up these drawing skills quickly—a great confidence builder for computer neophytes.*

## Integrated Software with Graphic Trends

RIK JADRNICEK: Not very long ago it was necessary to have a separate package of business-graphics software to produce graphs. With graphing capability now built into spreadsheet programs, these separate packages are becoming optional and primarily used only when more sophisticated graphs than available in integrated packages are wanted. Programs like 1-2-3 (p. 67) and SUPERCALC3 (p. 69) started the trend to integrate a simple business-graphics capability with spreadsheet programs. Now even more integration is taking place for other computers in the spirit of Lisa and Macintosh (see CHART, p. 129).

*Pictures change interactively...*

## SYMPHONY

IBM PC/XT compatibles; 320K; color graphics adaptor; $695 ($200 if exchanged for 1-2-3); copy-protected? YES; Lotus Development Corp., 161 First St., Cambridge, MA 02142; 617/492-7171.

RIK JADRNICEK: Integrates spreadsheet, word-processing, data-entry, database, communications, and business graphics capabilities into one software package. As you change the numbers, the pictures change interactively. You can transmit graphs over a regular phone line and share them with other computers using the same program. You can also print them out using a growing variety of printers and plotters. (Also see p. 111.)

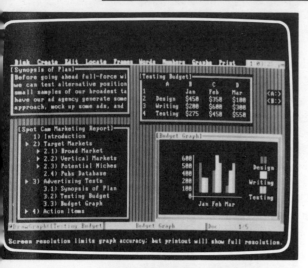

**With FRAMEWORK, unlike SYMPHONY, you get graphics and windows without having to add a color graphics board to your IBM PC. If you do have a color board, full color business graphs are one keystroke away.**

*Pictures worth a thousand numbers . . .*
## Business Graphics

RIK JADRNICEK: With all this software integration taking place, why do we need stand-alone business-graphics software? Simple. The software industry is in a state of transition. A good stand-alone business-graphics package produces sophisticated graphs from data files created by a variety of stand-alone spreadsheet software (in which you may have already invested quite a few hours). In addition, it might have editing features for more professional presentations, such as slideshows, if that is your need.

*Everything begins to happen graphically . . .*
## FRAMEWORK

**IBM PC/XT compatibles; 256K; $695; copy-protected? YES; Ashton-Tate, 10150 W. Jefferson Blvd., Culver City, CA 90230; 203/204-5570.**

RIK JADRNICEK: In FRAMEWORK everything, including text, is beginning to happen graphically. Windows appear like pieces of paper piled on your desktop. These pictures of your work can be expanded, contracted, organized in outline form, edited, transmitted by phone, sent to printers or plotters, and stored for later use. Again, be sure to keep an eye on the range of output devices these programs support. (Also see p. 110.)

*Basic business graphics plus slideshow . . .*
## FASTGRAPH

**IBM PC compatibles; 128K; color graphics board; supports Epson graphic printers, IDS Prism, HP 7470, HI plotter; copy-protected? NO; $350; Innovative Software, Inc., 9300 W. 110th Street Suite 380, Overland Park, KS 66210; 913/383-1089.**

PETER KIRKWOOD: With FASTGRAPH it is easy to build standard bar, line, and pie graphs from manually entered data or from DIF files generated by other applications software like VISICALC (p. 71), 1-2-3 (p. 67), SUPERCALC (p. 69), or DBASE II (p. 85).

The program is menu driven and logically organized. The documentation is clear and professional. Many display options are available, such as grid, 3-D symbols, pie-slice textures, and a high-quality graphics slideshow-presentation mode. No extra type styles or picture/logo symbols are available.

Graphs can be combined. For example, a line graph can be overlaid on a bar graph. Both the data and graphics screen can be edited directly; in fact, the data screen looks much like a spreadsheet. Graphics modification is limited. For example, you cannot expand or rotate graphs.

Math and statistical functions are not available with this software. Though FASTGRAPH tends to be a bit slow and at $300 seems expensive, it is similar in feel to the 1-2-3 graphics package, and is a professional and coordinated product that does just what it says it will, smoothly and efficiently.

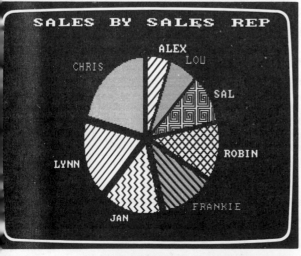

**BPS GRAPHICS can use data you move into the program from a spreadsheet, or you can enter data directly from the keyboard. Very easy to learn.**

*Easy to use, great for slide presentations . . .*
## BPS GRAPHICS

**IBM PC/XT compatibles; 128K ● TI PRO; 128K ● NEC APC-3; 256K; supports over 80 different printers and plotters; copy-protected? YES; $350; Business and Professional Software, Inc., 143 Binney St., Cambridge, MA 02142; 617/491-3377. Also available as WANG PC BUSINESS GRAPHICS for the Wang PC; $350; Wang Laboratories, Inc., 1 Industrial Avenue, Lowell, MA 01851; 617/459-5000.**

PAUL SCHINDLER: How high can I soar in praising this fantastic business-graphics package? You want pie charts? This program will draw you pie charts like you have never seen before. Bar graphs? Your bar graphs will sing. Projections never looked crisper, with lines, curves, and smooth-moving averages.

I came to the program cold, with one day in which to prepare fifteen slides for a presentation. Within 20 minutes I was doing colorful, professional-looking graphics. Unlike several cruder packages I glanced at,

BPS prepares presentation-quality graphics with no extraneous junk showing.

This program's best feature is its ease of use. Most graphics packages are so flexible they are useless. That is, before they will draw anything, the user has to make 20 decisions. BPS is different. It has default values for everything. These are easily changed, but if you are in a hurry, you give the program data and it gives you graphics. BPS has two alternating screens. One is full of data and instructions on what kind of chart to draw. The other is the drawing itself. The program has interfaces for a number of printers and plotters—smart interfaces: output on an Epson printer with Graftrax goes much more quickly than with some other programs.

Nothing is perfect, however. The editor, which is supposed to make it easy to change a piece of data or a heading, is balky and difficult to use. Still, it has the best title-handling routine I have ever seen. And of course BPS can accept data from other programs as input. In fact, I think it might even take your dog for a walk at night.

## Good, but no slideshow . . .

# GRAPHWRITER

Version 3.1; IBM PC/XT compatibles; P-system or MS-DOS; 128K; outputs to H-P, CalComp, IBM, or Mannesmann Tally plotters; $395 (Basic program) or $595 (extended program); Version 4.00 (features batch processing); MS-DOS; 192K; copy-protected? NO; $595; Graphic Communications, Inc., 200 Fifth Avenue, Waltham, MA 02254; 617/890-8778.

PETER KIRKWOOD: GRAPHWRITER offers a strong and sometimes imposing array of display formats, especially when the optional extension package is included. In addition to regular charts and graphs, some unusual chart styles are available, including bubble charts (circle size showing importance and location showing relationship), Gantt charts (project scheduling or time-line charts), organizational charts, and block diagrams. You are given considerable control of graph or chart elements, including axis labels, titles, and symbols.

The program can read Data Interchange Files (DIF) from both DOS and PASCAL disks. Regression lines can be plotted on a scatter chart, but otherwise the program is weak in standard statistical functions. (See Analyzing, p. 64, for graphics packages that handle statistical functions.)

GRAPHWRITER is written in p-System PASCAL and therefore doesn't need PC DOS to run, although there is a PC/MS-DOS version available now. The publisher provides a separate utility disk for formatting floppies, but since the program comes on ten disks, you would probably want to run it on a hard disk. Here's where the p-System causes problems. You must put the program into its own partition, and to get back and forth to PC DOS programs (like VISICALC, p. 71) you have to first back out to the floppy drive; files from the other program must be saved on the floppy drive before they can be used by GRAPHWRITER. The PC DOS version of GRAPHWRITER should eliminate these problems.

In general, the documentation is poorly organized, too wordy, and set in small type that is very difficult to read. The program menus seem to have the same problem. Despite these problems, though, GRAPHWRITER software is worth considering, because it will create professional-quality charts and graphs and drive a wider variety of printers and plotters than most other packages. Input forms are provided to aid in collecting data, as well as chart specifications for developing graphic presentations. We recommend the program for situations where input forms are best filled in by one department and then turned over to a graphics department that makes the final charts and presentations. The program focuses on the output of high-quality hard copy; there is no slideshow capability.

## Quick, efficient visuals . . .

# MICROSOFT CHART

Apple Macintosh; 128K; copy-protected? YES; $125; Microsoft Corporation, 10700 Northup Way, Bellevue, WA 98004; 206/828-8080.

STEWART BRAND: I agree with Andrew Fluegelman, founding editor of **Macworld**, that the Macintosh and software like CHART are going to gradually change the way we communicate. Illustration such as graphs no longer requires specialists, any more than typing does. Andrew found himself arguing points in his review of CHART with sparkling little graphs, quickly conjured on CHART and as quickly printed in publishable form on the ImageWriter printer.

Graphs are astonishingly efficient tools. They can convey broad understanding and great precision at the same time, of a variety of ideas at once, and in a tiny space. They help the brain meet numbers in the brain's terms—analog pictures rather than digital numbers; they tell quantity directly rather than through translation.

On the 128K Mac CHART is potent but slow. On the 512K Mac it should be a lot faster. You can enter data directly or pull it from MICROSOFT MULTIPLAN (p. 70). The charts can be fine-tuned with MACPAINT (p. 127), and they can be blended with text via MACWRITE (p. 54) or MICROSOFT WORD (p. 60) and telecommunicated with MACTERMINAL (p. 153). I particularly like some of the power available under the command "Analyze," which can take your

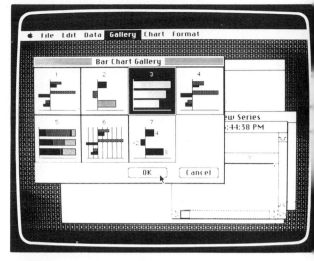

*"Gallery" on CHART on the Macintosh is a pull-down menu of 42 readymade chart formats. Enter your numbers, mouse-select a chart type, and—blink—there it is. You can quickly try on the various types to see which makes your point best. The program also offers the ability to create your own formats and tailor them extensively. It does not do curves, however.*

chart and render a second overlay showing Average, Cumulative Sum, Difference, Growth, Percent, Statistics, or Trend.

This program on this machine is an education.

## For presentation graphics . . .

# EXECUVISION

IBM PC; 128K; copy-protected? YES; $395; Prentice-Hall, Inc., Business and Professional Division, Route 9W, Englewood Cliffs, New Jersey 07632; 800/624-0023 or, in NJ, 800/624-0024

RIK JADRNICEK: EXECUVISION steps beyond the world of basic business graphics with a fantastic set of tools for preparing presentation graphics. You can freely edit the images you create and include them in slideshows. You can cut small sections out of an image, save them in a library on disk and then paste them into other images you create later.

The creators of EXECUVISION sell libraries of graphic shapes you can use, including decorative borders, initials and decorative designs, faces and figures, and maps and international symbols.

The documentation is very thorough and extensively illustrated (even showing the IBM and its keyboard every step of the way). Let the pictures speak for themselves . . .

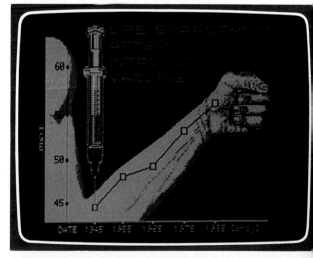

*This graph didn't pop up automatically from data. It's entirely hand-drawn, with numbers typed onscreen, using EXECUVISION.*

*This type of three-dimensional graphing will soon be commonplace on a desktop micro. Right now you need ISSCO mainframe software (they do offer an IBM PC interface) and a Tektronix 4691 inkjet printer.*

*Images you can grasp . . .*
## 3-D Business Graphics

RIK JADRNICEK: Three-D business graphics are downright exciting. Think about it—if a two-dimensional graph is worth a thousand words, a three-dimensional graph is certainly worth a thousand 2-D pictures.

A line graph that shows production on the *Y*-axis, time on the *X*-axis, and number of employees on the *Z*-axis coming out of the page, results in a contour map. Slicing the image through the *X-Y* axis gives you a 2-D production graph over time for any given number of employees. The possibilities are staggering. We may tend to think in these terms, but rarely do we see a clear, hard-copy representation of those thoughts. Higher resolution monitors will make 3-D images popular, but already some integrated business-software packages, like OPEN ACCESS (p. 109), are producing 3-D business graphs.

Now the question arises, "How do we edit and otherwise manipulate all these graphic images we create?" Business-graphics software usually lets you change only color, hatch patterns, font styles, graph types, and scale. With business graphics, most of the time we have to settle for what we get.

You can now take a screen picture created with another program and pull it into a graphics editor to manipulate it just as you would edit text with a word processor or modify a spreadsheet. Soon you'll be able to animate business graphics with a high level of precision.

---

*Monitor as canvas . . .*
## Painting Software

RIK JADRNICEK: Painting software is best suited for graphic artists (and also Sunday painters, doodlers, children, finger painters—anyone who likes to play with colors and patterns, who likes a bit of magic).

It's often called "pixel-based" software because the images are really made of hundreds of little dots of light—pixels, or picture elements. With painting software you can control each pixel on a graphics monitor. Manipulating groups of pixels "paints" an image on the graphics monitor, and manipulating groups of pixels creates animation over time. Depending on the quality of the software and hardware you are using, you may only be able to turn the pixel on or off, or you may be able to choose a color for the pixels from a palette of more than 16 million colors.

Your creation can usually be printed by a variety of dot-matrix printers, line plotters and ink-jet printers. However, since painting images make use of so many colors, the results are often less than satisfactory. One method of producing hard copy is to photograph the screen image using a camera on a tripod in a dark room (you need a long exposure time to avoid getting bars of light across the image), or by using various hardware devices, such as the Lang or Polaroid photo-monitor systems.

**(Videoslide 35 Computer Graphics Camera, includes camera, cables, manual; interfaces with most computers; $2599; interface modules $250-500; Lang Systems, Inc., 1010 O'Brien Drive, Menlo Park, CA 94025; 415/328-5555 ● Palette, includes 35 mm film unit, Polaroid print film unit, 35 mm slide processor, cables, slide mounts, software disk for Apple, IBM PC, DEC Rainbow; $1499; Polaroid Corporation, 575 Technology Square, Cambridge, MA 02139; 800/354-3535.)**

The next frontier is the marriage of computer graphics and video production. Already you can take an image recorded with a video camera and edit it on your computer (see EASEL/LUMENA, p. 132). The animation potential of this marriage is limitless and exciting.

*Scott Lewczek used the Artron PC-2000 software and hardware system ($19,995) for this painting. The subtle shading requires a wide palette of colors. The Artron software is also available for IBM PCs equipped with a Number Nine "Revolution" graphics board.*

---

*Automatic slide show . . .*
## FLYING COLORS

**Apple II family; 48K ● Commodore 64; game controller; color monitor; $39.95; copy-protected? YES; The Computer Colorworks, 3030 Bridgeway, Suite 201, Sausalito, CA 94965; 800/874-1888.**

KEN GOEHNER: Simply elegant. Or elegantly simple. This inexpensive hi-res graphics package brings new meaning to the word "nifty." You can use a joystick, trackball, KoalaPad, or other games controller in the paddle port, and a novice can figure out the entire system in five or ten minutes without consulting the documentation. It's that easy.

FLYING COLORS is a fast, interactive program with a good set of drawing features, including eleven brushtips, sixteen diagonal and cross-hatched color patterns, a smart fill-in mode that remembers the last color or pattern used, a point-to-point line function, a freehand drawing mode, and a "micro" mode for doing detail work and delicate corrections—all cursor controlled. And the Alpha function lets you add text.

With the Slide Projector you can stack images much as you would in a slide carousel, with a choice of cross-fading or successive display. This can be controlled either manually with the games controller or automatically by setting the time function for a period between 3 and 99 seconds. The "slides" can be loaded in any order with simple key commands. Each "slide tray" holds sixteen images and can be linked to other "trays" to present a formidable graphics program.

*The cursor splits into four brushes . . .*

## 4-POINT GRAPHICS

IBM PC compatibles; 128K (DOS 1.1), 192K (DOS 2.0); color graphics card ● Mindset computer; 196K; printers supported include Epson MX80, Diablo Series C Ink Jet, Mannesmann Tally, Quadram Quadjet, Sweet-P, Roland DXY 800, HP 7470; copy-protected? NO; $195; updates $29.25; IMSI, 633 Fifth Ave., San Rafael, CA 94901; 415/454-7101.

---

KATHLEEN O'NEILL: Circles, ellipses, straight lines, rectangles—all perfect. Fill them in with color; change to another color instantly. Add text, move it around, turn it upside down. Larger! Smaller! Hit another key. That was easy.

Like what you've done so far, but want to try something a little different without messing it up? Put it on one of the two buffers. It's there when you want it, faster and easier than using the disk, and it lets you combine separately drawn images.

The program's not perfect. It's hard to use the keyboard to draw free-form shapes (I didn't have a digitizer, and a joystick doesn't work). You can make curves by locating three points, but putting them together to draw something specific takes a lot of work. Also, the colors are very limited and brash.

I like being able to create my own brush. By using different colors for the brush, you can literally draw with a rainbow. Overlapping colors by addition or subtraction creates some pretty wild patterns and textures. There's also a demo mode that records every step you make, so you can animate your drawings.

It's fairly easy to learn the meaning of the keys, but best of all the documentation is really good. It's rare to find operating instructions this clear, logical, and well organized.

RIK JADRNICEK: 4-POINT deserves a gold star. Not only is it a good painting package, it can also edit pictures created by other programs. How? You call up a small 4-POINT utility program that automatically stores itself in RAM memory and gives you the A prompt back again. Take the 4-POINT disk out of the drive, go into another program, and while you're inside that program press two keys to store the screen picture on disk. For example, if you are in 1-2-3 (p. 67), while you have a graph on the screen simply hold the control key down and press F1 and a picture file will be written on the disk. Then, by starting up the 4-POINT software program, you can use it to draw on the 1-2-3 graph . . . a very powerful utility. I've used it with SUPERCALC3 (p. 69) and AUTOCAD (p. 134). Worked every time.

*Drawing tool for a variety of programs and machines . . .*

## KOALAPAD

Apple II family; 48K; $125 ● Atari; 48K ● Commodore 64; disk or cartridge; $110 ● IBM PC/PCjr; 128K; $150; copy-protected? YES; Koala Technologies Corp., 3100 Patrick Henry Dr., Santa Clara, CA 95050; 408/986-8866.

---

KATHLEEN O'NEILL: I've been drawing ever since I can remember, and any graphics software that makes me use the keyboard instead of a stylus leaves me quickly frustrated. If you're interested in drawing with your computer and don't want to jump into elaborate additions to your micro, the KoalaPad is an easy, wonderful place to start. The pad works with either your finger or a stylus and is surprisingly sensitive and accurate. I find it much quicker and easier to use than a joystick.

The menus are full-screen, showing both words and pictures, so you don't have to remember any codes. A button on the pad changes you to the drawing screen. Storage and retrieval are very simple and quick, so it's easy to save drawings or to rework ones you've started.

KOALAPAINTER (Apple II family) will draw in several pen shapes and do points, lines, connected lines, rays, circles, discs, erase, fill, frame, box, magnify (for correcting a pixel at a time), and "help."

KOALAPAINTER (Atari) will do all the basic functions above, plus mirror. It also has a color menu that allows you to mix colors, change colors on your drawing, and add a moving rainbow effect to parts of it.

KOALAPAINTER (Commodore 64) has the basic functions plus "Oops" (erases just the last part you did), X-color (changes one color in your drawing to another), Copy, Mirror, and Swap (lets you work on two screens and move parts between the two).

PC DESIGN (IBM PC) has the basics plus Copy, Text (adds typed words to images), Stamp (leaves a trail of images behind a moving cursor), and Bar and Pie (makes graphs a snap).

KOALAPAINTER (IBM PCjr) is far more fun than PC DESIGN. This program has lots more colors and, in addition to the basic functions, has X-color, three types of Mirrors (for symmetrical drawing), Copy, Swap, Zoom (besides seeing the enlarged pixels you get a small version of your drawing so you can see what you're doing), and last, but not least, Oops. KOALAPAINTER for the PCjr combines all my favorite parts of the other Koala software.

You can use the KoalaPad with many other programs (including games, 1-2-3 [p. 67], MULTIPLAN [p. 70] and DBASE II [p. 85]) instead of the keyboard or a joystick), and we're beginning to see new graphics software for it.

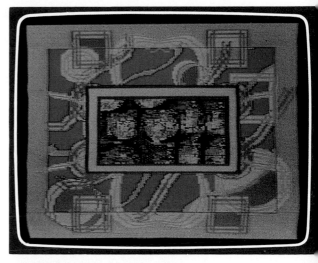

*All Koala's programs are easy to use and fun. KOALAPAINTER (for the IBM PCjr) has the most colors and functions—here demonstrated by Kathleen O'Neill.*

---

*A little animation . . .*

## MOVIEMAKER

Interactive Picture Systems; Apple II family; 48K ● Atari; 48K ● Commodore 64; $50; copy-protected? YES; Reston Computer Group, Reston Publishing Co., Inc., 11480 Sunset Hills, Reston, VA 22090; 800/336-0338; 703/437-8900.

---

ABE PETROW: Anyone who has had a course in animation will really appreciate this program. It takes time—there are too many features to learn in a week—but the manual is very good. This is a powerful program if you want to make short-action (5-second to 3-minute) moving graphics with six layers over a moving background, title scenes, and a four-voice sound track. Has zoom, duplication, mirror, and fill. Graphics Mode 7 (160 X 80) won't let you do Donald Duck, but with a little imagination and a lot of planning, you can probably do something better. The basic program will keep you interested and busy for months, and a professional version is available on a licensed basis.

---

*MACPAINT in color . . .*

## MOUSEPAINT

Bill Budge, Bill Atkinson; bundled with Apple's mouse; Apple IIc; $99; Apple IIe; $149; Apple Computer, 20525 Mariani Ave., Cupertino, CA 95014; 800/538-9696.

---

STEWART BRAND: Most of what you can do on the Macintosh with wondrous MACPAINT (p. 127) you can do on the Apple IIc and IIe with MOUSEPAINT. Resolution isn't as high, of course, but you have color. Prints out in nice black and white on the ImageWriter, rudimentary color on the Scribe (eats a lot of ribbon, though). DAZZLEDRAW, coming from Broderbund, will be competition for MOUSEPAINT.

After James Dowlen drew this landscape with LUMENA software on a Mindset (p. 126) computer, he printed it with a Diablo Inkjet printer ($1350). This is the printout. Inkjet printers, like dot matrix printers, print dots. The resolution matches what you would see on the monitor with this software—about 300 by 200 pixels.

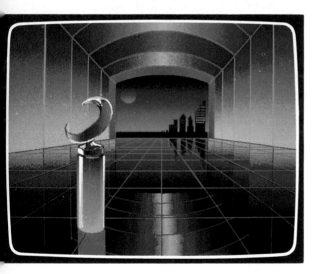

*The most professional painting package available . . .*

## LUMENA

IBM PC compatibles; 256K; RGB monitor (high-resolution), frame buffer; 2 disk drives or 1 disk drive and hard disk; $1250 (4000 colors, 16 simultaneous); $2500 (16 million colors, 4096 simultaneous) • Mindset computer; $400; accepts input from mouse or digitizing tablet (GTCO, Kurta or Summagraphics); copy-protected? YES; Time Arts, Inc., 3436 Mendocino Avenue, Santa Rosa, CA 95401; 707/576-7286.

## EASEL

IBM PC compatibles; 256K; RGB monitor; frame buffer; 2 disk drives or hard disk; input from digitizing tablet; copy-protected? YES; $1250 (4000 colors, 16 simultaneous); $2500 (16 million colors, 4096 simultaneous); Time Arts, Inc., 3436 Mendocino Avenue, Santa Rosa, CA 95401; 707/576-7286.

RIK JADRNICEK: EASEL turns the digitizer stylus into a variety of pens and brushes that includes an airbrush, a character brush, a brush that draws in four-way symmetry, and brushes you create yourself. You use a full palette of colors to paint, even mix and design your own. The colors available depend on the frame buffer (graphics board) being used. You can then freely edit and manipulate the images you create—in some cases, even images transferred from video.

*Artist James Dowlen created this image using LUMENA, and says, "If you have ever tried to draw a checkerboard tile floor in proper perspective, you know that even though it is simple perspective, it can be quite a task. With LUMENA you can lay out the tile pattern flat on the screen (as you would see it looking straight down), choose a horizon line and a vanishing point and the floor will lie down in perfect perspective."*

EASEL and LUMENA both include the following features, to name a few: moving and copying parts of an image, mirroring images, rotating, rescaling, temporary zoom, tapering, shadowing, perspective mapping, grid overlays, gravity lines, filling areas, masking, erasing, text, video digitizing, and merging images from disk. LUMENA is a version of EASEL software by Time Arts, Inc., that was developed for the Mindset computer (p. 126).

JAMES DOWLEN: I had absolutely no computer experience when I first tried my hand at the LUMENA graphics system, yet within only two or three hours I had created images. In that brief time I was hooked. Since the drawing is nearly all done with the electric stylus, the action is essentially the same as with pen or brush. You can even use the stylus to select menu items. You have several pen and brush choices: a "-1" pen has the feel of a fine-point detail pen; using a large brush feels like painting with thick paint.

The colors are beautiful and can be mixed at will, with very subtle adjustments of tone or value. Since you are dealing with light, you may need to alter your thinking when mixing colors: primary colors are now red, green, and blue rather than red, yellow, and blue. You'll catch on, it's not difficult. The luminosity is exciting—has the same emotional impact as stained glass lit from behind.

Special computer functions give you some rapid techniques you might never attempt with conventional mediums: rotate, reflect (to get a mirror image), automatic perspective (given horizon line and vanishing point), four-way symmetry, multicolor airbrush, perfectly horizontal or vertical lines, zooming for final cleanup. In my opinion LUMENA is sensational!

*Great precision . . .*
## Two-D Computer-Aided Design (CAD)

RIK JADRNICEK: Two-D CAD software is best suited for drafting applications and is often referred to as vector-based software. With pixel-based painting software, information on every dot of light (pixel) is saved and used to describe an element such as a line. Vector-based storage is more efficient, in that only the end points of a line need to be stored; the rest of the points are filled in automatically using a mathematical description of the line. A circle can be described with center data point and a specific radius.

The key difference between the two kinds of software is the physical size and detail of the drawing each is capable of producing. Painting software controls only the area appearing on the monitor display surface. Good 2-D CAD software lets you create a drawing larger than the monitor display surface—the monitor acts as a window onto smaller areas of the drawing. For example, you might define a 2-D *X* and *Y* coordinate system to be a 24 X 36 inch piece of paper. As you enter an element into the drawing on the screen, numbers (coordinates) and attributes (e.g., color, layer, line type) are recorded in a drawing database. This lets you then freely manipulate (edit), mathematically transform (move, copy, rescale, rotate), store, and transmit the drawing. You might zoom in so that one square inch fills the entire monitor screen, permitting you to draw very precisely. You might then zoom out so that the entire 36 X 24inch drawing fills the monitor screen, giving an overview of what you have drawn.

Good 2-D CAD software comes with ready-to-use drawing tools called "primitives": line, arc, circle, fill, array, and text—the more the better. These can be combined to produce curves, polygons, fillets (rounding corners), etc. Dimensioning and math calculations should also be included.

In addition, you ought to develop your own tools—for example, building a library of shapes and drawings you can save on disk to use in future drawings and save time. Good documentation, tutorials, ease-of-use, and user customization are also important considerations, since CAD software tends to be complex.

The more computers and supporting hardware devices (plotters, digitizers, graphics boards) the software supports, the more people you will be able to share your drawings with. This is, after all, the spirit of microcomputers.

Two-D CAD programs are beginning to communicate with other programs, such as spreadsheets and analysis programs. Some software (CADPLAN, p. 134) permits you to produce a parts list or bill of materials along with a database of specific drawing elements.

Video scanners are being developed that will enter drawings previously created manually into computerized parts libraries without requiring that they be redrawn. Designing and drafting functions are beginning to blend into one operation.

---

*Low price, good for simple drawings . . .*

## PC-DRAW

**IBM PC/XT compatibles; 128K (192K with DOS 2.0); color graphics card; supports light pens; optional plotter support for HP 7470A and HP 7475A; dot matrix printers supported include Epson MX & FX, IBM, Mannesmann Tally, Okidata 84A, NEC 8023, C. Itoh, IDS Prism; copy-protected? YES; $395; Micrografx, Inc., 1701 North Greenville, Suite 703, Richardson, TX 75081; 214/234-1769.**

BOB SOHR: Applause to Micrografx for an excellent, exceptionally easy-to-learn, well-documented program at the lowest price level. PC-DRAW has limited capabilities compared with state-of-the-art CAD software, but it's a quarter of the price. It has all you need to do flowcharts, office layouts, forms, circuit or graphic design, and business graphics (pie and bar charts, etc.). This is the way to start for the "just curious." You can use it as an educational tool or a toy (it's simple and should be fascinating for a child).

The tutorial and documentation are excellent—among the best I've seen and a model for other software vendors. The installation worked as advertised when I followed it line by line. An index in the manual would be a help, though. I made one phone call to the company (concerning printer support) and obtained immediate, friendly, and competent help.

You can freehand-draw from the keyboard using the cursor-control keys (limited to vertical, horizontal, and diagonal moves); draw lines point to point; create circles, arcs, and ellipses; or select symbols from two onscreen libraries, and you can create your own symbols and menu. Once in your drawing, you can move, expand, or reduce, replicate or dimension any symbol, however produced. Also, you can toggle on or off a background grid (size adjustable) and add text (provided or custom). Four abutting pages forming a square are in memory at any time (allowing you to create a drawing four times screen size). Symbols can be copied from one screen page to any other.

All this is enough to produce an amazing variety of drawings, although it would be nice to have unlimited freehand drawing (curves and angles). I didn't get to try a light pen, which presumably would help. Medium-resolution color is now supported with lots of color combinations onscreen, but of course it gives you less drawing on the same size screen.

PC-DRAW is highly recommended as an entry-level CAD package. For some applications, it will be all you ever need, and in any case it can serve as a tutorial and introduction to the 2-D graphics world.

---

*PC-DRAW's onscreen menus take the guesswork out of command and symbol selection. At $395 a bargain program and a good one to start with for 2-D technical drawing.*

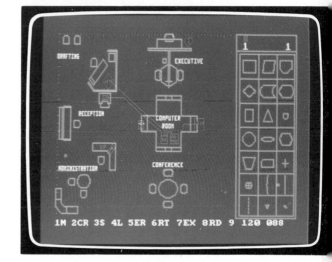

---

*Introductory program,
    good for isometrics . . .*

## ROBO GRAPHICS CAD-1

**Apple II family; 64K; includes joystick controller; supports Apple graphics tablet and Houston HI-PAD; supports all dot matrix printers with graphics dump; drives most plotters, including Hewlett-Packard, Houston Instruments, Roland, Amdek, Apple Color Plotter; copy-protected? YES; $1095; Chessell-Robocom Corporation, Robo Systems, 111 Pheasant Run, Newtown, PA 18940; 215/968-4422.**

RIK JADRNICEK: CAD-1 is for the Apple II or IIe owner who wants semi-professional CAD capability. It is best used for small drawings ranging from block diagrams to detailed architectural and isometric drawings, and is a good introduction and learning tool for computer-aided design with microcomputers.

A joystick with buttons is provided, and onscreen menus help you interact with the program. Good documentation and file-

management utilities help you through the learning process, but there is a tremendous amount of disk swapping in the process.

CAD-1 is written in fast assembly language, so things happen quickly. The program overcomes Apple's memory limitations by developing and using libraries of shapes. If a drawing gets too large and occupies too much memory, you can save a copy and then re-insert it in the drawing as a single entity requiring far less memory.

A strong point of CAD-1 is its ability to make precise isometric drawings, a feature often missing in 2-D CAD systems. You can rotate grids and snap to isometric grid points.

A few drawing niceties are missing, like the ability to draw on different layers and the support of high-resolution monitors, but CAD-1 is fast, powerful, and easy to use. As long as you understand that large drawings become an exercise in pre-organization and disk swapping, this package will do the job.

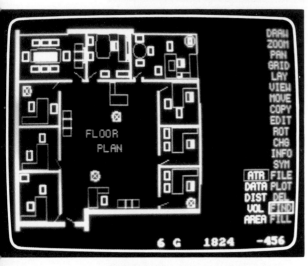

With CADPLAN, you can print a bill of materials based on information in the drawing—in this case a list of office furniture with costs automatically totaled for multiple items in the drawing. CADPLAN is one of the few drawing packages with this capability so far.

*Medium precision . . .*

## CADPLAN

**IBM PC compatibles; 320K; graphics card, color monitor; accepts input from Mouse Systems Mouse, GTCO, Kurta or Houston Instruments Digitizers; outputs to IBM, Calcomp, Houston Instruments or Hewlett Packard plotters and Epson or IBM dot matrix printers; copy-protected? NO; $1900; Personal CAD Systems, Inc., 981 University, Los Gatos, CA 95030; 408/354-7193.**

RIK JADRNICEK: CADPLAN has some interesting options: for an additional price you can have semi-automatic dimensioning (where the program tells you the distance between any two points according to the scale you set). Another CADPLAN option is a report generator utility that permits you to develop reports based on elements you place in a drawing. For example, you can produce a bill of materials or parts breakout from the drawing you just created—a powerful and useful feature often missing from CAD programs.

Most of the elements of a good CAD system are present, including multiple layers, line types and widths, color, symbol libraries, grids, grid snap, text, zooming, panning,

moving, copying, and editing of your drawing.

The program is excellent for space planning, block diagrams, and even freehand sketching, but if you want to do detailed architectural drawings and define points and angles in decimal units, it may not be precise enough.

You have 64,000 X 64,000 data points to work with, since the program is based on integer math (rather than floating-point math; see AUTOCAD, below). That means if you let each data point equal 1/1000th of an inch, you could create a drawing area of 64 X 64 inches accurate to 1/1000th of an inch, which may be adequate for most work. The capacity of a drawing using CADPLAN depends on the amount of memory available, so you have to do a little planning. With a large drawing you could run out of memory.

CADPLAN supports a variety of input and output devices and is very easy to use. But make sure it will suit your needs. The more basic version, called CADDRAFT ($495), may be all you need if you are primarily interested in space planning or block diagrams.

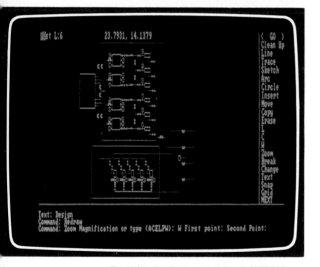

The piping drawing was created with AUTOCAD. You might put the entire drawing on one layer, the detail on a second. You could draw a picture of this page stuck on the 50-yard-line in the middle of a football field, then zoom in to one letter on the page and draw a house plan inside.

*Professional 2-D drawing, precise through 127 layers . . .*

## AUTOCAD

**CP/M-80 machines; 64K; 8″ disk format ● IBM PC/XT compatibles; 256K ● MS-DOS machines (DEC Rainbow, Eagle, NEC APC, TI PRO, Zenith Z-100); 256K ● Victor 9000; 384K; hard disk; 8087 chip; 512K memory recommended; supports many input devices (digitizers, mice, and light pens), and output devices (plotters and graphics boards); copy-protected? NO; $1000 for base program, $1500 for augmented program; AutoDesk, Inc., 150 Shoreline Blvd., Mill Valley, CA 94941; 415/331-0356.**

RIK JADRNICEK: AUTOCAD is capable of drawings ranging from simple flowcharts to large and complex architectural renderings. Your microcomputer becomes a drafting table with pencil, paper, T-square, compass, and more.

For example, with AUTOCAD you can simulate 127 layers of 24 X 36 inch tracing paper precisely registered one on top of the other, and you can draw on each piece of paper to an accuracy of less than one-trillionth of an inch (floating-point math). (Since the program becomes slower as the drawing grows larger, however, an 8087 numerical coprocessor chip ($260) is recommended to speed things up.)

All data and commands can be entered from the keyboard or (faster and easier) with a variety of input devices (digitizers, mice) supported by the program. Multicolored plots ranging from letter to architectural size can be printed.

A rich set of primitive commands enables various constructions of lines, arcs, and circles used for precision drawing. Editing features include erasing, moving, copying, scaling, and rotating of drawing elements. The $1500 advanced version provides semi-automatic dimensioning, cross-hatching, partial deletion, filleting, and a freehand sketch mode with its own set of editing commands.

User-definable menus, macros, and command files allow facile customization by users without programming knowledge (a very powerful feature). You can create and save libraries of shapes, then retrieve and place in drawings by selecting them from an onscreen menu or by touching pictures on the digitizer surface.

Zooming and panning capabilities turn the monitor into a window scrolling over the surface of a large drawing. Zooming into a small area enlarges that area and permits detailed drawing.

If you plan to do extensive work with the program, a hard disk drive is recommended to speed up disk input/output. Like a word processor, AUTOCAD is a picture processor, saving pages of drawings on disk as available RAM fills up.

AUTOCAD is a very sophisticated, mathematically precise program and an excellent choice for professionals. The only feature that seems to be missing is the automatic bill of materials report offered by CADPLAN.

*Professional drawings . . .*

## VERSACAD

**IBM PC/XT compatibles; 128K; input by Houston Instruments, Kurta or Summagraphic Digitizing Tablets; copy-protected? YES; $1995 ● HP 200; input by HP 9111A graphics tablet; $4995; all output to Houston Instruments or Hewlett-Packard plotters;**

## CADAPPLE

**Apple II family; 64K; input device and serial interface; ● IBM PC; 128K; 2 disk drives; graphics card; copy-protected? YES; $1795;**

**both from T&W Systems, Inc., 7372 Prince Drive, Suite 106, Huntington Beach, CA 92647; 714/847-9960.**

RIK JADRNICEK: VERSACAD for the IBM PC and CADAPPLE for the Apple II family are two versions of an extremely capable two-dimensional drafting program developed in 1977. A version is also available for Hewlett-Packard Series 200 computers. The program is written in Pascal and uses floating-point math for high-precision drawing capability.

Only 128K RAM is required on an IBM PC, because VERSACAD constantly pages the drawing to the disk; a hard disk drive and an 8087 numerical coprocessor chip are recommended to speed up program execution. As previously mentioned, professional microcomputer CAD software using floating-point precision tends to be inherently slow in zooming and panning a drawing, and VERSACAD is no exception. Speedy RAM-disk configurations can also be developed.

VERSACAD supports the Houston Instrument Hi-Pad and the Summagraphic bit-pad, along with a joystick input device. It also supports the full lines of both Houston Instrument's DM/PL series and Hewlett-Packard's HP-GL series of plotters as well as a variety of graphics boards, including the new Number Nine hi-res board and Conographic color board.

With either VERSACAD or CADAPPLE, you can create very professional drawings—from simple block diagrams to full architectural plots. All the basic editing and image-manipulation functions of a good CAD system are present. You can save "snapshot" zoomed views of your work, and a library feature lets you develop groups of 100 symbols and plot them out on a 10" x 10" symbol grid for later use in drawings.

A tiered menu structure appears on a separate monitor and online help is available. Most commands are executed with just a few keystrokes. The program is fairly easy to learn and use, and help and training are offered by T&W Systems, Inc.—worth looking into if you want to do some serious drawing on your microcomputer.

*Solids modeling . . .*
## 3-D Computer-Aided Design (CAD)

RIK JADRNICEK: Three-D computer-aided design software is often referred to as solids-modeling software. The solid image is normally constructed by linking a collection of polygons of various shapes and sizes. The more polygons used, the smoother and more representative the shape will be. Advanced software (see CUBICOMP, p. 137) will even smooth curved surfaces so that a sphere (actually made up of polygons) really looks like a sphere.

As with 2-D CAD, data points are stored in a database. Since a database is kept of each element used in creating an object, once created, the objects can be rotated in space, scaled, edited, stored, and transmitted. More advanced packages include hidden-line removal and surface shading, both of which contribute to the illusion of reality. This simply means that lines normally out of sight (falling behind other lines and surfaces) are removed and that the surface is shaded to mimic the way light would be reflected off a real object. With advanced software like CUBICOMP a palette of more than 16 million colors can be used to precisely shade an irregular shaped object while changing the light source. So a doughnut really looks like a doughnut.

Three-D software, although fascinating, is still in its infancy as far as practical applications go—in part because microcomputer processing speed doesn't yet allow the complex mathematical calculations necessary to create, shift, and rotate accurate solid models quickly and at a low price. It's a Catch-22 situation: 3-D software isn't yet sophisticated enough to be immediately useful, and because of that, the potential market isn't large enough to pay for software development.

### Who Should Use 3-D Software

BOB SOHR: There are those among us who if told they must learn some math to use a tool would just as soon pass and go swimming. It's the computers that should have the Ph.D.s in math—that's what they are for. It would be nice to run our hands over the imaginary curves in space and have them magically

*The CUBICOMP CS-5 system is expensive, but the kind of sophisticated surface and shading and smoothing you see in this 3-D drawing are very difficult mathematical feats.*

appear in holographic detail in midair. Unfortunately we ain't there yet. As a potential user of 3-D graphics software, you • should realize that something called analytic geometry starts to rear its head. Most of us can visualize things in three dimensions pretty well, but most present-day 3-D software requires you to describe an image using numbers representing points in a three-dimensional matrix. You may also have to know about things like local and global coordinates, sections of solids, and projections onto planes.

The computer is here to help. You'll end up doing a lot less per pound of end product than ever before. But you will have to learn the language. It would be a disservice to send you out to buy your new 3-D CAD package only to have you find you couldn't get past the first menu once you brought it home.

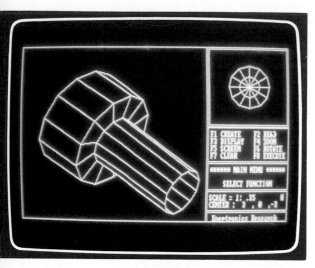

*This surface stick model is the result of a formula entered into the ENERGRAPHICS programs. The program can be an excellent way to visualize difficult mathematical concepts.*

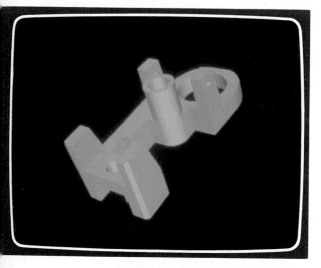

*Start with a "wire-frame" model. Remove the lines that would be out of sight. Shade and smooth the surface, and you have a 3-D image. CUBICOMP's CS-5 software even lets you punch holes and put objects inside.*

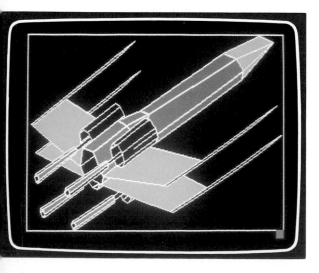

*Low price, requires math knowledge . . .*

## ENERGRAPHICS/PC

Version 1.3; IBM PC compatibles; 128K; color graphics board; RGB monitor; outputs to Epson MX/FX, C. Itoh, Okidata 92/93, Mannesmann Tally 160/180, NEC 8023, IDS Prism dot matrix printers; with $100 plotter option, supports HP 7470A/7475, Houston Instruments DMP 29 & 40, CalComp 84, Strobe 260, IBM 749/750, Sweet-P, Mannesmann Tally Pixie, Amplot II plotters; copy-protected? NO; $350; Enertronics Research, Inc., 150 North Meramec, Suite 207, St. Louis, MO 63105; 800/325-0174.

RIK JADRNICEK: ENERGRAPHICS is a surprisingly inexpensive package chock full of graphics surprises. It will do everything from business graphics to 3-D solids stick modeling. If you want a tutorial and extensive documentation on the state of 3-D graphics, this would be the least expensive entry package to get involved with. But prepare yourself for a mathematical journey into the third dimension. ENERGRAPHICS is more of a tutorial or learning experience than a software package for practical everyday use. You get a lot for your money.

*With the ADVANCED SPACE GRAPHICS hardware/ software combination you can trace a physical object in 3-D on the screen by moving the "Space Tablet" around the object's surface.*

*Inexpensive introductory package . . .*

## 3DESIGN

IBM PC/XT compatibles; 128K; color card; accepts input from mouse, digitizer, or joystick; Frieze Graphics by ZSoft available ($50) to support Epson, IDS, Okidata, C. Itoh or NEC dot matrix printers; copy-protected? NO; $249; Tr!tek Vision Systems, 4710 University Way N.E., Suite 1512, Box C-56789, Seattle, WA 98105; 800/392-9210.

BOB SOHR: 3DESIGN provides a good, low-priced introduction to the concepts and techniques of three dimensional design and has some practical application. Architects, engineers, and designers can create images of objects and then rotate, scale, translate, and view these images from different perspectives. It's like being able to walk around the image on the screen.

You can compose new objects using copies of images stored in libraries on disk. Unfortunately, the only input device is the keyboard. Using the keyboard, you can create vertical, horizontal, and diagonal lines, circles, arcs, and ellipses, but not curves or lines at arbitrary angles. Images tend to look

*With 3DESIGN software you can remove hidden lines and then take 3-D drawings one step past ENERGRAPHICS by adding elementary surface shading.*

fairly crude, with noticeable aliasing (diagonal lines look jagged). With the basic system, hard copy output capabilities are limited—no plotters are supported, and dot matrix printers are supported only with an extra-cost option.

The reference manual begins with a graphics-theory section and throughout makes an attempt to provide some academic background for the uninitiated. However, it falls short in not providing the kind of step-by-step feature presentation and practice tutorial that can get a new user up to speed fast and establish a friendly feeling toward a complex program.

Some nice features are a hidden-line removal routine (runs slow, as usual), rubber-band lines (get a starting point, then watch the line follow the cursor anywhere on the screen), a hierarchical structure for objects (the typewriter on the desk in your picture is "attached" to the desk and moves with it), and a "Z-axis indicator" that shows you, with a kind of depth gauge, how far in or out of the screen the current point you're describing is. A painting routine allows color filling of hidden-line drawings.

It appears that the current version will be phased out, so if you're interested in a cheap introduction to 3-D graphics, look into this one now.

*Stick modeling and 3-D
distance calculations . . .*

## ADVANCED SPACE GRAPHICS

**IBM PC compatibles; 128K; PC/XT compatibles; 192K; copy-protected? NO; $1695 including MCS 4-axis 3-D Space Tablet Digitizer; $1995 with package above and MCS HighRES A/D interface card; Micro Control Systems, Inc., 143 Tunnel Rd., Vernon, CT 06066; 203/872-0602.**

RIK JADRNICEK: ADVANCED SPACE GRAPHICS is both a 2-D and 3-D software package that comes with the only 3-D digitizer I know of, a novel idea. You can place a bowl on the digitizing tablet and enter its shape into the computer by touching a number of points on the surface of the bowl. These points are digitized and become data points on the circumference of circles whose centers fall on an axis of symmetry (see photo). When the data points are connected (automatically) to corresponding points on adjacent circles, the result is a "stick" representation of the surface.

Once the surface is defined, you can look simultaneously at a top, side, and front view of the object on the monitor. You can expand and shrink both the horizontal $X$ and vertical $Y$ axis scales to manipulate the object, rotate and move the shape, and even look at it from different perspectives. You can zoom in to enlarge parts of the shape for more detailed drawing. You can enter free-hand lines separately in three dimensions, place text labels within drawings, and print a precise representation of your work with a variety of dot matrix printers and pen plotters.

You cannot, as in more advanced systems like CUBICOMP (below), shade the stick surfaces or remove hidden lines for more realistic results. However, you can accurately measure distance—one of the best uses of the program. You can calculate $X$, $Y$, or $Z$ distances from point to point or as "as the crow flies" (the shortest distance between two points) with floating-point accuracy. Distances within the shape you create can be dimensioned, with values automatically increasing and decreasing as you rescale the drawing.

While ADVANCED SPACE GRAPHICS does not have the power and editing flexibility of a well-designed 2-D software package, it certainly is a sign of things to come. MCS plans a rewrite of the program in 1984 to change from advanced BASIC to the more powerful and flexible language C. More surprises in the area of 3-D digitizing are also in the works.

*Loaded with features,
priced accordingly . . .*

## CUBICOMP CS-5

**IBM PC compatibles; 384K minimum, 512K recommended; Intel 8087 math chip; high-resolution RGB monitor; Interface Adaptor box; supports most digitizing tablets, all mice and Summagraphics-type interface; outputs to Houston Instruments and Hewlett-Packard plotters, Diablo Color Ink Jet Printer, and to film recorders; copy-protected? NO; $9700; CubiComp Corporation, 3165 Adeline St., Berkeley, CA 94703; 415/540-5733.**

RIK JADRNICEK: For the price of an IBM PC plus hardware and software upgrades totaling about $10,000 you can have a 3-D system as good as many costing upwards to $100,000.

You don't need to calculate coordinate points, since you can enter data points by using a digitizer. You can create stick models of three-dimensional figures while scaling and rotating them in space. You can design complicated and irregular shapes and even punch holes in them using the keyboard and digitizing tablet. Also, you can remove the hidden lines, save the images on disk, and recall them at will.

A stick (often called a wire-frame) model can also be surface shaded so it looks like a real-world object, and if you change the light source, the shading of the object changes accordingly.

Special features of CS-5 are anti-aliasing and surface smoothing. Normally a diagonal line appears jagged on the monitor due to the small number of pixels representing it. Since 3-D images are composed of a collection of polygons, surface shading will often be jagged also. Special algorithms (mathematical processes) are used in CS-5 that help smooth the jaggedness of lines (anti-aliasing) and surfaces, making them appear realistic in spite of the coarseness of the monitor.

You can create animated sequences and presentations using files of stored keyboard commands (macros). The CS-5 software and available IBM PC RAM allow approximately 3000 polygons for creating shapes—just enough room to draw and shade a fairly detailed bicycle sprocket. Slow speed in regenerating images on the screen and limited capacity for drawings seem to be the current limitations of the program.

The advanced version of the program is fairly expensive for the average microcomputer user, but you can get their Techmar version for a more reasonable price. The manual is excellent and serves well as a tutorial in 3-D solids modeling. (You can buy the manual alone for $75.) The program is definitely worth the money . . . and it's still getting better.

Since CS-5 can work with EASEL (p. 132), professionals might want both. With this combination, you can create a 3-D image, shade it, leave the image on the screen, then use the sophisticated painting capabilities of EASEL to do some dramatic editing.

Since CS-5 can work with EASEL (p. 132)

*Books on Computer-aided Design*

## GRAPHICS FOR THE IBM PC

*Graphics for the IBM PC*; **B.J. Korites; 1983; 268 pp.; $28.50; $50 with disk; Kern Publications, 433 Washington Street, P.O. Box 1029, Duxbury, MA 02331; 617/934-0448; or COMPUTER LITERACY**

BOB SOHR: This book uses some advanced math concepts, and it requires knowledge of BASICA. Discussions include how to draw, translate, rotate, and scale objects in 2- and 3-D; elementary hidden line, perspective, shading, windowing, and clipping programs are all discussed. The sixty-two listings of BASICA programs range from placing a point on a page through an animated arcade game. An optional disk of programs discussed is available.

## GRAPHICS PRIMER FOR THE IBM PC

*Graphics Primer for the IBM PC*; **Mitchell Waite & Christopher Morgan; 1983; 430 pp.; $21.95; Osborne/McGraw-Hill, 2600 Tenth Street, Berkeley, CA 94710; 415/548-2805; or COMPUTER LITERACY.**

BOB SOHR: My personal preference. This book contains complete hardware sections and is an excellent tutorial on the use of BASIC graphics commands. It contains lots of color screens and diagrams along with program listings for a wide variety of pictures and geometrical shapes. The book is thorough on color use and contains a good animation section. Currently used as college text.

## PC GRAPHICS

*PC Graphics* (Charts, Graphs, Games and Art on the IBM PC); **Dick Conklin; 1983; 256 pp.; $15.95; John Wiley and Sons, 605 Third Avenue, New York, NY 10158; 212/850-6000; or COMPUTER LITERACY.**

BOB SOHR: The title says it. The authors pay particular attention to several types of charts, representing functions, curve fitting, animation, slideshows, and games, and include sections on text and high-resolution graphics, light pens, joysticks, and paddles—with problems and solutions in each chapter. For beginners—there's little in here about math transforms on images.

## GRAPHICS PROGRAMS FOR THE IBM PC

*Graphics Programs for the IBM PC*; **Robert Traister; 1983; 245 pp.; $14.95; Tab Books, Inc., P.O. Box 40, Blue Ridge Summit, PA 17214; 717/794-2191; or COMPUTER LITERACY.**

BOB SOHR: You need no previous experience to benefit from this book. Emphasis is placed on applications rather than theory—how to use BASIC to make the pictures you want. The book is written in an anecdotal style and includes a hardware overview, BASIC review, sections on text mode, random graphics, and color-graphics animation, and good details on how to get hard copy from printers.

## TELECOMMUNICATING

### Art Kleiner, Domain Editor

ART KLEINER: Someday everybody will communicate by computer, according to an emerging army of dreamers. Personal computer networking—exchanging text and pictures between terminals, over phone or cable—is so convenient that many expect it to become as widespread eventually as the telephone and television are now. The dreamers include corporations like AT&T, IBM, Sears, CBS, and the Knight-Ridder newspaper chain, but the systems these companies plan are still mostly unformed. These are still pioneer days, and personal computer owners are the pioneers.

Maybe the frontier feeling explains why computer networkers seem so fiercely individualistic. Or maybe the flexible nature of telecommunications inspires everyone who tries it to do something different. I've seen people play games (pp. 28-45), order products (p. 141), start small businesses that span continents on nationwide conferencing networks (pp. 146-147), retrieve public domain software from free bulletin boards (pp. 148-149), investigate background material about specific news stories (p. 144), seek romance (on bulletin boards, pp. 148-149), get stock quotations (p. 142), and work at home, sending their reports to the office by electronic mail (p. 145).

Most personal computer networks, such as The Source, CompuServe, and a dozen others reviewed in this section (pp. 141-147), give you a password and charge by the amount of time you're actually logged on (the "connect hour"). To reach them, you simply dial a local phone number that ties into one of several cross-country transmission services, which are cheaper long-distance carriers of computer signals than the regular phone lines.

Less expensive than national networks are local bulletin boards, which you can dial into to leave messages or take part in discussions. (Unlike national networks, bulletin boards aren't connected to cross-country transmission services; if you call one that isn't local, you must pay for the long-distance

---

## WHOLE EARTH RECOMMENDED TELECOMMUNICATING TOOLS

### (June 1984)

#### OVERALL GUIDE
**The Complete Handbook of Personal Computer Communications**, $14.95, p.140

#### ONLINE TRANSACTIONS (p.141)
Comp-U-Store (electronic shopping)
Source PUBLIC Files (user publishing)
BANK-AT-HOME (electronic banking)

#### ONLINE SERVICES FOR INVESTORS (p.142)
Dow Jones News Service
Independent Investors Forum
Source Unistox
CompuServe MicroQuote
The Desk Top Broker
Media General DataBank
Disclosure II
NAARS

#### TAPPING INTO DATABANKS (p.143)
**Omni Online Database Directory**
BRS After Dark
DIALOG Knowledge Index
**The Information Brokers**

#### NEWS SERVICES (pp.144-145)
CompuServe Information Service
Dow Jones News Service
Official Airline Guide Electronic Edition
NEXIS
Source UPI Newswire
NewsNet

#### ELECTRONIC MAIL (p.145)
MCI Mail
EASYLINK
International Electronic Mail Service (IEMS)
SourceMail

#### CONFERENCING (pp.146-147)
CompuServe Special Interest Groups (SIGs)
Participate-on-the-Source (PARTI)
Confer II
Electronic Information Exchange System (EIES)

#### ELECTRONIC BULLETIN BOARDS (pp.148-149)
**The Computer Phone Book**, $9.95
**Plumb**, $26.50/yr.
AMIS, $10
COMMUNITREE, $250
NET-WORKS, $99
COLOR-80, $150
COLORCOM/E, $50
IBBS, $50
CBBS, $50
THE BREAD BOARD SYSTEM (TBBS), $200
MULTILINK, $295
MIST/MIST+, $225-$495

#### TERMINAL PROGRAMS
MITE, $150-$195, p.150
CROSSTALK XVI and 3.0, $195, p.150
MODEM7, free, p.151
HAYES SMARTCOM II, $149, p.151
POST-PLUS, $195, p.151
PC-TALK. III, $35 donation, p.152
TELEPHONE SOFTWARE CONNECTION TERMINAL PROGRAM, $40, p.152
DATA CAPTURE IIe, $90, p.152
IN-SEARCH, $399, p.152
ASCII EXPRESS "The Professional," $130, p.152
AMODEM, $10, p.152
MACTERMINAL, $99, p.153
TRS-80 Model 100, $599, p.153
VIDTEX, $70, p.153
TRANSEND PC, $189, p.154
IBM PERSONAL COMMUNICATIONS MANAGER, $100, p.154
BUSINESS COMPUTER NETWORK, p.154

#### MODEMS (pp.154-155)
Volksmodem, $80
Atari 1030 Modem, $140
VICModem, $60
AUTOMODEM, $100
OPERATOR 103, $169
Visionary 100, $595
Signalman Mark XII, $399
Multi-Modem MT212AH, $549
Visionary 1200, $795

#### FILE TRANSFER (p.156)
**RS-232 Made Easy**, $17.95
MOVE-IT, $125/$150
KERMIT, $100
BLAST, $250

telephone call.) We review guides to existing bulletin boards on page 148, and software for starting your own on pages 148-149. To give an example of the bulletin boards' power: David Hughes of Colorado Springs entered onto his computer bulletin board the text of a pernicious city council bill outlawing professional work at home. Instead of tracking the bill down at City Hall, residents could dial in at their convenience and read the bill at home. Within a week, Hughes had gathered enough angry readers to storm the next city council meeting and influence council members to defeat the measure.

To begin telecommunicating, you need to buy a modem (p. 155) and a piece of communications software called a terminal program for your personal computer. The modem is an electronic box that first translates computer characters into sounds that travel through phone lines, and then untranslates them back into computer characters at the other end. The terminal program controls the modem, shunting text between it and your screen, disks, and printer. Compared with word processors, learning programs and organizing tools, modems and communications software don't vary much. We recommend a small selection of modems on page 155 and sixteen terminal programs on pages 150-154.

If you send a lot of programs and other files from one computer to another, you might also want file transfer software, reviewed on page 156. "An acquaintance regularly sends me spreadsheet files by phone," Louis Jaffe wrote us. "Loaded into SUPERCALC, they work just fine." Ultimate file transfer—local networks that allow several computers in one building to work with the same files simultaneously—is described on page 157.

Telecommunications is probably the most personal of computer applications, but it's also the most technically complex. The necessary tools—modems and communications software—are uneasy compromises between computers and phone lines, which weren't designed to work together. In practice, that means every computer network and software package you use will take a bit of fiddling until you get your connections right.

But don't be daunted; it's becoming easier. Programs are finally emerging that treat telecommunicating as a human activity instead of a technical obstacle course. Modems are getting cheaper and more reliable. A few computers—the TRS-80 Model 100 (see page 153), the PCjr (see page 17) and more to come—are appearing with built-in modems. And the networks are becoming more plentiful and reliable every week.

## WHY THIS IS THE LONGEST SECTION IN THE BOOK

**"A computer is a communications device first, second, and third."—Alan Kay**

STEWART BRAND: "Telecommunicating" is our founding domain. Three ways, in fact.

For me it was a cold plunge into teleconferencing that swerved my life toward personal computers and led directly to this book. In January 1983 I was invited by the Western Behavioral Sciences Institute in La Jolla, California, to participate as faculty in their School of Management and Strategic Studies. It was a six-month stint, nearly all of it conducted from my office on a Kaypro they loaned me to hook up to the 40 or so nationwide "students" (corporate executives) via the marvelous EIES network (p. 147). A success in its own right, the project also revolutionized my writing, my thinking, my work network, and my business.

People have been interested in this book's sizable advance, the $1.3 million from Doubleday, and in the fact that an eight-page proposal inspired it. What's more interesting to me is that it took only ten days for four coauthors to write that proposal and wrestle it through four drafts, even though one of us was traveling (Art Kleiner), one was on the East Coast (John Brockman), and two were jittering around in California (myself and Richard Dalton). The ectoplasmic bond was the EIES network. Its immediacy and convenience served admirably the need to make a single-voiced, enthusiastic, carefully proofed document. I'm not sure we could have managed it without telecommunications.

Art Kleiner is the living link between previous **Whole Earth Catalogs** and this project. He was Research Editor of the two editions of **The Next Whole Earth Catalog** (1981, 1982) and frequent Editor of our **CoEvolution Quarterly**. Building on his early involvement with EIES— he's been a user consultant since

*Art Kleiner*

Matt Herron

1979—he became Whole Earth's computer specialist, convener of the Personal Computer section in **The Next Whole Earth Catalog**. When this project came up, he had just left on sabbatical to do a book on the history of magazines and the invention of marketing. Returning to the rescue, he put together the network of friends and colleagues that initiated what you see here.

The telecommunications section is long because it covers online services as well as telecommunications software and hardware. Also, it is long because the subject is the most difficult in the book. Burdened by expertise, Art had the arduous task of triply distilling an already hard liquor.

## TYRANNY OF THE NEW

ART KLEINER: Necessity—the dire lack of good terminal programs for the Apple II family—mothered two new packages: PERSON TO PERSON from Trutec and the remarkable APPLE ACCESS II from Apple itself. APPLE ACCESS is slightly more versatile, but will only run on the IIc or the IIe with an Apple Super Serial Card. If you already have other hardware, get PERSON TO PERSON.

PFS:ACCESS, running on Apples and MS-DOS machines, is a good beginner's or busy executive's terminal program for accessing online networks—The Source, CompuServe, etc. It will replace HAYES SMARTCOM II (p. 151). Bulletin board browsers will feel limited: PFS:ACCESS only stores ten network numbers at one time. We're still evaluating CONEXUS, a bulletin board version of MIST, and KAMAS, a CP/M package.

## THE COST OF NETWORKING

| Name of Network | Initial Charge | Monthly Charge | Connect Charge (Per Connected Hour) Business Hours 300 BAUD | 1200 BAUD | Evenings & Weekends 300 BAUD | 1200 BAUD | Charge Per Transaction | Other Charges |
|---|---|---|---|---|---|---|---|---|
| CompuServe pp.142, 144, 146 | $19.95 (Includes one free hour) | None | $12.50* | $15* | $6* | $12.50* | None | $500-$1,000 per month for maintaining your own conference☆ |
| CONFER II p.147 | 20.00 per group (2 or more members) | 10.00 minimum per group | $21 | $21 | $18 | $18 | None | None |
| **Dow Jones News/Retrieval** pp.142, 144 (Any member can choose one of three plans:) | | | | | | | | |
| Standard | 75.00 | None | 72.00 | 72.00 | 12.00 | 12.00 | None | $24/hour extra free-text search |
| Blue Chip | 175.00 ($100 annual) | None | 72.00 | 72.00 | 7.80 | 7.80 | None | $16.29/hour extra for free-text search |
| Executive | None | 50.00 | 48.00 | 48.00 | 7.80 | 7.80 | None | $16.20/hour extra for free-text search |
| EasyLink p.145 | None | None | 14.40 | 27.00 | 14.40 | 27.00 | .15 per address, $2-5 per ★ overseas TELEX. | .15 extra for signing on from remote locations via WATS lines. |
| Electronic Information Exchange System (EIES) p.147 | None | 75.00 | 7.50 | 7.50 | 3.00 | 3.00 | None | $15/monthly (approx.) storage fees for each conference you create. |
| International Electronic Mail Service (IEMS) p.145 | $100 ($50 per account. IEMS has a 2-account minimum). | $5 per account | $3.00 | $3.00 | $3.00 | $3.00 | 25¢ per 1000 characters (a 250-word message costs 50¢); $2-4 per overseas TELEX.★ | None |
| MCI Mail p.145 | | None | None | None | None | Per message: $1 as electronic mail, $2 as first class mail, $6 and up as overnight mail or TELEX. | None | None |
| The Source pp.141, 144, 145, 146 | $100 | $10 ($1 fee plus $9 minimum connect change). | $20.75 | $25.75 | $7.76 | $10.75 | None | $10/monthly (approx.) storage fees for each conference you create. |

\* $2/hour surcharge if you use a different transmission network than CompuServe's own (will affect people in some small cities).
☆ Depends on whether the conference (SIG) includes extra text databases.
★ TELEX rate depends on destination.

*This table shows the relative costs for communication networks reviewed in this book. (Only those that you would actually subscribe to are included. Comp-U-Store, for instance, is available through three of the networks here—*

*CompuServe, Dow Jones News/Retrieval, and The Source.) Information and membership are available from: CompuServe, 5000 Arlington Centre, Box 20212, Columbus, OH 43220; 800/848-8990.*

*The Source, Source Telecomputing Corporation, 1616 Anderson Road, McLean, VA 22102; 800/336-3330. For addresses of the other services listed, see the individual reviews on the pages indicated.*

***Still the best guide . . .***

### THE COMPLETE HANDBOOK OF PERSONAL COMPUTER COMMUNICATIONS

*The Complete Handbook of Personal Computer Communications; Alfred Glossbrenner; 1983, 325 pp.; $14.95 postpaid from St. Martin's Press, 175 Fifth Avenue, New York, NY 10010; or COMPUTER LITERACY.*

ART KLEINER: This book covers much of the telecommunicating lore that nobody tells you about unless you know what to ask: how to compare networks, how to find the particular conference you need, how to connect your computer to someone else's typesetting equipment or directly to another computer.

Author Alfred Glossbrenner (he also wrote **How to Buy Software**, p.6) compares the major systems—The Source, CompuServe, Dow Jones News/Retrieval, bulletin boards, DIALOG, EIES, etc.—describes what they can do and how they fit into the general computer/networking culture. He also explains mysterious technical details, like parity and XON/XOFF, that you need not know about until something goes wrong.

**The Complete Handbook** is already somewhat out of date, but Glossbrenner promises to revise future editions. The book's enthusiasm and clarity will never age.

*Online discount shopping . . .*

## COMP-U-STORE

**$25/year membership; $23/hr (9-5 wkdays), $8/hr (eves & wkends), Comp-U-Card International, 777 Summer Street, Stanford, CT 06902; 203/324-9261.**

ELIZABETH M. FERRARINI: If you know what you want, don't need to touch the item beforehand, and want to save time and a lot of money, then let your micro shop at Comp-U-Store for everything from hair dryers to computer printers (mostly computer equipment and the kinds of products sold in mainstream discount houses). Most Comp-U-Store goods are 20 to 40 percent below the manufacturer's price; you also pay regular connect charges to CompuServe, The Source, or Dow Jones for the time you spend browsing online, plus an annual $25 membership fee.

You shop for one item at a time, proceeding through a series of menus that usually offer several selections and a "no preference." Beware of "no preference": specific answers help Comp-U-Store narrow the search to find exactly what you want. When you're done, Comp-U-Store lists all the products that meet your specifications. You can then see any product's list price, manufacturer's name, delivered price (including shipping to your area and all taxes), available colors, and description. You can purchase any by credit card or check. Most items come via United Parcel Service, and you can only return merchandise that arrives defective or broken. For the moment, Comp-U-Store is the only national electronic buying service. Since new regional electronic buying services are constantly expanding, that could change any time.

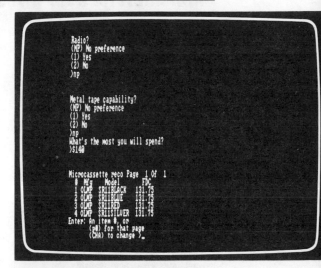

*Comp-u-Store takes you through a series of questions that narrow down your desires, then shows you a menu of choices—in this case, for a cassette tape recorder/player.*

*Publish on-line and get paid for it . . .*

## SOURCE PUBLIC FILES

**Available at normal Source rates (see table, p. 140); Source Telecomputing Corporation, 1616 Anderson Road, McLean, VA 22102; 703/734-7500.**

LEVI THOMAS: PUBLIC—a service within The Source—is the only place in computer networking where users publish their writing and get paid each time it's read. What you find there will vary in quality and intention; I found helpful information for navigating around the rest of The Source, plus entertaining stories such as "Published From a Bar-Stool: or, Saloon Journalism With the Model 100." My Great-Form-But-Too-Bad-About-the-Content award goes to a hillbilly-style newspaper called the **Par Mt. Telegraph**, containing cliché outhouse humor in an ingeniously interactive format, complete with comic strips. It takes very little time to learn PUBLIC's ins and outs and sample the selections there. The table of contents for each publication features the reading time of each entry and the number of times it's been read (for those interested in what's hot among other Source users). But each publication has different commands, which confuses most readers, who see several publications in one session. I don't know why The Source doesn't require a common Help command from its user-publishers.

PUBLIC is a great idea, and an open-ended opportunity to experiment with the format of computer communications. (Anyone can publish, but representatives of The Source must approve PUBLIC files for collecting a portion of readers' connect time charges.) If you don't find anything that interests you there, why not write something yourself?

## Home Banking

ART KLEINER: Many new home banking services are appearing, meaning that banking need no longer be locally based—a change that could have dire long-range effects on community investing. Still, home banking is an awfully big convenience. However, users should be sure to print out and monitor bank statements diligently. Some early home-banking systems have rinky-dink computer security, and if you don't notice that your money is missing, no one will.

*Online money tenders . . .*

## BANK-AT-HOME

**$7.50/mo, $.20 for each transaction plus $3-5/mo normal checking charge; United American Bank, P.O. Box 1959, Memphis, TN 38101; 901/766-2853.**

WILLIAM J. COOK (adapted from **The Joy of Computer Communications**, 1984, Dell books, $5.95): My personal computer has freed me from dealing with teller lines, paper checks, and all the other inconveniences of normal personal banking. I use the BANK-AT-HOME program operated by United American Bank of Memphis, Tennessee. I started by opening a checking and savings account over the phone. The opening deposit and signature cards went back and forth in the mail. I gave the bank a list of the people and companies I regularly pay; the bank contacted them and explained that they would receive their checks directly henceforth. I also told my empoyer to send my monthly paychecks directly to Memphis.

Now I pay $7.50 a month, plus 20 cents for each check the bank sends (to cover their first-class mail costs). Every time I log on, the service asks whom I want paid and how much; and it gives me a complete statement whenever I request it. If I feel a nostalgic urge to write a check the old-fashioned way, I can do that too—and I can set up a local checking or savings account as a cash drawer. When I need $100, I go to the local automatic teller machine, and then have BANK-AT-HOME replenish the cash by sending a check to my local bank.

## Online Services for Investors

*Stock quotes within 15 minutes...*

### DOW JONES NEWS SERVICE

Available at normal Dow Jones rates (see table, p. 140); Dow Jones News/Retrieval, P.O. Box 300, Princeton, NJ 08540; 800/257-5114 or (in New Jersey) 609/452-1511.

ELIZABETH M. FERRARINI: Want to keep frequent tabs on the value of your investment portfolio? Dow Jones News Service's extensive quotes on common and preferred stocks, corporate and foreign bonds, and composite options arrive from a variety of exchanges, within fifteen minutes of the latest transaction. Quotes from mutual funds and selected U.S. Treasury Bonds are updated several times a day. Also available is a database of historical quotes going back to 1978. The service is easy to use if you keep a list handy of Dow Jones's abbreviations for the particular stocks you have in mind. Dow Jones's commodities listings are quite limited; use National Computer Network's Nite-Line (8 a.m.-6 p.m. weekdays, 300 baud $20/hr, 1200 baud $26/hr; 6 p.m.-8 a.m. and weekends, 300 baud $9/hr, 1200 baud $15/hr; National Computer Network, 1929 North Harlem Avenue, Chicago, IL 60635; 312/622-6666) for comprehensive commodities updates.

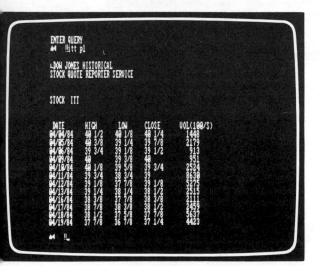

*Buy and sell...*

### THE DESK TOP BROKER

Available 7 a.m.-6 p.m. daily (PST). $6/hr (300 baud); $24/hr (1200 baud); $10 monthly minimum. C.D. Anderson and Company, 300 Montgomery Street, Suite 440, San Francisco, CA 94119; 800/822-2222.

ELIZABETH M. FERRARINI: The Desk Top Broker allows you to place orders via modem

*Most comprehensive of all...*

### INDEPENDENT INVESTORS FORUM

$360/year (includes $10/month free online time); $20/hr (9-5 wkdays); $14/hour (eves and wkends). Independent Investors Forum, 1128 East Bluff Drive, Penn Yann, NY 14527; 202/667-1719; or 3901 Cathedral Avenue, N.W., Washington, DC 20016; 202/244-4798.

ELIZABETH M. FERRARINI: Of all these services, the best value is the Independent Investors Forum, a conferencing system run on CONFER II (p. 147) by the American Association of Individual Investors in Chicago. The Forum allows you to exchange investment information with other callers and download free investment-analysis software for Apple and IBM PC-compatible microcomputers. Requests on the message board call for everything from help with a formula for exponential moving averages to tips for investing in the options market.

*Less expensive, less thorough...*

### UNISTOX

Available at normal Source rates (see table, p. 140); The Source, 1616 Anderson Road, McLean, VA 22102; 703/734-7500.

### MICROQUOTE

Available at normal CompuServe rates (see table, p. 140), with surcharge: $.25 for quotes on 25 stock symbols, $1.25 for report on any given stock; CompuServe Information Service, 5000 Arlington Centre Blvd., Columbus, OH 43220; 800/848-8990 or (in Ohio) 614/457-8650.

ART KLEINER: The Source and CompuServe also offer stock quotes; theirs are drawn from the news wires. The Source's is called UNISTOX, and is a service of UPI; CompuServe's service is called MICROQUOTE. They're less thoroughly updated than Dow Jones's but less expensive, especially if you access them at night.

*Dow Jones' historical quotes service answers questions such as, "How did International Telephone and Telegraph stock do in April?"*

to buy and sell stock at any time of day through its sponsor, C.D. Anderson and Company of San Francisco. What's more, the service automatically updates your C.D. Anderson accounts (including IRA and Keogh accounts), provides current stock prices, and monitors up to 18 stocks through a Stock Watch feature. Don't panic if you make an error; the Desk Top Broker always lets you confirm your order before sending it on to the Anderson wire room.

*Heavy on statistics...*

### MEDIA GENERAL DATABANK

Most detailed version: $15/hr plus $4.60 or less/seach; Business Information Systems, 747 Third Avenue, New York, NY 10017; 212/752-0831.
● Less detailed than BIS, above; $48-72/hr (9-5), $36-54/hr (eves and wkends); Dow Jones News/Retrieval, P. O. Box 300, Princeton, NJ 08540; 800/257-5114 or (in New Jersey) 609/452-1511.
● Less detailed than BIS, above; $39.75/hr (7-6 wkdays, local time); $34.75/hr (eves, wkends, holidays); Source*Plus (STOCKVUE); Source Telecomputing Corporation, 1616 Anderson Road, McLean, VA 22102; 800/336-3330. Produced by Media General, P.O. Box C-32333, Richmond, VA 23293; 800/446-7922.

ELIZABETH M. FERRARINI: If you need a lot of investment statistics, Media General will wire you to Wall Street. Updated weekly, this database contains information on corporate earnings, dividends, and comparative stock price performance. The database has two segments: companies and industry groups. You can easily search either one for companies that match your specific statistical need.

*Proxy statements, info in depth...*

### DISCLOSURE II

$51-102/hr (9-5), $18-36/hr (eves and wkends); $1.50-$3/request; Warner Computer Systems, Financial Systems Division, 605 Third Avenue, New York, NY 10158; 212/986-1919, and $48-72/hr (9-5), $36-54/hr (eves and wkends); $2-5/request; Dow Jones News/Retrieval, P.O. Box 300, Princeton, NJ 08540; 800/257-5114 or (in New Jersey) 609/452-1511, and other vendors. Produced by: Disclosure, Inc., 5161 River Road, Bethesda, MD 20816; 301/951-1300.

### NAARS

IBM PC; 64K; Bell 212-compatible modem (Hayes 1200, Racal-Vadic VA3451, Ven-Tel MD 212), and Mead Data Central Interface ($245); copy-protected? NO ● or a leased terminal from Mead (NEXIS) at $150/mo; Mead Data Central, 9333 Springboro Pike, Miamisburg, OH 45342; or P.O. Box 933, Dayton, OH 45401; 513/865-6800.

ELIZABETH M. FERRARINI: Two databases, Disclosure II and NAARS, provide in-depth business and descriptive information. Disclosure II offers corporate balance sheets for more than 6,000 companies, going back two years, plus their officers' and directors' names. Also, you can order the full texts of corporate filing documents through these databases. NAARS (the National Automated Accounting Research System), available through your PC or on NEXIS (p. 144), has annual reports and proxy statements online going back to the late seventies.

See page 77 for more on computers and investing.

## Tapping Into Databanks

*Best guide to information banks . . .*

## OMNI ONLINE DATABASE DIRECTORY

*Omni Online Database Directory*; Mike Edelhart and Owen Davies; 1983, 292 pp.; $10.95 postpaid from Collier Books, Macmillan Publishing Company, 866 Third Avenue, New York, NY 10022; 212/702-4212; or COMPUTER LITERACY.

---

ART KLEINER: Databanks provide hitherto ungatherable information: one service, called COMPU-MAP, calculates any route across the United States, warning of tolls and closed roads. Another, called AmericanProfile, describes the demographic, er, lifestyles of people who live along the way. There are law databanks, computer-industry databanks, lists of dormant oil wells, and lists of missing rare books. Nearly all are too expensive or too inaccessible for casual use. If you want to do some *serious* (i.e., professional) database searching, buy the encyclopedic **Omni Online Database Directory**. Its user-contributors describe the real purpose of each information bank. They even make something like the Bureau of Labor Statistics Consumer Price Index sound interesting. This book will help you find the databases, and offers a few clues for searching them. But to actually find what you need, you might be better off going to a librarian or information broker.

---

*Late-night,*
*low-cost data searching . . .*

## BRS AFTER DARK

Available Mon.-Fri. 6 p.m.-4 a.m., Sat. 6 a.m.-4 a.m., Sun. 6 a.m.-2 p.m. and 7 p.m.-4 a.m., all E.S.T. $75 initial charge; $12 monthly minimum; $6-14/hour, depending on which database is searched. Bibliographic Retrieval Service, 1200 Route 7, Latham, NY 12110; 800/833-4707 or (in New York state) 800/553-5566.

## DIALOG KNOWLEDGE INDEX

Available Mon.-Thurs. 6 p.m.-5 a.m., Fri. 6 p.m.-midnight, Sat. 8 a.m.-midnight, Sun. 3 p.m.-5 a.m., all caller's local time. $35 initial charge; $24/hour. DIALOG, 3460 Hillview Avenue, Palo Alto, CA 94304; 800/528-6050.

---

STEVEN LEVY: My first shock in telecomputing came when I realized that the Brave New World of getting information through your home computer did not yet exist for schlumps like me who aren't on some corporate tab. Though dozens of online databanks were available via modem—each derived from a bibliographic reference book like the **Science Citation Index** or **Index Medicus**—they typically cost $75 or more per hour, and using them well requires training. Then along came BRS After Dark—a cheaper, evening-and-weekend version of its parent, the Bibliographic Retrieval Service. I hooked up, admittedly a little worried that it would offer only abstracts, not the full text of articles I'd need.

One of my first searches was for information about the military-funded ARPAnet communications network. I had found very little in conventional libraries. Within five minutes (50 cents connect time), using the simple search function (BRS After Dark lobotomized the sophisticated commands used in its high-ticket day service), I discovered a 100-page report on the history of the ARPAnet. Its price wasn't listed, but the address of the research firm that prepared it was. I called them, and they sent it to me

gratis. Never would have found it otherwise.

I later tried BRS's competitor, Knowledge Index (child of DIALOG, the other main on-line data bank vendor). It had a great manual (clear without reverting to third-person-stupid, with sample sessions for each database) and more databases (hence more topics) than BRS After Dark. But it cost more.

If you plan well, a typical search on either service costs as little as one or two dollars, especially if you hone the wording of your request. Prices will drop when the masses use these services, but if you need information now, sign up.

Main complaint: neither allows you to search through all its databanks in one sweep. You have to hop in and out of menus, retyping your search strategy each time. (The daytime services let you store your search strategy online and check in every week or so to see what's new.) Even so, we're talking New Age bargain here. Highly recommended. You may never look at a card catalog again.

(Also, see IN-SEARCH, p. 152.)

---

```
TOPIC:  Find books on using personal computers in business.

  (1)  ?BEGIN BOOK1
       5/16/83  14:31:46 EST
       Now in BOOKS (BOOK) Section
       Books in Print (1490-1983) (BOOK1) Database
       (Copyright 1983 R. R. Bowker Co.)

  (2)  ?FIND PERSONAL AND COMPUTER?
                    5993 PERSONAL
                    7100 COMPUTER?
             S1    127  PERSONAL AND COMPUTER?

  (3)  ?FIND BUSINESS AND S1
                   15703 BUSINESS
             S2       8  BUSINESS AND S1

  (4)  ?DISPLAY S2
                       Display 2/L/1
       1075211   7797527XX
       Business Applications for the IBM Personal Computer
       Zimmerman, Steven; Conrad, Leo
       224p.
       R J Brady  06/1983
       Trade $16.95
       ISBN: 0-89303-243-3
       Status: Active entry
       Illustrated
       SUBJECT HEADINGS: MICROCOMPUTERS (00596668)

  (5)  ?LOGOFF
       5/16/83  14:32:44 EST
       Session Total: 0.021 Hours $   0.50  User U40003
```

*Knowledge Index has a clear, comprehensive manual; this excerpt shows how to refine your search in its database of Books in Print, which includes every available American published book.*

---

*How to sell information . . .*

## THE INFORMATION BROKERS

*The Information Brokers* (How to Start and Operate Your Own Fee-Based Service); Kelly Warnken; 1981, 168 pp.; $15.95; R. R. Bowker, 205 East 42nd Street, New York, NY 10017; 800/916-1600.

---

ART KLEINER: The Information Brokers explains how to turn databank searching and independent research into a cottage industry —a promising self-employment opportunity for liberal-arts educatees. People who search online now will have an inside track into strange new information-shepherding jobs in computer networks to come. This book tells how to learn the skills and sell them once you've got them.

## News Services

```
ENTER DEPARTURE CITY NAME OR CODE
    SAN FRANCISCO
ENTER DESTINATION CITY NAME OR CODE
    BOSTON
ENTER DEPARTURE DATE
    29 JUN
                    FARE MENU

FARES FOR                    FARES FOR
DIRECT FLIGHTS            DIRECT FLIGHTS
AND CONNECTIONS                    ONLY
---                                ---

1   COACH CLASS AND EQUIVALENT FARES    6
2   FIRST CLASS AND EQUIVALENT FARES    7
3   BOTH COACH AND FIRST CLASS FARES    8
4   ADVANCE-PURCH AND EXCURSION FARES   9
```

*Finding the cheapest fare from San Francisco to Boston with the OFFICIAL AIRLINE GUIDE ELECTRONIC EDITION. First you enter the departure city, target city and date; then choose what type of ticket you want. OAG shows you a list of fares; and (not shown) lets you expand any listing to find more information.*

*Superb weather and sports . . .*

## COMPUSERVE INFORMATION SERVICE

Available at normal CompuServe rates (see table, p. 140); CompuServe Information Service, 5000 Arlington Centre Blvd., Columbus, OH 43220; 848-8990 or (in Ohio) 614/457-8650.

ART KLEINER: CompuServe's news wire service only goes back one day, offering a few stories in each of a dozen or so categories. Though mediocre for news, it's the best place to find weather (superb land and maritime forecasts, keyed by locale, from the National Oceanographic and Atmospheric Administration) or sports results (Levy checks baseball box scores here).

*Four months of business news . . .*

## DOW JONES NEWS SERVICE

Available at normal Dow Jones rates (see table, p. 140); Dow Jones News/Retrieval, P.O. Box 300, Princeton, NJ 08540; 800/257-5114 or (in New Jersey) 609/452-1511.

ART KLEINER: Type in the code for a particular industry or corporation and scan a list of appropriate stories adapted from the **Wall Street Journal** going back four months. Choose the stories you want to read and they appear. You can make a search for particular words embedded within the stories, but it will cost extra and require a special manual. Nonetheless, Dow Jones is a good place to start research on any business-oriented topic. When I wrote about AT&T's new proposed computer network last fall, I depended on it. It's a good thing the service is so easy to use, because it offers almost no on-line help.

*Dial-Up Flight Information . . .*

## OFFICIAL AIRLINE GUIDE ELECTRONIC EDITION

$50 initial charge; $6/hour. Official Airline Guide, Attn: Electronic Edition, 2000 Clear Water Drive, Oak Brook, IL 60521; 800/323-3537.

ART KLEINER: This dial-up databank permits you to browse among commercial airline fares and schedules as easily as you'd browse among shirts in a department store. You choose your departing city, arriving city, and date; see the available fares; check the limitations on each fare; and print out the appropriate schedules. Then you log off and call the airlines to book your seats (you can't, unfortunately, make reservations online). A diligent travel agent might do more for free, but finding a good fare online will make you feel as triumphant as scoring well on a computer game. You can sample this database through CompuServe or Dow Jones News/Retrieval, but joining directly is much cheaper.

*Top of the line magazine, newspaper and wire service data . . .*

## NEXIS

$50/mo, $28/hour, $9-$18/each search request (9-5 wkdays), $4.50-$9/request (eves and wkends), $1.50-$3/search modification; IBM PC; 64K; Bell 212-compatible modem (Hayes 1200, Racal-Vadic VA3451, Ven-Tel MD 212); and Mead Data Central Interface ($245); copy-protected? NO ● or a leased terminal from Mead (NEXIS) at $150/mo; Mead Data Central, 9333 Springboro Pike, Miamisburg, OH 45342; or P.O. Box 933, Dayton, OH 45401; 513/865-6800.

ART KLEINER: If you spend $1000 or more worth of your time annually in library work, NEXIS is the best single tool to invest in; it not only saves time but opens up immense new research capabilities.

NEXIS keeps the full text of dozens of newspapers, magazines, specialized newsletters, and news wires, most going back several years, some to the late sixties: the **New York Times** and the **Washington Post**; the AP, UPI and Reuters wires; news services from Japan, Taiwan, and Britain; **Forbes**, **Computerworld**, and the **Almanac of American Politics**. (It has fewer newsletters than NewsNet, and no computer-oriented ones, but that will probably change.)

NEXIS is the smartest online information service, and the easiest to learn and use. Unlike the others, if you ask for "fortune telling" it will also find "telling fortunes." You can easily modify your request if it didn't hit right the first time. You can search all databanks simultaneously or move among

*History begins on Saturday . . .*

## SOURCE UPI NEWSWIRE

Available at normal Source rates (see table, p. 140); Source Telecomputing Corporation, 1616 Anderson Road, McLean, VA 22102; 703/734-7500.

ART KLEINER: The Source's service, based on the UPI news wire, lets you tag a particular topic and follow that day's stories about it, often while they're coming off the wire for the first time. Unfortunately, as veteran networker Steven Levy noted, The Source news history begins on Saturday, when they wipe the wire clean. So on Sunday morning, you can only look back to the previous afternoon. And while the news wire invites browsing, finding particular topics, especially obscure ones, is tricky. During the Democratic primaries last spring, I tried to learn about the IRS's new computer to track tax evaders. A Source search turned up two IRS stories, and neither matched to my topic; but I found 34 stories when I searched for Gary Hart.

*NEXIS browses through the newspapers, magazines, or newsletters you specify; then it presents one by one, the articles that include the combination of words you asked for. The KWIC feature highlights those words in each article, so you can see at a glance if the article matches your needs.*

them, your search request moving automatically with you. The best feature, called KWIC, pulls up each story with your search words highlighted within it, so you can instantly judge the story's value.

NEXIS has some limitations: You can't save incoming text on a disk, and can only print one screenful at a time, which slows down your sessions by a third. It runs only with its own IBM PC software (an Apple version may come soon). And even if you share an account, it's expensive. But worth it. Maybe even worth buying an IBM PC for.

*Two to three years' worth
of expensive newsletters . . .*

## NEWSNET

Rates vary depending on which newsletters are read: $24-$120/hr (9-5 wkdays), $18-$80/hr (eves and wkends); $15 monthly minimum; average session: $40. NewsNet, 945 Haverford Road, Bryn Mawr, PA 19010; 800/345-1301 or (in Pennsylvania) 215/527-8030.

ART KLEINER: NewsNet outrages me, just as many of its industry newsletters do: they're all too damned expensive, and only add to the cultish mystique of inside access. But these publications do help track specialized news, and they're cheaper and more current online than in print. The selection includes **Defense Industry Report**, **IBM Watch**, **Legislative Intelligence Week**, **Fiber/Laser News** and **Entrepreneurial Manager's Newsletter**.

Many go back two or three years. NewsNet's easy-to-use commands let you find articles by scanning titles or searching for key words. The best feature, called Flash, flags everything that comes in related to a particular topic and delivers it daily to your account. Use their On-Line Computer Telephone Directory to find someone's TELEX or SourceMail number.

# Electronic Mail

*A typical letter sent on MCI Mail: written and telecommunicated on a personal computer, printed out in MCI's offices in a remote city, and delivered as a local letter through regular first class mail. For an extra $10/month, you can store your letterhead and signature with MCI, and, with their laser printer, they'll print them on each letter.*

*Instant delivery at $1 per letter . . .*

## MCI MAIL

See table on p. 140 for rates; MCI Mail, 2000 M Street, N.W., Third Floor, Washington, DC 20036; 800/MCI-2255.

ART KLEINER: If you own a modem or telephone terminal, join MCI Mail—joining and receiving messages costs nothing. For $1 you can send an MCI Mail message to someone's terminal, and for $2, send a message that MCI prints out and drops off as regular first class mail. Higher rates ensure more rapid hand-delivery; for a short manuscript that *must* be across the country tomorrow, MCI Mail is probably the cheapest ($6) overnight message delivery service. Significantly, Purolator Courier works with, not against, MCI Mail.

I sent MCI Mail successfully two minutes after I signed on the first time. You can send messages over the TELEX network easily, for about $2 extra to most countries ($1 in the U.S.). Finding subscribers' addresses is tricky; MCI Mail needs a better directory. As with other electronic mail networks, you can send the same message to twelve people as easily as to one, but be wary: MCI Mail, unlike The Source, will charge you for twelve letters!

*(Suggested by Harry Newton)*

*Low-cost access to TELEX . . .*

## EASYLINK

See table on p. 140 for rates; EASYLINK Response Center, Western Union, 1651 Old Meadow Road, McLean, VA 22102; 800/336-3797 or (in Virginia) 703/448-8877.

## INTERNATIONAL ELECTRONIC MAIL SERVICE (IEMS)

See table on p. 140 for rates; International Electronic Mail Service, 21686 Stevens Creek Blvd., Cupertino, CA 95014; 408/446-4367.

ART KLEINER: Some of your would-be electronic mail correspondents may be reachable only via corporate mail systems—Tymshare's OnTyme, ITT's Dialcom, and the three or four interwoven international TELEX services. Corporations can afford the hefty minimum fees, but the rest of us can now link in through these two networks, which bundle their members into one "corporate" account

on each service, like a group chartering an airplane. Western Union's EASYLINK is also the only way to send your computer text as a telegram, and the cheapest way to send or receive TELEXes. At a reasonable cost to you, IEMS links to as many corporate mail networks as it can find.

EASYLINK has easy commands and one of the best manuals in the business. It lets you forward incoming messages to others with your own comments attached, and tag your sessions so that several users can share the same account. Unfortunately, it won't let you edit a mistake in a message before you send it. IEMS permits editing, but uses OnTyme's arduous commands (for instructions, you type EXE ** HELP instead of just ? or HELP). Both networks work well with the more automated communications software (pages 150-154), particularly MITE, CROSSTALK and ASCII EXPRESS, which provide the electronic confirmation (called an "answerback") required for TELEXing.

*Pay by the minute . . .*

## SOURCEMAIL

Available at normal Source rates (see table, p. 140); Source Telecomputing Corporation, 1616 Anderson Road, McLean, VA 22102; 703/734-7500.

ART KLEINER: The oldest electronic mail system for personal computers is still the most versatile. As with MCI Mail, with SourceMail you can learn to send and receive messages within minutes. You pay by the minute, but there's no extra charge for multiple copies. To cut costs, type messages on your word processor and then send them with your communications software. SourceMail offers a wide range of alternatives —you can reply to messages as you read them, send copies to other people, keep lists of groups who will all get one message, or "express mail" your message so it goes to the front of the receiver's incoming queue.

```
drive" type problems.  That's fine, I guess if you heavily
enjoy rapping on computers endlessly, but it got quickly
boring.  ...Richard
C866 CC251  Richard Dalton (wesc ed,334)  2/15/84   9:45
AM  L:6


C866 CC252  Anthony D. Fanning (TonyF,1608)   2/15/84
4:46 PM  L:7
KEYS:/BBS/TEN-YEAR-OLDS/

BBS's can follow the WALKIE-TALKIE pattern.  You know, with
the two ten-year-olds walking down opposite sides of the
street saying, "Can you hear me?"..."Yeah, can you hear
me?"...."Yeah, can you hear ME?" I see it a lot the day
after Christmas.  On the other hand, you can find useful
information on BBS's (if you're interested in computers,
that is).
C866 CC252  Anthony D. Fanning (TonyF,1608)   2/15/84
4:46 PM  L:7


C866 CC253  Larry Freeman (LarryF,1218)   2/15/84   7:01 PM
  L:13
KEYS:/MAC VS. KAYPRO/

On Monday, I stopped in to my "friendly" local computer
store and sat down to play the piano, I mean I sat down in
```

## A new kind of conversation . . .
## The Movable Electronic Computer Conference

ART KLEINER: Exchanging electronic mail among a group of people is like holding a seminar in a corridor—there's no centralized space where people know they should congregate. A computerized conference, on the other hand, supplies a focus: it maintains a transcript that keeps track of everybody's place and shows them new material automatically. Use conferencing to share research, to coordinate an ongoing project spread across the country, or to investigate new interests.

To find a local conferencing system in your area, use **The Computer Phone Book** (p. 148). Or set up your own system on a microcomputer and leave it hooked to the phone all day (see COMMUNITREE and MIST+, pp. 148-149). Or join established conferences on dial-up national computer networks. We list four national networks here, all somewhat complex but worth the time and money to explore.

*Wit and wisdom from EIES teleconference discussions. The Bulletin Board Systems remark is by Organizing Domain editor Fanning in Whole Earth's public conference on telecommunicating. The Lebanon comment, made just after the marine barracks fiasco in '83, is from a private set of conferences called the School of Management and Strategic Studies, run by the Western Behavioral Sciences Institute in La Jolla, California. Harlan Cleveland made this particular comment from Minneapolis, where he is director of the Hubert Humphrey Institute of Public Affairs at the University of Minnesota.*

```
C349 CC872  Harlan Cleveland (481)   10/27/83  11:50 PM  L:44
KEYS:/LESSONS FROM LEBANON..ONE/
A: 871

    In the 1960s those of us involved in fashioning
peacekeeping forces (mostly through the UN, at that time)
had one simple notion engraved on our minds: Superpower
forces had best not be used as international peacekeepers,
and sparingly even as mediators.

    If the mediator or peacekeeper shows up at the bargaining
sessions with a nuclear bomb sticking out of his rear pocket,
the disputants are going to tune their antennae toward the
middleperson rather than toward dialogue with each other.
The U.S. as peacekeeper cannot be credibly neutral.
Even if the superpower peacekeepers have the purest of
intentions, nobody will believe it.
```

*Dozens of subjects
—or create your own . . .*

## COMPUSERVE SPECIAL INTEREST GROUPS (SIGS)

**Available at normal CompuServe rates (see table, p. 140); CompuServe Information Service, 5000 Arlington Centre Blvd., Columbus, OH 43220; 800/848-8990 or (in Ohio) 614/457-8650.**

ART KLEINER: CompuServe's SIGs, or special-interest groups, are its most rewarding feature. The several dozen public SIGs on specific topics are like benevolent fiefdoms, each with a presiding duke (called a sysop, for "system operator") who manages the flow. Each SIG weaves up to eleven thematic threads; members choose which to follow. A beginner's menu makes the fairly complex commands masterable; regular users should switch to the expert menu and buy the SIG manual ($3.95 extra). The best SIG command (Read Thread) lets you easily follow a chain of responses; you can also

scan comment headers and mark items to retrieve in full later. The immense range of SIG topics includes every type of computer users' group imaginable plus such diverse interests as environmental issues, music, religion, animal care, and working at home.

You can start your own private CompuServe SIG for an absurdly overpriced $500-$1000 per month. CompuServe only stores about a month's worth of back discussion, so you can't use SIGs to keep archival records of a group's progress. But the sysop can archive some material. Most computer SIGs keep public-domain software for people to gather by phone; CompuServe's own software, VIDTEX (p. 153), is specially adapted for this. If you're curious about conferencing, check out CompuServe SIGs first.

*A giant information
department store . . .*

## PARTICIPATE-ON-THE-SOURCE (PARTI)

**Available at normal Source rates (see table, p. 140); Source Telecomputing Corporation, 1616 Anderson Road, McLean, VA 22102; 703/734-7500.**

LOUIS JAFFE: The most freewheeling of computer conferencing services, PARTI allows any user to start a public or private conference on any topic at any time. Despite frequent technical problems and a command structure that baffles even old hands, PARTI has become one of the most popular branches of The Source.

Both the 1983 Korean Airliner attack and the Grenada invasion spawned PARTI conferences that attracted hundreds of comments—some from well-informed military and intelligence people. These discussions subsided after a couple of weeks, but other PARTI conferences have gone on for months, on topics as diverse as UNIX, interpersonal relationships, and the nature of language.

Somebody in a PARTI conference once compared this system to watching TV. (If I knew where to begin looking, I'd retrieve that item and credit its author.) Scanning PARTI *is* like watching TV commercials—you find a jumble of briefly presented, often unrelated topics. As new conferences branch spontaneously from old ones, you can get pulled into the flow and lose track of time (which is how PARTI generates revenue for The Source). It's as if you were lost in the aisles of a giant information department store. By the time you find your way out, you're carrying a shopping bag full of ideas, assertions, and inanities.

*For connoisseurs and companies . . .*

## CONFER II

**See table on p. 140 for rates; Advertel Communications Systems, Inc., 2067 Ascot, Ann Arbor, MI 48103; 313/665-2612.**

## ELECTRONIC INFORMATION EXCHANGE SYSTEM (EIES)

**See table on p. 140 for rates; New Jersey Institute of Technology, 323 High Street, Newark, NJ 07102; 201/645-5503.**

ART KLEINER: These are the best conferencing systems for organizing projects or bringing together working groups of people. Both rooted in academia (the University of Michigan and New Jersey Institute of Technology, respectively), they have a wide range of complex capabilities. Both offer a diverse, warm community of people already in place who welcome new members. CONFER II is somewhat easier to learn and slightly more expensive; EIES is somewhat more perplexing (no one, not even designer Murray Turoff, knows all the EIES commands).

Both systems have features that really help people communicate. Detailed member directories let you learn more about the author of an intriguing comment before you contact him for follow-up. Pseudonyms permit anonymous comments (surprisingly useful for honest criticism). Elaborate search commands retrieve all items written by a particular author, in a particular month, or on a particular topic. Modifying commands let you change your mind, even after entering your words into public view.

CONFER II is available in customized versions for large groups and corporations. If you join as a small working group or individual, you choose an existing CONFER II arena, either

## THE PERSONAL EFFECTS OF NETWORKING

First there's uncertainty: "Did my message go through all right? Did I send it to the wrong person? Is it really private? How do I sign *off* this thing?"

As you feel more secure, pleasure takes over. The flow of ideas is exciting and flattering. "I posted my query at ten and by noon there were seven replies waiting!" You step into the rarefied atmosphere of a literary correspondence— but one faster, more immediately engaging, and easier to keep up with than that of the conventional world of letters. Mutual projects and opportunities blossom quickly, without regard for geographical distances.

Some people move on to addiction: signing on a dozen times a day ("maybe something is waiting"), cutting back offline relationships because they're less convenient ("if they're not on the network I don't want to talk to them"), running up unexpectedly large connect-time bills, merging work and home lives so they can sign on at night, and even dreaming about the network.

Fortunately, addiction is short-lived. You get overwhelmed by overload and cut back, learning to filter out material. You don't have to lose appreciation for the physical world; you can become more sensual elsewhere to compensate for the hours spent online. You use the telephone more sparingly, scheduling calls and exchanging agendas in advance.

Networking is catnip for people who communicate best by the written word. Good writers have charisma. Mediocre writers improve. Pushy or insensitive writers get ignored. People learn to articulate their emotions more explicitly to avoid being misunderstood. Race, gender, shyness, disabilities, age, and physical presence all lose importance.

Since you don't need an appointment to reach someone via computer network, you come to feel as if everyone is always accessible. But you also learn not to pressure people—they'll just shrug and ignore your message. For most participants, the increased contacts break down old hierarchies and make unforeseen relationships possible—as with the corporation vice-president and the college student who swap tips on playing ARCHON. The key impression is one of civilization—or, more precisely, a new way of being civilized.

*—Art Kleiner*

public or private. Public conferences are usually devoted to a broad subject like Computers or Law; within that, people initiate and respond to individual topics. You can join in as many arenas as you like, but be careful; CONFER II incites more give-and-take than any other system, and you may feel like you're drowning at first. With practice, you can easily choose which topics to follow and which to avoid.

As a nonprofit computer-based teleconferencing laboratory, EIES feels to its members like an online village, encouraging them to mingle messages with as many others as possible. One of EIES's main attractions is its unusually creative and knowledgeable membership. Though EIES's commands often feel tacked-on, its basic structure is simple enough. Both EIES and CONFER II are roughly masterable within a couple of hours.

The two systems charge differently but seem to cost about the same over a year. EIES's connect time rates are low, but accounts cost $75 per month. CONFER II has no monthly fee, but charges $15-25 per connect hour, making it better for casual use. Ultimately, your choice will depend on which system has the people you want to reach. I'm unabashedly biased towards EIES; we organized the **Software Catalog**, met many of our best contributors, and still share software evaluations there. After experimenting with CONFER II, I feel strongly drawn there, too. Had I but modem enough and time . . .

## A low-priced alternative to national networks . . .
# Electronic Bulletin Boards

### Favorite for Ataris . . .
## AMIS

$10 (public domain; cost of diskette, documentation & handling); or download from Atari SIG on CompuServe; Atari; 32K; Atari 850 interface ($220); GRAFex Company, Box 1558, Cupertino, CA 95015; 408/996-2689.

RIC MANNING: The most widely used Atari-based bulletin board system. It can switch between ASCII and ATASCII code, and handle several downloading protocols (see page 156).

### Choice software for groups . . .
## COMMUNITREE

Apple II family; 48K; 1-6 disk drives; Hayes Micromodem II ● IBM-PC with Hayes-compatible modem and hard disk ● TRS-80 Model III, 48K, TRS-80 modem; $250; copy-protected? NO; CommuniTree Group, 1150 Bryant Street, San Francisco, CA 94103; 415/861-8733; distributed by Softnet, Inc., P.O. Box 522, Berkeley, CA 94701; 415/548-8170.

RIC MANNING: Because CommuniTree's system can pack a lot of messages into only 48K of memory and can handle a variety of "branches" within one "tree" discussion, it's ideal for organizations. A Minnesota medical group, for example, divides their COMMUNITREE bulletin board by specialities such as surgery, radiology, and immunology. Callers append new comments to existing messages and thus build ongoing computerized discussions for each topic. At first the software is slightly intimidating, but once you're familiar with the full-word commands, it's easy to use.

### Four hundred fifty numbers you can call . . .
## THE COMPUTER PHONE BOOK

*The Computer Phone Book*; Mike Cane; 1983; 466 pp.; $9.95 postpaid from The New American Library, Inc., 1633 Broadway, New York, NY 10019; 212/397-8156; or COMPUTER LITERACY.

ART KLEINER: Free local bulletin boards often have the most interesting discussions. This detailed directory is the work of a strange madman named Mike Cane, who (apparently) actually called 1500 computer bulletin boards, of which he describes 450. When they bore him, he tells you ("There is nothing interesting on here. If you call this system, try to leave an interesting message.") When they enthrall him, he shows it ("If you stare at the stars and long to go into orbit, give this system a call to meet some kindred spirits.") When they're worth a long-distance phone call, he says so explicitly.

**The Computer Phone Book** contains an excellent guide to bulletin board commands, and to CompuServe, The Source, Dow Jones, and several dozen fascinating-sounding regional networks. Local bulletin boards are often short-lived, so supplement this book with up-to-date listings from **Plumb** (below) or **Computer Shopper** (p. 11).

### Monthly bulletin-board updates . . .
## PLUMB

Ric Manning, Editor; $26.50/yr (8 issues); Box 300, Harrods Creek, KY 40027; Source: STQ007; CompuServe: 72715,210.

STEVEN LEVY: Though many computer bulletin boards are technically oriented, I've come across a few that have little or nothing to do with computers. One of the first I tried was a New York City BBS devoted to astronomy (no astrology, please). Then there are lots of religious BBSs, plenty for dating, and a well-known one in Kansas with movie reviews. These and more are listed in this monthly newsletter, along with boards devoted to genealogy, rock and roll, ham radio, stocks, medicine, space, writing, jokes, and the occult.

### Bargain-priced, popular . . .
## NET-WORKS

Apple II family; 48K; 1 disk drive; Hayes Micromodem II; copy-protected? NO; $99; High Technology, Inc., 1611 Northwest 23rd Street, Oklahoma City, OK 73106; 405/524-4359.

RIC MANNING (editor of **Plumb**): The most popular of nearly a dozen Apple bulletin board programs. It's a good, general purpose, bargain-priced BBS program, easy for both the system operator and callers to use. NET-WORKS fits small, single-drive Apples or hard-disk-based bulletin boards like Pirate's Cove, which has more than 50 special interest sections.

### If you have a CoCo . . .
## COLOR-80

TRS-80 Color Computer; 64K; 2 disk drives and auto-answer modem; copy-protected? NO; $150; Silicon Rainbow Products, 1111 West El Camino Real, Suite 109, Sunnyvale, CA 94087; 408/749-1947.

## COLORCOM/E

TRS-80 Color Computer; any modem; $50; Copy-protected? YES; Eigen Systems, Box 180006, Austin, TX 78718; 512/837-4665.

RIC MANNING: There are dozens of CoCo systems across the country running on BBS Color 80. It is reliable, its download feature works particularly well with COLORCOM/E, a terminal package for the CoCo, and it includes a user log, handy for compiling mailing lists.

### $50 and loaded with features . . .
## IBBS

IBM PC & compatibles; 192K; 2 double-sided disks, hard disk preferred; auto-answer modem; copy-protected? NO; $50; Gene Plantz, System Software Services, P.O. Box 95638, Hoffman Estates, IL 60195; 312/843-2507.

RIC MANNING: Gene Plantz gave the IBM community a dandy present in 1983 when he made his BBS program available for $50. The program has all the features of the best bulletin board packages, including electronic mail, public bulletins, and a software downloading section.

*Grandaddy gets the job done . . .*

## CBBS

**CP/M machines; 48K minimum; 1 or 2 8″ disk drives with 500K or more, or 2 5-1/4″ disk drives, in Northstar Horizon or IBM PC format (requires program for reading other disk formats on your computer), Hayes, IDS, PMMI or other S100-bus modem; copy protected? NO; $50 (send check or money order); Randy Suess, 5219 West Warwick, Chicago, IL 60641; 312/545-8086 (modem).**

RIC MANNING: In 1978 in Chicago, Ward Christensen and his associate Randy Suess started the first computer bulletin board system. They went on to make the program available in public domain so others could create their own BBS. CBBS, written in machine language, is not particularly friendly to either the operator or the caller. But it gets the job done.

---

*State of the art . . .*

## TBBS

**TRS-80 NewDOS 80, LDOS, DOS+; $200; copy-protected? NO; Ebert Personal Computers, Inc., 4122 South Parker Road, Aurora, CO 80014; 303/693-8400.**

LOUIS JAFFE: THE BREAD BOARD SYSTEM, written by Phil Becker, is one of the few BBS that a nonprogrammer can operate. It does everything a BBS is expected to do and more, with unusually fast response time. The sysop can set up menus and submenus leading to any number of public or private message boards. There are four protocols for uploading or downloading software, including Christensen (p. 156). They're developing versions for the Kaypro and IBM PC.

---

*Double up on tasks . . .*

## MULTILINK

**IBM PC; 128K; copy-protected? NO; $295; The Software Link, Inc., 6700 23-B Roswell Road, Atlanta, GA 30328; 404/255-1254.**

KEVIN KELLY: MULTILINK allows two to eight other programs to run simultaneously on a single IBM PC. It comes supplied with its own bulletin board program, so you can run a BBS 24 hours a day while using the same computer for word processing, spreadsheets, and the like. If you hook up additional video terminals you can have, say, one person doing text, one doing a mailing list, and one doing accounting, all while folks call on the BBS. With this much going on the programs are slowed somewhat, but with two programs in operation you don't even notice. Though MULTILINK's documentation is meager, its bulletin board program is fairly sophisticated. Our local user group handles several thousand calls a month on it without much problem.

## STARTING YOUR OWN BULLETIN BOARD

ART KLEINER: If you have patience, a phone line, and some local people to link by computer network, why pay the connect time charges on a national system? Instead, dedicate a small computer to your own electronic bulletin board. You can publicize the phone number or keep it private.

Simple bulletin boards reflect their public domain tradition of "posting" notices and swapping software through the phone. More complex programs, like COMMUNITREE and MIST+, allow you to run your own elaborate conferencing or dial-up information jungle. Be prepared to spend time and money enduring some technical hassle in maintaining your network. Though your system can only exchange software with the same type of computer, any computer can call any BBS to leave or receive messages.

---

*Four packages rolled into one . . .*

## MIST/MIST+

**Peter & Trudy Johnson-Lenz; IBM PC; 256K; Hayes-compatible 1200 baud modem; hard disk recommended; $295; $495 w/optional database ● Kaypro or Vector; CP/M; 64K; Hayes-compatible 1200 baud modem; 2 disk drives or hard disk; $225; $375 w/optional database; copy-protected? NO; FoxHedge, Inc., 151 Potrero Avenue, San Francisco, CA 94103; 415/626-5903; or New Era Technologies, 2025 Eye Street, N.W., Suite 922, Washington, DC 20006; 202/887-5440.**

DARRELL ICENOGLE: MIST (called MIST+ in its 16-bit upgrade) is the most unique and powerful microcomputer communications product on the market. More than just a smart terminal program, it contains: (1) a full programming language with specifications for telecommunicating, (2) a database system called RESOURCES, and (3) a complete (albeit line-oriented) text editor.

MIST's optional RESOURCES database (nearly as extensive as DBASE II, p. 85) can be turned into a full-fledged computer teleconferencing system, complete with electronic mail, conferences, and your own online databanks. Call it up with your Radio Shack Model 100 to retrieve information while you're on the road, or to leave a midnight message for your secretary. You can also design your own MIST-based "groupware," programs that simplify an entire group's interactions with a remote online system.

I tailored a version of MIST that allowed me to train 50 Fortune 500 Chief Executive Officers (the ultimate challenge) to use EIES (p. 147) in three hours. They worked from a one-screen menu that I designed with MIST's programming language; its selections included composing text, dialing a remote network, sending text, receiving and storing text on disk, searching a series of conferences automatically, and manipulating messages.

```
Message 43
To:      SACTO FEMALES      Date: 04/23/84
From:    HARLEY271          Time: 07:41
Subject: FISHING PARTNER

I LIKE TO FISH THE AMERICAN RIVER AND FOLSOM LAKE AREA. I AM
LOOKING FOR A WOMAN WHO LIKES THE OUTDOORS AND ESPECIALLY
FISHING. DROP ME A LINE, HOOK, AND SINKER IF INTERESTED.
****HARLEY****


Msg# 9447 on 04/20/84 @20:52 (4)
Subj: planet earth..., To: randy keeling
From: KEN FYELDS, ORANGE

planet earth got crashed....the passwords were all totally
thrashed....megahertz may have taken the board down...i
havent called there in a while....
                                   ken fyelds
```

*Sample comments culled from computer bulletin board systems by bulletin board devotee Kevin Kelly.*

## Communications software . . .
## Terminal Programs

MITE's main menu. Each submenu in the bottom half allows you to customize different specifications. MITE is more easily adaptable to various computers, modems, and networks than any other terminal program.

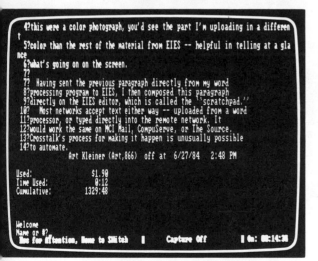

Following pre-programmed instructions, CROSSTALK XVI signs onto the EIES network while running unattended, and sends a file of text into the EIES message scratchpad. The "command line" at the bottom of the screen tells you that CROSSTALK is saving all incoming text to disk, and it reports how much time has gone by since the program logged in.

### Our benchmark program . . .
### MITE

8-bit CP/M or MP/M, $150; 16-bit CP/M, CONCURRENT CP/M (MITE/86) or MS-DOS (MITE-MS), $195; copy-protected? NO; Mycroft Labs, P.O. Box 6045, Tallahassee, FL 32314; 904/385-1141.

ART KLEINER: Finding MITE was like sailing into safe harbor after a violent storm. My first assignment for this section was to select one reliable terminal program that all our staffers could use with the same commands for a variety of networks. It had to perform the basic jobs of a good terminal program: dial a phone number (through a modem), log on to a remote network automatically, capture incoming text and save it on a disk (a process sometimes called downloading), send text from its disk to the remote network (called uploading), and hang up the phone. The program had to run on CP/M and as many other operating systems as possible.

There are several dozen CP/M terminal programs. Some don't work. Others take hours to install, or have no break key, or no automatic log-in commands. Some (like MICRO LINK II) work okay, but operate so illogically that using them takes constant concentration. Woody Liswood, who edited the Analyzing section of the **Software Catalog**, and Ward Christensen, who invented the XMODEM protocol (p. 156), both praised MITE. When it finally arrived, I realized neither had praised it highly enough.

MITE lets you write your own command sequences to log on to as many networks as you can use. With each network, you can meddle with (or ignore) a wide range of telecommunications specs, filter out

unwanted characters that might confuse your word processor, and customize the keys you use to operate MITE itself. MITE thus solves network-, protocol-, and modem-compatibility problems better than any other program I've seen. If you can't figure out the solution yourself, Mycroft offers excellent support.

MITE isn't quite as easy to use as SMARTCOM II (p. 151); you write MITE command sequences in a peculiar shorthand, and you must retype each sequence to make a small change. Some programs (CROSSTALK XVI, below; POST-PLUS, p. 151; and ASCII EXPRESS, p. 152) offer automated command languages that operate the program while it's unattended, dialing several networks in succession and performing specified jobs on each. MITE's new version (2.7) has such a language, but it's still weak and undocumented. Future versions may improve it.

MITE has the clearest manual of any telecom program (for instance many manuals describe Dow Jones News/Retrieval Service, but only MITE's describes how to filter out the CTRL UP-ARROW characters that mess up the way Dow Jones appears on your screen.) Once you know what to do you can bypass MITE's menus, but they're so explicit and logically sound that you may use them anyway. MITE is also the best terminal program for file transfer (see p. 156).

MITE is the meat-and-potatoes telecommunications software I recommend most often, especially when you need to use one program on several different computers. It will serve 70 percent of the readers of this section. For the other 30 percent, I've included alternative programs and the reasons to choose them.

### When you know enough to use the best . . .
### CROSSTALK XVI/CROSSTALK 3.0 (MS-DOS)

Version 3.41; most CP/M and MS-DOS computers; Bell-compatible modems; copy-protected? NO; $195; Microstuf, 1845 The Exchange, Suite 140, Atlanta, GA 30339; 404/952-0267.

ART KLEINER: For experts who want their networking more fully automated than MITE can offer now. With two keystrokes CROSSTALK logs me on to CompuServe and our Whole Earth conference there; it asks whether I want to see new items or print out old messages for our library files; if I request old messages, it asks me which message I want to start at, collects them, saves them on disk, and logs off when it's done. It took about three hours to program this sequence; now it saves me hours every week. CROSSTALK also lets you preset the screen colors, so at a glance you can differentiate the text you receive from the text you send and from CROSSTALK's own commands. (MITE

does this too, but not as elegantly.) CROSSTALK versions 1.0 and 2.0 are much less capable, and I don't recommend them.

JOHN MARKOFF: CROSSTALK doesn't force you to wade through vast levels of menus. You can summon all the program's commands from a single, unobtrusive command line at the bottom of the screen, while the rest of the screen shows what's happening on the network you've dialed up. The program can also function as a simple host system (with password protection), so I can dial my office and download files from my PC while I'm away. It supports both XMODEM and its own file-transfer protocols, and it controls file-transfer and micro-to-mainframe interaction as well as any program I've seen. But I enjoy CROSSTALK most because it has one of the cleanest user interfaces around: it feels right.

*Least expensive, most used,*
*and a standard . . .*

## MODEM7 (CP/M)

**Free; The Public Domain Software Copying Company, 33 Gold Street, C-13, New York, NY 10038; 212/732-2565; or NYACC, P.O. Box 106, Church Street Station, New York, NY 10008; or SIG/ M User's Group of ACG-NJ, P.O. Box 97, Iselin, NJ 08830; CBBS 201/272-1874, voice 201/272-1793; or CBBS 215/398-3937; voice 215/398-1634.**

ART KLEINER: The best bargain for an easy-to-use, somewhat hard-to-learn terminal program. It's also the cheapest easy file-transfer program (see p. 156). Modifying this public domain family of programs is a great tradition in CP/M hackerdom, and if you learn BASIC you could end up modifying yours. Versions vary in capabilities: "vanilla" (standard) MODEM7 sends and captures text fine, but can't automatically log on to networks. Documentation ranges from meager to none; the usual onscreen help is a cryptic list of one-key commands.

Get your first MODEM7 copy from a friend or user's group, or a mail-order source listed here (write for their catalogs first). With any version you can call up a local remote CP/M bulletin board (see **The Computer Phone Book**, p. 148) or CompuServe's CP/M users' group SIG (p. 146) and pull in newer versions —which might be only days old.

(Also, see "How to Get Free Software," p. 27.)

---

*Easy to learn, slow to use . . .*

## HAYES SMARTCOM II (MS-DOS)

**DEC Rainbow 100 ● IBM PC/XT ● Kaypro 2 ● Xerox 822; copy-protected? NO; $149; Hayes Microcomputer Products, 5923 Peachtree Industrial Blvd., Norcross, GA 30092; 404/441-1617.**

ART KLEINER: Like its closest competitor, PERFECT LINK (which is slightly easier to use but much less versatile), SMARTCOM II comes all figured out for you with prewritten command sequences for dialing all the popular networks. To dial a network that SMARTCOM's designers didn't anticipate, you just fill in a chart with prompts and replies. SMARTCOM II offers many technical choices, and the manual and menus explain them so well that using the program is an easy-to-swallow basic telecommunications course in itself—easier to start with than MITE or CROSSTALK XVI. But there's a price: the menus make SMARTCOM II slower to use. The program is sold alone or bundled with Hayes' Smartmodem 1200B, an IBM PC modem card. Hayes' SMARTCOM I, for the Apple, is simple and elegant but offers too few features to be recommended here.

---

## LOW COST NETWORKING

ART KLEINER: You don't need a $200 program, $600 modem, and $2000 computer to dial your local bulletin board. If you can find a used terminal (often for as little as $50-$100) with an RS-232 connector, you can hook it to a $70 Anchor Volksmodem (p. 155). It won't dial your phone, save text on a disk, or transmit files, but it will let you sign on to remote networks and participate.

Before you rush out to buy a communications package, see if your operating system disk contains a "dumb" terminal program (like that on the Kaypro 2, HP 150, and TRS-80 Models III and 4). You'll have to dial by hand (or with the modem's own commands) and you won't be able to save any text on disk, but the program will get you online.

If you have no computer and just want to network, consider a used portable printing telephone terminal, like the Texas Instruments Silent 700. They're advertised in **Computer Shopper** (p. 11) and other computer classifieds for around $300. They have good keyboards, print everything on thermal paper, and traditionally have had two rubber suction cups in the back for a phone handset. (New models, which connect directly to telephone jacks, sell for the same price as a TRS-80 Model 100, which we recommend instead.) Printing terminals can't save anything on disk, but they produce paper copies of everything—a mixed blessing.

---

*Read and write at the same time . . .*

## POST-PLUS (CP/M)

**CP/M 80 or TRS-DOS; modem; copy-protected? NO; $195; MCTel Corporation 3 Bala Plaza East, Suite 505, Bala Cynwyd, PA 19004; 215/668-0983.**

ART KLEINER: This is a split-screen program which lets you type a message on its word processor while you're logged on to an online network. As messages come in on the bottom screen (and get saved on a disk, perhaps), you type your replies on the top screen. The process feels as interactive as telecommunications can get, and it saves the connect-time charges you'd pay to type messages on most networks' clunky line editors. POST-PLUS is too complex for neophyte users (its extremely versatile command language is difficult to learn, but can automate all daily communications into one gargantuan command). The built-in word processor is limited but serviceable. CP/M-based expert networkers can customize POST-PLUS into a high-powered communications tool.

---

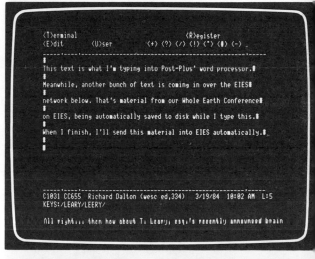

*POST-PLUS, the split-screen terminal program, divides the screen into three parts. At top are POST-PLUS's own commands; in the center, its word processor; at bottom, the terminal program, here showing a comment from the EIES network inquiring about Timothy Leary's new software.*

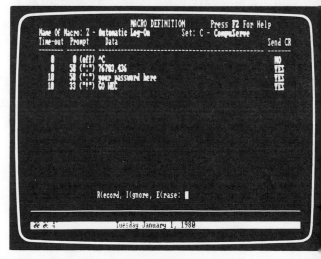

*The SMARTCOM II chart for creating an automatic log-in sequence. For each step, you fill in how long to wait for each prompt, the prompt character, what you type in reply, and whether or not to add a carriage return.*

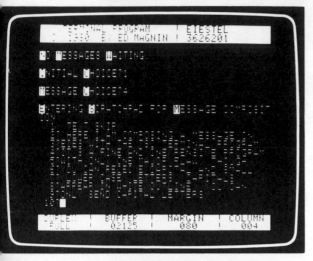

*Sending an EIES message with TERMINAL PROGRAM (the light-on-dark text in the center is all EIES). The program displays the phone number and network name at upper right ("EIESTEL" means "EIES via Telenet"), and how many characters have come through (at bottom under "BUFFER").*

*Almost free,
    but a bargain at any price . . .*

## PC-TALK.III

**IBM PC & most compatibles; most autodial & acoustic modems; 300-1200 baud; $35 suggested donation; Freeware/Headlands Press; Box 862; Tiburon, CA 94920.**

ART KLEINER: An inexpensive, easy-to-learn terminal program for the IBM PC which does everything MITE does except automatically log on to networks. Like SMARTCOM, it requires a lot of shunting back and forth among menus. You can only get PC-TALK by mail order (under his "freeware" concept, author Andrew Fluegelman asks for a $35 donation.) Fluegelman encourages owners to copy PC-TALK (but not for resale) and modify it, so there are dozens of public domain homebrew mutations, including a split-screen version, one allowing 450 baud transmission, and ones that make PC-TALK emulate various mainframe terminals. You can learn about the variations in the IBM PC SIG (p. 146) on CompuServe. A bargain for IBM PC owners curious about networking.

*Remembers your commands . . .*

## TELEPHONE SOFTWARE CONNECTION TERMINAL PROGRAM

**Apple II family; Hayes Micromodem or SSM Modemcard; copy-protected? NO; $40 by mail; $35 by modem (213/516-9432) and credit card; Telephone Software Connection, P. O. Box 6548, Torrance, CA 90504; 213/516-9430.**

## DATA CAPTURE IIe

**Apple IIe; all modems or serial cards; copy-protected? NO; $90; Southeastern Software, 7743 Briarwood Drive, New Orleans, LA 70128; 504/246-7937.**

ART KLEINER: Here's another bargain, this one from the Telephone Software Connection, a dial-up service that sends programs through the phone wires or by mail. You can get their TERMINAL PROGRAM either way. It has such an obvious method for setting up automatic log-on sequences it's amazing all programs don't ape it. You log on once by yourself, then type CONTROL-A; thereafter the program remembers how to do it.

TERMINAL PROGRAM only supports 40 columns and can only send capital letters. DATA CAPTURE IIe costs twice as much ($90), works as well, and offers lower case letters on an 80-column screen.

*Accessible, understandable
    DIALOG searching . . .*

## IN-SEARCH

**Version 1.01; IBM PC & compatibles ● TI Professional; 192K; 2 disk drives; Hayes 300, 1200 or 1200B Smartmodem or Novation 103, 212, Smartcat modem, or an acoustic modem; copy-protected? YES; $399; Menlo Corporation, 4633 Old Ironsides Drive, No. 400, Santa Clara, CA 95050; 408/986-0200.**

ART KLEINER: We don't recommend the DIALOG bibliographic service (parent of the KNOWLEDGE INDEX (p. 143), because it's too difficult and too expensive. But IN-SEARCH, the best of the "front end" databank-searching terminal programs, turns DIALOG's Byzantine codes and references into an accessible, understandable process reminiscent of flipping through a card catalog (but quicker and more fun). All DIALOG's databases and resources are cataloged within the software; you can easily revise your search midstream; and the software highlights the words you looked for in each reference, so you can instantly tell if you're warm or cool. IN-SEARCH comes with a DIALOG password; for $2000 a year you could use this and NEXIS (p. 144) and be as well-equipped for finding references since 1970 (when online databanks started) as any research library in the country.

*Works fine, but not for beginners . . .*

## ASCII EXPRESS "The Professional" (Apple II)

**Version 4.2; Apple II family; 48K, 1 drive; copy-protected? NO; $130; United Software, 1880 Century Park East, Suite 311, Los Angeles, CA 90067; 213/556-2211.**

ART KLEINER: The Apple II isn't a good computer for networking, only because the available software seems either too complex or too limited. If you have a CP/M card, get MITE. If not, ASCII EXPRESS is the best full-featured Apple II terminal program available. (Another package, SOFTERM 2, seems even more complete, and it handles APPLE DOS, CP/M, and PASCAL files. But it's so opaque, and its manual is so execrable, that I can't recommend it. Maybe next year.)

LOUIS JAFFE: ASCII EXPRESS has a built-in line-by-line text editor. It can answer and dial the phone unattended. You can leave it running and dial in from another computer to swap files. Its achievement, and its Achilles heel, is the procedure for setting up routines to log on to a remote system automatically. These routines are more powerful than those of most other programs, but to use them you must learn a mini-programming language. The manuals give this procedure only a brisk once-over. In general, the program is aimed at experienced users; if you're a novice, count on finding outside help.

*For Atari owners,
    the best is free . . .*

## AMODEM

**Versions 4.2 and higher. Atari 400/600/800, 800XL; 48K; 1 disk drive; 300/1200 baud modem; send $10 and specify which type of Atari and modem you have, or download from the BBS, 313/978-8087 at no charge above connect time; Jim Steinbrecher, 33220 Tricia, Sterling Heights, MI 48077.**

BERNIE BILDMAN: What a nice surprise is in store for Atari owners: the very best, most enjoyable terminal program is public domain . . . free! AMODEM 4.2 (written by Jim Steinbrecher) and its variations are the most popular. (I use AMODEM 4.9.) This program can capture incoming text and dump it to the device of your choice (disk drive, cassette, or printer). It will also transfer files with the XMODEM protocol (see p. 156). It runs at 300 or 1200 baud, sends text from disk or cassette, and toggles between phone and log-on automatically. One hitch: you need another public domain program, DISKLINK, to use AMODEM with the new Atari 1030 modem. You can obtain AMODEM and DISKLINK by mail, from the Atari SIG on CompuServe (p. 146), or from most any Atari bulletin board or local users' group.

*First for the Mac, great for graphics . . .*

## MACTERMINAL

**Apple Macintosh; Apple- or Hayes-compatible modem; copy-protected? YES; $99; Apple Computer, 20525 Mariani Avenue, Cupertino, CA 95015; 800/538-9696.**

ART KLEINER: The Mac's great telecom computer, and Apple's own MACTERMINAL (a melody on which many other companies will compose variations) excels at basic networking without automatic log-ons. The mouse navigates through the various menus

*As I understand the story, which unfolded on the Apple Users' SIG on CompuServe (go pcs-51), when Mac was first released, there was no way to hook it to a telephone line and no apparent way to write a terminal program. Apple had left it to Microsoft to write the necessary hooks into their BASIC and Microsoft had left it to Apple.*

*Anyway, one of the Apple SIGgers, now a local hero, broke open his Mac, traced the wires, and figured out how to address the machine language stuff that controlled the baud rate. He wrote a terminal program called MACTEP, downloaded it into CompuServe, and the rest is history.*

*MACTEP is now in its sixth or seventh version, has been distributed all over creation via BBS systems and ARPAnet, and whole packs of early Maccers are happily telecommunicating thanks to this selfless hacker, a gentle soul named Dennis Brothers.*
—Philip Elmer-Dewitt

that help you dial the phone and set communications parameters. Best features: you can split the screen, typing on the notepad while incoming text gets saved on the disk, and you can send graphic files to a distant Macintosh for a new type of greeting card.

*One of the terminal-setting menus in a prerelease version of MACTERMINAL. This one controls how incoming text looks when it appears on your screen. "Show LEDs" lets you check your modem status automatically.*

*When you can't run MITE . . .*

## VIDTEX (Commodore 64 and Radio Shack)

**Apple II family ● Commodore 64, Pet ● CP/M ● IBM PC; $70 ● TRS-80 Models I, II, III ● TRS-80 Color Computer; $40; copy-protected? NO; CompuServe, 5000 Arlington Center Blvd., P. O. Box 20212, Columbus, OH 43220; 800/849-8199.**

CHRISTOPHER DUNN: It has all the major functions—it stores incoming or outgoing text in a buffer, sends and receives from networks, controls baud rate and other transmission parameters, and has the CompuServe B protocol (which allows you to receive programs stored on CompuServe with their own scheme for eliminating transmission errors). I have used some other terminal programs, but VIDTEX beats them all. You can even arrange it to boot up, automatically dial and log you on, and take you directly to any area on any system.

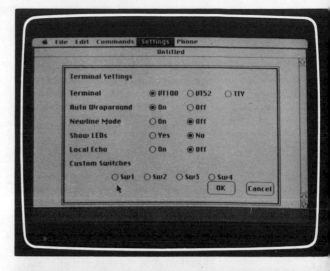

*The CompuServe VIDTEX main menu has as many features as other programs that cost three or four times as much. This is the IBM PC version; those for other computers are similar.*

*Traveling Communications . . .*

## RADIO SHACK TRS-80 MODEL 100

**8K, $799; 24K, $999; expandable to 32K with 8K RAM modules, $119.95 each; Radio Shack Division, Tandy Corporation, 1800 One Tandy Center, Fort Worth, TX 76102; 817/390-3700. (Also see p. 16 in hardware.)**

ART KLEINER: The best lap computer for telecommunications, especially while you're traveling. Its built-in modem and software can dial up and log on to networks automatically, and it sends and receives text easily. Its major disadvantage: no touchtone dialing, so it can't work with many office phone systems unless you hook it to another modem.

## TRS-80 MODEL 100 TIPS

HARRY NEWTON (**Teleconnect Magazine**): Here are our tips on getting maximum benefit from the Model 100 for telecommunications: Buy the maximum 32K size, so you have more room to store incoming text. Always keep the thing plugged in, so your rechargeable battery, which keeps your info in volatile memory, will stay charged and won't lose your data. Buy a two-foot "null modem cable" (a cable with two wires crossed, so you can send text from one computer to another as if there were two modems and a phone line between them). That way you can transfer your Model 100 files to your desktop personal computer, or attach your Model 100 to a 1200-baud modem. You'll probably need a male RS-232C plug on one end and a female on the other, but check. All computers are different.

Buy yourself a Radio Shack Modem Cable (Number 26-1410) to connect directly to the telephone network through any standard modular phone jack. Costs $20. Buy yourself a Radio Shack Acoustic Coupler (Number 26-3806). That will give you a 300-baud connection via coin or hotel phones, which have no modular plug. Costs $40.

*Cute mailing system, but limited . . .*

## TRANSEND PC

**IBM PC/XT & compatibles (not PCjr); Transend or Hayes-compatible modem; copy-protected? YES; $189; Transend Corporation, 2190 Paragon Drive, San Jose, CA 95131; 408/946-7400.**

ART KLEINER: Say you have people with IBM PCs spread over the country working on one project. They're not hackers; they can just about handle 1-2-3. You'd like them to exchange electronic mail—sometimes through The Source, but mostly by having each other's computers dial each other after the people have gone to bed. You want it to feel like walking down the hall and sticking a letter in the mail chute, not like engaging in "data communications." I recommend TRANSEND PC for this need, partly because

it's so damn cute. Its main screen looks like a desktop filled with in- and out-baskets. You pop in and out of the baskets like a mobile jack-in-the-box, typing letters on TRANSEND PC's facile word processor. Then, at your cue or at a preselected time, TRANSEND PC dials up a series of numbers, leaves messages where you want them and collects any that are waiting for you, tagging them separately. Each incoming message waits in your "in-box" until you read it and (if you wish) discard it. Then it goes to my favorite TRANSEND PC feature, a holding place called the "waste basket"; to delete it permanently, you must "shred" it. TRANSEND PC's iconic, nontechnical facade shows the direction that communication programs are taking; it also proves that Marshall McLuhan was right about new media imitating old.

You can only send TRANSEND PC mail to another computer running TRANSEND PC, to The Source, or to OnTyme (see IEMS, p. 145). There's a limited regular terminal program tacked on, but if you want to be compatible with a lot of different computers, don't get this program. Those who can use it, however, will chortle all the way to the keyboard.

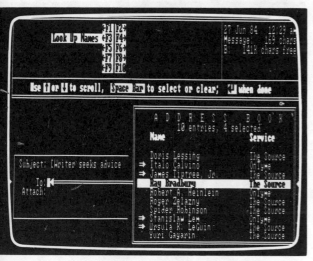

*First, you enter all the names and electronic mail addresses of your correspondents into TRANSEND PC. Then, when you address a letter, TRANSEND shows you everyone's name. You select the people who should receive this message. TRANSEND automatically figures out how to reach them—through The Source, OnTyme, or by dialing their computers directly.*

*jr calls the office . . .*

## IBM PERSONAL COMMUNICATIONS MANAGER

**IBM PC/XT, jr; 128K; 1 disk drive; IBM PCjr internal modem ($199) or IBM asynch. comm. adapter with auto-dial modem & RS-232 cable; copy-protected? NO; $100; IBM, P.O. Box 2989, Delray Beach, FL 33444; 800/447-4700.**

ART KLEINER: IBM's own program is the best for a PCjr or for PCs and PCjrs that must swap messages and files. It includes a good terminal program for dialing remote networks (similar to SMARTCOM II), and an electronic mail program like TRANSEND PC (but less captivating) for exchanging messages.

*Easiest way to get started . . .*

## BUSINESS COMPUTER NETWORK

**Version C.6; IBM PC/compatibles; 128K; Kaypro; 64K; Hayes-compatible modem; software free; copy-protected? NO; monthly membership, $5; first 20 sign-ons/month free; additional sign-ons $.25 each, plus regular online charges for each database; Business Computer Network, P.O. Box 36, 1000 College View Drive, Riverton, WY 82501; 800/446-6255 or, in WY, 800/442-0982.**

ART KLEINER: The software is free (for the Kaypro 2 or IBM PC), and it does all the work for you, automatically logging you on to a dozen online information systems. You don't even have to pay the networks' subscription charges or membership fees. Before each call, the software dials BCN's own toll-free number, instructs itself in the proper route, updates itself with any new BCN options, and adds 25 cents (plus regular connect-time charges) to your BCN bill. The rest is up to you; BCN doesn't make it easier to use CompuServe or DIALOG, just to get on.

BCN permits everything good telecom software should: capturing text on your disk, writing messages off-line and sending them on-line, sending any sequence to your printer. But there are caveats: you don't log on under the same account number each time, so you can't receive mail or messages on CompuServe unless you buy your ID number separately (it matters less with information services). BCN's software is worthless for networks that BCN hasn't signed up (like The Source, IEMS, CONFER II, EIES, Dow Jones News/Retrieval, or any local bulletin board). It's best for occasional database searching (on DIALOG, BRS, NewsNet and the Official Airlines Guide) and calling other BCN members' computers directly. Conferencers and frequent networkers are better off with MITE.

---

## *Between telephone and computer . . .*
# *Modems*

JIM STOCKFORD: Modems translate computer codes into sound signals that travel across telephone lines to other modems, allowing communication among computers of any brand. Some modems dial the telephone themselves; others require you to dial the telephone keypad. Many modems can also receive, or answer, a call.

Modems connect to the phone lines in two ways: directly, by cable to a jack, which is inexpensive and very reliable; or indirectly, with an "acoustic coupler," a device whose two suction cups fit on a telephone handset.

One important choice is the modem's baud rate—generally 300 or 1200 baud, figures that approximate the number of bits per second sent or received. Three hundred baud is just slow

enough to read as it scrolls by; 1200 is four times faster but still slow enough to skim. In areas where phone-line transmission is poor, a slow baud rate may be necessary to ensure correct reception (just as on a noisy phone line you speak more slowly to be understood).

A standalone modem works with most computer/software combinations, but it's on you to make sure they all work together properly. Standalone modems take up space on your desk or on top of your computer, but can be adapted to any new computer software you buy, or be sold later.

An in-board modem fits in a slot for your particular computer, and usually comes with software. However, it adds little to your computer's resale value, it takes up a slot you may need for something else, and you can't easily resell it. The several in-board modems we've seen are overpriced and machine-specific, so we don't recommend them. If you choose one, choose it according to the software that comes with it.

## Cheap, good . . .
## 300 Baud Modems

### A basic no-frills machine . . .

## VOLKSMODEM

$80; Anchor Automation, Inc., 6624 Valjean Avenue, Van Nuys, CA 91406; 213/997-6493

JIM STOCKFORD: The least expensive general purpose modem, the Volksmodem connects directly to standard modular phone connectors. It sends in full-duplex mode, which allows both connecting parties to transmit simultaneously, and half-duplex mode, in which only one party can transmit at a time. It automatically switches between Answer mode and Originate mode and its built-in speaker lets you hear if there's a busy signal, no answer, or lost carrier tone.

### Many features for Atari computers . . .

## ATARI 1030 MODEM

$140; Atari Corporation, 1265 Borregas Avenue, Sunnyvale, CA 94006; 408/745-2000.

The Atari 1030 modem allows status messages to be sent to the display and uses both pulse dialing (standard) and tone dialing (as in touch tone) from the keyboard. It is our choice for the Atari line. The software included is limited. A better software package is AMODEM (p. 152).

### Commodore modems . . .

## VICMODEM
## AUTOMODEM

$60 for VICModem; $100 for Automodem; Commodore Business Machines, 1200 Wilson Drive, West Chester, PA 19380; 215/431-9100

The VICModem is our choice for the VIC 20 because it's inexpensive, offers the same features as the Volksmodem, and fits the connectors. The software included is limited.

For the Commodore 64, the Automodem offers additional features: automatic call answering, status-information display (baud rate, parity configuration, and such), and number dialing from the keyboard. The software included is fairly good.

### Smart modem, great price . . .

## OPERATOR 103

$169; TNW Corporation, 3444 Hancock Street, San Diego, CA 92110; 619/296-2115.

Operator 103 offers a surprising number of features for the price. This is what is called a "smart" modem—it can sense phone line conditions and act intelligently. Its features include all discussed so far except tone dialing. It can also re-execute the previous command, or redial the last number. It allows keyboard control of parameters (parity, baud rate, stop bits)—very handy, as these controls are often switches buried in the modem case. While online, the user can send commands to the modem without breaking the connection.

### Low-cost message taker . . .

## VISIONARY 100

$595 for 2K model; $15 for each additional 2K up to 24K; Visionary Electronics, Inc., 141 Parker Avenue, San Francisco, CA 94118; 415/751-8811.

ART KLEINER: A modem with built-in communications software and memory. If you leave it alone hooked to a phone line all day people can dial it with their computers and leave messages (only for you; not for each other). Later you can connect it to any personal computer and pull those messages onto a disk. The Visionary also has a built-in clock and sophisticated commands for waiting until a certain hour, dialing into a remote network, saving incoming text in its own internal memory, and sending outgoing text from that same memory. That's a boon if your computer, like the Kaypro, has no internal timepiece. You can also use the Visionary as a TELEX terminal or a regular 300-baud modem.

### An aside on the Hayes standard . . .

Because the Hayes company has sold a lot of modems, communications software developers have made sure their programs work with Hayes modems. Once Hayes set the standard, other manufacturers designed their modems with similar commands and advertised "Hayes compatibility." Some modems are more "Hayes compatible" than others, depending on how well they fit the software. Hayes modems are good, but better, cheaper "Hayes compatibles" are available.

## Expensive, very good . . .
## 1200 Baud Modems

## Signalman Mark XII

$399; Anchor Automation, Inc., 6624 Valjean Avenue, Van Nuys, CA 91406; 213/997-6493.

This modem offers all the features of the previous machines plus the ability to send and receive at 1200 baud. It can also adjust automatically to the baud rate of another modem, sense a dial tone or a busy signal, and determine that its call is not being answered. This is the best choice for a low-cost 1200-baud modem.

## MULTI-MODEM MT212AH

$549; Multi-Tech Systems, Inc., 82 Second Avenue S.E., New Brighton, MN 55112; 612/631-3550.

This one offers a dazzling array of features. Besides all those previously mentioned, it will adjust to the baud rate or the parity of another modem, re-dial a number a specified number of times, dial another number if the first is busy or unanswered, dial a number in response to a single character, and store six phone numbers of up to 31 digits and keep them in its battery-powered memory.

### Best of the lot for businesses . . .

## VISIONARY 1200

2K, $795; 16K, $895; 32K, $995; 48K, $1095; Visionary Electronics, Inc., 141 Parker Street, San Francisco, CA 94118; 415/751-8811

The Visionary 1200 is the real prize. By far the best crafted, its capabilities reflect an elaborate design and lots of expensive circuitry. It is our favorite for a business tool.

In addition to nearly all features already mentioned, the Visionary 1200 comes with a microprocessor and 2K memory, expandable to 48K, which gives it the power of a computer. With a clock and calendar that can trigger calls, it will store phone numbers, incoming and outgoing messages, or log-on sequences, to the extent of its memory.

You can instruct it to call several numbers at any time in the future, leave any messages, store any responses, answer any incoming modem calls, and store their messages. It will not lose your data during a power-line failure. Take your computer elsewhere, and it will continue to do its job. Use it to collect your E-mail on CompuServe as part of its log-on routine.

Since its software is built in, the Visionary 1200 works with any file-handling communications software. It is unique on the market.

## Moving data from one computer to another . . .
## *File Transfer Programs*

ART KLEINER: The occasional transmission error produced by electronic noise over the telephone lines isn't noticeable in ordinary text, so you can ignore protocols—codes that check for errors—when you dial an online network for electronic mail, conferencing, or retrieving information. But if you send graphic files, database files, programs, or spreadsheets through the phone, you need to ensure that each chunk of data goes through intact, since a transmission error could ruin your work. File transfer programs move disk files between any two computers hooked directly by cable or through the phones. They can use any protocol, but it must be the same on both ends of the connection.

The XMODEM, or CHRISTENSEN, protocol (named after its inventor, Ward Christensen), is incorporated in nearly every public domain communications program (like MODEM7 and PC-TALK) plus many commercial packages: MITE, CROSSTALK, ASCII EXPRESS, and TSC TERMINAL PROGRAM. XMODEM lets you swap files with 75 percent of the personal computer telecommunicators you meet.

If communications software companies incorporated as many protocols as possible into their software, their users could swap files with more people using different software. Instead, too many companies make their software inaccessible by enshrining their own unique protocols as "standards." The exception, MITE (p. 150), offers seven protocols. I also recommend MOVE-IT, KERMIT and BLAST for specific uses, even though they only incorporate their own unique protocols.

---

### Making the connections work . . .
### RS-232 MADE EASY

*RS-232 Made Easy* (Connecting Computers, Printers, Terminals, and Modems); Martin D. Seyer; 1984; 214 pp.; $17.95 postpaid; Prentice-Hall, Inc., Box 500, Englewood Cliffs, NJ 07632; 201/592-2000; or COMPUTER LITERACY.

---

RACHEL UNKEFER: The first introductory book on the hardware aspects of data communications, especially the RS-232 interface, which is the standard for most personal computers. This book is best for people who have used a modem or printer, understand how to connect them to the computer, and want to know more about how the connection works. Author Martin Seyer uses an analogy between data communication and railroads to explain technical distinctions that would otherwise be hard to understand. The book's appendices contain charts of the pin assignments of RS-232 ports for about 270 brands of computers, terminals, modems, and printers (excluding Kaypro, Macintosh, and others), which can help you make your own cable. Even if your equipment isn't charted, the information about the interface in general (for example, what does DTR mean?) can help you figure out your hardware manuals' diagrams. Seyer could have gone into more depth about theoretical data communications, but on a practical level this is the best available guide.

---

### Micro, mini, mainframe moves . . .
### KERMIT

**Most mainframe and minicomputers ● Atari 800, 800XL; 1 disk drive; $100 ● IBM PC and most MS-DOS machines; 128K ● Most CP/M machines; 64K; copy-protected? NO; $100; KERMIT Distribution, Columbia University Center for Computing Activities, 7th Floor, Watson Laboratory, 612 West 115th Street, New York, NY 10025.**

---

MARK COHEN: KERMIT allows file transfer between a wide variety of different computers —micros, minis, and mainframes. In keeping with its grass-roots origins at the Columbia University Computer Center, KERMIT is in the public domain and its authors encourage its distribution. They sell complete, professional manuals and develop new KERMITs as fast as the computer companies can crank out incompatible machines. The program won't allow you to run Lotus's 1-2-3 on your Atari— it doesn't translate programs to new operating systems or languages—but it does allow you to transfer manuscripts or programs simply and efficiently.

---

### Big moves, less fuss, but expensive . . .
### BLAST

**Apple II family; 48K; 1 disk drive; RS-232 modem; ● All CP/M machines; 64K; 1 disk drive; RS-232 modem ● IBM PC and compatibles, most MS-DOS; 128K; 1 disk drive; RS-232 modem; copy-protected? NO; $250; most mainframes and minis (inquire for details); Communications Research Group, 8939 Jefferson Hwy., Baton Rouge, LA 70809; 504/923-0888.**

---

| IBM PC | | | Model 16 |
|--------|-----|-----|----------|
| Direction | Pin | Pin | Direction |
| N/A | 1 | 1 | N/A |
| From PC | 2 | 2 | From Model 16 |
| To PC | 3 | 3 | To Model 16 |
| From PC | 4 | 4 | From Model 16 |
| To PC | 5 | 5 | To Model 16 |
| To PC | 6 | 6 | Not used |
| N/A | 7 | 7 | N/A |
| To PC | 8 | 8 | To Model 16 |
| From PC | 20 | 20 | From Model 16 |

*An example of why you might need* RS-232 Made Easy: *the chart showing the cable connections between a Radio Shack TRS-80 Model 16 and an IBM PC.*

---

### Best for IBM PC clones and CP/M . . .
### MOVE-IT

**IBM PC/XT compatibles; most CP/M machines; copy-protected? NO; $125 (8-bit); $150 (16-bit); Woolf Software Systems, 6754 Eton, Canoga Park, CA 91303; 818/999-3135.**

WOODY LISWOOD: MOVE-IT has clear and extensive documentation, and it's designed to run on nearly every CP/M computer or IBM PC clone imaginable. If you get MOVE-IT up and running on a machine not listed in the documentation and are the first to call in to Woolf Software Systems with the methods or patches used, there is a small cash award for you. The feature I like most is the ability to control both machines from one keyboard.

ART KLEINER: Like many public-domain programs, KERMIT requires some hacking to use. BLAST allows file transfers between mainframes, minis, and micros, for people who don't want to fuss as much. Despite a terrible manual, BLAST is easy to learn and use. It's fairly expensive, but it doubles as a terminal program; if it fits your file-swapping needs, you can dial The Source with it too.

## LOCAL NETWORKS:
## STILL NEXT YEAR'S MODEL

ART KLEINER: Local computer networks may change how offices work more than any other computer use. These networks link small computers to share expensive hard disks and fast printers, mutually used databases and spreadsheets, and complex programs. I asked Richard Solomon, editor of **International Networks**, a newsletter on world telecommunications technology and policy ($375/yr; P.O. Box 187, Monson, MA 01057) and veteran networking consultant, to tell how to bring a local network into your business.

RICHARD SOLOMON: Business people often come to me with half-articulated local networking needs: Maybe they already have three Apples and an IBM PC in the office, with three more PCs and a Compaq on order, and they want them all to connect easily together. Unfortunately, no off-the-shelf product can do that yet, and I'd be skeptical of any manufacturer who said it could be simply done.

When you extend a web among computers, new complexities arise that you don't face when you try to interchange data between, say, SUPERCALC and DBASE II or between two ASCII word processors. First, there are no universal local network standards. Cable connections, operating systems, disk- access formats, and a host of other details are unpredictably incompatible. I once spent four days transferring WORDSTAR files from an Apple to an IBM PC. All sorts of problems arose that MicroPro seemed unaware of. Apple CP/M and PC DOS do different things with carriage return/linefeed. RS-232 serial-to-serial was out of the question without some extensive programming and resoldering of the Apple-Cat II. The modems or the software were not compatible at 1200 baud, so we had to settle for 300.

And the CP/M operating system stripped all the funny WORDSTAR characters, so the files required extensive manual manipulation. In the long run, rekeying would have been cheaper and faster—cheaper even than buying some untested software that promised the moon but, as usual, left out some small important detail.

A local network isn't going to do much for you where everything else is incompatible. But there are even more fundamental questions: How much wire can fit in your ceiling? How well can your office phone system carry computer signals? If it is an all-digital PBX, can it interface with your PC at all? (Probably not.) How well can your existing database software handle the tricky problems of access by more than one user? How compatible will your network be with the new equipment you'll want to buy next year, or with another local network you'll want to link it to later?

Local networks can have critical reliability problems. What do you do when your hard disk breaks? The smaller firms have neat products, but support is often terrible; you call them up and never get a straight answer. Their code is always proprietary, so you can't clean things up even if you know what you're doing. If all your data is on a hard disk and there was an error in their directory table, that can be catastrophic in a pinch. Too many companies have not graduated from the fun and games level of the microcomputer business and don't realize that people are using their toys for serious, money-making tasks. I dropped one vendor real fast when its hotline was answered on a Friday with a recorded message that said they only worked four days a week! Well, we often work seven days a week. That's why we use computers.

This year, you still need a consultant to set up a local network—someone skilled in using them who knows about several systems, who understands the economics involved, and who starts by asking what you do, how you do it, and why you want to change it. If a consultant starts off by saying, "I've got a super-duper product for you," look for someone else fast. Be wary of any scheme that costs more than 50 percent of the total cost of your computers and terminals.

The simplest local network is two computers connected by cable—for swapping files (see p. 156). Some programs will let both computers share files simultaneously on the same hard disk (if the operating systems are comparable). An alternative is expanding one microcomputer into a multi-user system, with other computers serving as terminals to the first. (They don't even have to be similar machines, since the other micros could emulate terminals when connected to the host machine.) Multi-user operating systems like UNIX (pp. 167-168) are more versatile, but may be overkill (especially in price) for most small businesses.

Most local networks use coaxial or fiberoptic cable, or ordinary telephone wire pairs, to link 3 to 25 machines. The more useful cable systems, like Ethernet, incorporate complex algorithms on interface cards so that each computer can sense when to send or receive a signal. Some office telephone systems are designed to carry data as well as voice, but require some special device for direct connection, since modems will not do. And next year telephone companies in many cities may offer AT&T's Circuit Switched Digital Capability, hopefully to be tariffed as a low-cost service sending data at 56 kilobits/second over ordinary telephone lines; this is fast enough to effectively extend your local network across a city or a continent.

Speed is important, because you won't just be sending files, you'll be interacting with a faraway program as quickly as if it were on your own computer.

I recommend waiting for the new products, which we'll review as good ones emerge. None of the popular PCs today were designed with digital high-speed (local or whatever) commmunications in mind. But some of the rumored offerings from AT&T (of course), IBM, Digital, and others will radically change the way software is written and micros are used. If you really need communications, you can probably assume that anything you buy now will be written off in less than three years, as these novel items come onstream.

CitiCorp in Manhattan sends its data locally by laser beams and microwave, coaxial cables, and fiberoptic lines running down the IRT subway line (which, as J.P. Morgan's bank, it financed back in 1904). Also, since 1918, the bank has had a pneumatic tube system in the IRT, still kept in very good shape. These are not department store tubes—they're large cylinders that carry their cargo between uptown and downtown at some 75 mph. Initially they carried paper, punched cards, and money, but now they transport floppy disks. When CitiCorp analyzed its various systems, it found that nothing was sending as much data faster than the pneumatic tubes.

## PROGRAMMING

### Gerald M. Weinberg, Domain Editor

GERALD M. WEINBERG: In 1905, when you went motoring, you took your mechanic. Twenty-five years later, mass production revolutionized the role of the automobile, but buying a Ford wouldn't have made sense if everyone still needed a mechanic on board.

In 1955, when you used your computer, you took your programmer. Twenty-five years later, mass production revolutionized the role of the computer, but buying a micro wouldn't have made sense if everyone still needed a programmer.

It was important to get rid of the mechanic in every car, but even after 80 years, we still need mechanics somewhere. Moreover, drivers who understand the mechanisms involved get a whole lot more satisfaction from their cars. Even if they don't make simple repairs themselves, their knowledge of the mechanical underpinnings makes them far more intelligent buyers of cars and service.

It's the same with programming, the technology that underlies all other software tools, the very instructions that drive the computer. The three most common problems software users face today are (1) selecting the right package, (2) understanding the documentation, and (3) coping with errors and shortcomings in the programs. If you use software—even though you never intend to write a program—you should read a few good books on programming. Why? A knowledge of programming (1) makes you a better shopper, (2) clarifies muddy manuals and foggy screens, and (3) suggests how to circumvent errors and shortcomings.

Some addicts say that programming builds character. If so, I must have built a lot of character in 30 years, but not enough to tolerate poor-quality software tools. Most of the tools available to the personal computer programmer are two decades behind the best that are available on mainframes. Fortunately, the micros are catching up fast, and they would develop even faster if the market were more sophisticated. Few personal computer users would recognize fine programming if they saw it.

One example: An enthusiast sent me a review of a tool for resequencing line numbers in BASIC. No doubt he finds it useful, but it's unforgivable that this tool wasn't provided as part of his BASIC interpreter. Even worse, why would a sensible programming language use line numbers in the first place? They're a throwback to the old days when the only terminals programmers could use were printers rather than monitors (BASIC and APL), or to the ancient days of punch cards (FORTRAN). A tool for resequencing line numbers in BASIC is like a blowtorch to light the pilot on your solar water heater.

Though unacquainted with good programming, personal computer users have been introduced to the consequences of poor programming in the software they buy—errors, incompatible interfaces, errors, clumsy designs, errors, poor performance, errors, wipeouts, and errors. None of this garbage is necessary, but the buyers think "that's just the way computers are." That's why this section emphasizes some of the classic books on programming—to accelerate the revolution of rising expectations. And that's why it emphasizes the entire programming process from conception to design to debugging, not just hacking code on the screen.

We have restricted the reviews of programming tools to a few of the best—partly owing to a lack of space, partly to a lack of more good tools, but mostly because it's time we learned from good examples. Unfortunately, some of the best programming tools are being treated as trade secrets within the software companies. Superior programming tools still have a small marketing potential, so they're more profitably used—like machine tools—to *produce* software products.

The market for software machine tools will always be smaller than that for prebuilt packages: There are a lot more Chevys than automatic milling machines. However, as hardware costs drop and user sophistication grows, the market for professional-quality programming tools will blossom. Some of these high-quality tools, like UNIX (p. 167), and object-oriented programming languages like SMALLTALK, are beginning to reach the personal computer market. As they do, their primitive imitations will be swept away. The sooner the better.

## DO IT YOURSELF SOFTWARE

STEWART BRAND: Software is beyond soft, beyond liquid, beyond even gas—it is utterly non-material. Yet it is completely accessible. That makes it a standing invitation to meddle. The stages are easy. First you install the commercial programs on your computer, customizing to suit. Then you combine a couple programs on one disk and blend them a bit. Then you enhance the keyboard with the likes of PROKEY and SMARTKEY (p. 93). Then you're messing with utilities (p. 174), further customizing your file and disk handling. You're programming. Keep it up and you'll be a programmer.

This section may be too technical for many (it's too technical for me), but those it's useful to will find matter of consequence. Programmers increasingly are programming our culture—the process needs to remain open and needs to keep getting better.

We're honored to have as domain editor a proponent of both, the distinguished author of **The Psychology of Computer Programming** (p. 170) and **An Introduction to General Systems Thinking** along with 20 other books. Jerry Weinberg has been working with computers for 28 years. At present he and his anthropologist wife Dani do consulting, training, and writing on the interaction between people and technology out of their base near Lincoln, Nebraska.

Matthew McClure

*Gerald M. Weinberg*

## WHOLE EARTH RECOMMENDED PROGRAMMING TOOLS

### (June 1984)

### BOOKS

**The Art of Computer Programming,** $32.95/volume, p.160
**The Elements of Programming Style,** $15.95, p.161
**Pascal From BASIC**, $12.95, p.162
**Machine Language for Beginners,** $14.95, p.165
**Learning to Program in C**, $25, p.165
**The C Programming Language,** $21.50, p.165
**Software Tools**, $18.95, p.166
**Software Tools in Pascal,** $18.95, p.166
**Notes on the Synthesis of Form,** $15, p.169
**Principles of Program Design,** $35, p.169
**Logical Construction of Systems,** $24.95, p.169
**Program Design and Construction,** $17.95, p.169
**Structured Design**, $26, p.169
**Standardized Development of Computer Software**, $54, p.169
**Microcomputer Software Design,** $12.95, p.170
**Rethinking Systems Analysis and Design**, $22.95, p.170

**Understanding the Professional Programmer**, $20.95, p.170
**On The Design of Stable Systems,** $34.95, p.170
**The Psychology of Computer Programming,** $16.95, p.170
**Hackers**, $17.95, p.171
**Fire in the Valley**, $9.95, p.171
**Software Engineering Economics,** $37.50, p.171
**Applying Software Engineering Principles with FORTRAN**, $27, p.171
**Program Modification**, $25, p.171
**Software Maintenance**, $41, p.171
**Techniques of Program and System Maintenance**, $26.95, p.171
**Tutorial on Software Maintenance,** $32, p.171

### PERIODICALS

**Software Maintenance News,** $15/yr, p.172
**Data Processing Digest**, $99/yr, p.172

### LANGUAGES

MBASIC, $350, p.162
BASIC COMPILER, $395, p.162
CBASIC, $150, p.162
CBASIC COMPILER, $500, p.162
COMPILER +, $60, p.162
TURBO PASCAL, $50, p.162
APPLE PASCAL, $250, p.163
NEVADA COBOL, $39.95, p.163
NEVADA EDIT, $39.95, p.163
PERSONAL COBOL, $395, p.163
CIS COBOL, $795, p.163
FORTH, p.164
MODULA-2, $40, p.164
MICRO-PROLOG, $295, p.165
OBJECTIVE C-COMPILER, $5000, p.166
VEDIT, $150/$195, p.167

### OPERATING ENVIRONMENTS

UNETIX, $130, p.168
CONCURRENT DOS, $295, p.174
OASIS 8, $850, p.174

### UTILITIES (p.173)

THE NORTON UTILITIES
POWER!
DU
COPY II PLUS
COPY II PC
MEMORY/SHIFT

## TYRANNY OF THE NEW

GERALD M. WEINBERG: This feature of the **Catalog** is Stewart's idea for dealing with his fear that people will think we're stupid if we don't mention the important new software products that are coming out every minute. In the area of programming tools, that's a bit like worrying that an important new opera might be written tomorrow and that you might miss it. There are more than 50,000 published operas, so why worry about one more? You can hear it next year, or the year after. It's true that you won't be able to impress your cocktail party friends or your computer club friends, but is that really important?

In applications such as word processing, which haven't been widely available for decades, what's new may be important, but programmers have been building their own tools for a long time. A truly new idea comes along only once every three or four years, so you're unlikely to miss a single one this year—in spite of what the software marketeers may say. Better you should get to know what's around now. Chances are, what you need already exists, both in operas and in software.

It's important to learn how to judge operas and software for yourself, so when you encounter something that's new to you, you can deal with it. I've tried to structure this section to prepare you to make that kind of critical judgment.

Even so, there are hundreds of programming tools that cannot be covered in a fourteen-page section. In preparing to edit this section, I held a brainstorming meeting with the University of Nebraska chapter of the Association for Computing Machinery, asking them what sort of tools they'd like to see available for their micros. At the end of the session, one programmer said that all he wanted was a simple tool that would help him keep BASIC under control. I told him that was easy—we each have a portable one that we carry around on one end of our spine. And it's easy to operate—the only thing the programmer gets to choose is which end of the spine.

## Why Bother Learning to Program?

PETER A. MCWILLIAMS: Teaching BASIC is a holdover from several years ago when there were no programs for personal computers. That time is past, but the habit of teaching the language of programming remains.

GERALD M. WEINBERG: Personally, I think everyone should learn to program, but that's not a problem, because all computer users *do* learn to program whether they want to or not. Any time you arrange your procedure for using a word processor or spreadsheet into a logical progression of steps, you are programming. In fact, even when you arrange your procedure into an *illogical* sequence of steps, you are programming. So the question is not whether you should learn to program, but whether you should learn to program *well*.

In short, the first reason to study programming is to improve your ability to think in terms of logical, efficient procedures, whether for using your computer or for using your own time without a computer.

GIRISH PARIKH: What if you are using a package or program that doesn't work the way you want it to? You might get it corrected by contacting the original author or vendor, but this can be time-consuming and expensive. If you know programming, however, you might tinker with the program (of course, after saving the original copy of the program in a safe place) and solve your problem. This is called "maintenance" programming.

GERALD M. WEINBERG: You may have a far greater need to maintain programs than to write new ones, but an even better reason for learning to program is to know how to solve problems without writing a single line of programming code. Let's face it. The state of the art in software is still a bit crude, and most packages are more heavily influenced by their programmers' concerns than by their intended audience. When you run into trouble with such a package, even a slight knowledge of programming may get you out of trouble by allowing you to figure out what's going on behind the scenes—the things the manual doesn't say explicitly.

GIRISH PARIKH: Learning a programming language, though important for programming, is only half the story. Before building a house, you first get a blueprint. To program effectively, before writing code you must first have a design.

GERALD M. WEINBERG: For most personal computer users, learning to design programs will probably be of much more value than learning to write code in some programming language. Those who understand design will make better decisions when buying software, just as those who understand architecture will make better decisions when buying a house. Fortunately for the beginner, there are now some excellent books on program design, which we review below.

GIRISH PARIKH: If you have learned programming, you can write short but important programs that you need but that are not available on the software market. And who knows? You might even get a software publisher interested, and make some money.

GERALD M. WEINBERG: Getting rich through programming is a common fantasy. If you intend to learn programming as a way of getting rich, try the lottery instead. Your chances are better. On the other hand, learning to program may help you get a job. But, as Parikh says, we still haven't reached that utopian state where only professional programmers need to write programs. Most of the programs you write will be trivial to everyone but yourself. Twenty lines of BASIC that change the format of all your files so you can use a new word processor may be worth thousands of dollars to you but not a penny to someone else.

To me, the ultimate reason for learning to program was perfectly expressed by Don Knuth as the first sentence of his monumental work, **The Art of Computer Programming** (Donald E. Knuth; Vol. 1, **Fundamental Algorithms**; 2nd ed., 1974; 634 pp.; Vol. 2, **Seminumerical Algorithms**; 2nd ed., 1981; 700 pp.; Vol. 3, **Sorting and Searching**; 1973; 722 pp.; $32.95/volume; Addison-Wesley Publishing Co., Jacob Way, Reading, MA 01867; 617/944-3700; or COMPUTER LITERACY):

The process of preparing programs for a digital computer is especially attractive, not only because it can be economically and scientifically rewarding, but also because it can be an aesthetic experience much like composing poetry or music.

GERALD M. WEINBERG: You don't need more reason than that.

---

*The tar pit of software engineering will continue to be sticky for a long time to come. One can expect the human race to continue attempting systems just within or just beyond our reach; and software systems are perhaps the most intricate and complex of man's handiworks. The management of this complex craft will demand our best use of new languages and systems, our best adaptation of proven engineering management methods, liberal doses of common sense, and a God-given humility to recognize our fallibility and limitations.*

—Frederick P. Brooks, Jr., Epilogue to
**The Mythical Man-Month**

*It goes against the grain of modern education to teach children to program. What fun is there in making plans, acquiring discipline in organizing thoughts, devoting attention to detail, and learning to be self-critical?*
—Alan J. Perlis

*I would rather write programs that write programs than write programs.*
—Anonymous graffitor at MIT

*Newton said he could see so far because he was like a midget standing on the shoulders of giants. Programmers, however, are like midgets standing on the toes of other midgets.*
—Richard Hamming

*As we progress through the different steps in the logical construction of systems, it's just good sense to review our products with a peer group of interested, competent people who may have a different perspective than we have. Viewing a product from these different perspectives will often find problems that the originator cannot see and the problems can be addressed and solved while it is still relatively cheap to solve them.*
—W. Clyde Woods

*One can only display complex information in the mind. Like seeing, movement or flow or alteration of view is more important than the static picture, no matter how lovely.*
—Alan J. Perlis

*Teaching by bad example . . .*

## THE ELEMENTS OF PROGRAMMING STYLE

*The Elements of Programming Style*; Brian W. Kernighan and P. J. Plauger; 2nd Edition, 1978; 160 pp.; $15.95; McGraw-Hill, 1221 Avenue of the Americas, New York, NY 10020; 212/512-2000; or COMPUTER LITERACY.

GERALD M. WEINBERG: For programmers, this is the one book to have if you're having only one. Like its namesake, Strunk and White's **Elements of Style**, the book concentrates on the essential practical aspects of style by example.

Collected into chapters under such names as "Expression," "Control Structure," "Common Blunders," and "Efficiency and Instrumentation" are real programs, not toys made up to illustrate a point. These bad examples serve as springboards for incisive discussions of the best ways to write correct and readable programs. Sad to say, these programs come primarily from programming textbooks, where our next generation of programmers is turning for guidance. Each of the examples gets rewritten, sometimes in more than one way, to illustrate the principles the authors espouse. The examples are in FORTRAN or PL/I, but few, if any, would be BASIC, COBOL, Pascal, or some other

common language. As the authors prove, "The principles of style are applicable in all languages, including assembly codes."

Each example is followed by an aphorism that captures the point: "Write clearly—don't be too clever"; "Choose a data representation that makes your program simple"; "Make it right before you make it faster." The rules are listed together at the end of the book. A programmer could do worse than paste the list on the wall.

This book could be used as a textbook for a programming course, yet the examples are sufficiently self-contained to allow you to open the book at random, read a few pages, and come away a better programmer. In fact,

that's not a bad way to work with the book on your second or third reading.

One of the strongest messages in this book is that programming is a holistic task. The error in the sine function is not with the formula or the numerical analysis—the first place many programmers would look—but arises from the simplest of all blunders, an uninitialized variable. Time and again, using subtle or surprising examples, Kernighan and Plauger lead us to sharpen both our reading and writing skills by discussing what is wrong in a given instance, how to correct it, and, most important, how to avoid it.

To whet your appetite, here's a single example from Chapter 5. It's supposed to read the sides of a triangle and compute the area. Before you buy the book and find out what the authors have to say, can you determine what in the example is wrong (and what's right)? (For assistance, see p. 208.)

```
READ (5,23) A, B, C
23 FORMAT (3F10.0)
S = (A + B + C) / 2.0
AREA = SQRT(S * (S − A) * (S − B) * (S − C)
WRITE (6,17) A, B, C, AREA
17 FORMAT (1P4F16.7)
STOP
END
```

## Which Language Should You Learn?

GERALD M. WEINBERG: When Jean Sammett wrote **Programming Languages: History & Fundamentals** in 1969, there were hundreds of known languages. Though a few of them have died, many more have been born, so now there may be thousands. When you add the multiple dialects of each language, and the multiple implementations of each dialect, the beginner has a big problem: which language to learn first?

In my opinion, there are two important rules to follow in choosing your first programming language:

1. It doesn't matter much, so choose something that's easily available to you.

2. Don't learn just one, learn at least two at the same time.

I have always trained new programmers by having them write every program in two languages as different from one another as possible. At the very least, this practice prevents extreme language chauvinism from developing. If you learn this way, you learn that *every* language has some good features and *every* language has some dreadful ones.

And since you're going to learn two, one of them might as well help you get a job—quite likely some form of BASIC, COBOL, Pascal, or some member of that family, like FORTRAN or PL/I. But don't choose two from this family. To save money, you'll probably choose the one that comes with your computer, which is quite likely some form of BASIC. Don't let it bother you; you're only learning.

DARRELL R. FICHTL: Let's set the record straight. I've worked with FORTRAN and own a C, a Pascal, and a BASIC compiler. All these work exceptionally well, but I like BASIC—it's the Chevy of the computer business. You'll also hear that BASIC is sloppy. That depends on the person doing the programming. The impression that nothing "serious" can be written in BASIC is totally erroneous. If you do a cross-section of programs currently on the market, you'll find that a good percentage of them are written in BASIC. In BASIC, you can make an efficient program that is a joy to work with. It depends totally on you.

MATTHEW MCCLURE: Most programming languages share certain fundamental concepts, such as variables, subroutines, arrays, loops, strings, conditional branching, input and output. Learn how one language, such as BASIC, implements these concepts, and it's usually not hard to learn how another language handles the same ideas. It gets more interesting when you have new concepts—structured/modular programming or extensibility, for example; then you get exposed to a whole new level of sophistication.

*High-quality BASIC . . .*

## MBASIC

Interpreter; release 5; CP/M 80 machines ● IBM PC/compatibles and MS-DOS machines; copy-protected? NO; $350; Microsoft Corp., 10700 Northup Way Box 97200, Bellevue, WA 98009; 206/828-8080.

TRS-80 BASIC; Microsoft Corp.; TRS-80 Models 4, 12, 16 (included with machine); Model 100 (comes loaded in ROM); copy-protected? NO; Radio Shack, 1700 One Tandy Center, Ft. Worth, TX 76102; 817/338-2392.

## BASIC COMPILER

Version 5.35; CP/M 80 ● MS-DOS; copy-protected? NO; $395; Microsoft Corp., 10700 Northup Way, Box 97200, Bellevue, WA, 98009; 206/828-8080.

## CBASIC

Version 2.8; Apple II family ● IBM 3740; copy-protected? NO; $150;

## CBASIC COMPILER

Version 2.0; Apple II family ● IBM 3740; copy-protected? NO; $500;

both from Digital Research, 160 Central Avenue, P.O. Box 579, Pacific Grove, CA 93950; 408/649-3896.

RICHARD L. MULLER: I chose MBASIC (called MS BASIC by some people) for a project because I wanted to develop a small application for the TRS-80, but wanted to do the development work on my Morrow Designs micro, a Z-80-based system running CP/M 2.2.

BASIC is a good language for beginners and experts alike. It differs from most other languages in that it is usually interpreted rather than compiled. The plus for interpreting is that one can arbitrarily stop an executing program, see what it's doing to variables of interest (even change them if desired), and then resume execution without waiting for a recompilation. The negative side of the interpreter approach is that programs execute far more slowly than with a compiler. Microsoft's compiler gives one the advantage of good development environment (interpreted BASIC) complemented with a tool to create an efficient final product (the compiler). (See also COMPILER PLUS, this page.)

I can strongly recommend Microsoft BASIC: It is a high-quality product. It works well and appears to be correct. Nevertheless, I would urge any potential purchaser to look too at CBASIC and CB80 from Digital Research, for I have friends who rave about them.

*Structured fundamentals . . .*

## PASCAL FROM BASIC

*Pascal From BASIC*; Peter Brown; 1982; 182 pp.; $12.95; Addison-Wesley Publishing Co., Jacob Way, Reading, MA 01867; 617/944-3700; or COMPUTER LITERACY.

MATTHEW MCCLURE: Pascal is the language most frequently taught in universities today. Descended from Algol 60 and designed by Niklaus Wirth, it is a block-structured language, so it is well suited for large programs—each block stands by itself and can be separately analyzed and debugged. Block-structured code is generally quite readable, which is nice when you come back to the big program you wrote a year ago and want to make some changes. Pascal is also faster and more portable than BASIC—a Pascal program written for one machine will usually run on another with little alteration.

LINDA K. PHILLIPS: This book is for all BASIC hackers who want to learn Pascal. It assumes you are familiar with BASIC programming and concepts, and explains how to "think" in Pascal. The book does *not* teach you how to "translate." Nor is it a textbook in the usual sense. Pascal can differ in different implementations, and Brown often refers the reader to specific implementation manuals.

*Easy speed . . .*

## COMPILER +

Jonathan Eiten; version 4.4; Apple II family; 48K; copy-protected? NO; $60; Hayden Software Co., 600 Suffolk St., Lowell, MA 01853; 617/937-0200.

TAM HUTCHINSON, JR.: We were programming our Apple II + to enter and store alphanumeric data on disk, and we noticed that Applesoft was very slow on string handling and disk access. After some searching through magazines and catalogs, we located COMPILER +. (Hayden rarely advertises the compiler, apparently, because many people don't know the value of a compiler.) We were very pleased with the results. Before we started using the compiler, searching for a string took ten to fifteen seconds. The compiler trimmed the time down to about one second. Disk reading and writing improved proportionately. High-resolution graphics seemed to plot two to three times faster.

Other advantages of the compiler are its ease of use and its ability to save and reuse the compiled version, to make overlays for large programs, to check the syntax of lines even when the program doesn't use them in a particular test run, and to produce software that can't easily be copied.

I'm not sure you could write a good program after reading this book alone, but that's not the purpose. The book aims at introducing the concepts of Pascal: the structured form, string and file handling, memory management, data types, and so on. It succeeds admirably.

My own decision after reading this book was that I am not yet ready to program in a new language. However, the IBM PC implementation of BASIC includes some of the Pascal concepts and allows for some structuring, so the structure that Pascal forces can be imposed to some degree on BASIC; I was surprised to find that reading the book has made me a better BASIC programmer.

*Outstanding value . . .*

## TURBO PASCAL

Version 1.0; CP/M 80 ● CP/M 86 ● Concurrent CP/M 86 ● IBM PC compatibles ● MS-DOS; copy-protected? NO; $50; Borland International, 4113 Scotts Valley Dr., Scotts Valley, CA 95066; 408/438-8400.

KEVIN BOWYER: I would recommend this product for anyone interested in Pascal; it has the best price/performance of anything I've seen. Because I've written a book [**Pascal for the IBM-PC (IBM DOS Pascal and UCSD p-System Pascal)**; Kevin Bowyer and Sherryl Tomboulian; 1983; 320 pp.; $17.95; book/ diskette, $45; diskette, $30; Robert J. Brady Co., Bowie, MD 20715; 301/262-6300] that uses as an example the DOS Pascal marketed by IBM, I tend to compare other Pascals to that one. TURBO PASCAL is smaller, easier to use, comes with its own full-screen editor, and is much cheaper—it's almost too good to be true.

TURBO PASCAL's editor allows you to reassign the editing commands to any keys you wish, making this editor look like whatever full-screen editor you already know. Moreover, this is not a bare-bones "standard" Pascal. It has all the normal extensions that make Pascal a convenient language for any task. At less than $50, even people who already own one Pascal compiler can afford to buy this tool.

*Complete toolkit . . .*

## APPLE PASCAL

**Version 1.2; Apple II family; 48K; copy-protected? NO; $250; Apple Computer, 20525 Mariani Ave., Cupertino, CA 95014; 408/996-1010.**

THOMAS MAYER: I bought an Apple to learn programming and for a long time experienced nothing but disappointment and frustration. Now I am fluent in Pascal and am paid big bucks for programming. All it took was hard work, a few good books, and APPLE PASCAL, the most used piece of software I own.

APPLE PASCAL has all the tools you need to program in Pascal. One purchase buys you a complete programming environment: an editor, a Pascal compiler, a linker, an assembler, and all the necessary file-maintenance utilities.

*COBOL? On micros? . . .*

## NEVADA COBOL

**Chuck Ellis; CP/M machines; 32K; copy-protected? NO; $39.95;**

## NEVADA EDIT

**John Starkweather; CP/M machines; 32K; copy-protected? NO; $39.95;**

**both from Ellis Computing, Inc., 3917 Noriega St., San Francisco, CA 94122; 415/753-0186.**

SHARON RUFENER: COBOL is an archaic mainframe computer language. So why bother to put it on micros? Here are several good reasons for implementing COBOL at the micro level: COBOL is the native tongue of most of the professional programmers in the world; most existing applications programs are written in COBOL; most of the programmers' jobs listed in the want ads require COBOL expertise. By knowing the language, you could write COBOL programs at home on your micro and then have them installed on the mainframe at work (why use the full might and heft of IBM to do a little job like debugging source code?).

Microcomputer enthusiasts sneer at COBOL. (They also display a snobbish attitude toward any but the latest language they have mastered.) They accuse COBOL of being clumsy and cumbersome. Not sufficiently oriented to the innards of any particular machine. Not sexy, chic, or *au courant*. Let's appreciate the fact that COBOL is a trusty old friend if you know it well. The source language is as portable as anything invented. It begs to be fashioned into structured and modular creations. And, when compiled, you have a tidy little bundle of machine language that will perform quite respectably.

The two manuals are for the experienced programmer; the beginner will need to supplement them. A lucid guide to the operating system is **Introduction to the UCSD p-System**, by Charles W. Grant and Jon Butah (1982; 300 pp.; $15.95); an excellent description of the Pascal language that covers the UCSD implementation is **Introduction to Pascal Including UCSD Pascal**, by Rodnay Zaks (2nd edition, 1981; 420 pp.; $17.95); both from Sybex Computer Books, 2344 Sixth Street, Berkeley, CA 94710; 415/848-8233.

The Apple implementation lacks some standard Pascal features, but it is more than sufficient for training and for most applications. The system library contains several useful routines, including a full set of graphics primitives, and is readily supplemented. Isn't it nice to have a language that grows with you?

I tried out two COBOL packages, one a Cadillac and the other a motorbike. The big one is PERSONAL COBOL (below). The little one, NEVADA COBOL, runs only on CP/M machines. You use your word processor or, better yet, NEVADA EDIT (also $39.95) to create source code.

NEVADA COBOL is a decently documented compiler for producing plain vanilla batch programs in ANSI 74 COBOL. You can compile fairly large programs—2500-5000 lines of instruction, depending on available RAM—and include almost limitless lines of comments as well.

Now, for $39.95 you know you're not going to get a lot of things. Approximately 20 percent of the standard instruction set is missing. NEVADA COBOL is set up to handle only data files that are sequential or direct access—nothing fancier. You don't get the SORT verb (that really hurts), which means you can't make your own tag files for homebrew file indexing, because you can't sort them!

And, strangest of all, NEVADA COBOL is not designed to let you write programs oriented toward a microcomputer's main input/output device, the monitor! You can do some clumsy interchanges of one data field at a time, using DISPLAY and ACCEPT statements, but that is inadequate for any serious data entry or display on microcomputer screens.

So what is NEVADA COBOL good for? It's a good tool for learning programming. It's student-priced and student-sized. It's also adequate for many small applications using pre-existing files, such as reports and file merges and extracts. It is mercifully free of the ornate complexities surrounding IBM mainframe programming. There is a certain clean elegance to this bare-bones compiler. If it can get you where you want to go, you couldn't do better.

*But seriously, folks . . .*

## PERSONAL COBOL

**IBM PC/XT compatibles; PC DOS 1.1; 192K; PC DOS 2.0; 256K; copy-protected? NO; $395;**

## CIS COBOL

**CP/M machines ● CP/M-86 machines ● PC/MS-DOS machines; copy-protected? NO; $795;**

**both from MICRO FOCUS, Inc., 2465 East Bayshore Rd., Suite 400, Palo Alto, CA 94303; 415/856-4161.**

SHARON RUFENER: Now, *here* is a COBOL for serious applications developers. It has just about everything one finds on mainframes, and then some. I have a friend who is using the CIS version of this package on his Osborne to develop an accounting system for the IBM PC market. His partners are coding other parts of the system on their various computers. This motley assortment of code will then be compiled for DOS, and another new software company will be launched.

This product is not a compiler, but a front-end source code development tool. It has a run-time module to execute your programs as though you had object code. Micro Focus also offers two (expensive) compilers which can handle just about any micro hardware/operating system combo. Or, you can cart your tested and debugged source code off to your mainframe shop and have it compiled there.

My friend, who is a true guru in matters computer, searched the marketplace for just the right COBOL tool. He was turned on to this one by contractor friends who are using PERSONAL COBOL at home to do coding for mainframes. They found the other prominent powerful COBOL for micros, COBOL 80 by Microsoft, not as useful for developing screen formats, and the documentation not as understandable; "you have to buy a book" was his observation.

PERSONAL COBOL is a package containing several products: COBOL II, FORMS-2 (a screen-forms generator), ANIMATOR (a debugging tool better than TRACE), a text editor, and a module that generates programs for maintaining ISAM files. Very useful stuff, and this is a full implementation of standard Level II ANSI COBOL. This product gives you a gamut of file types, including such exotic ones as Dynamic, Indexed I/O, and Line-Sequential (variable-length records). There is also a library for your source code COPY modules.

The documentation is quite well organized and readable, although a bit bewildering in its complexity. Even so, it is a great improvement over the manuals for mainframe COBOL. One would have to spend a few days getting acquainted with all the possibilities of the package. In sum, I would rather use PERSONAL COBOL with all its handy features than the version of COBOL I spent so many years with.

## Your Second Programming Language

GERALD M. WEINBERG: If you follow my recommendation and learn two languages simultaneously, try something a bit out of the mainstream for your second—something like FORTH, APL, SMALLTALK, Modula, LISP, C, or assembly language. Their approaches contrast sharply with those of the more commercial languages, so they will stretch your mind. One of my students, who cut her teeth on PL/I and APL, took a job as a COBOL programmer on Friday, studied COBOL over the weekend, and started work on Monday. Four weeks later, her bosses were so impressed with her work that they asked her to teach their Advanced COBOL course.

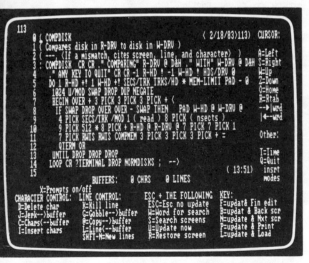

*The editing screen from MVP-FORTH. Surrounding the code are the editorial instructions; once you learn them, you can turn them off and concentrate on programming.*

*Compact, fast, extensible . . .*

## FORTH

**FORTH 64; Commodore 64 ● VIC 20; text editor & macro assembler included; copy-protected? NO; $39.95; Handic Software, Inc., 520 Fellowship Rd., Mt. Laurel, NJ 08054; 609/866-1001 ● GRAFORTH; Paul Lutus; Apple II family; $90 ● IBM PC compatibles; $125; copy-protected? NO; Insoft, P.O. Box 608, Beaverton, OR 97075; 503/641-5223 ● MACFORTH; Macintosh; copy-protected? NO; $149; Creative Solutions, Inc., 4701 Randolph Rd., Suite 12, Rockville, MD 20852; 301/984-0262 ● MASTERFORTH; Apple II family; 48K; copy-protected? NO; $100; floating point $40 additional; hi-res graphics $40 additional; MicroMotion, 12077 Wilshire Blvd., #506, Los Angeles, CA 90025; 213/821-4340 ● MVP-FORTH PROFESSIONAL APPLICATION DEVELOPMENT SYSTEM (PADS); Apple II family ● IBM PC/XT ● IBM PCjr; copy-protected? NO; $500; Mountain View Press, Inc., P.O. Box 4656, Mountain View, CA 94040; 415/961-4103 ● PC/FORTH; Version 2.0; IBM PC compatibles; 64K; copy-protected? NO; $100; PC/FORTH +; Version 2.0; IBM PC compatibles; 128K; copy-protected? NO; $200; both from Laboratory Microsystems, Inc., 3007 Washington Blvd., Suite 230, Marina Del Rey, CA 90290; 213/306-7412. ● POLYFORTH II; IBM PC compatibles; 64K; supports 8087 math coprocessor; copy-protected? NO; $295; FORTH, Inc., 2309 Pacific Coast Hwy., Hermosa Beach, CA 90254; 213/372-8493.**

MATTHEW MCCLURE: A program in FORTH is like a tower made of building blocks. The blocks are FORTH's "words," smaller programs themselves made up of FORTH words. Whereas most high-level languages are somewhat abstract—dealing with variables, relations, formulas—FORTH feels very direct: you have a processor, some memory and some storage space, and your job is to prescribe the series of movements of data from the computer's memory into the central processing unit (CPU) and back into memory when the CPU is through. Somehow, I never acquired such a direct feel for the machine using ALGOL, FORTRAN or BASIC.

FORTH generates very compact code, so it is good for putting large programs in small space. Because most implementations of FORTH are nearly identical, programs can be transported largely intact from one FORTH system to another without recoding, except for machine-specific features like graphics, which may need modification. FORTH also runs quite fast, which makes it a good language for games and for real-time applications involving control of other machines for industrial processes. It is not designed for simplicity of mathematical expression; I'd probably use another language if I were writing an accounting package or a complicated physics simulation.

FORTH is both a compiled and an interpreted language; you can give an instruction in FORTH and have it execute immediately, or you can write a long, complicated program and compile it for maximum speed and efficiency.

FORTH is also extensible. I've always wanted to be able to write a tool and then have it handy whenever I needed it. The freedom and power that comes from being able to create one's own language is common to all the fourth-generation languages—C, LISP, LOGO, and so on. Extensibility lets you have as much uniformity of expression and internal consistency as you please, since you define the input and output for every function you use. And since the programs tend to divide up into chunks, each one a FORTH word, even a large program can be reduced to a short series of words, each of which may represent a very complicated set of actions inside the computer.

FORTH gives you complete control over the machine, which is nice: anything you want to make the computer do, FORTH will let you. On the other hand, it is so wide-open that it also allows you to get away with poor programming practices. I actually find that well-chosen FORTH words create code that is easier to follow than many other languages, although, as in any language, it is possible to write incomprehensibly.

*The very next thing? . . .*

## MODULA-2

**Niklaus Wirth; Version 1.35; IBM PC compatibles and MS-DOS machines; 128K; copy-protected? NO; $40; Modula Research Institute, 950 N. University Ave., Provo, UT 84604; 801/375-7402.**

KEVIN BOWYER: Modula-2 was designed by Niklaus Wirth as a successor to his earlier languages, Pascal and Modula. It is touted by some folks as a competitor of C and ADA. This compiler offers a cheap and painless chance for IBM PC owners to learn about one of the contenders.

The documentation is, unfortunately, not so much an introduction to Modula-2 as a reference document for all the software that comes with the compiler. Using the compiler is not particularly convenient, nor are compilation or execution of programs particularly fast when compared with other language compilers that run directly under PC DOS, rather than under a command interpreter, as this one does. Despite some inconveniences, however, this product can give you a feel for the state of the art in one aspect of programming languages and environments.

*Real artificial intelligence on a micro . . .*

## MICRO-PROLOG

**Version 3.0; CP/M-80 machines; 64K ● IBM PC compatibles; 128K; copy-protected? NO; $295; Programming Logic Systems, Inc., 31 Crescent Dr., Milford, CT 06460; 203/877-7988.**

ERNIE TELLO: The programming language PROLOG has become a buzzword since the Japanese chose it to be the machine language for the dedicated hardware in their celebrated "Fifth Generation" project (see p. 199).

PROLOG, which stands for PROgramming in LOGic, is a specialized tool for artificial intelligence programming that chooses a first-order logic calculus and list processing as its main approach to machine-intelligence problems. MICRO-PROLOG is a very full implementation of PROLOG and is suitable for research into expert systems, intelligent databases, and natural language processing. This is a serious tool for accomplished and aspiring computer scientists who know what logic and logic programming are and what they intend to do with them.

MICRO-PROLOG is primarily written in assembler and as a result runs very fast, considering all the very high level things it is ready to do right out of the box. A nice plus is that large programs can be broken up into segments that are split between memory and disk or RAM-disk.

MICRO-PROLOG is a very specialized tool. If you want to develop an expert system that does not involve heavy math processing, it would be hard to find a package more ready to work for you "as is." MICRO-PROLOG implements a logic of relations that lets you describe the relationships between objects and define these relationships recursively. However, there are no trig or other math functions, and the input/output are as minimal as you could ever find. The Z-80 version has an assembly-language interface for custom extensions to the system, but at this writing the one for the 8088 is not yet available.

It is still a very open question what one can do using a tool like MICRO-PROLOG on 16-bit microcomputers with a megabyte of addressable memory, such as the IBM PC. If the ambitious work currently being attempted with microcomputer implementations of LISP in this environment is any indication, there may be some surprises for the hard-core skeptics.

*Good starting place . . .*

## MACHINE LANGUAGE FOR BEGINNERS

*Machine Language for Beginners*; Richard Mansfield; 1983; 350 pp.; $14.95; COMPUTE! Books, P.O. Box 5406, Greensboro, NC 27403; 800/334-0868 or, in NC, 919/275-9809; or COMPUTER LITERACY.

MATTHEW McCLURE: The instructions the computer actually follows are a series of 0s and 1s, binary code, called machine language. An assembler translates assembly language, which is much easier to write than binary code, into machine language for the computer's internal use.

GERRY WICK: If you know BASIC and want to learn machine language, this is the place to start. The book covers the popular computers that use the 6502 chip for their central processing unit—Atari, VIC-20, Apple II, Commodore 64, and Pet. Building on your experience as a BASIC programmer, Mansfield very gently takes you through the fundamentals of machine language.

The appendices include assembler and disassembler programs for all the computers

listed above, as well as memory maps and monitor programs, so you don't even need to buy an assembler. The tables for the individual instructions are well organized and useful but incomplete. The best tables I have found and use are in **Top-Down Assembly Language Programming for the 6502 Personal Computer** (Ken Skier; 1981; 434 pp.; $16.95; Byte Books/McGraw-Hill, 1221 Avenue of the Americas, New York, NY 10020; 212/512-2000; or COMPUTER LITERACY). The reference and comparison to BASIC will make this book easy for the beginner. But be careful. There are some errors in the programs.

*Structured, compact, powerful, portable . . .*

## LEARNING TO PROGRAM IN C

*Learning to Program in C*; Thomas Plum; 1983; 372 pp.; $25; Plum Hall, 1 Spruce Avenue, Cardiff, NJ 08232; 609/927-3770; or COMPUTER LITERACY.

## THE C PROGRAMMING LANGUAGE

*The C Programming Language*; Brian Kernighan and Dennis Ritchie; 1978; 228 pp.; $21.50; Prentice-Hall, P.O. Box 500, Englewood Cliffs, NJ 07632; 201/592-2000; or COMPUTER LITERACY.

DENNIS GELLER: C is a structured language in the same sense as Pascal, encouraging the user to build large programs in small, easy to understand pieces. C is a compact language that uses single symbols where others use whole words and that allows many shorthand notations. For example, + + i is a complete statement that increments i by one.

Unlike languages that try to hide the details of the underlying computer, C aims to expose the bit- and byte-level details, making it ideal for writing systems software where individual units of memory must be manipulated efficiently. C compares favorably with assembly languages in efficiency and flexibility, yet has the feel of higher-level languages, leading to lowered costs for both programming and maintenance. Costs are lowered even more by C's transportability. In C, it is easy for the programmer to isolate the machine-dependent parts of the program so that moving the software to new hardware takes relatively little work.

Kernighan and Ritchie's book is the standard reference for C, but Plum's careful introduction is a much better starting place for neophytes. It contains many careful program examples, all of which were run on three different machine architectures to ensure their wide applicability. Through special boldface references supported by extensive appendices, the book clearly indicates any material that might depend on the reader's machine, operating system, or C compiler.

Interspersed throughout the book is a small monograph on programming techniques and styles, plus a chapter on software development from design to documentation. Plum often presents two different C programs to solve the same problem, along with a discussion of their relative advantages. This is much more than an excellent introduction to the C language. It is also a primer on how to write a programming-language textbook.

*Hybrid vigor . . .*

## OBJECTIVE-C COMPILER

**Brad Cox; Version 2; IBM PC compatibles and MS-DOS machines; 64K; copy-protected? YES; $1000/user ($5000 minimum); Productivity Products International, 27 Glenn Road, Sandy Hook, CT 06482; 203/426-1875.**

MATTHEW MCCLURE: The "objects" that an "object-oriented" language manipulates can be anything from a flag in memory to a drawing on the screen to a whole set of programs. Operations on a class of objects all work the same way; for example, an operation to enlarge an image will work on a circle, a square, a rectangle, or a random shape, taking the shape as input and producing a new image, or object, as output. Thus we produce the icons of the new religion.

THOMAS LUBINSKI: If you have used the C language for anything from simple application programs to sophisticated systems, you will be amazed by the power of a few simple enhancements made to the language in OBJECTIVE-C. It uses the object-oriented techniques of SMALLTALK-80, the language developed at Xerox PARC and incorporated into Apple's Lisa and Mac, in conjunction with the extremely efficient C language. The result is an unsurpassed power tool for software crafters. What's more, the company provides excellent documentation and support.

Object-oriented programming is rapidly proving itself as an extremely powerful productivity aid. Quite simply, the technique reduces the size of a program and decreases the time required to build and test new programs. By organizing one's descriptions of data structures into categories referred to as "classes," and by extending the capabilities of a class through a technique known as "inheritance," one is able to re-use code to a degree that has been impossible up to now with traditional techniques. OBJECTIVE C relaxes many of the restrictions that a system normally places on the combinations of data types, so you can prototype diverse and complex application programs in a very short time. The result is a modular program structure in which "objects" are generally treated as independent of the rest of the system; both the data and the operations that can be performed on that data are encapsulated in a "class" description.

OBJECTIVE-C has proven to be a significant enhancement of our bag of tools. Bug-free, fast, and efficient enough for our own early-development phase, it is immediately applicable to the solution of numerous programming problems. In less than three months as a beta-test site user, we were able to produce a library of 3-D geometric modeling objects and an object-oriented interpreter for the manipulation of these objects, and have the entire system function with an existing C library. This no doubt attests to the productivity enhancement available with this tool.

The hybrid approach of combining the flexibility of "objects" with the highly efficient C language has certainly lived up to its expectations and claims. At any phase in the development of a program, one can select from the normal C programming statements (resulting in efficiency) or any of the object-oriented programming extensions (providing quick implementations).

*Top-notch tools teach good techniques . . .*

## SOFTWARE TOOLS

**Software Tools; B.W. Kernighan and P.J. Plauger; 1976; 286 pp.; $18.95;**

## SOFTWARE TOOLS IN PASCAL

**Software Tools in Pascal; B.W. Kernighan and P. J. Plauger; 1981; 366 pp.; $18.95;**

**both from Addison-Wesley Publishing Co., Jacob Way, Reading, MA 01867; 617/944-3700; or COMPUTER LITERACY.**

MATTHEW MCCLURE: These two books are very similar; the examples in **Software Tools** were written in RATFOR, a language based on FORTRAN, while those in **Software Tools in Pascal** are in Pascal. Essentially the same tools are developed and explained in both.

JIM FLEMING: The concept of software tools as developed by Kernighan and Plauger is a must for serious software developers. The tools in question are helpful programs that enable people to do things by machine instead of manually, and to do them well instead of badly. The specific tools developed in the books are useful in their own right, but of equal or greater importance are the underlying principles for developing suitable software tools whenever you are embarking on a significant development project.

The authors recognize that no one learns good programming simply by reading abstract statements about program constructs and data structures. They show how such concepts as top-down design, structured programming, and simple user interfaces can be combined to produce significant programs that are easy to write, easy to read, and easy to maintain.

Each of the software tools is introduced by a discussion of the class of problems it helps solve, followed by a discussion of the significant design considerations that went into creating it. The resulting code is exhibited along with a discussion of potential extensions.

I have found that building a software toolbox has saved me many months of work over the life of several software-development projects.

GERALD M. WEINBERG: As their needs and skills grow, serious users will eventually "hit the wall" on any system—be it programming language, word processor, spreadsheet, or database manager. The ability to compose complex tools from simple ones allows you to get through the wall and continue working in an ever more hospitable environment. This ability is so essential to programming that I wouldn't consider recommending any programming environment lacking it. Consider what Thomas Mayer has to say about VEDIT.

*Programming your text editor . . .*

## VEDIT

Version 1.38; CP/M machines; 64K; $150
• versions 1.38 or 1.16; IBM PC compatibles; 64K;
$150 • MS-DOS machines; 64K; $195; copy-
protected? NO; Compuview Products, Inc., 1955
Pauline Blvd., Suite 300, Ann Arbor, MI 48103;
313/996-1299.

THOMAS MAYER: Life before VEDIT was like
the Dark Ages. In its visual mode, VEDIT is a
lightning-fast text editor with all the
commands of a slick word processor. In the
command mode, a text-oriented
programming language enables you to
perform tasks impossible with a standard
word processor. For example, the following
command inserts a semicolon at the end of
up to four lines containing the word CASE:

4[FCASE$L-CI;$]$$

Translated, this means

Repeat the following task 4 times:

Find (F) the string CASE

Move to start of next line (L)

Move back one character (-C)

Insert (I) a semicolon

VEDIT provides ten text registers that allow
you to save a phrase and insert it with two
keystrokes, or to work on several files at once
by moving text between the registers and the
main work area. Text registers can also store
command sequences, and since you can save
text registers on a disk, you can develop a
library of complicated commands. Some
examples of my use of VEDIT:

• With a few keystrokes, I can take a
directory listing and turn it into a batch
command for my operating system to transfer
a list of files from one machine to another.

• When switching compilers, I had to
perform several nontrivial translations on
100K of source code in 30 files. I was able to
write a command to take a list of files to be
changed and make the changes in each file
without intervention.

• If I need to reformat a text file, it is easier to
use VEDIT than write a reformatting program.
I also use VEDIT for composing program
documentation. Since VEDIT works on
standard text files, it is easy to upload them to
another machine or read them from within a
program as help files. And, of course, I use
VEDIT for composing programs. This
function alone would earn it a place in my
programmer's toolbox. A fantastic product.

# Operating Environments

GERALD M. WEINBERG: Until recently, your choice of hardware
pretty much determined your choice of operating systems—and
vice versa. The situation is changing rapidly, largely because of
the influence of UNIX, which gave a new meaning to the term
"portability." For general use, there are other good operating
system choices. For instance, if you're running a small
business, the PICK operating system (PICK OPEN
ARCHITECTURE; Richard Pick; IBM PC/XT compatibles; 256K;
copy-protected? YES; $495; Pick Systems, 17851 F Skypark
Circle, Irvine, CA 92714; 714/261-7425) deserves careful
consideration. But if you're serious about programming, UNIX is
head and shoulders above the rest—even for developing
software that will run in other environments. You may not be
able to afford the machine resources, but those prices are
coming down daily. Moreover, other operating systems are
growing closer to UNIX with every new release, so whatever
your programming environment is called, it may eventually
be UNIX.

TOM LOVE: UNIX has three major advantages to programmers:
portability, modularity—pipes, filters, etc.—and support for
multiple users to communicate and coordinate their activities.

The best thing about UNIX is its portability. UNIX ports across a
full range of hardware—from the single-user $5000 IBM PC to
the $5 million Cray. For the first time, the point of stability
becomes the software environment, not the hardware
architecture; UNIX transcends changes in hardware technology,
so programs written for the UNIX environment can move into the
next generation of hardware.

JASON REBECK: UNIX is the software development religion of
the '80s, primarily because it's associated with the language C,
which is good for software development. And the 1980s are
apparently when applications for UNIX are going to be created
which may rival those of MS-DOS in general appeal and
availability.

TOM LOVE: The major impact of UNIX has been its modularity
and increased programmer productivity. Just as the ideas that
went into the OS 360 in the 1960s had a strong influence in the
1970s, UNIX grew up in the 1970s and will have a strong
influence in the 1980s. And the *next* decade will be influenced by
SMALLTALK. The current version of OS 360, MVS, has 11
million lines of code; UNIX accomplishes much of the same
functionality with 435,000 lines of code. SMALLTALK has
40,000 lines of code.

JASON REBECK: UNIX was created by software developers for
software developers, to give themselves an environment they
could completely manipulate. In addition to being a completely
masterable environment, UNIX is totally addictive to certain
kinds of people. UNIX makes them feel like God: They can do
anything they damned well please. This, of course, is UNIX's
great strength and weakness.

TOM LOVE: UNIX has a philosophy of sharing files, programs,
and utilities among users—distributed data. Other environments
have a philosophy of security. This openness turns out to be very
important. What we're seeing now is a temporary phase of
computing; we're just beginning to discover the advantages of
distributed processing and communications, and this is where
UNIX is appropriate. What we haven't yet seen are the
disadvantages of distributed data.

## UNIX COMPARED TO PC DOS

DAVID FIEDLER: PC DOS has many of the characteristics of a single-user UNIX system. The prime advantage of UNIX over PC DOS is its multi-user capability (although IBM's version, PCIX, is single-user).

JASON REBECK: The characteristics in common are I/O redirection, pipes, and hierarchical directories. I/O redirection means that everything, even a device, is a file, which makes it easy to reassign input and output processes. Pipes let the output from one part of a program serve as input for the next; this is often done with filters, whose implementation in PC DOS is different, but the effect of which is about the same. Since all I/O is a stream of characters passing by, you can create filter programs which modify the input character stream; for example, you can pass a file through a sort filter and the file comes out sorted. Join filters together and you have a pipe. The hierarchical directory just means there's a tree structure of directory and sub-directory items.

DAVID FIEDLER: With UNIX, you get hundreds of built-in utility programs for file manipulation and to make programmers' jobs easier along with communication facilities that let you talk to other UNIX systems all over the world, automatically.

JASON REBECK: The price for UNIX's complexity is the amount of storage it requires; seven to eight megabytes of associated files and programs for a complete system means you must have a hard disk. (You can cut down on the overhead by eliminating some of the parts, but you have to know the system to pick which ones.)

DAVID FIEDLER: UNIX costs a lot more than PC DOS; the least expensive version of UNIX that works on an IBM PC is COHERENT, and costs $500 (Mark Williams Co., 1430 W. Wrightwood Ave., Chicago, IL 60614; 312/472-6659). UNIX is much bigger than PC DOS: UNIX takes 100K RAM, PC DOS about 12K. Finally, the response time for UNIX is much slower than PC DOS because its multi-user kernel has to check many things before executing a file. UNIX is designed for faster disk drives than those on the IBM PC.

The great advantage to software developers is that they can develop programs under UNIX on an IBM PC, compile their programs on other computers, then sell the program in the UNIX marketplace. You can now buy extremely fast UNIX systems that support multiple users for less than $10,000, including the new Fortune XP 20, the Altos 586, and the Tandy Model 16.

*Is it possible that software is not like anything else, that it is meant to be discarded, that the whole point is to always see it as soap bubble?*
—Alan J. Perlis

*The fact is that we have so many changes to do today because we didn't control the changes yesterday. Changes are like rabbits. They beget changes.*
—W. Clyde Woods

## UNETIX

Version 1.0; IBM PC compatibles; 256K; copy-protected? NO; $130; Lantech Systems, Inc., 9635 Wendell Rd., Dallas, TX 75243; 214/340-4932.

ERNIE TELLO: This product is unique for small businesses and software-development outfits: a low-cost UNIX-like operating system for the IBM PC with multitasking and multiple windows in color.

This is the first product we know of that has implemented a multiple-window capability in a UNIX environment, improving the user interface of an otherwise notoriously hard-to-use system. The original idea behind windows was to simulate a desktop with various papers on it that were easy to get to. The multicolor windows of UNETIX are a breath of fresh air in the UNIX environment. If ever anything needed to be made easier to use, it's UNIX.

Another nice feature of UNETIX is the PC DOS emulator, which lets you run any program in DOS 1.1 format in the main window while retaining the ability to be doing other things in UNETIX in other windows.

Options available but not included are a terminal emulator and a C-language compiler. There are various ways to transfer information both between program windows and between the UNETIX and PC DOS file systems.

UNETIX is still a very young product. So far, it is not a fully equipped UNIX in the sense of having a huge arsenal of utilities and applications. Lantech wrote it "from scratch" without paying AT&T a license fee, which is why the firm can sell it for such an incredibly reasonable price. But what is there so far is generally of exceptionally high quality. The one qualification we have is in regard to speed. Generally, multiple-window products require lots of memory and processing time and end up losing time somewhere. UNETIX is no exception. DOS programs run noticeably slower under the emulation, and if you really push the multiple-window capabilities, then you pay in speed for concurrent operation in several windows.

## *A Design Library*

DENNIS GELLER: Almost anyone can learn to write a program of twenty lines, but a hundred line program is not five times as hard to write; it's more like twenty-five. Writing a large program is a difficult intellectual task, and programmers need all the help they can get.

The past decade has seen increasing attention to the problems people have in developing programs. The study of programming as a human activity was brought to public attention by Gerald M. Weinberg in **The Psychology of Computer Programming** (see p. 170).

A host of later books built upon the lessons of Weinberg and others in proposing specific ways to avoid the problems which he pointed out. Among these are books on design—the process of figuring out what you want to do in a program before you sit down to do it. Design carries a certain mystique, and is sometimes used by programmers as it is by architects, to encompass the whole problem of creating a piece of software that will stand up, do the job, and blend harmoniously with the work environment and the people who use it. It's no wonder that an underground classic among program designers is architect Christopher Alexander's **Notes on the Synthesis of Form** (1964; 216 pp.; $15; Harvard University Press, 79 Garden Street, Cambridge, MA 02138; 617/495-2480 or COMPUTER LITERACY). Alexander shows the deep correspondence between the form of a problem and the process of designing a structure that solves it—a lesson that applies at least as well to programming as to architecture.

Two simple concepts emerge from the literature on program design. First, programs that are designed as single monoliths tend to do mysterious and unpredictable things, like Arthur C. Clarke's creation in **2001**. To avoid this undesirable behavior, programs should be designed in small, understandable pieces. The second concept says to approach a problem slowly. Instead of rushing into details, the wise designer begins with a general statement of the program's function, then successively refines the statement to add more and more detail—in the process spinning off small, understandable pieces to perform well-defined tasks.

Michael Jackson's **Principles of Program Design** (1975; 310 pp.; $35; Academic Press, 4805 Sand Lake Road, Orlando, FL 32887; 305/345-2254; or COMPUTER LITERACY) applies this approach to data processing problems—those in which most of the work involves handling large masses of regularly structured data. Jackson provides a graphical method for displaying the structure of both data and programs, allowing the designer to reveal the structures as the design proceeds. Jackson would have us begin by diagramming the structure of the data on which the program is to work, then use that structure to express the general architecture of the program. Jackson's method can be applied to unraveling complex problems and to optimizing programs once they've been written.

Jean-Dominique Warnier's **Logical Construction of Systems** (1981; 192 pp.; $24.95; Van Nostrand Reinhold, 135 West 50th Street, New York, NY 10020; 212/265-8700; or COMPUTER LITERACY) also attacks problems with a data processing flavor, though his approach is distinct from Jackson's. For Warnier, what's important about a problem are the codes and data in the input, and the different decisions based on them. Warnier's book is an example of truly original thinking in the area of design, but it is difficult to understand because of translation problems.

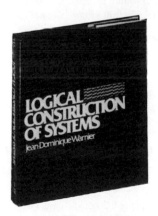

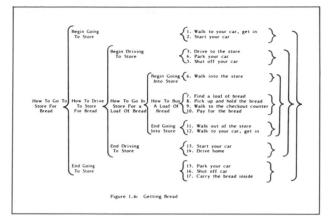

*A simple task like getting bread has more steps than one would expect, as shown in this diagram from* Program Design and Construction.

DENNIS GELLER: More complex problems call for complex approaches, such as that given in **Structured Design**, by Ed Yourdon and Larry L. Constantine (2nd edition, 1978; 464 pp.; $26; Yourdon Press, 1133 Avenue of the Americas, New York, NY 10036; 212/391-2828; or COMPUTER LITERACY). They start by looking at the structure of designs that have been developed by refinement, presenting a series of informal measures to evaluate the clarity and reliability of a design. Then they offer a unique method of developing a design by refinement. Rather than starting with the function of the program, they ask how data is to be transformed as it flows through the program. Tho parts of the program are then revealed as the transformations that change one form of the data into another.

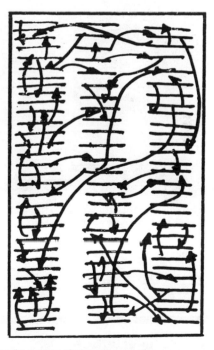

**Structured Design** *illustrates the structure of a large program after modularization. Imagine the spaghetti that would result if it were less carefully designed.*

GIRISH PARIKH: Possibly a better place to start understanding Warnier's approach is David Higgins's **Program Design and Construction** (1979; 189 pp.; $17.95; Prentice-Hall, P.O. Box 500, Englewood Cliffs, NJ 07632; 201/592-2000; or COMPUTER LITERACY), which describes a data-structure method derived from Warnier.

A careful exposition of program design techniques can be found in Robert C. Tausworthe's **Standardized Development of Computer Software** (Vol. 1, **Methods**; 1977; 379 pp.; $32.95; Vol. 2, **Standards**; 1979; 548 pp.; $32.95; or both volumes in one for $54; Prentice-Hall, P.O. Box 500, Englewood Cliffs, NJ 07632; 201/592-2000; or COMPUTER LITERACY), originally written for the engineers at the Jet Propulsion Laboratory and for

*(continued on p. 170)*

*(continued from p. 169)*

computer science students. For people who don't want to study computer science before writing programs, there is a simpler introduction, Sally Campbell's **Microcomputer Software Design: How to Develop Complex Application Programs** (1984; 227 pp.; $12.95; Prentice-Hall, P.O. Box 500, Englewood Cliffs, NJ 07632; 201/592-2000; or COMPUTER LITERACY). While I'd quarrel with some details in her material, Campbell's book is easy to read. Besides, any design is better than no design at all.

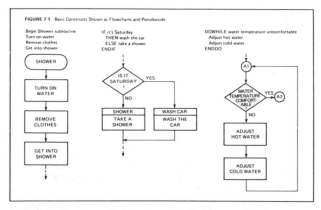

**FIGURE 7-1.** Basic Constructs Shown as Flowcharts and Pseudocode.

*Looking at a shower as a programming task in **Microcomputer Software Design.***

DENNIS GELLER: Jerry Weinberg has all the technical credentials you might need to believe that he understands software, but since the publication of **The Psychology of Computer Programming** (see review below) he has been giving most of his attention to the people side of software. Especially noteworthy in this regard are his **Rethinking Systems Analysis and Design** (1982; 208 pp.; $22.95); and **Understanding the**

**Professional Programmer** (1982; 288 pp.; $20.95); both from Little, Brown & Co., 34 Beacon Street, Boston, MA 02106; 617/227-0730; or COMPUTER LITERACY. I usually recommend these deceptively charming books as bedtime reading to people who want to get a little distance from their work. Each is a collection of short essays intermixed with little fables, like "The Natural History of White Bread," "The Goat and the Hippo," or "The Railroad Paradox." All in all, lots of fun.

But beneath the fun there is a deep, if not sinister, message: If we don't start doing things a lot better than we are now, we're not going to survive our own technology. Take the Railroad Paradox. When some suburbanites requested that a train passing through their station daily at 2:30 stop so they could go to the city, the railroad sent an observer to the platform every day for a week. Since there never were any commuters waiting for the train, the railroad declined to add the stop.

If you think the Railroad Paradox has nothing to do with computers, then you've never been near one. One of Weinberg's examples is the computer company that asked its engineers to investigate the addition of a new instruction that would make it easier for people to break their programs into subroutines. After some study, the engineers reported that almost none of the programs they examined ever used subroutines, so they saw no point in the modification.

Speaking of systems, I can't close without mentioning **On the Design of Stable Systems** (with Daniela Weinberg; 1980; 353 pp.; $34.95; John Wiley & Sons; 605 Third Avenue, New York, NY 10158; 212/850-6000; or COMPUTER LITERACY), a book so good I can't describe it properly. If you've read people like Ross Ashby, Kenneth Boulding, or Gregory Bateson, you'll know what I mean when I say that this is about systems. It addresses the question, Why is it that some things—objects, organizations, procedures—seem to persist for a long time, while others don't? The answer is as much philosophy as science, as much art as technology. When you read it—and you must if you're regularly engaged in the design of systems—you'll see that there is a small number of strategies which every system, whether animate or not, uses to prolong its own survival in the face of a hostile environment. (If you don't think hardware and users make for a hostile environment, you've had a very easy life as a programmer.)

I can summarize much of Jerry's work, and probably his self-chosen life mission, with my favorite Weinbergism, which should probably be called Weinberg's Zeroth Law: "If architects built buildings the way programmers build programs, the first woodpecker to come along would destroy civilization."

## THE PSYCHOLOGY OF COMPUTER PROGRAMMING

*The Psychology of Computer Programming*; Gerald M. Weinberg; 1971; 304 pp.; $16.95; Van Nostrand Reinhold, 135 W. 50th Street, New York, NY 10020; 212/265-8700; or COMPUTER LITERACY.

BEN SHNEIDERMAN: As a programmer, you're bound to be attracted to a book that lists a sense of humor as one of the "essential personality traits for programming." Jerry makes you laugh at the sometimes bizarre behavior of programmers as they wrestle with themselves, their colleagues, their managers, and awkward software tools. But Jerry's goal

in the book is more than laughter—he wants to make you a better programmer by helping you to understand the social structure in which programming is done.

In programming, independence has given way to interdependence. Jerry shows you why cooperation is a superior path, and explains how to collaborate effectively in "egoless" teams. When this form of communal utopia is attained, teamwork is a joy, productivity is high, and trusting relationships flourish. Building an effective team takes time, but many useful group processes, such as inspections and

walkthroughs, can be accomplished in hours or days.

Sometimes I see this book as a work of anthropology: the precise reports about a strange culture by a careful participant/observer/scientist. I especially appreciated the interdisciplinary style with the extensive annotated references to work in psychology, genetics, economics, sociology, feminism, general systems theory, mathematics, linguistics, and so on. If you are a programmer, work with programmers, or live with a programmer, this book will give you fresh insights.

## HACKERS

*Hackers (Heroes of the Computer Revolution);*
*Steven Levy; 1984; 672 pp.; $17.95; Doubleday &*
*Co., 501 Franklin Avenue, Garden City, NY 11530;*
*516/294-4400; or COMPUTER LITERACY.*

## FIRE IN THE VALLEY

*Fire in the Valley (The Making of the Personal*
*Computer);* Paul Freiberger and Michael Swaine;
*1984; 288 pp.; $9.95; Osborne/McGraw-Hill, 2600*
*Tenth Street, Berkeley, CA 94710; 415/548-2805; or*
*COMPUTER LITERACY.*

ART KLEINER: What makes personal
computer history fascinating? It's not just
unraveling which creative innovations begat
what multimillion-dollar companies.
Computer developers have wrestled for three
decades now with a dilemma that springs
from the heart of their technology: software is
a product of imagination, easily accessible
and changeable; but making a livelihood from
it requires fixing it relatively solid in order to
finish and sell it.

Steven Levy's **Hackers** is a *tour de force* of
storytelling, focused on what Levy calls the
Hacker Ethic—in which information is free
and the purpose of computing is making the
machines (figuratively) sing. The story picks
up the Hacker Ethic at its Massachusetts
Institute of Technology origins in the early

'60s, follows it through the home-brew
spawning of personal computers a decade
later, and chases it into the bizarre, esoteric
world of game programmers in the early '80s.

Levy, of course, is a major contributor to this
**Catalog**, but even if you distrust our
objectivity, take a glance at **Hackers**. It'll hook
you from the first page.

**Hackers** is a good introduction for anyone—
computer-involved or not—to the
contradictory forces battling within computer
peoples' souls. But it's not a comprehensive
history of the industry. **Fire in the Valley**,
written by two moonlighting **InfoWorld**
reporters (Freiberger and Swaine are now at
**Popular Computing** and **Dr. Dobb's Journal**,
respectively) tells the full story from the
transistor to the Macintosh. You see Bill
Gates programming minicomputers at age 13
and developing the IBM PC operating system
14 years later. A surprising number of people
in this infant industry have their innovative
roots in the '50s or '60s. Though dryly
written in places, **Fire in the Valley** is far and
away the best scorecard to date. If you're
already interested in computer gossip, this
book's treasure trove of reprinted
photographs will be worth the cover price.

STEWART BRAND: **Fire in the Valley** is the
most hilarious and thrilling book I've read in
years. The national economy winds up
pivoting on the misadventures, blind faith,
and blind luck of a bunch of techie hobbyists
and hippies with an obsession scorned by
corporate America.

---

## *Software Engineering*

GERALD M. WEINBERG: Though
software is a relatively new
phenomenon, it is not exempt from the
great systems laws that govern our
universe, such as

Everything changes but change itself.
—Heraclitus

Growth produces bigness.—Boulding

Over time, well-structured little
programs inevitably become muddled
big systems. The mainframe users have
learned this lesson the expensive way;
micro users have the chance to learn
from those experiences, which are
summarized in the evolving set of
practices called software engineering.
If you want to see into your own future,
take a look at Barry Boehm's monumental work, **Software Engineering
Economics** (1981; 768 pp.; $37.50;
Prentice-Hall, P.O. Box 500, Englewood
Cliffs, NJ 07632; 201/592-2000; or
COMPUTER LITERACY).

The survivors in software development
will be those who adopt good software
engineering practices **before** their need
becomes painfully evident.

## APPLYING SOFTWARE ENGINEERING PRINCIPLES

*Applying Software Engineering Principles with*
*FORTRAN;* David Marca; 1984; 270 pp.; $27; Little,
Brown & Co., 34 Beacon Street, Boston, MA
02106; 617/227-0730; or COMPUTER LITERACY.

DENNIS GELLER: This concise, well-written
book introduces the micro user to modern
principles of software engineering. Each
chapter contains a section called "For your
next project," containing the author's
suggestions for applying the chapter's
lessons to an ongoing software development
effort—either by adopting them on a small
scale or by using them to evaluate the work
being done. Too many books make the
assumption that once you've read the
material you'll be able to put it to work *in toto*.
By avoiding this assumption, Marca actually
increases the probability that his reader will
do something useful with his lessons.

Although the coding examples are based on
FORTRAN, Marca generally avoids clever
tricks, so the book will serve as a good model
no matter what language you happen to use.
Marca teaches his reader the process of
developing a program and its supporting
documentation—everything from basing a
design on stable building blocks to coping
with the restrictions of a compiler. He also
teaches technique—such as how to move
program complexity out of the code and into
the data structures.

A particular pleasure is the way Marca has
mixed technical and human considerations at
every level. He justifies his approach in terms
of the human limitations that affect the
programming task, and he also addresses the
needs of the program's consumer, as in his
chapter on "Building User Interfaces."
Overall, this is a well-done effort with
something to teach every programmer.

---

*The orientation of a programmer when doing*
*his or her own testing is to prove that the*
*program works. The orientation of a tester is*
*to make it fail.*
—*W. Clyde Woods*

## Software maintenance

STEWART BRAND: Some people save money fixing their own car. Others extend their personality by customizing their vehicles. You can do that with software.

GIRISH PARIKH: Microcomputer software packages, distributed by the tens of thousands, create new maintenance problems not previously experienced by the mainframers: distributing updates or corrections, answering customer queries, training users to make their own custom modifications. These problems have not been solved, and the micro user would be well advised to take self-protective steps, such as reading one of the small number of books on maintenance:

**Program Modification**; Jean-Dominique Warnier; 1978; 152 pp.; $25; Martinus Nijhoff, Kluwer Boston, Inc., 190 Old Derby Street, Hingham, MA 02043; 617/749-5262; or COMPUTER LITERACY.

**Software Maintenance (The Problem and Its Solutions)**; James Martin and Carma McClure; 1983; 472 pp.; $41; Prentice-Hall, P.O. Box 500, Englewood Cliffs, NJ 07632; 201/592-2000; or COMPUTER LITERACY.

**Techniques of Program and System Maintenance**; Girish Parikh, ed.; 1982; 300 pp.; $26.95; Little, Brown & Co., College Division, 34 Beacon St., Boston, MA 02106; 617/227-0730; or COMPUTER LITERACY.

**Tutorial on Software Maintenance**; Girish Parikh and Nicholas Zvegintzov; 1983; 360 pp; $18.75/members (Computer Society $34/yr; IEEE and Computer Society $90/yr), $32/non-members,

plus $4 shipping; IEEE Computer Society Press, Order Department, P.O. Box 80452, Worldway Postal Center, Los Angeles, CA 90080; 714/821-8380; or COMPUTER LITERACY.

Another approach is to subscribe to **Software Maintenance News** ($15/yr [monthly]; Data Processing Management Association, Special Interest Group on Software Maintenance, 141 St. Marks Place, #5F, Staten Island, NY 10301; 212/981-7842). Nicholas Zvegintzov, the newsletter's editor, says, "We have a single idea that unites us—the enhancement, adaptation, and correction of existing computer programs and systems. We have to find each other. We have to learn each other's tools, techniques, tactics, experiences, plans, and dreams." Zvegintzov makes interesting reading out of a subject that has been highly unpopular, and even hated by many programmers.

## Magazines to keep you informed

DEB WILLIAMSON: The marketplace is continually flooded with information on hardware and software so full of buzzwords that it's difficult even for seasoned programmers to digest. As a programmer with a great desire for the latest scoop but little time for research, I can scour the information I need out of a selection of magazines in a fraction of the time it takes to read books and visit computer stores. About five magazines allow me to get the tidbits of information I need before they become

obsolete: **InfoWorld** (p. 10), **Computerworld** ($44/yr [52 issues]; Computerworld, Inc., Box 880, 375 Cochituate Road, Framingham, MA 01701; 800/343-6474), **Datamation** ($42/yr [24 issues]; Datamation, 875 Third Avenue, New York, NY 10022; 212/605-9400), **Mini-Micro Systems** ($45/yr [15 issues] or free to managers who qualify; Cahners Publishing Co., 221 Columbus Avenue, Boston, MA 02116; 617/536-7780), and **Compute! (The Journal for Progressive Computing)** ($24/yr [12 issues]; COMPUTE! Publications, Inc., P.O. Box 5406, Greensboro, NC 27403; 800/334-0868).

### DATA PROCESSING DIGEST

*Data Processing Digest*; $99/yr (12 issues); Data Processing Digest, P.O. Box 1249, Los Angeles, CA 90078; 213/851-3156.

GERALD M. WEINBERG: My own list of regular magazines is similar to Deb's, but contains a few more entries because I am so involved in publishing. If I had to choose only one publication, however, I would pick **Data Processing Digest**. It's more than 30 years old and still going strong at $99 a year, though it's still unknown to many computer professionals. Here's how the magazine

describes itself: "**DPD** is written for the computer professional and the manager who uses computer technology for planning, control, and production. The editors regularly search many business, computer, industrial and educational periodicals to locate articles on all aspects of computer technology and its application to operations and management. Concise summaries of these articles and books appear in each issue." If it's important, you can be sure you'll know about it if you read **Data Processing Digest**, without having to read over a hundred periodicals each month.

# *Utilities*

DR. DOBB: Utilities are tool-tweakers; they make your computer easier to use, and let you do things you couldn't do before. The kind we're talking about here are the "diddlers," which show you what's going on inside your machine's entrails for medical or divinatory purposes. You might imagine that diddlers are only for serious programmers, but some of these should be in anyone's library.

*From a real expert . . .*

## THE NORTON UTILITIES

**Peter Norton; IBM PC compatibles; copy-protected? NO; $80; Peter Norton Computing, Inc.; 2210 Wilshire Blvd., #186, Santa Monica, CA 90403; 213/399-3948.**

DR. DOBB: Peter Norton is being promoted as a programming superstar, with his face in all his advertising. Nevertheless, he really does know a lot about the IBM PC, and has created a unique and useful package of utilities for the PC. If you want to change operating-system messages or recover from a disk crash, THE NORTON UTILITIES is just what you need.

*Operating systems made easy . . .*

## POWER!

**CP/M machines ● PC/MS-DOS machines; copy-protected? NO; $169; Computing! 2519 Greenwich Street, San Francisco, CA 94123; 415/567-1634.**

DR. DOBB: POWER! is one of the "shell" programs that hide the operating system from the user. These programs are supposed to relieve the user of tasks like decrypting operating system language like PIP PUB: = b:[EFG2UV].

POWER! supplies a handy bundle of operating system facilities in a form that is comparatively easy for a novice to use. You can format and copy disks, examine the contents of disks, and do the other things you expect an operating system to allow. You can also undelete files you have accidentally deleted, isolate bad sectors on the disk, and arrange files on the disk in logical groupings.

One of the decisive advantages of POWER! over some of the alternatives is that POWER! requires no installation. It is also available for the IBM PC, but its PC version is less powerful than the CP/M version.

*Perfect for hackers . . .*

## DU

**Ward Christensen; CP/M machines; public domain; Book 5, SIG M No. 91; catalog & sample disk $12; New York Amateur Computer Club, Inc., P.O. Box 106, Church Street Station, New York, NY 10008; or local CP/M users' groups.**

DR. DOBB: There is an ungodly number of utilities for CP/M systems, some atrocious but many excellent. One of the best is Ward Christensen's DU (stands for Disk Utility). A classic byte-level disk diddler, DU lets the wise and the unwary alike blithely finger the actual bytes of data stored on disk. With DU you can recover lost files, reconstruct scrambled disk directories, and read "unreadable" files. You can also lose files, scramble directories, and make readable files unreadable—somewhat scary symmetry.

The dangers inherent in the careless use of DU weigh heavily against recommending it to novices; on the other hand, it is tremendously useful. For example, you can use DU to recover a file you accidentally erased. It will run with little or no modification on virtually any plain-vanilla CP/M system. Christensen supplies the source code to the program, so you (or a hacker friend) can see just how it works, and modify it as you please. DU is not easy to use if you are not a programmer; its commands are cryptic and abbreviated. You may not be willing to spend time learning its logic and syntax. Get it anyway, and when you delete your entire electronic Rolodex, get your hacker friend to run DU for you. You can't beat the price.

*Apple doctor . . .*

## COPY II PLUS
## COPY II PC

**Apple II family ● IBM PC compatibles; copy-protected? NO; $39.95; Central Point Software, Inc., 9700 S.W. Capitol Hwy., #100, Portland, OR 97219; 503/244-5782.**

KATHY PARKS: One of my first acts as librarian at the **Whole Earth Software Catalog** was to accidentally destroy the master disk for the library's APPLE WRITER IIe. COPY II PLUS kindled hope and trepidation—it would be great if it worked, but how do you use it? The manual turned out to be a clearly written, outlined guide which enabled me to salvage the disk.

COPY II PLUS proved so simple to use that I prefer its copy function to the one provided on the Apple DOS 3.3 disk, and I usually recommend it to people who ask me how to format or back up a disk. The onscreen instructions, user's guide, and frequently updated supplements make it almost foolproof, inexpensive insurance for anyone's software collection. A version is also available for the IBM PC.

*Partitions memory to make a PC multi-user . . .*

## MEMORY/SHIFT

**Version 2.1; IBM PC/XT compatibles; 128K minimum, 256K recommended; $99; North American Business Systems, 642 Office Parkway, St. Louis, MO 63141; 800/325-1485.**

CHRIS GILBERT: MEMORY/SHIFT is a godsend for me in designing instructional materials for computer programs. I can place the program I'm writing about, say 1-2-3 or MULTIPLAN, in one partition, and do the writing/designing in another partition, using WORDSTAR. I've even gotten fancy and split the writing in two by creating a third partition: I use one for the instructor's class notes and the other for the participants' materials.

One very useful thing: MEMORY/SHIFT will check for a special name that you can assign each time it accesses a disk. That way, if you have changed disks while working in one partition, MEMORY/SHIFT reminds you to replace the correct disks for the work in progress in the other partition. This has saved me from innumerable possible disasters.

If you have a color/graphics card and a second monitor, MEMORY/SHIFT allows two different programs to be displayed on the two screens simultaneously. ("Not even Lisa can do that!" says the manual.)

**Dr. Dobb's Journal** (p. 13) was founded in 1976 by Bob Albrecht and Dennis Allison (Dennis and Bob became Dobb) of People's Computer Company, a non-profit organization that sprang from the same Portola Institute that gave us **Whole Earth Catalog**. The Dr. Dobb who wrote here about utilities is another many-headed beast. Contributors to this section were Bob Blum, Dave Cortesi, Nancy Groth, Gene Head, Thom Hogan, Ron Nicol, John Prather, Steve Rosenthal, Mike Swaine, Reynold Wiggins, and Steve Willoughby.

*You think you know when you learn, are more sure when you can write, even more when you can teach, but certain when you can program.*
*—Alan J. Perlis*

*Statistics show that only 50% to 70% of the errors in a software project are found by testing. Even testing by an independent, professional testing group finds no more than the high edge of this band. The answer lies in not putting errors into the code.*
*—W. Clyde Woods*

*One man's constant is another man's variable.*
*—Alan J. Perlis*

*Real live windows . . .*

## CONCURRENT DOS

AT&T ● CP/M-86 machines ● IBM PC/XT compatibles; 256K required, 512K recommended; 2 disk drives, hard disk recommended; copy-protected? NO; $295; Digital Research, Inc., 160 Central Ave., P.O. Box 579, Pacific Grove, CA 93950; 800/772-3545 or, in CA, 408/649-3896.

JONATHAN SACHS (author of **Osborne/McGraw-Hill CP/M-86 User's Guide**): Digital Research got caught flatfooted when Microsoft was anointed as supplier of the primary operating system for the IBM PC. For a while it looked as if the whole 16-bit computer market would go to Microsoft's PC/MS-DOS system, and Digital Research's CP/M would get the 8-bit scraps.

Digital Research is trying to catch up. With its new CONCURRENT DOS operating system, it's gone a long way toward succeeding.

"Concurrent" means that your computer can run several programs at once. At any time, one of these programs is in the foreground; that is, it's communicating with the keyboard and screen. The others chug along invisibly until they need keyboard input. Then each one waits until you put it in the foreground, which you can do at any time with one keystroke.

Concurrency is like a Post-It pad: seems like a gimmick until you use it. Then you can't get along without it. Concurrency will let you take intellectual side trips, play with alternatives, and stick notes to yourself where they're accessible but not in your way. Which, you'll suddenly realize, is how you did much of your work before your computer forced you to stop.

*CONCURRENT DOS lets you run up to four programs simultaneously. Here we have SUPERCALC3, WORDSTAR, and the system directory displayed on the screen.*

There's more. Digital Research sells a version of CONCURRENT DOS for the IBM PC that has windowing. You can divide the PC's screen into four rectangular parts of any size and position, each showing what's happening to one of four programs. Computer makers who want to use CONCURRENT DOS get a version with hooks that make it possible to develop similar windowing features on their own equipment.

Microsoft has been promising windows for MS-DOS Real Soon Now for about a year. Digital Research has been delivering them in CONCURRENT DOS (under its earlier name, CONCURRENT CP/M-86) since January 1984.

So far, the only other major windowing system actually available for the IBM PC is VisiCorp's VISI ON. CONCURRENT DOS has a major advantage over VISI ON: it works with *any* program that does screen I/O through system calls (instead of by talking directly to the hardware). VISI ON works only with programs designed specifically for it. This limits its usefulness if your work involves using non-VISI ON software. (On the other hand, VISI ON has a lot of attractive features, such as mouse control and pop-up menus, that CONCURRENT DOS lacks.)

CONCURRENT DOS has several advantages over MS-DOS besides windowing. Its time stamping facility is more elaborate than the one in MS-DOS. It lets you password-protect individual files, giving you a measure of security against friends or employees who might wish to use your private files.

What's the bad news? Unlike release 2.0 of MS-DOS, CONCURRENT DOS doesn't have subdirectories, a feature that lets you create several named areas on a disk and store a different group of files in each. Without subdirectories, managing lots of files on a hard disk is not easy.

Many applications run more slowly under CONCURRENT DOS than under MS-DOS—notably WORDSTAR. This appears to be a problem in the way the applications were converted to run under CONCURRENT DOS, not with CONCURRENT DOS itself. The latest version of CONCURRENT DOS can run MS-DOS programs, and on the IBM PC is said to run virtually any program that runs under PC DOS, including 1-2-3, WORDSTAR, and VISICALC. Perhaps running PC DOS programs under CONCURRENT DOS will diminish the speed problem.

If you feel a need for concurrency or windowing, CONCURRENT DOS may be just what you need. It offers almost everything you've now got, plus more.

*Fancy operating system for Z-80 micros . . .*

## OASIS 8

Version 5.6; Z-80 microcomputers (Onyx, IBC, NNC Electronics, Televideo, California Computer Systems); 64K; copy-protected? NO; $850; Phase One Systems, 7700 Edgewater Drive, Suite 830, Oakland, CA 94621; 415/562-8085.

PAUL SCHINDLER: OASIS has a slogan, "Makes micros run like minis." That about sums it up. For years, it has had features which the other operating systems are only now getting around to adding—time-and-date-stamping of files, log-on security, device drivers that really work, a sophisticated built-in telecommunications package, automatic backup of files—I could go on, about the re-entrant and compilable BASIC, the error-checking, the online help . . . but I think you get the idea.

OASIS has been held back in the marketplace by two problems. The system with its utilities takes up about 500K of disk space, which requires either multiple floppy disk drives or a hard disk; capacity increases and price reductions have made this less of a problem. The other problem has been its marketing; if Phase One were as good at marketing as they are at operating systems, no one would ever have heard of CP/M.

OASIS is *not* a good idea for people who are entirely dependent on software written by others. Although there are hundreds of packaged programs available for it, the number pales by comparison with the more popular operating systems. But if you want to write your own programs, and exchange them between machines from different manufacturers, OASIS is the best available environment to do that in—far better, even, than UNIX, which is famed for just these two capabilities.

# LEARNING

## Robert Scarola, Domain Editor

ROBERT SCAROLA: This section examines learning software—not all learning software, but a selection of the best that exists within some fairly distinct boundaries.

The first boundary is the age of the learner. The majority of the programs reviewed here are best suited for students up to thirteen or fourteen years old. This limitation comes partly from my own experience as an elementary school teacher for five years and as a computer lab instructor for first- through eighth-graders. It comes partly from the fact that in my opinion the most creative learning software is being developed for the under-fourteen age group, with a few exceptions in the area of simulations for adults—for example, THREE MILE ISLAND (p. 34) or FLIGHT SIMULATOR (p. 33). Learning software developed for teens and young adults tends, at this point, to be oriented towards a specific learning goal (an example is STOICHIOMETRY: MASS/MASS by Microphys Programs, Inc., which explores mass/mass relationships in chemical reactions). There may well be applications for this kind of software for high school or college students taking courses in a specific topic, but it tends to leave most home computer owners at a loss (see the review of CATLAB, p. 185, for an example of the best of this breed of software). Adults, with or without children at their sides, will enjoy WALL $TREET, ALGEBRA ARCADE, BASIC

PRIMER, D-BUG, VOLCANOES, the SEARCH series, BAFFLES, CATLAB, M_SS_NG L_NKS, and probably many others.

The second boundary is subject matter. I believe the best computer learning software doesn't waste its opportunity duplicating on the computer screen standard presentations of math, reading, science, social studies, or other academic disciplines. The best software crosses and merges disciplines to help individuals learn by (1) engaging in an accurate simulation, (2) solving a problem, (3) practicing a skill in a new way, or (4) creating an individualized tool. The Learning section is therefore organized around those four themes. A fifth legitimate learning theme is challenges and adventures—see the Playing section of the **Catalog** for programs that offer learning substance in an adventure format.

The third boundary is the audience. I have purposely not selected software for its classroom potential. In my experience, classrooms create special needs for learning software because teachers generally already have curriculums and methods in mind and are mainly interested in software that will help them achieve their teaching goals. I have selected learning software (with some exceptions, such as VOLCANOES and the SEARCH series) not so much for its value in the classroom as for its value to people who want to explore the educational possibilities of their computers at home.

*(continued on page 176.)*

## THE MOST PATIENT OF TEACHERS

STEWART BRAND: Learning, especially in kids, is greatly hampered by pace problems. Students are impatient to *get* something, but it takes repetition, and teachers become impatient with the repetition that for them rapidly becomes mindless. Matched frustrations. Add to that the variety of individual student paces being brutally standardized into an overall class pace, and you've got school-as-prison.

You can make computers pretend to be frustrated, but they never really are. Their forte is precisely mindless repetition. They don't drum their fingers or roll their eyes or breathe audibly through their noses while you take a long slow time coming up with the wrong answer to something. Fact is, they do the best possible thing for learners—they reward mistakes. Mistakes are trivial with a computer, who doesn't care, so you go ahead and make them, and then steer by them. Steering successfully is the reward. You're hooked.

We don't have a one-student-one-computer situation yet in most grade schools, but we will soon. It's coming rapidly in the colleges. Meantime the home, that traditional frontier of education, is a fine place for superior programs to prove their superiority, for sustained one-to-one between clever instructors and self-paced students. The blur between home and school can be blurred further by computers, and please do.

BARBARA ROBERTSON: Robert Scarola stopped by our offices one day last summer to ask if we needed a review of

ROCKY'S BOOTS (p. 188). That review appeared in the first issue of the **Whole Earth Software Review** and began a continuing relationship leading to this section of the **Catalog**.

For the past three years, Robert has been teaching LOGO (p. 191), word processing, and computer literacy to children and adults, and is currently working under a grant provided by the Marin County Computer Education Consortium to develop a science curriculum that uses computer software.

As a teacher (grades 1 through 6) in the alternative Pine Gulch School in Bolinas, California, Robert has an enthusiastic software testing lab readily available at school—and a second one at home, where he vies for time on an Apple II with two sons ages 8 and 10. In addition, his ties to the

Consortium gave him access to information collected by all the local educators interested in Learning software. In return, our library is now often populated with teachers looking for new software to evaluate and recommend—absolutely delightful to walk by and see full-grown adults watching frogs jump from one lily pad to another, or trains chugging around a track. Almost makes me want to learn algebra again.

Matt Herron

*Robert Scarola*

*(continued from p. 175)*

Within those three overall boundaries I had further criteria for selection. I avoided—and I strongly urge readers to avoid—most programs characterized as "drill and practice," "skill development," "skills reinforcement," and the like. They have titles like LONG DIVISION (Basics & Beyond), or PHONICS 1-3 (SRA), or ELEMENTARY ALGEBRA: POLYNOMIALS (Control Data), or COUNT AND ADD (Edu-Soft), or COUNT 'EM ( Micro-ED), and on and on. They typically use beeps and blats, smiles and frowns, laser shots and flashing signals on the screen to get across a basic right-or-wrong-answer statement in a drill format. They are little more than workbook pages put on a computer screen—a waste of time, energy, and money. They not only distort the value and potential of the computer and misplace its power, they reinforce the idea of computers as routinizing machines. And they make up 95 percent of all learning software programs on the market today. (The comprehensive publication **TESS: The Educational Software Selector**, 1984 edition, published by EPIE Institute and Columbia University Teachers College Press, lists nearly 6000 educational software programs currently on the market, the vast majority of them rote drill and practice programs.)

What I look for, and what I strongly urge you to look for when you shop for learning software (*always* try before you buy!), are programs that are:

● Alive—the program feels good to use. It makes you glad you own a computer and can do what you are doing with it (FACEMAKER, TRAINS, BUBBLE BURST).

● Clean—the program provides clear instructions, easy-to-use documentation, helpful screen menus (GERTRUDE'S SECRETS, BUMBLE GAMES, TEASERS BY TOBBS).

● Transparent—the program makes it easy to see and accomplish its objective (MAGIC SPELLS, EARLY GAMES FOR YOUNG CHILDREN, THE POND, MATH MAZE, LEMONADE).

● Interactive—the program engages attention by responding accurately and imaginatively (SNOOPER TROOPS, MAGIC SPELLS, BAFFLES, THE BASIC PRIMER, MUSIC MASTER).

● Expandable—the program allows itself to be easily modified to suit individual needs and purposes (M__SS__NG L__NKS, MONEY! MONEY!, PICTURE WRITER).

Such software programs I can use for my learning purposes; they don't use me for theirs. They permit things to happen in the world of learning that simply couldn't be done, or couldn't be done as well, in any other medium—things like:

● Simulations actively and accurately modeling an event that might otherwise never be touched upon by most of us (OREGON TRAIL, D-BUG).

● Simulations that might be important for us to practice before we engage the real thing (VOLCANOES, THE SEARCH SERIES, WALL $TREET, SIMULATED COMPUTER).

● Problem-solving experiences presented as a complex reality in a changing microworld under our control (ROCKY'S BOOTS, EARLY GAMES, MAKE-A-MATCH, THE INCREDIBLE LABORATORY, CATLAB).

● Tasks practiced without the fear of failure and made more enjoyable because of a lively and interactive presentation (STALKER, MASTERTYPE, ALGEBRA ARCADE, READER RABBIT, PIECE OF CAKE MATH).

● Creative acts allowed to happen because the computer's powerful ability to control, calculate, store, and retrieve information is made wonderfully accessible (BANK STREET WRITER, KOALAPAINTER/PC DESIGN, DELTA DRAWING, TURTLE TOYLAND, JR., LOGO).

### Hardware

Using this software will not and should not replace reading a book, hiking in the woods, being close with a friend or lover, or any of the tactile, emotional, imaginative, or spiritual experiences we have. But using such software can add significantly to those experiences by providing new ways to learn about life in this postindustrial, prerobotic late twentieth century.

1. If you have the money, buy an Apple IIe or IIc with a color monitor and two disk drives ($1600-1900 total, depending on where you shop). More quality learning software exists for the Apple than for any other computer on the market. The Apple IIe is tremendously versatile and expandable, with literally hundreds of devices and peripherals available to upgrade it as much as your wallet can stand over the years. The Apple is easily repaired—almost every chip on the mother board is socketed for easy removal and replacement. (This contrasts with the cheaper Commodore or Atari, for instance, in which nearly all the chips are dip-soldered to the mother board; if something goes wrong the computer must be either shipped back to the manufacturer or serviced by a professional technician—a cost that can go as high as half the original price of the computer.)

2. A color monitor is a must for using most learning software. You simply won't get as much out of using the programs in black and white if they are simulations, graphics, or adventure programs. With some programs you can't even tell what to do unless the symbols or graphics appear in color on the screen. Amdek and Commodore both make good color monitors at a reasonable price ($300-400). Though home computers all work with standard TV sets, monitors offer far better resolution—more detail in the image. If you do intend to hook up to a color television, you can buy a module for the Apple for about $40 that will do the job. But I would not personally want my children (or myself, for that matter) to sit twelve inches away from a regular color TV set for hours at a time. (For occasional use, however, it is a good cheap way to get access to a color screen.)

3. I suggest two disk drives for your Apple, since you will more than make up for the cost of the second disk drive ($300) quickly because of the ability to make back-up copies of programs. You will also be able to conveniently run a wide range of word-processing and other programs that require a data file disk.

If you are buying the computer for children younger than twelve years old and don't intend to use it yourself for business or writing purposes, or if you can't spring for an Apple, I would recommend next an Atari 800XL or Commodore 64 computer ($200-300). Atari currently leads Commodore in the amount and quality of learning software available, but Commodore is fast catching up. These are both basically "getting started" computers you can use for a year or two and let your kids explore on before you move up to the greater capacity and performance quality of something more expensive. Again, with these computers I strongly recommend the added expense of a color monitor. I would not go to the expense of disk drives for these computers, since many of the learning programs are available in cartridges.

The IBM PC, at around $2000, is mainly a business computer and at this writing has made few inroads on the educational market. Some learning software is being written for it, but the keyboard on the PC is not, in my opinion, as good as that on the much less expensive Commodore. I would not recommend buying it if you are primarily interested in the computer for home learning use. Only time will tell how much learning software will be developed for the IBM or the Apple Macintosh.

A joystick and a printer for any of these computers are great advantages for many learning programs. The joystick gives the learner easy control over the software and saves a lot of excited pounding on keys. Joysticks are inexpensive ($15-20 for Atari and Commodore, $35-75 for Apple; see p. 19) compared with the overall price of the computer or a service call for keyboard repair. Dot matrix printers make possible both graphics and text printouts. I recommend them for most learning uses, since they are faster, cheaper, and more reliable than letter-quality printers (which cannot print graphics), and most teachers will gladly accept papers written in dot matrix typeface. For the Apple, C. Itoh, Epson, Okidata, and especially the new, fast Apple Imagewriter are my favorites (all in the $500-600 range with cable and printer card), but check compatability with your software. Commodore and Atari both make their own brand-name printers, which sell for $300-400 and plug into a port on the computer, thus eliminating the need for a printer card and cable.

For starting cheap, you can get a complete starter system with Apple equipment including one disk drive and a color monitor (but no printer) for around $1300-1500. A comparable system for Commodore or Atari would cost about $1000-1200. If you forget about the disk drive on the Commodore or Atari and stick with cartridges, you can cut the price of your system by $300-400. Skip the monitor and use a TV, and you're under $400.

### *Magazines*

ROBERT SCAROLA: In the last five years alone, dozens of magazines have been published on learning with computers. It would take another section of the **Catalog** to sort out the useful wheat from the esoteric chaff. Next time around. For now, a few favorites, a few classics, and a few just worth knowing about.

**Classroom Computer Learning** [$15.95/yr (9 issues); Pittman Learning, Inc., 19 Davis Drive, Belmont, CA 94002]. High-quality articles and reports that have changed my views on learning software.

**Electronic Learning** [$19.00/yr (8 issues); Scholastic, Inc., 730 Broadway, New York, NY 10003]. In-depth coverage of new ideas, methods, and technologies; particularly useful for keeping current.

**ENTER** [$22.95/yr (10 issues); ENTER, One Disk Drive, P.O. Box 2686, Boulder, CO 80322]. Its name carries the theme of the magazine—gives primary grade children a wonderful entrance into the world of computers.

**DIGIT** [$12/yr (6 issues); DIGIT, Customer Service Dept., P.O. Box 27958, San Diego, CA 92128]. For teenage would-be hackers and programmers—a great "how-to" resource.

**Popular Computing** [$15/yr (12 issues); Popular Computing, Subscriber Service, P.O. Box 328, Hancock, NH 03449]. The **Popular Mechanics** of the computer world, it has everything from latest product news to lengthy technical articles (plus plenty of ads from manufacturers of hardware, software, and underwear in the burgeoning computer industry).

**Softalk** [$24/yr (12 issues); Softalk Publishing, Inc., 7250 Laurel Canyon Blvd., North Hollywood, CA 91605]. The all-encompassing source of what's new, nifty, and next for Apple owners. I own an Apple IIe and wouldn't be without this one.

### *Books*

ROBERT SCAROLA: Doing justice to what's out there is a hopeless task. I give up. Here are a few "classics":

**Mindstorms (Children, Computers and Powerful Ideas)** [Seymour Papert; 1980; 230 pp.; $15.95; Basic Books, Inc., 10 East 53rd Street, New York, NY 10022; 800/638-3030]. The bible of LOGO, and, for that matter, the unmatched visionary statement of the potential of learning with computers. This is a revolutionary manual on how to think about thinking.

**Apple LOGO** [Harold Abelson; 1982; 240 pp.; $14.95; BYTE/McGraw-Hill, Order Services, Manchester Road, Manchester, MO 63011; 314/227-1600, ext. 423]. A practical guide to the intricacies of LOGO presented by one of the masters.

**Discovering Apple LOGO (An Invitation to the Art and Pattern of Nature)** [David Thornburg; 1983; 145 pp.; $14.95; Addison-Wesley Publishing Co., Reading, MA 01867; 617/944-3700]. A wonderful exploration of the tie-in of LOGO graphics programming with the patterns of nature that underlie our existence.

**Learning with LOGO** [Daniel Watt; 1983; 365 pp.; McGraw-Hill Publishing Co., 1221 Avenue of the Americas, New York, NY 10020; 609/426-5254]. Presents many practical problems and possibilities for using and playing with LOGO in a tested, clear, usable format.

**Computer Literacy, A Hands-On Approach** [Arthur Luehrmann and Herbert Peckham; Apple II family; 32K; TRS-80 III, IV; 32K; $31.96 for disk and book; $13.28 for disk only; $6 school discount; copy-protected? NO; McGraw-Hill, 1221 Avenue of the Americas, New York, NY 10020; 800/223-4180]. Probably the best overall guide to discovering what computer literacy is through the achievement of it. Conceived and written by wise, thoughtful, twinkling scholars.

**Instant (Freeze-Dried Computer Programming in) BASIC** [Jerald R. Brown; 2nd edition, 1982; 200 pp.; dilithium Press, P.O. Box 606, Beaverton, OR 97075; 800/547-1842]. Clear, clean, readable, with appealing cartoons and clever graphics. What can I say? It's the one I learned on and it's still my BASIC favorite.

I will tread the turbid waters of magazines and books no further. If you need more help, I suggest a letter or phone call to the compassionate people at Computer Literacy Books and Magazines (520 N. Lawrence Expressway, Sunnyvale, CA 94086; 408/730-9955.) If they can't help you probably no one can. They carry every book reviewed in this **Catalog** and will take phone orders.

## WHOLE EARTH RECOMMENDED LEARNING TOOLS

### (June 1984)

MILLIKEN WORD PROCESSOR, $69.95, p.178
LEMONADE, $7.95/$48, p.179
OREGON TRAIL, $10 or trade/$49, p.179
SIMULATED COMPUTER, $29.95, p.179
T.REX, $50, p.179
THE HONEY FACTORY, $50, p.179
D-BUG, $35, p.180
TRAINS, $39.95, p.180
VOLCANOES, $50, p.180
SEARCH SERIES, $180/$240 each, p.181
JUKEBOX, $39.95, p.181
ALF IN THE COLOR CAVES, $39.95, p.181
BUBBLE BURST, $39.95, p.181
WALL $TREET, $24.95, p.182
SNOOPER TROOPS CASE #2: THE
    DISAPPEARING DOLPHIN, $50, p.182
TEASERS BY TOBBS, $49, p.182
MONEY! MONEY!, $39.95, p.182
APPLE BARREL, $10 or trade, p.182
STALKER, $10 or trade, p.182
THE POND: EXPLORATIONS IN PROBLEM
    SOLVING, $49, p.183

MAKE-A-MATCH, $29.95, p.183
THE BASIC PRIMER, $60, p.183
BANK STREET WRITER, $70/$80, p.184
M_SS_NG L_NKS: A GAME OF LETTERS
    AND LANGUAGE, $29.95/$59, p.184
KOALAPAD AND KOALA SOFTWARE,
    $100/$150, p.184
COLORING SERIES I, $29.95, p.184
PIECE OF CAKE MATH, $34.95, p.185
FRACTION FACTORY, $29.95, p.185
MUSIC MASTER, $34.95, p.185
CATLAB, $75, p.185
THE INCREDIBLE LABORATORY,
    $49, p.185
ALLIGATOR ALLEY, $44, p.186
ALIEN ADDITION, $44, p.186
DRAGON MIX, $44, p.186
METEOR MISSION, $44, p.186
VERB VIPER, $44, p.186
WIZ WORKS, $44, p.186
WORDMAN, $44, p.186

STICKYBEAR ABC, $39.95, p.186
STICKYBEAR NUMBERS, $39.95, p.186
STICKYBEAR OPPOSITES, $39.95, p.186
STICKYBEAR SHAPES, $39.95, p.186
ADDITION MAGICIAN, $34.95, p.186
NUMBER STUMPER, $39.95, p.186
READER RABBIT, $39.95, p.186
WORD SPINNER, $34.95, p.186
BAFFLES, $50, p.187
MASTERTYPE, $39.95/$50, p.187
GERTRUDE'S SECRETS, $45, p.188
BUMBLE GAMES, $39.95, p.188
PICTUREWRITER, $39.95, p.188
ROCKY'S BOOTS, $50, p.188
MAGIC SPELLS, $34.95, p.189
DELTA DRAWING, $39.95/$50, p.189
ALGEBRA ARCADE, $50, p.190
FACEMAKER, $29.95/$34.95, p.190
MATH MAZE, $39.95, p.190
LOGO, various prices, p.191
TURTLE TOYLAND, JR., $34.95, p.191

## TYRANNY OF THE NEW

ROBERT SCAROLA: The wheeled robots commercially available today can't discuss the weather with you, let alone save you from cosmic evil (as in **Star Wars** or **Battlestar Galactica**). But they can move independently, perform simple tasks, remember instructions, and even predict situations. These robots represent a significant servomotor step beyond the industrial robotic arms that perform routine picking, sorting, and welding tasks.

In April '84 I lucked out. RB Robot Corporation agreed to lend me an RB5X robot to use in my classroom for a month. I brought RB5X onto the K-8 school playground to cries of "Oh, my God, what *is* it?" and "I thought it was a vacuum cleaner!" The children nervously gathered around, half expecting to see Jawas and their Droid collector appearing over the horizon.

RB5X is a 30-inch-tall, 16-inch-wide, three-wheeled metal and plastic cylinder with a clear domed top. It has a speech synthesizer and can be programmed using an Apple computer with a super serial card (a LOGO translator package is currently being developed). It also has a built-in sonar detector ("Ex-cuse-me," it mutters when bumping into something) and an optional movable arm capable of picking up light objects.

The children loved programming RB (as they called him/her/it) to wheel around the classroom, lights blinking, motor whirring, arm extended, following a chalk line drawn on the floor. They learned quickly and unforgettably that even marvelous mechanical wonders of the late twentieth century operate according to programmed instructions that they could write.

I'm convinced that this kind of learning exploration is one of the major uses for robots like RB5X (another is cleaning house). Obviously, it will take a few more turns of the technological gears before robots become cheap enough for most schools and the likes of you and me . . . but then look what happened to computers.

**RB5X Robot; $2295; with options, $5,000; RB Robot Corporation, 18301 West 10th Avenue, Suite 310, Golden, CO 80401; 303/279-5525.**

Just as the **Catalog** goes to bed, Milliken Publishing Company has announced a word processor that appears to combine the best of HOMEWORD (p. 52) with the best of BANK STREET WRITER (p. 184), including features such as graphic icons for easy access, document editing without switching to an editing mode, typeface selection, and no disk dependency (boot up, remove the disk, and load another Apple or store the disk), freeing the disk drive for your data file disk. We'd like to hear from people using this program with children.

**MILLIKEN WORD PROCESSOR; Apple II family, 48K; copy-protected? YES; $69.95; Milliken Publishing Co., Computer Products Division, 1100 Research Blvd., P.O. Box 21679, St. Louis, MO 63132; 314/991-4220.**

*Old-timers with class . . .*

## LEMONADE

**Age level 7 to adult; Apple II family (ELEMENTARY VOLUME 3); disk drive; $48 ● Atari (THE MARKET PLACE); $46; MECC, 3490 Lexington Avenue North, Saint Paul, MN 55112; 612/481-3660 ● Commodore 64; cassette $14.95; disk (BUSINESS); $7.95; Commodore Computer Club, Commodore Business Machines, 1200 Wilson Drive, West Chester, PA 19380; 215/436-4200.**

## OREGON TRAIL

**John Cook; age level 7 to adult; Apple II family (ELEMENTARY VOLUME 6); disk drive ● Atari (EXPEDITIONS); 48K; $49; MECC, 3490 Lexington Avenue North, Saint Paul MN 55112; 612/481-3500. Or Apple Dissemination Disk #1; ● Commodore PET Dissemination Disk #6; $10/disk *or* free exchange: contribute your *original* program *on a disk* and they will send you one free disk of your choice; SOFTSWAP; Computer-Using Educators, San Mateo County Office of Education, 333 Main Street, Redwood City, CA 94063; 415/363-5472; (send $1 for their listing of program dissemination disks; they have hundreds of programs available (7-10 programs/disk) for Apple, Commodore Pet, Atari, TRS-80, and IBM PC computers).**

ROBERT SCAROLA: Somehow you have to begin getting your hands on software when you get bitten by the computer bug. Nowadays you can go to your local software dealer with your MasterCard and hock your future. Five or six years ago that was not the case. What software existed was pretty much passed around by users. And a lot of it was in the public domain. People wrote it for the fun of it, to make something new happen, not just to get rich. There are a few survivors of that time well worth knowing about, even though the graphics may seem outdated compared with the current cutting edge of software development, and even though there is no elegant packaging or grand promises.

LEMONADE and OREGON TRAIL were both created in 1979. They are classics—kind of like early Chaplin films. Some versions have passed into the public domain under different names—SELL LEMONADE and OREGON are common variations.

LEMONADE simulates the child's summertime activity of selling cool glasses of lemonade from a front-yard stand. The program has simple graphics depicting the kind of day it is—sunny, cloudy, rainy, etc.— and asks the learner to calculate the price of a glass of lemonade based on the cost of ingredients, the expected market, and available capital. The object, of course, is to make a profit. And, since two can play, you even get a chance to compete with that little twerp down the street. It's all done very sweetly—a lot like a parent would do who was helping a child set up such a stand.

I still like to play this game and so do a lot of adults I know. Especially when they allow themselves to let go of being adults.

The same is true of OREGON TRAIL. It showed lots of us the potential of learning software. There are minimal graphics in the public domain version I have—mostly just words that tell a story. You have to imagine that you are traveling the famous Oregon Trail with the early settlers. You have a stake to spend on various goods and equipment, and you must choose your purchases wisely at the beginning in order to make it all the way to the Pacific Coast. You get to hunt along the way by "shooting" with your joystick at a little stick creature on the screen. You might be attacked by Indians, starve, get sick, make it to a safe fort, and so on. All of the choices and most of the action are posed or described in words that appear on the screen.

OREGON TRAIL might be dull by today's graphics standards, but it is still worth knowing about for someone just getting into learning software because the plot is good, the challenge realistically presented, and the learning value of solving problems and making calculations to get West is high. Many programs being created today are not nearly as well done as either OREGON TRAIL or LEMONADE.

*Great graphics, scientifically correct . . .*

## T. REX
## THE HONEY FACTORY

**KERON Productions; Apple II, II + , 48K ● Apple IIc, 128K ● Apple IIe, 64K ● Commodore 64 ● IBM PC; copy-protected? YES; $50 each; CBS Software, 1 Fawcett Place, Greenwich, CT 06936; 203/622-2500.**

RICHARD DALTON: T. REX is a new direction for animated programs you maneuver with a joystick. This new focus is on simulation of natural science environments where you get to live out the daily challenges of being a dinosaur . . . or act as manager of a beehive (THE HONEY FACTORY).

Dinosaurs had a tougher time than you imagine. *Tyrannosaurus rex* had to wrestle with: water supplies; where to find other dinos to feed on (and conserve energy while tracking 'em down); the ambient temperature; and even whether the terrain he crossed could support his bulky body. If that doesn't sound tough, then why did they disappear?

KERON Productions, Inc., developers of T. REX, leave that answer to you as you maneuver the beast through environments they have created with scrupulous scientific accuracy. That's what simulations are all about and why personal computers are becoming more interesting—they can provide experiences that aren't possible any other way.

KERON's second program, THE HONEY FACTORY, offers four levels to match the skills of neophyte through expert honey producers. Natural hazards (like hungry birds) get increasingly difficult to cope with, too. Additional realistic simulations are expected from KERON and CBS.

*Here's* Tyrannosaurus rex *in his prehistoric home futilely pursuing dinner (he started the attack too far away). Players learn this costs energy without increasing food intake—shown graphically at the bottom of the screen.*

*The visible program . . .*

## SIMULATED COMPUTER

**Scott Steketee; age level: 12 and up; Apple II family; 48K ● Atari; 32K ● Commodore 64; 1 disk drive; copy-protected? NO; $29.95; EduSoft, P.O. Box 2560, Berkeley, CA 94702; 800/227-2778 or, in CA, 415/548-2304.**

JIM FRENCH: SIMULATED COMPUTER is the perfect introduction to the concepts involved in the inner workings of a computer. This program does not teach machine language or hexadecimal notation (those esoteric terms that refer to the on/off switching sequence by which the computer sends electronic signals

that transfer information). Instead, it uses the familiar decimal system to present graphically the components of the central processing unit (or CPU, the "brain" of the computer)—the accumulator, program counter, and instruction register. A limited number (twenty) of memory locations, instruction codes, and execution modes allow you to type in and then run simple programs while watching the whole process of fetching, incrementing, executing, and outputting your commands.

For the first time, using this program, I felt I really understood how it all works!

Follow Charlie Fix-it on the trail of the bug in the Central Processing Unit (CPU) of your computer. But keep an eye out for that chip-blowing enemy— Static Electricity! D-BUG is an in-depth, challenging (even enlightening) course in how computers work and how to fix the damn things when they don't.

*A computer fix-it game . . .*

## D-BUG

**Ramon Zamora; age level: 10 and up; Atari 400/800/XL, 48K • Commodore 64; 1 disk drive; copy-protected? YES; $35; Electronic Arts, 2755 Campus Drive, San Mateo, CA 94403.**

ROBERT SCAROLA: D-BUG has the unique format of a simple game overlying a complex, detailed, accurate, and colorful schematic of the inner workings of a computer. You team up with a computer repair technician—Charlie Fixit—and crawl inside your computer to make needed repairs.

You begin D-BUG with a simple game called Gotch-a, in which you and an opponent alternately trap bugs in a box on the screen. But at a random moment as you play, a problem (bug) occurs in the operating system of the computer, and it is up to you to travel into the guts of the computer (nicely imaged on the screen) and "repair" the problem with the assistance of Charlie Fixit.

As you make repairs and move back and forth from the game to the insides of the computer you learn not only a great deal about how a computer works—operations of its components, names of parts, etc.—but also about cause and effect and problem solving.

For me, playing D-BUG was something like a refresher course in computer repair. I had to find out what was wrong—faulty chips, bad connections, clogged fans—while avoiding that worst of all computer enemies: zzzzzzzzt—static electricity. When I succeeded I went back to the normal operations of my repaired machine and heaved a sigh of relief.

Thank God computers don't develop bugs as often as they breed in D-BUG. I would be completely bald from pulling my hair out. If your child masters this program he or she can probably make more money than you can.

*Railroading in the Old West . . .*

## TRAINS

**Eric Podietz, Guy Nouri; age level: 8 and up; Atari 800XL, 48K • Commodore 64; 1 disk drive; color required; copy-protected? YES; $39.95; Spinnaker Software Corp., 215 First Street, Cambridge, MA 02142; 617/868-4700.**

One of those rare simulations that's accurate, engaging and graphically excellent. You can start your travels on any Old West route you choose. Just remember, the higher the number, the harder the route and the better you have to be at managing time and money.

ROBERT SCAROLA: TRAINS presents a simulation of railroading in the Old West, complete with wonderful sound, graphics, and miniature steam engines. It also teaches basic principles of economics.

TRAINS has the catchiest musical/graphics introduction of any piece of software on the market—it immediately puts you in a mood to ride a train. Only you're the one running the railroad. You have to service industries in the Old West with your trains, moving from the easiest level to the hardest. On each of the eight levels you have a new track layout, new scenery, and a larger territory, complete with plains, mountains, deserts, cities, and drifting clouds.

It is up to you to manage the railroad's money: set priorities and meet deadlines in order to get ore from the mine to the factory or lumber from the forest to the sawmill. As you use your resources to meet the needs of the various industries, you can build new sections of track for your railroad and advance to the next level of the game. On the other hand, you can lose money and track by not fulfilling industry demands. And when you're out of money and coal, you're out of business and the game is over.

Plan your route, toot your whistle (sounds just like a model train whistle), watch your market update, keep your coal dry, stay on the track and don't crash, and play TRAINS. It's a great learning simulation for anyone who likes steam engines and railroading.

*Scientific method . . .*

## VOLCANOES

**Age level: 12-adult; Apple II family; 48K; 1 disk drive; copy-protected? YES; $50; Earthware Computer Services, P.O. Box 30039, Eugene, OR 97403; 503/344-3383.**

JIM FRENCH: VOLCANOES is a classic simulation that works best with groups but can also work with the individual learner. In VOLCANOES students study, conduct various scientific investigations, and make predictions of likely volcanic eruptions in a mythical land called Wrangelia. Both the software program and the support materials promote an understanding of the scientific method of inquiry and deduction, and both develop skills in record keeping and priority budgeting.

A player can gain a thorough understanding of the types of volcanic activity and methods of investigation with this well-thought-out simulation. As in real life, unpredictable events occur randomly that affect the playing of the game, including foul weather and a chance meeting with Bigfoot. I found VOLCANOES fascinating; it increased my own knowledge of what volcanists study and how they study it. Interacting with the software is easy, and the support materials include an excellent bibliography along with pre- and post-tests for students.

*Group explorations . . .*

## SEARCH SERIES

Tom Snyder Productions; age level: 10 to adult; Apple II family; 48K ● TRS-80 Models III, 4; 32K; disk drive; copy-protected? YES; $240 each ($180 with school discount); McGraw-Hill Book Co., Webster Division, 1221 Avenue of the Americas, New York, NY 10020; 800/223-4180; modules available: Geology, Geography, Community, Archaeology, Energy.

JIM FRENCH: In the SEARCH series for geology, geography, community, archaeology, or energy, while the subject matter is different in each program, all share features that make them unique and unparalleled in learning software. Each simulation can be played by a single learner, but they are vastly more effective and fun in a group situation. I have run several of the simulations with as many as 40 adults at a time with great success and much glee.

The five programs all have the same organizational format. The group of learners is first divided into subgroups of three to six people. Each subgroup must accomplish a task, such as navigate a ship in search of new lands and riches (GEOGRAPHY SEARCH), manage a power-producing utility (ENERGY SEARCH), find a new homeland for the tribe (COMMUNITY SEARCH), and so on.

The unique feature of all the programs is that the information given on the computer is only on the monitor screen for a short 30 seconds or so, forcing a collective/cooperative effort on the part of the participants to gather quickly the information needed to make their decisions. As the action proceeds, the computer announces various random events, such as attack by pirates, drought, or other disasters. In some of the programs interaction among subgroups is possible. If poor decisions are made your team can miss turns, lose money, fail in its task, or go bust and be out of the game.

All of this creates an atmosphere of great excitement and interest, in which an unusual amount of learning takes place. Ideally, a classroom teacher would use lots of supplementary activities and information with each program. The publishers of the SEARCH series make this easy by supplying with each package a set of workbooks that introduce the situation and provide glossaries, record-keeping forms, and reading material with background information. A teaching manual describing suggested activities to enrich the presentation is also included. (However, I recommend as little "teaching" intervention as possible.)

The one drawback for this exciting educational product is its price—$180 for each program in the series. Even though each comes with 20 workbooks and a teaching manual, the cost will discourage many people from acquiring a fine piece of learning software.

*No reading skills required . . .*

## JUKEBOX

Joyce Hakansson Associates; Atari; 16K ● Commodore 64; joystick; disk or cartridge; copy-protected? YES; $39.95;

## ALF IN THE COLOR CAVES

Joyce Hakansson Associates; age level 3-6; Commodore 64; joystick recommended; disk or cartridge; copy-protected? YES; $39.95;

## BUBBLE BURST

Joyce Hakansson Associates; age level: 4-8; Atari; 16K ● Commodore 64; joystick recommended; disk or cartridge; copy-protected? YES; $39.95;

all from: Spinnaker Software; 1 Kendall Square, Cambridge, MA 02139; 617/494-1200.

ROBERT SCAROLA: I know that Joyce Hakansson Associates—a team of artists, writers, educators, and programmers in Berkeley, California—had to have the help of children to design these programs. It's the only way they could have devised programs that are so colorful, musical, easy to use, appealing, and at the same so instructive in important early-learning concepts like direction, comparison, and interpretation.

The three programs are intended for very young learners, five to seven years old. In JUKEBOX the child tries to win gold records by moving as efficiently as possible from square to square on a simulated jukebox, with each move adding another record sale. In ALF IN THE COLOR CAVES the child moves a charming character named ALF down a variety of color lanes to match colors. And in BUBBLE BURST the child tries to stop the Zeboingers from breaking his or her bubbles by coordinating the direction and movement of a special bubble that can carry the Zeboingers away.

A fascinating aspect of these programs is that they are played with a joystick, have no written directions, and require no reading skills whatsoever. Yet their workings are easy for preschool children to grasp, the action is completely in the child's control, and the results are open-ended, without a hint of the old right/wrong carrot/stick mentality.

Joyce and her team are out there working like scholarly Santa's helpers. Expect to see many more exceptional learning software programs from this group.

*The time pressure is on to be efficient and coordinate eye/screen, hand/joystick movements to get from square to square. You can win a gold record if you're fast on your feet and find the pattern that collects the most records. Point those dancing shoes and try to jump your way into solid gold fame and fortune.*

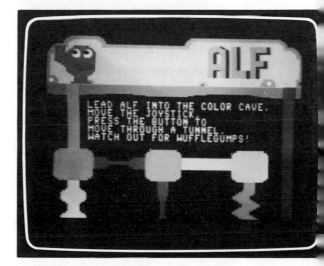

*Alf is no slouch when it comes to moving through the different colors and shapes in the color caves. When you finish steering him through the caves he'll do a little dance for you and zip back up to the top so you can play all over again. Very young children will get their matching skills exercised herding Alf around.*

*Heads Up! Here come two Zeboingers to burst your bubbles. Move the large clear bubble around with your joystick and you can disappear the diving Zeboingers and keep your bubble bath going. Pre-schoolers' eye/hand coordination and sense of direction get a lot of lively practice.*

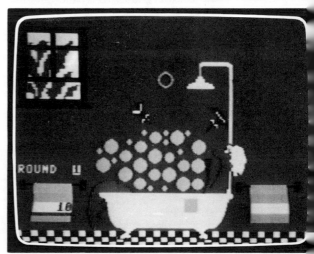

Socially approved gambling . . .

## WALL $TREET

**Age level: 10-adult; Apple II family; 48K ● Apple III in emulation mode; copy-protected? YES; $24.95; CE Software, 801 73rd Street, Des Moines, IA 50312; 515/224-1995.**

PAT BUCK: If you like Monopoly and acquiring fortunes you'll love WALL $TREET. From one to nine players can play, though one to four is the ideal number to avoid cumbersome complications. Each player starts the game with $10,000, using it to buy/sell 18 stocks in utilities, communications, oil, or manufacturing industries with real names— Apple, General Motors, RCA, and so on. The winner is the entrepreneur who accumulates the first $1,000,000, has the most money at the end of the game, or goes bankrupt last.

You control the action at all times. You buy, sell, take out loans, and get tips about the next day's market (for a price) while performing calculations and making investments. The program lacks explosive graphic displays, but more than makes up for it by accurately representing the up and down challenges of real world stock market investing.

Detective skills . . .

## SNOOPER TROOPS

## CASE #2: THE DISAPPEARING DOLPHIN

**Tom Snyder Productions; age level: 10-adult; Apple II family; 48K ● Atari; 48K ● Commodore 64 ● IBM PC compatibles; 64K; disk drive; color monitor recommended; copy-protected? YES; $50; Spinnaker Software, 1 Kendall Square, Cambridge, MA 02139; 617/494-1200.**

ROBERT SCAROLA: Kids have a natural love for solving mysteries, and the SNOOPER TROOPS series by Spinnaker gives them the opportunity to play detective and use mapping skills to hunt down suspected criminals. The series goes far beyond duplicating a board game like Probe by making special use of the animating and interactive abilities of the computer.

CLAIRE ANN GOULD: In SNOOPER TROOPS Case 2 you are assigned to crack the Case of the Disappearing Dolphin. Someone has stolen Lily right out of her pool and it is up to you to find the culprit. You have a manual to assist you with your record keeping of times, dates, and places as you engage in your search, questioning witnesses and suspects in the sleepy town of Costa Villa. The program uses the computer's capabilities for excellent graphics, sound effects, and information storage and retrieval to teach you mapping, note-taking, classifying, organizing, and reasoning skills while you seek a confession from Lily's kidnapper.

Thinking about numbers . . .

## TEASERS BY TOBBS

**Dr. Thomas C. O'Brien; age level: 8-adult; Apple II family; 48K ● Atari; 16K● TRS-80 Color Computer; 32K; ● TRS-80 Models I, III, 4; 16K; copy-protected? YES; $49; Sunburst Communications, Inc., 39 Washington Ave., Pleasantville, NY 10570; 800/431-1934.**

JIM FRENCH: This award-winning software promotes the best use of the computer. In a game format, with a character named Tobbs, the program reinforces arithmetic skills of a very high order in a way that is greatly superior to textbooks.

The program begins by presenting the players (as many as four) an arena for practicing addition and multiplication problems with sums and products of less than 100. This takes place on a simple grid. However, the students encounter six stepped-up levels of complexity, so by level 4 they have to begin working backwards to solve problems. This, of course, introduces in a very intriguing way the concepts of subtraction and division. Learners must begin making distinctions among what "must be, can be, and can't be . . ." and construct quite complex chains of thought to develop answers. The computer provides the format, generates random numbers, checks responses, and keeps records of correct answers. Real thinking skills are developed rather than mere rote memory.

I recommend this program highly, along with an excellent extension of it called TOBBS LEARNS ALGEBRA.

Civilization's basic skill . . .

## MONEY! MONEY!

**Jane Hartley; age level: 7-10; Apple II family; 48K; disk drive; copy-protected? YES; $39.95; Hartley Courseware, Inc., P.O. Box 419, Dimondale, MI 48821; 517/646-6458.**

AL MANN: Easy to use, imaginative, and effective, MONEY! MONEY! teaches a student to become proficient with money in fifteen lessons that move from recognizing and adding coins to buying from a clerk and counting change. The lessons begin with vocabulary reviews, and all have diverse and interesting scenarios. This package is ideal for working with disabled individuals (such as I am) because it contains a "mini-authoring" system that gives access to the graphics and enables a parent or teacher easily to design a lesson that meets a specific need. A record of each student's score is maintained for planning purposes, and limits can be placed on a program to reduce frustration or boredom.

For trade or $10 . . .

## APPLE BARREL

## STALKER

**Age level: 5 and up; both on Apple Dissemination Disk #9; 32K; disk drive; Integer BASIC; copy-protected? NO; $10/disk or free exchange: contribute your original program on a disk and they will send you one free disk of your choice; SOFTSWAP; Computer-Using Educators, San Mateo County Office of Education, 333 Main Street, Redwood City, CA 94063; 415/363-5472; (send $1 for their listing of program dissemination disks; they have hundreds of programs available [7-10 programs/disk] for Apple, Commodore Pet, Atari, TRS-80 and IBM PC computers).**

ROBERT SCAROLA: One of the best things learning software can do is take the drill out of "drill and practice." APPLE BARREL and STALKER are two early programs (1979) written with that intent.

Best of all, both are available from SOFTSWAP, a service for the barter of learning software programs (an original program of yours for a disk of their programs) or the purchase from their stock of programs for a minimal fee ($10 per disk). SOFTSWAP is part of Computer-Using Educators (CUE), an organization located at the San Mateo County Office of Education, in Redwood City, California. Much of SOFTSWAP's material does not meet current commercial software standards, but all of it is inexpensive, easily available, and a rich initial resource for someone just beginning to explore the learning possibilities of computer software.

APPLE BARREL offers practice in estimation by presenting an image of a wooden barrel on the screen that is randomly filled with apples (you can control the size of the barrel but not the final number of apples). Your job is to guess the number of apples in the barrel, with the computer hinting whether you are too high or too low. Eventually, when you get the answer, Farmer John sends you a greeting.

STALKER offers more of a game format. *After* you correctly answer a basic arithmetic problem in addition, subtraction, multiplication, or division, you compete with another player for the use of a color-coded fighter you then use to run into and destroy the appropriate Stalker marching across the screen. You select the level of difficulty by rank, from Private to General. The graphics are really excellent, and the play of the game, which is more cartoon than arcade in feeling, reinforces the learning of basic math calculations.

I like to point out to budding teenage programmers that STALKER was written by a fifteen-year-old student at the California School for the Deaf.

*Discovering patterns . . .*

## THE POND: EXPLORATIONS IN PROBLEM SOLVING

**Marge Kosel & Mike Fish; age level: 7-adult; Apple II family; 48K ● Atari (except 800XL); 32K; color ● Commodore 64 ● IBM PC compatibles; 64K; color graphics card ● TRS-80 Color Computer; copy-protected? YES; $49; Sunburst Communications, Inc., 39 Washington Ave., Pleasantville, NY 10570; 800/431-1934. Commodore and Atari versions also available from HesWare, 150 North Hill Drive, Brisbane, CA 94005; 415/468-4111.**

GEORGE RADDUE: Kids *love* this program. It's what I've been looking for: a concentrated activity that aims at building and honing an ability to detect and use pattern and sequence—that is, discovering logical steps in the solution of a problem.

In my primary school science classes much of our work is the construction of gadgets that exemplify concepts in the physical, biological, and behavioral sciences. Although these activities build critical thinking skills, most of the children I teach have had no prior experiences that help develop the concept of "knowing what to do next," and this inability poses one of my greatest challenges in helping the children construct their projects.

In THE POND, the goal is to learn a chosen pattern of lily pads well enough to program the leaps of a friendly frog from pad to pad without having him jump into the water (at which point he swims back to the beginning, and you have to start all over again). There is a practice mode for very young users and a more conceptual programming mode for older users. In the advanced mode, after a view of the presented pattern, the player must remember the number of leaps and their direction so the frog can make it to the final lily pad.

Last week I used THE POND with 160 kids from kindergarten through third grade. The kindergarten children had no difficulty using the program in the practice mode. The older children loved using their greater ability to decipher patterns in the programming mode. In one or another mode or difficulty level, the program was just right for all 160 little tigers.

There are two small problems: the player selects numbers by moving a cursor over a number on the screen rather than by pushing a number key—confusing for all the kids— and the instructions for how to leave the program and return to the main menu are hidden on the last page of the manual. But those problems are easily corrected and detract not at all from my strong feeling that this is the kind of learning software I've been waiting for.

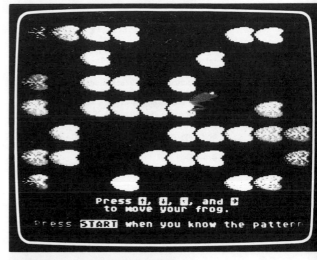

*That grinning frog is waiting to see if you've forgotten the pattern of lily pads and are going to dump him in the drink. With practice you can get him all the way to that great pink lily pad in the lake. If you make it, you just learned a lot about predicting, sequence and logical ordering (not to mention the rudiments of programming).*

---

*A magic electronic book . . .*

## THE BASIC PRIMER

**IBM PC/XT compatibles; 64K; copy-protected? NO; $60; IBM Customer Relations, P. O. Box 1328, Boca Raton, FL 33432; 800/447-4700.**

JIM STOCKFORD: You should learn BASIC. There are lots of terrific little programs out there on the bulletin boards, in books, available from user groups and libraries, nearly all written in BASIC. It is, after all, the lingua franca of the computer world. THE BASIC PRIMER is an excellent interactive tutorial for learning BASIC on the IBM PC. The software is presented as a magic electronic book.

Open the book to the table of contents and page through the lessons or refer to the extensive index by means of simple keystrokes on the computer. Each book lesson presents one concept of programming and a simple practice exercise. You then leave the tutorial, use BASIC in the computer to program for real, and return to the next lesson. It's the only tutorial I've found that provides this "exit to BASIC" feature.

As you page your way through the book, simple concepts build on each other and become more powerful. By the end you have the rudiments of BASIC programming firmly in your grasp and a feeling that you wish there were more, more! (There is more on BASIC on page 162.)

---

*Shapes, sizes, colors . . .*

## MAKE-A-MATCH

**Jane Adolf & Charles Brody; age level: 2-6; Apple II family; 48K ● Atari; 16K ● Commodore 64 ● IBM PC compatibles; 64K; color graphics card ● IBM PCjr; disk or cassette; copy-protected? YES; $29.95; Springboard Software, Inc., 7807 Creekridge Circle, Minneapolis, MN 55435; 800/328-1223.**

JIM FRENCH: A beautifully designed piece of software. This apparently simple program thoroughly engaged me as I worked my way through its various levels of complexity. The disk contains two types of problems. The first are matching problems using shapes and colors. The second are grouping/classification exercises using sizes and shapes.

Matching games begin at a very simple level; one matches a moving colored square with another of the same color. The child need only press a key on the keyboard or button on the paddles or joystick to make a correct match. If the child makes an error the computer gently demonstrates the correction and, if the learner is having trouble, adjusts the difficulty level. From this simple beginning the child can work through nine levels of color matching involving three shades of red, green, or blue, each with subtle variations.

One important feature of this "levels" approach is that the learner controls the response speed and jumps over the easy parts to more challenging material. I found I wanted to try all levels in order to gain insight into how children think about color discrimination.

The shape-matching level is even more useful and challenging, since here the child learns recognition skills needed for reading. You begin by matching basic shapes (circles, squares, etc.) and proceed to arrows with different orientations, faces with tiny differences of features (for instance, one arched eyebrow or a missing nose), boxes divided into segments, and easily confused letters such as d, b, and p.

Likewise, the grouping/classification problems go through levels of complexity, until eventually the child is classifying such shapes as circles, ovals, pyramids, and triangles of various sizes and degrees. The player does not even need to be able to read. A picture menu allows the child to control the choices while the program invisibly leads him or her to more and more discriminating tasks, giving what I call "soft" feedback for either errors or correct responses.

This is a top-notch early-learning program.

## BANK STREET WRITER

**Apple, Atari and Commodore versions by Intentional Educations, Inc., The Bank Street College of Education, and Franklin E. Smith; IBM PC version by Bank Street College of Education, Franklin E. Smith; age level: 8-adult; Apple II family; 48K ● Apple IIc; 128K ● Atari; 48K ● Commodore 64; $70 ● IBM PC compatibles; 64K (PC DOS 2.0, 128K) ● IBM PCjr; PC DOS 2.1; 128K; $80; copy-protected? YES; Broderbund Software, Inc., 17 Paul Drive, San Rafael, CA 94901; 415/479-1170.**

ROBERT SCAROLA: BANK STREET WRITER is not the most powerful word-processing program, nor the most versatile, nor the cheapest. But I believe it is one of the easiest to use if you are just beginning to learn word processing.

There are several reasons for BANK STREET WRITER's ease of use:

● A convenient, simple, and effective screen menu that lets you give commands quickly.

● The key to the program is the Escape (ESC) key—it gives you complete control over menus and functions. When in doubt just Escape and you will never find yourself lost in the backwaters of mysterious functions.

● Basic word processing functions—erase/unerase, move/moveback, find/replace, save/retrieve/delete files, print draft/final copy, initialize disks, clear screen—are smoothly incorporated into the work screen.

● The flip side of the disk contains a tutorial to introduce you to the program.

● You get a back-up disk with your purchase (by the way, don't buy the Scholastic version—it's much more expensive and comes with a completely unnecessary manual).

● BANK STREET WRITER is not disk-dependent, as are, for instance, both HOMEWORD and APPLE WRITER IIe. So you can load the program in one or several computers (if you are teaching word processing) and then remove the master disk and put it away for safekeeping. With other word processing programs the program disk must remain in the disk drive (so in effect you must have two disk drives—one for the program disk and one for your data disk), because the program periodically refers to it.

Eventually you will want to move beyond BANK STREET WRITER (for instance, see review of HOMEWORD by Stewart Brand on page 52). You'll want to be able to select typeface, underline, play more with margins, be able to store more text in memory, erase or move more than fifteen lines at a time, and so on. But you will find that these limitations of BANK STREET WRITER are not crucial when you are starting to learn word processing. And I don't know of a better entry into the word-processing world, which is already changing the way we think about writing. I used BANK STREET WRITER to write this section of the **Catalog**.

STEWART BRAND: We'd like to hear about other people's experience using BANK STREET WRITER versus HOMEWORD with first-time word-processor users, especially children. BANK STREET was designed with its cumbersome two modes (write, then change gears, then edit, then change gears, etc.) especially for teaching kids. HOMEWORD has its icons—little pictures for the same purpose. Which works best?

## M_SS_NG L_NKS: A GAME OF LETTERS AND LANGUAGE

**Chomsky & Schwartz; age level: 7-adult; Apple II family; 48K; disk drive; $49/disk ● Atari; 48K; disk drive; $49/disk ● Commodore 64; disk drive; $59/disk (English Editor not available) ● IBM PC; 64K; disk drive; $59/disk ● TRS-80 I, III, 4; 48K; disk drive; $59/disk; choice of seven disks: Young Peoples' Literature, Classics Old & New, MicroEncyclopedia, English, Spanish, French, and German Editors; copy-protected? YES; Sunburst Communications, Inc., 39 Washington Ave., Pleasantville, NY 10570; 800/431-1934; Atari and Commodore versions ($29.95) also available from HesWare, 150 North Hill Drive, Brisbane, CA 94005; 415/468-4111.**

JIM FRENCH: The title gives away the format of this program. Separately purchasable disks present encyclopedia information, foreign-language entries, entries you can make up, or passages from children's and adults' literary classics. The passages are offered in up to nine formats with various vowels, letters, parts of words, or words missing. Players make educated guesses about what is missing and in the process draw on their innate (and often surprising) knowledge about word structure, spelling, grammar, and meaning in context. They also get a sense of the authors' styles and develop one of their own as they practice reading skills and extend their vocabularies. Without conscious effort they therefore gain many language-related skills while the computer keeps score and records guessing accuracy.

The sources of the passages used in M_SS_NG L_NKS cover a wide range: they include the Bible, poetry, sports, animals, world records, and great literature in English, French, German, and Spanish. The software can be used by individual learners as a puzzle or exercise or by a group of students as a competitive/cooperative game. Either way, it achieves the author's purpose: "to help convey . . . some of the excitement and fun of Language."

## KOALAPAD AND KOALA SOFTWARE

**Age level: 4-adult; Apple II family; 48K; $125 ● Atari; 48K; disk or cartridge; $100 ● Commodore 64; disk or cartridge; $100 ● IBM PC compatibles; 64K; $150; color monitor recommended; copy-protected? YES; includes KOALAPAINTER program (entitled PC DESIGN for IBM PC versions);**

## COLORING SERIES I

**Apple II family; 48K; Atari; 48K; Commodore 64; copy-protected? YES; $29.95;**

**both from: Koala Technologies Corp., 3100 Patrick Henry Drive, Santa Clara, CA 95050; 800/562-2327.**

JIM DERICH: The KOALAPAD and its associated software offer the novice computer user a set of tools that makes drawing and learning on the computer entertaining and easy. Throw away the keyboard and interact with the computer freely and creatively.

The KOALAPAD itself is a six-inch-square, touch-sensitive graphics tablet with two buttons located conveniently at the top that function just like buttons on game paddles or joysticks. You interact with the computer solely by touching the pad with your finger or a stylus to select the needed drawing function from the screen menu—draw lines, circles, dots; change pen type; expand or reduce the drawing; frame it; and so on—and then pressing the appropriate button.

Several programs are designed to take advantage of the KOALAPAD's capabilities. The KOALAPAINTER comes with the KOALAPAD. It is a menu-driven, general purpose graphics utility that allows you to use the computer as a full-color electronic scratchpad. COLORING SERIES I is a storage disk replete with geometric designs intended for use with the KOALAPAINTER. It permits you to select a shape and modify it using the Fill, Draw, or other functions of the KOALAPAINTER. Children ages 6-11 love COLORING activities.

Other options for the KOALAPAD include a spelling-practice program called KOALAGRAMS SPELLING 1 that uses graphics and animation, and a musical-notation and tone-recognition practice program called SPIDER EATER. Both are excellent adaptations for the KOALAPAD. The only significant problem I found was that the pressure points on my KOALAPAD did not accurately correspond to the keyboard notation on the SPIDER EATER overlay.

The greatest benefit of the KOALAPAD is the easy access it provides even preschool children to the microcomputer's graphics capabilities. The pad is limited now only by the range of available software.

More on KOALAPAD on page 131.

*Musical notes and fundamental math . . .*

## PIECE OF CAKE MATH

Age level: 7-11; Apple II family; 48K; disk drive
● Atari; 16K; disk or cassette ● Commodore 64; disk
or cassette ● IBM PC compatibles; 64K; color
graphics card ● IBM PCjr; copy-protected? YES;
$34.95;

## FRACTION FACTORY

Age level: 8-12; Apple II family; 48K ● Atari; 16K
● Commodore 64 ● IBM PC compatibles; 64K; color
graphics card ● IBM PCjr; copy-protected? YES;
$29.95;

## MUSIC MASTER

Age level: 3-teen; Apple II family; 48K ● Atari; 16K;
disk or cassette ● Commodore 64 ● IBM PC
compatibles; 64K; color graphics card ● IBM PCjr;
copy-protected? YES; $34.95;

All from Springboard Software, Inc., 7807
Creekridge Circle, Minneapolis, MN 55435;
800-328-1223.

---

JIM FRENCH: In PIECE OF CAKE MATH,
fundamental math drills take place in an
imaginative simulated situation: a bakery. In
the first level, the child's task is to keep track
of how many cakes are baked and sold each
day over a week's time. Next, the child is
asked to predict the number of pieces there
will be if the bakers cut up the cakes in a
variety of ways, and the number of cuts
necessary to make to get a certain number of
pieces. If the child encounters problems, the
computer gently divides up the cakes until the
child can actually count the individual pieces
to get the correct answer. In so doing, he or
she catches on that multiplying and dividing
are actually meaningful labor-saving
operations—not an easy thing to convince
some children of. A second level contains
basic flashcard sequences of the four
fundamental math operations. The final level
is a game for up to four players called
Catchacake. The faster the child's reactions,
the higher the points add up. If the player

misses, another cake splats to the floor of
Fumble's Bakery (which itself is fun, but the
challenge of being the first to reach 1000
points overcomes the delight with splatted
cakes).

FRACTION FACTORY is a practice program
that sidesteps the familiar frustrations of
learning fractions (cutting up paper pies just
doesn't do it for some children). The program
has five games that reinforce the concepts of
fractions and sets, equivalency, finding
fractions of a number, and both adding and
subtracting unlike fractions. The child can
select the game of choice from a picture
menu, which means that even nonreaders can
use the program. The adding and subtracting
games are particularly well designed,
graphically leading the child to the correct
solution when wrong entries are made. It's a
great help for children having trouble with the
concept of fractions.

Finally, MUSIC MASTER is a program that
assists children in learning about and
generating music. For me, this is one of the
computer's most exciting potentials. I have
had even five-year-olds producing miniature
symphonies and self-created duets using this
program. MUSIC MASTER turns the
computer into a simple practice and
composing instrument. In the perform/
record/playback mode, the child can play
musical notes that appear on a piano
keyboard by pressing the number keys on the
computer. After creating a piece, the child can
instruct the computer to play it back, edit it,
modify it, and save it on a disk, all without a
musical instrument or adult assistance. The
child can also practice already created
programs in a "Simon Says" format, learn
musical notation using "Quido's Quiz," and
even add a graphics display that fills the
screen with randomly generated designs as
he or she composes. Children won't learn
intricacies of tempo or go much beyond one
octave, but they will get a wonderful
introduction into the world of music.

*A witches' brew of data to analyze . . .*

## THE INCREDIBLE LABORATORY

Marge Kosel & Jay Carlson; age level: 8-adult;
Apple II family; 48K ● Atari; 48K; disk drive;
joystick; color recommended; copy-protected?
YES; $49; Sunburst Communications, Inc., 39
Washington Ave., Pleasantville, NY 10570;
800/431-1934.

---

ROBERT SCAROLA: Kids love to make
monster shapes. It is this love that THE
INCREDIBLE LABORATORY uses as
motivation for learning strategies of scanning
and note taking.

The graphics on the screen are of a heating
laboratory retort to be filled with a variety of
chemicals. Each chemical added to the retort
modifies the witches' brew and adds a new
characteristic to the eventual monster. The
challenge for the learner is to work with the
computer (or a friend as the opponent) to
figure out which chemicals create which kinds
of monsters. To do that, the child must
develop strategies to gather information, look
for a pattern, analyze data, scan for clues,
focus, and gamble on a choice. Each time the
possibilities are there for a creating a horribly
interesting monster. It's what I call a learning
thriller.

Bubble, bubble, toil and trouble . . . Ben made his
monster out of four chemicals. Can he figure out
which chemicals cause which changes to make,
hee-hee-hee, more incredible monsters? It's a
learning thriller that takes development of record-
keeping and comparison skills in order to
succeed.

---

*Genetically valid kittens . . .*

## CATLAB

Judith Kinnear; age level: 14-adult; Apple II family;
48K; color monitor recommended; copy-
protected? NO; $75; CONDUIT, University of Iowa,
Oakdale Campus, Iowa City, IA 52244; 319/353-
5789.

---

GARY PORTER: CATLAB is for students at
least high school age or older who have been
introduced to the basics of Mendelian
genetics.

The simulation portion of the program
visually represents the coat color and pattern
resulting from the mating of domestic cats by
producing on the screen a genetically valid
litter of kittens. However, to use the program
you must keep accurate written records of the

mating cycle and use a scientific methodology
to control your experiments carefully.
Otherwise, as in life, the variables will quickly
get out of hand.

Used properly, CATLAB is an excellent tool for
developing skills in understanding genetic
ratios and recognizing the distinguishing
features of inheritance of monogenic traits—
dominant/recessive/codominant, autosomal/
sex-linked. The program also develops skill in
planning strategies for analyzing linkage,
gene interaction, and multiple allelic systems.

ROBERT SCAROLA: Whew, that's a
mouthful—but I figured we should
recommend at least one excellent piece of
learning software for high school and college
students.

*In STICKYBEAR NUMBERS, nine terrific little trains bring the digit 9 alive through colorful graphics reinforcement. Press a number key or the spacebar to answer—perfect for the youngest math beginners.*

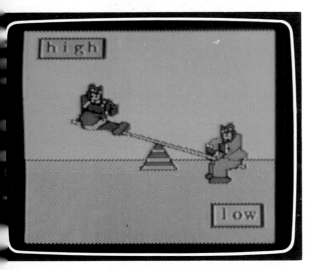

*Mr. & Mrs. Stickybear ride the teeter-totter—when one comes down the other must go up and the words "high"/"low" flash on the screen. Easy for early readers who want to learn all about those intriguing polarities we call opposites.*

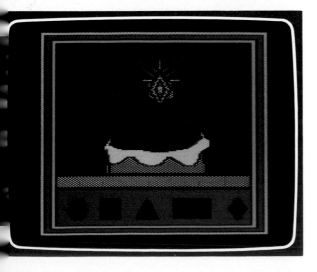

*Practice, practice, practice . . .*

## DEVELOPMENTAL LEARNING MATERIALS (DLM)

### ALLIGATOR ALLEY

Age level: 6-12; Apple II family; 48K; 1 disk drive; color recommended; copy-protected? YES, $44;

### ALIEN ADDITION

Age level: 6-9; Apple II family; 48K ● Atari; 48K ● Commodore 64 ● IBM PC compatibles; 64K (128K with PC DOS 2.0); color graphics card; copy-protected? YES, $44;

### DRAGON MIX

Age level: 9-12; Apple II family; 48K ● Atari; 48K ● Commodore 64 ● IBM PC compatibles; 64K; color graphics card; copy-protected? YES, $44;

### METEOR MISSION

Age level: 6-12; Apple II family; 48K; color recommended; copy-protected? YES, $44;

### VERB VIPER

Age level: 7-12; Apple II family; 48K; disk drive; color monitor recommended; copy-protected? YES, $44;

### WIZ WORKS

Age level: 6-12; Apple II family; 48K; 1 disk drive; color monitor recommended; copy-protected? YES, $44;

### WORDMAN

Age level: 6-9; Apple II family; 48K; disk drive; color monitor recommended; copy-protected? YES, $44;

all from: DLM, One DLM Park, Allen, TX 75002; 800/527-4747.

## XEROX EDUCATION PUBLICATIONS—WEEKLY READER FAMILY SOFTWARE

### STICKYBEAR ABC

### STICKYBEAR NUMBERS

### STICKYBEAR OPPOSITES

### STICKYBEAR SHAPES

Optimum Resources; age level: 3-6; Apple II family; 48K ● Atari; 48K; disk drive; color monitor recommended; copy-protected? YES, $39.95; Weekly Reader Software, Xerox Education Publications, 245 Long Hill Road, Middletown, CT 06457; 800/852-5000.

*Just light up the diamond shape at the bottom of the screen and press Return to get twinkling jewel—a simple and graphically brilliant recognition exercise.*

## THE LEARNING COMPANY

### ADDITION MAGICIAN

Dale Disharoon; age level: 6-10; Apple II family; 48K; Commodore 64; IBM PCjr; 128K; disk drive; color recommended; copy-protected? YES: $34.95;

### NUMBER STUMPER

Dennis Sorenson; age level: 6-10; Apple II family; 48K; color recommended; IBM PC compatibles; color graphics card; IBM PCjr; 128K; disk drive; copy-protected? YES, $39.95;

### READER RABBIT

Leslie Grimm; age level: 5-7; Apple II family; 48K; Commodore 64; IBM PC compatibles; color graphics card; IBM PCjr; copy-protected? YES; $39.95;

### WORD SPINNER

Dale Disharoon; age level: 6-10; Apple II family; 48K ● Atari; 48K ● Commodore 64 ● IBM PC compatibles; 64K; color graphics card; IBM PCjr; 128K; color monitor recommended; copy-protected? YES, $34.95;

all from The Learning Company, 545 Middlefield Road, Suite 170, Menlo Park, CA 94025; 415/328-5410.

ROBERT SCAROLA: These three software companies have all decided to develop series of software programs in the practice genre. Each attempts to use the capabilities of the computer to remove the routine from learning basics. Each has a different emphasis, however, and achieves a different degree of success.

DLM is my least favorite of the three because of the narrowness of its approach. DLM's software proceeds from the flashcard theory of teaching basic facts—that is, with repetition and time pressure the mind can be trained to retain all kinds of information, from the correct spelling of words to multiplication tables. DLM dresses up this basic theory in various disguises for the computer screen—spinning wheels that shoot correct numbers or words out of the sky (METEOR MISSION); alligators that eat proper grammatical sentence constructions or math facts (ALLIGATOR ALLEY); wizards that zap times tables (WIZ WORKS); vipers (VERB VIPER), aliens (ALIEN ADDITION), dragons (DRAGON MIX), and so on, all of which perform some operation on the screen, depending on the quickness of the learner's response to the problem.

That is both the constant curse and occasional value of the programs. For some children this kind of time-pressured practice works well. For others, it brings on panic, if not psychosis. I found I had a hard time performing within the time limits of some of the programs. Worst of all, there was no way to change the time limits to accommodate different learners' needs. So despite their use of appealing graphics, I only found one or two of these programs useable (my kids rated

VERB VIPER #1 and WORDMAN #2). If you like the DLM approach, most definitely try before you buy.

You are on safer ground with Xerox's STICKYBEAR NUMBERS, SHAPES, OPPOSITES, and ABC series. These programs are all for three- to six-year-olds and provide playful graphic images to reinforce the learning of basic letters, numbers, and concepts. What makes these programs stand out from the crowd is the imaginative detail of their graphic and sound presentations of the animals and objects that move and dance and play on the screen. The number and variety of such presentations on each disk are unusually large, so the youngster won't easily get bored. These would be among my absolute first choice of practice programs for the very young learner.

The Learning Company has produced a series of software that goes well beyond the simple practice routines of either the DLM or Xerox products. As with its stunning problem-solving programs, such as ROCKY'S BOOTS (p. 188), The Learning Company's practice programs always focus on the learner's ultimate control over the program. The Learning Company's programs are characterized by marvelous use of engaging graphics and are highly interactive. My personal favorite is READER RABBIT, which I think gives children an excellent opportunity to practice word patterns and sounds by running machines like a labeler, sorter, or train (see p. 189 for a discussion of MAGIC SPELLS, The Learning Company's magical spelling practice program). Another favorite is WORD SPINNER, which has a very effective fill-in-the-letter format. A + for The Learning Company.

*Deductive reasoning . . .*

## BAFFLES

**Jane D. Spain; age level: 10-adult; Apple II family; 48K; copy-protected? NO; $50; CONDUIT; University of Iowa, Oakdale Campus, Iowa City, IA 52244; 319/353-5789.**

JULIE ASKELAND: You play BAFFLES on a coordinate plane using "probes" to discover the hidden deflection points on the plane. If a probe is taken at 12 and comes out at 32 directly across from 12, most likely there are no deflectors in its path. But if a probe is taken at 10 on the vertical axis and exits at 27 on the horizontal axis, there must be a deflector to alter its course. And if a 10 should yield a 34, a point directly across and down 4, there must be two baffles to be found. A built-in point system encourages the learner to be shrewd in probing. The program can even be modified for competition with another player. One player hides baffles and the other tries to figure them out.

The format of BAFFLES allows for a trial run with the baffles in full view and then a choice of challenges with varying degrees of difficulty. The program exercises the learner's deductive reasoning powers while it challenges and delights.

*Which numbers add up to the right amount? With ADDITION MAGICIAN, you don't even have to write numbers well to be able to box the numbers in till they are all enclosed. Perfect for the frustrated beginner or the learning disabled.*

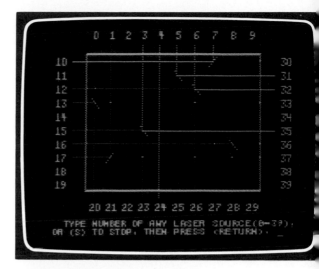

*Frustrated pool players can check out their angle shots. Predicting the baffling twists and turns gets you to the right number on the X or Y axis and sharpens your ability to estimate directions, patterns, and consequences.*

*Type for survival . . .*

## MASTERTYPE

**Bruce Zweig; age level: 6-adult; Apple II family; 48K; disk drive ● Atari; 32K; cartridge or disk ● Commodore 64; cartridge or disk ● all $39.95 ● IBM PC compatibles; 64K; $50; copy-protected? YES; Scarborough Systems, Inc., 25 North Broadway, Tarrytown, NY 10591; 914/332-4545.**

ROBERT SCAROLA: Why does MASTERTYPE succeed so well as a practice typing program? Possibly because its creator, Bruce Zweig, was careful to make sure the eye/hand coordination of typing is reinforced in a progression—from easy home keys, to more difficult symbol and number keys, to words. Most important, the learner can choose which lesson, speed, and difficulty to work with and can even make up target words.

Mastery at any skill level is determined by how quickly and accurately the learner responds by pressing the correct key or series of keys to shoot a looming letter or word spaceship (the graphics here are not so dramatic or overpowering that they get in the way of focusing on the represented letter or word). If the learner misses, the letter or word ship destroys one part of the learner's

home base. If the learner types correctly, the ship disappears, to be immediately replaced by another attacker. As the action goes on, the program evaluates speed and accuracy and gives a running account of the learner's performance—a summary of the number wrong and right, words per minute, and so on.

Learners younger than twelve might have some trouble with MASTERTYPE. If their hands aren't large enough to reach across the keyboard easily, they'll inevitably resort to a hunt-and-peck system. But the slight pressure and game aspects of the program will help older learners concentrate on and practice finding and remembering the keys quickly—which is what touch typing is ultimately all about.

STEWART BRAND: For a considerably more sophisticated typing instructor for $50, see TYPING TUTOR III on page 48.

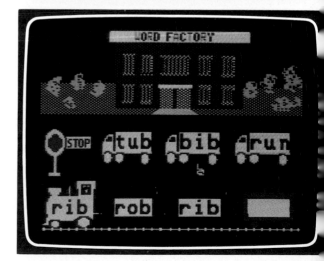

*Match words to pictures by inserting the correct letters; find the words with the same vowel sounds, fill the boxcars, and watch the train chug away. The theme in READER RABBIT is teaching reading skills with animated cartoons and toys—as non-threatening as being in a sandbox.*

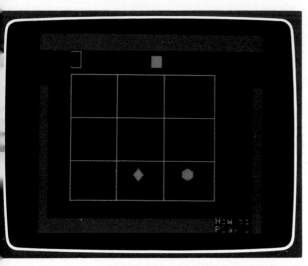

*Gertrude flew away and brought back this set of shapes to play with. Move them around till they are in the correct order (go to the "How to Play" room if you need help). Subtle Gertrude teaches sorting, classifying and logical ordering with a minimum of instruction and a maximum of exploration.*

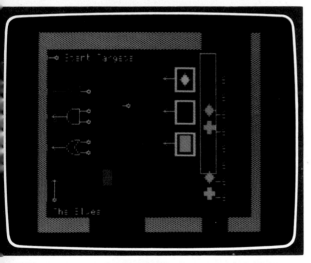

*ROCKY'S BOOTS makes it easy to solve problems and build all kinds of amazing machines that would otherwise be out of reach for kids to mess around with.*

*Controls drawing speed and direction . . .*

## PICTUREWRITER

**George Brackett; age level: 5-adult; Apple II family; 64K; disk drive; joystick; color, graphics printer recommended; copy-protected? NO; $39.95; Scarborough Systems, Inc., 25 North Broadway, Tarrytown, NY 10591; 914/332-4545.**

AL MANN: For these cerebral-palsied hands of mine, which occasionally spasm and create unwanted movements, PICTUREWRITER allows much more control over my drawing than the much-acclaimed KOALAPAD.

*Patterns and puzzles . . .*

## GERTRUDE'S SECRETS

**Teri Perl & Leslie Grimm; age level: 4-10; Apple II family; 48K ● IBM PC compatibles; color graphics card ● IBM PCjr; copy-protected? YES; $45;**

## BUMBLE GAMES

**Leslie Grimm; age level: 4-10; Apple II family; 48K ● Atari; 48K ● Commodore 64; copy-protected? YES; $39.95;**

**both from: The Learning Company, 545 Middlefield Road, Suite 170, Menlo Park, CA 94025; 415/328-5410.**

ROBERT SCAROLA: GERTRUDE'S SECRETS offers the same format for problem solving as ROCKY'S BOOTS, but instead of building machines the child must figure out the patterns of puzzles and then duplicate them by moving various shapes into a matrix of empty squares. The child accomplishes this with the aid of Gertrude, a friendly goose, picking her up by means of the floating cursor and moving her into the selected puzzle section, which contains arrays, trains, or loops. Gertrude then flies off to get a set of shapes that the child will use to duplicate the model pattern.

But that's not all. The child can also move into a separate room with the floating cursor and create new puzzles, or move into a third room and use the shape editor box to redesign the shapes used to make the puzzle patterns. GERTRUDE'S SECRETS thus gives the child the ability to control both the configuration of the problem and the selection of the tools used to solve the problem.

BUMBLE GAMES offers a series of simple thinking games in which the child finds a number on a scale or grid or plays tic-tac-toe using grid coordinates. What makes this program worth the money is the carefully designed musical and visual reinforcement and graphics, standard for most Learning Company programs. BUMBLE GAMES is the best of the firm's learning programs in this genre (much better than BUMBLE PLOT, incidentally, which also teaches grid coordinates but makes the unhappy error of introducing confusing negative numbers on the grid),

PICTUREWRITER has nearly every feature that the KOALAPAD has plus four additional features: First, PICTUREWRITER has a two-cursor system—one cursor tells me where I am while a second shows me where I am going. I can change the distance between the two cursors, thereby controlling my drawing speed. Another feature, Backup, allows me to erase my last steps. Edit lets me review my efforts and make modifications. Finally, with Redraw I can animate the picture. If you are a disabled individual, I highly recommend PICTUREWRITER for its ability to respond to your special needs.

*Rooms filled with wondrous tools . . .*

## ROCKY'S BOOTS

**Warren Robinett; age level: 9-adult; Apple II family; 48K; disk drive; color monitor; copy-protected? YES; $50; The Learning Company, 545 Middlefield Road, Suite 170, Menlo Park, CA 94025; 415/328-5410.**

ROBERT SCAROLA: ROCKY'S BOOTS has no stilted graphics, no "keybored" page turning with a hidden agenda. It's not a program that holds back the answers and puts the learner through the uninspiring exercise of finding out what is already known.

Instead, ROCKY'S BOOTS creates an open, moving, and changing environment filled with color (the program works on a monochrome monitor but color makes a wonderful difference) and sound that encourages exploration. The child moves a large floating cursor "off the screen" from one environment to another. Each environment is a room entered through a magic doorway and filled with tools, various parts, machines, and other surprises. There are cutters, clackers, electric arrows, sensors, and/not/or gates, flip-flops, clocks, and delays. Any of them can be "picked up" with the floating cursor and then rearranged, linked together, hooked to a power supply, turned on and off—used in as many different ways as there are children to think them up.

The instructions are clear, thorough, and simple enough for any second grader—or, for that matter, any self-conscious adult—to grasp with a little practice. The variety of combinations and the range of challenging tasks and games offered by the menu leave room for all kinds of experimentation with currents, switches, lights, and the rest—experimentation that is based on basic scientific principles. ROCKY'S BOOTS offers the learner a chance to use the very problem-solving skills we are trying so hard to teach these days—intuition, logical thinking, sequential ordering, rechecking, and debugging.

Most children, including myself, do the obvious first—build a machine that turns on and works: moves, honks, clacks, lights up, carries current, does something interesting that could not be done in the real world without a lot of expense, safety precautions, and time. Then we move from the concrete to the abstract and from the simple to the complex, all through the process of making something actually work. The only other times I have seen children learn similar skills with computers is when they work on programming in a language like LOGO or BASIC.

ROCKY'S BOOTS moves into another dimension, one reflective of the magical world children live in.

*Tailorable spelling . . .*

## MAGIC SPELLS

Leslie Grimm; age level: 6-10; Apple II family; 48K ● Atari with BASIC; 48K ● IBM PC compatibles ● IBM PCjr; 128K; color graphics card; copy-protected? YES; $34.95; The Learning Company, 545 Middlefield Road, Suite 170, Menlo Park, CA 94025; 415/328-5410.

ROBERT SCAROLA: MAGIC SPELLS meets my three criteria for good software in the practice genre.

First, it's engaging and clear. The letters are big, bold, and colorful; the graphics are simple but pleasing; instructions and command sequences are simple, effective, and accurate.

Second, it's friendly. The program gives students options: they can unscramble scrambled letters or use a simulated "flashcard" to learn correct spelling. Students are not rushed, and the program gently helps them spell words correctly. If the child misspells a word, the program shows the correct letters in the proper sequence below the misspelled word, leaving spaces for missing correct letters to be filled in. Learners win from or lose to a very happy looking demon, who appears on the screen when he wins points. When the student has worked through the word list, he or she gets part or all of a prize from the "treasure room" as a reward.

Third, the program is adaptable to particular needs. It allows the student or teacher to create individual word lists. A separate data file disk can be created containing a whole semester's worth of words. These words can be easy or difficult, making the program applicable for grades from kindergarten through sixth, seventh, and possibly even eighth grade (although it might look too "childish" to the age-conscious pre-teen).

MAGIC SPELLS makes learning to spell words correctly more enjoyable and rewarding than it could be without the help of a computer. How else could you play at substituting letters in words until you found the right combination? Impossible unless you happen to have controlling interest in an eraser company.

*Enter the Castle of Spells and spell your way to the fabulous treasure by getting all the words correct the first time. A deliberately uncluttered format completely in the control of the child—a compassionate way to practice spelling.*

*Absolutely wonderful . . .*

## DELTA DRAWING

Computer Access Corporation; age level: 4-adult; Apple II family; 48K; disk drive; $50 ● Atari; 16K; cartridge; $40 ● Commodore 64; cartridge; $39.95 ● IBM PC compatibles ● IBM PCjr; 64K; color graphics card; $50; copy-protected? YES; Spinnaker Software, 1 Kendall Square, Cambridge, MA 02139; 617/494-1200.

ROBERT SCAROLA: Welcome, all you kids (and grownups who still believe in fairies, sprites, and kids) to Spinnaker's DELTA DRAWING. Just boot it up and watch a letter of the alphabet become a magician's wand worked by you, an instant maestro playing in a powerful graphics world.

Hey, presto! Will a volunteer from the audience please step up to the keyboard? Thank you very much. Now, examine the keys closely. Check for hidden wires, invisible erasers, secret passages. Okay? Ready? Type D and watch the magic Delta draw a line. Type R. Ah ha, you just made a 30-degree right turn. Type M. Why, you moved without drawing a line. Type U and, whoops, you made a U-turn. Okay, try typing 4D,3M four times. A square is born (not you, of course). Now, press the 1 key. Hey, presto! The square disappears. Press 1 again. Hey, presto! The square reappears. Let's have a round of applause, ladies and gentlemen, for this very talented programmer from our audience. (What? You say you've never written a computer program before!!!?? Astonishing!! Another round of applause please and give the kid a silicon cigar!)

But don't stop now. Touch T and you can see the text of the program you wrote displayed on the screen. Type CONTROL-O and you can edit it. Try it! Nice, a quadrisomethingorother! Press the 2 and you just wrote another program! (Applause, applause.) Look, folks, he pressed 2 again on his own to make the program reappear! (The kid's a fast study.) CONTROL-F fills it in with any one of seven colors. (Purple? Yuk!) Ah, but never fear CONTROL-E and hey, presto! The screen is blank. CONTROL-Z and ZAP! so is everything else.

Let's have another round of applause and a second silicon cigar for . . . Oh, your mom doesn't let you smoke? Hey, a consolation prize for the kid. Give him a set of DELTA DRAWING Fast Start Cards so he can have all these magic tricks at his fingertips to impress his friends, amaze his teachers, and drive his parents nuts trying to figure out how their six-year-old just outdid Matisse.

*Eight-year-old Ben used one keystroke at a time to write the series of five programs that made this combination of arcs, circles and colors. (He couldn't duplicate it with paper and pen.) He can save it, modify it and print it out as easily as he wrote it. A simple but powerful child's programming tool based on LOGO.*

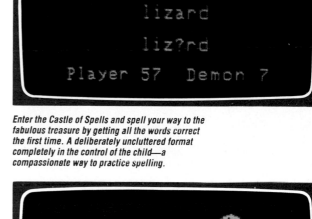

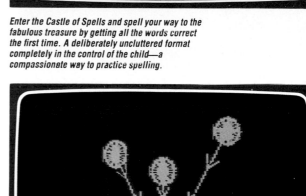

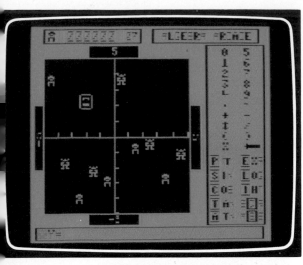

*The Algebroids are all in position, but watch out for the Graph Gobbler. He'll gobble the snakiest sine curve you can invent. A program that, at last, puts your equations in action. Math drill and practice without the drill.*

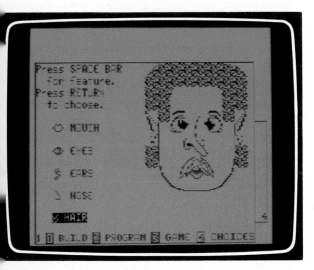

*Just one of many possible rubber FACEMAKER faces for kids to play with. Press the spacebar to program wiggles, winks, blats and frowns—an effective (and fun) way to teach elementary programming to the youngest child.*

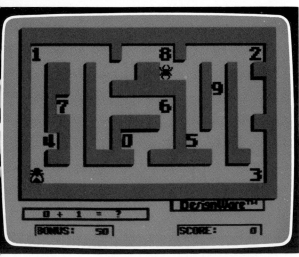

*"Come into my number parlor," said the lurking spider to the crafty fly. Basic math facts suddenly find themselves in a PAC-MAN world that kids enjoy being in. Arcade game meets learning, and maybe both can win.*

*Soaring equations . . .*

## ALGEBRA ARCADE

**Mick, Konemann, O'Farrell & Isaacs; age level: 12-adult; Apple II family; 48K ● Atari 800; 48K ● Commodore 64 ● IBM PC compatibles; 64K; copy-protected? YES; $50; Wadsworth Electronic Publishing Company, 8 Davis Drive, Belmont, CA 94002; 800/354-9606.**

JIM STOCKFORD: This excellent game develops an intuitive understanding of algebra. You are given vertical and horizontal coordinates on your display monitor, and little Algebroids march out and arrange themselves at random over the display.

TOM MACH: You need to wipe out these electronic monsters by suggesting an equation that results in a plotted line—curved, straight, wavy—along which your friend, Whirlwind, can move to destroy Algebroids and earn you points.

You also have to avoid the ghost who turns into the Graph Gobbler and eats your graph, leaving you scoreless and him satisfied. Then the Committee can impose a loss-of-turn penalty on you, and you've only got ten turns to eliminate the Algebroids, get the ghost into hiding, and plot a curve to destroy his hiding place and so win the game.

JIM STOCKFORD: You quickly develop a feel for creating formulas that will let you hit the Algebroids. Each formula lets you discover the graphic representation of a different algebraic equation. The game gives you the wonderful soaring sense of power felt by the inventors of all mathematical equations.

*Arithmetic on the fly . . .*

## MATH MAZE

**Age level: 8-12; Apple II family; 48K ● Atari 400/800/XL series ● Commodore 64 ● IBM compatibles ● IBM PCjr; 64K; color graphics card; copy-protected? YES; $39.95; DesignWare, Inc. 185 Berry Street, San Francisco, CA 94107; 800/572-7767.**

JIM DERICH: The object of this enticing and challenging game is mentally to solve the math problems presented in the four basic arithmetic operations and then to negotiate a fly through a PAC-MAN-like maze. The fly's job is to get the correct answer by retrieving the necessary digits (0-9) randomly scattered throughout the maze. The faster you solve the problem and retrieve the digits, the higher

*Animating Mr. Potatohead . . .*

## FACEMAKER

**Designware; age level: 3-8; Apple II family; 48K ● Atari; 48K; cartridge; $29.95 ● Coleco Vision; cartridge; 16K ● Commodore 64; cartridge; $34.95 ● IBM PC compatibles ● IBM PCjr; 64K; color graphics card; copy-protected? YES; Spinnaker Software, 1 Kendall Square, Cambridge, MA 02139; 617/494-1200.**

ROBERT SCAROLA: FACEMAKER gives the youngest children a chance to transform the solid adult world of serious faces into a crayon world they can control and change. In the process it gives them a chance to learn the computer keyboard, pick up a few simple commands, and achieve some sense of what programming is all about.

I like FACEMAKER because that's all it does. It's clean, simple, and easy, even for pre-schoolers. There are no potentially confusing commands and no "game" format or context to threaten the learning value of the program.

FACEMAKER puts a featureless outline of a face on the screen and the child uses the space bar to select a feature to paint on the face—eyes, nose, ears, hair, mouth—each one in a dozen or so comical variations. Once the face is built, the child can change any features easily by going through the same process again.

In addition, and this is a stroke of brilliance, the child can then write a short program, using single-letter commands, to animate the face: make the eyes wink or cry; the mouth frown, smile, or stick out its tongue (and blat); and the ears wiggle. Once done programming, the child can go on to play a game in which the computer makes the face perform several movements or sounds and the child is asked to list the sequence in a program—a good test not only of memory but also of early programming comprehension.

Someone at Spinnaker has, happily, spent time with children as well as with computers.

your score. You can select one of 40 different mazes provided on the disk or go to the maze editor to modify the maze you are using or create your own and save it on disk. Another option is to increase the difficulty level by introducing a spider into the maze. If the spider catches your fly, you return to the starting position and lose 40 points. You can further increase the difficulty by making the walls of the maze invisible. You still see the digits but can only detect a wall by bumping into it (incidentally, this program is easiest to play with a joystick).

MATH MAZE is a flexible, interactive, expandable, well-constructed learning program that has great potential to replace the rote memorization of math facts.

*Thinking about thinking, and drawing . . .*

## LOGO, IN ALL ITS MANIFESTATIONS

**APPLE LOGO II:** Apple II family; 128K; disk drive, color display, printer, and mouse recommended; copy-protected? NO; $175; Apple Computer, 20525 Mariani Avenue, Cupertino, CA 95014; 408/996-1010 ● **ATARI LOGO:** Atari; 16K; copy-protected? YES; $100; Atari, 1265 Borregas Avenue, P.O. Box 427, Sunnyvale, CA 94086; 800/672-1404 ● **COLOR LOGO;** TRS-80 Color Computer; disk drive for disk version; $50 (cartridge), $99 (disk); copy-protected? NO; Radio Shack, One Tandy Center, Fort Worth, TX 76113; 817/338-2392 ● **COMMODORE LOGO;** Terrapin; Commodore 64; disk drive; copy-protected? YES; $70; Commodore, 1200 Wilson Drive, West Chester, PA 19380; 215/431-9100 ● **DR. LOGO LANGUAGE;** IBM PC compatibles; IBM PCjr; PC DOS 2.1; 128K; $100; IBM PC/XT; PC DOS 2.0; 192K; color graphics card, RGB monitor; $150; copy-protected? PC/PCjr: NO; XT: YES; Digital Research, P.O. Box 579, Pacific Grove, CA 93950; 408/649-3896 ● **IBM LOGO;** IBM PC compatibles; IBM PCjr; 128K; disk drive; copy-protected? NO; $175; IBM Customer Relations, P.O. Box 1328, Boca Raton, FL 33432; 800/447-4700 ● **KRELL'S LOGO;** Apple II family; 64K; copy-protected? YES; $89.95; LOGO sprite board, $199.95; TURTLE PAK for schools, 20 disks, $500; 40 disks, $900; Krell Software Corp., 1320 Stony Brook Road, Stony Brook, NY 11790; 800/245-7355 ● **PC LOGO;** IBM PC compatibles; IBM PCjr; 64K minimum, 128K recommended; color graphics card; 8087 math processor chip ($200) optional; copy-protected? NO; $150; Harvard Associates, 260 Beacon Street, Somerville, MA 02143; 617/492-0660 ● **TLC-LOGO;** CP/M machines; copy-protected? NO; non-graphics; $100; graphics (requires graphics interface) $150; The LISP Co., P.O. Box 487, Redwood Estates, CA 95044; 408/354-3668. ● **TLC-LOGO;** standard version: Kaypro 2, 4, and 10; $100; deluxe version: Kaypro 2, 4, and 10; $130; with MicroSphere's color graphics board, $300 (external monitor needed for color application); copy-protected? NO; MicroSphere, P.O. Box 1221, Bend, OR 97709; 503/388-1194 ● **TERRAPIN LOGO;** Apple II family; 64K; copy-protected? YES; $100; Terrapin, Inc., 380 Green Street, Cambridge, MA 02139; 617/492-8816 ● **TI LOGO II;** Artificial Intelligence Laboratory; age level: 5-14; TI 99/4A; requires peripheral expansion box with 32K card; copy-protected? YES; $100; Triton Products, P.O. Box 8123, San Francisco, CA 94128; 800/227-6900, or in CA, 800/632-4777.

---

**ROBERT SCAROLA:** If Seymour Papert hadn't invented LOGO somebody would have to go out and do it now. For good reasons it has become one of the primary mechanisms by which novices learn how to program a computer.

The major reason is LOGO's unique ability to respond immediately to the programmer's effort, thus encouraging thinking about the very process of thinking and programming. In almost any other programming language—BASIC, Pascal, FORTH—the response is considerably delayed. First you write a set of instructions in the syntax of the particular language; then the computer interprets the instructions; next you instruct the program to RUN, and then stop to correct mistakes (de-

bugging). Not until then do you have a finished program.

A lot has already been written about LOGO as a computer learning tool. There have been both outrageous claims of success and outright cynicism. I suggest you ignore any outrageous claims—learning still takes effort, imagination, and attention, and nothing, not even LOGO, will enable anyone to attain overnight success. But I also suggest you ignore the cynicism. For two years, I have taught grades one through eight using LOGO, and my tempered point of view is that LOGO works.

LOGO places on the screen before you an upward pointing caret called a turtle. As you write a program on the screen using commands such as FD (meaning Forward) 20 (meaning 20 defined units of space on the screen, 1 unit having the value of about 2 mm), the turtle moves forward. Tell it BK and a number and the turtle moves backward that far. RT or LT and a number get you right and left turns, the number in this case indicating the degrees of the turn. You thus draw a square by typing in FD 20 (or any other number) RT or LT 90 (degrees), four times. As you type in the program, the turtle draws a line on the screen.

Simple enough, but just the beginning. Using other commands you can instruct the turtle to repeat something an endless number of times; you can use variables to change your number limits; you can write a program that becomes a primitive procedure like FD or RT and can then be used in other programs (a building block or "modular" approach to both programming and problem solving). You can use an editor to modify your primitive procedures and variables; and you can save your programs on a disk. In short, you can begin to get the feeling, very quickly, of the very powerful programming and graphics capabilities of the computer.

This basic format holds for any of LOGO's variations, whether you use Apple, Atari, Texas Instruments, Kaypro, Commodore 64, TRS-80, or IBM PC packages. (It is also the fundamental way in which Apple or Atari PILOT work.) In each case there are syntax differences and special capabilities. For instance, pre-constructed images called Sprites are available in TI LOGO and not Apple, while APPLE LOGO has more powerful programming capabilities than TI LOGO. (LOGO, by the way, is not limited to graphics: as with any powerful computer language you can also use it to perform calculations and devise entire systems of lists and variables.)

To get the full capability of the language you should spend the $100-140 to buy a version of LOGO with the complete set of instruction manuals. Learning to program in LOGO will make you feel like you just learned how the engine works in your car. And that's worth knowing even if you have no intention of ever becoming a mechanic.

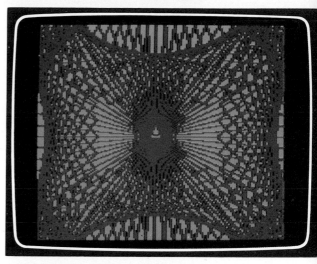

*The busy Turtle spins his web in this Apple LOGO program called "Web," by Russell, age ten. Russell wrote four nested procedures with variables to make the program. For Russell and other children, LOGO makes the difficult abstract process of thinking about thinking a concrete and powerful reality.*

---

*LOGO at its simplest . . .*

## TURTLE TOYLAND, JR.

Childware Corp.; age level: 6-adult; Commodore 64; joystick; copy-protected? YES; $34.95; HesWare, 150 North Hill Drive, Brisbane, CA 94005; 415/468-4111.

---

**JIM FRENCH:** LOGO can be used by preschoolers if a knowledgeable adult is there to help. For children who go it alone, HesWare has developed two LOGO-like programs intended for use by very young children. One, called TURTLE GRAPHICS II, I find limited in its usefulness because of an annoying screen-switching menu driven system and a painfully slow execution time.

HesWare's other product, TURTLE TOYLAND, JR., however, is a very different box of turtles. This is a self-teaching program in which the child selects from various options by means of a joystick and icons. A child need not be able to read or even know keyboard characters to discover and use the many options of the program.

The options are Playground, where the beginning students find out how to move the turtle around the screen; Training Land, where they create turtle designs; Music Land, in which they develop short musical interludes; Sprite Land, where they can make moveable shapes of their own design; and Toybox, where they can put all the pieces together. There are also some simple programming options, like loops and steps, in a procedure called Filmstrip.

## ET CETERA

### Barbara Robertson and Research Department, Domain Editors

STEWART BRAND: This is the "everything else" category, miscellaneous, unclassifiable, new, dubious, subversive, titillating. Where else would you put a slideshow control program and a track betting program? This domain should be the cutting edge, the realm of perpetual news. That the selection is so limited I think is a measure of the immaturity of the personal computer market and technology. People are still absorbing the basics covered in the other sections. Home computer use, where most of Etc. applies, is still a frontier.

Where are the medical self-diagnosis and self-care programs? Where are the dedicated databases for identification of birds, flowers, trees, butterflies? How about something besides a book (p. 198) to run household appliances? Where are the pet feeding and plant watering programs? Where's the weather prediction program?—give it cloud type, wind direction, barometer trend, and it gives you a prediction. How about a joystick that fights back, gives you motor feedback from the game or whatever that you're controlling? When you travel somewhere, you'd like to know what books in print, especially novels, are set in that locale—where's that database?

A regular feature in the **Whole Earth Software Review** (p. 11) is "Software That Ought To Be." Send us your needs and ideas—maybe we can help lever the proper software tools into existence. Software developers with odd and interesting new programs, do the same, send us what you've got—maybe we can help find customers for your originality.

There's a lot more revolution left in personal computers.

BARBARA ROBERTSON: This section of the **Catalog** was shepherded by the WESC/R research staff—Lyn Gray, Office Manager; Kathy Parks and Karen Hamilton, Librarians; Cliff Figallo, Hardware and Database Manager; Jim Stockford, formerly in charge of acquisitions, now Assistant Editor of the **Review**; with a good assist from Matthew McClure, formerly on the research staff, later Assistant Editor of the **Review**, now Managing Editor for the **Catalog**.

Without the research staff, the **Catalog** would still be an impossible dream. If you marvel at the quantity of information in this small book, remember that for each program and book reviewed, we have half a dozen more on our shelves in the library. Each one of those programs and books got to us because someone made a phone call or sent a letter. Each has been cataloged and shelved, checked out for review—and in—and out again, has warranty cards and invoices filed, disks and cassettes carefully removed, logged-in and stored away, and a thank-you letter sent. Each has information about it collected, distributed, and filed—from reviewers, from magazines (thank you Hank Roberts)—and perhaps the biggest task of all: each program and book that made it into the **Catalog** has access information. That little paragraph at the beginning of each review is the result of (sometimes many) phone calls to verify the facts. All of this, *all* of this, was done by the research staff. And more . . . they pay reviewers and send tear sheets to companies with products mentioned, take care of the hardware, answer the phones, distribute the mail, and somehow stay cheerful, enthusiastic, and interested. Why did they take on this section, too? For fun, and because no individual had the requisite range of interest.

Lyn and Kathy, who've provided food for many of our gatherings, took on cooking programs. Lyn also managed health, exercise and nutrition. Jim, a musician, reviewed dozens of music programs—and, innately curious (and prodded by Kathy), came up with some miscellaneous categories, as well. Cliff, a former house builder, examined programs that claim to manage houses. Matthew, a programmer, looks at and talks about the field he's most interested in—artificial intelligence.

Clockwise from front: Kathy Parks, Barbara Robertson, Matthew McClure, James Stockford, Lyn Gray, Cliff Figallo; center: Karen Hamilton.

Matt Herron

*Onscreen warp and weft . . .*

## VIDEO LOOM II

**Howard Harawitz; Apple II family; 48K; Grappler board recommended for printing; copy-protected? NO; $60 plus $4 handling; Howard Harawitz, 1472 Tower Rd., #827, Halifax, Nova Scotia, B3H 4K8; 902/429-3445.**

*A few keystrokes and the colors change in this traditional colonial overshot weaving pattern; threads can become thicker or the whole pattern can shift. With VIDEO LOOM II, the computer becomes a weaver's sketchpad for exact pattern drafting before struggling with loops and heddes.*

KEVIN KELLY: This program weaves colored textile patterns on a video monitor. At the same time, it sews a nifty circle in computer history: One of the very first programmable machines built was a loom run by sets of punched cards. That was about 1800. Now, with the touch of buttons, you can change thread thickness, color, spacing, and threading draft on a simulated loom with 32 harnesses and 64 treadles. Alter a choice and a new fabric unrolls down the screen. The color range is unnecessarily rudimentary, hampering sustained use for serious textile artists, but the program is fine as a tool for weaving instruction.

## Computers Can't Talk So Well, But They Make Fine Music

**JAMES STOCKFORD:** If you want to play music on a computer you have two choices. The Apple II family (except the can't-get-inside-the-box IIc) is good for beginners and the only option for professionals, who must buy sound boards that fit in the internal slots. The Commodore 64 has built-in sound—not quite professional quality, but the computer is much less expensive and provides more music capability than any other computer on the market. (The PCjr is nearly as good as the Commodore 64, but no good software is yet available for it.) I'm recommending five music programs I've found for these two machines—each the best of its class.

Budding musicians or budding programmers who want to write their own programs—a low-cost means of learning the rudiments of electronic music-making and computer architecture related to music-making—will want to buy the book, **The Commodore 64 Music Master** (James Vogel and Nevin B. Scrimshaw; $29.95; Softext, Inc., 380 Green Street, P.O. Box 2007, Cambridge, MA 02139; 617/876-2333; or COMPUTER LITERACY). It's an excellent tutorial that teaches BASIC programming and comes with a tape cassette of programs.

---

*Inexpensive software and circuit board combo play 16 voices . . .*

## MOUNTAIN COMPUTER MUSIC SYSTEM

Version 2.0; Apple II family; 48K; copy-protected? YES; $395; Mountain Computer, Inc., 300 El Pueblo Rd., Scotts Valley, CA 95066; 408/438-6650.

---

**JAMES STOCKFORD:** This board for the Apple II has sound-generating capabilities of professional quality. It's appropriate for serious students of computer-controlled music and for professional musicians as a sound-generating device.

**JOE WEST:** You use traditional notation to compose music that can play up to 16 simultaneous voices into a sound system. You can't hear the music while you type in the notes, and you must have an Apple Silentype printer to print your composition, but this system is reasonably priced for a high-quality sound-generating circuit board.

You can control the harmonic content of a tone, a complex amplitude and frequency envelope, and its stereo channel. The size of the note files decreases as the complexity of the tone parameters increases. The documentation includes clear and precise operating instructions, an understandable explanation of the physics of sound, and an excellent tutorial on assembly-language control of the music program. The manufacturer provides good customer support and moves quickly to resolve problems.

---

*Spectacular and immediately involving . . .*

## MUSICALC 1

Richard Wolton; Commodore 64; disk drive; monitor with speaker; copy-protected? YES; $50; Waveform Corp., 1912 Bonita Way, Berkeley, CA 94704; 415/841-9866.

---

**JAMES STOCKFORD:** This program—made for the Commodore 64—is a home entertainment music device for the curious and a low-cost sound generator, music-scale explorer, or controller of other intruments (drum machines, synthesizers, printers for sheet music) for budding musicians and computer/electronic music enthusiasts. However, it's not for teachers or professional musicians.

The Commodore 64 has three electronic sound chips, and MUSICALC 1 is the first program to use them. The slide controls and switches that monitor and manage each of the sound chips' voices are pictured onscreen. You can change all the voices' characteristics—pitch, tone, and so on—and see the results onscreen; even better, you hear them.

You get 32 sounds and 32 different song patterns, any one of which can have three voices. Each of the three voices can be made from a variety of waveforms and noises. You can change sounds and song patterns slightly or entirely by selecting menu options while a song is playing. When you like what you hear, you can save it. Print it out, if you like, with the program that prints music scores. The company also offers libraries of scale patterns from around the world and Afro-Latin and modern rock rhythms and sounds ($24.95 each).

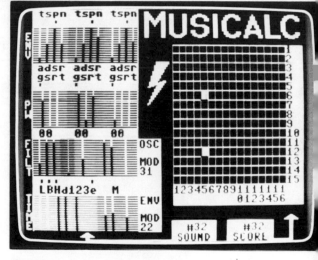

*MUSICALC 1 puts a synthesizer's console on the screen; you control it from the keyboard.*

---

MUSICALC 1 is complex—but worth it. (A file manager or word processor of this complexity would cost hundreds of dollars.) There's nothing else like it on the market.

**STEWART BRAND:** I've never seen a program generate instant glee in bystanders like this one. It bops out a tune and rhythms, you add a riff—random as you like—and it's transformed into interesting music, right on the beat.

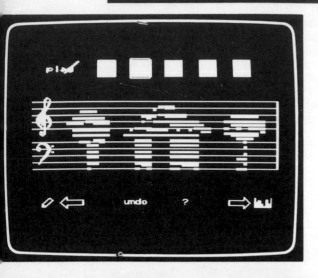

*The most wonderful, imaginative
music program we've found . . .*

## MUSICLAND

**Dr. Martin Lamb; Apple II family; 64K; KoalaPad or joystick; Mountain Computer Music System required; copy-protected? YES; $149 ($495 with Mountain System included); Syntauri Corp., 1670 So. Amphlett Blvd. Suite 116, San Mateo, CA 94402; 415/574-3335.**

JAMES STOCKFORD: It's a home-entertainment music game, an excellent tool for teachers, and a good sketchpad or toy for professional musicians.

*In MUSICLAND, you explore music by making pictures. The pictures and patterns become melodies and the colors determine the tones of the melodies.*

MUSICLAND has four game modules. In Music Doodles you use your KoalaPad or game paddles to draw pictures or patterns on a five-line staff. In Timbre Painting you dip into paint pots to color your doodles. Play your colored doodle and hear the sound of a pink smiley face, three blue birds, or any kind of pattern you have drawn and colored. The third module, Music Blocks, allows you to string many doodles together as a composition. The fourth, Sound Factory, presents the tools you need to make different tone colors, which you can store in the paint pots of the Timbre Painting module to color your doodles.

From the physics of sound to pitch, tone quality, and motif, all the fundamentals of music are treated in this supremely accessible program. I wish it were available for all computers.

*For professional musicians
and audio technicians . . .*

## PMS TYPE 201 WAVESHAPER

**Thomas Wilson; Apple II family; 48K; copy-protected? NO; $345; Pacific Micro Systems, 160 Gate Five Rd., Sausalito, CA 94965; 415/331-2525.**

JAMES STOCKFORD: This circuit board and software system for the Apple II is most appropriate for professional musicians, professional or semiprofessional studio owners and engineers, and audio technicians who want a low-cost, high-quality, design, emulation, and troubleshooting tool. It can also be used to control up to eight other

*Pure tech. PMS TYPE 201 WAVESHAPER allows some of the most flexible options for controlling waveforms, but you gotta know what you're doing.*

devices—digital equipment, other computers, industrial and medical simulations, and test devices.

You can create and send to a sound system a waveform in any shape you like. Each waveform can comprise up to 2048 points on an $X$-$Y$ axis with a time-base variable from 125 nanoseconds to one second per point. You can edit waveforms using the cursor, by coordinates, by utility, with your own BASIC program, or through the program's bit or byte mode. Utilities include online Help, Copy, Replicate, Invert, Print, Save to disk, Add and Subtract two waveforms, Fourier sinewave addition, and Scaling on the screen or an oscilloscope.

Most often used as an audio-frequency analyzing and development tool, the PMS 201 can replace frequency synthesizers costing thousands of dollars.

*You want a review of MUSIC CONSTRUCTION SET from Electronic Arts?*

*Warning: Do not buy this program. It is especially bad for the musical development of children. It will surely make piano teachers blossom and grow like the rain in little children's lives that they are.*

*When I was a little boy, they made me take piano lessons from a cruel, stuffy old lady. This program reminds me of my piano teacher. It's even got the same rap: "You may be an unheralded musical genius." That's what she told my parents about me. And they gave her money! That's what it says on the outside of the package about you. and you're supposed to give the man at the store money. That's what it's about.*

*The one purpose I can imagine for using this program is to instruct programmers and packagers what not to do. Everything wrong is included in this one thin package. Is one of the principal strategies of computer-oriented tutorials to provide rewards for "right" behavior? Then don't give the users any reward. As with virtue, make them wait, and wait, and wait for any reward, which, when it comes, will turn out to be their own doing. Is one of the best elements of computer-teaching immediate interaction of the user and the course? Then let's make this program as slow and unresponsive as possible. Is the delight of wide-open vistas one of the finest promises of computer training? Well, surely we can arrange to bore the user to tears with repetitive old musical wheezes and the most staid of compositional tools.*
—James Stockford

*For serious students and teachers . . .*

## MUSIC GAMES

**Lydia Bell; Apple II family; 48K; game paddles or joystick required; copy-protected? YES; $29.95; Howard W. Sams & Co., Inc., 4300 West 62nd St., Indianapolis, IN 46268; 800/428-7267 or, in IN, 317/298-5400.**

JAMES STOCKFORD: An expert set of electronic flashcards for the Apple, these games teach the fundamentals of music. Each concentrates on one aspect, such as pitch, recognition, rhythm, and sight reading. Variations of melody, rhythm and notation possible within each proficiency level keep beginning through advanced-intermediate students interested and challenged. The program stands head and shoulders above the dozen other contenders in this field.

## Good Eating

*Sophisticated recipe searching . . .*

### MICRO COOKBOOK

**Apple II family; 64K; 80 column card ● IBM PC/XT compatibles ● IBM PCjr; 128K; copy-protected? YES; $40; Virtual Combinatics, Inc., P.O. Box 755, Rockport, MA 01966; 617/546-6553.**

PAUL SCHINDLER: Until I saw MICRO COOKBOOK, I thought all cookbook programs were silly. What could they do that I couldn't do faster and better with a book? Well, the way I cook is to determine first what is fresh in the store or what spices I feel like having, and then search for appropriate recipes. MICRO COOKBOOK, really a database management system for recipes, works the same way. You enter a category, say Indian, and a spice, say curry powder, and it offers you a choice of all Indian recipes calling for curry powder.

The program is so well-designed I could use it immediately, without reference to the manual. You can print any recipe and a shopping list for selected recipes (and add items). Two reservations: It readjusts quantities when you change the number of servings, but doesn't convert them into more reasonable measurements (one teaspoon tripled is left at three teaspoons, not converted to one tablespoon). And it lets you add recipes more easily than any similar program I have seen or heard of, but limits you to 255 recipes per floppy. I know I have more recipes than that in my clip file.

BARBARA ROBERTSON: Paul uses MICRO COOKBOOK on an Apple II; the IBM PC version has a bit more power: There are 512 recipes on a double-sided disk, and the program searches through eight recipe files to find, for example, "all desserts that do *not* use sugar." I like it, too—I make up my own classifications, store my own recipes, and don't care about the 156 recipes they supply. Our office manager, Lyn Gray, prefers THE EXECUTIVE COOKBOOK—a pretty, tidy program (you can even order extra "designer" disks at $9 each) with lovely recipes. THE EXECUTIVE COOKBOOK is the easier to use of the two. It's more elegant and less flexible—recipes must fit on one 40-character by 14-line screen. More like a cookbook than a database program.

*Simple and elegant . . .*

### THE EXECUTIVE COOKBOOK

**Apple II family; 48K ● Commodore 64 ● IBM PC/XT compatibles; 128K; copy-protected? YES; $45; Executive Cookbook, P.O. Box 1717, Aptos, CA 95001; 800/227-3800.**

LYN GRAY: After ten minutes at the keyboard, I was ready to start printing out tasty and simple recipes. I got hooked and have been using THE EXECUTIVE COOKBOOK ever since.

The recipes are all in the gourmet category—things out of the ordinary, such as abalone chowder, eggplant mozzarella, fettucine prosciutto, jalapeno pasta salad, salmon in sour cream, and a turn-in-your-mother recipe for fudge (nothing weird like MICRO COOKBOOK's "Hot Dog Provençale"). Yet each is quick and simple to prepare—"do ahead" recipes are marked in the table of contents. It's perfect for busy professionals. There is no manual. All the instructions—they're simple ones—are onscreen.

You can add your own recipes and store them on as many new recipe disks as you want—the program even initializes blank disks. I have disks for desserts, appetizers, salads, and no longer keep scraps of paper tacked to the bulletin board, stuck in books, and stuffed in drawers. I can easily print recipes on sheets for use in the kitchen, on continuous-form index cards for recipe trading, or on large jam-jar labels.

## Right Eating

ELIZABETH MORGAN: For the past ten years, I've been calculating nutritional data by hand, and I really appreciate the speed and ease a good computer program provides. Of the more than a dozen programs I've tried, four stand out as the best of the bunch.

NUTRIPLAN is as refreshing as cool lemonade on a hot summer day— but doesn't analyze physical activity. HEALTH AIDE is the top banana—analyzes everything, but you pay the price in learning time, maybe more than you need. I-SHAPE and NUTRI-CALC are compromises. NUTRI-CALC adds a bit of physical activity to the nutritional analysis, has good nutrient information, but is more difficult to use than NUTRIPLAN. IN-SHAPE is fun to use, concentrates on physical activity, but utilizes only the four basic nutrients.

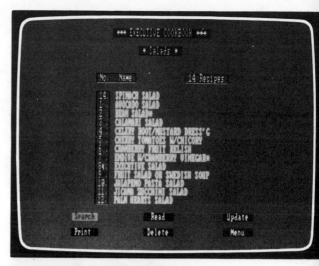

*All the instructions for THE EXECUTIVE COOKBOOK are on the bottom lines of the screen. The recipes are tasty and easy to prepare.*

This program does not increase a recipe by multiplying ingredient amounts by number of servings. I respect the authors' integrity in not adding such a "feature": Any experienced cook knows that doubling or tripling some spices and ingredients can be disastrous.

THE EXECUTIVE COOKBOOK has no flashy organizational tools—you can find recipes by title only (they're grouped into typical cookbook "chapters"—snacks/sandwiches, soups/stews, salads/dressings/sauces, etc.); you can print a recipe but not a shopping list. I don't mind, though. I prefer the simplicity.

*Counts calories for a week . . .*

### NUTRI-CALC

**Version 5.21; Apple II family; 48K ● Corvus Concept; 64K ● DECPro 350; 64K ● IBM PC/XT compatibles; 64K; Sage; 64K ● TRS-80 Models II, III, 4, 12, 16; 48K; copy-protected? NO; $129 (school discount rates available); PCD Systems, Inc., 163 Main St., P.O. Box 277, Penn Yan, NY 14527; 315/536-7428.**

ELIZABETH MORGAN: This program is divided into two sections, Nutri-Calc and Calorie. Nutri-Calc analyzes 821 food-directory items for 18 nutrients and water. You can't add foods, but you can replace ones on the list. It's more difficult to use than NUTRIPLAN—selecting the food items you want is a hassle, because you have to enter a code number from the manual for each—but you can store and analyze up to an entire week's worth of data. Line graphs compare your nutrient intake for protein, calcium, phosphorus, iron, vitamins A, $B_1$, $B_2$, and niacin to the RDA. With Calorie, you can find out how many calories you need to maintain a given body weight relative to physical activity. Or, if you enter the number of hours spent in five types of activities—vigorous work, walking, standing, sitting, sleeping—it tells you how many calories to cut each day to lose weight.

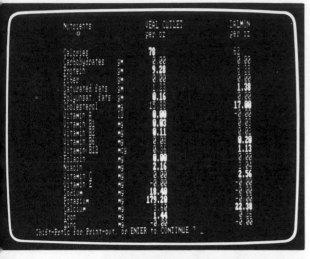

We were all surprised when NUTRIPLAN showed us that salmon was higher than veal cutlets in cholesterol; if you are what you eat, you might as well plan for it.

*Tracks a year's worth of data . . .*

## IN SHAPE

IBM PC compatibles; DOS 1.0 or 1.1, 64K; DOS 2.0, 96K; 80-column monitor; copy-protected? YES; $95; DEG Software, 11999 Katy Freeway, Suite 150, Houston, TX 77079; 713/531-6100.

ELIZABETH MORGAN: This program gives aerobic points for your choice of 23 exercises. It tracks performance, weight, and nutrient information on a daily, weekly, and annual basis. The food directory contains 1000 items, but analyzes for only the four basics: protein, carbohydrates, fat, and calories—no vitamins or minerals. Numerous line charts and bar graphs clearly show a year's worth of trends and progress—weight, what percentage of your diet is from one of the four basics, calories per food group, protein per meal, carbohydrates by weight, and more—52 choices in all.

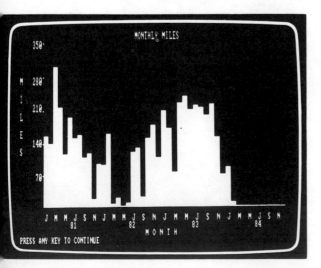

*Easy to use, one-day nutritional analysis . . .*

## NUTRIPLAN

Apple II family; 48K ● IBM PC compatibles; 64K ● IBM PCjr; 128K; copy-protected? YES; $75; Micromedx, 15 Caton St., East Northport, NY 11731; 516/735-8979.

ELIZABETH MORGAN: NUTRIPLAN is one of my favorites, even though it doesn't include exercise and only analyzes data for a meal or a day. It's easy to search through the 400-item food list and add to or change it. You can enter unlimited quantities of any food, analyze what you've eaten for 21 nutrients, and compare the results to the Recommended Daily Allowance (RDA). Screens are colorful and simple. You can compare two foods— say, ice cream and skim milk, or soybeans and chicken. NUTRIPLAN lists nutrients for both in green on a grey screen and highlights the higher amounts in white. This program is so refreshing—clear, easy to learn and use— and does such a good job of analyzing and presenting the information, I recommend it to everyone, from the occasionally curious to the health professional.

*For serious runners . . .*

## THE RUNNING LOG

IBM PC; DOS 1.1, 64K; DOS 2.0, 96K; 2 disk drives; color graphics card; copy-protected? YES; $39.95; Marathon Software, Box 26 Pinecrest, Clancy, MT 59634; 406/933-5783.

GAIL LAMPERT: If you're like me, a runner who likes to track her progress, this program is right up your alley. You can log in two runs a day. Tell the program the shoes you wear, temperature and time of day, morning pulse (whether you're running or not), and distance (or add your own categories); retrieve the information later by date. You can also get weekly, monthly, or annual mileage data, print tables or graphs, and do some analysis—for example, average length of runs over a designated time period or pulse rate versus mileage. A good program for people into rigorous training and tracking.

BARBARA ROBERTSON: A program to check out in this category is James F. Fixx's running program from MECA, unfortunately not available in a final version in time for our deadline. (THE RUNNING PROGRAM; James F. Fixx; IBM PC/XT compatibles, ● IBM PCjr; 128K; copy-protected? YES; $80; M.E.C.A., 285 Riverside Ave., Westport, CT 06880; 203/222-1000.)

*Runners in training—for marathons, aerobics or general conditioning—can track their progress over a five-year span using THE RUNNING LOG. The program even questions exorbitant performance claims to keep you honest.*

*The most complex and complete nutritional analysis . . .*

## HEALTH-AIDE

Robert Etheredge; Version 1.0; Apple II family; 48K ● IBM PC/XT compatibles; DOS 2.0, 128K; copy-protected? YES; $80; Programming Technology Corp., 7 San Marcos Place, San Rafael, CA 94901; 415/485-5601.

ELIZABETH MORGAN: If you really want to keep track of trends, nutrients, exercise, and calories, this program is your best bet. Be prepared to spend quite a few hours going through the manual and program just gaining familiarity, though. Here are some of the highlights: daily values for 35 nutrients, percent RDA, food cost, protein completeness, 700-item expandable food directory, monthly and yearly cycles, personal requirements for up to 40 people, weight loss, blood pressure data, pulse, running times, recipe files, shopping lists, and 150 exercises. There are graphs and charts (monthly and yearly) and lots of information in the manual—an entire chapter is devoted to nutrition education. This is a program for health professionals or someone really interested in details.

*See the night sky . . .*

## SKYMAP 2000

Commodore 64; copy-protected? YES; $39.95; Commodore, 1200 Wilson Dr., West Chester, PA 19380; 215/431-9100.

STEVEN LEVY: One of the niftiest programs I've seen for the Commodore 64 is SKYMAP 2000. What shows up on your screen is a view of the sky at night that is presumably the same view you'd get if you looked up at the sky that very night (unless you live in New York City, in which case you can see the sky only with your Commodore). Using the joystick, you move the cursor to a new star, press the button, and voila! It tells you what star it is and facts like how far from Earth it is. A much better tool for homebrew astronomers than a celestial atlas in hard copy. Only problem is getting an extension cord to bring the non-portable 64 and monitor outside.

*Use your Apple to control a slideshow . . .*

## APPLE/GEMINI LEISURE TIME EXPANSION (LTE) PACKAGE

Thomas Wilson; Apple II family; 48K; copy-protected? NO; $349;

## GEMINI 2000 PROGRAMMER/DISSOLVER

Includes handbook, AC adaptor; $549;

both from Pacific Micro Systems, 160 Gate Five Rd., Sausalito, CA 94965; 415/331-2525.

JAMES STOCKFORD: A slideshow set to music with voice overdubs can be a dazzling way to present a story, sales presentation, or travelog. But a mighty spectacle requires a mighty lot of editing.

With this package you get a hardware device (the Gemini 2000 P/D) that controls one or two projectors, a printed circuit board for the Apple II, and software on a floppy disk. You use the software to create the slideshow instructions, which you save on a cassette tape—in sync with a sound track if you want. Put the tape in the tape player, plug the Gemini 2000 P-D into the tape player and slide projector/s, and you have an automatic slideshow with music. The software can control three Gemini devices for a total of six possible projectors. You can switch from one projector to the other; set up a sequence of dissolves, cross-fades, and strobe effects; load slides from anywhere in any carousel in any order; control bulb intensity; cue timing to match music or speech; and repeat any of the sequence loops. Each instruction is called a cue—you're allowed 1500. Online help is available, as is an onscreen command page for reference. Works with Kodak and other projectors that have the same type of connectors. Compares favorably in price to LED-type single-purpose editing machines (Arion 828 at $2795, AVL Coyote at $1695), even when you add in the price of the Apple II—and is much more convenient, flexible, and powerful.

---

*Simple programs for astronomers . . .*

## CELESTIAL BASIC

*Celestial Basic (Astronomy on Your Computer)*; Eric Burgess; 1982; 300 pp.; $16.95; Sybex, 2344 Sixth Street, Berkeley, CA 94710; 415/848-8233; or COMPUTER LITERACY.

JAMES STOCKFORD: This book is a labor of love. Its backbone is two dozen program listings in BASIC divided into groups dealing with planets, moon, calendars, conversions, meteor showers, constellations, etc. Accompanying text is informative and graceful, with references to ancient astronomical practices, fundamentals of armchair astronomy, and careful suggestions for programmers.

The beauty of the printed BASIC listings is that they work for any computer with little or no modification. Program lines are simple, not condensed, to make modification easy for the beginning programmer. Each program is loaded with the expertise and data of an expert astronomer and his friends. The CELESTIAL BASIC users' group now has about 100 active members and publishes a newsletter, several cassettes for the Timex/Sinclair 1000, and a disk full of BASIC programs for the Apple II. Contact S & T Software Service, 13361 Frati Lane, Sebastopol, CA 95472, for more information.

---

*Calculates shipping costs . . .*

## POSTMAN

Version 1.71; Apple II family; 64K ● IBM PC compatibles; 64K; copy-protected? NO; $55 for full-featured program, $10 (refundable) for demo; Mom's Software, P.O. Box 19418, Portland, OR 97219; 503/244-9173.

LYN GRAY: For the office manager for the **Whole Earth Software Catalog** and **Review**, cost-cutting and efficiency are part of the job. I often find myself spending lots of time poring over the nine mail-service charts tacked to the mailing-area wall, just to determine the cheapest and/or timeliest way of sending letters, packages, and boxes.

POSTMAN helped me cut down on that valuable time. It displays the best method to ship—with alternatives—in bar-graph form. Calculates cost, zone, and number of days to deliver by United Parcel Service (UPS) ground, UPS second-day air, U.S. Postal Service (USPS) fourth-class parcel post, and USPS Priority services (first and air) when you enter the destination zip code and package weight. It lets you know if a zip code is nonexistent or if certain services are unavailable in the area in question (then it tells you what services are available). If only it could weigh, post, and deliver the mail as well.

*SIDEKICK let us put this review, a calendar, an appointment log from the calendar, and a calculator all onscreen at once. Handy for anyone who spends a lot of time in front of a screen.*

---

*A dashboard full of utilities for the IBM PC . . .*

## SIDEKICK

IBM PC/XT compatibles ● IBM PCjr; copy-protected? YES; $50; Borland International, 4113 Scotts Valley Dr., Scotts Valley, CA 95066; 408/438-8400.

JAMES STOCKFORD: This new windowing utility promises to be as indispensable as socks and underpants. No matter what program you're using, push a button and SIDEKICK's calendar, notepad, calculator, phone dialer, or ASCII conversion chart will immediately pop up on the screen.

Here's how it works. When you start your machine, boot up SIDEKICK right after you boot up your operating system. Then load any program you want to use and begin working. SIDEKICK sits invisibly in the computer's RAM memory. When you call SIDEKICK, the program you're working on stops dead in its tracks, leaving whatever you were doing on the screen. The SIDEKICK utilities you choose appear in windows on top (in various colors, if you have a color monitor). The perpetual calendar includes a daily appointment scheduler; the notepad is a simple word-processing program that uses WORDSTAR commands; the dialer is not a communications program but can (if you have a modem) dial any number stored in a phone list; the calculator includes basic arithmetic (binary and hexadecimal) plus nine nested levels of parentheses and logic operators. You can slide the windows around to peek at work underneath and run the cursor all over the screen as a pointer. When you've finished with SIDEKICK, you push a button and the main program begins again exactly where you stopped. Text and data entered into SIDEKICK can be moved into the program you're using, or saved in a file to be moved into another program later.

STEWART BRAND: Looks to me like SIDEKICK competes directly with THE DESK ORGANIZER (p. 114). We weren't able to race them. You may want to.

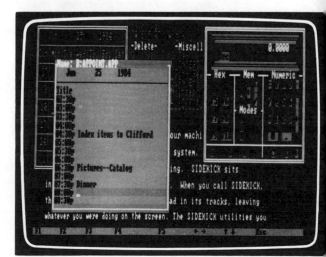

## Connecting your coffee pot to your computer . . .

### THE APPLE CONNECTION

*The Apple Connection*; James W. Coffron; 1982; 264 pp.; $14.95;

### THE IBM CONNECTION

*The IBM Connection*; James W. Coffron; 1984; 264 pp.; $16.95;

both from Sybex, 2344 Sixth Street, Berkeley, CA 94710; 415/848-8233 or COMPUTER LITERACY.

CLIFF FIGALLO: The computer is a digital creature, and though it lives on electricity, it cannot interact directly with the world of electrical switches and gauges. You can't plug an RS-232 cable into Mr. Coffee and program "turn on at 10:00." What you need is an *interface* between the computer's digital world and the analog world, where electricity is measured in volts instead of bits. A few software/hardware systems claim to provide home control, but I found none I could recommend. So far, if you want your computer to control the analog world, you'll have to arrange it yourself.

These books do a great job of clarifying the workings of digital systems and tell you how to program them to control the analog objects in your home. They are books for the seriously curious, not for the casual reader. And be forewarned that (1) the ability to write simple programs in BASIC is a prerequisite to making real use of these books and (2) the purchase of hardware is going to be another expense on the way to computer control in your home.

Virtually any job involving electrical switching, from turning on the lights at 9 o'clock, to designing a home-security system, to monitoring and maintaining critical environmental conditions in a greenhouse, can be handled using the fundamentals in these books.

## I got the horse right here . . .

### THE MASTER HANDICAPPER: THOROUGHBRED ENHANCED "GOLD" EDITION

Professor Jones; version 1.3; Apple II family; 64K ● Commodore 64 ● IBM PC/XT compatibles ● IBM PCjr; 128K ● TRS-80 I, III, 4; 48K; copy-protected? YES; $200; Professional Handicapping Systems, 1114 N. 24th St., Boise, ID 83702; 208/342-6939.

JAMES DONNELLY: If your life's dream is to make a living at the racetrack, get a job walking hots (sweaty horses). Eavesdrop. Advance to grooming. Keep your ears open. Become a blacksmith or, better, get a "vendor's" license and barn-area pass. Play gin rummy in the track kitchen all morning, every morning. Keep listening. Soon you'll be 56 years old and will enjoy a mutually friendly acquaintance with everybody from the racing secretary to the parking valets. And you'll know what and when to bet.

But if you're stuck in some lame-o job, like sitting in front of a computer, THE MASTER HANDICAPPER is worth a bet. THE MASTER HANDICAPPER series of eight programs gives you betting strategy, race analysis, data storage, and money-management programs

## Access to inner calm . . .

### CALMPUTE

Apple II family; 64K; copy-protected? NO; $90 (includes GSR monitoring device); HesWare, 150 North Hill Dr., Brisbane, CA 94005; 415/468-4111.

### RELAX

Apple II family; 48K ● Atari; 16K and up ● Commodore 64 ● IBM PC; 64K ● IBM PCjr; 64K; game control adaptor; copy-protected? NO; $140 (includes software for all machines listed plus connector cables); Synapse Software, 5221 Central Ave. Suite 200, Richmond, CA 94804; 415/527-7751.

DICK FUGETT: Handling more information faster is what computers are all about, and since "more" and "faster" are both key words in our society, it follows that folks think computers are wonderful. Mostly what people do faster with computers is manipulate their immediate environments, using all that speeding information to change their personal worlds. These programs emphasize "slow" and do absolutely nothing to modify your environment. They only let you work on yourself.

RELAX is based on EMG, the measure of muscle activity. You place a headband with conductive sensors on your forehead and the output shows up on the screen, allowing you to "see" your muscle tension. There's also a cassette with audio instructions to guide you through a muscle-by-muscle relaxation of your body. If you have ever experienced the

for betting thoroughbred, trotting, and dog races. Race analysis is based on **Racing Form** data—time and date for last race, track conditions, distance, purse, gender, workout time, etc. Type in this data and you get a bar graph showing the relative potential of each horse to win in a given race.

Hard-core handicappers might find the race-analysis section useful for historical records. Beginners will learn something about analyzing and handicapping strategy. For example, when I asked for information on the Daily Double, the program suggested two ways to bet: (1) If a horse in the first of the two races has clearly got it all over his competitors, you bet him and wheel the second half (bet on everything); (2) If the first race is real tight, box the four top picks for each race (bet all the combinations). Costs $32 (minimum bet) but can produce some real payoffs. My reaction, though, is, "Hmmph. Not if everybody is doing it. Which they mostly are."

The basic money management tips are most useful for heavy bettors, not the $2-window, "I like the name" players. The program keeps a running total of your win/loss rate—take your medicine!—but you'll still have to keep a separate account for hot dogs and flat beer: they'll screw up a running total every time.

rewards of *savasana*, the deep-relaxation pose, while practicing yoga, you know the benefits. For good measure, they've tossed in a feature allowing you to produce your own subliminal messages—little 1/60 second prompts to assist in guiding the subconscious in the ongoing attempt to clean up your act.

CALMPUTE is a simple program based on a hand-held monitor that amplifies galvanic skin response (best known for its application in lie detectors), showing the result on the screen. It is useful, but RELAX is more sophisticated, has better screens, and comes with a commendable and thorough 140-page manual explaining both principles and techniques. However, RELAX costs considerably more. If you want to start low, begin with CALMPUTE. You can later add to it (at extra cost) monitors for EMG as well as heart rate, body temperature, and electro-myograph—options not available with RELAX.

Whichever you choose, you'll be given the ability to take a quick look inside, where those two facets of the human condition labeled "mind" and "body" coincide. Observing the squiggly line on the screen freak out when some personal demon from the past is mentioned, or seeing it go smooth and calm after you exhale and relax your muscles, teaches awareness of the physical sensation of tension. Once identified, it becomes possible to consciously control what had before been both unnoticed and uncontrollable.

## Artificial Intelligence

MATTHEW MCCLURE: Artificial intelligence, or AI, is becoming a marketing buzzword; all sorts of programs claim to incorporate AI techniques, and some of them even deliver. What's the big deal?

The first attempts at AI centered around automated versions of such human activities as playing chess or checkers. A key concept arose from this early research: creating a computational model that could learn how to learn. Commonsense reasoning problems were attempted—classics like Missionaries and Cannibals—and solved. Similar techniques were applied to problems of perception—visual scene analysis by robots, for example, in which the robot deduces that the lighter-colored rectangle it sees must be a "door" because it goes all the way to the floor. Whole programming languages have been developed to handle the kinds of processing AI requires; LISP and PROLOG (see MICRO-PROLOG, p. 165) are two examples. Natural language processing, including speech synthesis and recognition, is one of the hottest areas of AI research today, and is yielding the greatest number of commercial applications, especially natural-language querying systems for database management.

At the high end of the price spectrum, complex expert systems imitate top-flight professionals in medicine, geology, agriculture, pest control. At the low end, ELIZA, Joseph Weizenbaum's early-'sixties experimental program that emulates a Rogerian psychologist, is an amusing illustration of how some of the simpler programs work.

*CP/M machines ● PC/MS-DOS machines; copy-protected? NO; $24.95; or as part of TOOLWORKS LISP/80, $39.95; The Software Toolworks, 15233 Ventura Blvd., Suite 1118, Sherman Oaks, CA 91403; 818/986-4885 ● Apple II family ● Apple III ● Commodore 64; cassette or disk; ● CP/M machines ● PC/MS-DOS machines; copy-protected? NO; $45 including source program; Artificial Intelligence Research Group, 921 North La Jolla Avenue, Los Angeles, CA 90046; 213/656-7368 or 213/654-2214.*

As powerful computation becomes increasingly inexpensive, some of the major obstacles to AI will be removed. Techniques like rule-based expert systems and hierarchically structured tree searches require enormous memory and vast numbers of comparison/computations, which is why the new "fifth generation" is so important: computers with megabytes of RAM, superfast processors and specialized languages will make today's machines look like pogo sticks next to tomorrow's rockets.

---

*Rule-based expert system for micros . . .*

## EXPERT-EASE

**Robbie McLaren; version 1.0; IBM PC compatibles; 128K; 2 disk drives; copy-protected? YES; $2000; Jeffrey Perrone & Associates, Inc., 3685 17th Street, San Francisco, CA 94114; 415/431-9562.**

BARBARA ROBERTSON: With EXPERT-EASE you can build a rule-based expert system that can solve problems and make decisions. If you have recurring problems for which consistent solutions would result in cost savings, the program will pay for itself in short order; it is also valuable where there's a high turnover of experts within a company, or where experts in a field are not always available.

EXPERT-EASE is remarkably easy to use. A decision tree is made up of examples, attributes and rules which you enter as the program prompts you. Then EXPERT-EASE uses the decision tree to solve your problem. Sample models come with the program, for tasks as disparate as predicting the stock market, diagnosing kidney disease, and deciding what to do on Sunday. If the program sold for less than $200, I'd buy it in a minute and recommend it without hesitation. As it is, the stiff price tag rules out buying it just for frivolous what-to-do-on-Sunday use.

---

*Learning to learn . . .*

## MACHINE LEARNING

*Machine Learning (An Artificial Intelligence Approach)*; Ryszard S. Michalski, Jaime G. Carbonell, and Tom M. Mitchell, eds.; 1983; 572 pp.; $39.50; William Kaufmann, Inc., 95 First Street, Los Altos, CA 94022; 415/948-5810; or COMPUTER LITERACY.

MATTHEW MCCLURE: This is perhaps the most advanced of the books covered here, which makes sense: its subject matter, essentially quantifying the learning process, is central to the idea of intelligence. Topics covered include learning from examples, modeling human learning strategies, knowledge acquisition, learning heuristics, and learning by analogy. If you can teach a computer to learn, you must have some understanding of what learning is. Read this book and you'll have it.

---

*Classic book in a young field . . .*

## BUILDING EXPERT SYSTEMS

*Building Expert Systems*; Frederick Hayes-Roth, Donald A. Waterman, and Douglas B. Lenat; 1983; 444 pp.; $34.95; Addison-Wesley Publishing Co., Reading, MA 01867; 614/944-3700; or COMPUTER LITERACY.

MATTHEW MCCLURE: **Building Expert Systems** gives a broad introduction to what is probably the most developed branch of the AI tree. It looks, for example, at eight different knowledge-engineering techniques applied to one common problem, revealing the strengths and weaknesses of each method. Authoritative and complete.

---

*Books on AI . . .*

## AUTOMATED REASONING

*Automated Reasoning (Introduction and Applications)*; Larry Wos, Ross Overbeek, Ewing Lusk, and Jim Boyle; 1984; 482 pp.; $28.95; Prentice-Hall, Inc., Englewood Cliffs, NJ 07632; 201/592-2000; or COMPUTER LITERACY.

MATTHEW MCCLURE: Written as a text for university students, **Automated Reasoning** takes you through the fundamentals of logic and introduces you to the techniques of puzzle-solving, symbolic execution, expert systems, and inference rules. Blessedly, no previous training in mathematics, logic, or programming is required to understand the concepts presented.

---

*Weighty tome . . .*

## PRINCIPLES OF ARTIFICIAL INTELLIGENCE

*Principles of Artificial Intelligence*; Nils J. Nilsson; 1980; 476 pp.; $30; William Kaufmann, Inc., 95 First Street, Los Altos, CA 94022; 415/948-5810; or COMPUTER LITERACY.

MATTHEW MCCLURE: As the Director of the Artificial Intelligence Laboratory at Stanford Research Institute, Nils Nilsson is an expert's expert. His book is not light reading, but if you want a strong foundation in AI, you should read it. Understand this book and you'll have the basics for natural language processing, automatic programming, robotics, machine vision, automatic theorem proving, intelligent data retrieval systems—nobody said it'd be easy, but at least it's terrifyingly clear.

## BUSINESS AS SERVICE

STEWART BRAND: Just because Point is a nonprofit foundation doesn't mean there aren't some potential conflicts of interest you should know about. A goodly amount of our working hardware was donated by the manufacturers—eight Kaypro 2s, two Kaypro 10s, ten Hayes Smartmodem 1200s, three Atari 800s, four Koala Pads. Other equipment we have on extended loan—a Hewlett-Packard 150 and HP ThinkJet printer and letter-quality printer; an IBM PCjr; a Coleco Adam; an Apple IIe and printer; a Dynax printer; an Infoscribe printer. Taking advantage of editorial discount (50%) we bought two Macintoshes and two Imagewriter printers. Some of these machines we praise in print, some we don't; all are put to good use and we're grateful for them.

Other confessions. One of our Board members, Doug Carlston, is president of a software company, Broderbund; he takes no part in our selection process. I own some stock in Apple Computer (worth $1,500 when I bought it in Jan. '84, based on no inside information). My wife, Patricia Phelan, is a part-time software agent working with John Brockman Associates, which is also Whole Earth's literary agent. Some of Brockman's software clients are reviewed here, some aren't. Though we are opposed to copy-protected software, when our staff or software reviewers work with programs from our library, they may neither keep nor copy them.

In 1968 I started the original **Whole Earth Catalog** as one activity of Richard Raymond's Portola Institute, a nonprofit public education foundation in Menlo Park, California. In 1971 Portola begat Point, which took responsibility for the over $1,000,000 that came in from sales of **The Last Whole Earth Catalog**. Most of the money was distributed in grants over the next three years. What little remained was used to found **CoEvolution Quarterly** (which still continues, with 22,000 subscribers—$18/year) and to make two more major incarnations of the **Whole Earth Catalog** in 1974 and 1980-81, all from Sausalito, California.

It's our custom to print—and try to explain—our finances in each of our publications. The cash report here shows expenditures and income for the first year of **Whole Earth Software Review** and **Whole Earth Software Catalog** taken together. The widely-reported $1.3 million advance from Doubleday for the **Catalog** came in two pieces—half (minus agent's commission) on signing (May, 1983), half (minus ditto) on delivery of film for the book (July, 1984). Likewise with the £40,000 advance from Corgi in England for the British edition. Point must sell 540,000 copies of the **Catalog** in the U.S. before we see any income beyond the advance.

The minus cash position in May '84 reflects borrowing against the second half of the advance. Income and expenses cover the first two issues of the **Review** as well as partial expenses on the **Catalog** (most of the contributors have yet to be paid). The advantage to the reader of Doubleday's handsome advance going to a nonprofit foundation is that all of the money was put to work on the research and publications; nobody got rich.

The title "Business as Service" comes from one of the courses we did with Point's year-long project, Uncommon Courtesy—School of Compassionate Skills. Business, we found, does best as business when it's performed as service. Service does best as service when it's approached as business. Each perspective keeps the other honest.

### CASH REPORT
May 1, 1983-May 31, 1984

### WHOLE EARTH SOFTWARE REVIEW & CATALOG

**INCOME**

| | |
|---|---:|
| Doubleday Advance | $567,500 |
| British Advance | 22,326 |
| Subscriptions | 123,067 |
| Back Issues | 1,505 |
| Direct Distribution | 4,456 |
| National Newsstand Distribution | 63,482 |
| Interest | 26,164 |
| Misc. | 290 |
| **TOTAL INCOME** | **$808,790** |

**EXPENSES**

| | |
|---|---:|
| Salaries | $285,175 |
| Writer/Contributor | 36,615 |
| Production Supplies | 8,657 |
| Printing (Magazine) | 87,060 |
| Subscription Fulfillment | 8,333 |
| Subscription Promotion | 136,909 |
| Distribution | 17,757 |
| Office, computer supplies | 22,421 |
| Equipment Rent/Maintenance | 2,676 |
| Telephone | 16,420 |
| Networks | 11,795 |
| Postage | 4,996 |
| Travel/Entertain./Auto | 23,139 |
| Rent & Maint./Utilities | 51,075 |
| Legal/Professional | 7,068 |
| Misc. Other | 9,112 |
| **TOTAL EXPENSE** | **$729,208** |

| | |
|---|---:|
| **POINT CORPORATE** | **$ 76,983** |
| **CAPITAL EXPENDITURES** | **61,175** |
| | |
| **NET CASH** | **– $ 58,576** |
| **Accounts Payable** | **– $ 72,988** |

# THE HARDWARE AND SOFTWARE THAT ASSEMBLED THIS BOOK

MATTHEW MCCLURE: People always ask, "Well, what do *you* use?" There's no short answer. After polling the staff, and ignoring hardware like a 1965 VW bug or "the telephone" and software like "my brain" and "sleep," here's most of what we found that we used.

*Hardware:* The most common computer was the Kaypro, both the 2 and the 10, for word processing and telecommunicating. We used IBM PCs for word processing and software testing, and the Macintosh for quick writing—memos, notices, forms, and previewing the chart on pages 50-51. Jim Stockford used his TRS-80 Model 100 for writing, telecommunicating, and keeping himself organized. Kathy Parks used the Apple IIe both for keeping track of the library (PFS:FILE) and for writing reviews (APPLE WRITER IIe). Line Editor Suzanne Lipsett used WORDSTAR on her Morrow Micro-Decision to transcribe the edited version of the Playing section. Cliff Figallo spent most of Spring '84 in front of a Compaq and Datamac hard disk, maintaining our research database with RBASE:4000. Jerry Weinberg came to Sausalito and edited the Programming section on a Commodore 64 with PAPERCLIP, the same word processor he uses on his SUPERPET in Nebraska. Robert Scarola did the Learning section with BANK STREET WRITER on his Apple II+ at home and brought the disk in for us to transform into typeset copy.

We did a lot of printing—draft after draft after draft. The Okidata Microline served me beautifully; so did Stewart's Gemini Star ("Not so beautifully" —SB) and the research department's Infoscribe 1100. We also used an Epson MX-80, an HP ThinkJet, an Apple Imagewriter, and the Dynax 15 made by Brother.

For telecommunicating, the Hayes Smartmodem 1200 was central to our operation, with an occasional assist from the Hayes Micromodem in the Apple IIe, the Visionary 100, and the VICModem from Commodore. We used EIES extensively, along with CompuServe and The Source. A Smartcable was indispensable for linking our Apple to the PC for transferring the Learning section to our standard format.

*Software:* Word processors WORDSTAR and NEWWORD were the mainstays, along with PERFECT WRITER (with PLU*PERFECT), THE FINAL WORD, and BUSINESSPAK+. For spelling checker it was THE WORD PLUS mostly.

Since much of our writing was done in teleconferences, we used a lot of telecommunications programs; MITE, MIST, CROSSTALK XVI, and SUPERTERM were the main ones.

Virtually all our typesetting was done by telecommunication from Sausalito to Mackenzie-Harris in San Francisco, using CROSSTALK on our IBM PC. Transforming text for this was one of the most interesting tasks in the production. For Jerry's Programming section, I used VIDTEX from CompuServe, uploading a file from the Commodore and downloading it to the PC. For Robert's Learning section, THE APPLE/IBM CONNECTION transferred the data, but slowly.

The prize for data transfer goes to three programs, XENOCOPY (PC/MS-DOS machines; 128K; copy-protected? YES; $98; Vertex Systems, 7950 W. 4th Street, Los Angeles, CA 90048; 213/938-0857), CONVERT (PC/MS-DOS machines; 64K, 2 disk drives; copy-protected? NO; $99; Selfware, Inc., 3545 Chain Bridge Road, Suite 3, Fairfax, VA 22030; 703/352-2977), and CROSSDATA (IBM PC compatibles; 128K; 2 disk drives; copy-protected? YES; $99; Award Software, Inc., 236 North Santa Cruz Ave., Los Gatos, CA 95030; 408/395-2773). These programs take a disk from a Kaypro, Morrow or a score of other CP/M formats and copy its data onto a PC-format disk; XENOCOPY and CROSSDATA also work vice versa. Since all our files were in WORDSTAR format, we wound up with a wonderfully compatible environment.

We used spreadsheets like MULTIPLAN, SUPERCALC2, and SUPERCALC3 to predict layouts and to design tables.

STEWART BRAND: Gawd. As you can surmise, the cacophony of software and hardware was made melodious by formidable application of fleshware. Barbara Robertson was the heroic intelligence in the middle of input traffic, Matthew McClure the heroic intelligence in the middle of output traffic; they made chaos cohere. Software is elusive, nasty, consequential stuff to review. This book is one-sixth the size of the most recent **Whole Earth Catalog**. It was twice the labor. Without the personal computers it might have been four times the labor, or impossible.

# ORDERING FROM COMPUTER LITERACY BOOKSHOP

**Send your book orders to:**

Computer Literacy Bookshop
520 Lawrence Expressway
Suite 310
Sunnyvale, CA 94086

**Please write "WESC" at the bottom of the envelope.**

*Shipping:* All books are shipped UPS for quickest turnaround time. Please add $2.50 shipping for the first one or two books. Add 25 cents for each additional book if you live west of the Mississippi; if you live east of the Mississippi, add 50 cents for each additional book.

Please give a street address—UPS cannot deliver to Post Office boxes.

*California:* Add 6% state sales tax; in BART counties, add 6½%.

*Foreign orders:* Sames as UPS. Add $3.50 per order for insurance if desired. Pay only in U.S. funds drawn on a U.S. bank.

*VISA/MasterCard orders:* Send card number, expiration date and name as it appears on the card.

*Telephone orders:* 408/730-9957 for credit card orders only. No C.O.D.'s.

*Hours:* 9:30-11:30 a.m. and 2:00-8:00 p.m. Pacific Standard Time.

## PRODUCTS REVIEWED FOR SPECIFIC COMPUTERS . . .

The following indexes were generated via our R:BASE 4000
database from information entered during library cataloging
and access checking. Since publishers often told us only
"many MS-DOS" or "most CP/M" machines, additional
programs for the HP-150 and IBM PCjr may be hidden in the
IBM PC index; additional programs for the DEC Rainbow in
the IBM PC index and the CP/M index. Look in the CP/M
index for Kaypro 2 (p. 16) and Morrow MD-1E (p. 16)
programs; in the IBM PC index for Sanyo 555 (p. 18),
Compaq (p. 18), NEC APC III p. 18), and Leading Edge (p. 18)
programs. Try any program out on your brand of computer
before you buy to be sure it works.

## APPLE II FAMILY (p.19)

Much of the software written for the Apple IIe will run on the
Apple IIc, but not all. The best way to tell is to try the
software in the store before you buy it.

# MAIN INDEX

Recommended products in bold

208

**SOLUTION TO QUESTION ON P. 161:**

*The problem is in not checking the input: suppose we try the "triangle" (3, 1, 1), or suppose A, B, and C are all negative numbers: the program will fail. Good programming involves envisioning the kinds of problems the program will run into before the fact.*